D1355637

OPEN SYSTEMS NETWORKING

Addison-Wesley Professional Computing Series

Brian W. Kernighan, Consulting Editor

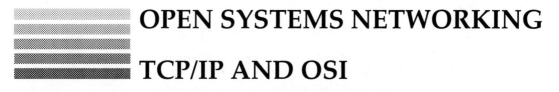

OPEN SYSTEMS NETWORKING

TCP/IP AND OSI

David M. Piscitello and A. Lyman Chapin

Addison-Wesley Publishing Company

Reading, Massachusetts   Menlo Park, California   New York
Don Mills, Ontariao   Wokingham, England   Amsterdam
Bonn   Sydney   Singapore   Tokyo   Madrid   San Juan
Paris   Seoul   Milan   Mexico City   Taipei

The publisher offers discounts on this book when ordered in quantity for special sales. For more information please contact:

Corporate & Professional Publishing Group

Addison-Wesley Publishing Company

One Jacob Way

Reading, Massachusetts 01867

Library of Congress Cataloging-in-Publication Data
Piscitello, David M.
    Open systems networking : TCP/IP and OSI / David M. Piscitello and A. Lyman Chapin.
        p. cm. - - (Addison-Wesley professional computing series)
    Includes bibliographical references and index.
    ISBN 0-201-56334-7 (alk. paper)
    1. OSI (Computer network standard) 2. TCP/IP (Computer network protocol) 3. Computer networks. I. Chapin, A. Lyman. II. Title. III. Series.
TK5105.55.P57 1993
004.6'2 - - dc20   93-17791
                                                                                            CIP

Copyright © 1993 by Addison-Wesley Publishing Company

All rights reserved. No part of this publication may be reproduced, stored in a retrieval system, or transmitted, in any form, or by any means, electronic, mechanical, photocopying, recording, or otherwise, without the prior consent of the publisher. Printed in the United States of America. Published simultaneously in Canada.

Cover photo by Steven Hunt, The Image Bank

Text design by Carol Keller

ISBN 0-201-56334-7

Text printed on recycled and acid-free paper.

1 2 3 4 5 6 7 8 9 10 MU 96959493

First printing, August 1993

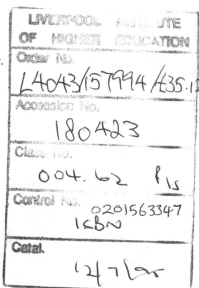

LIVERPOOL INSTITUTE OF HIGHER EDUCATION

Order No.
L4043/57994 /£35.12

Accession No.
180423

Class No.
004.62 Pis

Control No. 0201563347
ISBN

Catal.
12 7 95

CONTENTS

CHAPTER 13
THE NETWORK LAYER   **361**

CHAPTER 14
ROUTING   **413**

APPENDIX B
SOURCES

L. I. H. E.
THE BECK LIBRARY
WOOLTON RD., LIVERPOOL, L16 8NP

PREFACE

Why This Book, Now?

Open systems—in particular, Open Systems Interconnection (OSI) and TCP/IP[1]—are all the rage. There are plenty of books that discuss OSI and plenty more that discuss TCP/IP. However, despite the facts that the architecture and goals of OSI and TCP/IP are essentially the same, and that they are really just currently popular manifestations of the same fundamental principles and techniques, no previous book has examined the two in parallel. This book covers both Open Systems Interconnection and the Internet architecture and protocols, commonly known as TCP/IP. There are many compelling reasons for examining these architectures in parallel, which is what this book intends to do.

TCP/IP Has Strongly Influenced the Design of OSI   Many of the features and functions present in OSI trace their roots back to TCP/IP; for example, OSI's transport protocol class 4 and connectionless network protocol (CLNP) are functionally equivalent to TCP and IP. Furthermore, OSI's application services—Message Handling System, File Transfer Access and Management, the Directory, and Virtual Terminal—are all attempts to improve upon their TCP/IP ancestors; the OSI Message Handling System, for example, is intended to improve upon the highly successful electronic-mail facilities provided in the TCP/IP protocol suite by the Simple Mail Transfer Protocol by permitting facsimile, images, and voice to accompany text in a mail envelope. The OSI Message Handling

---

1.   Transmission control protocol (TCP) and internet protocol (IP) are the core protocols of the Internet architecture.

System also provides a platform for Electronic Data Interchange and Office Document Interchange, and the OSI Directory will provides a powerful, object-oriented, global information base that can be accessed by humans as well as by distributed applications such as electronic mail and network file and resource management, building on services hitherto provided by TCP/IP applications such as FINGER, WHOIS, and the Domain Name System.

OSI continues to profit from the experience accumulated during more than two decades of research on and real-world operation of TCP/IP networks, recorded (since 1969) in an on-line document series called the Internet requests for comments (RFCs). The RFCs constitute an archive of networking experiences that are in many cases directly applicable to OSI protocol design and the deployment of OSI-based networks as well as to the TCP/IP world that has been their traditional focus. This is particularly true, for example, in the area of transport protocol operation, in which OSI transport protocol class 4 and TCP share a common paradigm of "reliability through retransmission." OSI needs a research platform the likes of the Internet[2] not only to test and draw interest to its application services but to stress the limits of its routing and transport protocols.

OSI Has Also Influenced TCP/IP   TCP/IP's open shortest path first routing protocol is derived from OSI's intradomain intermediate system to intermediate system routing protocol (which was itself an adaptation of a link-state routing protocol developed for IP under the auspices of the Defense Advanced Research Projects Agency). OSI's data-definition language, Abstract Syntax Notation One, is used to define the Simple Network Management Protocol and its management information base. And OSI's Message Handling System and Directory are so promising that they are already operated over TCP/IP in large portions of the Internet.

OSI and TCP/IP Are Learning to Cooperate   Government open systems interconnection profiles (GOSIPs) and other computer and communication system procurement specifications mandate that OSI be introduced into the networking environments of government (particularly defense) agencies in Europe and the United States. Mandates such as these, al-

---

2.   The term *Internet*, with the initial *I* capitalized, refers to the worldwide interconnection of a vast number of backbone, regional, and local (enterprise) networks that operate TCP/IP, OSI, and other protocols. The Internet is a constantly growing entity, and although it is difficult to determine its exact size, well over 1.5 million hosts are (at the time of this writing) directly connected to the Internet using TCP/IP. A small, but growing, number of these hosts also use OSI protocols to connect to the Internet.

though highly criticized, have at least had the positive effect of causing developers on both "sides" to work together. Although the relationship between TCP/IP and OSI developers has ranged from quietly acrimonious to openly hostile in the past, the cold war is over (although, some highly vocal pockets of resistance remain), a period of *détente* is ending, and a *glasnost* has begun, as both sides see the benefits of working together. The number of "tweeners"—networking professionals who work on standards and development in both the OSI and the TCP/IP arenas—is growing, not because they think that it is important to cover all the political bases or because their positive self-image is enhanced by the broad-mindedness implicit in such an arrangement, but because the essential technical and organizational problems of networking (particularly internetworking) are the same everywhere and do not divide cleanly along party lines. The increased cooperation in areas of mutual concern—including interdomain (policy-based) routing protocols, OSI integration, and perhaps accredited standardization and government profiling of TCP/IP—will play an important role in the future of open systems networking.

The History of OSI Is Significant—Yet Largely Unknown   Having read several books about OSI prior to undertaking this project, the authors discovered that without the context of "having been there" to explain some of the seemingly irrational behavior of the OSI standards makers—and to translate the often impenetrable "standardese" of OSI— existing books either leave a false impression of OSI or fail to leave any impression at all, since they merely coalesce, condense, and regurgitate the OSI standards without separating what is important from what is not. The authors believe that one has a much better chance of understanding *how* something works if one knows how it got to be that way, if someone points out the issues that have been overblown, and if the unlikely scenarios are distinguished from the scenarios that are probable in real-world networks. The authors and contributors were present during the most significant periods of OSI standards development and remain active as architects of a future, multiprotocol Internet. They are in a much better position to sort the standards wheat from chaff than those who first encountered the issues only after the standards were published.

As Is the History of TCP/IP   To a large extent, the history of TCP/IP *is* the history of OSI. Those who are often perceived by the Internet community to be the "rational core" of OSI standards developers were, for the most part, weaned on TCP/IP: to the astonishment of some hardcore Internetters, they actually knew how to use and implement TCP/IP and its applications before they became involved in the development of OSI, but most important, they *respected TCP/IP* and appreciated the advantages of continued cross-fertilization between OSI and TCP/IP technology.

A Multiprotocol Global Internet Is Coming!   Open systems networking is the basis for the evolution of a truly global Internet. The significance of open systems networking cannot be understood by focusing attention on OSI or TCP/IP—or *any* "open" protocol architecture—in isolation. Only by examining both (eventually, all) of them in context can the history and likely future of internetworking be understood.

From these observations come the objectives of this book: make OSI intelligible, relate it to TCP/IP, and in the process, reveal the stories—the whys and wherefores—behind the standards. These objectives serve as the major differentiator between this and many other books that appear to cover some of the same material. *Open Systems Networking: TCP/IP and OSI* is not simply a reiteration or regurgitation of the OSI and TCP/IP standards, nor does it treat open systems networking as an adjunct to a book whose main purpose is to talk about data communications. Such reference material already exists and is not sufficient.

Several OSI-related books are *specialized*. Rather than examine OSI in a detailed manner from top to bottom (more often, bottom to top), they focus on a specific area of OSI: upper layers, lower layers, perhaps a particular OSI application such as the Message Handling System or the Directory. These are valuable but often can't serve as (nor do they pretend to be) a comprehensive primer. *Open Systems Networking: TCP/IP and OSI* attempts to present OSI and TCP/IP in a methodical, stepwise progression, beginning with basic architectural principles, the application of those principles to specific services and protocols, and the behavior of computer systems that operate the protocols and form open networks.

Open Systems Networking: TCP/IP and OSI further departs from the norm by adopting a "top-down," user-oriented approach. Electronic mail, for example, is discussed in the following contexts: What does it do? What does a network have to do to make it happen? How do these functions appear in OSI and TCP/IP (and why do they appear in that particular way)? A consequence of applying the "top-down" approach is that the text makes forward references (typically, toward more detailed explanations of what has been described at a conceptual level); a benefit is that readers deal first with aspects of open systems networking at a conceptual level (what something is) and later with the specific details of how something actually works.

Demystifying Open Systems

OSI and TCP/IP share concepts, even some culture, but they certainly do *not* share terminology! OSI and TCP/IP both suffer from "acronymania";[3] OSI, in particular, is far and away the most acronymaniacal technology yet inflicted on the world of networking. This book attempts to translate OSI (and TCP/IP) architecture and terminology from "ISO-ese" to "plain-speak." A major objective of *Open Systems Networking: TCP/IP and OSI* is to make it easier for readers to understand and apply basic networking concepts in the context of open systems. To some extent, the use of acronyms is unavoidable (as readers may already have noted). In this book, the use of acronyms is as much as possible abandoned in favor of more popular and accessible terminology; for example, the word *packet* or *frame* is preferred to the less intuitive OSI acronym *PDU* (which stands for "protocol data unit").

Equal Treatment

Open Systems Networking: TCP/IP and OSI compares and contrasts the OSI approach with the TCP/IP approach in what is intended to be an evenhanded and pragmatic fashion, taking sides on technical issues when appropriate but avoiding the political-party fervor with which the comparison is often fraught. For example, if the question "What does OSI's MHS add to message handling that TCP/IP's SMTP lacks?" is interpreted as biased in favor of OSI, the balance is eventually restored when the question "Why has SNMP, not CMIP, been so widely embraced by the industry?" is also posed and answered.

In some areas, the book may appear to be almost chaotically neutral, suggesting, for example, that TCP/IP's Simple Network Management Protocol might be used over OSI's connectionless transport protocol to manage OSI network resources or that the OSI Directory be used over TCP/IP to provide an array of information services. Although this might be interpreted as heresy (or at least disloyalty) by purists in the OSI and TCP/IP communities, the authors believe that it serves the user community much better than orthodoxy, since it demonstrates that open

3.   Acronymania \ ˈak-rə-ˌnim-ˈmā-nē-ə, -nyə \ *n*. [orig. Piscitello, D. 1991] madness over acronyms; also rage or eager desire for anything related to acronyms; insane or morbid craving for words formed from the initial letters of other words; mental disorder characterized by high, uncontrolled excitement over the creation of an endless stream of words formed from the initial letters of other words (Decidedly *not* Webster's . . .).

systems networking is about solving communications problems, not creating or complicating them.

Notwithstanding the goal of equal treatment, readers will find much more information in this book about OSI than about TCP/IP, for two reasons. The first is the extent to which the OSI architecture—the famous seven-layer model—has been adopted, even by its critics, as a way to *talk about* open systems networking, even when the subject is not OSI. The concepts and terminology introduced by the OSI reference model have in many cases become the standard *lingua franca* of network architecture, to such an extent that even a completely evenhanded treatment of OSI and another protocol suite is liable to sound like a treatise on OSI, with the other suite appearing to be short-shrifted. The authors know of no way, short of introducing yet a third "neutral" nomenclature, to avoid this and consequently have not tried to do so.

The second is the sheer volume of information that a truly complete presentation of the entirety of OSI and TCP/IP would represent, which could not possibly be contained within a single book such as this. In those cases in which it is simply not feasible to provide truly "equal treatment" to both the OSI and the TCP/IP variations of the same theme, the authors have elected to describe the OSI side in detail and to compare and contrast the corresponding TCP/IP component with the more detailed OSI description. This choice recognizes that a number of high-quality books describing TCP/IP are already widely available,[4] and that the technical specifications of the components of TCP/IP are not only available electronically on the Internet (at no cost beyond the network-access cost of retrieving them from one of the Internet document archives), but they are *much* easier to read and understand than their OSI counterparts. To successfully plow through the piles of OSI specifications (which must be purchased, at significant cost, from national standards organizations such as the American National Standards Institute without losing one's way simply requires more experienced guidance . . . and money! The authors can, at least, provide the former.

---

4.   Readers are encouraged to refer especially to Comer (1991), Stevens (1990), and Perlman (1992a).

Opinions Are Good!

The "value-neutral" approach adopted in many recent textbook-style treatments of OSI presents readers with the equivalent of an undifferentiated memory dump; by failing to distinguish between what is important and what isn't, these books serve the objective purpose of presenting the *facts* about OSI but make it very difficult for readers to *understand* it. A description of how each of the five OSI transport protocol classes works is a fine thing, but without knowing why there are five classes (why not just one? if more than one, why five?), and without being told that only two of the classes are ever used in practice, readers are not likely to come away with a very useful understanding of OSI transport services. The authors of *Open Systems Networking: TCP/IP and OSI* are in a position to make informed value judgments and to present the information in a format that leads to understanding rather than suffocation: like having an intelligent debugger, if you will, rather than a core dump.

Historical Asides and Authors' Insights

The historical and anecdotal observations made throughout the text are based on direct participation by the authors in the OSI and TCP/IP standards processes for the past 15 years, including participation in the Internet Engineering Task Force (IETF), the Internet Engineering Steering Group (IESG), and the Internet Architecture Board (IAB), as well as in many of the national and international standards committees. Many of the historical observations ("asides") concentrate on the standards process or the results of that process; by convention, they are italicized and proceeded in the text by the symbol $\boxed{\text{·AHA·}}$.

Readers familiar with *The Open Book*, by Dr. Marshall T. Rose, should not confuse these historical asides with the "soapboxes" used in Marshall's book. *The Open Book* is enlivened considerably by the use of soapboxes on which Marshall perches deliberately provocative, "not strictly objective" commentary on the material contained in the main text. Much of this commentary expresses Marshall's righteous indignation at the follies and pedantry of OSI and the OSI standardization process, claiming that since he wasn't there, he doesn't understand what really happened, but just *look* at the result! The net effect, of course, is to create and promote a pervasive negative impression about everything that carries the "OSI" label. (Some people, of course, believe that Marshall's negative impression of OSI is richly deserved . . .)

The purpose of the historical asides in *Open Systems Networking: TCP/IP and OSI* is not to use "pen up" observations to take sides in a contest between OSI and TCP/IP. The historical asides and authors' insights in this book do not rush to defend the OSI standards or the OSI standards-making process; in fact, they are often indictments of bad decisions that led to bad standards, since they reveal *how* the decisions were made, exposing the inherent flaws in applying a committee consensus process to the development of technology. (In some cases, of course, the authors themselves are wholly or partly to blame, since they *were* there and might have known better; those asides can be read as rueful self-criticism.) The asides and insights are also used to sort the good in OSI from the bad; often, criticism is accompanied by a recommended action—such as "Ignore this part of standard X," or "Implement only these functions of standard Y"—or a forecast of what will really matter in the future. It is worth noting that the asides and insights are not confined to OSI; the shortcomings and missteps of the "working code and rough consensus" process applied in the Internet community bring TCP/IP under fire as well. The authors have jostled the memories of several of the original DARPA researchers to add an historical perspective of TCP/IP as well.

Who Should Read This Book?

For networking neophytes, this book may serve as both a primer and a road map; it answers questions such as "How does it work?," "What is relevant and what is not?," and perhaps most important, "Why did they choose to do it this way?" For experienced networking professionals, especially those familiar with TCP/IP, this book demystifies OSI and in the process illustrates both its strengths and its weaknesses. For those involved in network planning and administration, especially in environments in which TCP/IP and OSI coexistence, transition, and migration are the buzzwords *du jour*, this book provides a basis for understanding not only how OSI and TCP/IP work but how they might peacefully and productively coexist in complex, multiprotocol internets, today and tomorrow.

Open Systems Networking: TCP/IP and OSI does not give an exhaustive explanation of the details of every protocol or service. The goal of this book is not to serve as the definitive "reader's companion" for every open systems networking standard but to present and answer the "why" and "how" questions of building open networks. The book therefore includes only as much protocol detail as is necessary to facilitate understanding; no one should expect to use it as a protocol implementation manual. However, the book should enable the system designer to understand the way in which OSI and TCP/IP systems work and the way in which a specific set of concepts and terminology is used to define the protocols. It should also assist anyone who has a fundamental understanding of data communications and networking to understand and apply the principles and protocols of OSI and TCP/IP to satisfy real-world computer-networking requirements.

Contributors

The authors are indebted to Lisa Phifer, Deirdre Kostick, Paul Francis (*née* Tsuchiya), and Yakov Rekhter, who made substantial contributions to the chapters on network management and routing. Lisa also contributed to both the text and the historical insights provided in the chapters on the OSI upper layers and the application service elements. It is no exaggeration to say that her timely and diligent review greatly improved the quality of this book.

Acknowledgments

No project of this magnitude can succeed without the assistance of friends and family. Radia Perlman deserves credit for insisting that we write this book and then alternately encouraging and chiding us until we had. Among our friends in the Internet community, we wish to thank Stephen Crocker, Jon Postel, and Vinton Cerf for their technical assistance and the contribution of anecdotal information on TCP/IP. Among the "tweeners," our thanks go to Ross Callon, John Burruss, Christine Hemrick, Kaj Tesink, Nancy Hall, Rob Hagens, Steve Hardcastle-Kille, Susan Hares, Mark Knopper, Hans-Werner Braun, Erik Huizer, and David Katz. We also wish to acknowledge our colleagues (past and present)—Jeff Rosenberg, Jim Hopkins, Gary Summers, Scott Stein, Tracy Cox, Larry Lang, Phil Karn, Ted Brunner, Kathy So, James Davin, Dave Oran, Chuck Wade, John Day, Bud Emmons, and Al Grimstead—who throughout our careers offered daily challenges and valuable insights, and enthusiastically supported our efforts. John Burruss, Radia Perlman, and Phil Almquist in particular deserve mention for having provided excellent technical reviews of the original manuscript.

We would certainly be remiss if we did not mention both the OSI and Internet communities as well; for more than 15 years, they have provided an immensely fertile testing ground for the formulation of networking ideas, and although the road has been somewhat rocky, we feel privileged to be a part of the process of developing networking technology.

Our wives and children demonstrated enormous patience and understanding, and offered support and encouragement that was simply remarkable. It will be difficult to repay the lost weekends and evenings, but a public acknowledgment of how much we love and appreciate them seems like a good start.

Finally, we'd like to thank Mark Taranto, who pounded the Byzantine principles of real analysis and metric space into Dave's head; he may not have contributed specifically to this project, but it's a good bet that Dave wouldn't be writing a book with Lyman without having completed his undergraduate degree in mathematics.

PART ONE

INTRODUCTION TO OPEN SYSTEMS

1

INTRODUCTION

Books that discuss computer communications invariably begin by drawing analogies between computer networking and earlier, landmark inventions that have had a profound impact upon, perhaps even "revolutionized," society. Andrew S. Tanenbaum compares the impact of computer networks to the mechanical systems accompanying the Industrial Revolution, while Douglas E. Comer likens digital communications networks to the great railroads of the nineteenth century. But neither the Industrial Revolution nor the railroad has made as great an impact on human civilization as "the marriage of the engineering of telecommunications to that of the computer industry" (Martin 1976, 2). Why? No previous technology has advanced quite so rapidly and with such unbounded horizons as the computer, and no previous technology has achieved anything close to the ubiquity of the modern telecommunications system.

James Martin accurately predicted that through this union, the telecommunications system would aid distributed processing, and the computer would facilitate telephony switching. The actual chronology of events in fact exceeded Martin's expectations, for shortly after his speculation in the mid-1970s, information processing was delivered to the desktop. A decade marked by increased computer speed, memory, and storage, accompanied by a proliferation of useful and distributed applications, has fundamentally changed the way in which much of society works and interacts: we now send mail, do our banking, and exchange documents electronically, from our business places and our homes. This change in human behavior has affected the telecommunications system more profoundly than Martin forecast when he suggested that computers would merely facilitate switching. It adds a level of sophistication to the equipment attached to the telephone network that could never have been achieved by a telephone handset with a 12-digit keypad. In addition to placing a voice call to conduct business, we increasingly seek to exchange images—files of immense size—and to animate them in the process, and we expect do so in *milliseconds*. In many respects, information has become as important a commodity to switch as voice. The traditional voice and data networks will undergo profound changes in the next decade, as both seek to integrate the services of the other.

Therein lies a problem with the marriage. As in the Houses of Montague and Capulet, the parents of voice and data don't get along. Rarely have computer and communications providers shared a common set of beliefs and purposes. In the House of Telephony, data switching has historically been viewed as a second-tier service, incapable of ever achieving the "cash-cow" status of voice, and therefore much less important to the "bottom line." In the House of Data, telephony providers have been criticized as being intolerably slow to respond to the increasing demand for bandwidth, willing only to focus on "dataphony,"[1] and the data services offered by "common carriers" have historically been much less powerful and flexible than on-premises, local area networking alternatives.

Never have these differences of culture and philosophy been more obvious than during the development of Open Systems Interconnection, during which the debates between the Houses of Voice and Data were often more religious and political than technical.[2] This is perhaps because, by the mid-1970s, the networking of computers had begun to look like a lucrative new market opportunity rather than an amusing academic toy. The notion of open systems networking became *interesting* to both the voice and the data worlds at nearly the same time, for profit's sake and no other; and both the House of Data and the House of Voice wanted to secure as big a slice of the new pie as possible.

But what exactly is "open systems networking"? There are, of course, many ways to answer this question. The answer certainly does not lie strictly within the reference model for Open Systems Interconnection (ISO 7498, 1984), because architectures and protocols other than OSI

---

1.   *Dataphony* is a term coined by Christine Hemrick, presently with Cisco Systems, to distinguish low-bandwidth, terminal-to-mainframe networking applications from high-bandwidth, distributed-processing applications—i.e., *real data networking*.

2.   OSI wasn't the first pretext for these debates. The initial experience of the conflict for one of the authors can be traced back to the first time a Bell Telephone employee marked the area surrounding a data access arrangement in a computer laboratory at a Burroughs development facility with red tape, plopped down a Bell modem and telephone, and said "Don't touch!" Shortly thereafter, it was necessary to move the entire wall without disturbing the tape. But OSI has certainly been the most visible and highly publicized example.

are widely acknowledged as bases for open systems networking. The publication of the OSI reference model is noteworthy primarily because it represents an internationally recognized effort at codifying what constitutes "openness." What is recorded in the OSI reference model as the definition of an open system is in fact far less significant than the events that motivated—in the minds of some, provoked—an international interest in open systems networking.

Even at this late stage in the evolution of open systems networking, *any* attempt at defining *open systems* is highly subjective. For the purposes of this book, however, *open systems networking* implies or suggests the following: multivendor, interoperable hardware and software systems, based on internationally recognized and publicly available documentation ("standards"), which can be acquired "off the shelf" (as a standard rather than special-order product).

Why is everyone so excited about open systems? Some are excited because the concept represents "safe networking": protection from proprietary networking solutions that lock users into dependence on the products and services of a single vendor (and thereby place users at the mercy of that vendor, in both an economic and a product- or feature-availability sense). Especially among government agencies that have spent millions of dollars (or the equivalent) on custom networking equipment, it is widely perceived that the enhanced interoperability brought about by openness and standards leads to a (desirable) highly competitive market, which will greatly reduce the cost of networking. Others have an altogether different concern: single-vendor solutions are not inherently evil, but information technology and distributed processing today span so many markets that no single vendor provides hardware and software solutions for every conceivable information technology application, and by necessity, companies with diverse needs *must* purchase information technology products from many vendors. Finally, some believe that open systems networking is the only way to achieve the service ubiquity of telephony for data.

Open systems networking and its associated standardization processes are an enormous undertaking that encompasses far more than establishing guidelines for data communications and information technology. Open systems standards have widely varying political and economic ramifications for users, equipment manufacturers, and network providers. For the network consumer, two very desirable effects of open systems standardization are to enhance interoperability and to foster a highly competitive market. For the vendor of a product line that interconnects via a proprietary networking technology, however, open systems standardization represents yet another opportunity for competitors to pry customers away from the hard-won market share that it has nurtured on that proprietary networking solution; the competitors, of course, view this as a major benefit. Finally, for the communications carriers in certain countries, standards are quite literally *enforceable laws* that govern the way in which public network resources may be used; standards offer them the means to extend their control over voice and postal services to data.

Today's open systems have different origins as well. OSI was, from the beginning, intended to be *the* open systems networking solution. TCP/IP[3] was not originally designed for such a lofty purpose; on the contrary, it began as a private networking experiment conducted within the U.S. computer science research community and supported by the Department of Defense Advanced Research Projects Agency (ARPA), with a potential for military applications. The ARPANET may have been the first operational packet-switching network, but few of those who designed and installed the original four-node network[4] in the fall of 1969 anticipated that in just over two decades, from such a humble beginning, a global Internet of over 1.5 million computers and an estimated 5 million users would evolve. And yet practically everything we know about packet switching, and a good deal of what we know about distributed processing, has been affected by the research and experimentation associated with the Internet. (A complete description of the history of TCP/IP is inappropriate here; for our purposes, it is sufficient to identify the landmark achievements in the history of TCP/IP [see Table 1.1].)

TCP/IP evolved into an open systems networking alternative largely due to the inability of the OSI standards developers to deliver the promised goods in a timely fashion, for the standards kept coming, and more were promised, but interoperable OSI implementations were hard to find. By 1984, so much hype had preceded the delivery of actual OSI-

---

3.   The term *TCP/IP* is commonly used to refer either specifically to the transmission control protocol (TCP) and internet protocol (IP) or generally to the entire suite of protocols that have been developed by the Internet community to operate in conjunction with TCP and IP in the capital-*I* Internet (the global interconnection of networks running the TCP/IP protocols) and in individual enterprise-specific "internets."

4.   The four original sites were the University of California at Los Angeles (UCLA), the Stanford Research Institute (SRI), the University of California at Santa Barbara (UCSB), and the University of Utah. According to Stephen Crocker, one of the graduate students who connected the first host—a SIGMA VII—to the first ARPANET interface message processor (IMP) at UCLA, "An RFP was released in the summer of '68, and Bolt Beranek and Newman (BBN) won. The contract called for delivery of a four node network in fall '69 with 50 (not 56) kilobit trunks. IMP 1 was delivered to UCLA prior to its scheduled delivery date of 9/1/69. SRI, UCSB, and Utah followed at monthly intervals" (Stephen D. Crocker, personal correspondence, December 1991).

TABLE 1.1   Landmarks in the History of TCP/IP

1969	RFC 1*	Network-control program (NCP) development First Internet RFC ("Host Software") IMP 1 delivered to UCLA
1971	RFC 114	First FTP, Telnet
1972	RFC 318	Telnet
1973	RFC 475	FTP† and (first) network mail system TCP development begins at DARPA
1974	RFC 675	First TCP implementations: SRI, BBN, UCLA
1979		Ethernet is born
1981	RFCs 786, 788 RFCs 791, 793	First mail-transfer protocol, first SMTP TCP and IP become Internet standards
1982	RFC 821	SMTP Internet standard (9/80: RFC 772)
1983	RFCs 882, 883 MIL-STD-1777 RFC 854	Domain Names U.S. DOD military standard for TCP Telnet Internet standard (6/80: RFC 764)
1985	RFC 959	FTP Internet standard (7/72: RFC 354)
1990	RFC 1157	SNMP Internet standard (8/88: RFC 1067)

* The network control program was completed and working prior to the introduction of the request for comments (RFC) document series. According to Jon Postel, who has been the editor of the RFC series since its inception, it was agreed at that time that the RFC series would include only "working documents" and that the ARPANET Network Information Center (NIC) would begin a standards series with NCP; somewhere along the line, NCP disappeared from the documentation. It is rumored that copies still exist in Stephen Crocker's documentation archives.
† According to Jon Postel, the origins of what we know as Internet mail are found in the "mail" command in this FTP specification.

compliant equipment, and so few interoperable products existed, that industry observers began to speak of it as a paper tiger. Proprietary networking solutions continued to dominate the market, and although manufacturers' marketing representatives talked a great deal about "conforming to the OSI reference model," their development groups managed to deliver only token products. The need for genuine open systems remained unfilled and was growing. Gradually, TCP/IP ate OSI's mideighties lunch, abetted in no small part by Dan Lynch's highly successful TCP/IP Implementers' Workshops, which evolved into the even more successful Interoperability Conferences and Exhibitions, sponsored by Interop, Inc. The first Implementers' Workshop was held in Monterey, California, in August 1986; the first Interop conference was held in Monterey, in March 1987, and by 1992, the attendance at the now semiannual Interop exceeded 50,000. Interop allowed TCP/IP vendors to demonstrate real products operating in a multivendor environment on real networks, while the OSI community endlessly debated the arcane merits of formal description techniques, conformance statements, and protocol implementation conformance statements.

Interop was just one of many enabling vehicles for the success of TCP/IP; the foremost was and remains the Internet infrastructure—the actual *Internet*, consisting of real networks and real systems—which facilitates experimentation and research on a global scale.[5] A grass-roots level of cooperation permeates the Internet, linking academics, network providers, and even the fiercest of competitors in the manufacturing sector: egos and company biases are frequently set aside to bring useful new technology into the Internet. This is the essence of what makes TCP/IP successful today.

Still, OSI keeps coming. The promise is quietly, but inexorably, becoming a reality. All of the critical-path protocol standards have been completed, and OSI X.400 message handling and X.500 directory applications are today operated over both pure-OSI stacks and hybrid stacks in enterprise networks and across the Internet. Real OSI products are now demonstrated alongside TCP/IP products at Interop as the industry attempts to shape the multiprotocol morass of today into the multiprotocol Internet of tomorrow.

Why has OSI failed to meet expectations? Unfortunately, OSI had to be all things to all people. It had to accommodate the needs of the teletex and videotex services; integrated services digital network (ISDN); and the government agencies and postal, telephone, and telegraph (PTT)

---

5.   According to Larry Landweber, who keeps track of Internet connectivity throughout the world, 109 countries (as of summer 1992) have some sort of connectivity to the Internet through IP, BITNET, UUCP, OSI, or FIDONET links; of these, 46 countries have direct IP connectivity (Landweber 1992).

agencies of 20 or 30 countries. Practically every innovation that came along in the early stages of OSI development had to be included, and this generous policy of inclusion played to the detriment of OSI, complicating it in some cases beyond reason, creating uncertainties among product planners, and most important, sapping valuable expertise that should have been devoted to implementing and testing it.

Despite these handicaps, OSI has managed to bring a variety of valuable new services to data networking: "white pages" directory services, a powerful network-programming language, multimedia messaging, and routing and addressing mechanisms that permit internets (and potentially, the Internet) to be scaled up to very large size. These may soon be appreciated as landmark achievements (see Table 1.2).

Open systems networking today is about OSI *and* TCP/IP, and perhaps other protocol stacks as well. Migration, evolution, and transition from TCP/IP to OSI—marching orders from the 1980s—are now widely regarded as irrelevant strategies; the operative words for the 1990s (and beyond) are *coexistence* and *integration*. The Internet is experimenting with OSI directory and message handling applications because they *add value*. Gateways are now provided between OSI and TCP/IP mail applications because they *serve the community*. OSI transport services provided by TCP and IP support OSI applications where OSI transport protocols have yet to be deployed, and transport service bridges are used where necessary because *it is a practical thing to do*. Backbone and regional networks switch OSI and TCP/IP datagrams, host implementations are becoming "dual-stack," and SNMP is run over OSI because *it all works*. In the Internet, conformance takes a back seat to interoperability, and OSI will be far more useful as part of the Internet than it has ever been on its own.

In *Open Systems Networking: TCP/IP and OSI*, the authors hope to provide an understanding of how the components of TCP/IP and OSI work, how they are similar and how they differ, how they came to be what they are today, and how they might play together in the future. There is much cause for optimism and enthusiasm, and the authors hope to impart some of this to the readers.

Organization of This Book

The remainder of Part One, "Introduction to Open Systems," describes the OSI and TCP/IP standards processes (and their key participants), and establishes the convention of examining OSI and TCP/IP in a fea-

TABLE 1.2   **Landmarks in the History of OSI**

1977		published articles on OSI RM
1978	CCITT X.200	First OSI standards meeting (TC 97/SC 16) First CCITT OSI RM (Grey Book)
1980	CCITT T series	Teletex (telematic services)
1983		First NIST OSI workshop
1984	ISO 7498 X.400 series	OSI reference model Message handling (MHS)
1987	ISO 8326/8327	Session service and protocol
1988	ISO 8571 X.500 series ISO 8822/8823 ISO 8072/8073 ISO 8473/9542 FIPS 146	File transfer (FTAM) The directory (ISO 9594) Presentation service and protocol Transport service and protocol Internetwork protocol and routing First release of U.S. GOSIP (8/88)
1990	ISO 9595/9596	Management service and protocol

Note: The dates shown in the left-hand column are the years in which the ISO Central Secretariat formally published the corresponding OSI standards. In many cases, the final version of a standard was widely available many years earlier (as an approved draft international standard; see Chapter 2).

ture-by-feature, side-by-side manner.

Part Two, "Open Network Architectures," examines the architectural models for TCP/IP and OSI. OSI promulgates a formal (and formidable) reference model; a single, readily identifiable "reference model" description of the TCP/IP architecture does not exist, so the authors compare the collection of TCP/IP architectural "folklore" to the more formal specification of the OSI reference model. Key concepts such as layering, services, and protocols are introduced, and the descriptive techniques used in OSI standards—the service model, state machines, and time-sequence diagrams—are covered here as well. OSI's data-definition and network-programming language, abstract syntax notation one, is described here, as are names and addresses and the roles they play in open systems networking.

An architectural characteristic of open systems networks (as opposed to proprietary networks) is the assumption of a set of generic, or generally available, applications that become building blocks (tools) for creating more complex distributed systems. In OSI, these are called *application service elements*; in TCP/IP, simply "applications." OSI and TCP/IP differ somewhat in the way in which applications are constructed. The differences between OSI and TCP/IP application "service" architectures are described in Part Three, "Upper Layers." Three "daily-use" application services that are common to TCP/IP and OSI—electronic mail, directories/information services, and network management—are presented here. An overview of the basic requirements of applications—synchronization, token control, connection management, activity management, remote operations, and reliable transfer—are introduced at a conceptual level here as well, so that readers have a general understanding of these capabilities to which they can refer when the specific mechanisms in the layers that provide these capabilities (presentation and session) are discussed later in the book.

Part Four, "Middle Layers," examines how end-to-end data transport, internetworking, and routing are performed in OSI and TCP/IP. The similarities and differences that exist between OSI and TCP/IP transport services, for example, are presented at a "bit level" of detail. The roots and history of the "connections versus datagrams" debate (which persists even today within the OSI community) are exposed here as well. Rather than include an exhaustive recapitulation of readily available information about existing point-to-point link and LAN technologies at the data-link layer, *Open Systems Networking: TCP/IP and OSI* focuses on *emerging digital technologies* that have been touted as broadband[6] platforms for advanced distributed applications: frame relay, FDDI, SMDS, and broadband ISDN.

Part Five, "The Future of Open Systems Networking," attempts a Hegelian *synthesis* of TCP/IP (*thesis*) and OSI (*antithesis*) by reviewing the guidelines for, and politics of, building a multiprotocol Internet. This part describes the status of the Internet activities that are directed at expanding the internetworking platform of the Internet to sustain its remarkable growth and examines issues related to evolving the Internet from its current TCP/IP core to a system that supports internetworking based on OSI, XNS/PX, and AppleTalk® as well.

---

6.   With apologies to electrical engineers—in particular, those who are familiar with the notion of broadband as it is applied in the world of local area networks—the term *broadband* is used here in the telephony sense of the word; i.e., transmission rates in excess of 1 megabit per second.

2 OPEN SYSTEMS STANDARDS

Both OSI and TCP/IP are guided by standards. The communities who develop standards for OSI and TCP/IP share some common practices. For example, both advance technology through a committee and consensus process using some form of parliamentary procedure. Both have a hierarchical infrastructure to coordinate work and enforce written (and unwritten) rules of conduct. Participation in both is international.

In other respects, these communities differ substantially, especially with respect to image and culture. To fully appreciate the differences, one must first understand the composition, scope, purpose, and practices of each community.

OSI Standards

In the late 1970s and early 1980s, the first OSI standards were developed under Technical Committee 97 (TC 97), Information Processing, of the International Organization for Standardization (ISO).

·AHA· *Why the acronym for* International Organization for Standardization *should be ISO, rather than IOS, is a mystery even to standards-committee insiders. The French version of the organization's name is* Organisation Internationale de Normalisation, *so the most common explanation for a mismatch between the name of an international standards organization and its acronym doesn't apply in this case. The best explanation the authors have heard is an analogy to the* Go Children Slow *traffic-sign con-*

vention: the most important word takes the place of honor (and in the case of traffic signs, of motorists' attention) in the middle.

As is the case with all ISO standards committees, the membership of TC 97 was composed of the national standards bodies of those countries that decided to participate: ANSI (the American National Standards Institute), for example, represented the United States; BSI (the British Standards Institute) represented the United Kingdom; AFNOR (the Association Française du Normalisation) represented France; and DIN (the Deutsches Institut für Normung) represented Germany. Within TC 97, which represented primarily the interests of computer manufacturers and users, Subcommittee 16 (TC 97/SC 16) was created for the express purpose of working on the new area of open systems interconnection.

Within Subcommittee 16, the OSI reference model and general architecture issues were studied in Working Group 1 (TC 97/SC 16/WG 1), and "layer-specific" activities were directed to the following WGs: transport and session to WG 6, application and presentation to WG 5, and sometime later, management of OSI systems to WG 4. Although most of OSI was brand new (and could therefore be assigned at will to the brand-new Subcommittee 16), its scope also encompassed aspects of telecommunications and data transmission for which standards work was already well under way. Responsibility for developing OSI-related standards for the network, data link, and physical layers were handed over to the existing Subcommittee 6 (Data Communications): physical interfaces to WG 3, data link layer to WG 1, and network layer to WG 2. This original committee structure for the development of OSI standards is illustrated in Table 2.1.

At the time, ISO TC 97/SC 6 and Study Group VII (SG VII) of the International Telegraph and Telephone Consultative Committee (CCITT)[1] worked closely on the development of public packet-switching standards (such as X.25, which is by far the best known). CCITT is a United Nations treaty organization and is composed primarily of telecommunication providers.[2] CCITT SG VII had begun work on a message handling service (which would eventually become the X.400-series rec-

---

1.   In this case, the acronym makes sense even though it does not correspond to the English-language representation of the name: *CCITT* expands to the French *Comité Consultatif International Télégraphique et Téléphonique*. The name of this group changed to *International Telecommunications Union-Telecommunications Standardization Sector* in March 1993, whereupon CCITT was officially superseded by the acronym ITU-TS; throughout this book, however, we use the more familiar CCITT nomenclature.

2.   Although there is nothing in the charter of either organization that says so, ISO has historically focused on the priorities of computer equipment manufacturers and users (the

TABLE 2.1   Original ISO OSI Standards Committees

Subcommittee	Working Group	Responsibility
16	1	OSI architecture
16	4	Management
16	5	Application,presentation
16	6	Session,transport
6	2	Network
6	1	Data link
6	3	Physical

ommendations), and ISO and CCITT agreed to coordinate their efforts to develop a single international reference model for Open Systems Interconnection.

Following an initial "feeling-out" period, these two standards bodies concluded that, as a parallel effort to the ISO standards for OSI, the CCITT would produce a corresponding series (the X.200 series) of CCITT recommendations. By 1984, the "joint" standards shown in Table 2.2 would be in place.

Over the years, an inordinate amount of time and energy would be devoted to ensuring that the contents, even the wording, of the two sets of what can be called "core OSI standards" would be identical. (It should be noted that the core set of standards expanded nearly exponentially from this modest beginning. The "References" list provides a cross reference of all ISO and OSI standards to their CCITT counterparts.)

Since 1984, the players, the process, and the number of OSI-related standards have grown, and the committee infrastructure itself has changed. ISO now carries out information technology standardization, including all of the work labeled "OSI," jointly with the International Electrotechnical

---

"host people"), whereas CCITT has focused on the priorities of the "common carrier" organizations (which, in many countries, are government-owned and -operated postal, telephone, and telegraph agencies) such as, in the United States, AT&T, Sprint, MCI, and theregional telephone operating companies. These two perspectives on how data networking should be organized are vastly different, as will be seen in later chapters.

TABLE 2.2   Cross-Reference of Initial ISO/CCITT OSI Standards

OSI Standard	ISO Standard Number	CCITT Recommendation
Reference model	ISO 7498	X.200
Service conventions	ISO TR 8509	X.210
Network service definition	ISO 8348	X.213
Transport service definition	ISO 8072	X.214
Session service definition	ISO 8326	X.215
Transport protocol	ISO 8073	X.224
Session protocol	ISO 8327	X.225

Note: The standards depicted here are those contained in the 1984 CCITT Red Book, Volume VIII, Fascicle VIII.5. Many other standards that are OSI related were jointly developed; notably, X.25/ISO 8208 at the network layer, as well as data link and physical layer standards too numerous to mention here.

Commission (IEC) in Joint Technical Committee 1 (ISO/IEC JTC 1), which has replaced TC 97. ISO/IEC still cooperates with CCITT. The TC 97 Subcommittee 16 has been replaced by Subcommittee 21 (Information Retrieval, Transfer, and Management for Open Systems Interconnection), and Subcommittee 6 has been renamed Telecommunications and Information Exchange between Systems. Typically, the participants in CCITT officially, the governments of countries that are signatories to the United Nations treaty that established the International Telecommunications Union ITU) and ISO/IEC "national bodies" have their own national committees, which submit national positions and contributions to the international standardization process represented by CCITT and ISO/IEC. In the United States, ANSI delegates the responsibility for actually producing standards to accredited standards committees (ASCs): Accredited Standards Committee X3 (Information Technology), for example, has responsibilities within the United States that are roughly equivalent to those of Joint Technical Committee 1, and within X3, X3T5 (OSI) and X3S3 (Data Communications) feed into SC 21 and SC 6, respectively. The Electronic Industries Association (EIA), Accredited Standards Committee T1 (Telecommunications), and the Institute of Electrical and Electronics Engineers (IEEE) also contribute to OSI standardization.

The OSI Standards Process

ISO OSI standards are initially introduced or created in committee as *working documents* that contribute to an existing *work item*. (In some cases, working drafts instigate new work items.) After some number of cycles of review, discussion, debate, and revision, working drafts are advanced through a committee vote to the status of *committee draft* (CD).[3] Committee drafts typically have a 60-day ballot period that offers national bodies the opportunity to review the material within their respective national committees. If a CD ballot fails, the document is revised according to comments submitted by members. (Loosely stated, the rules are as follows: a national body can't say "no" without providing comments that, if accepted, would enable that national body to change its ballot to a "yes"; i.e., in a CD ballot response, a national body can't really say, "This is a bad idea" [it happens, but with no effect]; if a national body really hates an idea, it should vote "no" on the original new work item ballot.) When a CD ballot is approved—i.e., a document is considered mature and stable—the CD is balloted as a *draft international standard* (DIS). Usually, although not always, a DIS represents a "substantially complete and accurate" specification, and folks are encouraged to implement it. A DIS ballot lasts six months, and in an ideal world, practical implementation experience *could* be obtained, although this has not historically been the case.

⬛ ·AHA· *There is a cautionary statement on a draft international standard that indicates that it may change. This has the unfortunate but practical effect among many organizations of inhibiting serious development until the document has become an international standard—unfortunate because it is at this very stage that the most serious implementation and testing should take place, so that what eventually becomes an International Standard is, in fact, implementable and highly likely to be useful.*

If a DIS ballot succeeds, the editor of the specification is assigned the responsibility of cleaning up the document and forwarding it to the ISO Central Secretariat in Geneva for processing as an *international standard*. The process is illustrated in Figure 2.1.

Of course, if one asked a hard-core Internetter, the perception of the process might be described more cynically, as is suggested in Figure 2.2.

CCITT operates somewhat differently. During a four-year *study period*, CCITT addresses new work items and performs revisions to recommendations made during the previous study period. At the end of the

---

3.   This step in the ISO standards process was, until a few years ago, called the "draft proposal" (DP) stage.

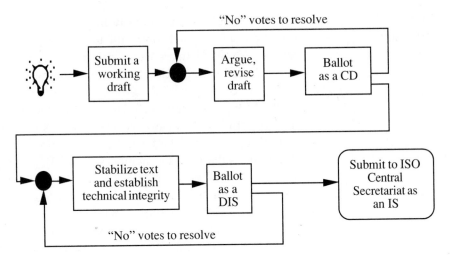

FIGURE 2.1   ISO OSI Standards Process

study period, a plenary assembly is held, during which CCITT *considers* (in the terminology that is common to all CCITT recommendations) specifications and, after careful consideration, grandly and *unanimously declares its view* that a specification benefits humanity (at least, that part of humanity that is involved in telecommunications) and directs editors to submit approved recommendations for publication in a series of books, fascicles, and volumes. Before the close of the plenary assembly,

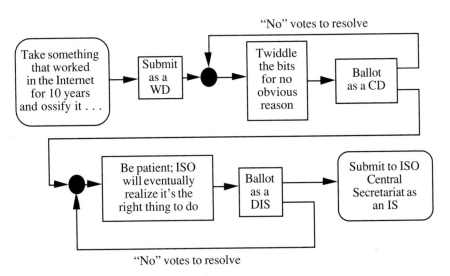

FIGURE 2.2   Internetters' View of ISO Standards Process

CCITT selects a pretty color for the entire series of books: thus far, primary (yellow in 1980, red in 1984, blue in 1988) and secondary (orange in 1976) colors have been selected. The 1992 recommendations will be published (sometime in 1993) in the White Books.

Beyond Base Standards: Profiles, Implementers' Agreements, and Conformance Testing

OSI standards offer *choices* in places where choices aren't always best for guaranteeing the interoperability of different implementations—which is presumably the purpose of having open systems in the first place. Shortly after it became evident that some of the choices in the OSI "stack" would result in serious noninteroperability, *profile groups* were established to whittle down the number of implementation possibilities from a frighteningly large number of combinations to a manageable few.

Profiles are combinations of protocol and service standards with (almost) all options either prescribed or proscribed. There are:

- *International standardized profiles (ISPs):* ISO Technical Report 10000 defines the framework and taxonomy of profiles for internationally recognized (and recommended) stacks.
- *Functional standards:* The European Committee for Standardization/European Committee for Electrotechnical Standardization (CEN/CENELEC) develops profiles for the European Economic Community (EEC).
- *Nationally standardized profiles:* Government (e.g., U.S., U.K.) OSI profiles (GOSIPs) identify nationally recommended stacks (U.S. GOSIP is illustrated in Figure 2.3).
- *Commercially standardized profiles:* Forums and consortia such as the OSI Network Management Forum and the North American Directory Association (NADA) identify stacks, services, and features for specific application services.

The problem with profile groups, and the entire ISP standards process, is that they remain corrupted by the same political maneuvering that gave us too many standards and choices in the first place. Rather than making the hard choices—i.e., defining one, mandatory OSI stack—they continue to permit many to coexist; seriously, now, is having four really that much better than having nine?

OSI implementation advances almost in spite of all this activity, although the result of the political in-fighting is that OSI offers islands—continents, really—of interoperability and must endure an embarrassing and seemingly endless stream of carping and abuse, even as it struggles to clean up its act. The National Institute of Standards and Technology (NIST) OSI Implementers' Workshop (OIW) and the European (EWOS)

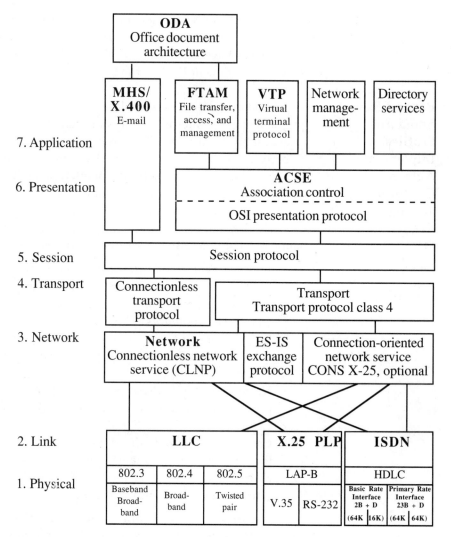

FIGURE 2.3   U.S. GOSIP (Version 2)

and Asian (AOWS) OSI workshops provide forums in which the base OSI standards are augmented by precise specification of the details that make for efficient and interoperable implementations and offer networks such as OSINET to allow vendors to test OSI equipment in a multivendor environment. The implementers' agreements that are produced by these forums are the raw material of the international standardized profile approval process.

Finally, there are organizations that define and provide *conformance testing,* a process in which vendors demonstrate compliance to an OSI profile and completeness of implementation against a "black-box" implementation. Organizations like the Corporation for Open Systems (COS) and the Standards Promotion and Applications Group (SPAG), although not strictly the analogues of Underwriters' Laboratory, provide such services.

Internet Standards

The development of standards for the Internet traces its ancestry to a research advisory group established by DARPA in 1980, the Internet Configuration Control Board (ICCB). For a time, the ICCB controlled all aspects of the development of the DARPA protocols. In 1983, DARPA restructured the ICCB and formed a central administrative committee called the Internet Activities Board (IAB). The IAB coordinated the design, engineering, and daily operational aspects of the Internet, which remains formally described as "a loosely-organized international collaboration of autonomous, interconnected networks, [that] supports host-to-host communication through voluntary adherence to open protocols and procedures defined by Internet Standards (RFC 1310,2)." In 1986, the IAB delegated responsibilities for the actual development of Internet standards to the Internet Engineering Task Force (IETF) and responsibilities for longer-term (hard-core) research to the Internet Research Task Force (IRTF) (see Figure 2.4). Until recently, the IAB had the final say in all Internet standards and research activities. With the formation of the Internet Society in 1992, the Internet Activities Board became the Internet Architecture Board and continued its role as a central coordinating body for Internet activities. The IAB now reports to the Internet Society board of trustees and supervises the Internet standards and research infrastructure. The composition of this infrastructure, and its relationship to other Internet Society activities, may be seen in Figure 2.5.

Like other standards bodies, the IETF is itself made up of working groups, which are composed of engineers and scientists from the academic, computer, and telecommunications communities. The working groups in the IETF are more fluid in nature than most standards bodies and tend to focus on one subject—perhaps a very specific one, such as extensions to a protocol, managed objects for a specific transmission facility, or a single routing protocol—and may meet, complete their work, and disband in less than a year. This is quite a contrast to the durability and longevity of, say, an ANSI-accredited working group such as X3S3.3, which has existed virtually forever and, after nearly 15

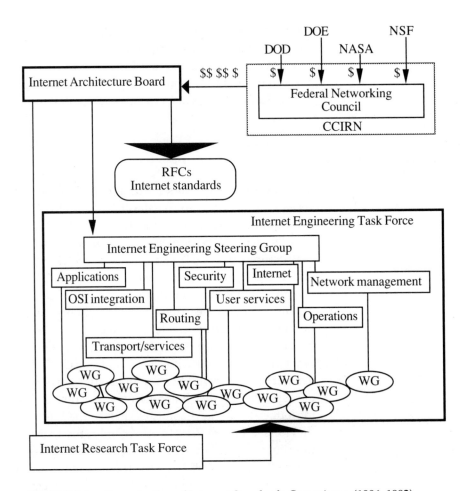

FIGURE 2.4   Organization of Internet Standards Committees (1986–1992)

years, continues to have responsibilities for providing U.S. national positions and contributions covering every aspect of the OSI transport and
network layers. (To be sure, there are WGs in the IETF, such as the SNMP
WG, that have had long lifetimes; the point is that they do not exist in
perpetuity.)

IETF working group activities are organized into specific disci-
plines: applications, Internet, network management, operational requirements, routing, security, service applications, transport, user services,
and standards management. These *areas* of activity are supervised by
directors; the directors, together with the IETF chairperson, comprise a
review and advisory committee called the Internet Engineering Steering
Group (IESG). IESG now makes all final decisions regarding Internet

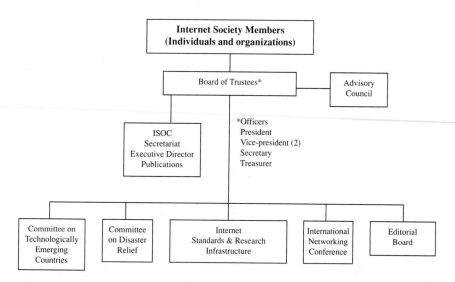

FIGURE 2.5   Internet Society Infrastructure

standardization. The Internet Standards Organization (not to be confused with ISO!) is depicted in Figure 2.6.

IETF "Friends and Family"

TCP/IP remains a predominantly U.S.-influenced protocol suite. However, with the growth in popularity of TCP/IP, and with the increased interest in expanding the Internet to accommodate OSI, international organizations have demonstrated a keen interest in contributing to the understanding, development, and deployment of internetworking technology. *RIPE* (Réseaux IP Européens) is a forum in Europe that nurtures expertise on IP networking. Working groups of *RARE* (Réseaux Associés pour la Recherche Européene) assist the IETF in integrating OSI application services and protocols into the Internet. RARE is loosely structured along IETF/IESG/IAB lines of control. Much of the message handling, directory, and internetworking protocol (CLNP) field experience obtained thus far on the Internet has been the result of cooperation between the IETF and RARE.

The Internet Standards Process

The core method of specification in the Internet is the *request for comment* (RFC). RFCs began as a means of documenting technical information shortly after DARPA started the ARPANET project in 1969. The RFC "process" begins when an individual or a party (including an external organization) makes a document publicly available for comment; such documents are called *internet drafts*. Internet drafts can be new ideas or

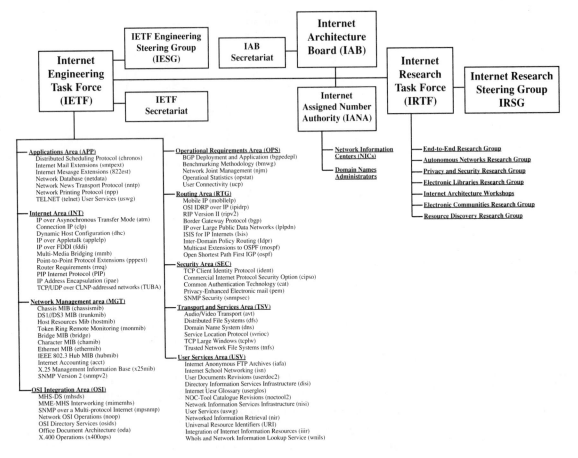

(Source: Internet Society)

FIGURE 2.6   Internet Standards and Research Infrastructure

existing RFCs that may require revision. They are made available to the public electronically as well as on paper. The technical or informational merit of internet drafts is discussed openly through regular IETF meetings and electronically through mailing lists. An internet draft that is expected to become an internet standard proceeds through a standards "maturity track" that is similar to the ISO standards track: loosely speaking, a "proposed standard (RFC)" corresponds to an ISO CD; a "draft standard (RFC)" corresponds to an ISO DIS; and a "standard (RFC)" corresponds to an ISO IS.

Strictly speaking, there is a significant difference in the process. As a rule, an internet draft may advance to a *proposed standard* once the

Internet community has reviewed and commented on the need for and stability of its contents. (In cases where a proposed standard may affect a core aspect of TCP/IP, implementation experience may well be required before an internet draft is advanced to a proposed standard.) Once an internet draft has been submitted to the IETF, recommended by the IESG, and approved for advancement by the IAB, it is forwarded to the Internet Assigned Numbers Authority (IANA), where it receives an RFC number.[4] A proposed standard must remain so for six months; during this time, experience must be acquired from at least two independent and interoperable implementations, and any results suggesting modifications must be addressed. If the proposed standard is demonstrated to be "mature and useful," it is advanced to a *draft standard*. A draft standard remains so for at least four months. Only after significant implementation and operational experience is acquired may a draft standard be advanced to a *standard* (STD). The process is illustrated in Figure 2.7.

Applicability Statements, Requirements RFCs

The IAB offers guidance to those who wish to produce interoperable implementations through *applicability statements*. There are three main classifications: if a technical specification is essential to achieving minimal conformance—for example, without IP, your implementation is pretty useless, and therefore IP is essential—the applicability statement that is applied is "required"; if the technical specification has been demonstrated to be truly useful and desirable, but not essential, the applicability statement that is applied is "recommended"; and if the technical specification is an enhancement bell or whistle, the applicability statement reads "elective." The requirements levels for all technical specifications are listed in the *IAB Official Protocol Standards* document, which is periodically issued as an RFC (e.g., RFC 1360).

Even in Internet standards, there are options and implementation considerations that are documented over a series of RFCs. Application of these RFCs contributes to the overall efficiency and performance of TCP/IP implementations. However, since RFCs, like ISO standards, are assigned numbers sequentially (chronologically), it is often difficult to know which RFCs are useful and which are not. To this end, a set of implementation requirements for host computers is documented (RFC 1122; RFC 1123 1989). These serve as a form of implementers' agreements for the Internet community. A similar set of requirements is to be developed for routers.

---

4.   Documents that are not expected to become or remain standards—those that are informational only, experimental, or have become obsolete and are hence "historical"—may have RFC numbers as well.

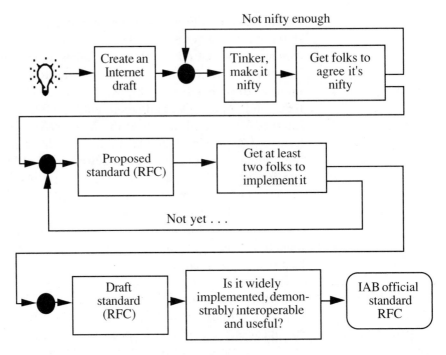

FIGURE 2.7   Internet Standards Process

Parting Comments on Open Systems Standards Processes

There is a perception (all too often accurate) that the OSI standards process is more apt to converge on a solution that is politically correct than one that is technically so. Within the OSI standards community, there also appears to be a tendency to compromise by embracing multiple solutions to a single problem as well as a tendency to create and tinker with new technology within committees often without the implementation and experimentation that is necessary (essential) to determining whether the technology is useful. These tendencies are inherently bad, and work progressed in this manner has a detrimental effect on the good work brought into OSI by organizations that went through the more rational process we associate with "R&D."

Committees are not laboratories for research, nor are they useful venues for field experimentation; all too often, ISO and CCITT standards committees hammer out compromises that have a significant impact on technology with regard only for the holy spirit of compromise (noteworthy examples here abound: the Ethernet type field versus the IEEE 802.3 length field, the selection of a 48-byte length for the ATM cell, multiple transport protocols for conformance). Committees should confine their activities to evaluating proposals of some demonstrated merit, with the aim of selecting those that are most likely to solve real networking problems. They should also contribute toward getting technology out of the laboratory and into the marketplace.

The TCP/IP standards community does a better job at this than the OSI community (although this, too, is changing: as the availability of OSI products grows, and OSI networks grow as well, a competence in OSI operations is slowly forming, and there is an increasing emphasis on interoperability). In the Internet, whether it is OSI or TCP/IP or hybrids thereof, the community attempts to perpetuate the rich tradition and image of "research and technology first." Quite often, even internet drafts have had some, albeit limited, field experience. And there is considerably less willingness to compromise in the TCP/IP community; here, there is more of a "winner-take-all" attitude, and those who have competing technologies often conduct what have become known as implementation "bake-offs" to test the mettle of the alternatives. The Internet has become a very good place for folks interested in acquiring OSI field experience.

The OSI standards community also suffers from an excessive concern for general applicability. Because of its international exposure, and partly because some of the participants don't know when to stop, OSI must support everything, and in a glorious and ultimate manner. In OSI, it often seems that solutions exhibit the properties of a gas, expanding to fill any container in which they are placed. In TCP/IP, solutions are often more modest and incremental; you'll never see the word *simple* or *trivial* as part of the name of an OSI protocol, but Internet standards developers covet those modifiers and are proud to include them, whenever possible, in the names of Internet standards.

Some of the differences between the two communities can also be attributed to *size.* In his defeat of the Spanish Armada in 1588, Sir Francis Drake demonstrated that small and maneuverable corsairs could defeat significantly larger warships. The TCP/IP community has a similar advantage over the OSI standards community. Although it is growing—and even today is facing some of the same difficulties that have faced the OSI standards community—the TCP/IP community has remained at a very manageable size, which allows standards makers considerable latitude in coming to closure on specific issues. OSI standards makers inherited the enormous bureaucracy that facilitated the construction of a global telephone service and established standards for mundane items such as wineglasses and prophylactics as well. A bake-off is a reasonable and eminently practical way to select a management or routing protocol partly because the community remains small enough that nearly everyone can understand and accept the results of a handful of implementations on technical merit alone. Bake-offs aren't as easy to conduct when countries that have either recently or forever been at war are involved, especially if they happen to be proponents of competing technologies.

Another difference lies in composition; participation in international standards making is expensive and time-consuming. Few members of the research community have the budget (or for that matter, the stomach) for standards work (even if more of them had, the politics of open systems would remain an exasperating and significant deterrent); hence, only the big guns from the commercial sector and public providers attend.

It is also true that the stakes in standardization are different. For the moment, TCP/IP is a cash cow. From an economic standpoint, the entire TCP/IP community—network providers, equipment manufacturers, and end users—stands to profit by rapid closure on issues. At an international level, however, what is profitable for one country may be unprofitable for another, and hence, a national delegation, or *community* of delegations, attending an ISO or a CCITT meeting may have a stronger incentive to thwart or impede progress as a protectionist act than any vendor attending the IETF could imagine. To accommodate the needs of a larger and considerably more diverse community, OSI standards makers often have little choice but to compromise in ways that in other circumstances might be considered incomprehensible.

There is also a difference in *process*. Here, the agility factor again plays in favor of the TCP/IP community. OSI is an international effort. The Internet community is largely a U.S. effort, and although the effort is becoming more international in nature, there remains a decidedly Caesarian attitude in the IETF—the governors of remote outposts were expected to come to Rome to visit Caesar and not vice versa (this, too, is changing, but slowly). Advancement of standards in OSI requires collaboration and consensus across a very wide variety and number of individual standards bodies. This translates into an overload of liaisons and meetings. ISO/CCITT standards goers and doers have to attend dozens of meetings a year to get something done, if only to see the advancement of a standard through the process without any damaging results. ISO standards preparation also involves translation among three languages (English, French, and Russian), which tends to slow things down—particularly near the end of the process.

Finally, there is a difference in document *distribution* and *availabilty*.

TCP/IP standards are free. They can be obtained electronically through the Internet itself, 24 hours a day, or requests can be made for postal delivery. There are on-line help facilities to get interested parties through the process. There are useful informational RFCs like the *Hitchhiker's Guide to the Internet* (RFC 1118), and helpful information services organizations such as the Internet network information center (InterNIC). Furthermore, members of the Internet can use the existing network infrastructure to conduct useful work between meetings through mailing lists, using the very technology they standardize. ISO and CCITT standards are difficult to identify, hard to acquire, challenging to read, and hideously expensive. Consider that the full set of CCITT Blue Books is "discount packaged" by resellers for approximately $3,000! Even the OSI MHS package alone costs $363. This simply doesn't make sense: if standards makers want open systems, then they should be doing everything possible to make standards freely available and easy to access. ISO and CCITT, and their associated national standards bodies (such as ANSI), are doing exactly the opposite. The Internet has the right idea. International standards organizations should wake up and smell the coffee brewing.

PART TWO

OPEN NETWORK ARCHITECTURES

3

CONCEPTS AND TERMINOLOGY OF OPEN SYSTEMS

Introduction

Throughout *Open Systems Networking: TCP/IP and OSI*, the terminology and concepts of OSI are used to describe open systems architectures. Although its terminology is certainly original, most of the basic concepts of OSI—the layered model, service definitions, hierarchical naming and addressing, internetworking, and subnetworks—are derivative, having been derived from principles that were established by other architectures, especially TCP/IP, and documented in different ways. The important contribution of OSI is not the concepts but the way in which they have been expressed in the form of a comprehensive "reference model" of open systems interconnection—the *Basic Reference Model of Open Systems Interconnection* (ISO/IEC 7498:1993).[1] The use of the descriptive tools of the OSI architecture as the basis for describing the general open systems principles of layering, naming and addressing, protocol specification, and service definition throughout this book recognizes not that OSI as a whole is worthier than TCP/IP or other protocol suites but that the OSI architecture is widely known, and its terminology and concepts are readily accepted as the basis for architectural descriptions.

The terminology and specification of TCP/IP present a striking contrast to OSI. The ARPA researchers (at the time they built it, DARPA was actually ARPA) who built the first TCP/IP networks freely admit that they were not terribly concerned with defining an architectural model. Of course, over time, the urgency of formally documenting the

---

1.   The new second edition of ISO/IEC 7498 will be published in 1993. It has already been published by CCITT as Recommendation X.200-1992.

TCP/IP architecture has waned; unlike OSI, TCP/IP is defined by the real networks (including the vast Internet) that implement it, not by the relatively few documents that describe it. Thus, although there are several landmark journal articles that describe the architecture of TCP/IP (Cohen and Postel 1983; Cerf and Cain 1983) and a retrospective RFC (RFC 871), much of what is known about the architecture of TCP/IP remains folklore.[2]

This chapter avoids attributing basic architectural principles to any particular open systems architecture, focusing instead on the way in which those general principles are expressed by OSI and by TCP/IP. It examines the pleonastic[3] terminology of OSI and compares it to the blue-collar language of TCP/IP and identifies the core set of terms and definitions that are used throughout this book. Readers will note that the authors owe no strict allegiance to either OSI or TCP/IP. Although OSI and TCP/IP terms are used when protocol-specific terminology is necessary, the authors use what they believe to be the best terminology from the entire field of networking for the general discussion of the characteristics and principles that are common to both protocol suites.

Architectures

An *architecture* is an abstract model of some part of the real world—in this case, a model of the organization and behavior of networks consisting of interconnected, communicating computer systems and applications. Because it is an abstraction, it is a useful device for describing concepts and relationships in a clear and concise fashion, without cluttering the description with references to the characteristics of specific systems or applications. The utility of such an architectural description depends on the power of the abstraction (how successfully the architecture ex-

---

2.   In an electronic-mail exchange, Jon Postel assisted the authors' archaeological dig for TCP/IP architectural artifacts but warned us that "any writing about the ARPANET protocol architecture is after the fact (probably revisionist) history." The authors interpret Jon's comment not as an implication of TCP/IP writers in an Orwellian scheme to present a deliberately spin-controlled version of the architectural origins of TCP/IP but rather as a recognition that, for example, a paper written seven to ten years after the fact may perceive an "architectural principle" in what was really just good fortune or the result of a series of hits and misses. In fact, of course, Jon Postel *is* the TCP/IP architecture; any attempt to "improve" the documentation of TCP/IP by replacing Jon with a document, however well constructed and thorough, would be an enormous step backward.

3.   At the risk of being accused of pedantry, the authors feel the word *pleonastic*, derived from *pleonasm*, or "the use of more words than are necessary to express an idea," is simply too accurate to eschew.

presses important concepts and relationships and suggests new ones) and on its relevance (how useful the architecture proves to be in the development of real systems and networks).

For designers and builders of networks and the distributed applications that use them, the development of an architectural description of the environment in which the many individual components of their designs and implementations will interact serves two essential purposes. First, it creates a global conceptual framework within which the relationships among individual components can be studied and explored at a common level of abstraction. This framework encourages broadly based solutions to problems, since it places each component in an abstract context that illuminates its interactions with other components. Second, it serves as the basis for formal descriptions of the characteristics of individual components, becoming a "global functional specification" for the distributed environment. Like any functional specification, it establishes a common reference point for the behavior of the designs and implementations that follow from it.

Open Systems

Open systems are "open" by virtue of their mutual adherence to one or more open systems standards, which specify those aspects of the behavior of an open system that are directly relevant to its ability to communicate with other open systems. There are many open system specifications and standards, each of which belongs to a particular architecture (e.g., OSI or TCP/IP). An architecture is typically described by a *reference model*, which expresses the organizing principles of the architecture (the reference points) and provides a framework (a model) within which the various services and protocols, and the relationships among them, may be defined. Thus, for OSI, we have the *OSI reference model* (OSI RM);[4] for TCP/IP, the Internet architectural model or, simply, the Internet architecture.

The term architecture suggests an analogy between a reference model and the elements of the more familiar architecture of buildings. A building-construction manual is concerned with generally applicable truths about building: "The roof goes on the top, and the basement goes

---

4.   Or simply *RM* for short. One often encounters the equivalent acronym *ISORM*, for "ISO reference model" (reflecting the provenance of both the OSI architecture and the associated standards), as in "ISORMites" (devout disciples and defenders of the OSI faith).

on the bottom," or "Plumbing is good." This is just the accumulated wisdom, or perhaps common sense, of the builder's craft. A local building code is much more specific: it specifies the use of a particular grade of 4-inch PVC pipe supported at no less than 1-foot intervals (etc.), or it mandates conformance to an American Society for Testing Materials standard for the flammability of roofing material. The blueprints for an office building are even more specific: they specify, very precisely, every detail of the construction of an actual building, giving the length and placement of every piece of 4-inch PVC pipe and the brand name and stock number of the roofing material.

The principles of construction that are collected in the manual are assumed to be universal. There are, however, a great many local building codes, each of which "conforms" to the generally accepted principles of construction. And within the jurisdiction of a single building code, an almost infinite variety of actual buildings can be constructed.

The OSI reference model describes both the general principles of open systems networking and the specific prescriptions for open systems that follow the OSI architecture. Like the building-construction manual, the OSI reference model collects "universal truths" about open systems: layers are good; internetworking accommodates many different types of real-world networks; addresses must be unambiguous. Like a building code, the OSI reference model also defines an abstract model of an open system: not only are layers good, but OSI has seven of them; internetworking functions are in the network layer; and addresses in OSI are not only unambiguous, they are constructed in a particular (hierarchical) fashion. However, just as a building code doesn't describe any particular building, the OSI reference model doesn't describe any particular implementation of a real open computer or communications system.

In fact, it could be argued that the scope of the OSI reference model is even more limited than that of a building code, since it specifies only the externally visible behavior of an open system and carefully avoids issues that are not directly relevant to the ability of the system to communicate with other open systems. A building code might prescribe PVC pipe for drain lines in residential construction, although the requirement is actually for pipe with certain characteristics (thermal stability, resistance to corrosion, etc.), whether made of PVC or an equally suitable material. The OSI reference model specifically refrains from defining the characteristics of an open system, such as how to manage buffers or pass information from one process to another, that are not relevant to the interconnection of open systems. This restraint is essential, since such restrictions would be based on assumptions about the current state of the art. In addition to reducing opportunities for competitive differentiation among open system vendors, they might easily deter innovation in computer hardware and software design.

Architecture Wars

The "architecture wars" between OSI and TCP/IP involve primarily the building-code aspects of open systems. Very few people get into arguments about whether or not plumbing is a good thing or whether or not it is useful to organize the functions of an architecture into layers; many plumbing contractors, however, are quite willing to debate the merits of copper pipe over PVC, and similarly, network engineers will debate whether security functions belong in the transport layer or the network layer. Anyone associated with the construction business knows how many different variations on the same basic theme can be captured by different codes; nevertheless, buildings constructed according to codes in Massachusetts and Pennsylvania are (presumably) equally habitable. The differences between the OSI and the Internet architectural models are almost entirely variations on themes that are common to all open system architectures: layers, services, protocols, and other generally applicable concepts from the open system cookbook.

Layers

Many functions must be performed above the transmission media (the "wires") to support useful communication between computer systems. For example, it is often necessary to ensure that the information sent from one computer to another arrives in order, uncorrupted, and without loss or duplication. If the two computers are physically attached to different transmission media (e.g., one to an Ethernet local area network and another to a public, packet-switching network), it is also necessary to define a function that selects a route and forwards data over multiple "hops" from source to destination. Additional functions encode and preserve the semantics and context of information as it is understood by a distributed application (a networked file service, electronic mail, or a directory service) running on several communicating computer systems.

As an example, consider this partial list of the functions that might be performed by communicating computers (real-world open systems) to accomplish the transfer of a file from one system to another:

- Access to the local file transfer service
- Identification of the application (and destination computer) to which the file is to be transferred
- Establishment of communications between the peer applications that will be involved in the file transfer
- Determination of a common representation of the information to be transferred, including both file and data structure
- Access via the local file storage facility to the contents of the file to be transferred
- Selection of the network service and/or transmission media through which the contents of the file must travel (routing and forwarding)
- Data fragmentation and reassembly
- Physical-level signaling and bit transmission
- Reliable transportation of the contents of the file from source to destination, resulting in an exact duplicate of the original file at the destination

Although it would be possible to do so, specifying one humage[5] protocol to deal with all these functions would be inefficient, inflexible, and inordinately complex; in fact, just plain silly. Imagine, for a moment, what the state machine would look like!

The principle of *layering* solves this problem by collecting functions into related and manageable sets. For example, the functions associated with reliable data transport (detection and correction of lost, misordered, duplicated, or corrupted packets) logically form one set; those that handle routing and forwarding, another; and those that handle data representation, a third. In the process, the sets of functions are organized in a hierarchy. Data representation, typically viewed as an application-oriented or "end-user" function, sits on top of the reliable delivery or "end-to-end transport" functions, so that the end-user functions can make use of the end-to-end functions (i.e., they won't have to duplicate them). Both the OSI reference model and the Internet architectural model call the related and manageable sets *layers*.

Layers are good, but how many layers? The OSI reference model specifies seven (Figure 3.1), which have gradually assumed an almost

---

5.   The origin of this word is attributed to Matthew Piscitello (age 4 at the time), who could not discriminate between daddy's use of humongous and mommy's use of huge, so he created his own.

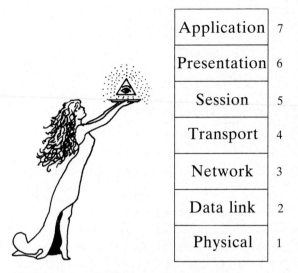

Application	7
Presentation	6
Session	5
Transport	4
Network	3
Data link	2
Physical	1

FIGURE 3.1   OSI Reference Model

holy significance and to which other, less sacred architectures are often compared.

The Internet architecture specifies five layers (Figure 3.2), combining the functions of the OSI application, presentation, and session layers into a single application layer.

⌸·AHA·⌸ *One might suppose that the people responsible for the OSI reference model believed that seven is, in fact, the "right" number of layers for an open systems architecture or that the Internet architects, after careful analysis, determined that five is the "right" number. Precedent, of course, argues for the mystical properties of the number 7; there are, after all, seven dwarfs:*

7	*Sneezy*
6	*Sleepy*
5	*Dopey*
4	*Doc*
3	*Grumpy*
2	*Bashful*
1	*Happy*

. . . *and* seven *deadly sins:*

7	*Wrath*
6	*Sloth*
5	*Lust*
4	*Avarice*
3	*Gluttony*
2	*Envy*
1	*Pride*

Application
Transport
Internet
Network interface
Physical

FIGURE 3.2   Internet Reference Model

But in fact, the architects of both OSI and the TCP/IP protocol suite had never seriously worried over the fact that their respective architectural models had a particular *number of layers and certainly never anticipated that the number of layers in the OSI reference model would become, one day, the only thing that many people would remember about the architecture.*

Needless to say, there is nothing special about the number 7, nor is the fact that the OSI reference model has seven layers and the Internet architecture has five deeply significant. What *is* important is the way in which the OSI and Internet architectures allocate functions among the layers and the ensuing consequences for the operation of OSI and Internet systems and the development of distributed applications.

A Quick Tour of OSI's Seven Layers

The application, presentation, and session layers of the OSI model are collectively referred to as the *upper layers* (Figure 3.3). They provide end-user services: the functions that enable applications to share and manipulate information. Not surprisingly, the remaining layers (transport, network, data link, and physical) are collectively referred to as the *lower layers.*[6] They provide an end-to-end data transport service, organizing the communication resources that exist in the real world to carry information from any source system to any destination system.

The upper layers are *application oriented;* they focus on the application processes that are the ultimate "end users" of OSI. They operate as though they were directly connected to all their peers at the transport service boundary, without regard for the way in which their communication is actually accomplished. The lower layers are *communications oriented;* they focus on the job of supporting the upper layers' complacent fiction

---

6.   In some circles, the transport and network layers are referred to as the middle layers.

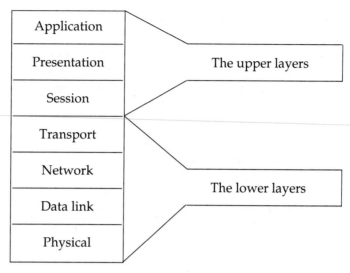

FIGURE 3.3   The Great Divide

that they are directly connected by arranging for data to be transported out of one host computer or *end system*; across the arbitrarily complex and heterogeneous real world of wires, fiber, ether, carrier networks, bridges, and routers; and into another end system.

The *application layer* provides access to OSI services. It is also (conceptually) the place in which distributed applications reside and in which they access the networking environment.

The *presentation layer* isolates applications from concerns about the representation (syntax) of the data they exchange, allowing them to deal only with their meaning (semantics). It defines a common or *canonical* form for the representation and manipulation of application information. Some computers use EBCDIC as the native character encoding, and others use ASCII, and different computers and operating systems store information in memories or disk files in different ways. Presentation layer functions allow applications to represent their data in a machine-independent fashion by providing a universal language in which to describe abstract data structures. By offering what is often called a common network programming language, the presentation layer allows applications to exchange structured information rather than raw bit strings. It also defines the way in which elements of that language are actually transmitted from one system to another. The presentation layer is thus responsible for transforming information from machine-specific data structures common to the source computer into machine-independent data structures for transmission, and from machine-independent data structures for transmission to machine-specific data structures common to the destination computer as data are received.

The *session layer* provides mechanisms for organizing and synchronizing the exchange of data between application processes. Session permits an application to mark its progress as it sends and receives data (synchronization points), provides ways for applications to control the direction of information flow (turn management), coordinates multiple independent exchanges ("activities") within the overall context of a single session, and allows applications to inform each other about the occurrence of errors and the steps to be taken to resynchronize part or all of the affected dialogue(s).

The *transport layer* provides "transparent transfer of data from a source end open system to a destination end open system" (ISO/IEC 7498: 1984). Transport is responsible for creating and maintaining the basic end-to-end connection between communicating open systems, ensuring that the bits delivered to the receiver are the same as the bits transmitted by the sender: in the same order and without modification, loss, or duplication.

The *network layer* provides "a path between transport entities, relieving the upper layers from dealing with the way in which data are transferred from one end open system to another" (ISO/IEC 7498: 1984). Network determines the path or route that the data must take from original source to final destination and forwards the data over that route. It provides a service that is independent of the underlying transmission media and includes all of the routing, relaying, and interworking functions needed to get from source to destination, regardless of the number or type of transmission resources that may be used in tandem or in parallel.

│◦AHA◦│ *The boundary between the transport and network layers was originally conceived by early telephony-oriented OSI developers as a representation of the traditional regulatory boundary between customer premises equipment (CPE) and a public carrier network: CPE contained transport and the upper layers, and the carrier network implemented the network and other lower-layer functions. This model assumed a pervasive global carrier network to which every end system was directly attached. The popularity of LANs and other privately deployed networks based on the concept of "internetworking" had made this model obsolete even before the work on the OSI reference model was completed. The result is a network layer with an extensive internal structure, containing both internetworking functions (which are independent of any particular network technology) and network-specific functions (which vary depending on the type of real-world network involved). The Internet architecture captures this distinction much more clearly, by defining separate "internet" and "network-interface" layers.*

About all the OSI reference model can think of to say about the *data link layer* is that it "provides for the control of the physical layer, and detects and possibly corrects errors which may occur" (ISO/IEC 7498: 1984). The data link layer couples to a particular physical access method whatever functions are necessary to recover bit-stream errors that may be introduced during transmission (due to "noise," clock jitter, cosmic rays, and other forms of signal interference).

The *physical layer* provides "mechanical, electrical, functional, and procedural means to activate a physical connection for bit transmission . . ." (ISO/IEC 7498: 1984), which is OSI's attempt to dress up the unvarying role of the physical layer in any network architecture: to transform bits in a computer system into electromagnetic (or equivalent) signals for a particular transmission medium (wire, fiber, ether, etc.).

┌───────────┐
│ ⋄AHA⋄ │ *The data link and physical layers appear in the OSI reference*
└───────────┘ *model primarily for the sake of completeness (during the deliberations over the text of the reference model, it often seemed to the authors that somewhere, someone with considerable authority had declared, "Let there be nothing in the world of communication for which OSI has no layer"). Since these two layers deal with functions that are so inherently specific to each individual networking technology, the layering principle of grouping together related functions is largely irrelevant. This has not, of course, prevented endless arguments about whether there is or is not an addressing function in the data link layer or whether medium access control for an IEEE 802 local area network is a data link layer function or a physical layer function.*

For most real network technologies, it is both impractical and unnecessary to determine where the boundary between these two layers lies or even whether to describe the functions of the real network as "data link layer functions" or "physical layer functions." Since many real networks also include functions that are, from the technical standpoint of the OSI architecture, "in the network layer," the TCP/IP model of real networks as simply individual network services is much better. OSI recognized this after the fact by introducing what amounts to a codicil to its reference model[7]—namely, the "subnetwork" concept, which collects everything below the OSI internetworking protocol into a single abstraction, forgoing formal discrimination of network layer functions, data link layer functions, and physical layer functions.

A Quick Tour of Internet's Five Layers

How does the OSI allocation of functions among seven layers compare to the layering applied in the Internet architecture? In *Internetworking with TCP/IP*, Douglas Comer (1991) characterizes the TCP/IP architecture as comprising application-level and network-level internet services. This distinction between upper layers (actually, in the Internet architecture, a single upper layer) and lower layers follows the same logic for TCP/IP as for OSI (see Figure 3.4).

The application-level internet services are a set of application programs that operate across a TCP/IP-based internet. All of the end-user functions, which are divided among three OSI layers, are incorporated in the TCP/IP architecture into each application program individually. TCP/IP applications, therefore, are designed to operate directly over a raw transport interface.

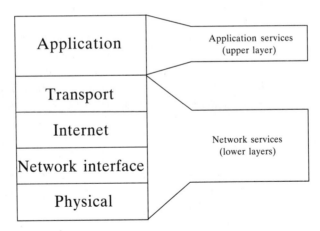

FIGURE 3.4   Upper Layer/Lower Layers Distinction in TCP/IP

---

7.   The codicil is the *Internal Organization of the Network Layer* (ISO/IEC 8648: 1988), which was published five years after the reference model as a way of "burying the hatchet" in the war between two factions, each of which painted the other in extreme terms. Faction 1, the network-centrics, saw the world as composed of powerful, pervasive public data networks that graciously suffered the attachment, for a fee, of relatively insignificant pieces of end-user equipment; faction 2, the host-centrics, saw the world as composed of a global fraternity of vigorous, autonomous computer systems and LANs, filled with important end-user applications, which occasionally, when it could not be avoided, permitted the public networks to carry some of their communication.

The network-level internet services correspond more or less directly to the services provided by OSI's lower layers. The OSI transport layer provides much the same end-to-end communications service as the TCP/IP transport layer. OSI offers both virtual circuit (connection) and datagram network layer services (see "Connections and Connectionless," later in the chapter); TCP/IP offers only a datagram internetworking service. The network interface layer in the TCP/IP architecture corresponds to a combination of the OSI data link layer and the network-specific functions of the OSI network layer. The physical layer, of course, does what the physical layer must do.

The monolithic upper layer in the Internet architecture reflects the deliberate involvement of the TCP/IP architecture in the way in which distributed applications are organized. In this respect, OSI provides a more comprehensive model. On the other hand, the correspondence between the lower layers of the Internet architecture and real-world internetworks is much clearer and more accurate than it is in the OSI case. It has been suggested that OSI is the "better" model of distributed applications and that TCP/IP is the "better" model for the networks that support their communication.

Terminology

The principles applied to the development of the OSI reference model are similar to those of the TCP/IP architecture; unfortunately, the terminology is not. The OSI architects were convinced that none of the familiar terms of network engineering, freighted as they were with preexisting real-world connotations, would suffice for the highly formal and precise descriptions they imagined for their reference model. The elusive and mystifying world of "OSI-speak" was created to insulate the ethereal and pure concept space of OSI from contamination by the existing networks of mortals. The resulting terminology reads more like German existentialism than Tanenbaum's *Computer Networks* (1988).

OSI is unquestionably encumbered with too many obscure terms with confusing definitions. A definition is supposed to be "a brief and precise description of a thing by its properties" (Thatcher and McQueen 1977). OSI's definitions are far from brief and are often imprecise; in many cases, brevity and clarity are sacrificed for the sake of either precision or political compromise. The language of TCP/IP ("Internet-ese"), on the other hand, is disarmingly accessible and bears a striking resemblance to terms that one might use to describe real networks.

Nevertheless, it is difficult to understand either OSI or TCP/IP without first becoming familiar with some of the most frequently used terminology. In some cases, readers need to be familiar with a term because it expresses an important concept; in other cases, they need to be familiar with a term because they will encounter it in the OSI standards and will otherwise be inappropriately intimidated by it. Since most of the difficult terminology belongs to OSI, most of what follows applies to that architecture; except where noted, the terminology of TCP/IP is intuitive.

 The situation regarding terminology is similar to that in which Owl finds himself in the House at Pooh Corner:

Owl explained about the Necessary Dorsal Muscles. He had explained this to Pooh and Christopher Robin once before, and had been waiting ever since for a chance to do it again, because it is a thing which you can easily explain twice before anybody knows what you are talking about (Milne 1954).

Entities

In the OSI architecture, the service provided by a layer is, conceptually, the result of the collective activity of all the computer systems that participate in OSI. Each open system contains components (vertical slices) of each layer that OSI calls *subsystems*. A subsystem represents the functionality of a single layer that is actually present in an individual open system. An open system therefore contains seven subsystems, each one corresponding to one of the seven layers identified in Figure 3.1. Collectively, subsystems of the same rank form a layer.

All the functions present in a given subsystem may not be active at the same time. For example, if a layer offers both a datagram and a virtual-circuit type of service, but only the datagram service is being used, then only the datagram-oriented functions of that layer are active. The active elements within a subsystem are called *entities*.

In effect, an entity is the "stuff" inside a layer. Informally, the terms *layer entity*, *entity*, and *layer* are used interchangeably, with the understanding that the formal meaning is "an active element within a hierarchical division of an open system" (ISO/ICE 7498: 1984).

⋅AHA⋅ *Given the multinational composition of the standards organizations responsible for OSI, it is not surprising that a great deal of energy is expended in the selection of universally acceptable names for the "things" to which open systems networking standards must refer. Early in the OSI work, it became clear that an architecturally neutral term for the "thing" that sits in an OSI layer and represents the activities that take place there would be needed. Process, module, and other terms borrowed from the realms of programming languages and operating systems all carried the implication of implementation, and the OSI architects were particularly concerned to avoid the impression that every "thing" in the OSI architecture necessarily finds its counterpart in an implementation. They came up with the wonderfully metaphysical term* entity, *which the* Oxford English Dictionary *defines as "Being, existence, as opposed to non-existence; the existence, as distinguished from the qualities or relations, of anything." Perfect! Then, returning from the meeting in Berlin at which the agreement on this term was reached, Lyman noticed the following posted on the underside of the toilet cover in the lavatory of the airplane, which added an entirely unique perspective to OSI terminology.*

```
┌─────────────────────────────────────────────┐
│           DO NOT THROW                       │
│  ☐    cups          towels    ☐              │
│  ☐    bottles       napkins   ☐              │
│  ☐    razor blades  diapers   ☐              │
│              entities                        │
│            IN TOILET                         │
└─────────────────────────────────────────────┘
```

Notation

The notations *(N)*, *(N + 1)*, and *(N – 1)* are used to identify an arbitrary layer entity and the layer entities hierarchically adjacent to it (Figure 3.5). Typically, the value of (N) is an integer (1 through 7; the physical layer is numbered 1, and the application layer is numbered 7). In many OSI standards, the first letter of the name of a layer is used for (N) rather than an integer. Thus, the terms *layer-4-entity, (4)-entity, transport entity,* and *T-entity* all refer to the same thing.

Services

The relationship between (N)-entities in adjacent layers is expressed in OSI by the following concepts and terms:

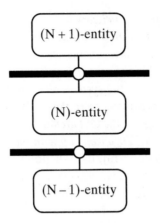

FIGURE 3.5   Entity Notation

- Each (N)-entity performs *(N)-functions.*
- The (N + 1) entities assume that a well-defined set of *(N)-facilities* is provided by (N)-entities.
- The set of (N)-facilities that (N)-entities provide to (N + 1)-entities is called the *(N)-service.*

Thus, the transport layer performs transport functions and provides a set of transport facilities that constitute a transport service to the session layer. Similar terminology applies to the TCP/IP architecture; for example, the TCP/IP internet layer provides a datagram service to the transport layer.

OSI takes great pains to formally define services, and a service-definition standard is provided for each layer. The purpose of the service definition is to formally identify the functions to be performed (and the facilities to be provided) by a layer, so that a protocol can be developed to provide a well-defined and manageable set of functions. The existence of a formal (N)-layer service definition also assists in the design of layer (N + 1), since it can be assumed that certain functions are already performed in layer (N) and (in theory) should not be duplicated at any layer above (N). For example, if the transport service provides end-to-end reliable delivery, the session layer should not.

Services provide a formal way to express the relationship that exists between an entity in one layer and an entity in a layer immediately above or below it. The OSI service model contains the following elements:

- A user of the service provided by layer (N) resides at layer (N + 1), and is called an *(N)-service-user.*

- The elements involved in the provision of the (N)-service are called (N)-entities (as described in the preceding section).
- The (N)-entities that actively participate in providing the (N)-service are collectively referred to as the *(N)-service-provider.*
- The (conceptual) point at which an (N)-service is provided to an (N + 1)-entity by the (N)-service provider is called an *(N)-service-access-point,* or (N)-SAP.
- The information exchanged at an (N)-SAP is called *(N)-service-data,* and individual units of that data are called *(N)-service-data-units,* or (N)-SDUs.

These relationships are illustrated in Figure 3.6.

Applying these principles to the specific example of the interaction between the session and transport layers, we have the following:

- A session entity, a user of the service provided by layer 4, the transport layer, resides at layer 5 and is called a transport service user.
- The elements involved in the provision of the transport service are called transport entities.
- The transport entities that actively participate in providing the transport service are collectively referred to as the transport service provider.
- The (conceptual) point at which the transport service is provided to a session entity by the transport service provider is called a transport service access point, or TSAP.
- The information exchanged at a trasport service access point is called transport service data, and individual units of that data are formally called transport service data units, or TSDUs.

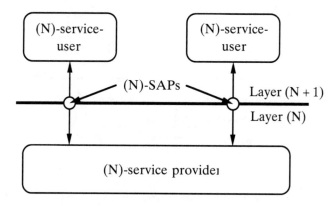

FIGURE 3.6   Generic Service Model

The Queue Model

The OSI service model provides a convention for describing the interactions between adjacent entities. The exchanges across a service boundary are modeled as a pair of queues, where each exchange represents an atomic (simultaneous) interaction at two (N)-SAPs (see Figure 3.7). Objects, called *service primitives*, are placed in or removed from a queue by the service users and by the service provider. The service primitives indicate some action that must be (or has been) performed by one of the other participants in the service interaction.

As an example, imagine that (N)-service-user A wishes to establish an (N)-connection to (N)-service-user B. An object, the (N)-CONNECT service primitive, is submitted by (N)-service-user A to the (N)-service-provider in the form of a *request* primitive; i.e., it is placed in an imaginary queue that exists between service users and the service provider. This is step 1 in Figure 3.8. The queue is accessible via A's (N)-service-

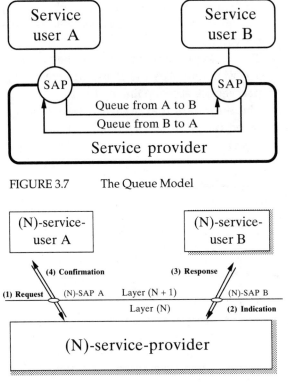

FIGURE 3.7   The Queue Model

FIGURE 3.8   Confirmed Service

access-point. The (N)-service-provider removes the request primitive from the queue and informs (N)-service-user B of the request by inserting an (N)-CONNECT *indication* primitive in the queue (step 2). (N)-service-user B accesses the queue via its own (N)-service-access-point. B removes the indication primitive from the queue and accepts the connection request by placing a positive (N)-CONNECT *response* primitive in the queue (step 3). The (N)-service-provider removes the response primitive from the queue and places a *confirmation* primitive in A's queue (step 4). OSI calls this a *confirmed service*.

There is also an *unconfirmed service*. Here, only the request primitive is available to (N)-service-users, and only the indication primitive is available to the (N)-service-provider. (N)-service-user A places the request primitive in a queue when it wishes to send (N)-service-data to (N)-service-user B. The (N)-service-provider places the indication primitive in a queue to:

- Notify (N)-service-user B of a request from (N)-service-user A.
- Notify one or more (N)-service-users of an event or action instigated by the (N)-service-provider (hence, the term *provider-initiated*).

The unconfirmed services are illustrated in Figures 3.9 and 3.10.

Connections and Connectionless

One of the most basic concepts of network architecture is the distinction between the *connection* and *connectionless* models of communication. The connection model is based on the establishment and maintenance of "state information" that is held in common by the communicating par-

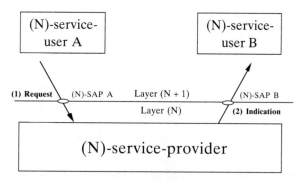

FIGURE 3.9   User-initiated Unconfirmed Service

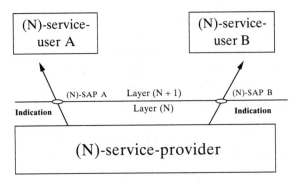

FIGURE 3.10   Provider-initiated Unconfirmed Service

ties and the underlying service provider; the state information establishes a context within which the parties interact with the service provider and communicate with each other. The connectionless model is based on individually self-contained units of communication (often called "datagrams"), which are exchanged independently without reference to any shared state (that is, there is no "connection" between the communicating parties). In the connection model, each individual unit of communication is interpreted by reference to the shared state of the connection (which captures information such as the identity of the communicating parties, the current status of flow-control variables, the way in which data have been encoded for transmission, and the sequence numbers of data units that have not yet been mutually acknowledged). In the connectionless model, each unit of communication carries within it all the information that each party needs to interpret it, since there is no shared state to refer to.

◆AHA◆   *The OSI reference model terms* connection-oriented *and* connectionless, *describing virtual circuit and datagram modes of operation, were coined by Lyman Chapin and John Gurzick during the production of the first draft of the connectionless addendum to the OSI reference model on the roof of The Pointe resort in Phoenix, Arizona, in 1981. Sometime between 1983 and 1987, the connection-oriented "X.25 crowd," who were not about to hyphenate the noun* connection *(to create an adjective) without attaching a similarly demeaning shackle to the rival* connectionless, *succeeded in changing the "official" term to* connectionless-mode—*an injury to English grammar that at least had the dubious virtue of leaving everyone equally dissatisfied. A few reminders of the original terms persist; the standard acronym for the "connection-mode network service," for example, is* CONS, *not* CMNS, *and the title of ISO/IEC 8073 is "Connection-oriented Transport Protocol."*

A common mistake is to assume that either the connection model or the connectionless model must be used uniformly throughout a network architecture; that is, if one layer is defined using the connection model, then all the other layers must also use the connection model. In fact, the two models are complementary: it is appropriate to use the connection model to define a protocol in one layer (e.g., the transport layer) and the connectionless model to define a protocol in a different layer (e.g., the network layer), the combination of which can be used to provide a connection-oriented (transport) service to a higher layer.

The TCP/IP and OSI architectures employ both models in all layers, with one important exception: in TCP/IP, only the connectionless model is used to define the services and protocols of the internet layer. The Internet architecture refers to the two models as simply "connections" and "datagrams." The OSI reference model, with its penchant for "precise" terminology, uses the terms *connection-mode* and *connection-oriented* for the connection model and the term *connectionless-mode* for the connectionless model.

·AHA·   *In the earliest work on OSI, communication between peer entities was modeled exclusively in terms of connection-based interactions, which were* de rigueur *among the telephony-oriented people[8] who dominated early OSI standardization activity. Consequently, the assumption that a connection is a basic prerequisite for communication in OSI permeated early drafts of the reference model, and came to be perceived as a dominant and prerequisite feature of the OSI architecture. This widely held perception caused many people who were familiar with the use of the connectionless model for internetworking in TCP/IP and other architectures to dismiss OSI as applicable only to X.25 and other connection-oriented networks. The pejorative association of OSI with X.25 has been hard to shake, despite the fact that the connectionless internetworking model has been fully incorporated into the OSI architecture,*

---

8.   The temptation to attach a descriptive collective label to people with perspectives or beliefs different from one's own is usually irresistible, albeit deplorable; wherefore, those who came to OSI from traditional telephony backgrounds have been dubbed "wire stringers." Wire stringers believe in connections (there being no such thing as "connectionless telephony") and are skeptical of what they call "lossy datagrams"; internetworks built on the connectionless model were therefore dismissed as "academic toys." Not surprisingly, computer nerds are as likely as normal people to succumb to petty variations on the Lee Atwater syndrome.

and a complete set of protocols and services to support it has been defined and standardized.

Communication using a connection proceeds through three distinct phases:

1. *Connection establishment*, during which the parties that intend to communicate negotiate and agree on the terms of their interaction and perform any necessary "setup" functions (such as the allocation of buffers, the establishment of underlying communication links, and the initialization of state variables).
2. *Data transfer*, during which information is exchanged according to the rules established during connection establishment.
3. *Connection release*, during which the context established for communication is dismantled (buffers freed, underlying links torn down, state data structures deallocated).

Connection-mode operation is based on the familiar model of a telephone conversation:

1. Dial the phone.
2. Talk to the party at the other end.
3. Hang up.

In contrast, connectionless communication has just one phase of operation: transmission of a single, self-contained unit of data in a package that contains all relevant information. It is based on the equally familiar model of the basic postal mail service: put all necessary information (address, return address, postage, "airmail" label, etc.) on the envelope and drop it in the mailbox slot.

Connectionless data transmission has been described disparingly as "send and pray"; but is more accurately described as "best-effort delivery." A service provider, be it a datagram network or a postal authority, wouldn't last long if its users truly believed that packet or mail forwarding and delivery could only be accomplished through divine intervention.

What about Protocols?

A protocol is a well-defined set of rules for what amounts to a "conversation" between computer systems. The OSI architecture defines an [N]-*protocol* as "a set of rules and formats (semantic and syntactic) which determines the communication behavior of (N)-entities in the performance of (N)-functions" (ISO/IEC 7498: 1984).

Imagine how a typical telephone call is structured. Fred dials Wilma's telephone number. Wilma answers with a "Hello?" Fred says, "Hello, Wilma, this is Fred." Wilma replies (and implicitly acknowledges that Fred has indeed reached Wilma) with "Oh, hello, Fred." This is more or less the equivalent of a connection establishment. Fred and Wilma exchange pleasantries, Fred tells Wilma he'll be late for dinner, etc.; i.e., they transfer data. They exchange good-byes and hang up, the equivalent of connection release. In general, the caller intuits a great deal about the nature of the phone call before actually dialing; most callers anticipate that they will share a common language with the party called, it is considered rude or suspicious if one does not identify oneself or say hello, and most understand that an "uh-huh" or a "yep" is an explicit acknowledgment that the listening party has heard and understood what the speaking party has said. Although these semantics of a conversation are (thankfully) not written in ISO standards, they do constitute an implicit set of rules that people generally adhere to when calling one another, at least in the United States. The same is true for the mail system. There is a convention applied to identify the sender and intended recipient of a letter. (Conventions certainly exist to simplify the processing of mail, but the degrees of latitude that the U.S. Postal Service and PTTs extend to postal patrons are often nothing shy of remarkable.)

Computers establish connections and send datagrams in much the same manner, but the semantics and syntactical elements are more rigorously defined. The normal flow of a computer conversation is a highly structured sequence of actions. Possible exceptions to the normal flow must be considered and accommodated by introducing some action to be taken in response to the exception. And of course, the words exchanged must be understood by the systems that exchange them. The set of actions that define an (N)-protocol defines the *state machine* for the protocol. The words exchanged between communicating (N)-entities are called *(N)-protocol data units* or *(N)-PDUs*. Since computers must be able to distinguish between words that convey actions to the bit level of detail, the structure of each (N)-PDU exchanged is defined for each (N)-protocol. The bits that (N)-protocols interpret to determine what actions to take are collectively called *(N)-protocol-control-information,* or *(N)-PCI*. The data that an (N)-service-provider moves from one (N)-service-user to another are called *(N)-user-data*.

A generic illustration of the relationships among many of these terms is provided in Figure 3.11, and a concrete example is provided in Figure 3.12. Note that the terminology is different in the Internet architecture; in fact, it is different for each layer. Figure 3.13 illustrates that the same principles can be applied.

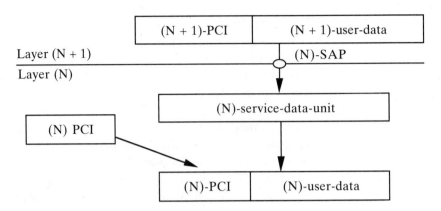

FIGURE 3.11   Relationships among Protocol and Service Terminology

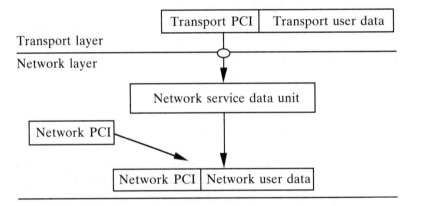

FIGURE 3.12   Protocol and Service Terminology: A Concrete Example

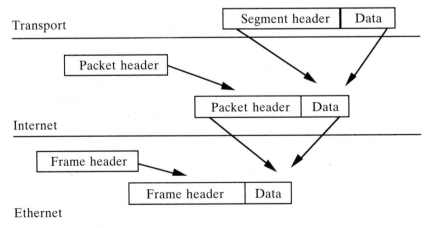

FIGURE 3.13   Terminology of the Internet Architecture

Protocol Headers and User Data

A more familiar term for (N)-protocol-control-information is *protocol header*. As one progresses iteratively down the layered architecture, the formal "rules of thumb" for the association of protocol headers with user data are:

- The (N) user data to be transmitted/transferred are prepended with (N) PCI, forming an (N) PDU.
- One or more (N) PDUs are passed across an (N) SAP as one of a set of service parameters that comprise an (N)-SDU, called (N)-service-user-data.
- The (N)-service-user-data themselves are prepended with (N − 1)-PCI, forming one or more (N − 1)-PDUs.

All of which basically says that at each layer, in order to exchange user data, a protocol is operated. To convey the rules of the protocol from sender to receiver, PCI or header information is attached to the user data to describe them, distinguish them from other data being exchanged, and tell the receiver what to do with them. The header information is meaningful only to the peers of a given layer, so when the combination of header and data is passed down to an adjacent, lower layer, it is treated like one lump of user data. Entities at the lower layer also have a job to do and rules to follow, so the process continues until you get to the lowest layer, where electrons follow nature's course (see Figure 3.14).

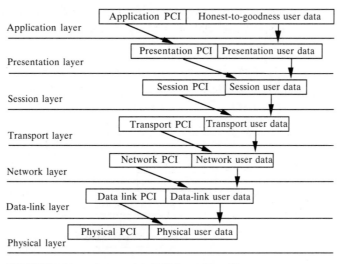

FIGURE 3.14   Separating PCI from User Data

There are certainly those who would conclude that the developers of OSI were a bit too obsessed with protocol control information, and wry comments made during OSI standards meetings, such as "Remember, we're in the header business, not the data business . . . ," provide anecdotal substantiation of this claim. OSI is by no means fit and trim. The expectation is that feature for feature, OSI brings enough that is new and helpful toward the goal of open distributed processing to encourage its development and use.

Relating Service to Protocol

The relationship between a service and a protocol is straightforward: for every primitive action, there is a related set of protocol exchanges that enable the service provider to accomplish what it has been directed to do by its service users (or to notify its service users of exception situations that arise during the provision of service). This relationship is illustrated in Figure 3.15.

Note that for certain service primitives, there may be no explicit exchange of (N)-PDUs between the (N)-entities that comprise the (N)-service-provider. In this situation, the service primitive exchange models a local action taken by a service user or the service provider; e.g., passing locally significant parameters. For other service primitives, several exchanges of (N)-PDUs might follow the issuance of one primitive request before the associated indication is generated. In the data transfer phase of the transport layer, for example, a transport PDU containing transport user data is sent by the transport entity serving A to the trans-

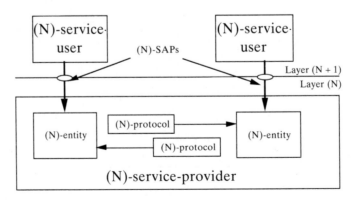

FIGURE 3.15   Relating Service to Protocol

port entity serving B as a result of the issuance of a T DATA.request primitive by transport user A. A transport PDU containing an explicit acknowledgment of receipt of those data is returned by the transport entity serving user B prior to the issuance of the T-DATA.indication primitive to user B.

Time-Sequence Diagrams

A second model applied nearly as often in OSI standards as the queue model is the time-sequence diagram. The time-sequence diagram again attempts to represent the interaction of service users and a service provider but adds the dimension of time. Compare the time-sequence diagram in Figure 3.16 to the queue model example in Figure 3.7.

The time-sequence diagram is actually more powerful than the queue model when extended to illustrate both protocol exchange and service primitive interaction, as shown in Figure 3.17.

This extension does not appear in (m)any OSI standards but is used extensively in this book because it is effective in demonstrating the order in which things occur.

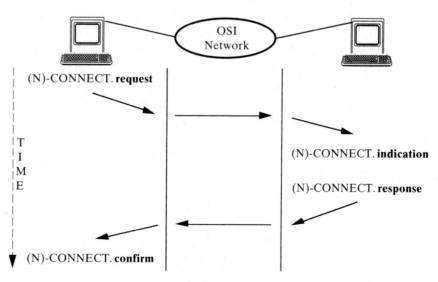

FIGURE 3.16   Time-Sequence Diagram

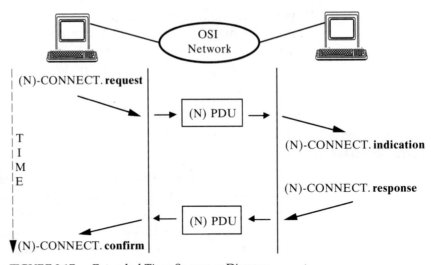

FIGURE 3.17   Extended Time-Sequence Diagram

A Final Fling with OSI Fundamentals

Applications typically deal with arbitrary-length octet streams, and information exchanged between applications ranges from single keystrokes to
multimegabyte images. Transmission media used in networking today
vary widely in the maximum transmission unit size that can be accommodated with tolerable and detectable loss, from several hundred to several
thousand octets. Computer bus technologies have similar physical limitations but can handle tens of thousands, even millions of octets. Thus,
when the octet streams exchanged between applications are physically
larger than an offered maximum transmission unit size, functions must
be present to chop up the stream into small pieces and then put the pieces
back together again. *Segmentation* is the process of breaking an (N)-ser-
vice-data-unit into several (N)-protocol-data-units; *reassembly* is the process of recombining the (N)-PDUs into an (N)-SDU (see Figure 3.18).

Sometimes, it is useful to clump together small pieces of informa-

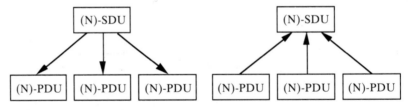

FIGURE 3.18   Segmentation and Reassembly

tion and transmit them in one swell foop. Two forms of this processing exist in OSI. If the combining process occurs across two adjacent layers, the terms *concatenation* and *separation* apply. Concatenation is the process of combining several (N)-PDUs into one (N – 1)-SDU; separation is the reverse function of concatenation (see Figure 3.19). If the combining process occurs within a layer, the terms *blocking* and *unblocking* apply. Blocking is the process of combining several (N)-SDUs into a single (N)-PDU; unblocking is the reverse function (see Figure 3.20).

A similar formal terminology is defined for connections. *Multiplexing* is the process of supporting several (N)-connections using a single (N – 1) connection or (N – 1)-association; *demultiplexing* is the reverse function. Correspondingly, *splitting* is the process of using several (N – 1)-connections to support a single (N)-connection, with *recombining* being the reverse function. These are much harder to draw, so this is left as an exercise for readers.

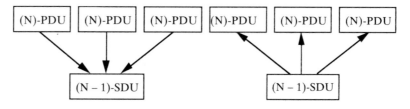

FIGURE 3.19   Concatenation and Separation

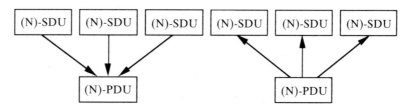

FIGURE 3.20   Blocking and Unblocking

Conclusion

This chapter has provided an overview of the formal methodology used to describe OSI, and has compared this to the accumulated folklore that describes the Internet architecture. The authors observed that many architectural "fundamentals" are common to both the OSI and Internet architectures and that it is in the application of these fundamentals that the architectures often diverge. This chapter has also identified the terminology readers will most frequently encounter in ISO/IEC, CCITT, and Internet standards, first defining terms in the context of their native architectures and then relating the formal and often impenetrable OSI terms to their more commonly encountered Internet counterparts.

The ISO reference model provides a nearly complete description of OSI architecture and terminology. To obtain a complete description of Internet architecture and terminology, readers must "trawl" the RFC directories. Two noteworthy sources for information on this subject are *Perspective on the ARPANET Reference Model* (RFC 871) and *Hitchhikers Guide to the Internet* (RFC 1118).

4 THE LANGUAGES OF
OPEN SYSTEMS

Introduction

Traditionally, data exchanged between applications across networks have been treated as arbitrarily long strings of "*n*-bit" bytes (typically, in TCP/IP and OSI, $n = 8$; hence, the term *octet* is used throughout). Applications did not distinguish how data were represented as an end (user) form from the way they were transferred. This was (and remains) especially true for the Internet application protocols, where the support of ASCII as the principal character set for providing human-to-terminal interfaces evolved in such a fashion that ASCII became the *de facto* programming language used for defining commands and replies (protocols) for computer-to-computer applications such as electronic mail and file transfer.

Parallel to the development of the OSI protocols, a set of nonproprietary languages has been developed and standardized for open systems to accommodate data representation ("abstract syntax notation") and a corresponding encoding for data transfer ("transfer syntax"). They provide a universal language for network application programming that enables applications to exchange values of data without losing the semantics of those data (how they are structured, what types of data are present in a complex data structure, how long the structure is). These languages are covered in some detail in this chapter, as they illuminate a number of differences in the approaches that have been applied to open systems networking by the OSI and TCP/IP architectures. Readers will also note that the languages ostensibly created for OSI have been applied to more recently developed Internet applications, most notably in the area of network management.

Equally important to the study of languages are the practices of naming and addressing; the definition and representation of names are discussed in this chapter, while the details of the overall naming and addressing strategies of OSI and TCP/IP are described in Chapter 5. A subpractice of naming—protocol identification ("protocol IDs")—is described in chapters in which this practice is relevant.

"Open" Languages—Breaking Language Barriers

A computer vendor promoting a proprietary network architecture based on its own products can define and use whatever terms it likes, name things without worrying about conflicts or ambiguity, and document its work using the descriptive notations and syntaxes that are most convenient for its technical writers and customer-training people. When you own the show, you can make the rules, and anyone who wants to participate has to learn to speak your language. The architectural "language barrier" is a powerful argument for network homogeneity—one that many computer vendors have used to effectively exclude their competitors' products from participation in networks based on their proprietary architecture. Homogeneity, of course, is precisely the prison from which the open systems networking concept promises to release the builders and users of networks. In order to do so, it must define and use terminology, naming schemes, and descriptive techniques—*languages*—that are universally understood.

| ·AHA· | *It is hard to overemphasize the importance of languages in the development of open systems. During a meeting in 1988 of the* |

ISO/IEC standards committee concerned with network-layer standards (ISO/IEC JTC 1/SC 6/WG 2), the editor for one of the OSI routing protocol standards, Dave Oran, was engaged in a discussion with another delegate about the relationship between level-1 and level-2 intradomain routing. Across the table, three Japanese delegates were following the discussion intently with the help of a Japanese-English dictionary. Repeatedly, Dave attempted to make what seemed to him an obvious point; the other delegate continued to disagree with equal resolve. After several iterations, it suddenly dawned on Dave that the other delegate's understanding of the situation was radically different from what he had assumed, at which point he sat back and said, "Well, if that's what you mean, then we're really in deep sneakers!" During the brief silence that followed, one could hear the pages flipping in the dictionary as the Japanese dele-

gates searched for the word sneakers; *then a buzz of whispered consultation among the three in Japanese and more page flipping to confirm that they had indeed found the correct definition of* sneakers. *Finally, the head delegate turned to Dave and, with an expression of intense consternation, asked, "Excuse me, Mr. Editor, but please explain* deep sneakers."

The work of all the major international standards organizations, including ISO and CCITT, is conducted almost exclusively in English; non–English-speaking delegates are expected to either learn to cope in "English-as-a-second-language" mode or provide their own translations of documents (a daunting prospect, considering the enormous amount of documentation that attends even the simplest standardization effort). The result is to give a significant practical advantage to native English speakers—and fluent non-native English speakers—in the formal standards-development process. In effect, ISO and CCITT have adopted English as the "standard" language for standards development, with a significant penalty for noncompliance.

Data Representation

Five thousand years ago, the Sumerians, Babylonians, and Egyptians encountered a problem conducting commerce in ancient Mesopotamia: although they generally agreed on the representation of simple numbers (*1*, *2*, and *3*) as recognizably similar stroke or cuneiform numerals, they did not agree on the representation of larger numbers and did not (originally) agree on syntactic markers for place value or the way in which graphic symbols for basic units (such as *10* and *60*) should be composed to represent a numerical sum (such as the value "80" represented by the composition of symbols for *60 + 10 + 10*). In the years since then, the problem of unambiguously representing numerical and non-numerical data has grown steadily worse, as the number of things demanding unambiguous representation has kept pace with the increasing complexity of social and economic intercourse. The absolute literal-mindedness of the computer turned this problem into a genuine nightmare, but it took networking to turn the problem into a nightmare of global proportions.

Although we have introduced a formal language and grammar— mathematics—the general issue of dealing with numbers has changed little since the time of ancient Mesopotamia. Even those who have had little formal education in mathematics understand the notion of a whole number or an integer—no fractional parts, positives and negatives, remember? Someone says "integer," and we think {. . . , –2, –1, 0, 1, 2, . . .}:

517 is an integer, *67,190* is an integer, and Avogadro's number[1] is an integer. We can pretty much grasp this without advanced degrees. The notion of integer in this context is *abstract*.

Generally speaking, programming languages such as C and Pascal have a model of "integer" that is less abstract than the pure number-theory concept of "integer" but more abstract than the way in which a particular operating system stores things that are labeled "integers" into containers (memory locations). Consider that when a mathematician says "integer," she is dealing with the entire unconstrained concept of integer (abstract); but when a programmer says "integer" to the UNIX 4.2bsd C compiler by declaring a variable to be of type short, she gets a signed 15-bit container capable of expressing "integer" values in the range −32,678 through 32,767, and if she declares the variable to be of type unsigned long, she gets a 32-bit container capable of expressing "integer" values in the range 0 through $2^{32} - 1$. These represent a more *concrete syntax* of integer—i.e., one that is semantically bound to the machine and operating system architecture on which the C program is compiled. And finally, when the C compiler generates machine-language instructions for a particular computer, the concept of "integer" is not even present—there is only the concept of binary numbers (a concrete representation) constrained to fit into containers of a certain size.

As a rule, when people discuss numbers, they don't think of "containers" for integers. Computers, and folks who program them, do (a preoccupation inherited in part from times when memory was a scarce and precious resource, and by today's standards, outrageously expensive). Now, containers have built-in limitations on ranges of numbers; for example, encoded in hexadecimal, the value "517" requires a 2-octet container; the value "67,190" requires 3 octets; and the value of Avogadro's number requires many. By and large, folks who program computers don't expect ranges of values as broad as Avogadro's number when they define data constructs in programming languages like C and Pascal as part of the process of writing applications. Typically, they define containers that appear to satisfy near- and modestly long-term needs. This is true for protocols as well (protocol headers are, after all, merely another form of data structure). A version field of a protocol doesn't appear to require more than an octet; heaven forbid we ever reach 255 versions of any single protocol and require yet another octet to encode version 256! On the

---

1.   The number of atoms in a mole—the amount of any substance whose weight in grams is numerically equal to its atomic or molecular weight. Avogadro's number is 6.02 × 10^{23}.

other hand, a 16-bit container for the window-size field of TCP, which allowed for a 65,535-octet window, and the 32-bit sequence-number field seemingly satisfied long-term needs in the 1970s; with multimegabit, fiber "data pipes," these containers are now generally regarded as too small.[2]

There is another complication when dealing with the representation of numbers in computers and programming languages: even within the context of the same programming language, different machine architectures may interpret a data structure in an entirely different manner. Take the `int` example. Compiling the same C program containing `int` declarations on two different machines may produce two different results: on a DEC PDP-11, an `int` without qualification is 16 bits, whereas on a VAX 11/780, an `int` without qualification is 32 bits, effectively begging the question of whether either interpretation matches the programmer's intent.

Of course, such problems extend beyond the world of whole numbers; only some of the data we represent in computers are integers. The variation among machine architectures in their representation of more complicated data types—real numbers, complex numbers, characters, graphic strings—is even worse. This introduces yet another issue: how to preserve the semantics of information as well as the value when it is exchanged between two computers.

All of these factors make for pretty messy networking; clearly, there can be no networking of open systems without a standardized, machine-independent language in which it is possible to represent basic information elements in such a way that (1) the information can be interpreted unambiguously in any context; (2) the values of data structures can be, in principle, unbounded; and (3) the information can be conveyed between computer systems without loss of semantics.

OSI captures the meaning (semantics) of data exchanged between open systems (the *abstract syntax*) independently from the specification and internal representation of that data in a computer (the *concrete syntax*) and the bit patterns used to transmit the data structure from one computer to another (the *transfer syntax*). The separation of abstract from

---

2.   In RFC 1323, *TCP Extensions for High Performance*, Jacobson, Braden, and Borman discuss the problem of dealing with "long delay paths"—links with high bandwidth × delay products; over such links (e.g., SONET OC-3C [155 Mbps] and future gigabit transcontinental U.S. fiber links), the 32-bit sequence number can "wrap" dangerously close to or faster than the 2-minute maximum segment limit assumed by TCP, and the 16-bit window size, which limits the effective bandwidth to $2^{16/RTT}$ (round-trip time) is insufficient to "fill the pipe." (Here, the U.S. transcontinental delay, approximately 60 milliseconds, represents a hard-and-fast lower bound on RTT, which cannot be defied.)

concrete and transfer syntax is significant in the sense that data can be represented without concern for the container size for the data or the manner in which they are recorded in any given computer.

Abstract Syntax Notation

Abstract Syntax Notation One (ASN.1 ISO/IEC 8824: 1987, which is equivalent to CCITT Recommendation X.208) is arguably the most widely accepted language for the representation of data for open systems networking. ASN.1 was originally developed as part of the work on OSI upper-layer standards to serve as a uniform canonical representation of any data type (both predefined, or standardized, data types and user-defined data types), so that *objects* in the OSI environment—protocol headers, electronic-mail message headers and bodies, directory entries, management information, and virtual filestores—might be conveyed from one system to another in a form that could be understood without reference (adherence) to any specific machine or operating system architecture. ASN.1 has since been adopted as the specification language of choice by people working in areas other than OSI, including TCP/IP, despite the fact that it is frequently criticized as expensive, in terms of processor cycles, to perform the transformation between a system's native (hardware- and operating system–specific) representation of data and ASN.1.

Readers who are familiar with the terminology of database management will recognize ASN.1 as a *data-description language*. ISO/IEC 8824 defines the language itself and the many predefined data types that it standardizes. A companion standard, ISO/IEC 8825: 1987 (CCITT Recommendation X.209), defines *basic encoding rules* (BER) for encoding the abstract data types of ASN.1 as actual bit streams that are exchanged by open systems. Although the standards do not require the exclusive use of the ISO 8825 basic encoding rules to encode ASN.1, in practice almost every encoding of ASN.1 is specified according to the basic encoding rules.

As a general-purpose data-description language, ASN.1 can be used in many different ways. Its original use, especially in its earliest incarnation as CCITT X.409-1984, was to specify the contents of the headers of the OSI Message Handling System and upper-layer protocols; ASN.1 descriptions are used to specify protocol data units, to define objects that can be used to manage network resources, and to define objects and object attributes that can be registered and entered into a global database or directory. ASN.1 offers the equivalent of programming tools of grammar. Using ASN.1, one can construct arbitrarily complex data structures and retain the semantics of these data structures across many and diverse computer (operating) systems. One can think of protocol data units encoded in ASN.1 as verbs (they request actions such as get, set, modify, read, open, close, search, and initialize) and their objects as nouns—one "gets" the value of a management object, for example, or "reads" an attribute from a directory entry. There is even a means of assigning proper names—object identifiers.

ASN.1 Data Types and Tags

Like many programming languages, ASN.1 provides the means to identify the type of data structure. The data types that are predefined by ISO/IEC 8824 cover most of those types that are required for the specification of protocols (see Table 4.1).

In ASN.1, data are typed as either *simple* or *structured*. Simple data types are rather intuitive; they are data types that are defined by the set of values that may be specified for that type, for example:

- A BOOLEAN has two distinguished values ("true" and "false").
- An INTEGER may be assigned any of the set of positive and negative whole numbers.

TABLE 4.1   ASN.1 Data Types

Number (Tag)	Type	Number (Tag)	Type
1	BOOLEAN	17	SET, SET OF
2	INTEGER	18	NumericString
3	BITSTRING	19	PrintableString
4	OCTETSTRING	20	TeletexString (T61String)
5	NULL	21	VideotexString
6	OBJECT IDENTIFIER	22	IA5String
7	ObjectDescriptor	23	UTCTime
8	EXTERNAL	24	GeneralizedTime
9	REAL	25	GraphicsString
10	ENUMERATED	26	VisibleString
11	CHOICE	27	GeneralString
12–15	Reserved for Addenda		
16	SEQUENCE, SEQUENCE OF	28	CharacterString

- A REAL may be assigned any of the members of the set of real numbers—i.e., a number that can be stored in floating-point processors and represented by the general formula $mantissa \times base^{exponent}$.
- BITSTRING and OCTETSTRING may be composed of an ordered sequence of 0 or more bits and octets, respectively (and similarly for other character-string types—e.g., NumericString, Printable-String).
- The ever-interesting NULL may be assigned the singular value "null."
- An ENUMERATED type is one for which a list of values is identified as part of the type notation.

Structured data types are constructed from the simple data types. The availability of so many simple types alone provides for a wealth of combinatorial possibilities. Commonly used structured types are:

- SET, a fixed, unordered list of distinct types, some of which may be optional.
- SET OF, an unordered list of zero or more of the same type.
- SEQUENCE, a fixed, ordered list of distinct types.
- SEQUENCE OF, an ordered list of zero or more of the same type.
- CHOICE, like SET, a fixed, unordered list of distinct types, but in which any instance of a CHOICE takes the value of one of the component types.
- The nefarious ANY, a CHOICE type bounded not by a list of distinct types but by anything that can be defined using ASN.1, which is often used to indicate "I dunno" or "for further study".

Figure 4.1 provides examples of simple and structured data types.

The *OBJECT IDENTIFIER* data type serves as the basis for a general-purpose naming scheme that can be used to identify anything that can usefully be represented in an open systems architecture as an "object." As one might expect, there are a great many "things" in a network that can usefully be modeled as objects (borrowing at least some of the information-theoretical "object" model that has been used in, for example, object-oriented programming languages). *Object identifiers* (OIDs) serve as a uniform way to refer unambiguously to any of these "things" (this is examined more closely in Chapter 5).

Each data type is assigned a unique numeric *tag* for unambiguous identification within the domain of types. These are intended mainly for machine use, and they provide the data-stream identification of a data type. There are four classes of tags. The UNIVERSAL tags are defined in ISO/IEC 8824 and shown in Table 4.1. Tags that are assigned in other OSI standards—e.g., tags that identify protocol data units of applications

```
brainDamaged         ::= BOOLEAN

numberOfEmployees    ::= INTEGER    -- one typically hires integral numbers of employees

avogadrosNumber      ::= REAL { 602, 10, 23 }

                                -- value of Avogadro's number is 6.02 × 10^23

digitizedVoice       ::= BITSTRING

G3NonBasicParams     ::= BITSTRING {
                              twoDimensional(8),
                              fineResolution(9),
                              unlimitedLength(20),
                              b4Length(21),
                              a3Width(22),
                              b4Width(23),
                              uncompressed(30) } -- from CCITT X.411-1984

UMPDU                ::= OCTETSTRING     -- from CCITT X.411-1984
                                    -- no enumerated values, can be any length

sevenDeadlySins      ::= ENUMERATED { pride(1), envy(2), gluttony(3), avarice(4),
                              lust(5), sloth(6), wrath(7) }
                     -- corresponds to seven layers of OSI


messageBody          ::= SEQUENCE OF BodyPart
                     -- every element of "Body" is of type messageBodyPart, defined as follows:
messageBodyPart      ::= CHOICE {
                              [0] IMPLICIT asciiText, -- an IA5STRING
                              [1] IMPLICIT telex,     -- an OCTETSTRING
                              [2] IMPLICIT voice,       -- a BITSTRING
                              [3] IMPLICIT G3Facsimile, -- a SEQUENCE
                              [4] IMPLICIT teletex,   -- an OCTETSTRING
                              [5] IMPLICIT graphicalImage } -- a BITSTRING
-- the use of the keyword IMPLICIT indicates that the tag of the tagged types in the CHOICE need
    not be
-- encoded when data type is transferred; results in minimum transfer of octets without loss of
    semantics

TeletexNonBasicParams   ::= SET {
                              graphicCharacterSets [0] IMPLICIT T61String OPTIONAL,
                              controlCharacterSets [1] IMPLICIT T61String OPTIONAL,
                              pageFormats [2] IMPLICIT OCTETSTRING OPTIONAL,
                              misTerminalCapabilities [3] IMPLICIT T61String
                                   OPTIONAL,
                              privateUse [4] IMPLICIT OCTETSTRING OPTIONAL }
-- OPTIONAL indicates that there is no constraint on the presence or absence of the element type
```

Note: The double hyphen is used by ASN.1 to denote a comment.

FIGURE 4.1   Examples of ASN.1 Data Type Definitions

such as the X.500 Directory or the X.400 Message Handling System—are
assigned APPLICATION-specific tags. Tags that have context within a

type (that is, within an already tagged type)—e.g., members of a set, elements of "fields" of a protocol data unit—are as-signed CONTEXT-SPECIFIC tags. Finally, ASN.1 has provisions for organizations and countries to define additional data types; types of this origin are distinguished from others of like origin by PRIVATE tags.

Modules

A set or collection of ASN.1-related descriptions is called a module. A module of ASN.1 statements can be compared to a source file from a library of files that are included in a C or Pascal program. Rather than labor through the fairly intuitive syntax of a module, a fragment of an ASN.1 module is illustrated in Figure 4.2 (the keywords and relevant elements of the module definition are in boldface type).

Note that like other programming languages, ASN.1 permits the import and export of modules of ASN.1 (absent in this example). Thus, if another application service would find it useful to import the FTAM defi-

```
ISO8571-FTAM DEFINITIONS ::=
BEGIN
PDU ::= CHOICE              { InitializePDU, FilePDU, BulkdataPDU }
InitializePDU ::= CHOICE    { [APPLICATION 0] IMPLICIT FINITIALIZErequest,
                           [1] IMPLICIT FINITIALIZEresponse,
                           [2] IMPLICIT FTERMINATErequest,
                           [3] IMPLICIT FTERMINATEresponse,
                           [4] IMPLICIT FUABORTrequest,
                           [5] IMPLICIT FPABORTresponse }
FINITIALIZErequest ::=      SEQUENCE {
                           protocolId[0] INTEGER { isoFTAM(0) },
  versionNumber[1] IMPLICIT SEQUENCE { major INTEGER,
                           minor INTEGER },
                           serviceType[2] INTEGER { reliable (0), user correctable
                           (1) }
                           serviceClass[3] INTEGER { transfer (0), access (1),
                           management (2) }
                           functionalUnits[4] BITSTRING { read (0), write (1),
                           fileAccess (2),
-- definitions continue . . .
FINITIALIZEresponse ::= SEQUENCE . . .
-- definitions continue . . .
END
```

Source: ISO 8571, "File Transfer, Access, and Management" (1988).

FIGURE 4.2   Example of an ASN.1 Module

nitions, it could do so rather than defining these same ASN.1 types again.

Note that in addition to a module reference or name, the DE-SCRIPTION statement may include an *object identifier* to provide a globally unique identifier for this module. (Object identifiers are rather unique ASN.1 simple types that provide a universal identification mechanism and are covered under the general rubric of naming and addressing; see Chapter 5.)

Transfer Syntax—Basic Encoding Rules (BER) for ASN.1

Constructing the bit-stream representation of the number *255* is a relatively simple task—eight binary 1s, and you don't even have to worry about the order of bit transmission. It is quite another issue to indicate along with this bit-stream representation whether the originator of these eight binary 1s intended that they be interpreted as the integer *255* or 1 octet of a much larger integer or the "true" value of a BOOLEAN data type or the mantissa of a real number. To preserve semantics of a data type, to accommodate values of indefinite length, and to accommodate the transmission of complex data structures in which component data types may be present or absent (OPTIONAL), encoding and transmitting the value are simply not enough.

The bit patterns used to transmit ASN.1-encoded data types from one computer to another—the *transfer syntax*—are defined in ISO/IEC 8825: 1987, *Specification of Basic Encoding Rules for Abstract Syntax Notation One (ASN.1)*. There are three components to an encoding: the identifier or *tag*, the *length*, and the contents or *value*; the term *TLV encoding* is derived from the names of the fields of encodings (Rose 1990).

To say that the basic encoding rules are arcane is an understatement. Like so many aspects of OSI, the efficiency of BER has been compromised by the perceived need for backward compatibility with its ancestor, CCITT X.409-1984. The identifier octets, which convey the type class and number (tag), are encoded in one of two manners. Bits 8 and 7 of the initial identifier octet indicate the *class*—UNIVERSAL (00), APPLI-CATION (01), CONTEXT-SPECIFIC (10), or PRIVATE (11). Bit 6 identifies whether the data type is primitive (0) or constructed (1). The remaining bits of this octet contain the tag number if the number is in the range $0 < \text{tag number} < 31$:

Bits 8 and 7	Bit 6	Bits 5, 4, 3, 2, and 1
Class	Primitive/constructed	Tag number

For example, the identifier octet of the BOOLEAN "brainDamaged" from Figure 4.1 should convey the following information: UNIVERSAL, primitive, tag number 1. It is thus encoded in the following manner:

Bits 8 and 7	Bit 6	Bits 5, 4, 3, 2, and 1
00	0	00001

If the tag number exceeds 30, then the tag number field in the initial identifier octet is populated with the value "31," indicating "There are more identifier octets." Bit 8 of every subsequent octet is reserved as a flag, where the value "1" is used to indicate "More octets follow," and the value "0" indicates "This is the last octet of the tag number, I promise!" Thus, if an application had a protocol data unit with a tag number of 32, the identifier octets would look like this:

Initial Identifier Octet			Subsequent Octet	
Bits 8 and 7	Bit 6	Bits 5, 4, 3, 2, and 1	Bit 8	Bits 7–1
01	1	11111	0	0100000

There are two methods for encoding the length octets: using the *definite form*, 1 or more length octets indicate the length in octets of the value field. More bit cleverness is used to extend the length octets: here, bit 8 of the initial octet is reserved as a continuation/termination flag. A single length octet is used to indicate contents field lengths up to 127 octets (in such cases, bit 8 of this octet is 0); for contents fields with lengths greater than 127 octets, bit 8 of the initial octet is set to 1, and bits 7 through 1 indicate the number of subsequent octets in the length octets field. Thus, if the contents field of a data type is 202, the length octets are encoded as follows:

Initial Length Octet		Subsequent Octet
Bit 8	Bits 7–1	Bits 8–1
1	0000001	11001010

For the *indefinite form*, the initial length octet serves as the initial delimiter of the contents field: bit 8 of this octet is set to 0, bits 7 through 1 to 1—i.e., represented in hexadecimal as 01111111. The contents field follows this octet and is variable in length. An *end-of-contents* field follows the contents field: it is encoded as 2 octets containing binary 0s (treated as a basic encoding of a UNIVERSAL tag value zero of zero length).

Do I Really Have to Deal with All This?

Just as programmers are no longer expected to deal directly with low-level machine languages, protocol implementers are not expected to deal directly with ASN.1 and certainly not with BER unless they wish to. Public-domain and commercial ASN.1 compilers are available that accept a formal ASN.1 specification as input and produce reasonably machine-independent high-level language code (most commonly C code) for the programming language data structures that result from applying the basic encoding rules (or in some cases, any other encoding rules specified by the user) to the ASN.1 input stream. This permits implementers to deal with familiar elements of their favorite programming language to process protocol headers and other data items originally specified using ASN.1.

Running the protocol header specified formally by the ASN.1 statements shown in Figure 4.3 through an ASN.1 compiler might produce the C data structure shown in Figure 4.4.

This code would typically be incorporated into a program that would use it to construct outgoing protocol headers and to parse incoming ones. The actual bits transmitted and received would depend on the values given to the individual elements of the data structure in each instance.

It is possible to dig much deeper into the world of ASN.1; readers who are interested in doing so should consult Steedman (1990), which is entirely concerned with ASN.1. Other fertile but predictably harshly critical sources for acquiring more knowledge about ASN.1 are Rose (1990, 1991).

```
simpleDatagram DEFINITIONS ::=
BEGIN
PDU          ::= SEQUENCE {
                        protocolIdentifier [0]   INTEGER,
                        versionNumber [1]      INTEGER,
                        sourceAddress [2]      INTEGER,
                        destinationAddress [3]   INTEGER,
                        userData [4]           OCTETSTRING }
END
```

FIGURE 4.3   simpleDatagram Protocol Header in ASN.1

```
# define maxUserDataLength 255
struct _pduStruct_t {
                unsigned long           protocolIdentifier;
                unsigned long           versionNumber;
                unsigned long           sourceAddress;
                unsigned long           destinationAddress;
                userData                char[maxUserDataLength]
} pduStruct-t
```

FIGURE 4.4   simpleDatagram Protocol Header in C

Languages and the TCP/IP Community

Most of the applications written for TCP/IP are written in a programming language and compiled to an executable format suitable to the machine and operating system on which the application will reside. Application protocol data units are often plain-text ASCII with specific guidelines for the interpretation of keywords, "white space," special characters, and escape character sequences (see, for example, Internet mail, discussed in Chapter 8). Although this may not at first seem particularly elegant, it has the very desirable characteristics of (1) being nearly universally understood and (2) getting the job done.

Some TCP/IP applications make use of machine-independent data-definition languages. The popular Network File System (RFC 1057; Sandberg 1988) uses External Data Representation (RFC 1094), which, although admittedly highly optimized for translation to and from UNIX/C data representations, is easily ported to operating systems such as MS-DOS. ASN.1 is used in the definition of the Simple Network Management Protocol (SNMP; see Chapter 9) and in the definition of managed objects for the SNMP; and of course, the OSI upper-layers implementations that run on top of TCP/IP are encoded in ASN.1.

Only a subset of ASN.1 is used to define SNMP. The full comple-

```
IfEntry ::=
    SEQUENCE {
      ifIndex
         INTEGER,
      ifDescr
         DisplayString,
      ifType
         INTEGER,
      ifMtu
         INTEGER,
      ifSpeed          --a gauge is an application-specific ASN.1 data structure in SNMP
         Gauge,        --it is a 32-bit INTEGER that can increase or decrease but will not "wrap"
      ifPhysAddress
         OCTETSTRING,
      ifAdminStatus
         INTEGER,
      ifOperStatus
         INTEGER,
      ifLastChange     --timeticks is an application-specific ASN.1 data structure in SNMP
         Timeticks,    --it is an INTEGER; each increment represents .01 second of time
      ifInOctets       -- a counter is an application-specific ASN.1 data structure in SNMP
         Counter,      --it is a 32-bit INTEGER that monotonically increases and "wraps"
      ifInUcastPkts
         Counter,
      ifInNUcast Pkts
         Counter,
      ifInDiscards
         Counter,
      ifInErrors
         Counter,
      ifInUnknownProtos
         Counter,
      ifOutOctets
         Counter,
      ifOutUcastPkts
         Counter
      ifOutNUcastPkts
         Counter,
      ifOutDiscards
         Counter,
      ifOutErrors
         Counter,
      ifOutQLen
         Gauge,
      ifSpecific
         OBJECT IDENTIFIER
}
```

FIGURE 4.5   SNMP Table ifTable in ASN.1

ment of ASN.1 data types was considered to be burdensome to impose on computer systems that had roles in life other than performing management operations. The predominant sentiment in the Internet community is that like many OSI efforts, ASN.1 tried to be all things for all people, for all time, and the result was something certainly general but too complex. SNMP uses the simple types INTEGER, OCTETSTRING, OBJECT IDENTIFIER, and NULL, as well as the structured types SEQUENCE and SEQUENCE OF (basically, everything you could construct using the standard C programming-language data structures, int and char). The other data types that are needed are emulated using this reduced set. A BOOLEAN, for example, is represented as an INTEGER with two values, true and false; relative time is represented as an INTEGER as well, with each INTEGER value representing a hundredth of a second, or a "timetick." The rest of the ASN.1 types, it is argued, are inessential (and expensive) luxuries.

An example of ASN.1 use in the SNMP is shown in Figures 4.5 and 4.6. The SNMP table ifTable was compiled using an ASN.1 compiler; the compiler creates an "include" file, which contains the C data structure shown in Figure 4.6.

```
typedef
struct _ifEntry_t {
    long                ifIndex;
    OctetString         *ifDescr;
    long                ifType;
    long                ifMtu;
    unsigned long       ifSpeed;
    OctetString         *ifPhysAddress;
    long                ifAdminStatus;
    long                ifOperStatus;
    unsigned long       ifLastChange;
    unsigned long       ifInOctets;
    unsigned long       ifInUcastPkts;
    unsigned long       ifInNUcastPkts;
    unsigned long       ifInDiscards;
    unsigned long       ifInErrors;
    unsigned long       ifInUnknownProtos;
    unsigned long       ifOutOctets;
    unsigned long       ifOutUcastPkts;
    unsigned long       ifOutNUcastPkts;
    unsigned long       ifOutDiscards;
    unsigned long       ifOutErrors;
    unsigned long       ifOutQLen;
    OID                 *ifSpecific;
} ifEntry_t;
```

FIGURE 4.6   ifTable in C, as Generated by an ASN.1 Compiler

Conclusion

This chapter has described the formal way in which data are represented in OSI applications and the means by which not only the values of data but the semantics associated with them are transferred between distributed applications. The authors have described only enough of ASN.1, the data-definition language used in the development of OSI application services, to enable readers to understand some of the protocol examples given in the text. Readers interested in the details and intricacies of ASN.1 are encouraged to read Steedman (1990). This chapter has also described the way data are represented and manipulated by TCP/IP applications and how ASN.1 is applied in the Internet as well as the OSI community, but with an economy of data-type definitions (see also RFCs 1155, 1157, and 1213). And finally, the chapter has introduced the notion of object identification; in the following chapters, readers will appreciate the important role that object identifiers play in the open systems "name game."

5

NAMES AND ADDRESSES

John Schoch's well-known differentiation of names, addresses, and routes (Schoch 1978) unintentionally spawned widespread misunderstanding of the role of naming in network architectures. It asserts that names and addresses are fundamentally different and that routes and addresses are unrelated. In fact, anything that serves semantically to identify is, by definition, a name. An address is simply a name with special properties: an address is also a name (of a point within a specified coordinate system), but not all names are addresses. A route is not an identifier at all, but a specification of a path from one point to another in a graph that represents the topology of a particular network at a particular point in time.

To understand the role that they play in open systems networking, it is not important to recognize a high-level distinction between names in general and the names of network locations (addresses). In this chapter, the discussion of "names" applies as well to the special class of names that are addresses. Routes, since they are not identifiers, are covered elsewhere (in Chapter 14). We also discuss the role of registration authorities in the administration of open system naming schemes and describe the most important classes of names and addresses (some of which are covered, in much greater detail, in the chapters that describe the network components that actually use them).

Names

The importance of naming schemes should be intuitively obvious to anyone who has ever dealt with a large distributed system of any kind (such as the postal mail system, a motor-vehicle registry, or a computer network). A naming scheme specifies the structure and significance of names and the way in which a name is allocated (selected from the set—the "name space"—of all possible names) and assigned (associated with, or "bound to," the particular object for which it is the identifier).

A naming scheme may be characterized according to a number of basic criteria, including:

- *Scope:* whether a naming scheme is intended to apply globally to an entire class (or to entire classes) of objects or is intended to be understood only within and with respect to a particular local context
- *User-friendliness:* whether a name must be intelligible to and usable by a human user or is intended only for communication among "nonhuman" network elements
- *Scale:* the ability of a naming scheme to accommodate an increase in both the number and (potentially) the internal complexity of names as the size of the corresponding system increases
- *Permanence:* whether the binding of a name to an object is transient (and whether or not the name may be reassigned to another object after its association with one object has ended) or persistent (and if the latter, whether or not the name or some part of it must be registered with a formal registration authority in order to ensure that it can be used unambiguously throughout an open system)

The way in which a particular type of name will be used determines the importance of each of these criteria to the design of an appropriate naming scheme. For example, a system of names for houses along a street ("street numbers") will generally be designed for limited scope (the context is provided by the street; different houses on different streets may have the same street number without ambiguity); a high degree of user-friendliness (since human "users" will be writing these street numbers on envelopes; they should probably not, for example, start at 5,354,201 or some other large number); the ability to scale to at least the number of houses that might reasonably be built along the street, coupled with an assignment rule that leaves enough space between adjacent house numbers to accommodate the future construction of new houses on side lots; and of course, permanence (for which the guarantor is often the town's tax assessor).

Hierarchy

The most straightforward way to keep track of the names that have been allocated from a particular name space is simply to enumerate them in a list, in which each name appears once. If the number of names that have been allocated is "small enough,"[1] this is also a perfectly practical way to keep track of them and to advertise them if necessary (so as to make the names, and their object bindings, known to potential users); but if the number grows too large, the cost of maintaining and distributing the simple enumerated list of names eventually becomes excessive. However, for a "flat" name space, from which names with no discernible structure are allocated, there is no alternative: every reference by name to a set of objects must name every member of the set individually.

If the names associated with a particular name space do have a discernible structure, however, they can be grouped accordingly. The structure may be syntactic or semantic, or some combination. In the case of street numbers, for example, it is common to allocate only odd numbers to houses along one side of the street and only even numbers to houses along the other side, which creates a discrimination that is based on a semantic attribute of the house number. In order to make a statement about the entire collection of houses on one side of the street, it is not necessary to enumerate every house number; it is sufficient to refer to "the houses with odd [or "even," as the case may be] house numbers." In large condominium complexes consisting of more than one building, it is also common to name individual condominium units by means of a two-part identifier, the first part of which names the building and the second part of which names the unit within the building (such as "B-42" for unit 42 in building B). The syntax of the name creates a discrimination that allows the local fire department, for example, to determine which building to train its hoses on without individually identifying all the units contained within that building (all of which, in the case of a building fire, share a common fate).

The second example illustrates the usefulness of *hierarchy* as a way of structuring an address space. In a hierarchically structured name space, individual names (and the objects to which they are bound) can be effectively grouped into larger and larger aggregations based on some property of the objects that is reflected in a corresponding hierarchical property of the name space. Such a structure, which is commonly represented by an inverted tree diagram, makes it possible to refer to a collec-

---

1. "Small enough" is, of course, a subjective measure; what is "small enough" for a computer's database-management system may be "too large" by far for a human administrator with a clipboard.

L. I. H. E.
THE BECK LIBRARY
WOOLTON RD., LIVERPOOL, L16 8ND

tion of objects by giving just the name of the collection (the subset, or "subtree," of the structure that contains all the objects that share a common property of interest) rather than exhaustively naming the individual elements of the subset.

Although hierarchies are generally established according to criteria that are related to some property of the named objects—their location within a network, for example—they may also be established purely for administrative convenience, without reference to any essential property of the named objects. It might be convenient, for example, to define a hierarchy within a hitherto flat name space in order to distribute the job of allocating and assigning names among several managers, even though a hierarchically structured name space does not confer any benefit with respect to dealing with the named objects; in such a case, there is no practical significance to the fact that the name of an object appears in one part of the hierarchy or another.

Occasionally, the desire to establish a hierarchical structure based on the corresponding real-world organization of the named objects collides with an equally strong desire to establish a hierarchical structure based on the administrative convenience of the registration authority or authorities responsible for the task of managing the assignment of names. More often, however, there is a natural relationship between the way in which objects are organized (the practical hierarchy) and the way in which their names are most readily managed (the administrative, or naming, hierarchy).

The difficulty of managing a flat name space increases linearly with its size. The difficulty of managing a hierarchical name space can be made to increase at a much slower rate by judicious selection of the hierarchy. As we will see in the chapters on the network layer (Chapter 13) and routing (Chapter 14), the selection of an appropriate hierarchy determines whether or not a network architecture *scales* well—that is, whether it supports a network that can continue to grow in size and extent or creates practical upper bounds on size and extent that inhibit the network's growth.

OSI Naming Architecture

The OSI naming architecture is described in part 3 of the OSI reference model (ISO/IEC 7498-3: 1989), *Naming and Addressing*. In the layered architecture of OSI, *entities* represent the active agents that operate within a layer to carry out its assigned functions (see Chapter 3); entities are named by *entity titles*, or simply *titles*. Service access points (SAPs) represent the logical interfaces between adjacent layers, at which the lower-layer service is conceptually presented to and received by the upper layer. Service access points are named by *service access point addresses*.

In principle, each of the seven layers of the OSI reference model contains named ("titled") entities, and each of the six layer service boundaries (there is no application-layer service boundary) is speckled with addressable service access points. In practice, however, the only important titles are those associated with entities in the application and network layers: application entity titles (AE-titles), because they are the basic unit of identification for OSI applications (the "end users" of an OSI network), and network entity titles (NETs), because routing information is exchanged among network entities independent of any particular data flow between network service access points. None of the other layers contains entities that need to refer to each other independent of the service access points to which they provide access. The truly important addresses are the network, or network service access point (NSAP), address (which identifies individual hosts connected to the network), and the subnetwork address (which identifies a point at which any system—host or router—is logically or physically attached to a real network).

Service access point addresses above the network layer are constructed by simply concatenating a *selector* to the next-lower-layer service access point address. The selectors are used to accomplish a "fan-out" at the layer service boundary to (potentially) multiple entities in the layer above. The presentation address is the culmination of this process of address composition—it identifies an application entity, which is as far up the stack as you can go in the OSI architecture. The presentation address is particularly significant as the point at which the names associated with applications are coupled to the addresses that are used by OSI-defined services and protocols (see Chapters 7 and 11). Below the network layer, the abstract concepts of "service access point" and "service access point address" bear only a forced and awkward relevance to the technology-specific data link and physical components of real networks and are best left unexplored.[2]

Application Entity Titles	Since the ultimate sources and sinks of information in an OSI network are application entities, every end-user interaction in an OSI environ-

2.   This is an excellent example of the benefit of knowing what is and is not important! The ISO and CCITT committees concerned with data link–layer standards have spent endless hours debating the existence and properties of data link addresses without coming to any satisfying conclusions that apply to the data link service in general (rather than to one or more data link technologies in particular). This unproductive exercise has been pursued because the groups involved failed to recognize a very basic point: that the concept of "service access point address" is not useful in the context of the data link service (notwithstanding the reference model mandate that all service boundaries have SAPs and all SAPs have addresses).

ment depends, at some point, on the identification of the participating application entities by their application entity titles, and by implication, the presentation address associated with that title.

Prior to the development of the X.500-series standards for the OSI Directory, the syntax of application entity titles was poorly defined. However, this caused very few problems because, in the absence of a directory, the early end users of OSI were unlikely to make use of any of the application-layer features that would have required them to know what an application entity title was. The ASN.1-encoded, generic form of application entity title, contained in early drafts of the OSI standard for registration authorities (ISO/IEC 9834-1: 1991), was both very simple and not very useful:

```
AE-Title ::= SEQUENCE {
             AP-Title,
             AE-Qualifier }
```

The registration authority standard also defined an all-numeric form of application entity title, in which the application process title (AP-Title in the ASN.1 definition) part is syntactically an object identifier, and the application entity qualifier (AE-Qualifier) part is an integer:

```
AP-Title ::= IMPLICIT objectIdentifier
AE-Qualifier ::= INTEGER
```

The agreements reached by ISO/IEC and CCITT on the 1988 (and subsequent) directory standards (see Chapter 7) included the recognition of two well-defined forms for the application entity title, one of which is the object identifier form just shown. The other, much more useful, form is one in which the application entity title is syntactically equivalent to a directory distinguished name:

```
AP-Title ::= RDNSequence
AE-Qualifier ::= RelativeDistinguishedName
```

A relative distinguished name sequence (RDNSequence) is just a sequence of relative distinguished names of entries in the directory information tree; in this second form of application entity title, the application process title contains the relative distinguished names of the directory entries from the root down to (but not including) the entry that represents the application entity, and the application entity qualifier adds the relative distinguished name of the application entity entry itself. This makes it easy to list an application entity in the directory and to refer to it by a distinguished name that may be used as a valid title for the application entity.

System Titles

Recognizing that applications—even OSI applications—necessarily reside in systems, and that people have become accustomed over the years to thinking about applications as "running on" a particular computer system, the OSI naming scheme defines the concept of *system title*, the effect of which is to bring the decomposition of the application entity title, begun in the previous subsection, even closer to the real world.

The concept of system title is equivalent to the familiar concept of *host name* in TCP/IP; it is a permanent identifier for a particular OSI end system (host), and the identification of applications running on that end system can be based on it by further decomposing the application process title in either its object identifier form or its relative distinguished name form:

Generic form:

```
AP-Title ::= SEQUENCE {
                System-Title,
                AP-Qualifier }
```
Form 1:

```
System-Title ::= RDNSequence
AP-Qualifier ::= RelativeDistinguishedName
```
Form 2:

```
System-Title ::= objectIdentifier
AP-Qualifier ::= INTEGER
```

The entire process of application entity title formation can now be traced back to the registration of system titles, or host names. The distinguished name form of an application entity title begins with a high-order sequence of relative distinguished names registered (implicitly, as a simple consequence of being entered in the directory information base, or explicitly) by a system-title registration authority, to which another relative distinguished name is concatenated to form an application process title, to which another relative distinguished name is concatenated to form an application entity title—*et voilà!* A similar process of concatenation of subidentifiers to a base system-title object identifier creates the object identifier form of an application entity title.

By convention, registration authorities for system titles and application process titles require the simultaneous allocation of both forms (object identifier and relative distinguished name sequence), which ensures that the values of both forms are (1) interchangeably available for use (they appear, logically, in the same place in the register) and (2) protected from allocation as the value of any other title.

TCP/IP Naming Architecture

The naming architecture of TCP/IP, being less deliberately abstract than that of OSI, is correspondingly simpler. It is entirely captured by the Domain Name System, which is discussed in Chapter 7.

Addresses

In the context of open systems networking, an address identifies a specific point in a graph that represents the topology of a particular logical network. That's pretty general, but in the OSI architecture, the concept of "address" is even broader, including the identification of points on the interfaces between the layers of the OSI reference model.

It turns out that the only OSI addresses worth talking about are the ones that are concerned with network and subnetwork topologies. In the TCP/IP architecture, which has never been encumbered by addressable points on its layer interfaces, the interesting addresses are the TCP/IP equivalents of OSI's network (NSAP) and subnetwork addresses: the IP (internet) address and the addresses of network interfaces. Both OSI network addresses and IP addresses are best understood in the context of the network layer and the routing protocols that use them and are thus discussed in more detail in Chapters 13 and 14. Subnetwork and interface addresses are inherently technology-specific: no matter how wonderful and/or pervasive a particular network is, there is always, somewhere, another (different) network to which it eventually must be connected, wherefore no subnetwork-specific address is a substitute for an internetwork address.

Registration Authorities

In order for names to be useful, there must be a way to ensure that the allocation and assignment of names is unambiguous and that the relationship between a name and the "thing" it names is maintained in such a way that users can find out what it is (by "looking it up"). The latter function is performed by a directory service and is covered in Chapter 7; the former is performed by a *registration authority*.[3]

A registration authority plays two important roles with respect to a

---

3.   It should be pointed out here that the term *registration* can imply either simple "listing," in which a name-to-thing relationship is recorded in a list (but about which the listing

particular class of names: it administers the name space, managing the actual allocation of values from the name space and the assignment of those values to things that are entitled to be identified by a name of that class; and it maintains a record of the name-to-thing bindings that it has created. This record of bindings may then be incorporated into a directory (see Chapter 7). It is important to recognize, however, that registration and directories are separate systems (although in some cases, as we shall see in our discussion of the Domain Name System in Chapter 7, they are inextricably linked). Registration may proceed whether or not there is a directory in which the registered names are listed. A directory, however, implies at least an informal or implicit registration authority responsible for the names that appear in the directory.

Registration Authority Procedures

In the OSI world, the way in which registration authorities operate is defined by an international standard, ISO/IEC 9834-1: 1991, which is (intentionally) identical to CCITT Recommendation X.660. This standard specifies a tree-structured name-registration hierarchy, within which individual registration authorities operate, exercising hegemony over that part of the global name space that is represented by the subtree for which the authority is the root. The topmost levels of the registration hierarchy are defined by ISO/IEC 8824 (CCITT X.208) and ISO/IEC 9834-1 (CCITT X.660), which together specify the registration hierarchy shown in Figure 5.1.

In the world of open systems, there are a great many identifier types that must be registered in order to ensure that they can be used unambiguously. In the OSI world, these include:

Document types
Standardized object identifiers
Virtual Terminal profiles and control objects profiles
AP titles and AE titles
Abstract syntaxes

---

agency makes no assertions of any kind), or "formal registration," in which the registering agency not only records and lists a name-to-thing relationship but also confers "legitimacy" on it—guaranteeing, for instance, that the name is not bound to any other object or that the person or organization registering the name has some legal right or entitlement that is expressed by the fact that the name is registered with the agency. At this time, it is not clear which model of "registration" applies to the registration authorities that have been and are being formed in support of open systems networking. It is likely, however, that registration authorities established by international standards or, within countries, by national governments or national standards organizations will operate in accordance with the "formal registration" model but that the directory systems in which name-to-thing bindings are recorded for others to "look up" will operate according to the "listing" model.

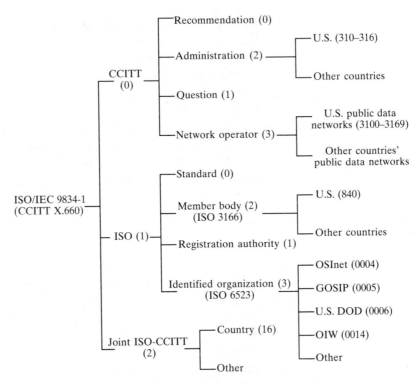

FIGURE 5.1   The OSI Name-Registration Hierarchy

Transfer syntaxes
Application context identifiers
System titles
Organization identifiers
Administration (public) messaging domain/private messaging
    domain (of X.400 MHS) names for message handling systems

Many of these identifiers are registered statically by the specification of
one or more ISO/IEC and/or CCITT standards or by national standards.
Others are registered dynamically, as necessary, by registration authorities constituted specifically for that purpose.

**The U.S.
Registration
Authority**

The American National Standards Institute (ANSI) operates a registration
authority that assigns organization names in two forms: (1) an alphanumeric form, which may consist of from 1 to 100 characters chosen from a
specified character set,[4] and (2) a numeric form, which consists of a posi-

4.   The character set is defined as registration number 102, the Teletex Set of Primary

tive decimal integer greater than or equal to 113,527 and less than 16 million. The numeric form may be obtained with or without a corresponding alphanumeric form, but the alphanumeric form is always accompanied by (and in the register, associated with) a numeric form.

·AHA· *Many people have wondered why ANSI decided to begin the assignment of numeric organization names at the nonintuitive value "113,527," which is not, among other things, a power of 2 (or any other interesting number). Realizing that they had to specify some value as the starting point (and hoping to avoid conferring any special cachet on the recipients of the first few numbers by starting at, say, "1"), the members of the U.S. registration authority committee were about to pick a "logical" number ("1,000," perhaps, or "2,048") when Jack Veenstra, the chairman of the committee, shouted "113,527!"—which was promptly dubbed the "Veenstra constant" and written into the registration authority procedures. Later, the members of the committee arranged for AT&T (Veenstra's employer) to receive the numeric organization name "113,527" in Jack's honor.*

An organization name may be used in several different ways to form unambiguous identifiers. The alphanumeric form is most often used as the organization name in an electronic-mail address (as, for example, the value of the "organization" or "organizational unit" elements of an X.400 originator/recipient address containing "/C = US"; see Chapter 8). The numeric form may be used as the value of the "organization" field in an OSI NSAP address constructed according to ANSI Standard X3.216-1992 (see Chapter 13) or as part of an object identifier prefix for constructing unambiguous object identifiers for organization-specific objects (such as, for example, organization-specific management information base variables for use with a network management system). The registration authority does not specify or constrain the way in which an organization name may be used, nor does it guarantee the legal right of an organization to actually use the name. Only one guarantee comes with an organization name obtained from ANSI's registration authority: that ANSI has not previously assigned the same name to anyone else and will not do so in the future.

Until recently, the U.S. name-registration authority conducted its business under the { iso (1) member-body (2) us (840) } arc of the registration hierarchy (see Figure 5.1), registering names for ANSI

Graphic Characters, of the ISO International Register of Character Sets to Be Used with Escape Sequences, plus the space character.

standards, private organizations with U.S. national standing, and the names of U.S. states and "state equivalents." In 1991, however, changes in the registration authority procedures standard—adopted as a result of joint efforts by ISO/IEC and CCITT to align their registration procedures, leading to a single standard (ISO/IEC 9834 | CCITT X.660)—invalidated this procedure; they required that private organization names with national standing be registered under the { joint-iso-ccitt (2) country (16) us (840) } arc of the registration hierarchy. This had two immediate, significant consequences: organization names already registered under the { 1 2 840 } arc were suddenly "homeless," and policy control over the assignment of organization names—previously vested solely in ANSI, which owns the { 1 2 840 } arc as the U.S. member body in ISO, under the old rules—became the joint responsibility of ANSI and the U.S. Department of State (which is the official U.S. representative in the CCITT arena).

The solution to this problem was, fortunately, straightforward; Figure 5.2 illustrates the way in which the new { 2 16 840 } subtree will be jointly administered.

The Federal Information Processing Standard 5 (FIPS-5) subtree will be managed by the existing U.S. government FIPS-5 commission (U.S. Department of Commerce 1987), which defines the names of "states and state equivalents" within the United States. Under the old rules, these names had been "imported" from FIPS-5 directly into the first 100 numeric name slots of the { 1 2 840 } arc; however, since no name assignments were ever made under these values, they have simply been abandoned. Under the new rules, the FIPS-5 state names are expected to be available for use as the values of the stateOrProvince attribute in relative distinguished names in the X.500 Directory (see Chapter 7).

The existing register of private organization names will move, intact, from the { 1 2 840 } arc to the { 2 16 840 2 } arc, which will also be administered by ANSI. This "copy" operation, however, will not invalidate existing names (such as organization identifiers and applica-

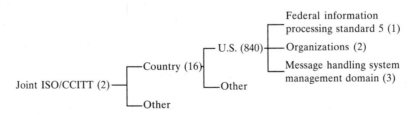

FIGURE 5.2   The U.S. Name-Registration Subtree

tion entity titles) that may already have been constructed using the { 1 2 840 } prefix; in effect, two equivalent prefixes will exist (in perpetuity) for currently registered organization names. New registrations will be made only under the new { 2 16 840 2 } arc, and organizations possessed of an "old" registration will be encouraged (but not required) to construct no new identifiers under the { 1 2 840 } arc but to use the { 2 16 840 2 } arc instead.

The numeric organization names under { 2 16 840 2 } will be used as values of the "organization" field in the construction of NSAP addresses with authority and format identifier values of 38 or 39 and an initial domain identifier value of 840, according to American National Standard X3.210-1992, just as they were under the old rules (see Chapter 13); this usage is not affected by the switch to a new subtree, since only the numeric organization name, without the qualifying { 1 2 840 } or { 2 16 840 2 } prefix, is used in the construction of NSAP addresses.

Since the rule change covers only "private organization names with national standing," the existing mechanism for registering the names of American national standards under the { 1 2 840 } arc is unaffected and will remain in place.

The creation of a new arc for message handling system management domain names recognizes the apparently unreconcilable difference between the general registration of organization names and the registration of names that will be used as administration messaging domain and private messaging domain names for X.400 (see Chapter 8). This is unfortunate, since it means that organization names registered under the organizations arc—including those names that have already been registered under the "old rules"—cannot be used as administration messaging domain or private messaging domain names in an X.400 originator/ recipient address unless they are also registered under the new message handling system management domain arc. The very different requirements associated with the registration of organization names that are intended for use in an X.400 context make this situation unavoidable.

AHA _The designers of the original registration authority for the United States recognized that their general-purpose registry, which permitted great flexibility in the formation of an acceptable organization name (it could consist of up to 100 characters chosen from a very large character set), could not enforce the constraints that might be applicable to the use for which a registered name was intended. Message handling system management domain names, for example, are constrained by CCITT Recommendation X.411 to be no longer than 16 bytes and must be constructed from the "Printable-_

String" character set defined by ISO/IEC 8824. They hoped, however, that these additional constraints could be observed in practice without creating application-specific registries for different types of organization name. The difficulties of doing so, at least in the case of organization names that will be used as MHS administration or private domain names, have proved to be too great.

The U.K. Registration Authority

The United States is not, of course, the only country with a need to register names with national standing under the various arcs of the ISO/IEC 9834 registration hierarchy. ANSI's counterpart in the United Kingdom, the British Standards Institute, operates a similar U.K. Registration Authority (UKRA),[5] which is governed by British Standard (BS) 7306 (1990). The U.K. registration authority is more specific than ANSI's; whereas ANSI hands out organization names that can be used for a wide variety of purposes, BSI has elected to assign organization names that can only be used in the construction of OSI network-layer addresses (see Chapter 13) and in fact the UKRA (see Chapter 13) includes the following specific disclaimer: "Users of an X.400 service therefore obtain their O/R addresses through mechanisms provided for that purpose, independently of any allocations that may be made under this standard."

The GOSIP Registration Authority

In the United States, ANSI operates the U.S. registration authority (in conjunction with the Department of State with respect to some of the arcs below { 2 16 840 }; see the subsection entitled "The U.S. Registration Authority," earlier in the chapter), but it is not the only organization registering "national standing" identifiers. The U.S. General Services Administration, acting for the National Institute of Standards and Technology (NIST), administers a GOSIP registration authority that assigns identifiers for use in two specific contexts:

1. GSA will provide U.S. government agencies with strings (all of which begin with the characters "GOV+") that can be used in X.400 mail addresses as part of constructed private management domain or organization names, under a delegation from ANSI to NIST that is registered as the arc { iso (1) member-body (2) us (840) gov (101) }.
2. GSA will provide, to anyone who asks, a numeric value that can be used in the administrative authority identifier field of U.S. GOSIP version 2 NSAP addresses (see Chapter 13), under a delegation of authority from the ISO 6523 part of ISO's subtree that is registered as the arc { iso (1) identified-organization (3) NIST (5) }.

---

5.   In fact, BSI has delegated the responsibility for actually operating the U.K. Registration Authority to the Electronics and Business Equipment Association.

Fortunately, these identifiers are in every case readily distinguishable, in context, from identifiers registered with ANSI under other arcs of the registration hierarchy. ANSI has agreed not to allocate message handling system management domain names beginning with "GOV+" under its { 2 16 840 3 } arc, and the administrative authority identifier values allocated by GSA, although they are semantically equivalent to the organization field values allocated by ANSI, can appear only in NSAP addresses that follow the GOSIP version 2 format (with AFI = 47 and IDI = 0005), whereas the org values can appear only in NSAP addresses that follow ANSI Standard X3.216-1992.

The Internet Assigned Numbers Authority

In the Internet world, the list of names that are formally registered is (remarkably) even longer than it is for OSI. The Internet Assigned Numbers Authority (IANA) is responsible for assigning and registering names (which, in Internet jargon, are simply called "numbers," since that's what they are) of the following types:

Version numbers
Protocol numbers
Port numbers
Internet multicast addresses
The Internet Ethernet address block
IP type-of-service parameter values
IP time-to-live parameter values
Domain Name System parameter values
BOOTP parameter values
Network management parameter values
ARPANET and MILNET logical addresses
ARPANET and MILNET link numbers and X.25 address mappings
IEEE 802 numbers of interest
XNS protocol types
PRONET 80 type numbers
Ethernet numbers of interest
Ethernet vendor address components
UNIX port numbers
Address resolution protocol parameters
Reverse address resolution protocol parameters
Dynamic reverse address resolution protocol parameters
X.25 type numbers
Public data network numbers
TELNET options

Mail encryption types

Machine names

System names

Protocol and service names

Terminal type names

These number registrations are published periodically in an Internet RFC entitled *Assigned Numbers*.

The preceding list does not include the most visible Internet registration activity: the Internet registry, which assigns Internet network numbers (the high-order part of a 32-bit Internet address, from which individual IP host numbers are generated). This activity is formally the responsibility of the Internet Assigned Numbers Authority, but the actual assignment task has traditionally been carried out by the Internet's Network Information Center (NIC). The Network Information Center was operated for many years by SRI International in Menlo Park, California, but was recently reassigned to Network Solutions, Inc., operating under contract to Government Systems, Inc. (GSI), operating under contract to the Defense Information Systems Agency (DISA, which was formerly the Defense Communications Agency, or DCA).[6] In most cases, a public or commercial network operator (service provider) will apply to the Internet registry for network numbers on behalf of its clients; in some cases, the registry preallocates blocks of numbers to a service provider, which is then free to further assign them to its clients as needed.

Object Identifiers

Of the data types predefined by the Abstract Syntax Notation One (ASN.1) standard (see Chapter 4), one—the OBJECT IDENTIFIER data type—is particularly important to naming in OSI. The value of an object identifier names an information object; it is an ordered set of nonnegative integer values whose root is defined in ISO/IEC 9834-1 and whose branches or arcs are derived from the registration authorities described earlier and depicted in Figure 5.2.

What are information objects? Applications and systems are objects. The documents that define OSI protocols and services are objects. OSI Directory entries and attributes of those entries (see Chapter 7); X.400

---

6.   If you followed all that, you might be qualified for a career in Internet name assignment; see Appendix D for the address and phone number of the Internet Network Information Center.

Message Handling System mail addresses (see Chapter 8); and the sets of counters, gauges, and status indicators used in the management of network resources by OSI's Common Management Information Service and TCP/IP's Simple Network Management Protocol (see Chapter 9) are among the many things OSI considers objects. Essentially, anything in a network can be modeled as an object; among these, objects that require a name for unique and unambiguous identification are registered by a naming authority.

Conclusion

This chapter has described the roles names play in OSI and the formal composition of OSI addresses. (The roles of names in TCP/IP have intentionally been deferred to Chapter 7, where the Domain Name System is discussed, and the details of network addresses have been deferred to Chapter 13, where OSI network service access point addresses and IP addresses are discussed.) The names most relevant to understanding how OSI applications identify each other for the purpose of conducting information exchange have been specified as well. The authors have also explained that the means by which identifiers in general are guaranteed uniqueness is through the establishment of registration authorities recognized by ISO/CCITT and that a similar infrastructure exists for TCP/IP— i.e., the Internet Assigned Numbers Authority. The chapter concluded with a discussion of the role played by object identifiers in the "name game" and the relationship of this ASN.1 data type to name registration.

PART THREE

UPPER LAYERS

6

OPEN SYSTEMS APPLICATIONS

An architectural characteristic of open system networks (as opposed to proprietary networks) is the assumption of a set of generic, or generally available, applications that serve as building blocks or "tools" for constructing more complex distributed system applications. These are generally regarded as "applications" in the TCP/IP world; in OSI, they are called *distributed application services*.

Distributed application services, whether OSI- or TCP/IP-based, share some characteristics in common. For example, irrespective of whether one describes a file transfer application that uses TCP/IP's File Transfer Protocol (FTP) or OSI's File Transfer, Access, and Management (FTAM), the file transfer application will have at least the following characteristics:

- An end-user interface that provides a human or another application with the means to enter commands that direct the application to send files to and receive files from a remote host, list or change directories, rename or delete files, move files from one directory to another, etc. (There will also be a means for the application to inform the end user of the results of the actions, successful or failed.)
- The means of performing input to and output from mass storage device(s) (disk-tape).
- The means of transferring the files and file-related information between hosts.

Thus, for both OSI and TCP/IP, there are local and communications components to every distributed or end-user application. The *local component* of an application consists of the end-user and/or programmatic interfaces to the application, functions that access local input/output resources such as disk, and access to computing resources of a host machine. The *communications component* consists of the entity that provides distributed communications capabilities to the distributed application; OSI calls the communications piece an *application entity* (AE) and the sum of the parts that comprise a distributed application an *application process* (AP). (See Figure 6.1.)

Although the notion of an application process is common to both TCP/IP and OSI, their approaches to constructing application entities is different. In TCP/IP, each application entity is composed of whatever set of functions it needs beyond end-to-end transport to support a distributed communications service—e.g., the exchange of mail, remote file access, or file transfer—into the protocol(s) of that particular application; in other words, each application process builds in its own, often unique, set of tools, commands, and exchange mechanisms. File Transfer Protocol, for example, has an entirely different set and way of exchanging commands and replies than "Internet mail" (sometimes called "SMTP/822" mail, referring to RFC 822, which describes mail message contents, and RFC 821, Simple Mail Transfer Protocol [SMTP]; see Chapter 8). There is no common notion of establishing application "connections" among Internet application services,[1] and no common reliable

An end-user application (mail, file transfer, etc.)

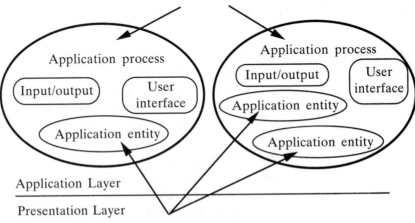

FIGURE 6.1   Application Process Structure

---

1.   In the implementation of the original set of application or *host protocols*, the *initial*

transfer and dialogue-control service, nor is there a true, common network-programming language or a common remote procedure call mechanism. (The *external data representation* [XDR; RFC 1014] and *remote procedure call* [RPC; RFC 1059], developed in conjunction with *Network File System* [NFS; RFC 1094; Sandburg 1988], are, in a sense, application service elements but are not formally used as such outside of NFS.) This is not intended as a criticism but merely to illustrate that, by and large, each Internet application process builds in what it needs and assumes only that an underlying transport mechanism (datagram or connection) will be provided.

In OSI, each distributed application service selects functions from a large common "toolbox" of *application service elements* (ASEs) and complements these with application service elements that perform functions specific to a given end-user service—e.g., mail (message handling) or file transfer (see Figure 6.2). Conceptually, application entities in TCP/IP have a single service element, whereas application entities in OSI may have many.

An application entity that supports OSI's File Transfer, Access, and

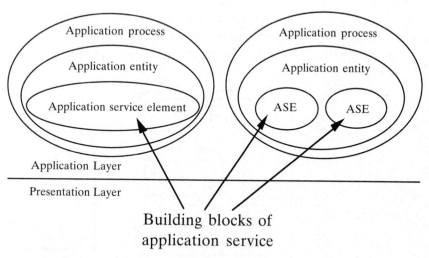

Building blocks of
application service

FIGURE 6.2   Composition of an Application Entity

connection protocol (ICP; RFC 1230) conceptually served this purpose, which we shall see in Chapter 10 is provided by the association control service element in OSI. While the initial connection protocol was implemented separately in a few implementations, most folks implemented the functions used from this conceptual "inner protocol" directly in FTP, Remote Job Entry, and TELNET rather than using it as a layer or independent module on top of the connection-oriented, host-to-host protocol, which later evolved into TCP.

Management thus has at least one application service element (FTAM) that is different from OSI's Message Handling System (MHS) but both use the same "tool" for establishing communications (the association control service element discussed in Chapter 10). Similarly, the OSI Directory service and common management information service elements use the association-control "tool" as well as a common remote procedure call "tool" (the remote operations service element, also discussed in Chapter 10). In such configurations, one application service element is a *user element* of other ASEs (see Figure 6.3).

Extending the "tool" analogy a bit further, to tighten a screw or bolt on an automobile, a mechanic (the end user) uses tools like an electric screwdriver and a ratchet wrench (ASEs); both of these require another tool (another ASE) to complete the task: the electric screwdriver requires a bit, and the ratchet wrench requires a socket. The screwdriver and wrench are thus user elements of the bit and socket ASEs, respectively. Absent the bit and socket, these tools may be useful, perhaps, but only as hammers.

Note that in OSI, application service elements that provide intuitively obvious "end-user" application services—message handling, directories, file transfer—can themselves be regarded as tools of multifunction distributed applications; a messaging application may, for example, make use of both message handling service and directory service elements, the latter invoked for the purpose of obtaining inter–mail application routing

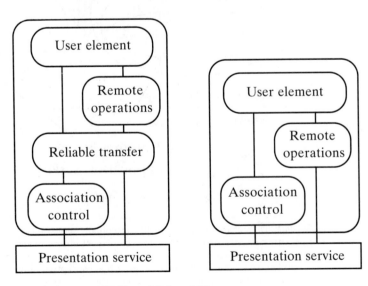

FIGURE 6.3   ASE Use of Other ASEs

information or mail addresser. Moreover, an application service element such as a message handling service element in one instance provides an "end-user" application—mail handling—but also acts as a "tool" for other application services, such as electronic data interchange and office document interchange. Finally, an end-user application is not restricted to using only those application service elements that are made standards by CCITT and ISO/IEC: "home-brew" user service elements can be written in ASN.1, and these, too, may use standard application service elements.

Given the contrast in styles, the TCP/IP approach to building applications has sometimes been called a vertical one: each application was developed independently, "top" (i.e., end-user application service) to "bottom" (i.e., transport). The OSI approach, consistent with the pervasive notion of layering, has been called a horizontal approach (end-user applications developed using a common application-development infrastructure; see Figure 6.4).

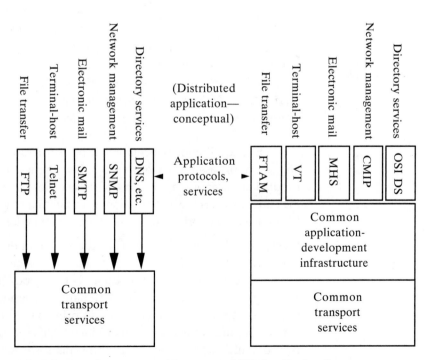

FIGURE 6.4   Comparison of Internet and OSI Application Structure

Distributed Application Services

OSI is clearly not the exclusive distributed applications environment for all forms of distributed applications services. Applications developed over TCP/IP and other protocol suites tending toward "openness" satisfy many essential end-user needs and are likely to continue to satisfy these needs along with OSI. This diversity is not a truly bad thing (see Chapter 17), since, historically, diversity and competition have often led to improvements and landmark developments in computer communications. It is also important to note that the applications-development infrastructure of OSI—the upper layers—may easily be ported over to existing transport service infrastructures; this is especially true for TCP/IP, and the success of enterprises of this sort is discussed in subsequent chapters.

·AHA· *The generality and flexibility of the OSI applications-development infrastructure is not without cost, and detractors continue to berate it, criticizing it for its complexity (in both specification and implementation) as well as the excessive processing and memory overhead that is associated with operating distributed applications in this environment. Some of this criticism must be tempered by the fact that many of the existing implementations are "first-generation," and it is to be expected that further field and implementation experience will yield leaner, faster software. Some of the criticism is well-founded, and one can only hope that those who have implemented OSI-based applications will work to see that the standards are revised to correct major shortcomings. Despite the criticism, OSI continues to be a catalyst for the development of protocol and service frameworks for interesting distributed services.*

OSI's applications-development infrastructure provides a convenient and multipurpose framework for the development of a wide range of distributed applications; a sampling of these is described briefly in the following subsections. Some are variations on a familiar "theme"—electronic mail, file transfer, directories—whereas others are more forward-looking.

Electronic Mail and Message Handling System (MHS)   "E-mail" is the ability to send and receive the electronic equivalent of written correspondence typically delivered through a postal agency. In addition to simple textual mail messages, OSI message-handling services facilitate the electronic exchange of documents that, in principal, can be comprised of facsimile, graphics, or even speech or video. OSI's Message Handling System is also likely to provide a distribution platform for office and electronic document exchange.

Electronic Data Interchange (EDI) The ability to exchange bus. documents—e.g., standard "forms," such as invoices, purchase orde ᴗ, payment orders, and customs declarations/reports—is an international concern, especially for the European Economic Community. OSI standards for these forms are consistent with the United Nations/EDIFACT Standard, and the forms can be transferred using OSI's Message Handling System (see Chapter 8).

Office Document Architecture Interchange (ODA/ODIF) The ability to exchange documents containing text and graphics—spreadsheets, page layouts from desktop-publishing applications, papers produced using word-processing applications—between like and dissimilar applications (e.g., from brand X word processor to brand Y) without losing any of the document's contents is accommodated within OSI's office document architecture, also known as the CCITT T.400-series Recommendations for document Transfer, Access, and Manipulation (DTAM). The office document architecture specifies document structures, interchange formats, character content architectures, and content architectures for raster, tile raster, and geometric graphics (ISO/IEC 8613: 1989), in many parts).

Directory Services Like the operator-assisted directory services offered through the telephone network this service includes the ability to match names with addressing information. In addition, OSI offers a comprehensive registration and identification infrastructure that helps individuals, applications, and organizations acquire information ("attributes") that provides a more detailed characterization of things ("objects") that are named. The OSI Directory is expected to serve as a repository for information that characterizes people, applications, mail systems, management systems—virtually any information that one wishes to register and make publicly available.

Distributed File Systems The ability to access and manage file systems mounted on remote computers is an integral part of distributed processing today. OSI offers new tools in this area and also an equivalent environment upon which to run existing and eminently popular tools such as Network File System.

Network Management Network management provides the ability to monitor the status and use of resources of a distributed processing environment—hosts, bridges, routers, the transmission facilities that interconnect them, and software (application as well as protocol processes) resident on these machines—as well as the ability to detect, isolate, and

circumvent problems that might arise in any of these network components. OSI has a comprehensive "common management" applications
infrastructure that provides monitoring, analysis, accounting, and diagnostic services and more.

Remote Database Access   OSI provides a generic remote database architecture—protocols and services—for client/server interactions (dialogue,
transaction, and data-resource management) and also provides for a set
of "specializations" that allow one to further define the parameters of
remote database access operations to accommodate a specific remote
database language—e.g., the standard query language SQL (ISO/IEC
9579 1992).

   These are but a few of the areas of distributed processing and information technology that can use OSI. Of course, many of the capabilities
OSI offers have easily identifiable TCP/IP counterparts. Applications
based on the Simple Mail Transfer Protocol (see Chapter 8) offer textual
electronic-mail correspondence similar to that offered via OSI's Message
Handling System and, with recent extensions that are today experimental, may enable multimedia messaging as well. The Domain Name System
offers a host name– to–IP address service similar to an application-
name–to–presentation-address capability offered by the OSI Directory;
other Internet applications—such as WHOIS, FINGER, Archie, the Wide
Area Information Service, and the WorldWideWeb offer a variety of resource locators and information services (see Chapter 7).

   In certain application areas—messaging and directory services—
many believe that OSI adds value to existing TCP/IP applications. In
other areas—for example, distributed file services and window-based
systems—existing services like NFS are considered superior to application services developed specifically for OSI. In fact, the utility and widespread application of services such as NFS and the X Window System
have provided the basis for the development of conventions and eventually standards for operating these applications over OSI stacks.

   This is true in the area of network management as well. Although
there are those who believe that OSI's "common management" is superior
in many ways to the Simple Network Management Protocol, applications
based on the SNMP are sufficiently popular that they are now used to manage dual-stack (OSI and TCP/IP) internets (actually, the Simple Network
Management Protocol framework provides network management for large-
scale internets that are IP- as well as XNS/IPX, AppleTalk-, and OSI-based).
And recent extensions to the Simple Network Management Protocol
arguably improve on an already useful and proven commodity.

There are also areas where OSI will offer application services that are to date not addressed in TCP/IP: OSI's progress on transaction processing, office document architecture, and electronic data interchange standards is followed with great interest by the Internet community.

Conclusion

This chapter has described how OSI and TCP/IP differ significantly in their approaches to constructing distributed system applications. OSI asserts that distributed applications operate over a strict hierarchy of layers and are constructed from a common tool kit of standardized application service elements; TCP/IP makes no such assertion, insisting only that distributed applications operate over a common end-to-end transport service. Which approach is better? OSI's is general and flexible, and its emphasis on modularity and reuse of common mechanisms comports well with current object-oriented models of application development; but generality costs, and as is the case with many aspects of OSI, the inefficiency of a too-literal implementation may outweigh the theoretical benefits. TCP/IP's "apply to affected area as needed" approach is more application-specific and may lead to the redundant implementation of the same function in many different applications; but in most cases, the greater efficiency and performance of the resulting applications outweigh the potentially greater inefficiency of application software development. It is interesting to observe that the most promising new work on the implementation of the "upper layers" of OSI (see Chapter 11) combines the functions of the application, presentation, and session layers into a common library of modules that are included—or not included—in applications, as each demands. This is yet another example of OSI's learning and borrowing from TCP/IP—an exchange that takes place in both directions much more readily (and frequently) than most people suspect (or are willing to admit).

The remaining chapters in Part Three examine application services and upper layers in a "top-down" fashion. Although this may seem contrary to the customary flow, a top-down approach has the advantage of allowing readers to deal first with easily recognizable and practical examples of services encountered on a daily basis—the use of a telephone, a postal service, a telephone book, or directory assistance—and gradually learn the technical aspects of how equivalent "electronic" services are provided across complex internets. Thus, Part Three continues by providing a comparison of application services offered by both architectures, focusing on function and high-level operation. Chapters 7, 8, and 9 examine three distributed application services—directories, electronic messaging, and network management. These are chosen because they are popular and easily recognized distributed applications and because there is considerable overlap between the OSI and TCP/IP counterparts with respect to services offered. From this sampling, readers are expected to gain an overall understanding of distributed processing in OSI and TCP/IP.

Chapter 10 examines three application service elements—association control, remote operations, and reliable transfer—that provide essential, or "core," services for distributed applications in OSI, and Chapter 11 describes the OSI presentation and session layers. A consequence of the rigid layering in the OSI upper layers is that many of the functions that an application may use or invoke are accessed through application service elements but performed elsewhere in the architecture (e.g., in the session layer). Chapter 10 introduces such functions at a conceptual or metalevel, whereas Chapter 11 describes how these functions are provided.

It should be noted that Chapters 10 and 11 diverge from the side-by-side analysis that is a convention elsewhere in the text, as the functions corresponding to the OSI upper layers are embedded in the Internet applications described in Chapters 7, 8, and 9 on an "as-needed" basis.

7

DIRECTORIES

In a conversation with Richard Cambridge in 1755, Samuel Johnson made the now famous remark that "Knowledge is of two kinds. We know a subject ourselves, or we know where we can find information upon it" (Boswell 1791). In a large network, it is neither possible nor desirable for every network element[1] to know everything about every other network element—impossible because there is too much to know, and undesirable because much of the information is constantly changing, and the more widely distributed it is, the more difficult it is to maintain synchronization among all the many places in which it is replicated.

Since we cannot invest every network element with complete knowledge, we must provide a system whereby they "can find information upon it." This is the role of the network directory, which—as anyone who has ever used a telephone directory might easily surmise—is simply a place to store lots of information about the elements of a network. By doing so, the network directory not only solves the problems of "There's too much information to store everywhere" and "The information changes too often to be kept current everywhere" but also permits references to network elements to be made indirectly, through the directory, by name, rather than by some other attribute (such as network address, geographic location, or organizational affiliation) that might not be as permanently or reliably attached to the element as its name.

---

1. Intuitively, we think of network elements as the computers—PCs, workstations, bridges, routers—that provide network and host services. In the context of directories, however, the notion is extended to applications, to users of the network, and even to more fundamental pieces of such network elements including the information stored in these elements; in fact, very nearly every object we *name* within a network may be characterized and accessed by the use of directories.

Given such a general definition of *directory*, it is easy to imagine the network directory as a general-purpose database system—and in principle, it could be. In practice, however, the directory services that have been developed for open systems networking have been designed for the more specialized purpose of relating a particular class of names to a particular set of attributes associated with them—for instance, mapping Internet host names (such as "`nic.switch.ch`") to IP addresses (such as "`130.59.1.40`"). In this chapter, we will concentrate on the open systems directories whose core service is name-to-address mapping (although they provide other services as well): OSI's X.500 Directory and the Internet's Domain Name System. However, we will also take a look at a number of "directorylike" utilities and introduce the field of *networked information retrieval*, which began with a directory model but has evolved far beyond it.

The basic function of a directory service is deceptively simple, but the way in which directory services are used in open systems networks is not. The telephony model of a directory is a good place to begin our discussion of the design criteria for a network directory service, precisely because it is *not* a good model for such a service.

The Telephony Model

For many people, the term *directory* suggests the local telephone company's printed telephone directories and dial-up "directory assistance."[2] The telephone directory system is simple and straightforward: given the name and address of a telephone subscriber, it returns the subscriber's telephone number (unless the subscriber has paid a surcharge to the telephone company for an "unlisted number"—in which case, the information is available only to duly authorized law–enforcement personnel). This service is possible because the telephone companies jointly and exclusively administer a common pool of telephone numbers, for which the boundaries of local jurisdiction are (with rare exceptions) well-established and universally accepted.

This directory service has three limitations that argue strongly against its applicability to a worldwide open systems Internet. First, it is

---

2.   Directory assistance was widely known as "information" until the telephone companies, for which providing "information" is an expensive gratuity to customers who are "too lazy to look it up in the book," successfully stamped out the familiar term in favor of one that subtly suggests infirmity on the part of the user.

able to provide a telephone number only when given the subscriber's name and address. Lacking either a complete name or a sufficiently detailed set of attributes to disambiguate entries for the same name in the same locality, no other information that characterizes or distinguishes an individual can be used to facilitate a query. (Some printed directories, such as the yellow pages, may contain additional information provided by the subscriber; this is not always accessible "on-line" through directory assistance. For example, it is possible to ask for "a florist in Horsham" and obtain the name and telephone number of at least one in that city, but it is unlikely that an operator will be able to tell you whether the florist is a member of FTD or Teleflora, or which credit cards the florist accepts.) Second, it is not uniformly accessible. In order to obtain directory assistance, one must first know the appropriate country, city, and/or area codes, as well as the number for directory assistance itself, and construct one's query according to the appropriate local conventions—for example, in the appropriate local language. Third, the telephone directories—particularly the printed versions—are typically distributed no more frequently than once a year and thus inevitably contain a significant amount of incorrect (outdated) information.

The telephone directory system benefits enormously from a key feature of the telephone network: the fact that there is a direct relationship between the hierarchical structure of telephone numbers (with their country, city, area, and exchange components) and the geographic location hierarchy within which the telephone subscribers live. Data networks typically do not share this characteristic, despite being organized hierarchically. The corporate network of a large multinational company, for example, is likely to be organized according to the company's operating hierarchy (divisions, departments, cost centers, etc.), which may place the London and Hong Kong sales offices close together and the sales and personnel departments geographically colocated in Hong Kong far apart. Further, the affiliations and service relationships of data networks are (to date) neither as uniform nor as tightly regulated as telephony networks.

Directory System Principles

Given that the simple telephony model is not appropriate for a large-scale network directory, what *are* the characteristics that such a directory should have?

- Both the directory database and the mechanisms for operating on it must be distributed; the size of the database and the frequency with which directory information must be updated preclude centralization.

- However, the directory must appear to its users to be a single, consistent database. The same query, originating from any point in the network, should return the same information.[3]
- The directory must be organized hierarchically, so that the responsibility for managing the information in the directory can be delegated to different organizations as self-contained "subtrees." The hierarchy must be extensible, since the way in which organizations allocate and apportion responsibility among and within themselves in a large open systems network is certain to change over time.
- The directory must be organized in such a way that it is possible to formulate unambiguous queries; that is, it must not be the case that two different information elements contained in the directory cannot be distinguished by the directory's query mechanism.
- Because the directory for a large-scale network is necessarily itself a large-scale distributed system, it must not be application-specific—that is, it must be capable of storing information about objects for many (ideally, all) of the applications for which the network is used. This argues strongly for a directory information model based on the definition of *object classes* (families of objects sharing certain characteristics) and *attributes* (information about an object that either describes the object or distinguishes it from other objects), so that two different applications that refer to the same type of object do not require that the directory store two separate (application-specific) sets of information about the same objects.

Open System Directories

The world of open systems networking has produced two large-scale, open directory systems. *The Domain Name System* (DNS) is the established

---

3.   Actually, the consistency requirements for a network directory are not as stringent as they typically are for a distributed database system. It is reasonable and acceptable, after an update, for the directory to exhibit local inconsistencies for some period of time until the change has propagated throughout the system. A directory query is almost never an end in itself but is followed by an attempt to use the information obtained, with a strong likelihood that the inconsistency will be exposed. Since the directory query and the subsequent network access based on it are not synchronized, it matters little whether the information changed before or after the directory query if it changes before the information is actually used.

Internet directory, and the *OSI Directory*, which is also known as "X.500" (after the first of the set of CCITT Recommendations that defines it) is both the standard for OSI networks and a candidate for use within the Internet (although not necessarily as a replacement for the Domain Name System).

The OSI Directory is deliberately comprehensive; it is intended to capture the relationship between an arbitrary name and an arbitrary list of attributes for virtually any network application. The Domain Name System is—particularly in practice—more narrowly focused: it associates the names of two specific resources (electronic mailboxes and Internet hosts) with two specific corresponding pieces of information about them (mail server addresses and IP addresses, respectively), although its design permits extension to other uses. Although the generality of the OSI Directory invites its application to other problems—it is used, for example, to store *universal document identifiers* for some of the networked information retrieval projects described at the end of this chapter—we are concerned here primarily with its deployment as a traditional "name lookup" service in both OSI networks and the multiprotocol Internet.

The Domain Name System

In the beginning, there were just four nodes in the only Internet around (the ARPANET), and maintaining a table of mappings from host name to network address was not a problem. In the early years of the ARPANET, growth was modest, and the host-name–to–address mappings were maintained by the Network Information Center (NIC) in a single file (hosts.txt), which was periodically retrieved (by using electronic file transfer or, in extreme cases, by requesting a magnetic or even paper tape) by each host or site administrator and loaded into each host attached to the network. Each host would then search through the file whenever it needed to find the network address for a named host.

This system worked well while the ARPANET was small, but as it grew, and as the composition of the network changed, the bandwidth consumed by the periodic and increasingly frequent electronic file transfers to retrieve the hosts.txt file from the NIC, and the disconnect between site administrators' management of their local names and addresses and the appearance of changes in the NIC's definitive hosts.txt file, made it clear that the centralized scheme was impractical and that an alternative would have to be found.

The Domain Name System began as a class project at the University of California at Berkeley and has, in recent years, been released by the Berkeley UNIX group as part of the Berkeley Software Distribution. Paul Mockapetris—first at Berkeley and later at the Information Sciences Institute of the University of Southern California—conceived an alternative to `hosts.txt` based on (1) a distributed database containing generalized *resource records* and (2) a naming scheme based on hierarchically structured *domain names*. His original design was published in November 1983 in RFCs 882 and 883; after experience with several implementations, the Domain Name System (DNS) was formally specified in RFCs 1034 and 1035 in November 1987.

The deployment of DNS in the Internet is, to say the least, nonuniform. Different versions of BIND—the *Berkeley Interactive Name Demon*, the UNIX software for name resolution—are bundled with different releases of UNIX software, and host-name lookups are done in a variety of different ways, depending on the vendor and on individual site philosophy. Some networks—including, for example, the entire U.S. federal MILNET—have decided not to use DNS and to rely instead on the old `hosts.txt` file for host-name–to–IP-address translation for the simple reason that there is no DNS security model to support the authentication of users and providers of DNS services. Nevertheless, DNS is one of the most important services in the Internet, and most of the strategic plans for the evolution of the Internet and the TCP/IP architecture depend on the near-universal deployment of DNS or a successor.

The DNS is a distributed system, with distribution based on the concept of *delegated authority* for the administration of individual domains and subdomains. This means that local system administrators maintain files containing information about their local hosts and networks, and this information is made available to users of the DNS through *name servers* that are locally configured and maintained.

Domain Names

The DNS name space is hierarchical, consisting of a set of nested domains, each of which represents an administratively related set of Internet hosts. Directly below the root of the hierarchy is a set of *top-level domains*, which originally referred to logical parts of the U.S. ARPANET:

`arpa:`	for the U.S. Department of Defense Advanced Research Projects Agency itself
`com:`	for commercial organizations
`edu:`	for educational institutions
`gov:`	for U.S. nonmilitary government agencies
`mil:`	for U.S. military agencies

`net:` for organizations directly involved in the provision and support of ARPANET and its services

`org:` for "other" organizations

With the expansion of the modern Internet outside the United States, additional top-level domains have been added, corresponding to individual countries; for example, `au`, `ca`, `us`, `uk`, `se`.

These country-code domain names are normally chosen from the two-letter codes registered in ISO 3166, *Codes for the Representation of Names of Countries* (ISO 3166: 1988).

AHA

The introduction of country-code domain names came about not because the DNS architects believed that it was the right way to register domains in countries outside of the United States but because they could not convince most of the non-U.S. network and site administrators that the established `com`, `edu`, *and other domains were not exclusively for U.S.-based organizations. The introduction of country-code top-level domains in parallel with the old nongeographic domains has led to some interesting anomalies. RARE,[4] for example, administers the domain* `rare.nl` *under the top-level domain for the Netherlands; RIPE,[5] which is organizationally affiliated with RARE, administers* `ripe.net`. *In the United States, the Corporation for National Research Initiatives (which operates the IETF secretariat, among other things) operates* `nri.reston.va.us`; *Bolt Beranek and Newman (which built the first IMPs and routers for the ARPANET, among other things) operates* `bbn.com`. *Observing the benign chaos with which the original top-level domain scheme has been infected by the introduction of country-code domains, Paul Mockapetris introduced the* `int` *top-level domain—for which Paul is the administrator—specifically for "people who don't understand that* `org` *isn't just for U.S. organizations."*

Below the top-level domains, names are constructed hierarchically by identifying subdomains, sub-subdomains, and so on to (in principle) any desired depth, until the final name (at a leaf of the tree; see Figure 7.1) completes the identification of an individual Internet host. Thus, within the top-level domain `uk`, the subdomain `ac.uk` is administered on behalf of U.K. academic institutions; within `ac.uk`, the subdomain `ucl.ac.uk` is administered by University College, London; and within

---

4. *Réseaux Associés pour la Recherche Européene*. RARE is the principal sponsor and coordinator of academic and research networking in Europe.

5. *Réseaux IP Européens* (literally, "Research IP for Europe").

the subdomain `ucl.ac.uk`, the host name `murphy.ucl.ac.uk` identifies a workstation sitting on the desk of Professor Suzanne Chapin in her office in Whitehead Hall at University College, London.

The rules for the formation of names are straightforward: a name may be no longer than 63 characters; it must start with a letter; it must end with either a letter or a digit; the rest of the name may consist of letters, digits, and hyphens; and both upper- and lowercase letters may be used (although name lookups in the DNS are defined to be case-insensitive).

How the DNS Works

The DNS is implemented as two distinct components: DNS *servers* (usually called *name servers*), which contain information about one or more *zones*; and DNS *clients* (usually called *resolvers*), which interrogate name servers on behalf of local host processes.

The DNS Server   Each DNS server provides name-to-address mappings for one or more *zones*. A `zone` is a set of contiguous domains beginning at some point in the DNS naming hierarchy and comprising that point and all the subtrees below it, as far, in each subtree, as either the leaves of the subtree or the point at which another (subordinate) zone is defined. In practice, an actual name server may be responsible for serving more

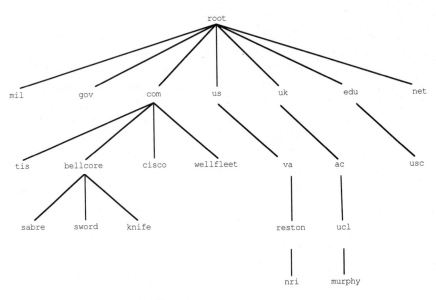

Figure 7.1   A Partial DNS Tree

Note: The word `root` is used merely to illustrate where, conceptually, the root of the name tree begins; domain names do not have the explicit identifier `root` as a component.

than one zone and will generally also serve the reverse `in-addr.arpa` zones (see "'Reverse' Lookups," later in the chapter) that correspond to its local domains.

Secondary name servers can be identified for each zone, so that name resolution for that zone is not cut off when the primary name server, or the links to it, are lost.

The DNS Resolver   A DNS name server not only stores and manages information about domains; it also responds to queries concerning that information from client processes or *resolvers*. A resolver is typically a set of library routines that are invoked by an application program when it needs to resolve a name reference. In BSD UNIX, for example, the routines are `gethostbyname` and `gethostbyaddr`. The resolver takes the name and uses it to query either a local table[6] (if the reference is to a locally maintained name or to a name that the resolver has maintained in a local cache) or one or more DNS servers for corresponding *resource records*.

The resolver's most significant task is to formulate a proper query. Since the DNS works with fully qualified names, this may involve a bit of interpretation on the part of the resolver, which may be presented by its user with a name that is not fully qualified. Some resolvers abdicate this responsibility entirely and are capable of looking up only the name string exactly as provided by the user. Others are able to recognize a less than fully qualified name and supply the missing high-order domain specification automatically (defaulting, for example, to the domain in which the user's own host resides).

Clients and servers use a common format for DNS queries and replies. Basically, a client provides a unique *identifier* (so it can later match responses to queries) and poses a number of *questions* the server should attempt to resolve. In the case of name-to-address lookups, each question is an entry of the form {query domain name, type, class}; in this example, the domain name to be resolved is provided, the query type is set to a value indicating that the client is looking for an IP address, and the query class is set to a value indicating which object class (Internet domain names) is to be interrogated. The server returns a similarly formatted

---

6.   Many resolvers have sophisticated methods of caching domain names, to reduce delay in resolving DNS queries. A frequent practice is to request and copy an entire DNS server's name information, then periodically send consistency-check inquiries to the DNS server. Two benefits are introduced when hosts practice caching: first, the processing of a DNS inquiry is faster, because there is no DNS client/server (protocol) interaction; second, if a server becomes unreachable, the local resolver can continue to satisfy lookups using the cache.

message with *answers* in a general form (a *resource record*). The resource record again contains a domain name, type, and class and, additionally, provides a suggested *time to live* for the information contained in this resource record and a variable-length *resource data* field, preceded by a length indicator field (see Figure 7.2).

Although the principal users of a DNS resolver are host applications, most host operating systems allow human users to present a query

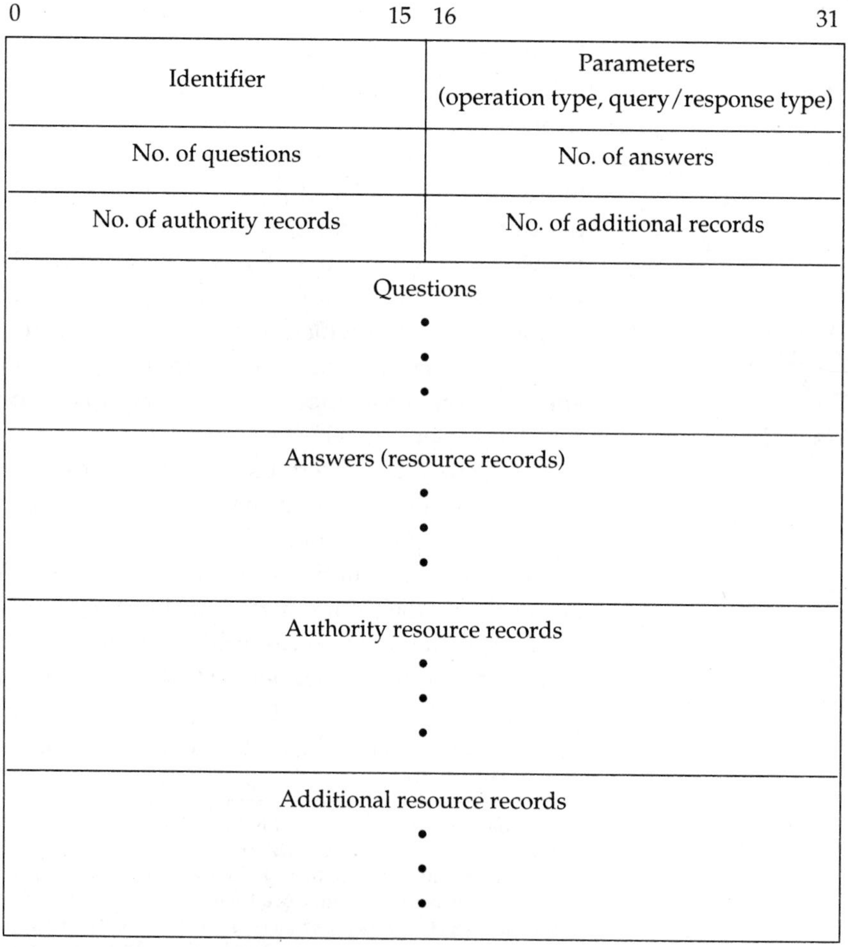

0	15	16	31
Identifier		Parameters (operation type, query/response type)	
No. of questions		No. of answers	
No. of authority records		No. of additional records	
Questions • • •			
Answers (resource records) • • •			
Authority resource records • • •			
Additional resource records • • •			

FIGURE 7.2 DNS Message Format

directly, using, for example, a command such as the UNIX *nslookup*, which, in the SunOS version, looks like this:

```
% /usr/etc/nslookup
Default Server: nameserver.bbn.com
Address: 128.89.1.2

> nic.ddn.mil
Server: nameserver.bbn.com
Address: 128.89.1.2

Name: nic.ddn.mil
Address: 192.112.36.5


>exit
```

Most Internet applications, including common ones like FTP and TELNET, accept a domain name from the user and call a resolver internally, so it is rarely necessary for a user to query the DNS directly (except out of curiosity and perhaps to trouble-shoot networking problems).

"Reverse" Lookups

A special domain within the domain name space, in-addr.arpa, provides a mechanism for performing "reverse" lookups—that is, finding the name associated with a given address. The entries in the in-addr. arpa domain are constructed by reversing the order of the components of a network number (the first 1, 2, or 3 bytes of an IP address, depending on whether the address is a class-A, class-B, or class-C address; see Chapter 13), and appending the in-addr.arpa domain name. Thus, for example, the entry for BBN's class-B network number, 128.89.0.0, would be 89.128.in-addr.arpa; a lookup on this entry would return the domain name bbn.com. Individual host systems, such as the Macintosh on the desk in Lyman Chapin's office at BBN, appear as subdomains of the network-number domain; for example, 224.16.89.128.in-addr.arpa.

Mail Exchange

The DNS also plays an important role in electronic-mail service (see Chapter 8). A host acting as a mail transfer agent must know the host name and IP address of the host to which a mail message is to be delivered before it attempts the delivery. It extracts the domain name part from the destination mail address (again, see Chapter 8), and creates a query with a *question* of query type *MX* (for "mail exchange"). The DNS server returns an answer with one or more MX resource records. Each MX record identifies a host to which mail may be forwarded, with each host domain name accompanied by an indication of how desirable it is to use this host for forwarding mail relative to others in the list (a *preference field*).

The OSI Directory

The OSI Directory is both a logical database of information about a set of objects in the real world and a system of agents and protocols that manage the information and support a variety of queries and searches by directory users. It is not intended to be a general-purpose database system, although an actual implementation of the Directory might be built upon such a system. It is an expressed architectural goal of the OSI Directory that it be capable, in principle, of accommodating the information-storage and -distribution needs of every network and every host throughout the world of open systems networking:

ISO/IEC 9594 [the ISO equivalent of CCITT Recommendation X.500] refers to The Directory in the singular, and reflects the intention to create, through a single, unified name space, one logical directory composed of many systems and serving many applications. Whether or not these systems choose to interwork will depend on the needs of the applications they support. Applications dealing with nonintersecting worlds of objects may have no such need. The single name space facilitates later interworking should the needs change. (ISO/IEC 9594-1: 1990)

The X.500-Series Standards

In 1988, the first jointly-developed ISO/IEC/CCITT standards for a worldwide directory system, generally known as "X.500," were published. Although the term *X.500* is commonly used to refer to the directory standards, they in fact consist of eight separate specifications, which are listed in Table 7.1. (The ISO/IEC 9594 series of standards are referenced in subsequent subsections; refer to this table if you wish to find the

TABLE 7.1   The X.500-Series Directory Standards

CCITT Recommendation	ISO/IEC Standard	Title
X.500	9594-1	Overview of Concepts, Models, and Services
X.501	9594-2	The Models
X.511	9594-3	Abstract Service Definition
X.518	9594-4	Procedures for Distributed Operation
X.519	9594-5	Protocol Specifications
X.520	9594-6	Selected Attribute Types
X.521	9594-7	Selected Object Classes
X.509	9594-8	Authentication Framework

corresponding subject in an X.500-series Recommendation.)

Work on the directory standards continues as a joint enterprise of ISO/IEC and CCITT. By the end of 1992, several critical areas of study were completed, among them:

- A model for replication of parts of the directory information base and, in particular, definition of a standard replication protocol. Hitherto, replication protocols used between directory system agents were proprietary.
- A list-based access-control mechanism. The X.500-1988 and ISO/IEC 9594: 1990 versions of the OSI Directory have well-defined authentication mechanisms but no standard means of restricting access to specific parts of the directory information base; thus, anyone who is currently authorized to use the directory is authorized to look at *everything* in the database.

Architecture

The principal architectural features of the OSI Directory are:

- *Decentralized maintenance:* Each system providing an OSI Directory service is responsible for the maintenance and integrity of only its own local part of the directory information base; wherefore updates and other management operations can be carried out independently by "keepers of the directory information," formally known as directory system agents.
- *Structured information model:* The OSI Directory defines an object-oriented model and database schema that applies uniformly to all the information stored in the directory.
- *Hierarchical global name space:* The hierarchy of distinguished names depends uniformly from a single, global root, providing a homogeneous name space for directory users.
- *Extensive search and retrieval capability:* Directory users may construct arbitrarily complex queries and perform highly complex interactive searches of the directory information base.

The X.500 standards define the directory in terms of "models":

- The *information model* specifies the contents of directory entries, how they are identified, and the way in which they are organized to form the directory information base.
- The *directory model* describes the directory and its users, the functional model for directory operation, and the organization of the Directory.
- The *security model* specifies the way in which the contents of the

directory are protected from unauthorized access and updates to the directory information base are authenticated.

The Directory Information Model

The information contained in the OSI Directory is organized as a set of *entries*; the set of all such entries constitutes the *directory information base* (DIB). The entries in the DIB are arranged hierarchically and can be represented in the form of a tree (the *directory information tree*, or DIT). The acronyms *DIB* and *DIT* are often used interchangeably;[7] a useful way to think about the relationship between the "database" and the "tree" is to consider that every entry in the database occupies a position in the tree—the tree therefore expresses the hierarchical relationship that the OSI Directory defines for the entries in its database, as illustrated in Figure 7.3.

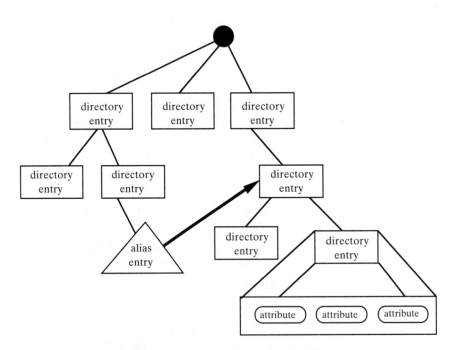

FIGURE 7.3   Structure of Directory Information and of Entries

---

7.   The X.500 standards always refer to the complete set of entries in the directory as the DIB, reserving the equivalent term *DIT* for those circumstances in which it is important to emphasize the hierarchical tree structure of the database.

Directory Entries and Attributes   The ASN.1 encoding of a directory entry is:

```
Attribute ::=
    SEQUENCE {
        type      AttributeType,
        values    SET OF AttributeValue }

AttributeType ::= OBJECT IDENTIFIER

AttributeValue ::= ANY
```

Each directory entry consists of a set of *attributes*, each of which consists of an *attribute type*, which identifies the class of information given by the attribute, and one or more corresponding *attribute values*, which are particular instances of that class of information (see Figure 7.4). An entry may not contain more than one attribute of a given type.

What sort of things are attributes? Virtually anything that describes an object for which a directory entry is created. Some attribute types are

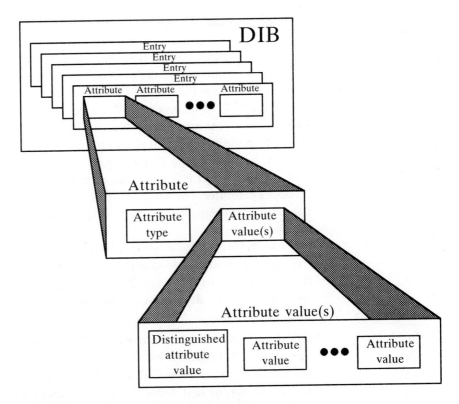

FIGURE 7.4   Directory Entries and Attributes

internationally standardized. A set of "selected attribute types," considered by the standards committees to be widely applicable, is provided in ISO/IEC 9594-6: 1990; they include:

- *Labeling attribute types:* Common Name, Surname, Serial Number
- *Geographic attribute types:* Country Name, Locality Name, State or Province Name, Street Address
- *Organizational attribute types:* Organization Name, Organizational Unit, Title
- *Postal-addressing attribute types:* Postal Address, Postal Code, Post Office Box, Physical Delivery Office Name
- *Telecommunications-addressing attribute types*: Telephone Number, Telex Number, Teletex Terminal Identifier, Facsimile Telephone Number, X.121 address, ISDN Number, Registered Address
- *OSI application attribute types:* Presentation Address, Supported Application Context

This is but a sampling. Other attributes are defined by national administrative authorities or private organizations. For example, it is perfectly appropriate to imagine a set of attributes for the medical profession, including residency or attending physician attributes (where? how many years? under whom? area[s] of specialization? publications, honors received, recommendations, evaluations, hours of practice?) and malpractice attributes (insurance carrier, annual premium, suits pending, suits settled). In other words, you can assume that organizations or individuals can create an attribute type for anything they wish to use to distinguish an individual or an object from another of its class.

In order to ensure that attribute types are assigned in such a way that each is distinct from all other assigned types, they are identified by an object identifier. The syntax (and hence, the data type) of attribute values for a particular attribute type is specified when the attribute type is defined.

An *attribute value assertion* (AVA) is a proposition—which may be true, false, or undefined—concerning the value(s) (or in some cases, only the distinguished values; see the following paragraphs) of an entry; it is usually expressed as a sequence of one or more statements of the form `AttributeType = AttributeValue`.

Directory Names   At most, one of the values of an attribute may be designated as a *distinguished value*—in which case, the value appears in the *relative distinguished name* (RDN) of the entry. Every entry has a unique relative distinguished name, which consists of a set of attribute value assertions (each of which is true) concerning the distinguished values of attributes of the entry. The set contains exactly one assertion about each distinguished value in the entry. By far the most common case is that in which an entry has just one distinguished value, and the relative distinguished name therefore consists of a single attribute value assertion; however, this need not always be the case.

The *distinguished name* (DN) of a given object is defined as the sequence of relative distinguished names of (1) the entry in the directory information base that represents the object and (2) All of the entries superior to it in the directory information tree, in descending order. A distinguished name can be used as the primitive name (see Chapter 5) of the object it identifies. Object identifiers can be transformed in a simple way into distinguished names for access to an X.500-based directory service, either by a direct mapping (in which the object identifier value corresponds directly to a distinguished name of which the components are values of a directory attribute of type object-identifier-component-value) or by ensuring that object identifier component values are allocated together with corresponding relative distinguished name values.

Figure 7.5 illustrates the relationship between relative distin-

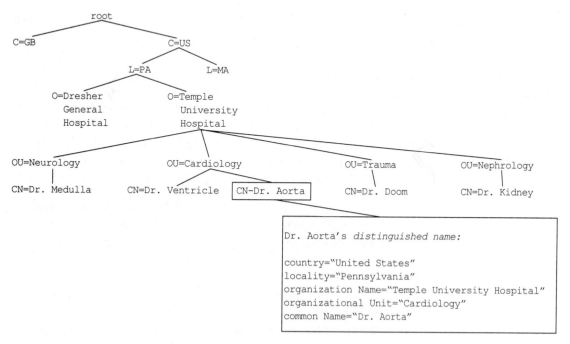

FIGURE 7.5   The Directory Information Tree

guished names and distinguished names. Entries at leaves of the tree are sometimes *alias* entries. They are pointers to object entries and provide alternative names for the objects to which they point.

> ⟦·AHA·⟧ *It is important to recognize that directory distinguished names are not necessarily user-friendly; user-friendly naming is a property of the directory service, not of distinguished names per se. Thus, "user-friendly naming" occurs not as a natural result of the use of directory distinguished names but as a consequence of directory user agents making judicious use of the directory system to ensure that those distinguished names for which the property of "user-friendliness" is important have it.*

Object Classes   Conceptually, a family of objects that have in common a well-defined set of attributes constitutes an *object class*. Object class definitions provide (detailed) "characterizations" so that individual objects (object instances) may be associated with a particular object class. ISO/IEC 9594-7, *Selected Object Classes*, provides an initial set of object classes for use in the Directory. As an example, most people can be associated with a `residentialPerson` object class, which is itself a subclass of *person*. A directory entry for a `residentialPerson` must contain a locality name attribute and may optionally contain any of the following attributes: a locale attribute set (locality name, state or province name, street address); a postal attribute set (physical delivery office name, postal address, postal code, post office box, street address); a preferred delivery method; a telecommunications attribute set (fax, ISDN, telex number, etc.); and a business category. Similarly, many people can be associated with the `organizationalPerson` object class; a directory entry for an `organizationalPerson` may contain a locale attribute set, an organizational unit name, a postal attribute set, a telecommunications attribute set, and a title (position within the organization).

Role of the Directory   Like the Domain Name System, the Directory plays an important role in name-to-address resolution; in particular, the Directory may be used to determine the addressing information required for applications to communicate. Two object class definitions—`applicationProcess` and `applicationEntity` (see Figure 7.6)—allow directory providers a means to create entries in the Directory to enable application "lookups" (the usefulness of this service, and the importance of the attributes of these object class definitions, becomes more apparent in Chapters 10 and 11).

```
applicationProcess OBJECT-CLASS
     SUBCLASS of top                        -- all object classes are subclasses of "top"
     MUST CONTAIN {
        commonName }
     MAY CONTAIN {
        description,                         -- a textual description of the application
        localityName,                       -- geographic/physical location of application
        organizationalUnitName,             -- unit with which application is affiliated
        seeAlso }                           -- name(s) of other directory objects that
                                            -- describe this application

applicationEntity OBJECT-CLASS
     SUBCLASS OF top
     MUST CONTAIN {
        commonName,
        presentationAddress }               -- see Chapter 5 and Chapter 11
     MAY CONTAIN {
        description,                         -- a textual description of the application
        localityName,                       -- geographic/physical location of application
        organizationName,                   -- organization with which application is affiliated
        organizationalUnitName,             -- unit with which application is affiliated
        see Also,
        supportedApplicationContext }       -- see Chapter 10
```

FIGURE 7.6   `applicationProcess` and `applicationEntity` **Object Class Definitions**

The Directory Model

The directory information base is distributed throughout the worldwide collection of directory system agents that form the OSI Directory. In the general model, queries are forwarded from a directory user agent, which acts as the agent for a real user, to a directory system agent, which attempts to satisfy the request. In many instances, a local directory system agent can do so by using information it maintains in its own local piece of the directory information base; in cases where the query refers to a part of the directory database for which the local agent has no information, it passes the request to an agent that does (see Figure 7.7).

The organizational mapping and administration of the OSI Directory follow the model applied to the X.400 Message Handling System (discussed in Chapter 8). Directory system agents may operate singly or together as a group to provide a directory service to one or more directory user agents, under a single administration called a *directory management domain* (DMD). If the management domain is operated by a public telecommunications provider, it is referred to as an *administrative directory management domain*, and if the management domain is operated by a company or noncommercial organization, it is referred to as a *private*

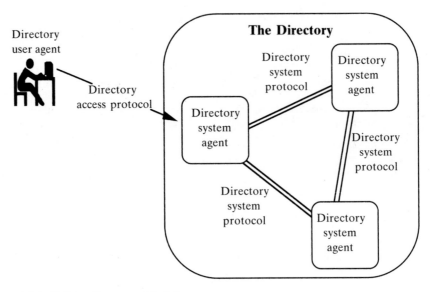

FIGURE 7.7   Directory Model

directory management domain. The organization that administers a directory management domain is responsible for overseeing the creation and modification of directory entries in its DSAs, allocating names to entries, and ensuring the integrity (and privacy, if applicable) of the entry information.

AHA   *ISO/IEC 9594-2: 1990 and the X.500 Recommendations say little about the rules governing the interconnection of private and administrative directory management domains. One might assume that the politics and economics that determined the "correct" methods for interconnection of publicly and privately administered Message Handling Systems apply to directory systems as well. Not so. Having learned just how constricting the guidelines were during the early deployment of X.400, those responsible for the definition of the X.500 Directory backed off considerably, and generally speaking, providers of OSI Directory services are encouraged to interconnect in whatever fashion is most appropriate (and legal within the constraints of particular national regulations!).*

The Directory Service

The directory service is provided to users through access points called *ports.* Different types of ports exist for different directory services. A *readPort* is available for reading attributes of a directory entry, comparing an attribute of a directory, and canceling a previous directory inquiry. A *searchPort* may be used to obtain a list of subordinates of a specified, named directory and to search the directory information base for the set of entries that satisfy some filter. Like a "yellow pages" service, this facility enables a user to get a list of entries that all have a common attribute—for example, all organizational persons having the same organizational unit name within an organization or all residential persons sharing the same postal code. Both list and search capabilities of the searchPort facilitate browsing through the database. The *modifyPort* provides the means to add and remove a "leaf" entry from the Directory Information Base, as well as the means to add, delete, or replace attributes of an existing directory entry and to modify the relative distinguished name of a leaf entry. The ASN.1 macros for these ports are shown in Figure 7.8.

```
directory
      OBJECT
            PORTS {
            readPort[S],        -- the directory is treated as an object
            searchPort[S],      -- it is a supplier [S] of services through
            modifyPort[S] }     -- these ports
::= id-ot-directory

dua
      OBJECT
            PORTS {
            readPort[C],        -- the directory user agent is treated as an object
            searchPort[C],      -- it is a consumer [C] of the services provided
            modifyPort[C] }     -- through ports by the directory
::= id-ot-dua

readPort
      PORT {
            CONSUMER INVOKES {
                        Read, Compare, Abandon }
::= id-pt-read

searchPort
      PORT {
            CONSUMER INVOKES {
                        List, Search }
::= id-pt-search

modifyPort
      PORT {
            CONSUMER INVOKES {
                        AddEntry, RemoveEntry,
                        ModifyEntry, ModifyRDN }}
::= id-pt-modify
```

FIGURE 7.8   ASN.1 Macros for the readPort, searchPort, and modifyPort

To access the Directory, a directory user agent *binds* to one of the types of ports offered on behalf of an end user. The BIND ASN.1 macro is used to create an *association* (see Chapter 10) between the Directory and the local directory user agent. To execute a bind operation, an end user indicates the type of port needed and may be required to provide *credentials*; these may be as simple as the user name, or the directory service may require that the user provide stronger credentials, which can be employed to authenticate the user (see "Directory Security Model," later in this chapter). If the bind operation is successful, the user may perform any of the remote operations available through the port type requested.

Using the *read* operation, for example, the user may specify as an argument to the remote operation an object name from which information is requested (e.g., the name of a residential person) and a selection of information that is associated with that name (e.g., the name of the locality in which the person resides). The result expected from the read is the selected entry information; unexpected results (e.g., errors resulting from the incorrect specification of attributes or violation of an access control in the read request) are also accommodated via the read remote operation.

Once a user no longer requires the services of a port, he or she uses the *unbind* operation to release the association between the Directory and the directory user agent that provided access to the Directory.

Directory System Agent Interaction

ISO/IEC 9594-4, *Procedures for Distributed Operation*, describes a framework within which directory system agents may work cooperatively to provide wide distribution of information maintained in the directory database. (Here, each DSA that works in cooperation with other DSAs to provide a directory service is modeled as a single object, and the Directory is modeled as a set of objects.) In circumstances where a directory system agent does not have the information requested by an end user locally available, the agent may use *chained service ports* to communicate with other DSAs and "pass a request" to another DSA.[8] The chained service ports offer DSAs the opportunity to use *chaining*, in which the local DSA, in effect, puts the user "on hold" while it communicates with another DSA to find the requested information, which it then passes back to the user; or *referral*,

---

8.   Although the directory standards admit to the need to replicate information among DSAs, the current ISO and CCITT X.500 standards do not define protocols to support replication, nor do they describe the methods for keeping replicated information current; these are expected in the 1992 extensions (see also Radicati [1992]). During the interim, OSI directory implementations have resorted to proprietary means of propagating information as well as managing how to distribute information or "knowledge" about how directory information has been distributed/replicated.

in which the DSA responds to the user's request immediately with a message to the effect that "I can't answer your question, but here is the name of a DSA that can—go talk to that DSA yourself." A third form of DSA-DSA interaction, *multicasting*, is effectively an extension of chaining; it allows a DSA to issue the same request to multiple DSAs, either simultaneously or sequentially. The ASN.1 macros for the *refinement* of the DSA directory object to include these ports are shown in Figure 7.9.

The chainedRead, chainedSearch, and chainedModify ports complement the read, search, and modify ports in DSAs but are only

```
DirectoryRefinement ::= REFINE directory AS
  dsa  RECURRING
              readPort[S],   VISIBLE    -- the DSA provides this port to DUAs
              searchPort[S], VISIBLE    --the DSA provides this port to DUAs
              modifyPort[S]  VISIBLE    --the DSA provides this port to DUAs
              chainedReadPort    PAIRED WITH dsa    -- provided to DSAs only
              chainedSearchPort  PAIRED WITH dsa    -- provided to DSAs only
              chainedModifyPort  PAIRED WITH dsa    -- provided to DSAs only


dsa
  OBJECT
      PORTS {
          readPort[S],
          searchPort[S],
          modifyPort[S],
          chainedReadPort,
          chainedSearchPort,
          chainedModifyPort }
::= id-ot-dsa

chainedReadPort
  PORT {
      ABSTRACT OPERATIONS {
                      ChainedRead, ChainedCompare, ChainedAbandon }
::= id-pt-chained-read

chainedSearchPort
  PORT {
      CONSUMER INVOKES {
                      ChainedList, ChainedSearch }
::= id-pt-chained-search

chainedModifyPort
  PORT{
      CONSUMER INVOKES {
                      ChainedAddEntry, ChainedRemoveEntry,
                      ChainedModifyEntry, ChainedModifyRDN }}
::= id-pt-chained-modify
```

FIGURE 7.9   ASN.1 DirectoryRefinement Macros

supplied to other DSAs (and not to directory user agents). The distributed aspects of the directory model are illustrated in Figure 7.10.

The interaction between DSAs is similar to the DUA-DSA interaction. DSAs use a `DSABind` operation to establish an association with other DSAs, then make use of the services provided through the chained port type—chained read, search, modify—to which they have been bound. When a DSA has completed use of a chained port, it releases the association using a `DSAUnbind`.

Directory Protocols

The OSI Directory standards define a protocol for communication between a directory user agent and a DSA (the directory access protocol [DAP])[9] and a protocol for communication among peer DSAs (the directory system protocol [DSP]); these are defined in ISO/IEC 9594-5, *Protocol Specifications.* The protocols are described in terms of the remote operations the user agent and system agent may perform. Specifically, the directory access protocol is defined in terms of three application service elements—the `readASE`, `searchASE`, and `modifyASE`—which are consumers of the corresponding operations shown in Figure 7.8. The directory service protocol is defined in terms of three other application service elements—`chainedReadASE`, `chainedSearchASE`, and `chainedModifyASE`—which are consumers and suppliers of the corresponding operations shown in Figure 7.9. Figure 7.11 illustrates the way in which these elements are related by the directory protocol model.

Directory Security Model

The directory security model provides for both authentication services and access control. *Authentication services* are provided to verify the ini-

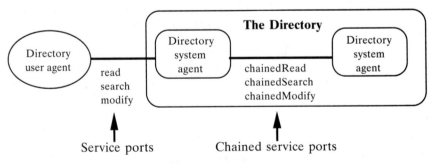

FIGURE 7.10   Distributed Directory Model

9.   Note that in cases where a directory user agent and directory service agent are located in the same system, use of the DAP may not be necessary.

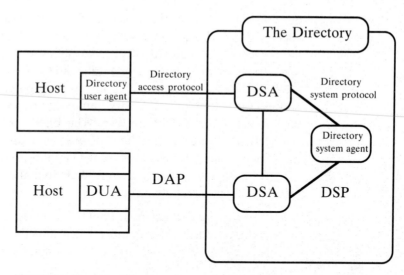

FIGURE 7.11   The Directory Protocol Model

tiator of a directory request; *access controls* are provided to keep parts of the directory information base private from directory users who have not been given the privilege of accessing that information. ISO/IEC 9594-8: 1990, *Authentication Framework*, provides for two levels of authentication. A *simple authentication* uses a password mechanism to verify the identity of a directory user, whereas a *strong authentication* uses cryptographic mechanisms based on a public-key encryption cryptosystem (Diffie and Hellman 1976). The strong authentication specified for the Directory may be used in both the directory-access and system protocols to authenticate the initiator of a request as well as the responder to a request. This is useful in protecting against identity interception, masquerading, and replay. A basic access control—one in which access to directory entries, attributes, or attribute values of an entry can be controlled—is specified in the 1992 version of X.500 and post-1990 revisions to ISO/IEC 9594.

The Relationship Between the OSI Directory and Message Handling Services

The most immediate consumer of the services of a global OSI Directory is the X.400 Message Handling System (see Chapter 8). The Message Handling System requirement for a directory service, which was implied but not stated in the 1984 version of the X.400-series Recommendations, is explicit in the 1988 and later versions. In the 1984 version, the *originator/recipient* (O/R) name used to identify the sources and destinations of mail messages could be only one thing: an O/R address. In the 1988 and later versions of the standard, an O/R name can be either an O/R address (as before) or a directory name (that is, a distinguished name in the context of the X.500 Directory). The 1988 and later versions require that a directory service be either directly or indirectly accessible to the message transfer systems of a message handling system.

A message handling system is likely to make use of a directory system for at least the following services:

- *User-friendly O/R names:* If the O/R names for mail users may only be O/R addresses, users must deal directly (and frequently!) with lengthy, cumbersome, and pedantic strings such as
- `/c=us/admd= mcimail/prmd=nermc/o=bbn/s=Chapin/g= Lyman`. If, on the other hand, a relative distinguished name in the Directory may be used as an O/R name, then mail users may deal directly with much friendlier (for one thing, shorter!) strings, such as "Lyman Chapin" (a clear improvement). In this example (and assuming that the Directory has been properly configured to place the "Lyman Chapin" relative distinguished name at the appropriate place in the directory information tree), a distinguished name entry would appear in the directory for `c=us@o=nermc@ou=bbn@ commonName=Lyman Chapin`, which can be transformed in a straightforward (and standardized) way into an O/R address.
- *Expansion of distribution lists:* When multiple recipients of electronic mail are combined in a distribution list, the name of the list can appear as the O/R name in a mail message. The Directory can be employed to support the use of a user-friendly directory name, rather than an O/R address, for a distribution list, in the same way as it supports the use of directory names for individual message recipients. It can also be used to support the expansion of a distribution list by the message transfer agents responsible for it, since the Directory can store all the O/R addresses for the message recipients included in a distribution list under the single relative distinguished name of the distribution list.
- *Message Handling System user searches:* A Message Handling System user who lacks sufficient information about a message re-cipient to properly address a message may—outside of the Message Handling System itself—use the search capabilities of the Directory to find the missing information (for example, the recipients full "common

name") based on whatever partial information the user may have (such as, perhaps, the recipients first name and phone number).

The components of the X.400 Message Handling System use the Directory in the same way as any other Directory user; there are no special protocols linking X.400 components to X.500 DUAs or DSAs. The directory service required by the 1988 and later X.400 standards need not, therefore, be provided by X.500, nor indeed by any "global" directory. Each Message Handling System component deals with a local DUA or DUA equivalent, and no formal coupling between the Message Handling System and the Directory is required as a matter of conformance to the standards.

The OSI Directory in the Internet

The X.500 Directory is potentially far more powerful and comprehensive than the patchwork combination of `hosts.txt` files, Domain Name System, and other information services and locators that are currently used to perform directorylike functions in the Internet. Since the approval of the 1988 X.500 Directory Recommendations, there has been considerable interest in the use of the OSI Directory in the TCP/IP Internet.[10] A very large number of "pilot" projects—experiments in the use of the OSI Directory service in the Internet—are today operational and interconnected. They share a common global `root` directory maintained at the University of London Computer Centre by the PARADISE project.

PARADISE

PARADISE, the COSINE X.500 Directory service pilot, was launched in November 1990 to coordinate an international directory service for the European research and development community. PARADISE provides some services itself, such as a user interface to the directory service, and as of November 1991, also serves as a link between national pilots in the 18 countries that are participating in COSINE. PARADISE is managed by University College, London, and involves the University of London Computer Centre, X-Tel Services, and a group of public service providers, including PTT Telecom in the Netherlands, PTT Switzerland, and Telecom Finland.

---

10.   The use of the term *TCP/IP Internet* here is intentional; it refers to the use of the OSI Directory to maintain information about the traditional TCP/IP protocol suite in the Internet, in addition to its use to maintain information about OSI protocols that may be supported by a multiprotocol Internet.

One of the PARADISE services is a public-access interface to the Internet OSI Directory system. The interface, called "de" (for "directory enquiries"), is distributed with ISODE (the ISO Development Environment) releases 7.0 and later. Users of "de" can find information about people and organizations that are listed in the directory, using a query model that supports approximate matching and a variety of "wild cards." Users can also list entries in the Directory—people within a department, departments within an organization; organizations within a country, or countries represented in the Directory.

The public-access interface is easy to use. Users with access to the Internet can use TELNET to connect to the host `paradise.ulcc.ac.uk`. A sample interactive session is shown in Figure 7.12. (Note that user-entered text is in bold typeface.)

```
SunOS UNIX (found.paradise.ulcc.ac.uk)

login: dua
Last login: Thu May 28 17:46:52 from 134.246.150.51
SunOS Release 4.1.1 (DUA) #4: Tue Apr 21 11:37:06 BST 1992

        Welcome to PARADISE - the COSINE Directory Service

Connecting to the Directory - wait just a moment please ...
You can use this directory service to look up telephone numbers and electronic mail addresses of
people and organisations participating in the Pilot Directory Service.
You will be prompted to type in:

:- the NAME of the person for whom you are seeking information
:- their DEPARTMENT (optional),
:- the ORGANISATION they work for, and
:- the COUNTRY in which the organisation is based.

On-line HELP is available to explain in more detail how to use the Directory Service. Please
type ?INTRO (or ?intro) if you are not familiar with the Directory Service.

?                       for HELP with the current question you are being asked
??                      for HELP on HELP
q                       to quit the Directory Service (confirmation asked unless at the request
                            for a person's name)
Control-C               abandon current query or entry of current query

Person's name, q to quit, * to browse, ? for help
:- p kirstein
Department name, * to browse, <CR> to search all depts, ?
                            for help

:-
Organisation name, * to browse, ? for help
:- univ london
Country name, * to browse, ? for help
:- uk
United Kingdom
```

```
Got the following approximate matches. Please select one from the list by typing the number
  corresponding to the entry you want.

United Kingdom
  1 Brunel University
  2 University College London
  3 University of London Computer Centre
Organisation name, * to browse, ? for help
:- 2
United Kingdom
                          University College London
                            Computer Science
                              Peter Kirstein
                                description           Head of department
                                telephoneNumber       +44 71-380-7286
                                electronic mail       P.Kirstein@cs.ucl.ac.uk
                                favouriteDrink        not while on duty
                                roomNumber            G01
                                X.400 mail address    /I=P/S=Kirstein/OU=cs/O=ucl/
                                                        PRMD=UK.AC/ADMD=GOLD 4
00/C=GB/

Person's name, q to quit, <CR> for 'p kirstein', * to browse, ? for help
:-
```

FIGURE 7.12   Sample PARADISE Interactive Session

X.500 Implementations

Interoperability among X.500-based directory systems is primarily a matter of lineage; the many different systems deployed in the Internet today are the direct descendants of just a handful of original implementations. The most widely used implementation of the OSI Directory is called QUIPU (Hardcastle-Kille 1992), originated from University College, London, a product of the Integrated Network Communication Architecture (INCA) project. A rival X.500 implementation, developed at the Institut National de la Recherche en Informatique et Automatique (INRIA) in France under the auspices of the ESPRIT project Thorn, is called, not coincidentally, "Pizarro."

A list of currently available implementations of X.500-based directory systems, with particular emphasis on implementations that are designed to operate in the Internet TCP/IP environment, is contained in RFC 1292, *A Catalog of Available X.500 Implementations.*

Other Internet Directory Utilities

Only two of the formal directory services and their application in the Internet have been discussed thus far. These services are relatively new.

In the rich history of the Internet, two earlier directory applications—
WHOIS and FINGER—are noteworthy, as they represent earlier attempts
at providing "name-to-attribute" services.

WHOIS

The WHOIS service supports a limited form of name-to-attribute mapping for IP networks and IP network administrators in the Internet. It is
primarily used by system postmasters or other administrators to find the
"point of contact" for an Internet site. A centralized WHOIS database is
maintained by the Internet's Network Information Center at host `nic.`
`ddn.mil`. WHOIS servers are also distributed throughout the Internet
wherever individual sites choose to run the BSD "whois" program for
access to local and/or remote WHOIS databases. WHOIS (formally,
"NICNAME/WHOIS") is specified by RFC 954 (1985).

X5WHOIS, developed as part of the FOX project,[11] is a variant of
the WHOIS server program that provides access to information in the
`@o=Internet@ou=WHOIS` subtree of the X.500 Directory. (One of the
activities associated with the deployment of X.500 pilots in the Internet
has been to load the contents of the NIC's master WHOIS database into a
subtree of the Internet X.500 directory.) SRI International, in Menlo Park,
California, provides a public-access X5WHOIS server that may be
reached in one of two ways:

1. Through the regular BSD `whois` program:
   ```
   % whois -h inic.nisc.sri.com <search string>
   ```
2. Through TELNET to `inic.nisc.sri.com`:
   log in as `x5whois` (no password) and type one-line `<search`
   `string>`s

The X5WHOIS server looks like a normal directory user agent to
the X.500 Directory and uses the standard X.500 directory access protocol to query X.500 DSAs with the user-supplied `<search string>`.

FINGER

The FINGER protocol (formally, "NAME/FINGER") is specified in RFC
1288, updated in December 1991. The FINGER protocol has been implemented for UNIX systems (i.e., the `fingerd` daemon), and for a small
number of non-UNIX systems, to provide an informal (and highly idiosyncratic) mechanism for discovering information about a user logged in
on a local or remote Internet host. When invoked on one host—with, for

11.   FOX—Field Operational X.500—is a pilot X.500 directory project funded jointly by
the Department of Energy (DOE), the National Aerospace Science Agency (NASA), the
National Science Foundation (NSF), and DARPA; and coordinated by USC/ISI; and operated jointly with Performance Systems, Inc., Merit, Inc., and SRI International.

example, the command line `finger dave@mail.bellcore.com`—it returns information about "Dave Piscitello" obtained from the remote host's `mail` operating system and (optionally) from that user's `.plan` and `.project` files:

```
[Mail]
Login name: dave          In real life: Dave Piscitello

Office: 1C322, x2286      Home phone: n/a

Directory: /u/dave        Shell: /bin/ksh

Last login: Tue Apr 7 10:12 on type from thumper.bellcore.com

Project: all manner of fast packet technologies

Plan: to make public networks a "safe space" for datagrams
```

The usefulness of this service is severely limited by the fact that one must already know a person's user name and host name in order to obtain information from FINGER; by the fact that few non-UNIX systems support the service; by security concerns, which cause many site administrators to disable it; and by the very restricted query model, which supports FINGERing only a specific user on a specific host.

Resource Location

The proliferation of information that is stored "somewhere in the Internet" has promoted a familiar problem to the top of many current networking research agendas: how does one locate the specific information that one needs? A directory service can help to identify the potential sources of information, but it is impractical to construct a directory that is both efficient in the performance of its principal task (that of mapping various identifiers, such as mail user names, to a list of attributes, such as the address of the mail transfer agent to which mail for that user name should be forwarded) *and* capable of processing complex, incompletely specified queries such as "Where can I find information about research on low-temperature fusion in Great Britain since 1991?"

As the library science community discovered the convenience and boundless opportunities associated with the networking of libraries, the new field of *networked information retrieval*—the term generally used for the problem of locating and retrieving information resources that are accessible by means of a network—was born. The authors can only scratch the surface here, but the following projects are particularly interesting examples of the way in which systems designed to discover "information about information" far beyond the capabilities of traditional directories have been designed.

Archie

Archie (a play on the word *archive*) began as a project at McGill University to address the problem of how to quickly and easily scan the offerings of the already bewildering and rapidly growing number of anonymous FTP sites scattered around the Internet. The current system—which is accessible through an interactive TELNET session,[12] by electronic mail, and through command-line and X-window clients—accepts queries such as "Where can I find the following file . . . ?" and returns a list of anonymous FTP archives that contain the named file; for example, the request

```
% archie rfc-index.txt
```

returns the host names and directory locations where the `rfc-index.text` file resides, i.e.,

```
Host nic.ddn.mil
  Location: /rfc
     FILE -rw-r-r-    20166 May 28 1992 rfc-index.txt
Host nnsc.nsf.net
  Location: /rfc
     FILE -rw-r-r-    20224 May 28 1992 rfc-index.txt
```

and so on. (There are a fairly large number of Internet sites that maintain a copy of the `rfc-index.txt` file!)

The shortcomings of such a service are obvious: it searches only for specific file names (and you have to know the exact name of the file—"fuzzy" matches are not supported), and it searches only Internet anonymous FTP archive servers. It is, however, a dramatic improvement over nothing at all.

Wide Area Information Service

The goal of the Wide Area Information Servers (WAIS) project is to facilitate the growth of a distributed system of information servers and clients based on the ANSI standard bibliographic search and retrieval protocol

---

12.   There are public-access Archie servers all over the Internet, including:
archie.mcgill.ca (the first Archie server, at McGill University in Montreal)
archie.funet.fi (in Finland)
archie.ans.net (in New York)
archie.au (in Australia)
archie.doc.ic.ac.uk (in the United Kingdom)
archie.rutgers.edu (at Rutgers University in New Jersey)

(ANSI Z39.50-1988). WAIS is a much more ambitious undertaking than Archie; it is a general-purpose search and retrieval system with two significant characteristics:

1. It uses the standard Z39.50 protocol to search documents and document indexes stored in a wide variety of repositories (not just Internet anonymous FTP archives).

2. It supports a unique, user-oriented search model that closely matches the searching strategy with which people are already familiar: (a) start with a few key words or phrases; (b) see what WAIS retrieves; (c) tell WAIS which of the retrieved articles, or sections of articles, are most relevant to the subject of your search and ask it to search again using your selections as models; and (d) repeat the process until you've found what you want.

The "search from a good example" strategy makes WAIS a very powerful tool, since it not only provides appropriate feedback to the user during the search but also permits the scope or even the original purpose of the search to be changed, iteratively and interactively, as the search proceeds. WAIS also has a built-in accounting system: the client search screens include an explicit "cost" field, which presents both a statement of what it costs (or would cost) to make a particular query and a running decremented count of "how much money you have left."

WAIS uses Z39.50 over TCP/IP, modem, OSI, and other networks; the motivation for using a standard protocol is to eventually be able to work with a wide variety of standard bibliographic search and retrieval systems that are being developed by the library science community. It was originally developed at Thinking Machines Corp. in Cambridge, Massachusetts, by Brewster Kahle, who turned it over to the WAIS Clear-inghouse at the nonprofit Center for Communications Research at Research Triangle Park near Charlotte, North Carolina.

A simple WAIS public-access interface is supported by the NSFnet Network Services Center; connect using TELNET to `nnsc.nsf.net` and log in as `wais`, with no password.

WorldWideWeb

The "WorldWideWeb" project is an ambitious attempt to make all online information readily accessible to users as a "web" of documents and links among them. It was originally developed in 1989 by Tim Berners-Lee, Robert Cailliau, and Jean-François Groff at CERN for use by the high-energy physics community but has expanded far beyond its original target audience.

The goal of WWW is to merge the techniques of "hypertext," in which links between pieces of text (or other information, such as video frames) emulate human associations among related ideas, and text retrieval, which allows associations to be formed based on the content of text or other information media.

WWW "browsers," as the client interfaces are called, are designed to make it easy for users to pursue the links that are displayed from current information to other information, as this example from a simple line-mode browser illustrates:

```
WORLD WIDE WEB

     The WorldWideWeb (W3) is a wide-area hypermedia[1]
     information retrieval initiative aiming to give univer-
     sal access to a large universe of documents.

General Project Information

     See also: an executive summary[2] of the project,
     Mailing lists[3] you can join, Policy[4] , latest W3
     news[5] , Frequently Asked Questions[6] .

Project Status[7]        A list of project components and
                         their current state. (e.g. Line
                         Mode[8] , X11 Viola[9] , X11
                         Erwise[10] , NeXTStep[11] ,
                         Daemon[12] )

People[13]               A list of some people involved in
                         the project.

Bibliography[14]         Paper documentation on W3 and ref-
                         erences.

History[15]              A summary of the history of the
                         project.

How can I help[16] ?     If you would like to support the
                         web.

1-29, Back, <RETURN> for more, Quit, or Help:
```

Wherever a link exists to related information (shown, in this example, as square-bracketed numbers), the user can follow the link by typing the number at the prompt; other browsers use a "point and click" interface, which would show links by highlighting the words or phrases to which they were attached (rather than by assigning a number to them, as in the terminal-oriented interface used for this example).

Conclusion

The Domain Name System is used in the Internet today principally to perform a mapping from some form of name to an Internet (IP) address. As the Internet evolves to a multiprotocol environment, it is desirable that the DNS and/or other directory systems evolve to a system in which the information returned by a name-based query includes multiprotocol (not just IP) addresses, other names, security parameters, protocol-stack information, and other "attributes." The desire to generalize DNS is quickly tempered by the realization that the basic "name-to-address" translation is a fundamental and real-time operation, that it lies in the critical path for real-time applications, and that it cannot be generalized at the expense of efficiency. By contrast, the "name-to-arbitrary-object/attribute-list" translation is not as time-critical, and the OSI Directory accommodates this aspect of directory services nicely, with the potential for providing a platform for many if not all of the information and resource locators mentioned earlier. One of the issues the Internet community faces as the Internet becomes ever more multiprotocol in nature is how to evolve DNS alongside X.500 Directory services. DNS simply can't—and won't—go away: the fact that the X.500 architecture does not currently break out the two different classes of "directory" capability nicely makes it difficult to "simply use X.500" in situations in which a name must be matched with an Internet address very quickly. The DNS, however, is expanding to accommodate OSI network addressing, and although it is easy to speculate how X.500 might evolve so that it serves two different purposes—real-time name-to-address translation (the function of the DNS) and non–real-time white pages and yellow pages services (both to human users and to distributed-system applications)—it appears that both directory applications will play important roles in the Internet.

8

OPEN SYSTEMS MESSAGING: ELECTRONIC MAIL

"E-mail"—the ability to send and receive the electronic equivalent of written correspondence typically delivered through a postal agency—is the most popular and powerful distributed application in use today. It is used for personal correspondence; with the creation of mailing lists, it is used for electronic "conferencing" and it can be used to post large documents to mailing lists for review. In many cases, it is a convenient alternative to file transfer. For those individuals who have no other file-transfer mechanisms available—i.e., those who may have only terminal access to a network—this form of *messaging* is not only convenient, it is an essential means of acquiring electronic documentation.

The postal service is the obvious paradigm for electronic mail: one composes mail, places it in an envelope, addresses the envelope, and passes it to a postal handler—a carrier, a mailbox, or a postal worker stationed at a service window in a post office. The postal handler is one of many "handlers" in the postal delivery system who will attempt to deliver the mail to the addressee identified on the envelope. Both OSI and Internet mail follow this basic model, although the mechanisms, protocols, and message formats of the two mail systems are different.

What is "mailed" through a postal service is not limited to personal correspondence; in addition to letters, people mail bills, invoices, and other business "forms"; photographs; books and catalogs—in short, all sorts of "stuff." Similarly, electronic mail has evolved from the basic transfer of textual mail messages to encompass a variety of electronically encoded messages, including facsimile, graphic images, office documents and forms, digitized voice, telex, and potentially even more. The OSI Message Handling System and the Internet's Simple Mail Transfer

Protocol (SMTP) with recently defined extensions make electronic mail a powerful medium as well.

OSI Message Handling System (X.400 MHS, MOTIS)

The OSI Message Handling System is defined in the CCITT X.400 series recommendations; the ISO standards reference MHS by the less familiar name *Message-Oriented Text-Interchange System* (MOTIS) (ISO/IEC 10021: 1990, in many parts). They describe essentially the same functional model: a distributed system that provides end users with the ability to send and receive electronic messages.[1]

The distributed system that comprises the OSI MHS has the following functional entities:

- An *end user*, identified by an originator/recipient name (O/R name). The end user employs the message handling service to compose, send, and receive messages.
- A *user agent* (UA), an entity that provides an end user with the ability to compose and send messages and also delivers messages to an end user. User agents typically offer some form of local message "management" as well—that is, an end user is customarily provided with the ability to store copies of messages sent/received locally (i.e., in folders, or directories, for subsequent retrieval) and to receive notifications that mail has arrived (the notorious `biff y` in UNIX).
- *Message transfer agents* (MTAs), which forward messages from the originator to the recipient UAs. Where circumstances prevent the immediate delivery of a message to a recipient, MTAs often provide temporary storage of messages and will repeatedly attempt to deliver a message for some predetermined period of time. (Thereafter, the message will be discarded, and the mail system will attempt to notify the originator of the failure.) The conceptual model for "store-and-forward" messaging is illustrated in Figure 8.1.
- MTAs combine to form the *message transfer system* (MTS), and the distributed system composed of the UAs and MTAs is the Message Handling System (MHS). (See Figure 8.2).

---

1.   ISO/IEC 10021 and the 1988 CCITT X.400 Recommendations are nearly identical. The earlier model for message handling services X.400-1984 is now obsolete; however, as there remain many implementations of the 1984 version in use today, both are described here.

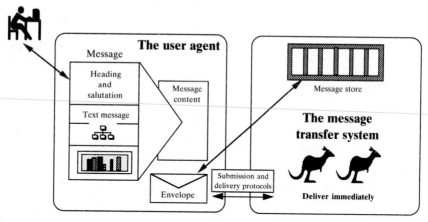

FIGURE 8.1   Store-and-Forward Messaging

In the early X.400 (1984) model of an MHS, the user agents operate at a sublayer above the MTAs, as follows. A mail *originator* (mail user X in Figure 8.3) calls upon a user agent (application) to compose a mail message to mail user Z. The UA application provides mail user X with prompts, menus, etc., that enable X to compose a message, in the process providing the UA with information essential for the preparation of an interpersonal message (IPM); i.e., X provides both heading information (to, from, subject, carbon copy, blind carbon copy) and body information (an ASN.1-encoded text message, accompanied perhaps by an ASN.1-encoded facsimile).

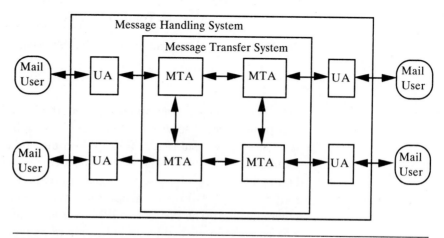

Source: Data Communication Networks Message Handling Systems: X.400 (1984)

FIGURE 8.2   MHS Model

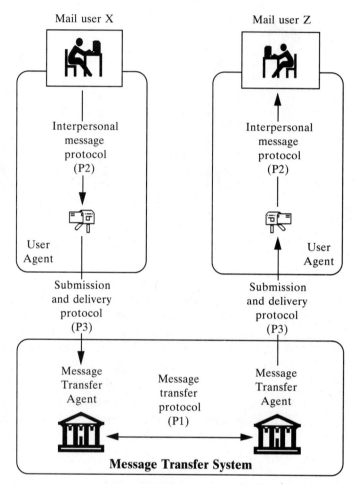

FIGURE 8.3   MHS Protocol Architecture (1984 version)

The message is communicated from the UA invoked by X to the UA that provides mail service to mail user Y through the use of the *interpersonal messaging protocol* (P2) (CCITT Recommendation X.420 [1984], [see ISO/IEC 10021: 1990]). The ASN.1-encoded header of this message (see Figure 8.4) is very nearly self-explanatory (comments in addition to those found in the X.420 recommendation have been added for clarification where needed). The body of an IPM may have multiple parts (see Figure 8.5), each distinguished by an indication of its type. Since the body types represent different electronic media, the OSI Message Handling System is often referred to as providing "multimedia" mail capabilities.

```
Heading ::= SET {
IPMessageId,                    -- a unique and unambiguous message identifier, contains a
                                -- PrintableString and may include an O/R name
originator                      [0] IMPLICIT ORDescriptor OPTIONAL,
                                -- the name of the message sender; e.g., a mail user X's O/R name
AuthorizingUsers                [1] IMPLICIT SEQUENCE OF ORDescriptor OPTIONAL,
                                -- only if not the originator
primaryRecipients               [2] IMPLICIT SEQUENCE OF Recipient OPTIONAL,
copyRecipients                  [3] IMPLICIT SEQUENCE OF Recipient OPTIONAL,
                                -- a list of other folks who are to receive this IPM (more O/R names)
blindCopyRecipients             [4] IMPLICIT SEQUENCE OF Recipient OPTIONAL,
                                -- a list of other folks who are to receive this IPM (more O/R names)
                                -- but whose names should not appear in the heading delivered to
                                -- other recipients
inReplyTo                       [5] IMPLICIT IPMessageId OPTIONAL,
                                -- the message identification of the message to which this IPM refers
obsoletes                       [6] IMPLICIT SEQUENCE OF IPMessageId OPTIONAL,
                                -- the message identifiers of any messages this IPM renders
                                -- obsolete
crossReferences                 [7] IMPLICIT SEQUENCE OF IPMessageId OPTIONAL,
                                -- the message identifiers of any messages this IPM references
subject                         [8] CHOICE {T61String} OPTIONAL,
expiryDate                      [9] IMPLICIT time OPTIONAL,
                                -- represented as UTCTime, the date/timestamp beyond which the
                                -- delivery of this message becomes meaningless
replyBy                         [10] IMPLICIT time OPTIONAL,
                                -- represented as UTCTIME, the date/timestamp beyond which a
                                -- reply to this message is meaningless
replyToUsers                    [11] IMPLICIT SEQUENCE OF ORDescriptor OPTIONAL,
                                -- a list of folks who should be included in any reply to this message
importance                      [12] IMPLICIT INTEGER { low(0), normal(1), high(2) }
                                DEFAULT normal,
sensitivity                     [13] IMPLICIT INTEGER { personal(0), private(1),
                                companyConfidential(2) } OPTIONAL,
autoforwarded                   [14] IMPLICIT BOOLEAN DEFAULT FALSE
                                -- an indication that this message has been forwarded automatically
                                -- by the MHS to the addressee "delegated" to receive this mail
                                }
```

(Source: Adapted from X.420 (1984), *Interpersonal Messaging User Agent Layer)*

FIGURE 8.4   ASN.1 Encoding of an Interpersonal Message

```
BodyPart ::= CHOICE {
                [0] IMPLICIT IA5Text,
                -- vanilla ASCII strings of characters
                [1] IMPLICIT TLX,
                -- 5-bit code assignments of ITA2 for conveying telex info
                [2] IMPLICIT Voice,
                -- bit string representing digitized voice
                [3] IMPLICIT G3Fax,
                -- a page count, followed by a sequence of bits, each representing a
                -- page of a group-3 facsimile
                [4] IMPLICIT TIF0,
                -- a document encoded according to T.73 text-interchange format
                -- (used by group-4 fax class-1 terminals)
                [5] IMPLICIT TTX,
                -- body part is a teletex document (sequence of T61 charstrings)
```

```
[6] IMPLICIT Videotex,
-- body part is a videotex document (T.100- or T.101-encoded)
[7] NationallyDefined,
[8] IMPLICIT Encrypted,
-- a body part that has been subjected to encryption
[9] IMPLICIT ForwardedIPMessage,
-- a body part where an IPM has been subsumed within an IPM
[10] IMPLICIT SFD,
-- character-encoded information organized as a sequence of
-- paragraphs, the details of which are specified in CCITT
-- Recommendation X.420, called a "simple formatted document"
[11] IMPLICIT TIF1
-- a document encoded according to T.73 text-interchange format
-- (used by group-4 fax class-2 and -3 terminals)
}
```

(*Source:* Adapted from X.420 (1984), *Interpersonal Messaging User Agent Layer*)

FIGURE 8.5   IPM Body Types

      Continuing with the example in Figure 8.3, the UA invoked by mail user X logs onto a message transfer agent and submits the interpersonal message through a series of service requests. Using the abstract LOGON service, the user agent provides the MTA with the name of the mail originator and a password to validate the UA. (In some electronic-mail applications, the end user provides log-on information once, at application start-up.) Once validated, the user agent invokes the message-submission service (SUBMIT) to transfer messages to one or more recipients. In practice, the detailed operation of the message-submission service is hidden from the end user. Although user interfaces differ across E-mail applications, many offer a menu of mail-creation operations (create new message, forward message, reply to message, attach file); once a message is composed, the user may queue it for submission or send it immediately, often by the simple act of hitting a "send" key or clicking on an equivalent "button." The E-mail application composes the information needed to submit the message to the message transfer system for the mail user (recipient, message content and content type, options such as deferred delivery time, priority, and delivery notice). If the MTA is remote from the UA—i.e., the UA cannot communicate with the MTA via a local (Interprocess communication) interface—the interpersonal message is forwarded to the MTA in a `submissionEnvelope`, one of a set of message protocol data units (MPDUs) of the *submission and delivery protocol* (P3). The P3 protocol uses a remote operations service and optionally a reliable transfer service to submit messages (interpersonal as well as operations messages) to the MTA (CCITT Recommendation X.410-1984)[2]; note that embedding this func-

---

2.   At the time of publication of the X.400 (1984) Recommendations, the application-

tionality in the MHS elements was quite controversial and is inconsistent with the current structure of the OSI upper layers (see Chapter 10).

The submission and delivery protocol provides the MTA with the addressing and message-processing information it needs to forward (or store and later forward) the IPM through the MTS. Thus, either by decomposing the protocol or by directly parsing the parameters of the SUBMIT.request, an MTA will have acquired the addressing and processing information it needs to forward (or store) the IPM. The MTA composes a user MPDU, consisting of an *envelope* and *content*, to carry the interpersonal message toward its destination.[3] (See Figure 8.6.)

```
UserMPDU ::= SEQUENCE { UMPDUEnvelope, UMPDUContent }
UMPDUEnvelope ::= SET {
                MPDUIdentifier,
                -- a global domain identifier—country name, administrative
                -- domain, and optionally, a private domain identifier, plus a
                -- printable ASCII string—uniquely identifies this UMPDU
                originator ORName,
                originalEncodedInformationTypes OPTIONAL,
                ContentType,
                -- the class of UA used to create the content—e.g., a value of
                --IPM or P2
                UAContentID OPTIONAL,
                -- a printable string
                Priority DEFAULT normal,
                -- can be nonUrgent, normal, or urgent
                PerMessageFlag DEFAULT { } ,
                -- handling directives: disclose recipients, conversion prohibited,
                -- alternate recipients allowed, content return request
                deferredDelivery [0] IMPLICIT Time OPTIONAL,
                -- UTCTime
                [1] IMPLICIT SEQUENCE OF PerDomainBilateralInfo
                OPTIONAL, [2] IMPLICIT SEQUENCE OF RecipientInfo,
                TraceInformation }

UMPDUContent ::= OCTET STRING
```

(Source: Adapted from X.411 (1984), *Message Transfer Layer)*

FIGURE 8.6   ASN.1 Encoding of the UserMPDU of the P1 Protocol

layer structure described in Chapter 10 was not complete. Remote operations and reliable transfer mechanisms were incorporated into the MHS model to support the submission and delivery protocol and message transfer protocol. The term *server* was used to describe these remote operations and reliable transfer mechanisms. The structure of the application layer for the MHS was revised and aligned with the OSI application-layer structure following the publication of the CCITT Red Books in 1985; the "servers" were removed, and the MHS model now makes use of the remote operations and reliable transfer service elements.

3.   This discussion of X.400-1984 focuses primarily on the submission and delivery of messages. The X.400-1984 Recommendations describe the operational behavior of UAs and MTAs and, in particular, describe mechanisms and protocols that MHS elements may use to perform status inquiries, detect routing loops, etc. Discussion of these aspects is beyond what the authors hope to cover here.

Conceptually, an IPM with a multipart body, encapsulated in the P1 protocol, looks like Figure 8.7.

When the user MPDU of the P1 protocol arrives at the message transfer agent that provides delivery service to mail user Z's user agent, notification and delivery of the interpersonal message are accomplished through the use of the message-delivery service (DELIVER). If the MTA is remote from the recipient's user agent, the `deliverEnvelope` *MPDU* of the submission and delivery protocol (P3) is used to deliver the message from the MTA to mail user Z's user agent. Z's user agent extracts the interpersonal message from the envelope and makes it available to Z. As with message submission, the details of this operation are hidden

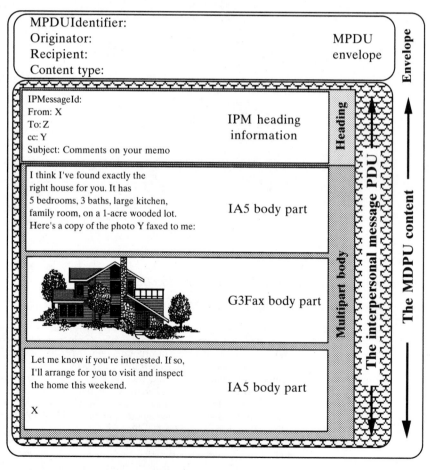

FIGURE 8.7   Conceptual Message Structure

from the mail user. (An audible or visible notice of mail arrival is common to e-mail applications. The mail user then "opens" his or her mailbox to view the new mail that has arrived.)

Organization Mapping— Administration of Message Handling Systems

Like telephony, electronic mail is most powerful if it crosses organizational, national, and international boundaries. And like the global telephone network, an infrastructure must be associated with this power to see that it is operated effectively and responsibly. OSI MHS describes a hierarchy that enables public and private administrations to cooperate in providing message-handling services.

A collection of message transfer and user agents is said to constitute a *management domain* (MD). MDs may provide both message-transfer and interpersonal message services. Publicly administered MDs—i.e., those operated by a PTT or regulated telecommunications carrier—are called *administration management domains* (ADMDs, or AMDs); MDs operated by a company or noncommercial organization are called *private management domains* (PRMDs or PMDs). Both may offer user agent services to their subscribers. For reasons both political and economic, a PRMD is considered to operate wholly within a single country; hence, a multinational company will have multiple PRMDs. According to the letter of the X.400-1984 Recommendations, private management domains may connect to multiple administrative management domains (e.g., a PRMD in the United States may connect to message handling services offered by several local, independent, and interexchange companies, if they were all indeed permitted to offer such *information services*). PRMDs are not allowed to forward mail between ADMDs (e.g., act as a mail gateway between countries), and of course, a private management domain in the United States, for example, must forward messages to a PRMD in the United Kingdom through ADMDs. The relationship between administrative and private management domains, and correct methods of interconnection are shown in Figure 8.8.

·AHA·	*Although such heretical notions are not codified in CCITT Recommendations, PRMDs within a country may connect their MTAs without an intervening ADMD in that country. In the United States, we call this dreaded notion "by pass," or simply "enterprise mail."*

Names and Addresses in MHS

Every subscriber to the MHS is potentially an originator and recipient of messages; hence, the term *originator/recipient name*, or *O/R name*, is used to describe an MHS user. An O/R name is supposed to be *descriptive*; i.e.,

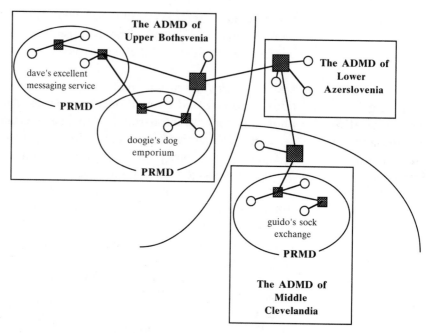

FIGURE 8.8   Administration and Private Management Domains

it uniquely and unambiguously identifies an MHS user. O/R names are composed of attributes that provide sufficient specific information to distinguish every mail user from every other mail user. For example, suppose there is a Dr. Aorta who is a hematologist on staff in the Temple University Hospital, Philadelphia, Pennsylvania, U.S.A. (see Figure 7.5 in Chapter 7). This attribute list uniquely distinguishes Dr. Aorta from Dr. Ventricle, who is also a hematologist on staff in the hospital of Temple University, Philadelphia, Pennsylvania, U.S.A. However, if Dr. Bert Aorta and Dr. Ernie Aorta are both on staff in the same hematology department, then the attribute list is not sufficient to distinguish Bert from Ernie; a given-name attribute is needed.

The same logic is supposed to be applied to O/R names, and the organizational mapping of the OSI Message Handling System provides insight into the construction of O/R names. Management domains are responsible for ensuring uniqueness of O/R names within the MD. The standard attributes of an O/R name are:

- *Personal:* nominally a personal name, perhaps composed of surname and given name, initial, and generational qualifier.
- *Organizational:* the name and unit of the organization (company or noncommercial enterprise).

- *Architectural:* ADMD or PRMD name, an X.121 *public data network number,* or a unique UA identifier.
- *Geographic:* nominally a country name; may also include street name and number, town, and region.

For compatability with telematic services—in the 1984 version of the OSI MHS, O/R names are sometimes more address than name. From the attribute lists, MDs may create O/R names of several forms. These are illustrated in Table 8.1 (consistent with X.400, the optional attributes are distinguished by the use of square brackets).

An example of one of the more commonly encountered forms of O/R name is C=US/ADMD = ATTMAIL/PRMD = DNA6L/ORG = UNISYS/PN = JudyGertz.

O/R names identify users; to forward messages, however, user agents must provide the message transfer system with the address of the destination UA so that the MTS can select the route the message must take to arrive at the destination UA. In X.400 (1984), O/R names describe elements of the MHS architecture, and some variants go so far as to embed network addressing information in the attribute list. In a kinder, gentler world, O/R names would not have such routing information; names would be independent from addressing entirely, and the bindings between O/R names and O/R "addresses" used for routing would be acquired from a directory service. Fortunately, UAs of mail-processing systems typically offer users a means of creating personal lists of aliases or abbreviated names, so rather than having to remember and type "C = US," "ADMD = ATTMAIL," "PRMD = DNA6L," "ORG = UNISYS," "PN

TABLE 8.1   Forms and Variants of O/R Names

Form 1, Variant 1	Form 1, Variant 2	Form 1, Variant 3	Form 2
Country name ADMD name	Country name ADMD name	Country name ADMD name	X.121 address Teletex Terminal identifier
[PRMD] [Organization name] [Organization unit]	UA unique identifier	X.121 address	
[Personal name] [Domain-defined]	[Domain-defined]	[Domain-defined]	

= JudyGertz," it is quite possible that you'll be able to type or select "JudyGertz."

Refinements to the MHS—X.400 (1988)

The 1984 version of the MHS predated the completion of the OSI upper- and application-layer structures described in Chapters 6 and 10, respectively. Some of the facilities identified in entirely separate application service elements—notably, remote operations, reliable transfer, and association control—were embedded in the message handling service, along with the specification of presentation transfer syntax (X.409-1984 is actually a precursor to ASN.1/BER). The X.400-1984 MHS model also suggested an altogether unnecessary layering relationship between the UA and MTA service elements.

Deployment of X.400-1984 revealed some serious limitations. It did not readily accommodate mailing lists, and no security features had been defined. The naming structure was poorly defined, as was the "store" component of store and forward. None of these limitations seemed insurmountable, and certainly, remedies could be found in four years. Remarkable what field experience reveals . . .

The 1988 version of the MHS describes a restructured MHS model, more closely in line with the OSI upper- and application-layer structures. Specifically, open systems behaving as user agents, message store, message transfer agents, and access units—the *functional objects* in the Message Handling System—are described as application processes (APs). Central to each AP is the application entity, which consists of a set of MHS-specific application service elements that perform message administration (the MASE), submission (the MSSE), delivery (the MDSE), retrieval (the MRSE), and transfer services (the MTSE). These ASEs use the supporting "core" ASEs described in Chapter 10—remote operations, reliable transfer, and association control. Conversion to/from abstract/transfer syntax has migrated to the presentation layer.

The user agent and message transfer agent are part of a set of what are called *consumers* and *suppliers* of message handling services. Consider Figure 8.9. A user agent application entity that consumes services that perform message submission, delivery, retrieval, and administration services consists of a user element (UE) plus the four ASEs that provide these services. These services are supplied by the MTA along with an explicit message archive called the *Message Store.*

The relationship between the functional objects and the consumer/supplier ASEs is illustrated in Table 8.2.

Some of these changes are reflected in the MHS protocols (the revised protocol architecture is depicted in Figure 8.10). A message store

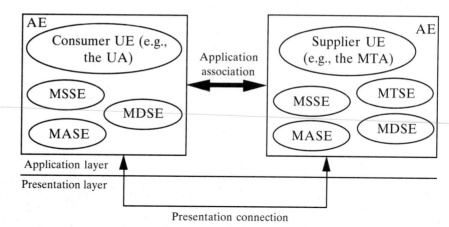

FIGURE 8.9   MHS Application Entity Structure (1988)

access protocol (P7) has been introduced to enable the UA to contact the message store directly. The submission and delivery (P3) protocol, used by both the message store and user agents to access the message transfer service, now has *extension fields* to accommodate the identification of mail users through directory names, the use of object identifiers to identify content type, and the ability to specify external encoded information types. The structure of the IPM remains the same, and the P2 message content remains OCTETSTRING, but some of the body parts identified in 1984 are eliminated (telex and simple formatable document, found to be redundant). A new value for the content type (22) is defined to distinguish X.420-1988–encoded contents from ones that are entirely consistent with content types that might have been generated using X.420-1984. (In such cases, the value of this data type remains 2.)

X.400-1988 introduces new functionality as well. It is now possible

TABLE 8.2   Relationship between the MHS Functional Objects and the Consumer/Supplier ASEs

	Functional Objects of the MHS			
ASE	*UA*	*MS*	*MTA*	*AU*
MTSE	—	—	Consumer/supplier	—
MSSE	Consumer	Consumer/supplier	Supplier	—
MSDE	Consumer	Consumer	Supplier	—
MRSE	Consumer	Supplier	—	—
MASE	Consumer	Consumer/supplier	Supplier	—

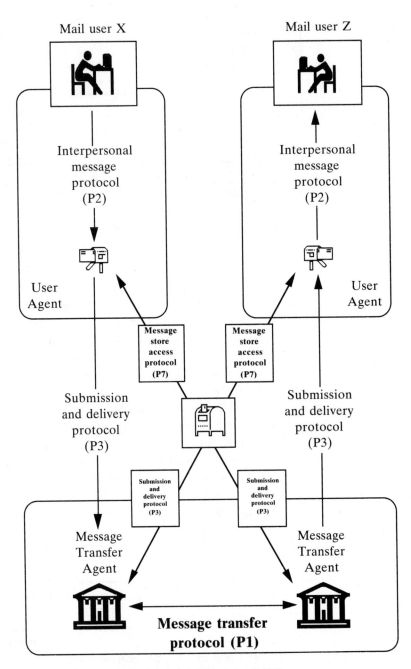

FIGURE 8.10   MHS Protocol Architecture (1988)

to create distribution lists and, within this context, closed user groups. Distribution lists provide mail users with the ability to send messages to a group of mail users using a single O/R name (which is the name of the list). A mail user who is authorized to send mail to a distribution list sends a single message to the distribution-list O/R name; the message transfer system sees that a copy of this message is forwarded to all members of the list (this process is called *expansion*). Typically, a single user manages the distribution list and is responsible for adding members to and removing members from the list. The distribution list identifies the recipients of messages but imposes no restrictions on who may post messages to the distribution-list O/R name, once that name is discovered by a nonmember. An administrator of a distribution list may also limit who is allowed to send messages to that list (the constituency of who may post messages to a distribution list is called a *closed user group*).

X.400-1988 provides a means of introducing privacy to electronic mail. Using the security mechanisms developed for the X.500 Directory, a public-key encryption system can be used to generate an electronic signature. The means of decoding the signature are understood only by the communicating parties and the public-key administrator. With the signature, a recipient can, for example, authenticate the origin of a message, verify the integrity of the message content, and authenticate the message partner (peer). Using mechanisms also recommended in X.509, a message can be encrypted and thus kept confidential. (A thorough discussion of the security aspects of X.400-1988 is provided in Plattner et al. 1991.)

MHS and the Directory

X.400-1988 introduces the use of X.500 directory names as a complementary way of identifying mail users (O/R names as composed in X.400-1984 can still be used). Directory distinguished names, which can be entirely free of "addressing" attributes, can be used by the UA to access the MS or MTA, and between the MS and an MTA as well; for routing between MTAs, however, a directory name-to-UA address mapping must be performed. Specifically, either the user agent of the originator of a message or the first message transfer agent on the path from the originator to the recipient must perform the directory name to O/R address mapping by querying the OSI Directory whenever the originator uses a directory name rather than an O/R address. Such mappings can be registered in the OSI Directory by the administrator of a management domain; thereafter, MTAs may search the OSI Directory for the name-address mapping. The name-to-address mappings may also be modified by an administrator if, for example, a mail user moves from one management domain to another. If directory naming is done independently of

UA addressing, the migration of the mail user from one management domain to another is entirely transparent to all other mail users.

Message Handling System use of the OSI Directory is not limited to name-address resolution. MHS elements may use the OSI Directory to expand distribution lists (i.e., to obtain the UA addresses of all the UAs that provide service to members of the list) and to learn what services and functions MHS components support.

MHS Use of Remote Operations and Reliable Transfer Facilities

In configurations in which an MTA is remote from a UA, the submission and delivery protocol (P3) provides the means by which an MTA and the user agent accomplish what would otherwise be signaled across a local interface, perhaps in something as simple as a procedure call; i.e., the UA invokes operations at the MTA (literally "store and forward the message"), and similarly, the MTA delivers messages to the UA (deliver it to the user). In OSI, procedure calls that are performed across a distributed interface (i.e., across an OSI connection between two applications) are called *remote operations*.

Interpersonal messages containing graphic, digitized voice, or facsimile body parts can be quite large. Generally speaking, if communication between UAs and MTAs is disrupted during the transfer of a large message, restarting from the beginning of the message is time-consuming and, in some cases, expensive. For such messages, the ability to provide checkpoints during message transfer so that UAs and MTAs can recover from (temporary) communications failures, resynchronize to a common point to restart, and continue from that point with a minimum amount of retransmission is an important aspect of message forwarding and delivery. In OSI this is called *reliable transfer*. OSI provides both reliable transfer and remote operations capabilities as part of the communications toolbox described in Chapter 10, *'Core' Application Service Elements*. In the 1984 version of the MHS, remote operations and reliable transfer were embedded in X.400 (1988), the MHS application service elements make use of the remote operations and reliable transfer services provided by the core ASEs to operate the MHS protocols.

Interworking between X.400 (1984) and X.400 (1988)

By the time the 1988 version of MHS was available, a modest but growing installed base of 1984 implementations existed. Eventually, these will go away. However, with the extensions to the MHS and protocols, with the introduction of new naming conventions, and in particular, with the considerable modifications to the OSI upper layers over which MHS would operate, a fair number of incompatibilities exist.[4]

---

4.   The mechanisms to assist in negotiating the correct OSI upper layer protocol environment are described in Chapter 10.

From the perspective of the 1988 MHS user, interconnecting 1988 and 1984 MHS implementations is a process, however temporary, of lowering one's expectations and is called *downgrading*. The extensions introduced in the 1988 version were done so that the MHS would run without them (they are encoded as additional elements of protocol). X.419-1988 Appendix B notes that unless the extension is marked as critical for transfer or critical for delivery, it can simply be deleted; otherwise, "downgrading" cannot be performed, and message forwarding/delivery will fail. (A particularly disappointing aspect of downgrading is that it prevents the use of the security features.) Directory names cannot be used, and X.419-1988 suggests that downgrading be accomplished by deleting the directory name and the O/R address. The Internet community has spent considerable time and effort piloting the use of X.400 and has some practical solutions to dealing with "downgrading." As a general approach, RFC 1328 suggests the use of a domain-defined attribute, always a standard O/R name as defined in RFC 1327.

RFC 1328 also suggests several alternatives that may be applied when dealing with the issue of downgrading interpersonal messages. Depending on gateways and their configuration, it will in some cases be necessary to downgrade from an X.400-1988 content type to one conforming to X.400-1984. In such circumstances, only protocol control information and addressing that can be parsed by a 1984 MHS implementation can remain in the IPM that is to be forwarded. Body-part conversion is another story. Five scenarios exist:

- Some of the information encoded in the 1988 body part is lost.
- The 1988 body part is converted without loss (not always in the "a miracle occurs" category, but close).
- Conversion is simply not possible, and the message must be discarded.
- The body part can be discarded and replaced with a (typically IA5 text) message.
- The body part can be encapsulated as an external 1984 body part.

Although these scenarios paint a somewhat bleak picture when downgrading, the net effect is more positive. Mail users on 1984 MHS may still exchange primarily textual messages with 1988 MHS mail users. The bottom line on downgrading: avoid it if possible.

Internet Mail

Although there are many mail systems in operation across the TCP/IP

Internet, the most popular is based on the Simple Mail Transfer Protocol (SMTP, RFC 821), a protocol used to reliably transfer mail, and the standard for Internet text messages (RFC 822), which specifies a syntax for text messages. SMTP uses an interprocess communication paradigm for mail submission, relay, and delivery; since mail transfer is expected to be reliable, SMTP operates over a TCP connection (see Chapter 12) between hosts. Hosts in the mail system provide mailboxes for mail users, behaving in this role like MHS user agents.[5] Hosts attached to more than one network relay mail messages between hosts that are not connected to the same network; their behavior in this role can be compared to MHS message transfer agents. The collection of hosts involved in these activities forms an SMTP-based mail-delivery system, as shown in Figure 8.11.

RFC 822 defines the syntax and composition of mail messages. As with MHS, mail consists of an envelope containing information necessary

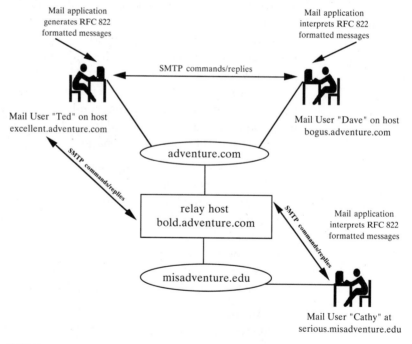

FIGURE 8.11   SMTP Model for Mail Delivery

---

5.   The analogy is not intended to suggest that Internet based its architecture on MHS; it is merely an artifact of having elected to describe MHS first. It is probably safer to assume that while developing the X.400 MHS recommendations, CCITT and ISO experts may have happened across the Internet mail standards among the many they researched, and some are likely to have used Internet mail during the MHS development period.

to forward and deliver mail, and a message content. Mail consists of a header and a single body part consisting of lines of text; standard "822" mail doesn't address how one might encode graphics, facsimile, voice, etc. Through years of experience, folks in the Internet have applied "ad hack" means of transferring documents more complex than mere 7-bit ASCII text; common ways to transfer binary information include programs that expand each digit of a binary octet into two 7-bit ASCII bytes or encode 3 octets as 4 plus control information (e.g., UNIX *uuencode*) RFC 1113. More recent extensions to SMTP provide a wider range of possibilities and are discussed later in the chapter.

The RFC 822 mail header consists of single lines of ASCII text called header fields.[6] Each field contains a field name and a field body. A field name is separated from the field body by a colon (":") and may not contain any SPACE or control (CTL) characters including the colon. The field body is terminated by a carriage return character followed by a line feed character (CRLF). RFC 822 does not require that the fields in the mail header appear in a particular order, except that all header fields must precede the body of the mail message.[7] The general form of mail in the metasyntax used by RFC 822 is shown in Figure 8.12. Figure 8.13 provides an "annotated" example:

```
field    = field-name ":" [ field-body ] CRLF

field-name = 1*<any CHAR, excluding CTLs, SPACE, and ":">

field-body = field-body-contents
            [CRLF LWSP-char field-body]

field-body-contents =
<the ASCII characters making up the field-body, as
defined in the following sections, and consisting
of combinations of atom, quoted-string, and
special tokens, or else consisting of text>
```

(*Source:* RFC 822 (1982), *Standard for the Format of ARPA Internet Text Messages*)

FIGURE 8.12   Metasyntax of "822" Mail

---

6.   The notion of a "single" line is slightly deceiving, since it is more accurately interpreted as a set of ASCII characters terminated by a carriage return/line feed (CRLF) combination.
7.   RFC 822 does recommend that, if present, header fields should be sent in the following order: "Return-Path," "Received," "Date," "From," "Subject," "Sender," "To," "cc."

```
Replied: Wed, 20 Jan 93 16:16:04 -0500            % date this mail reply was sent
Replied: "Christine Hemrick <hemrick@cisco.com>"  % identifies who replied to mail
  Return-Path: hemrick@cisco.com                  % information about the address and
                                                  % route back to mail originator,
                                                  % provided by final transport system
Received: by mail.bellcore.com;id 9301202023.AA05391  % a copy of this field is added by each
                                                  % transport service that relays the
                                                  % message—used for trace
Received: from ash.cisco.com by breeze.bellcore.com (5.61/1.34)
  id AA06912; Wed, 20 Jan 93 15:20:49 -0500
Message-Id: <9201202020.AA06912@breeze.bellcore.com>.  % unique message identifier
Received: by ash.cisco.com; Wed, 20 Jan 93 12:20:44 -0800
From: Christine Hemrick <hemrick@cisco.com>       % sender of message
Subject: RE: meeting time and venue               % subject
To: dave@.bellcore.com (Dave Piscitello)          % intended recipient
Date: Wed, 20 Jan 93 12:20:43 PST                 % time message was received by
                                                  % transport system serving recipient
In-Reply-To: <9201201625.AA17281@sword.bellcore.com>;  % identification of message to which
  from "Dave Piscitello" at Jan 20, 93 11:25 am   % this message replies
X-Mailer: ELM [version 2.2 PL16 mips 1]           % user-defined field name
```

FIGURE 8.13   Sample "822" Mail Header

Mail is composed according to this syntax and submitted by an end-user application to a mail facilitiy—e.g., UNIX *sendmail*—for forwarding; in this example, the sendmail facility uses "ARPANET" mail format and SMTP commands.

SMTP commands and replies are also encoded as 7-bit ASCII characters. The core aspects of sending and receiving mail are straightforward. Suppose that mail user Ted at host "excellent.adventure.com" wishes to send mail to user Dave at host "bogus.adventure.com" and that Ted's computer is able to establish a TCP connection to Dave's computer. Ted uses a mail application to create and send an 822 mail message. The mail application at excellent.adventure.com initiates a mail transaction with host bogus.adventure.com by invoking a local sender SMTP process, which establishes a TCP connection to a receiver SMTP at host bogus.adventure.com at service port 25. To indicate that the TCP connection was successful, the receiver SMTP at bogus.adventure.com returns the SMTP reply "220 bogus.adventure.com Service Ready." The sender SMTP process at excellent.adventure.com next sends the command "HELO excellent.adventure.com"; the receiver SMTP accepts the mail connection by returning the reply "250 bogus.adventure.com, Hello excellent pleased to meet you" to the sender SMTP.[8] At this point, the sender and receiver SMTP

---

8.   The three-digit reply code is used by SMTP; any text that follows is meant to assist postmasters . . . or humor them.

processes have completed greetings, and mail transactions may proceed. The sender SMTP at `excellent.adventure.com` issues the command "MAIL FROM: <Ted@excellent.adventure.com>." The receiver SMTP at `bogus.adventure.com` acknowledges the identification of the sender by replying "250 <Ted@excellent.adventure.com> ...Sender OK." The sender SMTP then submits the recipient information for the mail in the command "RCPT TO: <Dave@bogus.adventure.com>." The receiver SMTP at `bogus.adventure.com` indicates that it knows about the mailbox "Dave," so it replies "250 <Dave@bogus.adventure.com>... Recipient OK." The sender SMTP now sends the mail message "DATA," indicating that it wishes to forward a mail message. The receiver SMTP replies "354 Start mail input; end with <CRLF>. <CRLF>" and will treat the text lines that are transferred as mail data until it receives a mail data termination sequence; i.e., a CRLF, followed by an ASCII period character ("."), followed by a CRLF. If the message transfer is successful, the receiver SMTP at `bogus.adventure.com` replies "250 OK" and attempts to notify Dave that mail has arrived. (If this were the only message that the mail system at `excellent.adventure.com` had to send to `bogus.adventure.com`, it would then issue a "QUIT" command, and the receiver SMTP would close the mail service connection [reply code 221]; otherwise, the mail sequence is repeated.)

Note that if there were multiple recipients for this mail, the sender SMTP would issue one "RCPT TO: <forward-path>" command for each recipient, where the <forward-path> argument indicates a single mail recipient's address (a source route to a mail recipient may accompany the address as part of the argument).

This example illustrates only the scenario in which the host systems involved are able to establish direct connectivity—e.g., within a single domain (`adventure.com`). In configurations in which mail-delivery hosts cannot directly connect using TCP (e.g., for policy/administrative reasons, an enterprise network may not allow all mail systems within its domain to exchange mail directly), mail must be forwarded through multiple mail-delivery systems. (This is also true, and even more complicated, when mail application "gateways" are used to send and deliver mail between mail users operating over different mail systems—e.g., MHS and Internet mail, discussed later in this chapter.) Suppose, for example, that Ted tries to send mail to Cathy's mailbox at `serious.misadventure.edu`, and `excellent.adventure.com` must relay mail through `bogus.adventure.com` to do so. The sequence of mail commands and replies might be as shown in Figure 8.14.

```
SMTP Process        Command/Reply
{excellent.adventure.com is the source host, and bold.adventure.com the relay host,see Figure 8.11}
sender              (opens TCP connection to host bold.adventure.com)
receiver            220 bold.adventure.com Service Ready
sender              HELO excellent.adventure.com
receiver            250 bogus.adventure.com, Hello excellent pleased to meet you
sender              MAIL FROM: <Ted@excellent.adventure.com>
receiver            250 <Ted@excellent.adventure.com>...Sender OK
sender              RCPT TO: <@bold.adventure.com:       Cathy@serious.misadventure.edu>
receiver            250 <@bold.adventure.com:
                    Cathy@serious.misadventure.edu... Recipient OK
sender              DATA
receiver            354 Start mail input; end with <CRLF>.<CRLF>
sender              Date: 14 MAY 1993 10:10:11
sender              From: Ted@excellent.adventure.com
sender              Subject: reschedule conference time & venue
sender              To: Cathy@serious.misadventure.edu
sender
sender              I have a conflict; can we reschedule to Tuesday at 9 am?
sender
sender              .
receiver            250 OK
sender              QUIT
receiver            221 excellent.adventure.com Service closing transmission channel
{relay host bold.adventure.com now becomes the sender, and destination host serious.misadventure.
   edu, the receiver}

sender              (opens TCP connection to host serious.misadventure.edu
receiver            220 serious.misadventure.edu Service Ready
sender              HELO bold.adventure.com
receiver            250 serious.misadventure.edu
sender              MAIL FROM: <@bold.adventure.com:       Ted@excellent.adventure.com>
receiver            250 OK
sender              RCPT TO: <Cathy@serious.misadventure.edu>
receiver            250 OK
sender              DATA
receiver            354 Start mail input; end with <CRLF>.<CRLF>
sender              Received: from excellent.adventure.com by
                    bold@adventure.com; 14 MAY 1993 10:11:45
sender              Date: 14 MAY 1993 10:10:11
sender              From: Ted@excellent.adventure.com
sender              Subject: reschedule conference time & venue
sender              To: Cathy@serious.misadventure.edu
sender
sender              I have a conflict; can we reschedule to Tuesday at 9 am?
sender
sender              .
receiver            250 OK
sender              QUIT
receiver            221 serious.misadventure.edu Service closing transmission channel
```

FIGURE 8.14   Relayed Mail Scenario

It is important to note that, while sending, mail-delivery systems keep a copy of the mail they forward until they have successfully transferred it to the destination system (the host of the recipient); in the case of relaying, a sender only keeps a copy until it has successfully transferred the mail to the relay (and the process iterates as each relay acts as a sender). The positive aspects of using a reliable transport service like TCP to transfer mail in these circumstances is sometimes negated: mail can be misrouted or lost by mail systems, and it is often difficult if not impossible to provide a failure notification to the originator.

Mail Addresses   In its simplest form, a mail address—or mailbox—is by convention of the form {"local part," "@," "domain"}. The local part may be as simple as the name of a user; e.g., Ted, Dave, or Cathy in the earlier examples. The local part may be decidedly complex, especially if used at gateways to convey mail addresses of mail systems other than SMTP/822 systems (e.g., UUCP or proprietary mail systems). "Domain" always names a host in the mail system (see Chapter 7); it is typically constructed as a sequence of {"element$_1$," "." "element$_2$," "." . . . "element$_n$"}. The nth elements (e.g., "com" and "edu") are "top-level" name domains that share a common root—the Internet naming domain—and elements $n - 1$ to 1 are children of the root; for example, "serious" is a host in the "misadventure" name domain, which itself is in "edu."

Most mail applications allow users to create nicknames or aliases that are easier to remember—i.e., "user-friendly." The UNIX *mail* processing system permits users to create single-name aliases and personal distribution lists using an alias command line; e.g., the entry "alias Ted `Ted@excellent.adventure.com`" will allow a user to type "Ted" rather than the full mail address.

Distribution Lists   SMTP provides distribution-list capabilities by means of an EXPAND (EXPN) command, which has a single argument <string> that identifies a mailing list. A sender SMTP process that must forward mail containing an unrecognized "To:" argument—one that is neither a legitimate mailbox nor a locally maintained alias—opens a TCP connection to a host that knows the mailing list and, following the exchange of greetings, sends an "EXPN <string>" command; if the host indeed knows how to expand the string, it returns a succession of positive-completion "250" replies, each conveying one mail address. The sender SMTP process concludes this mail session and begins another, sending a succession of "RCPT TO <forward-path>" commands to identify each of the members of the mailing list who should receive copies of the mail. This example, of course, presupposes that the sender SMTP actually *knew* that the argument of the "To:" was in fact a mailing list.

MIME—Multipurpose Internet Mail Extensions   RFC 1341 defines mechanisms for generalizing the message content of 822 mail to include multiple body parts, which may be both textual and nontextual; i.e., like OSI MHS, the mail contents can be combinations of voice, graphics, and text, and the text can be multifont and multicharacter set. The extensions include:

- A MIME-version header field (like the P2 content-type field in X.400 MHS), to distinguish MIME message contents from 822 message contents.
- A content-type header field, to specify the type and native representation of data in the body of a message.
- A content-transfer-encoding header field, to specify an auxiliary encoding applied to the data to allow them to pass through mail-transport mechanisms incapable of transferring the data in their native representation.
- Content-ID and content-description header fields, two optional header fields to further describe the data in a message body.

MIME will support the following content-types:

- *Text:* textual information in many character sets, and possibly formatted.
- *Multipart:* several body parts, possibly of differing types of data, combined in a single message.
- *Application:* application-specific or binary data.
- *Message:* an encapsulated mail message.
- *Image:* still images, "pictures".
- *Audio:* audio or voice.
- *Video:* video, composite audio/video, or moving image data.

MIME specifies two encodings for the extended content types. Where data largely consist of octets that correspond to printable ASCII characters, MIME recommends a *quoted-printable* encoding; mail systems will process such encodings without modification, leaving the encoded version in a mostly human-readable form. Where data consist of arbitrary octet strings, MIME recommends *Base64*, a variant of the encoding scheme from RFC 1113; briefly, and proceeding from left to right, 24 bits are grouped together, represented as output strings of four encoded 6-bit characters, and then translated into a single alphabetic character from the base-64 ASCII set.

MIME also describes extensions that permit the use of character sets other than ASCII in text tokens of 822 header fields such as "Subject" or "Comments," within a comment delimited by "(" and ")," and in a word or phrase in a "From," "To," or "cc" header field. Both the header and body contents extensions are intended to be compatible with existing mail implementations. MIME uses the mail header fields defined in RFC 822, leaving the field names intact and in ASCII, but extends the encoding of the field body by introducing the notion of an *encoded word*, which, although transparent to mail systems that do not implement MIME, conveys semantics in addition to the header field—e.g., a character set and encoding. Specifically, an encoded word begins and ends with an ASCII "=, "and three arguments—character set, encoding, and encoded text—are bounded by an ASCII "?" (there are thus always four "?"s) and terminated by a SPACE or new line. The *character sets* include US-ASCII and the ISO/IEC 8859 (1987) ISO 8859 family of character sets. Like the MIME message body parts, the *encoding* is either an ASCII "B," for Base64, or "Q," for "quoted-printable." The *encoded text* is any printable ASCII character string. (Using "Q," however, there are some constraints; i.e., you cannot embed a "?" or SPACE in the string, and other characters—"/," "|," "<," ">," and "@"—are illegal in header fields, where they are significant.) Thus, using encoded text in the field body of the "To:" header field in the following fashion

```
To: =?ISO8859-1?Q?Andr=E9_?= Pirard <PIRARD@vm1.ulg.ac.be>
```

allows one to encode the name "André Pirard" without sacrificing the accent mark over the *e*. The loss of transparency in field bodies is small in comparison to the gain for mail users who benefit from the extensions.

MIME is a promising and valuable method of enhancing the interworking between Internet mail and the OSI Message Handling System: with it, the multimedia aspects of MHS can be extended to environments where Internet mail is preferred.

Security

RFC 1113, *Privacy Enhancement for Internet Electronic Mail: Part I—Message Encipherment and Authentication Procedures*, describes how to provide confidentiality, authentication, and message integrity as-surance using cryptographic techniques on messages exchanged between originator and recipient user agent processes in environments where RFC 822 mail messages are used. Like many extensions to TCP/IP applications having a large embedded base, privacy-enhanced mail (PEM) is designed so that the mail-transfer agents—SMTP processes or any message-transfer system that supports RFC 822 mail message formats—aren't affected by the deployment of the extensions. PEM provides data confidentiality (protection against unauthorized disclosure of a message and certain mail header fields); sender authentication (corroboration that the originator of a mail message is indeed who he or she claims to be); message integrity (proof that the message has not been tampered with); and if asymmetric key management is used, nonrepudiation of message origin (proof of the integrity and origin of the message). These privacy facilities are provided by encoding a set of header fields to carry the cryptographic control information and an encrypted message and conveying these as the text portion of an RFC 822-formatted mail message (the encrypted message is encoded in printable form). (See also RFC 1422, *Privacy Enhancement for Internet Electronic Mail: Part II—Certificate-based Key Management*, RFC-1423, *Privacy Enhancement for Internet Electronic Mail: Part III—Algorithms, Modes, and Identifiers*, and RFC 1424, *Privacy Enhancement for Internet Electronic Mail: Part IV—Key Certification and Related Services*, which supercede RFCs 1113, 1114, and 1115.)

Interworking between MHS and Internet Mail

In general, interworking between mail applications involves any or all of the following:

- Mail address translation—e.g., from OSI MHS O/R names to Internet mailbox addresses.
- Protocol mapping—e.g., from RFC 822 Internet text message format to an X.400 interpersonal message (P2), or SMTP to X.400 message transfer access protocol (P1).
- Message content handling—the preservation of content type of all message content parts supported in one message transfer system to another—e.g., the preservation of the text content of an RFC 822 message across an X.400 MHS as content type 2.

Much of the useful work in interworking between OSI MHS and Internet mail systems has been performed in the IETF message-handling working groups and documented by Steve Hardcastle-Kille (RFC 987, RFC 1026, RFC 1137, RFC 1327), who has also done extensive work in the development of mail interworking for the U.K. academic community, which uses the Joint Network Team or Grey Book mail system (Kille 1984a, 1984b). The most recent proposed standard, RFC 1327, defines interworking or mapping between X.400-1988 and RFC 822, with backward compatibility with earlier mappings to X.400-1984–based mail systems.

A comparison between Figures 8.4 and 8.13 suggests that the "header information" used when composing electronic mail in these two systems is quite similar. The mappings between the RFC 822 message header and the interpersonal message system protocol (P2) described in X.420-1988 when an 822 message system is the point of mail origin are accomplished by mapping the RFC 822 header into an extension field in the IPM. When an X.400 MHS is the point of mail origin, mappings are accomplished by (1) mapping existing RFC 822 header fields onto corresponding IPMS protocol information and (2) introducing extension header fields where required. Currently, multipart bodies are supported, but with some loss of information; with MIME extensions, however, it is anticipated that further investigation into interworking between MIME and the OSI MHS will yield mappings that will preserve multipart messages, as well as messages containing multimedia body parts.

Mapping of an RFC 822 mail address is onto an X.400 O/R address. The simplest incarnation of this mapping assumes that the country, ADMD, PRMD, organization, and organizational unit attributes in an O/R address are present; these are mapped to elements in the domain part of an 822 address. The personal name is mapped to the local or user part. For example, it isn't that difficult to see how the following e-mail addresses can be converted into equivalent O/R addresses:

S.Kille@cs.ucl.ac.uk	**mdavies@nri.reston.va.us**
C = "GB"	C = "US"
ADMD = "GOLD 400"	ADMD = "ATTCOM"
PRMD = "ac"	PRMD = "va"
O = "UCL"	O = "reston"
OU = "cs"	OU = "nri"
PN = "S.Kille"	S = "mdavies"

Of course, when attributes corresponding to local and domain parts are absent or ambiguous—e.g., a mail address of the form "`dave@mail.bellcore.com`" or "`tredysvr!dvnspc1!dvncnms !lap@gvlv2.gvl.unisys.com`"—things get stickier. RFC 1327 devotes considerable attention to the details of providing gateway mappings between complex RFC 822 addresses and O/R addresses and also describes methods of mapping between directory names and RFC 822 addresses.

RFC 1327 is unlikely to be the last of the 822-to-MHS interworking documents; the current incarnation of interworking does not yet address security extensions or dealing with different and multiple message content types. These are likely to be more important as field experience with X.400-1988, MIME, and privacy-enhanced mail increases. In any event, don't be surprised if you begin to receive via your Internet mailer mail headers such as those shown in Figure 8.15.

```
From Alf.Hansen@delab.sintef.no Tues May 18 07:27:58 1993
Return-Path: <Alf.Hansen@delab.sintef.no@sabre.bellcore.com>
X400-Received: by mta mhs-relay.cs.wisc.edu in /PRMD=XNREN/ADMD= /C=US/;
      Relayed; Tues, 18 May 1993 06:21:04 +0000
X400-Received: by /PRMD=uninett/ADMD= /C=no/; Relayed;
      Tues, 18 May 1993 06:18:10 +0000
X400-Received: by /PRMD=uninett/ADMD= /C=no/; Relayed;
      Tues, 18 May 1993 06:18:06 +0000
Date: Tues, 18 May 1993 06:18:06 +0000
X400-Originator: Alf.Hansen@delab.sintef.no
X400-Recipients: non-disclosure:;
X400-Mts-Identifier: [/PRMD=uninett/ADMD= /C=no/;930518131806]
X400-Content-Type: P2-1984 (2)
Content-Identifier: 2483
Conversion: Prohibited
From: Alf Hansen <Alf.Hansen@delab.sintef.no>
To: Erik Huizer <Erik.Huizer@surfnet.nl> (IPM Return Requested)
Cc: dave <dave@sabre.bellcore.com> (IPM Return Requested),
  skh <skh@merit.edu> (IPM Return Requested),
    "Kevin.E.Jordan" <Kevin.E.Jordan@mercury.oss.arh.cpg.cdc.com> (IPM Return Requested),
  "S.Kille" <S.Kille@cs.ucl.ac.uk> (IPM Return Requested),
    "Harald.T.Alvestrand" <Harald.T.Alvestrand@delab.sintef.no> (IPM Return Requested),
    sjt <sjt@gateway.ssw.com> (IPM Return Requested),
    Megan Davies <mdavies@nri.reston.va.us> (IPM Return Requested)
In-Reply-To: <9305151310.AA20876@survival.surfnet.n>
Subject: Re: Boston IETF scheduling
Status: RO

Erik,
  . . .
```

FIGURE 8.15   822 Headers from an 822–MHS Relay

Conclusion

This chapter has examined the electronic mail and message handling services of OSI and the Internet. The evolution of the OSI MHS functional model and protocol architecture was traced from the 1984 version to that described in X.400-1988. (Readers should note that the inability on the part of standards makers to arrive at a consensus on the OSI application-layer structure in 1984 introduced perturbations not only in the MHS architecture but in the entire OSI upper-layer architecture; these are discussed in Chapters 10 and 11.) The 1988 version of the OSI MHS is a substantial improvement over its 1984 ancestor, providing a useful, scalable, and secure framework for multimedia messaging.

SMTP/822, or "Internet mail," has evolved from a humble text-only platform to a message handling service that is seemingly feature for feature the equal of OSI MHS by the introduction of privacy enhanced mail and MIME. When PEM was introduced, and MIME shortly thereafter, hard-line Internetters were quick to proclaim X.400 dead, while equally hard-line OSI types dismissed these SMTP extensions as yet another hack. There is, in fact, more posturing than truth in such statements. Readers are asked to consider whether it is really important that there be a winner or whether the true benefit of having two equally powerful message-handling services is that interworking between them will result in a considerably more robust and globally interconnected electronic mail system.

9 NETWORK MANAGEMENT

Why all the interest in network management, and why all the effort? Part of the answer lies in the ever-increasing importance of networks and internetworking. Today, the phrase *mission critical* applies not just to networks that support space-exploration applications but also to those that support sales, airline and hotel reservation systems, health care, commodity and stock exchanges, commerce, and finance. Nearly every business depends on the health of its network to remain in operation. Like the dial tone in the voice network, the availability of facilities for data communications is now taken for granted, and there is an increased incentive to keep networks healthy.

Part of the answer lies in the actual number and size of networks. Data network operation is no longer a matter of managing one site, with one vendor's equipment and one vendor's proprietary management tools. And increasingly, as enterprises connect their networks to share information, "operations" crosses administrative boundaries as well.

These observations address the question "why all the interest?" The answer to the question "why all the effort?" lies in the fact that until recently, with only a handful of noteworthy exceptions, management and diagnostic tools for data networks were either proprietary or homebrewed. There is thus both opportunity and incentive for those who wish to become involved in a new technology that can be put to practical use in a short time frame.

The OSI and Internet communities have each developed technologies to solve the problem of network management. The Internet approach is based on a management protocol called *Simple Network Management Protocol* (SNMP), designed with the philosophy apparent from its name: keep it simple. The OSI approach is based on a management protocol called *Common Management Information Protocol* (CMIP), also designed with the philosophy apparent from its name: provide a common protocol flexible enough to solve all problems.

This fundamental difference in design philosophies created the predictable result. SNMP was designed and deployed quickly, solving the immediate problem of managing the Internet and then moving beyond to other networking environments. CMIP took longer to design, and its deployment is slowed both by its inherent complexity and by the market success of SNMP. Nevertheless, both SNMP and CMIP technologies exist today and will likely continue to be deployed in future network- and systems-management products. And it is also true that these two management models do not address the entirety of the issues related to network management. It is therefore advisable to explore what each tool has to offer and to construct complete management solutions that solve real-world user needs based on whatever combination of technologies is appropriate.

The Internet Approach: Keep It Simple

While the Internet remained a modest collection of hosts, gateways, and users, network management was an "ad hack" practice, and home-brew management, abetted by the sturdy ICMP "ping" facility, was the norm. As the Internet grew both in size and in importance to its users, and as TCP/IP-based internetworking expanded outside the research community, the need for network management capabilities grew. By 1988, research and experimentation by the Internet community led to the definition of two management systems and associated management protocols: the *High-Level Entity Management System* (HEMS) (Partridge and Trewitt 1988; RFC 1021; RFC 1022) and the *Simple Network Management Protocol* (RFC 1157).

Both of these management protocols were designed to operate over the TCP/IP protocol suite. However, because of a strong desire on the part of U.S. government agencies to have a graceful transition from TCP/IP to OSI, the research community agreed to abandon the longer-term HEMS effort in favor of a management framework based on OSI CMIP standards (the trials, travails, and tragedy of OSI Common Management over TCP/IP are discussed later in this chapter).

SNMP was initially viewed as an interim step on the road to the longer-term OSI solution; of course, nothing is ever truly interim. SNMP proved to be an especially adaptable management framework. Executable code for SNMP fit into literally anything containing an embedded microprocessor and was rapidly implemented into a wide range of networking components, from mainframe host systems to PCs, routers, bridges, data/channel service units, even uninterruptable power supplies. The immediate success and subsequent widespread deployment of SNMP have caused folks to reconsider even mentioning SNMP and the word *interim* in the same breath.

SNMP and the SNMP-based network management framework are described in the following sections.

What Is Managed in an Internet?—Internet SMI and MIBs

In the SNMP management framework, shown in Figure 9.1, there are four basic elements: the managing entity, the managed entity, the management protocol used between the two entities, and the management information base. The *managing entity* is an application residing in a network management station (NMS). The network management application monitors, and in some cases controls, the operation of network resources (e.g., routers, bridges, and hosts). The *managed entity* that resides in the managed network resource is called an SNMP *agent*; it is responsible for responding to management operation requests received from the NMS. In addition, the SNMP agent may asynchronously send messages called *traps* to NMSs when the SNMP agent detects certain predefined events, such as a link failure, in the managed network resource. The *management protocol* used between the NMS and the SNMP agent is, of course, the simple network management protocol. The *management information base*,

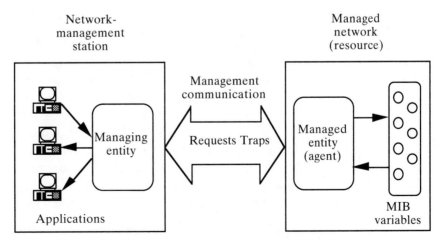

FIGURE 9.1   Internet Management Model

or MIB, is a logical store of information used to support network management (RFC 1213).

SNMP-based network management is based on a philosophy of keeping the required management overhead and functionality at a minimum for both the network and the managed resources (this is referred to in *The Simple Book* as the Fundamental Axiom of Network Management [Rose 1991]). In the SNMP model, the network-management station is expected to perform more network management–related processing than the managed resource since (1) the network management station's primary job is to support network management, and (2) generally speaking, the network management station and its users have a clearer understanding of the "big picture" of the network than any individual managed resource. The NMS usually has applications that may show maps of the managed network, chart various statistics (received/sent packets, error packets, etc.), and notify an operator of errors via audible or visible alarms. The NMS may even perform some rules-based analysis—also hyped as artificial intelligence or applied learning—to help the network manager maintain the network and resolve network problems.

The managed network resource's primary function is not network management: routers should route, bridges should bridge, and hosts should host applications. For these resources, network management should be secondary. In the SNMP model, the agent is expected to devote less to network management processing than the NMS, and typically performs management operations in response to requests from the NMS. With SNMP, network management is based on the NMS *polling* the agents in a network for information; it is expected that generating responses to polls should impose less processing at a managed resource than the often computationally complex process of diagnosing problems.

SNMP-based network management further refines the notion of polling by applying a network management paradigm known as *trap-directed polling*. In trap-directed polling, the NMS polls an SNMP agent in response to an asynchronously generated alarm called a *trap message*[1] it receives from the SNMP agent (as opposed to continually polling for information from the SNMP agent or expecting the SNMP agent to download information on a regular basis). Trap-directed polling relieves the SNMP agent from the burden of monitoring for thresholds or maintaining schedules for downloads, and relieves the network of the traffic caused by frequent polling for information. Trap messages, however, are

---

1.   The trap message indicates that a noteworthy event has occurred; e.g., a link has failed, a link has been restored, or a managed resource has re-booted.

not delivered reliably, so it is not advisable to eliminate polling in the SNMP management model and rely solely on event notifications for direction. A prudent management practice is to poll for information that describes the operational status of all managed resources, in a "round-robin" fashion.

Polling is useful for some aspects of network management—especially fault detection, isolation, and recovery—but there are other occasions when large amounts of network data must be collected for subsequent review and analysis. Frequent requests for large amounts of network data impose a heavy load on managed resources, and are discouraged. Polling can indeed be a two-edged sword; if it is applied incorrectly, by polling too frequently, network managers (especially those with new tools) can figuratively bring a network or managed resource to its knees.

>·AHA·> *One network manager the authors know tried polling network resources for eight pieces of information on every interface every 30 seconds. The managed network resources were spending more time responding to network management queries than to routing network traffic. At the end of a day of intensive polling, the network manager had a gigabyte of network information, a network with lousy performance, and very irritable users. With a little more experience, the network manager now polls for less information less frequently.*

The Management Information Base

The initial Internet efforts focused on three aspects of network management: defining the minimum set of information that is useful and necessary for managing the Internet and its components; identifying how that set of information would be defined; and finally, the management protocol itself.

The management information base (MIB) is the logical store of information used to support network management of the Internet. The goal in designing the MIB was to identify a minimal set of useful information that could be implemented quickly without unduly burdening the managed network resources. The first MIB (or MIB I) was described in RFC 1066 in 1988. MIB I contained 114 *objects,* or types/pieces of information that were viewed as essential for managing TCP/IP-based networks. After additional work and experimentation, some objects were deleted and new objects were added to the MIB, which is now called MIB II (RFC 1213).

MIB II contains over 170 objects organized into nine groups: *system,* interfaces, ip, icmp, tcp, udp, egp, transmission, and snmp (RFC 1213). The system group includes general information on the managed network resource; examples include system name and location. The interfaces group contains information relevant to specific interfaces on a managed resource; examples include interface index, interface type, and interface description. The ip, icmp, tcp, udp, egp, and snmp groups contain information relevant to the protocols, such as counts of protocol packets sent and received.

The transmission group is one of the extension mechanisms that allow graceful addition of network management information to MIB II. It is structured to allow for addition of MIB subsets (called modules) specific to transmission media. For example, MIB modules for access to the digital transmission facilities of the telephony network (DS1- and DS3-based access; see Chapter 15) are defined in separate RFCs but are considered to exist as branches of the MIB II transmission group. Other examples of media-specific transmission MIB modules include the token-ring and token-bus LANs, FDDI, the SMDS interface protocol, and frame-relay modules (again, see Chapter 15). This modularity in the MIB structure is one mechanism for supporting the various, changing technologies that underlie the Internet, while leaving the fabric of network management unchanged.

Even with all the information identified in MIB II and in the transmission MIBs, more information is available for information-hungry network managers. Managed objects that are applicable to a specific vendor's products or protocols may be identified and posted electronically as enterprise-specific MIBs. "It's raining MIBs" is a phrase frequently used to describe the tremendous growth in the number of MIBs available for SNMP-based network management.

| ·AHA· | *Why are there so many MIBs and so many objects to manage?* |

Engineers rather than network operators have traditionally composed MIB modules. All too often enamored with their (well, our) technologies, they (we) get carried away. As one participant in the IEEE 802.6 subcommittee once suggested, they (we) "count everything that moves, and even things that don't move, just to be sure that they stay in the same place." Staff at the NSF Network Operations Center have often suggested that "any more than six [objects] is too many." A downside of having so many objects to keep track of is that the essence of SNMP management is ultimately compromised; despite good intentions, managed resources are spending too much time counting things!

The Structure of Management Information

The second aspect of network management addressed by the SNMP designers was the structure and definition of the information. When the designers tackled the "How should information be defined?" issue, they recognized that the basic rule of simplicity was joined by another fundamental need—the need for extensibility. Knowing that the Internet was a growing beast and that initial efforts to manage the beast would also grow, the designers of SNMP were concerned that the information structure accommodate future growth. These efforts resulted in the definition of the *Structure and Identification of Management Information for TCP/IP-based Internets* (RFC 1155).

The information needed for network management is modeled as a collection of *managed objects*. As described in RFC 1155, the managed objects for SNMP-based management are defined using a subset of OSI's abstract syntax notation one (ASN.1; see Chapter 4). Objects are classified into types, with each object type identified by a name, a syntax, and an encoding. The *name* uniquely identifies the object *type*; the representation of the object type name is an OBJECT IDENTIFIER, as discussed in Chapter 5. For example, the Internet subtree (shown in Figure 9.2) is assigned the object identifier { iso(1) org(3) dod(6) internet(1) } —or more descriptively, "ISO, organization, Department of Defense, Internet."

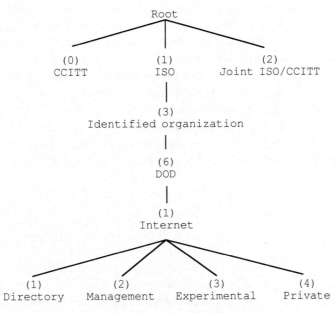

FIGURE 9.2   Internet Object Identifier Tree

Under the Internet subtree, there are four nodes: directory (1), management (2), experimental (3), and private (4). The MIB II standard objects for SNMP-based management are defined in the management branch. Proposed objects are classified under the experimental branch, and objects appropriate for specific products are defined in the private branch. By allocating the fourth branch to "private," the SNMP designers provided a mechanism for extending the naming structure to include information that was pertinent to specific products but not required for general use in the Internet or for network management. It is under the private node that companies attempt to distinguish their agents from their competitors' by identifying even more objects to manage!

The *syntax* is an ASN.1 data structure used to describe a particular object type. Examples of syntax include INTEGER, OCTETSTRING, and NULL. The *encoding* identifies how instances or specific occurrences of an object type are specified using the syntax.

It is the object instances, not object types, that are of interest during network management operations. When an interface is causing networking problems, a network manager needs to know specifically which interface is misbehaving, not just that an interface object type exists. The instance is identified by its object type name and an instance identifier, which is specified in the MIB containing that object. For example, in the *interfaces* table—the ifTable group of MIB II (RFC 1213)—instances are identified by ifIndex, which is a unique integer value assigned to each interface. The instance is depicted as the object identifier with the generalized format x.y, where *x* refers to the object type identifier and *y* is the instance identifier (Rose 1991). Consider, for example, the object ifOperStatus of the interfaces table of MIB II. The ifOper-Status value indicates the status—up, down, or testing—of an interface. For this example, assume that the network manager has received a trap message indicating a link-down condition on interface 7 and that the network manager wants to verify the operational status of the interface. The object identifier for ifOperStatus—or the "x" part of x.y—is { iso(1) org(3) dod(6) internet(1) mgmt(2) mib-2(1) interfaces(2) ifTable(2) ifEntry(1) ifOperStatus(8) }, numerically represented as "1.3.6.1.2.1.2.2.1.8." The object identifier for the specific instance, interface 7, is "1.3.6.1.2.1.2.2.1.8.7." The NMS polls the router's SNMP agent for the value of this instance using this object identifier; the SNMP agent responds with a value indicating that the interface-7 operational status is down. (Note: The pairing of the name of an object or a variable with the variable's value is called a variable binding, or *VarBind*.) Based on this knowledge, the network manager would begin additional troubleshooting procedures, focusing on interface 7.

How Do I Manage It?— SNMP Protocol

SNMP consists of five message types: `GetRequest-PDU`, `GetNextRequest-PDU`, `SetRequest-PDU`, `GetResponse-PDU`, and `Trap-PDU` messages. There are two basic formats for these message types. The first format is used for the `GetRequest`, `GetNextRequest`, `SetRequest`, and `GetResponse` (see Figure 9.3). The information contained in these messages includes: request ID, error status, error index, and a list of object names and values. A second format is used for the `Trap-PDU` message. The information contained in this message includes: the object identifier for the sending SNMP agent, SNMP agent network address, trap identification, enterprise-specific trap identification, time-stamp, and any associated objects and values.

The `GetRequest-PDU` and `GetNextRequest-PDU` are sent by the network management station to the SNMP agent to request retrieval of network management information. The `GetRequest-PDU` includes an object identifier (or a list of object identifiers) that identifies the information needed by the NMS. If the receiving SNMP agent does not have that specific object, the SNMP agent will respond with a `GetResponse-PDU` with a packet format identical to the `GetRequest-PDU`, indicating "noSuchName" in the error-status field. If the SNMP agent does maintain a value for the object named by the object identifier, it populates the value field of the VarBind and returns the packet to the transport address of the originator of the `GetRequest-PDU` (the network-management station).

```
GetRequest-PDU ::=
    [0] IMPLICIT SEQUENCE {
    request-id
    RequestID,
    -- an INTEGER, used to distinguish among outstanding requests
    error-status -- an INTEGER, always 0
    ErrorStatus,
    error-index -- an INTEGER, always 0
    ErrorIndex,
    variable-bindings
    VarBindList
    -- a SEQUENCE of VarBinds, where each VarBind is a name
    -- (objectName) and value (objectSyntax); here, values are always 0  }
```

FIGURE 9.3   GetRequest-PDU

The `GetNextRequest` is processed differently by the SNMP agent. The `GetNextRequest-PDU` also includes the object identifier (or list of object identifiers) for the requested information; however, the SNMP agent will respond to a `GetNextRequest-PDU` with the next lexicographical instance in relation to the sent object identifier. The `GetNext Request-PDU` is referred to as the "powerful GetNext operator" (in particular, see Rose [1991]) because of this feature and the relative ease of its implementation.[2]

The `SetRequest-PDU` is used by the network management station to request that the value of an object instance be changed by the SNMP agent. For example, the network management station may use a `Set-Request-PDU` to request an update to a routing table entry or to change the desired status of an interface to "testing." For sets, the SNMP agent designers and implementers must do additional work to identify the correct combination of information needed from the NMS for the set and to ensure that the set is performed correctly in the managed resource. Upon completion of the set operation, the SNMP agent returns a `GetResponse-PDU` with the value in the VarBind indicating the result of the set operation.[3]

There are security concerns related to SNMP; for example, changes to values of configuration-related managed objects, introduced either by malicious intrusion or by error, can disrupt the performance of a network, even bring it to a halt, and monitoring of network management traffic can reveal user behavior patterns and perhaps help an intruder identify critical (frequently used) resources. (The security aspects of SNMP are discussed later in this chapter.) For these reasons, the set operation is considered the "least simple" of the SNMP management operations.

The `Trap-PDU`, unlike the `GetRequest-PDU` and `GetNext Request-PDU` messages, is initiated by the SNMP agent. A small number of predefined events, which are identified in MIB modules, are triggers for the SNMP agent to send the `Trap-PDU` message to authorized network management stations. RFC 1213, "MIB II," defines five trap messages: cold start, warm start, link up, link down, and authentication failure (i.e., attempts by an unrecognized NMS to get or set values of managed ob-jects); others have been identified in enterprise-specific MIBs. After the event is detected by the SNMP agent, it makes a "best-effort"

---

2.   If the SNMP agent does not have a "next lexicographical instance" to return, then a `GetResponse` message indicating the "noSuchName" error will be returned.

3.   Note that since SNMP is datagram-based, the `GetResponse-PDU` may be lost; i.e., the NMS may receive no confirmation of the completion of the set operation. To determine the results of a set operation, implementations are likely to run a timer following an attempt at a set operation; if the time expires and no `GetReponse-PDU` has arrived, the NMS will issue a `GetRequest-PDU` to determine the value of the object upon which the set operation was performed.

attempt to notify the NMS. The underlying transport protocols (e.g., UDP, TCP) determine whether the network will attempt resends, etc., to transport the message to the destination. (Note that the recommended transport for SNMP, User Datagram Protocol [UDP], is an unreliable datagram protocol and that, typically, there are neither retransmissions nor notifications of loss of a Trap message.)

Examples of Trap-Directed Polling When an SNMP agent in a router detects that it can no longer send or receive traffic across a physical interface, it sends a link-down trap to the network management station. After receiving the trap at the NMS, a network operator will initiate trouble-resolution steps—or follow a "recipe" of actions—to identify the source of the problem. First, the operator may use the NMS application to poll for the interface's operational status to verify that the status of the interface is indeed "down" (i.e., the NMS will send a `GetRequest-PDU` requesting the value of the object `ifOperStatus` in MIB II and may receive a `GetResponse-PDU` with the value of `ifOperStatus` set to "down"). If the operator elects to diagnose the fault in a "bottom-up" fashion, she may poll for physical-layer information from the transmission MIB for this particular interface type. For example, if this were a 1.544-Mbps link based on the DS1 signal, the operator might request values from the *DS1 configuration table* (RFC 1232), which contains information on the alarm and loopback states of an interface, and the *DS1 current table*, which contains counts of DS1-related errors (RFC 1232). If these polls yielded information that isolated the fault to the satisfaction of the network operator, the NMS might proceed by calling in a trouble report to the telephone company; if not, the NMS might continue polling for errors until the reason for the error condition is found.

Note that although fault isolation can be trap-directed, it need not be so; in fact, since there are no guarantees that Trap messages will be delivered, NMS applications often rely on repeated polling of one or more specific objects—e.g., the `ifOperStatus`—and monitor for a change in value. In practice, more than a handful of NMS applications still rely on an echo packet or a ping facility to determine loss of reachability to a managed resource; if the `ifOperStatus` changes, or the echo requests fail to elicit an echo reply after a given number of attempts, the NMS application informs the operator that the status of a managed resource has changed or cannot be determined, and the operator will then proceed with the troubleshooting previously described.

The network-management applications in the NMS may automate some of the protocol exchanges with the SNMP agent so that the network operator does not have to manually initiate polling for trouble resolution. Also, some applications automatically monitor the status of the managed network resources. For example, some SNMP-based applications can display the managed network as a diagram of links and nodes. The links and nodes are shown in different colors to indicate their status; some applications show links that have gone "down" in red and links that are "up" in green. These applications generally poll the SNMP agents for the ifOperStatus values of the relevant interfaces on a regular basis (or alternatively, use ping). The ifOperStatus values are then used as the variable to determine the color changes for the maps. This allows for proactive monitoring of the network while minimizing the traffic exchange required across the network. Other applications allow the network manager to select statistics to be displayed in a graph. The output graphically depicts trends in error and usage counts, allowing the network manager to develop a clearer notion of trends.

SNMP and the Protocol Stack

SNMP is an application-level protocol. To avoid forced retransmissions and to minimize the use of network bandwidth, SNMP was originally specified to run over the user datagram protocol, a connectionless transport protocol in the TCP/IP suite (see Chapter 12). Use of SNMP has expanded outside of TCP/IP-based networks. Standards for its use over other transport protocols such as AppleTalk, IPX, and OSI's connectionless transport protocol—the so-called SNMP "over foo"[4] effort—have been developed and are discussed later in this chapter.

Security and SNMP

The current, "community-string–based" SNMP offers what is known as a trivial authentication service. A *community string* is an OCTETSTRING that provides an authentication service similar to passwords. If the receiving SNMP entity "knows" the community string received in an SNMP message, the message is considered authentic. Implementations are also encouraged to check that the IP address received in the SNMP message is the correct IP address for that community string.

There are four main security concerns with community-string–based SNMP: message modification, unauthorized monitoring of messages, masquerades, and replay. Each of these concerns is related to the results of unauthorized access and possible changes to network-management information that may harm the functions of the network or a managed network resource.

To address these concerns, the Internet community has specified an

---

4.   Literally, "SNMP over anything."

enhancement to the SNMP protocol that provides for additional security features (RFC 1351; RFC 1352; RFC 1353). The *secure SNMP* described in this enhancement provides four security services: data-origin authentication, data-integrity verification, privacy, and protection from replay.

One of the challenges in defining the secure SNMP protocols was to leave the basic SNMP messages unchanged. The designers accomplished this by identifying procedures that left the basic packets intact and added "wrappers" containing the enhanced security-related information to the message formats. Obviously, even with the basic packet headers left unchanged, there are some changes to SNMP to accommodate the security features. These changes involve the use of SNMP parties, a data-authentication algorithm, a data-privacy algorithm, and loosely synchronized clocks. Instead of using community strings, secure SNMP uses *SNMP parties*. An SNMP party represents a role that an SNMP entity takes when performing SNMP management operations. Associated with each SNMP party is a set of information specific to that party; this information includes SNMP party identifier, transport address, acceptable message size, and secret keys for the protocols. The secure SNMP protocol provides for use of both an authentication protocol and a privacy protocol for protecting SNMP messages. Currently, the message digest 5 (MD5) algorithm (RFC 1321) is suggested for the authentication protocol, and the U.S. national data-encryption standard (DES) is suggested for use as the privacy protocol. However, the structure of the protocols is modular, and alternate authentication and privacy protocols may be used. The secure SNMP documents outline a system using private keys with placeholders established for future public-key system use. The secure SNMP documents also outline a mechanism for key management using SNMP.

OSI Common Management: Flexibility, At A Price

ISO began developing a network management extension to the OSI reference model in the early 1980s, but did not complete this initial design phase until almost a decade later. Many factors contributed to this delay, but perhaps the single biggest factor was that—unlike the authors of SNMP, who had a mutual, clearly defined objective ("manage the Internet")—the many, varied ISO members who developed CMIP had no single, common objective. As is the case with so many ISO standards, the OSI Network Management Framework (ISO/IEC 7498-4: 1989) describes a model that is incredibly general and can essentially mean almost anything to anyone.

This model subdivides the network management problem space into five *systems management functional areas* (SMFAs)—fault, performance, configuration, security, and accounting—and enumerates tasks that are relevant to each area. This model was originally intended to organize development of individual standards that would define technologies to implement and automate each identified task. In practice, however, it was found that most tasks are common to several areas, and the concept of developing standards for each functional area has since been abandoned. The current approach is to develop standards representing *systems management functions* (SMFs), each of which defines a self-contained tool that can be used by a number of management applications. For example, the event-report management function (ISO/IEC 10164-5: 1991) defines a mechanism that can be used to forward an identified set of event reports to a given destination under specified conditions; the events themselves might be relevant to any area of management.

Like SNMP, the OSI management framework and a model known as the *systems management overview* (ISO/IEC 10040: 1991) identify a number of components that together provide management capabilities (see Figure 9.4). The components include a *managing system* (which plays the *manager role,* similar to an SNMP network management station), a *managed system* (which plays an *agent role,* similar to an SNMP network element), a *management communications protocol* (CMIP), and *management information.* An OSI *managing system* serves as the interface between management applications with which network administrators deal, and the network or system to be managed. On the other side, an OSI *managed system* provides an access point to the resources to be managed, receiving

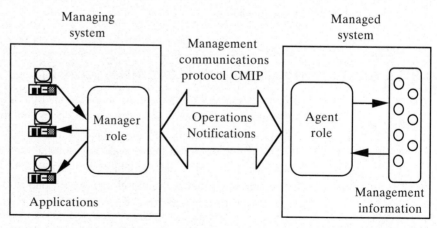

FIGURE 9.4   OSI Management Model

and carrying out management *operations* directed at specific resources and forwarding *notifications* that indicate events pertaining to those resources. The resources themselves are modeled as *managed objects*; the collection of all managed objects (conceptual) is known as the *management information base* (MIB).

> **·AHA·** *Although these OSI concepts are similar to those described previously for SNMP, the details and usage can be quite different, as the authors show in this chapter. In fact, most of the difference—and hence, the debate between "simple" and "common" management—lies neither in the concepts nor in the protocol bits; rather, it lies in the management paradigm.*

What Do I Manage?—OSI Management Information Model and GDMO

Like the designers of SNMP, the architects of OSI management also recognized that the resources to be managed were many and varied and that a common representation would be necessary to manage them in a multivendor environment. The challenge was again to find a method of abstractly representing resources in a manner that would allow for common understanding but also facilitate vendor extension and future enhancement. The resulting approach, defined in the *management information model* (ISO/IEC 10165-1: 1991) and based on object-oriented technology and techniques, is extremely flexible; flexibility, however, does not come without cost.

Using the management information model, resources such as systems, protocol layer entities, and devices are modeled as *managed object classes*. Each managed object class has a number of properties that are made visible over the management interface. Properties include:

- *Attributes:* detailed information that is known (or that might be configured) about the resource
- *Notifications:* significant events that might occur during the lifetime of the resource
- *Operations:* management requests that can be performed on the resource
- *Behavior:* rules that describe the way the resource can be managed

These properties are encapsulated in a single, self-contained definition that is assigned an object class identifier. This identifier—which may be an OBJECT IDENTIFIER, as described in Chapter 5, or a simple integer—serves as the target or source of all CMIP data units. Each property—attribute, notification, or operation—is also assigned a unique identifier to be included in CMIP data units.

For example, a managing system sends a CMIP packet to retrieve the `octetsReceived` counter attribute for all resources that are protocol layer entities. However, there are many kinds of protocol layer entities, and it would be impractical to represent them all as the same object class with exactly the same set of properties. Since all protocol layer entities receive octets of incoming data, it would be nice to be able to capitalize on this so that you could develop one piece of code capable of handling this property. Thus, what is really needed is one object class that represents the properties that are common between all protocol layer entities and many specific object classes that contain both that which is common and that which is unique to a given layer. This can be accomplished using a technique known as *inheritance*, in which what is common is represented as a *superclass* and what is specific/unique is represented as one or more *subclasses*. This technique can be applied iteratively, refining and combining superclasses into more complex and specialized subclasses. Inheritance can also be handy for adding vendor extensions to a standard object class or for enhancing object classes of an old product with new features added in the next release. Even when inheritance is not used, properties that have previously been defined can be reused in other managed-object class definitions.

Another tool—*allomorphism*—can be used to take advantage of commonality between object classes. Allomorphism allows an actual resource (known as a managed-object instance)[5] to behave as several managed object classes. For example, a product that provides OSI class 4 transport service (see Chapter 12) might be viewed as a generic communications entity and connection-oriented protocol machine or as a specialized transport-layer entity and connection-mode protocol machine (see Figure 9.5). These specialized views correspond to object class definitions that are subclassed from the generic views. The view taken in a particular management interaction depends on the level of detail in which an administrator is interested. Using inheritance when defining managed object classes makes allomorphism easier but is not required—any classes that share common properties can take advantage of allomorphism, so long as the class designers reused the same attribute, notification, operation, and/or behavior definitions.

---

5.   A managed-object class defines the type of resource to be managed; a managed-object instance is a particular resource of that type. For example, all OSI transport connections can be considered instances of the same OSI transport connection class.

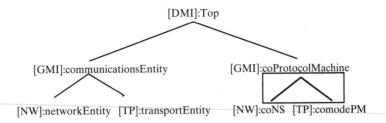

[DMI] = ISO/IEC 10165-2: 1991, *Definition of Management Information*
[GMI] = ISO/IEC 10165-6: 1990 *Generic Management Information*
[NW] = ISO/IEC 10737: 1993 *OSI Network Layer Management Information*
[TP] = ISO/IEC 10733: 1993 *OSI Transport Layer Management Information*

FIGURE 9.5   Example of an Inheritance Tree

> **·AHA·** *The term* object *is used very differently in the OSI and Internet models. OSI managed object classes are similar to Internet object groups, whereas OSI attributes are similar to Internet object types. These "similar but different" terms can be confusing and misleading. For example, it is not uncommon to see a comparison between the number of "objects" defined in OSI and Internet MIBs: an OSI MIB may define only a dozen or so object classes but probably contains attributes numbered in the hundreds—in the same ballpark as the number of object types defined by the Internet MIB II. However, beneath this terminology lies a fundamental difference between the two models—in the Internet model, individual variables are addressable units of information; in the OSI model, variables are encapsulated within classes that are addressed as a whole.*
>
> *To illustrate, consider the difference between "flat" programs, which contain a simple list of statements, and structured programs, which contain a nested hierarchy of function calls or modules. Modular programs can be more complicated to develop but can be easier to update and reuse. The same can be said of Internet and OSI "objects."*

Managed object class designers have a number of tools available to them. The management information model also defines structuring techniques like *containment* (a method of hierarchically organizing class definitions; refer to the discussion of naming in the following section) and *conditional packages* (a method of clumping together related properties and assigning a condition that indicates when the properties will be present—for example, OSI transport class 4 properties are contained in a conditional package that is present only if class 4 operation has been negotiated for a transport connection). Each class definition is documented using a format called *Guidelines for the Definition of Managed Objects*, or GDMO (ISO/IEC 10165-4: 1991).

GDMO contains a number of *templates*—blank forms that are filled in to represent specific managed object classes and their properties. The OBJECT CLASS template lists the packages that make up the class. The PACKAGE template lists the properties included in the package. Each property is defined using an ATTRIBUTE, ATTRIBUTE GROUP, NOTIFICATION, ACTION, PARAMETER, or BEHAVIOR template. Containment relationships between classes are represented using a NAME BINDING template. The filled-in GDMO templates define how the object class and its properties are represented in CMIP data units. For example, the ATTRIBUTE template that defines octetsReceived refers to an ASN.1 type called "Count," which is defined as an ASN.1 INTEGER (ISO/IEC 10165-2: 1991). A CMIP request packet that retrieves the octetsReceived attribute (identified by its OBJECT IDENTIFIER) causes the agent to return a CMIP response packet containing the octetsReceived attribute, the OID, and an INTEGER value. Unlike the Internet structure of management information, the OSI guidelines allow any ASN.1 type to be used when defining managed object class properties.

The object-oriented philosophy of subclassing/allomorphism and reuse described in the OSI management information model has been used to define many resource-specific MIBs in GDMO format. Unlike the Internet community, which initially developed MIB I to manage the resources of the Internet, ISO has not focused its MIB[6] development efforts on managing OSI stack resources. Initial MIBs, such as the OSI Network Management Forum Library, published in 1990, were developed based on preliminary versions of the *Guidelines for the Definition of Managed Objects*. The *Definition of Management Information* (DMI; ISO/IEC 10165-2: 1991) and *Generic Managed Information* (GMI; ISO/IEC CD 10165-5: 1992), published in 1992, were the first MIBs based on the final (IS) version of the GDMO; these might be considered the ISO equivalent of Internet MIB II (RFC 1213) because they provide the foundation on which all other resource-specific MIBs are built. For example, the *Definition of Management Information* defines an object class called "Top," which is the ultimate superclass—it contains attributes that are inherited by all other managed object classes. The "definitions" and generic man-

---

6.   In this chapter and throughout the industry, the term *MIB* is often used to refer to a collection of definitions. ISO standards have no single term for this concept, although *management information library* is often used. ISO/IEC 7498-4: 1989 defines the term *MIB* as a conceptual collection of management information.

aged information model also define object classes such as "System" and "Network," which are positioned at the top of the managed object tree visible to each agent. Now that the underlying management information model and GDMO standards have been published, dozens of resource-specific MIBs are expected to appear by the end of 1993. The first of these—the OSI transport- and network-layer MIBs (ISO/IEC 10737-1: 1992 and ISO/IEC 10733: 1992)—have already been completed.

As might be expected with a general model and format, the management information model and GDMO are being used by a wide variety of organizations throughout the industry, including standards bodies (ISO, CCITT, ANSI, IEEE, even the IETF), consortia (OSF, UI, X/Open), implementers' workshops (OIW), procurement specifiers (NIST, U.S. Air Force), and vendors (telecom, datacom, systems). In the absence of a single governing body like the IETF, it is more difficult to keep track of MIBs under development, where they are published, how they are registered, etc. To address this problem, *management information catalogs* are being developed to provide both paper and on-line listings for publishing organizations, MIBs, and object classes. Also, since any registration authority can provide object identifiers for GDMO-based MIBs, most organizations act as their own registration authority; other MIB definers use a *public registration service,* such as that provided by the OSI/NM Forum.

> ┌─────────┐
> │ ·AHA· │ *ISO GDMO-based MIB development got off to a slow start,*
> └─────────┘ *but all signs indicate that an "MIB explosion" will occur in*
> *the 1993–94 time frame as the industry enters the "publish or perish" phase.*
> *Because MIBs to some extent dictate the choice of management protocol, avail-*
> *ability of Internet MIBs for many technologies may already have locked OSI*
> *management out of some potential markets (most notably, management of devices*
> *critical for internetworking, such as routers and bridges). Thus, the eventual*
> *market success of OSI management rides largely on the ability of MIB definers to*
> *publish a comprehensive set of implementable GDMO-based MIBs—quickly!*

How Do I Manage It?— CMIP/CMIS and SMFs

Given an MIB that defines what you want to manage, the next obvious question is "How do I manage it?" In the traditional ISO style, the authors of the *Common Management Information Service* (ISO/IEC 9595: 1990) answered this question by defining a set of abstract service primitives and parameters. CMIS can be thought of as a collection of function calls or methods that can be invoked to perform operations on or receive notifications from managed-object classes. The CMIS services are: M-GET,

M-SET, M-EVENT-REPORT, M-CREATE, M-DELETE, M-ACTION, and M-CANCEL-GET.

- The CMIS *M-GET* service can be used to retrieve the attributes of network and system resources—for example, to get the `octets-Received` counter attribute. This is similar to the "service" that is provided when the SNMP `Getrequest-PDU`, `GetResponse-PDU`, and `GetNextRequest-PDU` messages are used.
- The CMIS *M-SET* service can be used to modify attributes—for example, to configure OSI transport layer timer values. This is similar to the service provided via the SNMP `SetRequest-PDU` (and corresponding) `GetRequest-PDU`, `GetResponse-PDU`.
- The CMIS *M-EVENT-REPORT* can be used to signal a noteworthy occurrence—for example, an excessive number of retransmissions occurring in the OSI transport layer. This is similar to the SNMP trap message.
- The CMIS *M-CREATE* and *M-DELETE* services allow the manager to request that managed-object instances be added or removed—for example, an event-forwarding discriminator might be created to control the flow of events from the agent to the manager (more on this subject later in the chapter). There are no comparable SNMP messages, although MIB designers may define tables in which rows can be added or deleted using the SNMP `SetRequest-PDU` message.
- The CMIS *M-ACTION* service allows a manager to request that any arbitrary operation be performed on or by a resource—for example, an ACTION might be used to activate or deactivate protocol layer entities. There are no comparable SNMP messages, although, again, MIB designers might provide a variable that, when set, would initiate an operation.
- The CMIS *M-CANCEL-GET* service allows a previously requested M-GET to be aborted; the reason for this will become obvious later in the chapter, when multiple replies are discussed. There is no comparable SNMP message.

Each service primitive is converted into protocol data units by the *common management information protocol* specification (ISO/IEC 9596-1: 1990);[7] Figure 9.6 illustrates the CMIP GET packet, which is used to convey the semantics of the M-GET service.

---

7.   CMIS and CMIP version 1 were published in 1989, vendor experimentation began, a few show demos were held, and defects discovered during this process were reflected in

```
CMIP-1 {joint-iso-ccitt ms (9) cmip (1) modules (0) protocol (3)}
DEFINITIONS ::=
BEGIN
m-GET OPERATION
   ARGUMENT      GetArgument
   RESULT        GetResult
   ERRORS        { accessDenied, classInstanceConflict,
                 complexityLimitation, getListError, invalidFilter,
                 invalidScope, noSuchObjectClass, noSuchObjectInstance,
                 operationCancelled, processingFailure, syncNotSupported }
   LINKED        { m-Linked-Reply }
::= localValue 3

GetArgument ::= SEQUENCE { COMPONENTS OF BaseManagedObjectId,
                    accessControl    [5] AccessControl OPTIONAL,
                    sychronization   [6] IMPLICIT CMISSync
                                         DEFAULT bestEffort,
                    scope                [7] Scope DEFAULT baseObject,
                    filter               CMISFilter DEFAULT and{},
                    attributeIdList  [12] IMPLICIT SET OF AttributeId
                                         OPTIONAL }

BaseManagedObjectId ::= SEQUENCE { baseManagedObjectClass    ObjectClass,
                                   baseManagedObjectInstance ObjectInstance }

AccessControl ::= EXTERNAL
CMISSync ::= ENUMERATED { bestEffort (0), atomic (1) }

Scope ::= CHOICE {
            INTEGER { baseObject (0), firstLevelOnly (1), wholeSubtree (2) },
            individualLevels    [1] IMPLICIT INTEGER,
            baseToNthLevels     [2] IMPLICIT INTEGER }

CMISFilter ::= CHOICE {
            item [8] FilterItem,
            and  [9] IMPLICIT SET OF CMISFilter,
            or  [10] IMPLICIT SET OF CMISFilter,
            not [11] CMISFilter }

AttributeId ::= CHOICE { globalForm [0] IMPLICIT OBJECT IDENTIFIER,
                localForm [1] IMPLICIT INTEGER }
ObjectClass ::= CHOICE { globalForm [0] IMPLICIT OBJECT IDENTIFIER,
                localForm [1] IMPLICIT INTEGER }

ObjectInstance ::= CHOICE { distinguishedName [2] IMPLICIT DistinguishedName,
                nonSpecificForm [3] IMPLICIT OCTET STRING,
                localDistinguishedName [4] IMPLICIT RDNSequence }
```

version 2, published in November 1990. At this point, to eliminate churn and provide a stable base, ISO "froze" CMIS/CMIP for the next four years. Because version 2 is the basis for most existing and future CMIS/CMIP-based products, this chapter discusses only version 2.

```
FilterItem ::= CHOICE {
    equality    [0] IMPLICIT Attribute,
    substrings [1] IMPLICIT SEQUENCE OF CHOICE {
                        initialString    [0] IMPLICIT SEQUENCE {
                                          attributeId AttributeId,
                                          string      ANY DEFINED BY attributeId },
                        anyString         [1] IMPLICIT SEQUENCE {
                                          attributeId AttributeId,
                                          string      ANY DEFINED BY attributeId },
                        finalString       [2] IMPLICIT SEQUENCE {
                                          attributeId AttributeId,
                                          string      ANY DEFINED BY attributeId }},
    greaterOrEqual    [2] IMPLICIT Attribute,
    lessOrEqual       [3] IMPLICIT Attribute,
    present           [4] AttributeId,
    subsetOf          [5] IMPLICIT Attribute,
    supersetOf        [6] IMPLICIT Attribute,
    nonNullIntersection [7] IMPLICIT Attribute }

Attribute ::= SEQUENCE { attributeId  AttributeId,
                         attributeValue   ANY DEFINED BY attributeId }
-- The following are IMPORTed from X.500 Info Framework...
DistinguishedName ::= RDNSequence
RDNSequence ::= SEQUENCE OF RelativeDistinguishedName
RelativeDistinguishedName ::= SET OF AttributeValueAssertion
AttributeValueAssertion ::= SEQUENCE { AttributeType, AttributeValue }
AttributeType ::= OBJECT IDENTIFER
AttributeValue ::= ANY
```

END
Source: ISO/IEC 9596-1: 1990

FIGURE 9.6   ASN.1 Definitions for the CMIP M-GET.request PDU

> ⟨·AHA·⟩ *CMIS services and SNMP messages, at the surface level, are
> not all that different. CMIS provides a few additional services
> built into the protocol, whereas these operations can (mostly) be accomplished
> using SNMP and a cleverly defined MIB. One must dig deeper yet to see where
> the true differences lie . . .*

**CMIP and the
Protocol Suite**

The OSI common management application service elements use CMIP, a
connection-oriented application-layer protocol, as the means to distribute
management function and information. Like other ISO-defined application service elements, the CMIP ASE uses association control (see Chapter 10) to establish, release, and abort the underlying association. CMIP
defines a small amount of user information that gets carried in the association-control protocol to allow the common management service user to

negotiate what the association is to be used for, but otherwise relies on the normal association-control routine to set up management dialogues. The *Systems Management Overview* (ISO/IEC 10040: 1991) defines a single application context that is used between management application service elements (see Chapter 10). When used over a full OSI stack, CMIP assumes reliable data transfer, allowing managers and agents to go about their business without worrying about detecting loss or retransmission. Insulation from the transmission characteristics of the underlying network has many benefits—management applications and agents don't need to be fine-tuned to "behave nicely" in each installation, and alternative transport mechanisms can be used with minimum disruption (for example, vendors deploy CMIP over proprietary transports as well as OSI). However, as noted in the discussion of SNMP and UDP, connection-oriented transport implies unsolicited retransmission, which can be costly—perhaps even fatal in times of network crisis, and more overhead for brief management exchanges or interrogations (i.e., one must establish a connection, exchange requests and responses, and tear down a connection, as opposed to "simply" using datagrams).

CMIP and Remote Operations

OSI common management uses the invoke/result paradigm of remote operations; the CMIP protocol relies on an application service element called *remote operations* (see Chapter 10). Every CMIS request maps to a remote operations service. The CMIP data units also map into remote operations protocol data units. These can be thought of as "envelopes" into which CMIP data units are inserted for transmission. CMIS also makes use of the linked-reply facility defined by remote operations to cover the case in which multiple replies are generated in response to a single invoke (see Chapter 10). Because CMIP is built on top of remote operations, CMIS can be used in synchronous or asynchronous modes, as described in Chapter 10.

All CMIS operations are directed to a particular resource by including in the request a managed object class ID and a managed-object instance name. The managed object class can be an OBJECT IDENTIFIER (global form) or a simple integer (local form), although the "local form" can only be used when the manager and agent have a common understanding—for example, to reduce overhead when using CMIP to manage a private or proprietary network. The managed object instance name can be either an X.500-style *distinguished name*, a *local distinguished name* (LDN), or a simple OCTETSTRING (limited to use in a well-defined context). Recall from Chapter 7 that distinguished names (DNs) are composed of a sequence of relative distinguished names (RDNs); each RDN consists of an *attribute value assertion* (AVA) containing an attribute ID and value. This syntax allows unambiguous names to be constructed in any multivendor environment by using something called a *containment tree,* an example of which is shown in Figure 9.7.

The containment tree organizes managed-object classes into a hierarchy, with the containing class being called the "superior" and the contained class being called the "subordinate." Each instance in the tree has its own name, unique within the context of its superior—this is the RDN. By concatenating all RDNs in a branch of the tree, you can derive a globally unique distinguished name that identifies one and only one managed object instance. A local distinguished name is the name derived from concatenating all RDNs in a branch of the subtree contained by the "System" managed object class.

⸬AHA⸬ *Internet naming is based on statically defined object identifiers, whereas OSI naming is based on dynamically generated distinguished names. Internet naming is always local to the agent, whereas OSI naming may be local to the system (LDN) or global (DN). As might be expected, OSI naming is more general and flexible than Internet naming, but at a cost— DNs and LDNs are typically longer than OIDs and, hence, more expensive to construct, process, and transmit.*

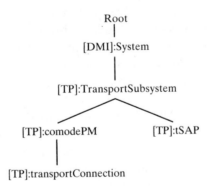

Root

[DMI]:System

[TP]:TransportSubsystem

[TP]:comodePM   [TP]:tSAP

[TP]:transportConnection

Note: Names for an instance of the transportConnection managed object class
  RDN = { Id = "1," Value = "A" }
  LDN = { TransportSubsystem RDN + comodePM RDN + transportConnec
  DN = { System RDN + LDN }

FIGURE 9.7   Example of a Containment Tree

CMIS allows, as an option, *scoping* and *filtering* capabilities, which enable the same operation to be performed on several resources by issuing a single request. The scope parameter identifies a part of the containment tree (a subtree)—for example, all instances contained by system X. The filter parameter carries a conditional statement or predicate that can be tested against attribute values to further limit the operation—for example, all instances of class "transport connection" with operational state "disabled." A *synchronization* parameter allows the operation to be treated as *atomic* (do it all or do nothing) or *best effort* (perform the operation on as many instances as you can, and inform me of the result). These optional fields allow for the composition of very powerful CMIS requests, such as "Delete all transport connections in system X that are disabled." Figure 9.8 demonstrates how remote operations linked replies

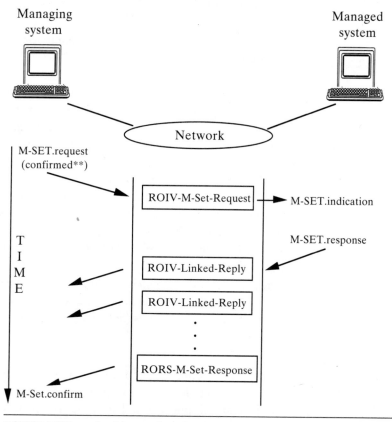

**CMIS M-SETs can be either confirmed or non-confirmed, at user discretion

FIGURE 9.8   Sample M-SET Operation

might be used by CMIP to return the results of such an operation, one reply per managed object instance (linked replies and parent-child operations are discussed in Chapter 10). In the figure, a managing system calls upon a managed system to perform the sequence of change operations associated with the M-SET.request "delete transport connections in your system that are disabled." A single CMIS request is transferred by invoking remote operations. The M-SET.request is conveyed in a remote operations packet (in the figure, the ROIV-M-Set-Request packet). As the agent at the managed system deletes each transport connection (each managed-object instance), a successful result is returned using remote operations linked replies (in Figure 9.8, one ROIV-Linked-Reply packet would be returned for each deleted managed-object instance). The completion of the management operation would be signaled back to the managing system by the arrival of a remote operations (successful) result packet (in Figure 9.8, the RORS-M-Set-Response).

⌈·AHA·⌉ *CMIS scoping and filtering provide capabilities that go beyond the "all-powerful" SNMP GetNext but have been criticized as costly to implement and support. This is one example of a key philosophical difference between the authors of SNMP and CMIP—SNMP places the burden of management operations on the network management station, whereas CMIP allows for distribution of the load between manager and agent. It is important to note that CMIP does not require load distribution—it can be implemented without scoping or filtering capability. Further, it can be argued that scoping and filtering must be provided for somewhere and that providing this capability as part of the management protocol simplifies management application development and reduces network management traffic. With SNMP, the management application issues many GetNext messages, sifts through the results, and figures out what is really of interest; with CMIP, the management application issues a single scoped M-GET, and the agent does the sifting, returning only the interesting stuff. Finally, it is impossible to provide the same semantics without scoping and filtering—attribute values change, and testing them as close to the resource as possible minimizes (but does not eliminate) temporal flux.*

System Management Functions

System management functions (SMFs) provide tools—protocols and managed object classes—to implement routine management tasks common to many applications. The initial batch of SMFs, published in late 1991, provide the following services:

- The *"Object-Management Function"* (ISO/IEC 10164-1: 1991) provides pass-through services corresponding to all CMIS operations,[8] and a few common notifications: `attributeValueChange`, `object-Creation`, and `objectDeletion`. These notifications are defined in ISO/IEC 10165-2: 1991 and appear in many GDMO-style managed object classes.

- The *"State Management Function"* (ISO/IEC 10164-2: 1991) provides a few common state attributes and a common notification that can be used to signal changes in state. For example, most resources can be operational or disabled, some allow administrative control over use of the resource, and some can tell whether or not they are in use. The SMF allows this information to be represented in the same way, in any managed object class, allowing common management applications to be developed to monitor and manage the status of any resource.

- The *Attributes For Representing Relationships Function* (ISO/IEC 10164-3: 1991) provides common relationship attributes and a change notification that allow the interrelationship between managed object classes and instances to be captured in a consistent manner.

- The *Alarm-Reporting Function* (ISO/IEC 10164-4: 1991) defines common notifications to signal faults detected by the agent system. Again, common representation of this information facilitates development of common fault monitoring applications.

- The *Event Report Management Function* (ISO/IEC 10164-5: 1991) and *log control function* (ISO/IEC 10164-6: 1991) allow managers to control which notifications will be sent as CMIS M-EVENT-REPORTs or logged by the agent system.

Many other SMFs are currently available or under development, including those aimed at security, performance, and accounting management. For example, *Objects and Attributes for Access Control* (ISO/IEC 10164-9: 1991) allows security to be provided at the management object class, instance, and even operation level.

The event report and log control functions enable manager control by using object-oriented techniques. For example, the event report management function allows a manager to turn event forwarding on or off or temporarily suspend it, to specify primary and backup destinations to

---

8. Basing management applications and agents on the object management function (OMF) pass-through services is intended to insulate them from the underlying protocol (CMIP) and therefore allow substitution (for example, to use a local RPC mechanism instead). In practice, it turns out that there is another big advantage to using OMF instead of CMIS—OMF allows an implementation to conform to only the agent "half" of CMIS, whereas CMIP requires support for both roles.

which the events should be sent, to indicate dates and times during which forwarding should be enabled, and to specify detailed filters that can be used to selectively forward only a few events. Similarly, the log control function allows control over logging of notifications at the agent system, for subsequent retrieval by the manager.

·AHA· *Another key philosophical difference between OSI and Internet management is event handling. As mentioned previously, SNMP uses (but does not rely upon)* trap-directed polling, *in which only a few critical events are detected by the SNMP agent, to be supplemented by periodic or trap-initiated polling by the SNMP NMS. On the other hand, OSI might be considered* event-driven *(recall that CMIP operates over a transport connection; hence, the delivery of events is reliable). GDMO-based managed object classes tend to be defined with a number of notifications intended to signal changes in the resource. The event report and log control functions provide management control over forwarding and logging so that every little notification doesn't end up being transmitted or stored. The end result is enormous flexibility for managers and thus for the management application—network or system administrators can pick and choose what they want to poll for and what they want to be notified about. And—you guessed it—an enormous cost for the agent, which must detect, filter, throw away, store, and/or forward these notifications. Cost can be reduced by clever implementations that propagate filter criteria back into the resources themselves and pragmatic MIB design (use conditional packages to allow implementation flexibility, avoid notifying about anything and everything you can think of). Finally, it is possible to use CMIP in a polling mode, without being event-driven. In fact, most initial implementations of CMIP did just this, for the sake of simplicity—and because the event report and log control functions (ISO/IEC 10164-5: 1991; ISO/IEC 10164-6: 1991) were completed after CMIP (ISO/IEC 9596-1: 1990).*

Profiles

It is impossible to conclude any discussion of OSI without mentioning *international standardized profiles* (ISPs) for CMIP. International standardized profiles identify a collection of base standards, select options contained within the standards, and specify pragmatic constraints (for example, limiting field lengths; see Chapter 2). Because OSI standards are layered and have so many options, ISPs are necessary to enable vendors and users to build and buy products that can interoperate. For OSI management, final ISPs are available for CMIP, and draft ISPs are available for the system-management functions. For example, the *Enhanced Management Communication* profile (ISP 11183-2) specifies detailed requirements for CMIP, ROSE, ACSE, presentation, and session protocols. The *Basic Management Communication* profile (ISP 11183-3) specifies similar requirements but excludes scoping and filtering features. Any vendor providing a CMIP-based product today can be expected to claim conformance to one or both of these profiles.

Putting It All Together

Having discussed the capabilities that Internet and OSI management ASEs have to offer, it is certainly appropriate to mention that, by and large, network and systems administrators really don't care a whit about management paradigms, robustness, elegance, or which "ASE" they use (if, in fact, they even know what an ASE is). They care about managing their enterprise. Today more than ever before, it is vital to provide "plug-and-play" technologies that work together to solve customer problems. Some of the strategies that have thus far been developed for integration, coexistence, and migration of management technologies are mentioned in the following subsections.

Mix-and-Match Protocols: SNMP over Foo, CMIP for the Internet

Over the past few years, there have been several attempts to "bridge the gap" between CMIP and SNMP, including the following:

- *CMIP for TCP/IP-based internets* (RFC 1095) was originally intended as a long-term management solution for the Internet. CMOT defined the use of CMIP/ROSE/ACSE over a specialized version of the OSI presentation layer (RFC 1085) over TCP/IP. This approach has since been discarded by the Internet community following a network-management "bake-off."

$\boxed{\cdot\text{AHA}\cdot}$ *At a point during the parallel development of SNMP and CMOT at which no further progress could be made in committee, the SNMP and CMOT camps decided to end the debate with a bake-off. It was jointly agreed that following several months of development, the implementation worthiness of the two proposals would provide the final input. According to Internet folklore, the SNMP camp was able to demonstrate multiple, interoperable implementations, and the CMOT camp had none.*

- More recently, the IETF considered a full-blown CMIP for the Internet (RFC 1189), which would eventually obsolete the original

CMOT effort. This approach glued the entire OSI CMIP upper-layer stack (down through session) onto TCP/IP using RFC 1006. A GDMO-based version of the Internet MIB II, called the *OIM MIB II* (RFC 1214) was to be developed. This MIB was intended to allow management of Internet resources using CMIP protocols. This activity came under IESG review in the spring of 1992, and the working group was disbanded due to inactivity. Members of the X/Open and OSI Network Management Forum expect to produce a CMIP over TCP/IP using RFC 1006 as described earlier; however, RFC 1214 will be abandoned in favor of the CMIP profiles mentioned in the preceding subsection.

- *"SNMP over OSI"* (RFC 1418) and, more recently, *"SNMP over Foo"* (read "anything") RFCs have been developed by the IETF to glue SNMP over non-UDP/TCP transport technologies. This approach allows a single management protocol (SNMP) to be used in virtually any networking environment. The MIBs are different from those developed for CMIP, but for multiprotocol networks, and for those configurations where SNMP agents cannot be reached using UDP, these extensions are expected to serve the Internet community quite well.

- Although little standards activity is involved, CMIP network management systems vendors, cognizant of the market availability of communications equipment that supports SNMP agents, have developed proxy elements in their CMIP-based products to gather information and alarms from SNMP agents and integrate them into the management capabilities they offer.

Dual-Stack Approach: Hide It Under the API

It is possible, and in some circumstances, quite pragmatic, to offer "dual-stack" products, which provide for concurrent application use of more than one technology (OSI and TCP/IP). In fact, "dual stack" is increasingly becoming "multistack," in which supporting technologies are not limited to Internet and OSI protocols but include RPC-based communication environments and the like. When more than one technology is used, applications can be insulated from this fact by using a common, transparent *application programming interface* (API). For example, the X/Open management protocol API provides programmatic interfaces to both SNMP and CMIP and makes some attempt at limited transparency, at least for services that are common to both management protocols—for example, an mp_get_request "C" function call is provided that can initiate an SNMP Get message, a CMIS M-GET.request, or perhaps even a local RPC query.

Unfortunately, the way in which a MIB is defined often precludes application transparency—for example, a MIB that uses CMIS M-ACTION cannot be managed using SNMP unless it has been translated to an Internet SMI-style MIB and a gateway function is built to map between the two MIBs below the level of the API. This approach is currently undergoing specification and development by consortia such as X/Open and the OSI/NM Forum.

On the Horizon: Simple Management Protocol (SMP) ... or Is That "SNMPv2"?

Like most tools, network management isn't very useful if it's not deployed. As a practical consideration, the authors and advocates of SNMP carefully guarded the protocol and management framework against the sort of meddling that caused the OSI common management effort to become bogged down in definition so that it could be widely deployed as quickly as possible. The advent of the secure SNMP enhancements, however compatible with the present SNMP standards, clearly called for revisions to existing implementations. This posed a problem of no small measure to the SNMP community: there were other minor deficiencies that the Internet community would eventually wish to address, and the thought of two revisions and accompanying transitions was, to say the least, troublesome. Following a March 1992 IESG call for contributions on the future of network management for the Internet, a proposal for a *Simple Management Protocol* was presented to the IETF in August 1992. The proposal, currently a set of seven Internet drafts, provides a strategy for coexistence with the current SNMP, addresses some of the identified weaknesses of the SNMP framework, and claims to improve SNMP performance. SMP uses the secure SNMP enhancements but, as an outgrowth of implementation experience, it has exposed and consequently solved some operational problems encountered. (The result is that SMP implementations deviate from the secure SNMP RFCs, and the changes the SMP introduces to secure SNMP are now under consideration in the IETF; once approved, the secure SNMP RFCs will be made historical, and there will be only one transition for internetwork management; i.e., from SNMP version 1 to the eventual SMP/SNMPv2 RFCs.)

The more visible SMP enhancements to the SNMP include a change in the composition of the Trap message (it is now identical in structure to the other SNMP data units). A new message type, dubbed the "awesome" GetBulk operator, improves the way an SNMP manager retrieves large numbers of managed objects. A large set of error codes has been identified to improve exception reporting. Transport mappings of the SMP onto OSI, AppleTalk, and Novell/IPX as well as the recommended UDP are provided. There are also a considerable number of changes to the structure of management information, including some new data types (enumerated BITSTRING and 64-bit counters, an OSI network address data type). Finally, and notably, an *Inform Request* message has been introduced, with an accompanying MIB, to be used for manager-to-manager communications; the `InformRequest-PDU` can be used as an acknowledged event notification and to transfer information between network management stations. Network management stations can thus operate in a dual role—manager of resources as well as a resource or subordinate to other NMSs. A very fortuitous side effect of the timing of the introduction of SMP is that extensions for security, as well as improvements both desired and necessary, can be incorporated into existing implementations in a single version change, and with a well-defined coexistence plan.

·AHA· *During recent deliberations about SMP, an IETF member preferring anonymity suggested that SMP "is kinda like a datagram version of CMIP, but without scoping and filtering." Indeed, SMP seems to have addressed many of the much-ballyhooed shortcomings and deficiencies, and it will likely refuel the SNMP versus CMIP fire. If the existing base of SNMP agent implementations can be upgraded quickly, and the claims of improved and more robust functionality are warranted, SMP as SNMP version 2 will extend the market lead it currently holds over CMIP. Given that transport mappings are provided to allow SNMP to operate over OSI, AppleTalk, and Novell/IPX, and taking into consideration the practical difficulties of managing a multiprotocol Internet, the argument that there exists a single management framework to manage* all *aspects of a diverse Internet may be a bit premature and somewhat overstated, but it remains compelling.*

Where To from Here?

Most of the attention paid to network management is focused on the management protocols—SNMP and CMIP—and frameworks. However, if you ask a network administrator about products based on these protocols, you will find that although having standard protocols for network management is important, daily operations staff are still concerned that many aspects of network operations remain unattended, and network administrators will quickly tell you that reachability programs like ping, traceroute, netstat, and similar utilities continue to be important components of daily network operations.

The UNIX *ping* command uses the echo request datagram of the Internet control message protocol (ICMP; see Chapter 13) to evoke an echo reply datagram from a designated host on a TCP/IP network. It is by far the most commonly used fault-isolation tool. Ping provides a means of determining whether a host is "IP-reachable" and is useful for obtaining (a coarse measure of) round-trip times; many network management stations use ping in an automated fashion to monitor network connectivity.[9] An OSI version of echo/ping is described in RFC 1139[10] and will be incorporated as two new packet types (request and reply) in the second edition of ISO/IEC 8473, the *OSI Connectionless Network Layer Protocol* (CLNP; see Chapter 13), providing OSI network operations folks with a tool whose features are equivalent to the ICMP-based ping.

Traceroute is a program that determines the route an IP packet would follow from a source to a designated host by issuing a series of user datagram protocol (UDP) packets directed to a bogus destination port and with the internet protocol "time to live" set to intentionally small values, to elicit error messages from gateways that are attempting to forward the UDP packet. A gateway that receives the UDP packet but cannot forward it because its time to live has expired must return an ICMP error message "time exceeded." From these messages, the traceroute program constructs a list of gateways that comprise the route between the sender and the destination. The "probes" begin with a time to live of 1 and increase by 1 until an ICMP message "port unreachable" is returned, indicating that the host has been reached, but the specified port is an incorrect one. Traceroute is an effective diagnostic tool for network operations; a companion OSI traceroute program has been developed by members of the Network OSI Operations (NOOP) group within the IETF.

Network administrators are also quick to point out that there is too much effort directed at "managing everything that moves . . . ," and MIB mania has left vendors with little alternative but to continue to focus their efforts on the development of new MIBs. At the agent level, MIB mania increases the management burden; equally problematic is that additional MIB development in network management applications is performed at the expense of creating better diagnostic aids and applica-

---

9.It is interesting to note that in the manual pages of some UNIX OSs, automating ping is discouraged; for example, the manual page for ping that accompanies the MACH[Ten] UNIX® system from Tenon Intersystems says ping "should be used primarily for manual fault isolation. Because of the load it could impose on the network, it is unwise to use ping during normal operations or from automated scripts."
10.This RFC is soon to be obsoleted; the replacement RFC will eliminate one of the two elective ways to ping and align exactly with the ISO standard.

tions that "heal" networks without manual intervention. There is also altogether too much effort directed at simply presenting information to network administrators in the jazziest manner; graphic user interfaces aside, most of the network management systems today offer little to simplify the task of managing. SNMP and CMIP can provide solicited events or traps, but all too often, a human must still intervene to identify and solve the underlying real-world problem. Tools now exist to measure network utilization, but more and better tools are needed to assist in network analysis and capacity planning and provisioning.

If you are in network operations, before getting all worked up about which protocol you use, be forewarned: you won't be giving up your pager any time soon.

A closing commentary on SNMP versus CMIP: It should be apparent that entirely different perspectives and mind-sets drove and still drive SNMP and CMIP. CMIP is to a large extent telephony-driven and based on a telco view of the composition of packet and fast-packet networks. This view is inherited in part from telephony operations and managing voice connections. In this view, switching systems are comprised of two components: the switching or network elements and computers that are used to manage groups of network elements, called supervisory *systems.* Supervisory systems are themselves managed by yet another and typically more centralized tier of operations systems. In this environment, the OSI common management framework is imposed between the supervisory and operations systems (the management framework and protocol used between supervisory systems and network elements is often proprietary). The popular term for this is management of managers. In theory, the network elements—the equivalent of routers and bridges of the public networks—don't bear the burden of CMIP/CMIS (in practice, counting and reporting often take their toll). From this example, it can be seen that advocates of OSI common management may have based their framework on the assumption that the managed resources themselves do an awful lot of management. In SNMP, which was developed with a datagram internetworking paradigm in mind, there is an assumption that management is not the principal function of the managed resource—routers, bridges, and hosts all have better things to do with their CPU/links/memory than manage themselves, and so management overhead for these resources should be small (in fact, it can be argued that left to manage themselves, they would inevitably miss the bigger picture of the network and screw up). Is this insight enough to appreciate the differences? Hardly enough to fully appreciate them, but enough to start.*

Conclusion

This chapter has compared the "simple" network management framework for the Internet to OSI's "common" management approach. Both SNMP and CMIP base services on interactions between a manager and its agents and, by extension, interactions between managers. Both model management information in an object-oriented fashion and use abstract syntax notation one for object typing, identification, and encoding. The similarities end there. Through examples, the authors demonstrated that the management paradigms of SNMP and CMIP are vastly different and showed how SNMP attempts to place the burden of network management on the managing side, while CMIP distributes the burden between a manager and its agents. It was suggested that this difference is partly attributable to what the Internet (traditionally and decidedly a *data* community) and OSI (strongly influenced by the *telephony* community) interpret as managed network resources. Finally, the chapter called readers' attention to the fact that even after one decides which management framework is best for his or her networking environment, there are other, equally important management tools to consider and briefly described what TCP/IP and OSI offer as management instrumentation to complement network management protocols.

10 "CORE" APPLICATION SERVICE ELEMENTS

Open any toolbox—irrespective of whether it belongs to a plumber, a carpenter, an electrician, or an automobile mechanic—and you will find a common, or "core," set of tools: subtleties aside, a pair of pliers, a screwdriver, and a wrench are useful and necessary tools, whether the application is plumbing, carpentry, electrical work, or automotive repair. In general, distributed applications also rely on a set of core capabilities; i.e., service elements that provide:

- The ability to initiate and terminate communications across a network (in this case, the OSI networking environment) and to ascertain prior to attempting to transmit data that the called application has all the facilities and capabilities required to interpret and operate on the data about to be sent. In OSI, the *association control service element* (ACSE) provides these capabilities.
- The ability to structure conversations between distributed applications (for example, providing the ability for applications operating over a full-duplex connection to "take turns") and the ability for an application to recover from disruption of underlying communications services without loss of data (for example, providing the ability for peer applications to indicate "Yes, I heard what you said up to the point where we were disconnected, and I've committed it to memory [written it down]"). In OSI, the *reliable transfer service element* (RTSE) provides application access to the complement of dialogue control capabilities offered in OSI: activity and turn management, synchronization, and resynchronization.
- The ability to perform functions at remote computers (remote oper-

ations, remote procedure calls). In OSI, the *remote operations service element* (ROSE) enables an application operating at one computer to request or direct an application operating at a second computer (or multiple computers) to share part of the processing burden. Conceptually, a remote operation might say, "Do this for me and inform me of the result when you've completed the task," or "Do this for me while I go off and do something equally important. Don't interrupt me unless something goes wrong."

These application service elements are the nucleus of an OSI application tool kit. (Readers are left with the exercise of determining which application service element corresponds to the pair of pliers, the screwdriver, and the wrench.)

·AHA·   *Identifying only these application service elements as "core" elements is admittedly subjective. OSI tried to do so formally in the early stages of application layer standardization and failed because no consensus could be reached. In theory, the set of basic application service elements is open-ended; many others—notably, commitment, concurrency, and recovery (CCR); remote database access (RDA); and message handling—might eventually be included. Association control, reliable transfer, and remote operations, however, are likely to be included in nearly everyone's view; the treatment of "core" application service elements in this chapter, then, represents a minimalist's view.*

Association-Control Service Element

The association control service element is included in all application context specifications[1] and is used to form a connection (called an *association*) between application entities. In fact, the *facilitating* aspects of establishing an association—notably, the exchange of naming information (especially application entity titles) and negotiation of the facilities that the communicating applications will need in order to communicate—are ACSE's primary role.

It is useful to continue with the analogy of association control's playing the role of a facilitator in OSI application-to-application commu-

---

1.   Technically speaking, the ACSE service definition *strongly suggests* this, stating that "it is expected that the ACSE will be included in all application context specifications" (ISO/IEC 8649: 1988). The OSI *application layer structure* standard (ISO/IEC 9545: 1989), written a year later, states that the ACSE "is a necessary part of AEs." The reason for this ambiguity is revealed in a later discussion of *modes* of ACSE operation.

nications. In creating an application association, the association control service element truly facilitates a conference session; it identifies:

- Who will be talking (which application entities)
- What subjects will be discussed (which application service elements)
- The language(s) that will be spoken during the conference session (what abstract syntaxes will be exchanged)
- The "props" required for the conference session (what the presentation and session connections should look like)

Once it has established an association between two or more application entities, the association control service element fades into the background, reappearing only to assist in closing the conference session (and in extreme cases, to interrupt or cancel it).

The ACSE Service and Protocol

The formal mechanisms for establishing an application association are described in a service definition (ISO/IEC 8649: 1988) and a protocol specificaiton (ISO/IEC 8650: 1988). There are four association control services: *A-ASSOCIATE* provides "connection" establishment, *A-RELEASE* provides an orderly "disconnect," and the *A-P-ABORT* and *A-U-ABORT* services offer provider- and user-initiated disruptive "disconnects." Formally speaking, in establishing an association, 30 parameters are defined for the A-ASSOCIATE service. Simplified greatly, application entities use the parameters of the A-ASSOCIATE service primitives to identify:

- Themselves
- The application context required for this association
- The presentation context required for this association
- Presentation service requirements
- Session service requirements

(The complete set of A-ASSOCIATE service parameters is presented in Table 10.1.)

To invoke the service, an association control user (a.k.a. the requester) issues an *A-ASSOCIATE.request* primitive. The requester may be another standard application service element or a user element. In the *normal mode of ACSE operation*, association control uses some of the parameters passed in this request to construct the A-ASSOCIATE.request packet (in Figure 10.1, the AARQ APDU); most of the parameters conveyed in the AARQ APDU are identifiers. Application entities identify themselves through the exchange of their names—their *application entity*

TABLE 10.1   A-ASSOCIATE Service Parameters

Parameter Name	Request	Indication	Response	Confirm
Mode	User option	Mandatory(=)		
Application-context name*	Mandatory	Mandatory(=)	Mandatory	Mandatory(=)
Calling AP title*	User option	Conditional(=)		
Calling AE qualifier*	User option	Conditional(=)		
Calling AP invocation identifier*	User option	Conditional(=)		
Calling AE invocation identifier*	User option	Conditional(=)		
Called AP title*	User option	Conditional(=)		
Called AE qualifier*	User option	Conditional(=)		
Called AP invocation identifier*	User option	Conditional(=)		
Called AE invocation identifier*	User option	Conditional(=)		
Responding AP title*			User option	Conditional(=)
Responding AE qualifier*			User option	Conditional(=)
Responding AP invocation identifier*			User option	Conditional(=)
Responding AE invocation identifier*			User option	Conditional(=)
User information	User option	Conditional(=)	User option	Conditional(=)
Result			Mandatory	Mandatory(=)
Result source				Mandatory
Diagnostic*			User option	Conditional(=)
Calling presentation address	See ISO 8822	See ISO 8822		
Called presentation address	See ISO 8822	See ISO 8822		
Responding presentation address			See ISO 8822	See ISO 8822
Presentation context definition list*	See ISO 8822	See ISO 8822		
P-context definition result list*		See ISO 8822	See ISO 8822	See ISO 8822
Default presentation context name*	See ISO 8822	See ISO 8822		
Default presentation-context result*			See ISO 8822	See ISO 8822
Quality of service	See ISO 8822	See ISO 8822	See ISO 8822	See ISO 8822
Presentation requirements*	See ISO 8822	See ISO 8822	See ISO 8822	See ISO 8822
Session requirements	See ISO 8822	See ISO 8822	See ISO 8822	See ISO 8822
Initial synch point serial number	See ISO 8822	See ISO 8822	See ISO 8822	See ISO 8822
Initial assignment of tokens	See ISO 8822	See ISO 8822	See ISO 8822	See ISO 8822
Session connection identifier	See ISO 8822	See ISO 8822	See ISO 8822	See ISO 8822

*Not used in X.410-1984 mode of operation.
Note: In this table, the notation "(=)" is used to indicate that the value of the parameter (when it is present) in an indication or confirm primitive must be the same as the value of the same parameter in the corresponding request or response primitive (respectively). The notation "See ISO 8822" is used to indicate that the requirements for the parameter are specified in the service definition for the presentation layer (ISO/IEC 8822: 1988; see Chapter 11).

titles—which are defined as having two components: an *AP title* plus an *AE qualifier* (see "Names," in Chapter 5). Application entities further qualify this identification with *AE invocation identifiers,* which distinguish application entities at the process or run-time level.

```
AARQ-apdu ::=              [APPLICATION 0] SEQUENCE
{ protocol-version         [0] IMPLICIT BIT STRING
                               { version1 (0) }
                               DEFAULT version1,
application-context-name   [1] Application-context-name,

called-AP-Title            [2] AP-title
                               OPTIONAL,
called-AE-Qualifier        [3] AE-qualifier
                               OPTIONAL,
called-AP-Invocation-identifier  [4] AE-invocation-identifier
                               OPTIONAL,
called-AE-Invocation-identifier  [5] AE-invocation-identifier
                               OPTIONAL,
calling-AP-Title           [6] AP-title
                               OPTIONAL,
calling-AE-Qualifier       [7] AE-qualifier
                               OPTIONAL,
calling-AP-Invocation-identifier [8] AE-invocation-identifier
                               OPTIONAL,
calling-AE-Invocation-identifier [9] AE-invocation-identifier
                               OPTIONAL,
implementation-information [29] IMPLICIT Implementation-data
                               OPTIONAL,
user-information           [30] IMPLICIT Association-information
                               OPTIONAL
}
```

(Source: ISO/IEC 8650: 1988)

FIGURE 10.1   ASN.1 Definition of the AARQ APDU

Why are AE invocations and AP invocations identified? Suppose an association is formed between an application entity "Fred" on a computer "Flintstone" and an application entity "Barny" on a computer "Rubble." An integer is assigned to identify the run-time process (the application process, or AP) executing application entity Fred on Flintstone and similarly for application entity Barny on Rubble. Suppose the process containing Fred is unexpectedly terminated, but Barny continues. When Fred is resurrected as a new run-time process, new invocation identifiers are assigned so that in subsequent communications, Barny will know that it is communicating with a different process than before and hence can determine that the interruption in communication was due to a run-time process failure at Flintstone. Conversely, if communication between Fred and Barny is interrupted, and both processes continue, once communication is restored between Flintstone and Rubble, both application entities will be able to recognize that they are communicating with the same invocation of their peer.

A singularly important parameter passed in the A-ASSOCIATE.request primitive is the *application context name*. The application context name identifies the set of application service elements required by the distributed application initiating this communication.

The information passed to ACSE in the A-ASSOCIATE. request primitive is used to construct a corresponding A-ASSOCIATE request protocol data unit. The ASN.1 definition of this PDU is given in Figure 10.1.

An application that uses the directory system protocol (described in Chapter 7), for example, uses the association control service element and a set of defined remote operations. The application context `directorySystemAC` that describes this is "named" by the OJBECT IDENTIFIER `id-ac-directorySystemAC`; the ASN.1 definition for this application context is:

```
directorySystemAC
APPLICATION-CONTEXT
APPLICATION SERVICE ELEMENTS {aCSE}
BIND DSABind
UNBIND DSAUnbind
REMOTE OPERATIONS {rOSE}
OPERATIONS OF {
chainedReadASE, chainedSearchASE,
chainedModifyASE}
ABSTRACT SYNTAXES {
id-as-acse, id-as-directorySystemAS}
::= {id-ac-directorySystemAC}
```

Thus, when creating an association between two (directory) application processes that wish to use the directory system protocol, the requesting application entity assigns the information object `application-context-name` (one of the data in the AARQ APDU, shown in Figure 10.1) the value of the OBJECT IDENTIFIER `id-ac-directorySystemAC`. Using the application context name, the called application entity determines the set of application service elements that must be available to support this distributed application.

The requester also identifies the abstract syntaxes (modules of

ASN.1 "code"; note that this, too, is derived from the application context), the presentation services that are required, and the presentation address of the called association-control user (a.k.a. the "accepter") in the A-ASSOCIATE.request primitive. These parameters are not conveyed to a remote association control "peer" using the association control protocol. They are submitted in the A-ASSOCIATE.request by the requester so that the association control service provider can make appropriate requests when establishing a presentation connection to support the distributed application; they are used to compose a P-CONNECT.request primitive (see Chapter 11).

> AHA *Why should the association control service user have knowledge of both the presentation and session service requirements, and why must these be indicated in an A-ASSOCIATE.request? Part of the reason lies in the parallel development of the CCITT X.400 Message Handling System recommendations and the OSI upper layers. CCITT had developed message handling standards with the understanding that the T.62 protocol developed for teletex would be used at the session layer. What Marshall Rose describes in a "soapbox" as "largely hysterical reasons" were simply political: accommodating the perceived (exaggerated) "embedded base" of teletex terminals in X.400 was considered "strategic," and T.62 functions were effectively "grandfathered" into the OSI session layer, rendering moot any argument about correct placement of these functions elsewhere.*
>
> *What would have been a "correct" solution? There are at least two schools of thought on this subject: (1) the session and presentation functions are in the wrong layers and should have been identified as application layer functions in the first place, perhaps to the extreme of eliminating the session layer entirely; and (2) the functions of the upper layers are not inherently hierarchical, and a complete rethinking of the upper layers was appropriate. In fact, aspects of both schools of thought exist: the pass-through of presentation and session requirements is a concession to the first school of thought (the application layer ultimately controls what goes on in the session layer, and where the protocol operates is a formality) and the definition of application service elements in the OSI Application Layer Structure standard is a concession to the second school of thought (you have building blocks in the application layer).*

Association control and presentation connection processing are "piggybacked": the association control APDUs for A-ASSOCIATE, A-RELEASE, and A-U-ABORT are conveyed as user data in corresponding presentation service primitives (P-CONNECT, P-RELEASE, and P-U-ABORT, respectively). The sequence of primitives and application proto-

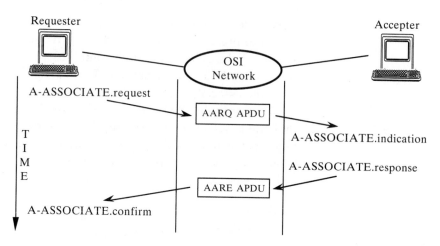

FIGURE 10.2   Association Establishment

col exchanged between a requester and an accepter during association establishment is depicted in Figure 10.2.

A-ASSOCIATE is a confirmed service; thus, in the normal sequence of events, the A-ASSOCIATE.request is processed by the requester, which composes an AARQ APDU and submits it to the presentation layer (via the P-CONNECT.request primitive). The AARQ APDU is delivered (as user data of the P-CONNECT.indication primitive), and the information conveyed in the APDU is passed to the accepter via the A-ASSOCIATE.indication. The accepter may accept or reject the association (admittedly, having an accepter "reject" something seems counterintuitive, but that's what the standard says); this result, together with a reason code, is indicated in the *result* and *diagnostic* parameters[2] of the A-ASSOCIATE.response. The result and diagnostic, together with the identifiers of the responding application entity, are used to compose the A-ASSOCIATE response packet (in Figure 10.2, the AARE APDU). The response packet is delivered to the requester (via the P-CONNECT.confirm primitive). The ASN.1 definition of the AARE APDU is shown in Figure 10.3.

---

2.   According to the standard, the reason for rejection may be "permanent" or "transient," but what constitutes permanent or transient is not discussed. The choice of diagnostic codes defined in the ACSE protocol includes "application context name not supported" and a set of codes indicating "title/invocation/qualifier not recognized." The OSI folks did try to standardize the use of these and additional reason codes but failed. Transient is typically used for no-resource conditions, and permanent is used for cases in which the named AP/AE doesn't exist or requested session user requirements, for example, aren't supported.

```
AARE-apdu ::=                  [APPLICATION 1] IMPLICIT SEQUENCE
{ protocol-version                 [0] IMPLICIT BIT STRING
                                           { version1 (0) }
                                           DEFAULT version1,
application-context-name           [1] Application-context-name,

result                             [2]    Associate-result,

result-source-diagnostic           [3]    Associate-source-diagnostic,

responding-AP-Title                [4]    AP-title
                                          OPTIONAL,
responding-AE-Qualifier            [5]    AE-qualifier
                                          OPTIONAL,
responding-AP-Invocation-identifier    [6]    AP-invocation-identifier
                                          OPTIONAL,
responding-AE-Invocation-identifier    [7]    AE-invocation-identifier
                                          OPTIONAL,
implementation-information         [29]   IMPLICIT Implementation-data
                                          OPTIONAL,
user-information                   [30]   IMPLICIT Association-information
                                          OPTIONAL
}
```

(Source: ISO/IEC 8650: 1988)

FIGURE 10.3   Abstract Syntax of AARE-apdu ASN.1 Definition of the AARE APDU

No "data packets" are defined for the association control service element. Once an association is established, no association control protocol is exchanged until the association is released or aborted; only the protocol of other application service elements, including the user element, is exchanged by the application processes.

The *A-RELEASE* service (Figure 10.4) is used to terminate an association in an orderly manner; the communicating application entities typically see that all information exchanges have been completed prior to releasing the association. This is a confirmed service. It uses the A-RELEASE request and A-RELEASE response packets (in Figure 10.4, the RLRQ and RLRE APDUs, respectively), and the service primitive and protocol action is similar to that of the A-ASSOCIATE service.

The *A-U-ABORT* service (Figure 10.5) is disruptive; it is invoked when one association control user chooses to terminate an association abruptly. No attempt is made to assure that all information exchanges have been completed. *A-P-ABORT* occurs when the association control service provider releases, either due to errors internal to the association control service provider or when the association control provider determines that services below the application layer have failed in some man-

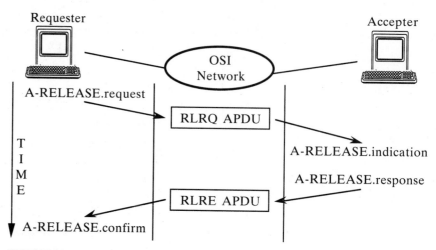

FIGURE 10.4   Association Release

ner. Both ABORT services use the A-ABORT packet (in Figure 10.5, the ABRT APDU) when protocol is exchanged; A-P-ABORT does not involve protocol exchange when occurring as the result of communication failure.

Modes

ISO/IEC 8649 defines two "modes" of ACSE operation: in the *normal mode,* implementations use the association control service and protocol as defined in ISO/IEC 8649 and 8650; in the *X.410-1984 mode,* however, implementations are required to pretend that the association control protocol doesn't exist for the sake of communicating with CCITT X.410-1984 implementations. In such circumstances, implementations pass the presentation and session service requirements through to the presentation

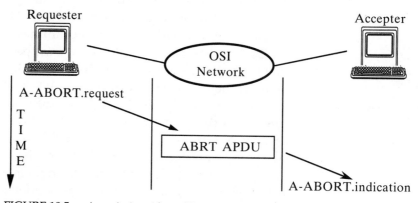

FIGURE 10.5   Association Abort (User-initiated)

layer and use only the presentation kernel (see Chapter 11). No association control protocol is exchanged; the mode of operation is conveyed during the presentation connection establishment (see Chapter 11).

Only a handful of the parameters of the A-ASSOCIATE service are used in the case of X.410-1984 mode (those that are not marked with "*" in Table 10.1). The conformance statement for the association control protocol says that either or both modes must be implemented.

> ┌─────────┐
> │ ·AHA· │ *The X.410-1984 mode of operation is named after the 1984*
> └─────────┘ *version of the CCITT X.400 Message Handling System re-*
> *commendations. The history behind the existence of two modes of ACSE opera-*
> *tion is simple. In 1983, the CCITT was in the process of completing its recom-*
> *mendations for message handling services; at the time, however, the disposition*
> *of function between the application and presentation layers of the message han-*
> *dling architecture was still a subject of great debate in the ISO OSI community.*
> *Since leap years were historically "publish or perish" times for CCITT—the*
> *member organizations had to agree upon recommendations during a plenary*
> *session or wait another four years for the next plenary—it was determined that*
> *the best interests of the CCITT community would not be served by waiting for*
> *the OSI upper layer organization to be completed. Applying the changes*
> *throughout the MHS architecture could be done in 1988, with only the small*
> *issue of "backward compatibility" to consider—and how hard could that be?*

Reliable Transfer Service Element

There are very few occasions when you have the luxury of reading a book uninterrupted, or "cover to cover." More often than not, you find time to read several pages, perhaps a chapter or two, but inevitably, your reading time will be interrupted, or you'll fall asleep. You might dog-ear the last page read or use a bookmark to locate the point where you should continue when you once again find time to read. You do so because you would certainly prefer to continue reading from the page where you left off rather than begin again from page 1. In such situations, you and the book have formed an association, and your use of a bookmark, for example, provides a *synchronization* point (or "checkpoint"). Similarly, if you engage in a telephone conversation with someone and your call is unexpectedly disconnected, you redial and typically continue, or *recover*, the conversation from the point at which you were interrupted. Again, you and the party you call are engaged in a (voice) application, and your ability to remember the last subject under discussion serves as a synchronization point in the conversation in the event that the underlying telephone connection fails. In both examples, large amounts of information are exchanged between communicating entities. And although the two forms of dialogue illustrated differ—the first is monologue, the latter two-way alternate—there is a strong incentive in both cases to avoid repetition.

End users of applications that exchange large amounts of data—multimedia message handling, image transfer/retrieval, office or electronic document interchange, plain old bulk file transfer—share this incentive; they don't want to "start from scratch" if network connections fail. It wastes time and resources and is potentially costly. The *reliable transfer service element* (RTSE) (ISO/IEC 9066-1: 1989; ISO/IEC 9066-2: 1989) provides services that enable application entities to (1) synchronize and later recover from (temporary) communications failures between end systems with a minimum amount of retransmission, and (2) conduct both monologue and two-way alternate conversations without having to deal directly with the mechanics of providing such services.

The reliable transfer service element relieves the user from having to worry about the details of association establishment and release. This service does not provide low-level control of associations the way that association control does; rather, it initiates and terminates an association for a reliable transfer service user with the primary purpose of transfer ring data. The reliable transfer service effectively bundles several layer of service features into a single service. Using the RTSE primitives, a re¹ able transfer service user can:

- Coordinate information exchange within an association (turn management)
- Confirm that a remote reliable transfer service user has received and secured data before sending more data (synchronization)
- Recover from the temporary loss of a presentation connection
- Ensure that an association is closed without loss of any information that might have been in transit when the close was requested (the popular term for this mechanism is *graceful* close)

The foregoing can be accomplished with three simple service requests: RT-OPEN, RT-TRANSFER, and RT-CLOSE.

As an example, consider a medical-imaging service, one that enables physicians to retrieve X rays or magnetic resonance images (MRIs) from a central database across a network providing application-to-application throughput of 1 Mbps. MRIs are very large, measurable in megabytes of data. In a worst-case scenario—all but the last 1,000-byte fragment of the image is transferred, and the network connection fails — retransmission of a 10-megabyte (80-megabits) MRI "from scratch" could cause nearly 80 additional seconds of delay in the transfer. Now, a physician's time is precious, and such delays might not be tolerated. The reliable transfer service could be used by this medical-imaging service element to assure that the precise image is delivered to the physician without excessive retransmission. In this example, retransmission could begin from the point of failure (the last 1,000 bytes), and the delay would be greatly reduced.

The reliable transfer process, from request to completion of transfer, is composed of the functions discussed in the following sections.

Association Establishment

A physician makes a request for an MRI from a remote image database. The user element of the remote image database application invokes the RT-OPEN service, which uses the Association-Control Service Element to form an association between the computer hosting the database and the physician's local computer (see Figure 10.6). Note that in this example, the information object `.application-context-name` of the AARQ APDU would be assigned the OID value for the association context name of the mythical MRI application "davesExcellentMRIs." Since the origin and location of this name information are not obvious, let's consider the example a bit further. Suppose "Dave's Excellent Software" is a U.S.-based company, and suppose further that the firm decides to obtain a globally unique identifier from the U.S. registration authority (see Chapter 5). The organization identifier is given the alphanumeric representation of "davesExcellent" and assigned a numeric value of "22345." When Dave's Excellent Software develops the MRI application, it uses the branch of the object identification tree `iso (1) member-body (2) US (840) davesExcellent (22345)` to uniquely identify application entities, abstract syntaxes, application context names, etc., for its applications. Thus, depending on how the company decided to write ASN.1 definitions for its applications, the application context name of the application davesExcellentMRIs might look like this:

```
davesExcellent-MRIs-ac OBJECT IDENTIFIER
::= { iso (1) member-body (2) US (840) davesExcellent (22345)
     MRIs (01) applicationContext (03) }
```

This application context name identifies the user element[3] and, by impli-

---

3.   The term *user element* refers to the consumer of ASE services. (ISO/IEC 7498-1: 1993).

cation, the set of application service elements that the user element requires[4] (in this case, association control service element and RTSE).

TABLE 10.2   RT-OPEN Service Parameters

Parameter Name	Request	Indication	Response	Confirm
Dialogue mode	Mandatory	Mandatory(=)		
Initial turn	Mandatory	Mandatory(=)		
Application protocol	User option	Conditional(=)		
User data	User option	Conditional(=)	User option	Conditional(=)
Mode	A	A		
Application context name	A	A	A	A
Calling AP title	A	A		
Calling AE qualifier	A	A		
Calling AP invocation identifier	A	A		
Calling AE invocation identifier	A	A		
Called AP title	A	A		
Called AE qualifier	A	A		
Called AP invocation identifier	A	A		
Called AE invocation identifier	A	A		
Responding AP title			A	A
Responding AE qualifier			A	A
Responding AP invocation identifier			A	A
Responding AE invocation identifier			A	A
Result			A	A
Result source				A
Diagnostic			A	A
Calling presentation address	P	P		
Called presentation address	P	P		
Responding presentation address			P	P
Presentation context definition list	P	P		
P-context definition result list			P	P
Default presentation context name	P	P		
Default presentation context result			P	P

Note: In this table, the notation "A" is used to identify parameters that appear in the RT-OPEN primitive so that their values can be "passed through" RTSE to corresponding ACSE primitives, and the notation "P" is used to identify parameters that are similarly "passed through" to the presentation service.

4.   Note that the term *application protocol data unit* is used generically here. Depending on how the application is written, the APDU may be an ASN.1 SEQUENCE consisting of

The abstract syntaxes that the presentation layer would have to manage would include ACSE, RTSE, and the APDUs defined for the MRI transfer. Thus, the abstract syntax component of the *presentation context definition list* parameter of the A-ASSOCIATE.request would contain the following object identifier value:

```
davesExcellentMRIs-as OBJECT IDENTIFIER
::= { iso (1) member-body (2) US (890) davesExcellent
    (22345) MRIs (01) abstract syntax (02) }
```

It would also contain the object identifier values for the ACSE and RTSE abstract syntaxes.

The protocol necessary to establish an association via the reliable transfer service—the RT-OPEN request and accept packets (in Figure 10.6, the *RTORQ* and *RTOAC APDUs*, respectively)—is conveyed as user data in the A-ASSOCIATE service primitives and "piggybacked" onto the *AARQ* and *AARE APDUs*. In effect, the reliable transfer protocol "header" merely adds to the list of parameters negotiated during association control; it does not create an additional association. The state machine of the RTSE protocol is wedded to that of the association control protocol during association setup and release. The additional parameters include *checkpoint size*, the number of kilobytes of data that may be sent between synchronization points, and *window size*, an upper bound on the amount of data that can be sent. Checkpoint size is an indication of how frequently you want to insert synchronization points in the data stream; window size indicates how many units of checkpoint size you'll send before you will wait to hear that the receiver has secured the data you have transmitted—in effect, how far you are willing to press your luck.

Once an association is established, the image is transferred using the RT-TRANSFER service.

RT-TRANSFER: Activity Management, Checkpointing, and Synchronization

A reliable transfer service user can submit arbitrarily large amounts of data—as a single, encoded user element APDU value—in a single RT-TRANSFER.request. In our medical image transfer example, an entire image of perhaps several megabytes of data might constitute a single user element APDU. The RT-TRANSFER service accepts such arbitrarily large quantities of user data and treats each submission as a separate transfer *activity*. Within the context of this transfer activity, a sending

---

an operator (e.g., FETCH-IMAGE), followed by the arguments patient name (OCTET-STRING) and patient number (INTEGER). An associated medical image (GRAPHICS STRING or BITSTRING) might be retrieved by using the patient information to identify which image "instance" is requested.

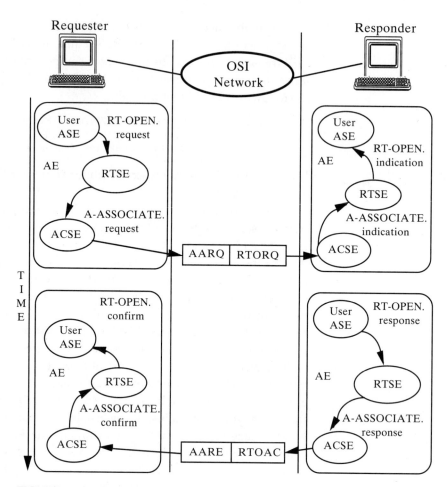

FIGURE 10.6   Reliable Transfer Open

RTSE fragments the medical image into octet strings of length {check-point size × 1,024} and then invokes the following presentation services (see Chapter 11):

- P-ACTIVITY-START.request to signal the beginning of a user element APDU (an activity) to the receiver
- P-DATA.request to transmit the first fragment as a RELIABLE TRANSFER APDU (in Figure 10.7, the initial RTTR APDU)

The sending RTSE then alternately sends:

- A P-MINOR-SYNCHRONIZE.request to insert a checkpoint into the information stream

- A P-DATA.request to transmit the next (final) fragment as a RE-
  LIABLE TRANSFER APDU (in Figure 10.7, the subsequent RTTR
  APDUs)

until all the user data (the entire medical image) have been transferred.
Finally, the sending RTSE uses the P-ACTIVITY-END.request primitive
to mark the end of the activity when the last fragment of the medical
image has been sent.

On the receive side, the RTTR APDUs arrive as user data transferred across a presentation connection. The receiving reliable transfer
service element secures data extracted from each RTTR PDU received
and confirms this by responding to the P-MINOR-SYNCHRONIZE.indi-
cations. The receiving RTSE user (the user element of the physician's
medical-imaging application process) is informed when transfer of the

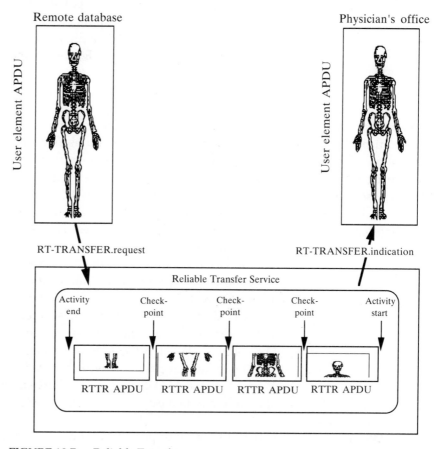

FIGURE 10.7   Reliable Transfer

entire image is complete (the end of this transfer activity) via the RT-TRANSFER.indication primitive. If the transfer activity is completed within a *transfer time* indicated by the sender (a "catastrophic failure" time-out value), the sending RTSE user (the remote image database application) is informed that the user data have been secured by the receiving RTSE via the RT-TRANSFER.confirmation primitive. If the transfer is not completed within the specified transfer time, the sending RTSE gives up, invokes the presentation activity discard service (see Chapter 11) to clean up the mess, and aborts the association.

Turn (Token) Management

The medical image transfer example considers only the case in which reliable transfer is a one-way operation (from remote database to physician). Other applications might want to organize information exchange into dialogues (two-way alternate). In such communications, elements familiar to telephone conversations—politely waiting one's turn to speak, asking for a turn to speak, interrupting, resuming after an interruption—are implemented using RT-TRANSFER services in conjunction with RT-TURN-PLEASE and RT-TURN-GIVE services; these services make use of the turn-management presentation (and session) services discussed in Chapter 11.

Reliability Mechanisms: Exception Reporting/Transfer Retry, Association Recovery/Transfer Resumption

The reliable transfer service attempts to mask several types of error conditions from reliable transfer service users during a transfer activity. For example, the reliable transfer service performs recovery of a single activity without user intervention: if a receiving RTSE encounters an error that is procedural or local to the receiving RTSE and is recoverable, it will discard the present activity and retry the transfer using exception and activity-management presentation services. The reliable transfer service also recovers from the temporary loss of an association between two reliable transfer service users by resurrecting the association (here's where invocation identifiers are handy) and resuming an activity interrupted by the communications failure from the last checkpoint. Of course, when the error detected by a receiving RTSE is "severe," or when an association cannot be resurrected within a user-specified *recovery time*, the service will be aborted. The RT-ABORT service is also available to allow abrupt termination of an association between two reliable transfer service users (in Figure 10.8, the ABORT packet for reliable transfer, the RTAB APDU, is piggybacked onto the association control ABORT APDU, ABRT).

RT-CLOSE: Association Release

The RT-CLOSE service provides a "graceful" termination of an association. Any outstanding RT-TRANSFER.request must be confirmed (in

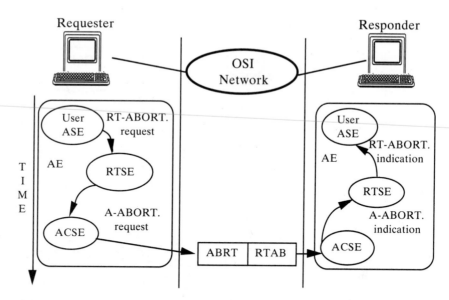

FIGURE 10.8   RT-ABORT (User-initiated)

both directions) before the association can be closed; i.e., any activities in the process of being transferred must be completed. Figure 10.9 illustrates how the RT-CLOSE service maps onto the A-RELEASE service. Note that no explicit RTSE protocol is used in the close process (recall that the RLRQ APDU is part of the association control protocol); user data from the user element are passed as user data in the A-RELEASE primitives and protocol. Although this might appear to be a curious departure from the user-initiated RT-ABORT, in which an explicit RTAB APDU may be used, it's really OK; the RTAB APDU allows user elements to convey an APDU that might provide a more detailed explanation of the reason for abort than the Abort-reason "user-error" specified in ISO/IEC 9066-2.

> ⟦AHA⟧ *One might expect that OSI file transfer, access, and management would make excellent use of the reliable transfer service. Unfortunately, FTAM was developed before the reliable transfer service, and FTAM manages presentation services directly. There are some who consider this "a good thing," since FTAM makes extensive use of presentation services beyond those used by the RTSE.*

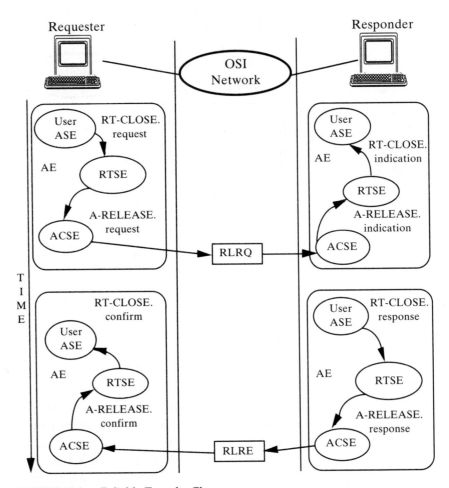

FIGURE 10.9   Reliable Transfer Close

Remote Operations Service Element

As the name implies, the remote operations service element (ROSE) allows an application process on one computer to invoke an application process on a different (remote) computer to perform some set of operations. The concept is a powerful one and is used in applications where client/server, manager/subordinate (agent), or multipeer, shared processing relationships are necessary.

Remote operations, often called *remote procedure calls*, appear in many distributed-processing applications today. The Network File System (NFS; Sandberg 1988) applies a client/server remote operation paradigm in providing a networked or distributed UNIX file system. Client workstations (often diskless) invoke the services of a "disk-full" computer, called a file server, to read information from, and write information to, long-term storage. Network management applications based on OSI common management use remote operations to invoke the services of subordinate or agent applications that run on manageable network resources to isolate and correct faults, configure those resources, and collect management information through some set of management operations. And both the OSI Message Handling System and the OSI Directory (see Chapters 7 and 8) make extensive use of remote operations in the somewhat similar user agent/transfer agent relationships.

Some distributed operating system applications—e.g., DUNE (Alberi and Pucci 1987), LOCUS (Walker et al. 1983)—apply the client/server paradigm to a group of networked computers, whereas other distributed operating systems behave as if they were a single "monster" multiprocessor, multitasking (super)computer, with each computer possessing the ability to pass off a task or procedure to another, less busy computer and each having "equal access" to the others' resources (CPU, disk, etc.).

Just as the reliable transfer service element simplifies the process of reliable data transfer between computer systems, the remote operations service element simplifies the process of distributing operations across multiple computer systems. Like RTSE, ROSE relieves user elements from having to worry about the details of association establishment and release (it either invokes association control itself or allows the reliable transfer service element to do so) and bundles several layers of service features into a single service. Within the context of an association, ROSE allows an application process on a local computer to invoke an application process on a remote computer and request that it perform an operation. The operations themselves are treated as ASE services and are defined as abstract syntaxes in standard application service elements like the MHS and Directory ASEs or in user-programmed application service elements. (Remote operations in OSI thus operate on abstract rather than concrete data types.) OSI collectively labels the set of ASE services available to a user element of an application entity an *operations interface* (Figure 10.10).

In the figure, each "user ASE" represents some remote operation(s) the user element may invoke. The user element may use the ACSE directly to establish associations between itself and other user elements. The user element may optionally use the reliable transfer service element to handle association control and reliable transfer if information transfer between user elements would benefit from this additional facility.

Synchronous and Asynchronous Operations

In some distributed applications, the invoking user element may wish to wait for the operation to be completed (remote operations performed in this "lockstep" fashion are classified as *synchronous operations*), or the user element may invoke a remote operation and continue processing while the operation is performed (*asynchronous operation*). In both cases, the performer can be directed to return indications of whether or not the requested operation was successful (a result and/or an error). The matrix of synchronous/asynchronous modes and reply possibilities is illustrated in Table 10.3; each combination is known as an *operation class*.

TABLE 10.3   ROSE: Operation Classes

Operation Class	Synchronous	Asynchronous	Report Result	Report Error
1	✓		✓	✓
2		✓	✓	✓
3		✓		✓
4		✓	✓	
5		✓		

Linked Operations   In some distributed applications, the performer of a remote operation may find it necessary to invoke a related operation from the user element that originated the remote operations relationship (the "parent" of the remote operation). Remote operations *linked* to the parent remote operations are called "child" operations. Figure 10.11 illustrates this concept.

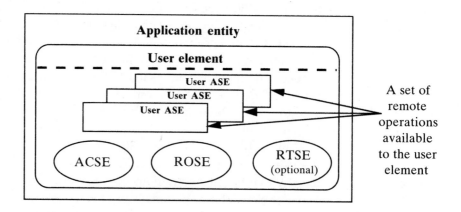

FIGURE 10.10   Operations Interface

FIGURE 10.11   Linked Operations

Distributed applications correlate linked operations using the *invoke ID*. A concrete example: remote operations invoke IDs are used to correlate OSI common management information service requests and responses—in other words, management applications assign unique numbers to their requests and use these numbers to decipher later responses from managed systems. For example, when a management application issues an M-GET.request with invoke ID "42," the manager sends an ROIV-M-GET request packet. The agent on the managed system responds with an RORS-M-GET response PDU, also containing the invoke ID "42" (these common management information services call the RO-INVOKE and RO-RESULT ROSE services, which are described later in this chapter). If multiple replies are needed, the agent responds with several ROIV linked-reply packets (each containing the linked ID "42"), concluded by the final RORS-M-GET response packet.

Relationship of ROSE to Other "Core" Application Service Elements

ROSE may use ACSE directly to establish associations. In such configurations, the ROSE user invokes association control to establish and release associations, as illustrated in Figures 10.2 and 10.4, respectively, and uses the presentation layer to transfer data. ROSE users may wish to take advantage of the services of RTSE; in this case, the ROSE user establishes and releases associations by invoking the services of RTSE (RT-OPEN and RT-CLOSE, illustrated in Figures 10.6 and 10.9, respectively) and uses the RT-TRANSFER service (Figure 10.7) to transfer data (see Figure 10.12).

ROSE Services and Protocol

The ROSE services provide the basic elements for interactive (inquiry/ response) communications:

- *RO-INVOKE* allows an AE to request that another AE perform an

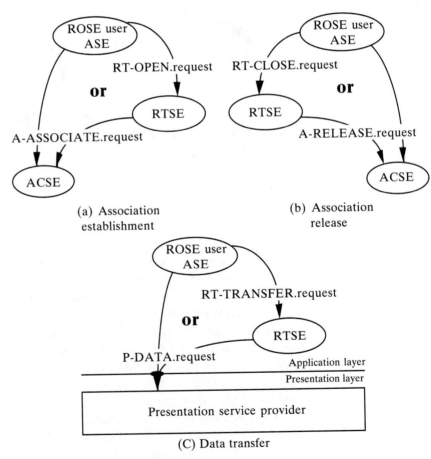

FIGURE 10.12   ROSE Use of "Core" Application Service Elements

operation; the requesting AE is called the *invoker*, and the AE responsible for the grunt work is called the *performer*.

- *RO-RESULT* and *RO-ERROR* allow performers to indicate whether the operation succeeded or failed.
- *RO-REJECT-U* and *RO-REJECT-P* are exception services initiated by the performing AE or ROSE, respectively.

All ROSE services are described in the standards as "unconfirmed" (except RO-REJECT-P, which is provider-initiated). (Table 10.4 illustrates the primitives and parameters of the ROSE.) A more accurate description is that RO-RESULT, RO-ERROR, and RO-REJECT are "confirmations" for operations that are RO-INVOKEd. A typical sequence of ROSE events, for example, is "Send an RO-INVOKE and get back an RO-RESULT or RO-ERROR." RO-RESULT means complete and successful, whereas RO-ERROR means something went wrong—either partial or total failure occurred (for example, the operation may have been performed with a diagnostic returned).

TABLE 10.4   ROSE Primitives

RO SERVICE	Parameter Value	Request	Indication
RO-INVOKE	Operation value	Mandatory	Mandatory(=)
	Operation class	User option	
	Argument	User option	Conditional(=)
	Invoke ID	Mandatory	Mandatory(=)
	Linked ID	User option	Conditional(=)
	Priority	User option	
RO-RESULT	Operation value	User option	Conditional(=)
	Result	User option	Conditional(=)
	Invoke ID	Mandatory	Mandatory(=)
	Priority	User option	
RO-ERROR	Error value	Mandatory	Mandatory(=)
	Error parameter	User option	Conditional(=)
	Invoke ID	Mandatory	Mandatory(=)
	Priority	User option	
RO-REJECT-U	Reject reason	Mandatory	Mandatory(=)
	Invoke ID	Mandatory	Mandatory(=)
	Priority	User option	
RO-REJECT-P	Invoke ID	ROSE provider option	
	Returned parameters	ROSE provider option	
	Reject reason	ROSE provider option	

The ROSE user APDUs are the basis for *the actual work to be done.* The ROSE protocol is merely a "wrapper," present primarily to convey parameters of the service. Specifically, the remote operations invoke packet (ROIV APDU) is used to convey the *invocation identifier, linked invocation identifier,* and *operation value* from the RO-INVOKE.request. The ASN.1 data type identified in the ARGUMENT clause of the remote operation may be included in the ROIV APDU as well. Other parameters (the *operation class* and the relative *priority* of this operation with respect to other invoked operations) are not carried in protocol but affect handling by the local ROSE provider.

The remote operations *result* (RORS) and remote operations error (ROER) packets convey the invocation identifier as a means of correlating the ASN.1 data type identified in the RESULT and ERROR clauses of an OPERATION to a given invocation of that remote operation.

The remote operations reject (RORJ) packet again conveys the invocation identifier as a means of correlating a user or provider rejection of an operation. A reason for rejecting the operation is encoded as an ASN.1 data type called *problem* (for which ISO/IEC 9072-2 provides a list of standard values).

RO-Notation

ROSE provides a set of ASN.1-defined macros—BIND, OPERATION, UNBIND—to facilitate association establishment, RO invocation, and association release. Two additional macros—APPLICATION-CONTEXT and APPLICATION-SERVICE-ELEMENT—assist programmers in defining the application context for a distributed application and in defining ROSE user elements, respectively.

Let's assume that the object identifier for the whimsical user element "dish drying" from Figure 10.11 is as follows:

```
dishDryingService OBJECT IDENTIFIER
::= { iso bogus (999) example (999) dishDrying (99) }
```

The APPLICATION-CONTEXT macro might then look like this:

```
dishDryingContext                      APPLICATION-CONTEXT
    APPLICATION SERVICE ELEMENTS       { aCSE }
    BIND                               dishDryerEnslave
    UNBIND                             dishDryerFreeToCruise
    REMOTE OPERATIONS                  { rOSE }
    INITIATOR CONSUMER OF              { dishDryingASE }
    ABSTRACT SYNTAXES                  { aCSE-abstract-syntax,
                                         dryTheDishes-abstract-
                                         syntax }
        ::= { iso bogus (999) example (999) dishDrying (99)
            application-context (2) }
```

```
-- the OID value for the abstract syntax --
dryTheDishes-abstract-syntax OBJECT IDENTIFIER
    ::= { iso bogus (999) example (999) dishDryer (99)
           abstract-syntax (1) }
```

In this example, the application context identifies association control, the BIND and UNBIND macros, the ROSE (as the remote operations provider), and the ROSE user application service element "dish-Drying ASE" (the definitions of the actual remote operations to be performed by the initiator and responder). In this example, the INITIATOR CONSUMER OF clause indicates that the ROSE user that establishes the association may invoke "dishDryingASE". The clauses RESPONDER CONSUMER OF and OPERATIONS OF (not used in this example) could be used to indicate ROSE user application service elements that only the responder, or both the initiator and the responder (respectively) may invoke.

The object identifier value for the application context is passed as a parameter in association establishment (as the application context name parameter of the A-ASSOCIATE.request primitive). Similarly, the abstract syntaxes of all the application service elements—representing the set of APDUs required for this application—are passed as a parameter in association establishment (the OIDs of aCSE-abstract-syntax and dryTheDishes-abstract-syntax are enumerated in the presentation context definition list parameter of the A-ASSOCIATE.request primitive).

The "dishDryingASE" is defined using the APPLICATION-SER-VICE-ELEMENT macro:

```
dishDryingASE             APPLICATION-SERVICE-ELEMENT
    CONSUMER INVOKES        { dryTheDish }
    ::= { iso bogus (999) example (999) dishDrying (99)
           application-service-element (3) }
```

Here, the clause CONSUMER INVOKES identifies the parent remote operation "dryTheDish"; this is the only remote operation that Mom can ask the SUPPLIER (son Billy) to perform. If there were parent operations that son Billy could invoke, they would be identified using the SUPPLIER INVOKES clause, and if there were parent operations that both the CONSUMER and the SUPPLIER could invoke, they would be specified using the OPERATIONS clause.

The BIND and UNBIND macros for this example might look like this:

```
dishDryerEnslave
    BIND
            ARGUMENT ::= bindArgument
            RESULT ::= bindResult
            BIND-ERROR ::= bindError
```

```
dishDryerFreeToCruise
    UNBIND
            ARGUMENT ::= unbindArgument
            RESULT ::= unbindResult
            UNBIND-ERROR ::= unbindError
```

In this example, both the BIND and UNBIND macros are defined as synchronous operations: Mom asks son Billy to dry the dishes, expecting compliance or an argument, and also expecting an indication that the task is completed before she will allow Billy to "cruise." There are, of course, error situations (the actual definition of the parameters for these remote operation macros is left to the readers' imagination).

The BIND macro hides the details of establishing an association from the ROSE user, irrespective of whether the association control service element is used directly (Figure 10.2) or the association is established via the reliable transfer service (Figure 10.6). All the information necessary to establish an association is identified in the APPLICATION-CONTEXT and APPLICATION-SERVICE-ELEMENT macros noted earlier. The UNBIND macro is used to release the association (once the dishes are dried).

Linked Operations

One expects to find several linked operations associated with the parent operation "dryTheDishes" identified in the CONSUMER INVOKES statement of the application service element definition:

```
dryTheDishes ::= OPERATION
    BIND
        ARGUMENT ::=
        RESULT ::=
        ERROR ::=
        LINKED ::= { askForTowel, askForDish, howManyLeft }
        ::= 0

askForTowel   AskForTowel   ::= 1
askForDish    AskForDish    ::= 2
howManyLeft   HowManyLeft   ::= 3
```

The linked operations identify work that the CONSUMER (Mom) may be called upon to do by the SUPPLIER (Billy). Note that each parent OPERATION may have local or globally unique values; i.e., the data type of operations may be INTEGER (as illustrated) or OBJECT IDENTIFIER. The linked operations are identified within the context of the parent operation.

The ASN.1 specification of each OPERATION formally defines the work a performer must attempt to complete, in a machine-independent fashion. There are two ways that ROSE might be used to invoke these operations:

- The consumer can pass the identification of a remote operation (and associated results/errors) to a supplier, which effectively points the supplier to a concrete set of procedures to execute. The input to these concrete procedures and anticipated replies (results/errors) accompany this identification (the ARGUMENT, RESULT, and ERROR clauses).
- The consumer can pass the identification of a remote operation and accompany this with an ASN.1-encoded copy of the machine-specific software that is to be executed. For example, one computer in a UNIX-based distributed operating system might use ROSE to schlepp a user C program fragment off to a less busy peer as the ARGUMENT data type in the OPERATION.

Putting It All Together

Relating all the pieces in a normal sequence of events:

1. A user element invokes a remote operation via the BIND macro.
2. If reliable transfer service is identified in the APPLICATION-CONTEXT macro, ROSE establishes an association between an initiator and a responder using the RT-OPEN service. If reliable transfer service is not identified in the APPLICATION-CONTEXT macro, ROSE establishes the association using the A-ASSOCIATE service. (Note that a BIND could be disrupted by any underlying ABORT service.)
3. If the BIND is successful, the initiating or responding user element may invoke remote operations as described in the {CONSUMER INVOKES, SUPPLIER INVOKES, OPERATIONS} clauses of the APPLICATION-SERVICE-ELEMENT macro using the OPERATION macro. ROSE processes the OPERATION macro using the RO-INVOKE, RO-RESULT, and RO-ERROR services. If RTSE is used, the RO-INVOKE service is mapped onto the RT-TRANSFER service; otherwise, the ROSE makes direct use of presentation data transfer.
4. The invocation of any of these parent operations may result in the invocation of linked operations. Child operations may appear as multiple replies, resulting in a sequence, for example, that begins with sending an RO-INVOKE, continues with the receipt of several RO-INVOKEs, and is concluded by one final RO-RESULT or RO-ERROR.
5. An OPERATION may be disrupted via the RO-REJECT service if

ROSE or a ROSE user cannot process the OPERATION. (An OPER-
ATION could also be disrupted by any underlying ABORT service.)

6. When the user elements have exhausted their use of ROSE, the
UNBIND macro is used to release the association. If the reliable
transfer service is used, ROSE invokes the RT-CLOSE service; otherwise, ROSE invokes the A-RELEASE service. (Again, association
release can be disrupted by any underlying ABORT service.)

ROSE is arguably the most powerful and frequently used application service element (ACSE is frequently used but not nearly as powerful). The whimsical dish-drying example illustrates how one goes about
constructing remote operations. Figure 10.13 presents the ASN.1 definition of the directory system protocol, which was ROSE as an example.

```
DirectorySystemProtocol {joint-iso-ccitt ds(5) modules(1) dsp(12)}
DEFINITIONS ::=
BEGIN

EXPORTS
    directorySystemAC, chainedReadASE, chainedSearchASE,
    chainedModifyASE;

IMPORTS
    distributedOperations, directoryAbstractService
        FROM UsefulDefinitions {joint-iso-ccitt ds(5) modules(1)
            usefulDefinitions(0)}
APPLICATON-SERVICE-ELEMENT, APPLICATION-CONTEXT, aCSE
            FROM Remote-Operations-Notation-extension {joint-iso-
ccitt
                remote Operations(4) notation-extension(2)}
    id-ac-directorySystemAC, id-ase-chainedReadASE,
    id-ase-chainedSearchASE,
    id-ase-chainedModifyASE, id-as-directorySystemAS, id-as-acse;
        FROM ProtocolObjectIdentifiers {joint-iso-ccitt ds(5) mod-
ules(1)
            protocolObjectIdentifier(4)}
    Abandoned, AbandonFailed, AttributeError,
    NameError, SecurityError, ServiceError, UpdateError
        FROM DirectoryAbstractService directoryAbstractService

    DSABind, DSAUnbind,
    ChainedRead, ChainedCompare, ChainedAbandon,
    ChainedList, ChainedSearch,
    ChainedAddEntry, ChainedRemoveEntry, ChainedModifyEntry,
    ChainedModifyRDN,
    DSAReferral
    FROM DistributedOperations distributedOperations;

directorySystemAC
    APPLICATON-CONTEXT
        APPLICATION SERVICE ELEMENTS {aCSE}
        BIND          DSABind
        UNBIND        DSAUnbind
```

```
REMOTE OPERATIONS {rOSE}
OPERATIONS OF {
      chainedReadASE, chainedSearchASE,
      chainedModifyASE}
ABSTRACT SYNTAXES {
      id-as-acse, id-as-directorySystemAS}
::={id-ac-directorySystemAC}
```

```
chained ReadASE
      APPLICATION-SERVICE-ELEMENT
            OPERATIONS {chainedRead, chainedCompare, chainedAbandon}
      ::= id-ase-chainedReadASE

chainedSearchASE
      APPLICATION-SERVICE-ELEMENT
            OPERATIONS {chainedList, chainedSearch}
      ::= id-ase-chainedSearchASE

chainedModifyASE
      APPLICATION-SERVICE-ELEMENT
            OPERATIONS {  chainedAddEntry, chainedRemoveEntry,
            chainedModifyEntry, chainedModifyRDN}
::= id-ase-chainedModifyASE
```

```
chainedRead              ChainedRead           ::=1
chainedCompare           ChainedCompare        ::=2
chainedAbandon           ChainedAbandon        ::=3
chainedList              ChainedList           ::=4
chainedSearch            ChainedSearch         ::=5
chainedAddEntry          ChainedAddEntry       ::=6
chainedRemoveEntry       ChainedRemoveEntry    ::=7
chainedModifyEntry       ChainedModifyEntry    ::=8
chainedModifyRDN         ChainedModifyRDN      ::=9

attributeError           Attribute Error       ::=1
nameError                NameError             ::=2
serviceError             ServiceError          ::=3
dsaReferral              DSAReferral           ::=9
abandoned                Abandoned             ::=5
securityError            SecurityError         ::=6
abandonFailed            AbandonFailed         ::=7
updateError              UpdateError           ::=8
```

```
END
```

(*Source:* ISO/IEC 9594-5: 1990), "Protocol Specifications.")

FIGURE 10.13   ASN.1 Definition of the Directory Service Protocol

"CORE ASE Wanna-bes"

The application tool kit is growing. A number of application service elements recently completed by ISO and CCITT offer capabilities that appear promising enough to speculate that they may ultimately become members of the "core." Although it is beyond the scope of this book to address every application service element, there is a growing number of application service elements that one might classify as "core ASE wannabes." In the area of transaction processing, for example, there are three candidates. The OSI *commitment, concurrency, and recovery* (ISO/IEC 9804: 1990; ISO/IEC 9805: 1990), *distributed transaction processing* (ISO/IEC DIS 10026: 1992), and *remote database access* (ISO/IEC DIS 9579: 1992) services provide ways to associate a sequence of operations (a transaction or an atomic action) performed on remotely accessed data, such that either the entire sequence of operations must be performed on the data or the effects of all the operations must be undone. This "all or none" characteristic is referred to as *atomicity*. Assuring that the effects of the operations leave the data in either the original or the revised state (but no other) is called *consistency*. Another characteristic of processing a transaction is *data isolation*: from the time a transaction is initiated until it is completed, all data involved in the transaction may not be accessed by any other transaction.

A final characteristic of transaction processing is that once the data are changed, the changes endure failures of any subsequent transaction performed on the data. For example, if a transaction "foo" succeeds and results in a counter's value being changed from 1 to 2, the subsequent failure of a transaction "bar" cannot "undo" the effect of "foo" by leaving the counter with a value other than 2.

Commitment concurrency and recovery, transaction processing, and remote database access service elements are enabling vehicles for distributed-processing applications such as electronic banking (automated teller machines), point-of-sale inventory control, purchasing using debit cards, electronic brokering, and remote database access.

Early in the development of the OSI application layer, the terms *common application service elements* (CASE) and *specific application service elements* (SASE) were abandoned because no consensus could be reached on what criteria should be used to distinguish what was common from what was specific. This problem exists only if you persist in believing that the classification of an application service element is something static rather than dynamic. The true measure of whether an application service element is among the "core" set of application tools is how extensively it is used. Although the OSI Message Handling System and the Directory may be considered specific end-user applications today, in the future—as standards for office document management, banking, electronic data interchange, document filing and retrieval, and electronic library applications emerge—these, too, may become "core ASEs."

Conclusion

This chapter concludes the discussion of the application layer. It has examined the most frequently used application service elements—ACSE, RTSE, and ROSE—and illustrated how these ASEs provide services, individually and collectively, to the application service elements described in Chapters 7, 8, and 9. In the process, the authors have attempted to demonstrate the modularity of the OSI application layer and the flexibility afforded a user element (a specific application service) when a set of general-purpose mechanisms are made available to a developer of distributed application services.

11 THE PRESENTATION AND SESSION LAYERS

The presentation and session layers collaborate to provide many of the distributed-processing capabilities presented to user elements by the service elements of the application layer; for this reason, they are discussed together.

Presentation Layer

Chapter 4 describes how ASN.1 provides the application programmer with a tool for creating data structures that are syntactically independent from the way in which data are stored in a computer and from the way in which they are transferred between computer systems. Transforming these abstract syntaxes into "concrete" data structures appropriate for a given operating system (e.g., UNIX, DOS, VMS, MVS) is typically handled by tools such as *ASN.1 compilers*. The task of preserving the semantics of the data exchanged between a sender and receiver across an OSI network is handled by the presentation layer, which performs the transformations from the local (concrete) syntax used by each application entity to a common *transfer* syntax. This leads us to the discussion of the notion of a presentation *context set*.

Context Set Definition

The presentation layer is responsible for managing the transfer syntaxes associated with the set of abstract syntaxes that will be used by application entities as they exchange information across a presentation connection. As part of presentation connection establishment, application entities must be sure that the presentation layer can support a transfer syntax for every abstract syntax required by the distributed-processing application(s) that will use this connection. A *presentation context definition list*, consisting of a presentation context identifier and an abstract syntax name, is created by the application entity that initiates the presentation connection establishment. The responding application entity determines whether the list is complete and whether it can be supported, on a "per-entry" basis. The set of presentation contexts resulting from this negotiation is called the *defined context set* (DCS).[1]

Presentation Service

The presentation service (ISO/IEC 8882: 1988) is presented in terms of the *facilities* it provides. The *connection establishment* (P-CONNECT) and *connection termination facilities* (P-RELEASE, P-U-ABORT, P-P-ABORT) provide presentation connection management between communicating application entities. Within the context established for a presentation connection, and through the use of the *context management facility* (P-ALTER-CONTEXT), the presentation layer preserves the semantics of data as they are transferred between applications.

In OSI, certain functions reflected by application service elements are performed in the session layer—e.g., token management, synchronization, and checkpointing. When these session layer services are invoked, and because the rigid layering prescribed by the OSI reference model does not allow one to "skip layers," the presentation layer is seemingly "in the way." The presentation layer does not provide the service directly but instead passes these service primitives between the application and session layers; thus, the so-called *pass-throughs* were born. For applications that require direct manipulation of session services, the presentation layer offers applications "pass-through" facilities to services offered by the session layer. Collectively identified under the rubric *dialogue control*, they consist of 21 services that directly reflect session layer token management, activity management, data synchronization, and exception reporting services.

(The complete set of primitives and parameters of the presentation service is illustrated in Table 11.1.)

Note that although the presentation layer service primitives suggest that the presentation layer has some active role in providing activity and token management, synchronization, and exception services, this is not

---

1.   A default context is always known by the presentation service provider and the service users. The need for a default context arises (once again) from the need to support the X.410-1984 mode of the OSI Message Handling System; when no presentation protocol is exchanged, the default context is assumed. The *default context name* may also be passed as a parameter during presentation connection establishment.

TABLE 11.1   Presentation Service Primitives

Presentation Primitive	Parameter Name	Request	Indication	Response	Confirm
P-CONNECT	Calling presentation address	M	M		
	Called presentation address	M	M		
	Responding P-address			M	M
	P-context definition list	U	C(=)		
	P-context definition result list		C	C	C(=)
	Default context name	U	C(=)		
	Default context result			C	C(=)
	Quality of service	Pass through	Pass through	Pass through	Pass through
	Presentation requirements	U	C	U	C(=)
	Mode	M	M(=)		
	Session requirements	Pass through	Pass through	Pass through	Pass through
	Initial serial number	Pass through	Pass through	Pass through	Pass through
	Initial token assignment	Pass through	Pass through	Pass through	Pass through
	Session connection identifier	Pass through	Pass through	Pass through	Pass through
	User data	U	C(=)	U	C(=)
	Result			M	M(=)
P-RELEASE	User data	U	C(=)	U	C(=)
	Result			M	M(=)
P-U-ABORT	User data	U	C(=)		
P-P-ABORT	Provider reason		M		
P-ALTER-CONTEXT	P-context addition list	U	C(=)		
	P-context deletion list	U	C(=)		
	P-context addition result list		C	U	C(=)
	P-context deletion result list			U	C(=)
	User data	U	C(=)	U	C(=)
P-DATA	User data	M	M(=)		
P-TYPED-DATA	User data	M	M(=)		
P-EXPEDITED-DATA	User data	M	M(=)		

L. I. H. E.
THE BECK LIBRARY
WOOLTON RD. LIVERPOOL

TABLE 11.1   Presentation Service Primitives continued

Presentation Primitive	Parameter Name	Request	Indication	Response	Confirm
P-CAPABILITY-DATA	User data	U	C(=)	U	C(=)
T-TOKEN-GIVE	Tokens	Pass through	Pass through		
P-TOKEN-PLEASE	Tokens	Pass through	Pass through		
P-CONTROL-GIVE	User data	U	C(=)		
P-SYNC-MINOR	Type	Pass through	Pass through	Pass through	Pass through
	Synch point serial number	Pass through	C(=)	U	C(=)
	User data	U	C(=)		
P-SYNC-MAJOR	Synch point serial number	Pass through	Pass through	U	C(=)
	User data	U	C(=)		
P-RESYNCHRONIZE	Resynchronize type	Pass through	Pass through		
	Synch point serial umber	Pass through	Pass through	Pass through	Pass through
	Tokens	Pass through	Pass through	U	C(=)
	User data	U	C(=)	C	
	P-context identification list		C		
P-ACTIVITY-START	Activity identifier	Pass through	Pass through		
	User data	U	C(=)		
P-ACTIVITY-RESUME	Activity identifier	Pass through	Pass through		
	Old activity identifier	Pass through	Pass through		
	Synch point serial number	Pass through	Pass through		
	Old session connection ID	Pass through	Pass through		
	User data	U	C(=)		
P-ACTIVITY-END	Synch point serial number	Pass through	Pass through		
	User data	U	C(=)	U	C(=)
P-ACTIVITY-INTERRUPT	Reason	Pass through	Pass through		
P-ACTIVITY-DISCARD	Reason	Pass through	Pass through		
P-U-EXCEPTION-REPORT	Reason	Pass through	Pass through		
	User data	U	C(=)		
P-P-EXCEPTION-REPORT	Reason				Pass through

the case. In all instances where the words "Pass through" appear in Table 11.1, all the presentation service provides is access to the corresponding session service. Note also that the presentation service provides (access to) four forms of *information transfer* services: normal, typed, capability, and expedited data. These, too, are best explained in the context of the underlying session service.

Connection Establishment   The presentation connection establishment service is invoked via the association control service element (Chapter 10), which supplies presentation (called and calling) addressing information, presentation and session requirements, mode of operation (normal or X.410-1984), and lots more.[2]

The semantics and composition of the *presentation addresses* used in presentation connection establishment are discussed in Chapter 5; they identify the application entities that will use the presentation connection. Note that if an application entity is represented as a Directory object (see Chapter 7), the ASN.1 definition of a presentation address in an entry of "application entity object" class looks like this:

```
applicationEntity OBJECT-CLASS
SUBCLASS OF top
MUST CONTAIN{
        commonName,
        presentationAddress }
MAY CONTAIN {
        description,
        localityName,
        organizationName,
        organizationUnitName,
        seeAlso,
        supportedApplicationContext }
 ::= {objectClass 12}

presentationAddress ATTRIBUTE
    WITH ATTRIBUTE-SYNTAX
        PresentationAddress
    MATCHES FOR EQUALITY
    SINGLE VALUE
    ::= { attribute Type 29 }
```

2.   A comparison of Tables 10.1 and 11.1 demonstrates how much of the information required to establish an association between OSI applications "trickles down, percolates up" through several service boundaries. The volume of information that is passed is daunting, and the repetition and cross-referencing between the service and protocol definitions of several layers is one aspect of OSI standardization that contributes to much of the confusion and dismay that afflict the OSI upper layers. The authors hope that readers will be sufficiently comfortable by now with the concepts of the functions provided by the OSI upper layers that the repetition will be recognized as an artifact of the rigid layering approach prescribed by the OSI reference model.

```
PresentationAddress ::= SEQUENCE {
    pSelector      [0]     OCTET STRING OPTIONAL,
    sSelector      [1]     OCTET STRING OPTIONAL,
    tSelector      [2]     OCTET STRING OPTIONAL,
    nAddresses     [3]     SET SIZE (1...MAX) OF OCTET STRING }
```

(*Source:* ISO/IEC 9594-6: 1990), "Selected Attribute Types."

Presentation requirements are identified in terms of *functional units*, a logical grouping of services somehow distinct from facilities. There are three presentation functional units:

- The *kernel* consists of connection establishment, release, abort, and normal information transfer (P-DATA service only).
- The *context management* facility provides the ability to alter the defined context set (to add or delete a presentation context).
- The *context restoration* facility, used in conjunction with the resynchronization service, allows the defined context set to be recorded at specified points during data transfer. If the presentation connection is resurrected following a temporary failure, the DCS can be restored to one known at the specified "restart" point (i.e., to one that both presentation users remember).

Session requirements, also identified in terms of functional units, represent a checklist of the session services that will be used by the distributed applications. They are provided in the P-CONNECT primitives (see Table 11.1) so that they can be used in the negotiation of a session connection to support the distributed application.

⟦·AHA·⟧ *The grouping of presentation services into both facilities and functional units is an artifact of the CCITT/ISO "mind-meld." CCITT speaks of services in terms of facilities, and initially, the presentation service was described in these terms. Later, when CCITT and ISO attempted to merge several notions of the session layer into a single "service," the term functional unit was introduced to better describe the relationship between seemingly disjoint services. Although the presentation service is initially described in terms of facilities, the term is abandoned midway through ISO/IEC 8822 and never used again.*

In the *normal mode* of operation, these parameters are conveyed in the connect presentation packet and the negotiated parameter values are returned in the connect presentation accept packet (in Figure 11.1, the CP and CPA PPDUs, respectively). Recall from Chapter 10, however, that no

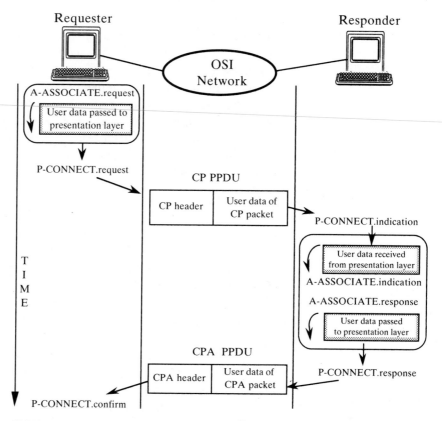

FIGURE 11.1   Presentation Connection Establishment

protocol is exchanged above the session layer to establish an application association with the X.410-1984 mode of operation; under these conditions the presentation context definition list, default-context name, and presentation requirements are always absent from presentation connection establishment primitives, since their values are fixed and understood *a priori* by implementations that support the 1984 version of X.400 and are not needed to create a CP or CPA PDU. The connect presentation reject packet (the CPR PPDU, not shown) is used by the presentation service provider or the called application entity to refuse the presentation connection. (If the provider refuses the connection request, it offers a reason—default context not supported, incorrect protocol version, etc.—in the CPR PPDU.) The application protocol associated with association establishment (the AARQ and AARE APDUs; see Chapter 10) are typically submitted as user data—a presentation data value in the P-CONNECT primitives—and "piggybacked" in the presentation protocol, as illustrated in Figure 11.1.

Many of the parameters used by association control during presentation connection establishment are really intended for use in session connection establishment. Among these are session requirements, session connection identifier, initial assignment of tokens, and initial synch-point serial number. These are used to negotiate a "proper" session connection—one that ensures that all the tools required for communication are present. For example, if the reliable transfer service element is used by an application process, synchronization services and activity management would be included in the session requirements.

Release and Abort Services   The presentation layer provides application entities with access to the orderly (nondestructive) release service offered by the session layer; parameters passed in the P-RELEASE service primitives (user data and result, see Table 11.1) are used in the corresponding session release service primitive. In the normal mode of operation, the application protocol used to support the A-RELEASE service is passed directly as user data to the S-RELEASE service; no explicit presentation protocol is used. (In Figure 11.2, the RLRQ and RLRE APDUs are conveyed as user data in the session finish packet, the FN SPDU.)

The abort service operates in much the same manner as the presentation release service. The application protocol used to support the A-ABORT service is conveyed as user data in P-U-ABORT primitives and subsequently transferred in the abort release user packet (in Figure 11.3, the ARU PPDU). The presentation provider may also abort the presentation connection if a protocol error is detected; here, the abort release provider packet (the ARP PPDU, not shown) is sent by the presentation entity that detected the error. (This, of course, begs the question of whether the presentation entity that generated an erroneous packet remains capable of interpreting the ARP packet, but it does provide closure.)

Context Set Negotiation   When a presentation connection is established for a single application service element—the message transfer service element of the OSI Message-Handling System, for example—the negotiation process is a formality: all entries in the presentation-context definition list should be supported. When an attempt is made to allow two or more application service elements to share a single presentation connection, the situation becomes more complex. If, for example, the initiating user element wants to allow both the Directory and the common management information service to operate over a single presentation connection, but the responder doesn't support the directory service, the responder can

TABLE 11.2   Session Service Primitives

Session Primitive	Parameter Name	Request	Indication	Response	Confirm
S-CONNECT	Session connection identifier	U	C(=)	U	C(=)
	Calling session address	M	M		
	Called session address	M	M		
	Responding session address			M	M
	Result			M	M
	Quality of service	M	M	M	M
	Session requirements	M	M(=)	M	M(=)
	Initial serial number	C	C(=)	C	C(=)
	Initial token assignment	C	C(=)	C	C(=)
	User data	U	C(=)	U	C(=)
S-RELEASE	User data	U	C(=)	U	C(=)
	Result			M	M(=)
S-U-ABORT	User data	U	C(=)		
S-S-ABORT	Provider reason		M		
S-DATA	User data	M	M(=)		
S-TYPED-DATA	User data	M	M(=)		
S-EXPEDITED-DATA	User data	M	M(=)		
S-CAPABILITY-DATA	User data	U	C(=)	U	C(=)
S-TOKEN-GIVE	Tokens	M	M(=)		
S-TOKEN-PLEASE	Tokens	M	M(=)		
S-CONTROL-GIVE	User data	U	C(=)		
S-SYNC-MINOR	Type	M	M(=)		
	Synch point serial number	M	M(=)	M	M(=)
	User data	U	C(=)	U	C(=)
SY-SYNC-MAJOR	Synch point serial number	M	M(=)	M	M(=)
	User data	U	C(=)	U	C(=)
S-RESYNCHRONIZE	Resynchronize type	M	M(=)		
	Synch point serial number	C	M(=)	M	M(=)
	Tokens	C	C(=)	C	C(=)
	User data	U	C(=)	U	C(=)

TABLE 11.2 Session Service Primitives continued

Session Primitive	Parameter Name	Request	Indication	Response	Confirm
	S-context identification list		C	C	M
S-U-EXCEPTION-REPORT	Reason	M	M(=)		
	User data	U	C(=)		
S-S-EXCEPTION-REPORT	Reason		C(=)		
S-ACTIVITY-START	Activity identifier	M	M(=)		
	User data	U	C(=)		
S-ACTIVITY-RESUME	Activity identifier	M	M(=)		
	Old activity identifier	M	M(=)		
	Synch point serial number	M	M(=)		
	Old session connection ID	M	M(=)		
	User data	U	C(=)		
S-ACTIVITY-END	Synch point serial number	M	M(=)		
	User data	U	C(=)		
S-ACTIVITY-INTERRUPT	Reason	U	C(=)	U	C(=)
S-ACTIVITY-DISCARD	Reason	U	C(=)		

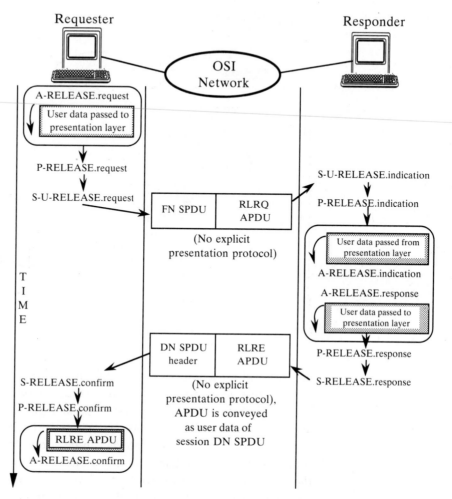

FIGURE 11.2   Normal Release of a Presentation Connection

selectively reject all the entries on the list that are associated with the Directory, and the initiator can determine that only common management information service can be supported over the resulting presentation connection. (Situations such as this are the exception rather than the norm.)

Negotiation and Renegotiation of Transfer Syntax   For those situations in which a presentation connection is to be shared or reused by different application service elements, the presentation layer provides an "alter context" service—a user element can add entries to and delete entries from the defined context set (using the presentation context addi-

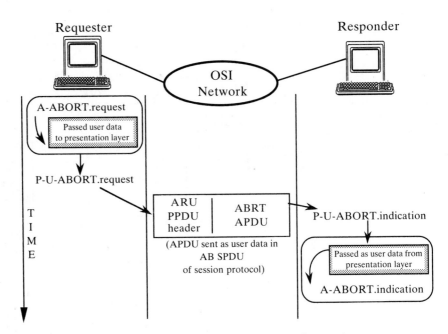

FIGURE 11.3   User-initiated Abort of a Presentation Connection

tion list and presentation context deletion list parameters, respectively). When is this necessary? Consider the scenario in which an FTAM association exists between two open systems, and a user on one system decides to make use of the OSI Directory. Using the P-ALTER-CONTEXT service, the necessary presentation contexts can be added to the defined context set of the presentation connection that already exists. The initiator sends the revised presentation context in an alter context packet, and the responder acknowledges the revisions using the alter context acknowledgment packet. In Figure 11.4, these are the AC and ACA PPDUs, respectively.

Is this useful? It's yet another form of multiplexing, and only time and experience will demonstrate whether the savings in performance is worth the implementation complexity.

Data Transformation to and from Transfer Syntax   Transforming data to and from transfer syntax is the basic and essential service of the presentation layer. Data submitted by a sending application service element are transformed from the local syntax to the common *transfer* syntax, transferred from the source system to the destination system, then transformed into the local syntax understood by the receiving application service element at the destination system. This is performed for all transfers

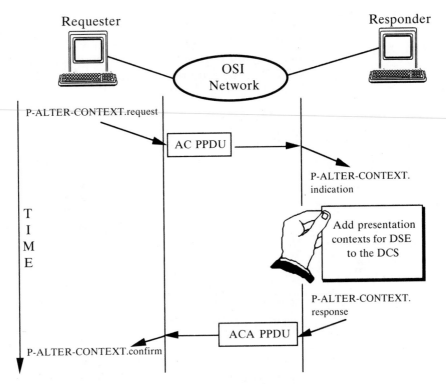

FIGURE 11.4   Changing the Defined Context Set

of presentation data values (user data). This encoding/decoding is normally provided in one of two ways: either the application provides for encoding/decoding itself, perhaps assisted by ASN.1 compiler tools, or the encoding/decoding is provided within the presentation layer. (Although the second alternative would seem to be the obvious choice, the first is more efficient because it avoids "double encoding": encode data in the local syntax, then in the transfer syntax.)

Information Transfer, Dialogue Control   The intention to use session services—including mode of data transfer (duplex, half-duplex), activity management, and synchronization services—is indicated in the P-CONNECT.request primitive (see Table 11.1). This is the setup process for an application to use pass-through services. The list of required session services continues on its "trickle down, cross the network, percolate up" journey from the initiating user element to the target user element in two forms. Information is passed to the presentation entity to request "additional" session services during session connection establishment, discussed later in this chapter. The session service requirements of the requester may also be conveyed in the optional *User session requirements* field (Figure 11.5) of the connect presentation packet (in Figure 11.6, the CP PPDU) by setting the appropriate bit of the ASN.1 BITSTRING data structure to a value of 1.

```
User-session-requirements ::= BIT STRING {
                        half-duplex          (0),
                        duplex               (1),
                        expedited-data       (2),
                        minor-synchronize    (3),
                        major-synchronize    (4),
                        resynchronize        (5),
                        activity-management  (6),
                        negotiated-release   (7),
                        capability-data      (8),
                        exceptions           (9),
                        typed-data           (10)  }
```

(*Source:* ISO/IEC 8823: 1988)

FIGURE 11.5   Abstract Syntax of User-session-requirements field of the Connect Presentation Packet

If session synchronization services are requested, an *initial serial number* may be provided (a session user option; see the discussion of session synchronization services, later in this chapter). The initial direction of information transfer—requester side first, accepter side first, accepter side chooses—may also be specified to indicate "who speaks first." These values are used locally, in the creation of an S-CONNECT.request.

When the connection establishment process is completed, the session services negotiated during that process are available via the pass-through presentation services. The following section examines the session layer and its services in more detail.

⌐AHA⌐   *This all seems rather unnatural. Why not have application service elements perform the very capabilities they present to user elements? The reasons are largely historical and political. Early in the development of OSI, CCITT and ISO agreed that sharing a single reference model for open systems was a good thing. Having two very large, consensus-driven organizations participate in joint development of a single set of protocols and services, however, was not. Setting aside the issue of cultural differences, coordinating—and particularly, sequencing—the development of standards proved daunting from the outset. Committees were formed in both standards bodies for all seven layers (and then some), and these proceeded in parallel; under such cir-*

cumstances, it turned out to be impossible to define standards using a top-down or bottom-up approach. At first, coordination seemed a minor inconvenience; the OSI RM, after all, was there to guide all the standards committees. But the OSI RM itself was revised on several occasions to accommodate "pre-OSI" CCITT recommendations such as the T.62 session protocol for teletex communications and the X.25 packet-level protocol. The result? Functions that arguably should lie in the application layer were assigned to the session layer because the X.400 MHS recommendations were "ready to ship" before the application layer structure was completed (see Chapter 8).

How bad is the resultant upper-layer architecture? Although pass-throughs preserve architectural purity, they are inconvenient: application service elements pass parameters for session in procedure calls to presentation, which copies or passes pointers to the same parameters in procedure calls to session, resulting in what one OSI implementer describes as "silly little no-op pass-through routines, slowing down the whole stack. . . ."[3] Exaggerated? Only in the sense that in the overall performance of OSI implementations, this is probably not the killer. An alternative? OSI might have adopted the "tool-kit" philosophy from the application-layer structure earlier in the process, but that's another case of "hindsight."

Session Layer

Information exchange between computer systems can be viewed as having two fundamental components. The first is information *transfer:* moving the information from its origin or source to its destination. In OSI (and TCP/IP), this aspect of information transfer is the responsibility of the *transport service.* Now, the transport service moves data between open systems *transparently;* that is, the transport service is only responsible for the transfer of an unstructured or "raw" bit stream of information from one open system to another, and it doesn't know or care where application data begin and end. Applications, however, do. The second fundamental component—preserving the *structure* of data defined by communicating application processes—belongs to the *session service* (ISO/IEC 8326: 1987). Thus, in addition to the expected connection management services—connection establishment, release, and abort—the session layer provides application processes with the synchronization, checkpointing, and resynchronization mechanisms to organize and

---

3. From an electronic-mail conversation about the presentation layer with Lisa Phifer.

impose structure on data exchanged. These are collectively referred to as *dialogue-control* facilities.

A further aspect of transport service transparency is that the transport service isn't expected to know or care whether transport service users take turns sending data or do so simultaneously, or even whether consecutive data are submitted by the same application. The responsibility for maintaining *control* of the conversation(s) that take place between communicating application processes also belongs to the session service. The session layer provides application processes with the following mechanisms to control the conversations, or *dialogues,* conducted by communicating application processes:

- Facilities that enable applications to "take turns" exchanging data or otherwise influence information exchange. The coordination of a *half-duplex* method of information exchange, synchronization services, and activity management services are governed by the assignment of *tokens.* Token-based facilities also enable application processes to coordinate the "graceful" release of associations; they enable applications to make sure that all information transfers are complete before their communication is terminated (if this was the way they chose to behave).
- Facilities that allow application processes to conduct several exchanges in the context of a single session connection. Since the unit of application exchange is called an activity (see Chapter 10), the facilities that enable applications to "distinguish between different pieces of logical work" (ISO/IEC 8326: 1987) are collectively referred to as *activity management.*

Session Services   There are more than 20 session services (see Table 11.2). For identification during connection negotiation and also for convenient identification by other standards (notably the presentation service, where session service requirements must be indicated by application entities during association establishment), session services that are related are logically grouped into *functional units.* Each functional unit is examined separately in the following sections.

The Kernel Functional Unit The *kernel* functional unit consists of session connection establishment; "normal" data transfer (half- or full-duplex); graceful, or orderly, release; and user- and provider-initiated abort services. All session connections require use of the kernel. During *connection establishment,* the availability of the session services required by the application entities that will use the session connection is determined by the session service users (the presentation entities).

There are actually four steps associated with the session functional unit *negotiation* process, and the actions performed are best described by examining the OSI upper layers together:

1. Formally, the calling application entity invokes the association control, in the process identifying the application's session requirements for communication (see Chapter 10); these are "trickled down" to the presentation entity in the P-CONNECT.request and to the session entity in the S-CONNECT.request. In practice, this might be implemented as a series of procedure calls within an "association/connection management" module, with each call passing as a "user data" parameter the protocol data unit(s) of the higher-layer entity. Armed with the cascaded set of CONNECT. request packets, the calling session entity establishes a transport connection (see Chapter 12), and a session connect packet (a CN SPDU) is constructed and submitted to the transport layer in a data request. If shorter than 512 octets, the connect presentation packet (the CP PPDU) is conveyed in the user data parameter of the session connect packet; if between 513 and 10,240 octets, it is conveyed in the extended user data parameter of the session connect packet (available in session version 2 only). Otherwise, only the first 10,240 octets of the CP PPDU are sent in the extended user data parameter of the CN SPDU, followed by one or more connect data overflow packets (CDO SPDUs). (Note that Figure 11.6 and this discussion show only the scenario in which everything fits in a single CN SPDU.)

2. The called session entity receives the CN SPDU, parses it, and generates an S-CONNECT.indication, passing among the parameters the set of session functional units indicated by the called presentation entity (and encoded in the CN SPDU), and session service user data (containing the CP PPDU). The called presentation entity extracts the connect presentation packet (the CP PPDU) and uses the encoded data to generate a P-CONNECT.indication (see Figure 11.1 and the accompanying text). The user session requirements from the calling application entity are identified to the called application entity in the indication ("percolating up" of parameters). The called application entity may make adjustments to user session requirements, based on (a) options left for the called application entity (for example, the calling application entity might have proposed both half- and full-duplex modes of transfer, effectively say-

ing to the caller "You choose") or (b) known limitations to the underlying session implementation (e.g., if a session functional unit requested by the calling application entity is not supported).

If the resulting list still satisfies the application requirements as understood by the called application entity, it uses association control to accept the association, and the revised session requirements are "trickled down" in the presentation and session CONNECT. response primitives, again in the manner described in step 1. The revised requirements are encoded in the session accept connection packet (in Figure 11.6, the AC SPDU), which is returned over the transport connection to the calling session entity. Note that the session functional units that will be used over the session connection are defined as the intersection of what the called and calling session entities exchange in the session user requirements field of the CN and AC SPDUs. Negotiation is thus a "whittling down" rather than a "bartering" process.

4. The calling session entity parses the AC SPDU, determines (and records) the session functional units that will be used across the session connection, then percolates the revised set up as per step (2).

This entire sequence is illustrated in Figure 11.6.

·AHA· *Even though the OSI upper layers are formally organized in a hierarchy, from an examination of the information passed through the presentation layer it is obvious that a purely "clinical" interpretation of the interactions among application, presentation, and session entities would be extremely inefficient. Well-behaved implementations of the OSI upper layers frequently lump association, presentation, and session connection management together as a single process that is aware of, for example, the complement of session functional units available in a particular implementation, the available application service elements, and the requirements they impose on both the presentation layer (what presentation syntaxes) and the session layer (what services). In such implementations, connection management is far from the scavenger hunt the standards depict.*

The Many Faces of Data Transfer (Full-Duplex, Half-Duplex, Expedited, and Capability Functional Units)　There are two modes of normal data transfer: *full-duplex* (both directions at the same time) or *half-duplex* (either direction, only one direction at a time, with the choice of direction being controlled by the session service users). The half-duplex functional unit uses the give tokens and please tokens services (S-TOKEN-GIVE, S-TOKEN-PLEASE): a *data token* is exchanged between

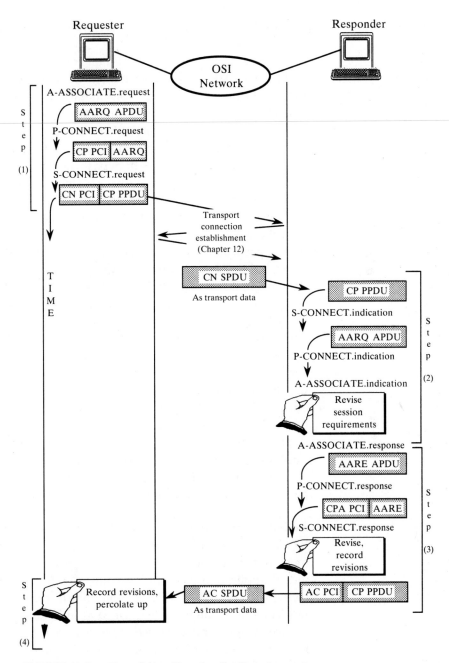

FIGURE 11.6   Negotiating User Session Requirements

the two communicating session service users to control the direction of information flow.

The notion of token-based data transfer is a pretty simple one: if you hold a token, you can use the service governed by that token (in this case, you can use the normal session data service); if you don't have the data token, you can request it using the please tokens service, or you can wait until the data token is yielded via the give tokens service, but you can't use the normal session data service until you hold the data token.

There are several ways to bypass the data token. In addition to the normal data transfer service, there is an *expedited data transfer* service. Expedited data are uninhibited by token/flow control but extremely limited in size (a mere 14 bytes). Originally, this data service was perceived to facilitate virtual terminal services, but outside of this, it's not especially useful, particularly since virtually nothing can be BER-encoded in 14 or fewer bytes. *Typed data transfer* can be used even if you don't hold the data token; it's sort of a "token be damned, I'm sending data" service. Of course, restrictions apply: the typed data service is available only when the half-duplex mode is selected. It is used by commitment, concurrency, and recovery (ISO/IEC 9804: 1990) and the Virtual Terminal (VT; ISO/IEC 9040: 1990). CCR uses typed data to request a restart, whereas Virtual Terminal uses typed data to switch VT profiles. Both CCR and VT use the half-duplex mode and clearly find occasions when it might have been wiser to use full-duplex, if only to have it available for exception cases. (This probably argues strongly for having standardized a full-duplex-only session service rather than a full-duplex service *plus* a half-duplex service with a patchwork exception service.)

A fourth data functional unit, *capability data*, is best understood, and only applicable, in the context of activity management.

Activity Management Functional Unit   Chapter 10 discusses how the RT-TRANSFER service accepts arbitrarily large user data from a user element and treats each submission as a separate transfer activity (an individual application protocol data unit). At the session layer, the activity concept is preserved: APDUs submitted to the presentation layer in P-DATA.requests can be distinguished as individual activities by using the services that comprise the *activity management functional unit*. In particular, activity services are used to identify the beginning and end of an activity (S-ACTIVITY-START, S-ACTIVITY-END), to interrupt and later resume an activity (S-ACTIVITY-INTERRUPT, S-ACTIVITY-RESUME), and to discard an ongoing activity, (a transfer that for some reason has become expendable and can be trashed [S-ACTIVITY-DISCARD]).

Session activity management services are accessed by application entities using activity pass-through facilities of the presentation layer. The P-ACTIVITY-START and P-ACTIVITY-END primitives, for instance, map directly onto the S-ACTIVITY-START and S-ACTIVITY-END primitives. As an example, Figure 11.7 illustrates the sequence in which an activity is started by the application entity using the P-ACTIVITY-START primitive; the request is passed through to the session service in the form of a directly mapped S-ACTIVITY-START, which is communicated across the network via the activity start packet (in Figure 11.7, the AS SPDU).

If a single application entity is using a presentation connection, activities aren't very interesting. If the presentation connection is shared between two application entities between ASEs of the OSI Message Handling System and the Directory, for instance—activity management can play an interesting role. Consider, for example, a situation in which the MHS and the Directory share a presentation connection between two computers, "Michaelangelo" and "Donatello." The message transfer application service element at Michaelangelo is in the process of forwarding a jumbo mailgram to Donatello when a directory user attempts to retrieve some naming/ addressing information (perhaps the name of a bodacious pizza parlor). Rather than delay the directory request until

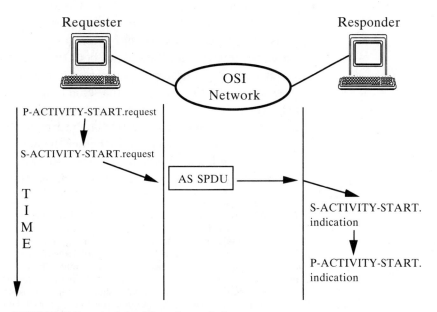

FIGURE 11.7   Activity "Pass-throughs"

the jumbo mailgram is transferred, the sending application entity can interrupt the mail activity using the S-ACTIVITY-INTERRUPT service (via the P-INTERRUPT pass-through). The progress of the mail activity is suspended, and a directory activity is started. When the directory activity is ended, the progress of the mail activity is resumed using the S-ACTIV-ITY-RESUME service (via the P-ACTIVITY-RESUME pass-through).

The S-ACTIVITY-INTERRUPT service may also be used in situations in which an application process is temporarily unable to continue processing the activity in progress (its ability to continue to receive data is compromised). In such cases, a new activity may not be started (a reason for interrupting the ongoing activity may be provided to the session layer via the pass-through mechanism; this is conveyed in session protocol, and no presentation protocol is involved).

Figure 11.8 illustrates the sequence in which an activity is interrupted. An activity "foo" is started (an AS SPDU is sent), data are transferred (via the normal data-transfer mode, DT SPDU), then "foo" is interrupted (in this case, to start an activity "bar"). The initiator sends an activity interrupt packet (AI SPDU), and the responder acknowledges the interrupt request using the activity interrupt acknowledgment packet (AIA SPDU). The initiator then starts activity bar, sends data, and resumes activity "foo" using the activity start, normal data and activity resume packets (AS, DT, and AR SPDUs, respectively).

Activity management is a token-based service; only the holder of the *major/activity* token may interrupt or start an activity.[4] Whenever an activity is started, an *activity identifier* is assigned to that activity. If an ongoing activity is interrupted, the state of both the "old" and "new" activities is maintained. If, for example, major, minor, and/or resynchronization services are in use, the value(s) of the serial number(s) significant to the (old) activity at the point at which it was suspended is (are) stored for that activity, and the serial number(s) may be used for the new activity.

In case readers wondered whether the designers of the OSI session layer had overlooked *anything*, rest easy—they did not. Leaving absolutely nothing to chance, they even considered the scenario in which an

---

4.   When transport expedited data service is available, a special SPDU, called a prepare (PR) SPDU, is used to "warn" the peer session provider that something "big" is about to happen—a major synchronization acknowledgment, resynchronize, or resynchronize acknowledgment packet (MHA, RS, or RA SPDU) is coming. The PR SPDU is sent on the transport expedited flow, indicating that incoming SPDUs received on the transport normal data flow may be discarded under certain circumstances. For example, when an activity is interrupted, a PR SPDU is used to signal "prepare to resynchronize," letting the peer session provider know that it can ignore incoming normal data flow until the AI SPDU is received.

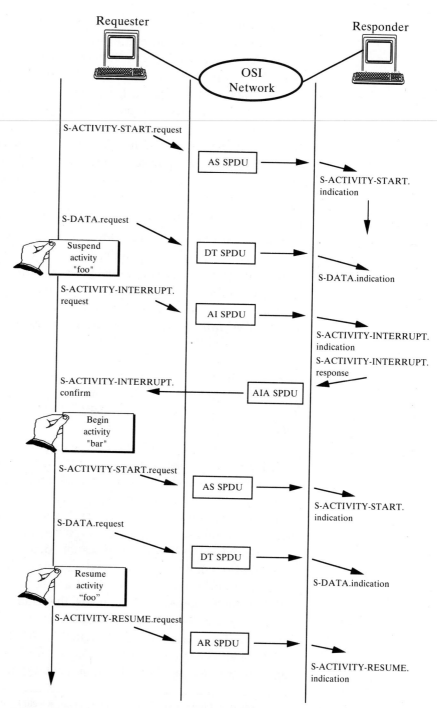

FIGURE 11.8   Interrupting an Ongoing Activity

activity has just ended, and before another activity is started, there might arise a need for an application to send a small amount of information— say, a nice, round number like 512 octets—prior to invoking the ACTIV-ITY-START service. (Hey, who knows? It could happen. Really.) *Capability data transfer* offers just such a service. It can be invoked only when activity services are available but no activity is in progress, and only if one holds the major/activity token and has the right to start the next activity (if available, one must also hold the data and/or minor synch token as well). Capability data transfer is sort of like a TV commercial: it can only be invoked "between" activities. Unlike the other data transfer services offered by the session layer, it is a confirmed service. This is necessary to ensure that the data transfer is completed before a new activity is started.

Major and Minor Synchronization Functional Units   Chapter 10 introduced the concept of checkpointing, a facility that enables applications to identify during data exchange "points" in the transfer to which they may return in order to recover from (temporary) communications failures with a minimum amount of retransmission. The session *S-SYNC-MAJOR* and *S-SYNC-MINOR* services are used to provide the checkpointing, and the session *S-RESYNCHRONIZE* service is invoked to recover from temporary communication failure with a minimum of retransmission. As with the other pass-through services, these session services are indirectly accessed by application service elements via the corresponding presentation services (P-SYNC-MAJOR, P-SYNC-MINOR, and P-RESYNCHRO-NIZE, respectively).

All of the synchronization services use a *serial number*, a binary-coded decimal number between 0 and 999,999, to identify points in the byte stream. The decimal number bears no relationship to the octet position of the data being transferred; rather, it has a specific and somewhat different meaning or purpose for each synchronization service. In the major synchronization service, for example, the serial number indicated in an S-SYNC-MAJOR service invocation identifies both the end of a previous unit of communication called a *dialogue* and the beginning of the next. An important characteristic of a *dialogue unit* is that once an S-SYNC-MAJOR.request has been made, the requester can make no further service requests—especially additional data-transfer requests—of any kind until it receives the corresponding S-MAJOR-SYNC.confirm. The S-SYNC-MAJOR.request demands that no further action be taken with regard to transferring data within this activity[5] until both the sender and

---

5.   Note that if the activity functional unit is not selected, there is, in effect, one and only one activity transmitted over the session connection.

the receiver share a common understanding that previously transferred data have been secured (note that the current activity can be interrupted or discarded, or the session connection can be aborted).

The S-SYNC-MINOR service provides secondary or finer granularity to the checkpointing within an activity. Minor synchronization is distinguished from major synchronization in the following ways:

- An S-SYNC-MINOR.request may be issued as a confirmed or an unconfirmed service, at the sender's discretion.
- While an S-SYNC-MINOR.request is outstanding, any other service can be requested, including additional S-SYNC-MINOR.requests.
- The confirmation of an S-SYNC-MINOR.request or an S-SYNC-MAJOR.request implicitly confirms any outstanding S-SYNC-MINOR.requests.

Just as major synchronization points structure data exchange within an activity, minor synchronization points structure data within a dialogue unit. An example of a properly structured activity is illustrated in Figure 11.9.

Both the major and minor synchronization functional units include the give tokens and please tokens services; these are used to assign control of the *major/activity* token and *synchronize-minor* token. Only the session service user that holds the major/activity token may invoke the S-SYNC-MAJOR service; similarly, only the session service user that holds the synchronize-minor token may invoke the S-SYNC-MINOR service.

Symmetric Synchronization Some applications can operate in full-duplex mode. A set of computers that form a constantly replicating database, for example, could exchange information bidirectionally. In such scenarios, each application must have the ability to checkpoint both directions of information flow independently; the synchronization services should be symmetric. At the session layer, this translates into pro-

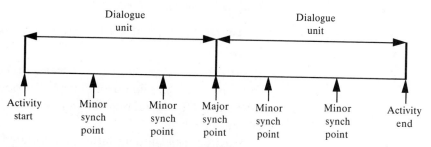

FIGURE 11.9   Structured Exchange of Data

viding a capability for both session service users to insert checkpoints into their "send" flow. When symmetric synchronization is used, a session entity maintains two serial numbers—one to checkpoint what it sends and one to checkpoint what it receives. ISO/IEC 8326 Addendum 1: 1987 and ISO/IEC 8327 Addendum 1: 1987 identify the extensions to the major and minor synchronization services to accommodate symmetric synchronization. Basically, two serial numbers are identified/ negotiated/exchanged at connect time and during activity start or re-sume. The values of both serial numbers are used to identify a major synchronization point or an activity end/interrupt. If resynchronization services are selected, resynchronization can be invoked independently on either direction of information flow or simultaneously (here, both serial numbers must be provided).

·A·H·A· *The original session service and protocol standards were designed to be compatible with the CCITT Recommendation T.62 session protocol for Teletex services, and the agreement between ISO and the CCITT was that the 1984 X.215/X.225 recommendations and the ISO/IEC 8326/8327 session standards would contain identical text. Now, T.62 session services were designed to operate in a half-duplex mode. Since only one of the session service users transferred data at a time, there was a need for only one session synchronization serial number. When full-duplex operations were introduced into the session standard, a second serial number was required to enable session service users to control each direction of information flow independently— to operate minor synchronization and resynchronization services. This is all well and good, but the timing of this "discovery" was unfortunate. Since CCITT closed the 1984 study period while symmetric synchronization was still under study, the Red Book versions of the CCITT recommendations and the ISO session standards were published without it. Symmetric synchronization services and protocol were introduced as addenda to the session service (ISO/IEC 8326 Addendum 1: 1987) and protocol (ISO/IEC 8327 Addendum 1: 1987) and in the 1988 Blue Book recommendations.*

Resynchronize Functional Unit   The *S-RESYNCHRONIZE* service is used to:

- Recover from temporary loss of a transport connection with a minimum of retransmission. Here, the *restart* option is indicated in the S-RESYNCHRONIZE.request and conveyed in the session resynchronize packets.
- Discard or *abandon* data hitherto associated with the current dialogue unit.

- *Set* the synchronization-point serial number to any valid value.

In all forms of the S-RESYNCHRONIZE service, the requester may propose a (new) assignment for the available tokens (or it may indicate that the accepter is allowed to assign token ownership). In the case of a "restart" request, the requester indicates the serial number at which the restart is to commence; it is effectively saying, "I'm confident that the transfer state is reliable to up to this point; let's resume transfer here." The accepter sets the lowest serial number to which a synchronization point confirmation is expected; it also sets the next serial number expected to the restart serial number indicated in the session resynchronize (restart) packet (RS-r SPDU). At this point, the accepter has modified its state machine to reflect that of the requester, so it sends a resynchronize (restart) acknowledgment packet (the RA-r SPDU). Upon receiving the RA-r SPDU, the requester may retransmit data (see Figure 11.10). The accepter may discard any data secured and associated with a serial number greater than the serial number indicated as the restart serial number; from the requester's perspective, these are "suspect" or unconfirmed data.

In the case of an "abandon" request, the requester does not send a serial number, since it's effectively saying, "Let's start over." In response to the session resynchronize (abandon) packet (the RS-a SPDU), the accepter returns a session resynchronize (abandon) acknowledgment packet (the RA-a SPDU), discards all data of this dialogue unit that were previously secured, and awaits "new" transfer. In this case, the accepter expects to proceed as if resynchronization hadn't happened at all. The serial number indicated in the next major/minor synchronization request will be the "next expected serial number" indicated in the RS-a SPDU, and the lowest serial number to which a resynchronization restart may be set becomes 0.

In the case of a "set" request, the requester selects any valid serial number and sends this in an RS-s SPDU. The accepter sets the next expected serial number to the value received in the RS-s SPDU, and returns an RA-s SPDU. Following receipt of the RA-s SPDU and confirmation of the S-RESYNCHRONIZE.request, the requester will use the "set value" in subsequent synchronization requests, and the lowest serial number to which a resynchronization restart may be set becomes 0.

Like the major and minor synchronization services, application entities access the session resynchronization service via a pass-through service of the presentation layer (P-RESYNCHRONIZE).

Exceptions Functional Unit Considering how complicated the session protocol can be, it seems only fitting that a service was designed to allow

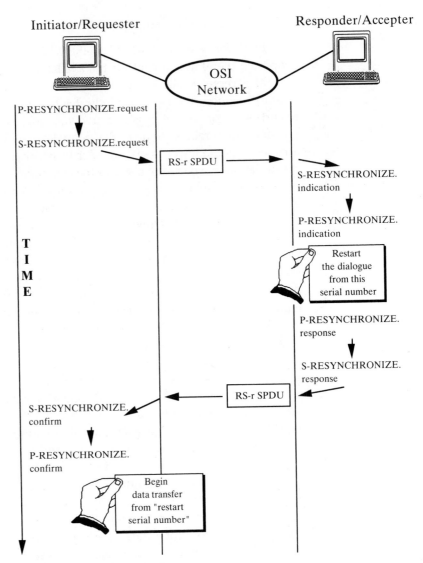

FIGURE 11.10   Resynchronization "Restart"

the session service provider to notify session service users of "unantici-
pated situations not covered by other services" (from ISO/IEC 8326:
1987). The presentation exception reporting service (S-P-EXCEPTION-
REPORT) can be used to signal a protocol or "nonspecific" error to session service users. If a protocol error has been detected by either session
protocol machine (SPM), that SPM may attempt to transfer an exception
report packet (an ER SPDU), which contains as a parameter the SPDU

that the session protocol machine has identified as objectionable. Following an indication of this sort, the session service users are encouraged to resynchronize, interrupt or discard the current activity, or abort the session connection. (Note that only if the transfer and interpretation of the ER SPDU are successful will both session service users receive an indication that an exception condition has been detected.)

An exception reporting service is also available to the session service users. If a session service user encounters an exception condition, it can issue an S-U-EXCEPTION.request. The local session protocol machine will attempt to transfer an exception data packet (an ED SPDU) to the remote SPM containing an indication of the sort of physical, emotional, or psychological problem the requester is experiencing. If the ED SPDU arrives and can be processed, an S-U-EXCEPTION.indication may be generated.

Although it is possible to attempt to resynchronize, interrupt, or discard the current activity, or even yield tokens to a session service user that thinks it can solve the problem if only it could send data, it's generally a good idea for the session service user to follow exception service requests with an abort. Dynamic, self-recovering protocol implementations are hard to find.

Negotiated Release Functional Unit   The negotiated release functional unit consists of orderly release and the give tokens and please tokens services. The *orderly release* service (S-RELEASE) resembles the graceful close offered by TCP (see Chapter 12); both session service users cooperate to ensure that all data in transit have been delivered (acknowledged) before the session connection is closed. Orderly release is influenced by the *release token*; if an S-RELEASE.indication arrives and the release token is available, the accepter may refuse to release the connection (once again belying the term *accepter*). This situation might occur when a mail application "foo" has nothing more to send to its peer "bar" and wishes to release the association, but "bar" still has messages to forward to "foo".

Orderly release is initiated using the S-RELEASE.request service primitive. A session finish packet (an FN SPDU) is sent to the accepter; if the accepter agrees to close the session connection, it returns a session disconnect packet (DN SPDU), confirming the S-RELEASE. A *transport disconnect* parameter in the DN SPDU may be used to indicate whether the transport connection hitherto supporting this session connection is to be reused, and the session protocol machine will proceed according to what is indicated. If the accepter wishes to maintain the session connection, it responds to the FN SPDU with, appropriately, a session not finished packet (NF SPDU), resulting in a rejection of the S-RELEASE service. This is permitted only if the negotiated release functional unit was accepted when the session was established.

Abort Services   The *session abort* service (S-U-ABORT) of the kernel functional unit supports the abort services of the association control service element and the presentation layer. What more can one say? An application entity has observed that things have gone to hell in a handbasket and indicates that it wants to tear down the connection. The *presentation abort* service (S-P-ABORT) is used to indicate that something disastrous has occurred in or below the session layer; the protocol implementation is broken, for example, or the transport connection has disconnected. If the latter is true, the session layer initiates an S-P-ABORT.indication to notify the presentation layer.

Session Protocol

Most of the descriptions of the session protocol have been vicious and unkind. Regrettably, they are deserved, and no amount of historical perspective can alter the fact that the session protocol, from encoding to operation, is neither elegant nor efficient.[6] In version 1, there are 29 states in the protocol machine, further complicated by 75 predicates—and this doesn't take into account additions to accommodate unlimited user data (ISO/IEC 8327 Addendum 2: 1987) or symmetric synchronization (ISO/IEC 8327 Addendum 1: 1987). The encoding of the session protocol itself is a "fixed-field format" lover's worst nightmare. For starters, all session protocol data units have the following components:

SPDU identifier (SI)	A single octet; identifies the type of SPDU
Length indicator (LI)	A single octet; specifies the length of the SPDU in octets
Parameter identifier (PI)	An individual or a group parameter (variable-length)
User information	(Variable-length)

---

6.   Upon first examination, it almost appears that its creators were a divided camp, half insisting on a "TLV" approach similar to ASN.1, the other half insisting on specification by the bits and bytes "as we've always done it in the lower layers." The true reason is not nearly this simple. The session protocol is arguably the worst example of design by committee; faced with multiple base documents to consider (one from ECMA [ECMA75], one from CCITT [CCITT T.62], others too embarrassing to mention), confronted with a commitment to align OSI and the CCITT Teletex protocols, and expected to come to closure on a standard prior to the completion of the 1984 CCITT study period, the committee collapsed under pressure and, "in the spirit of compromise," adopted a combination (not quite the union) of the services of the documents under consideration. At the service level, this was a sizable enough pill to swallow; the ramifications to the protocol (of course, everyone insisted on perpetuating their own bits as well) were nearly ruinous.

The *parameter identifier* (PI) specifies either an individual parameter or a parameter group. Individual parameters have the following components:

Parameter identifier	A single octet; identifies the parameter
Length indicator	A single octet; specifies the length of the parameter in octets
Parameter value	The value assigned to the parameter

whereas *parameter groups* are sets of logically related individual parameters:

Parameter group identifier (PGI)	A single octet; identifies the parameter group
Length indicator (LI)	A single octet; specifies the length of the parameter group in octets
PI_1	Identifier of first parameter in group
LI_1	Length of first parameter in group
PV_1	Value assigned to first parameter in group
•	
•	
•	
PI_n	Identifier of nth parameter in group
LI_n	Length of nth parameter in group
PV_n	Value assigned to nth parameter in group

This encoding style is decidedly complex; the composition of the sample session connect packet (CN SPDU) in Figure 11.11 illustrates how quickly the protocol header becomes littered with "nested" parameter identifiers and length indicators (LI).

Octet No.	CN SPDU	Meaning/Significance	AC SPDU	Octet No.
0	SI = 13	SPDU identifier for connect SPDU	SI = 13	0
1	LI = 723	Total length of SPDU (does not include the SI or LI)	LI = 726	1
2	PGI = 1	Connection identifiers parameter group identifier	PGI = 1	2
3	LI = 138	Length of connection identifiers parameter group	LI = 138	3
4	PI = 10	Calling (CN) or called (AC) SS user reference	PI = 9	4
5	LI=64	Length of SS user reference ($0 < n \le 64$ octets)	LI = 64	5
6–69	<Value>		<Value>	6–69
70	PI = 11	Common reference parameter	PI = 11	70
71	LI = 64	Length of common reference (here, 64 octets)	LI = 64	71
72–135	<Value>		<Value>	72–135
136	PI = 12	Additional reference information parameter	PI = 12	136
137	LI = 4	Length of additional reference information	LI = 4	137
138–141	<Value>		<Value>	138–141
142	PGI = 5	Parameter group identifier for connect/accept item	PGI = 5	142

143	LI = 64	Length of connect/accept item parameter group	LI = 64	143
144	PI = 19	Protocol options parameter	PI = 19	144
145	LI = 1	Length of protocol options parameter	LI = 1	145
146	<Value>	Ability to receive extended concatenated SPDUs	<Value>	146
147	PI = 21	Transport service data unit (TSDU) maximum-size parameter	PI = 21	147
148	LI = 4	Length of TSDU maximum-size parameter	LI = 4	148
149–152	<Value>	Maximum size of TSDUs (for both directions)	<Value>	149–152
153	PI = 22	Version number	PI = 22	153
154	LI = 1	Length of version number	LI = 1	154
155	<Value>		<Value>	155
156	PI = 23	Initial serial number parameter	PI = 23	156
157	LI = 6	Length of initial serial number parameter	LI = 6	157
158–163	<Value>	A BCD-encoded value between 0 and 999,999	<Value>	158–163
164	PI = 26	Token-setting item parameter	PI = 26	164
165	LI = 1	Length of token-setting item	LI = 1	165
166	<Value>	Four "bit pairs" representing initial holder of token	<Value>	166
	n/a	Token item parameter	PI = 16	167
	n/a	Length of token item	LI = 1	168
	n/a	Indication of which tokens are requested by caller	<Value>	169
167	PI = 20	Session user requirements parameter	PI = 20	170
168	LI = 2	Length of session user requirements parameter	LI = 2	171
169–170	<Value>	Each bit represents a session functional unit requested by SS user	<Value>	172–173
171	PI = 51	Calling session selector parameter	PI = 51	174
172	LI = 16	Calling session selector length ($0 < n \le 16$ octets)	LI = 16	175
173–188	<Value>		<Value>	176–191
189	PI = 52	Called (responding) session selector parameter	PI = 52	192
190	LI = 16	Session selector length ($0 < n \le 16$ octets)	LI = 16	193
191–206	<Value>		<Value>	194–209
207	PI = 193	User data parameter	PI = 193	210
208–210	LI = 512*	Length of user data parameter	LI = 512	211–213
211–722	<Value>	User data—contains CP PPDU, AARE APDU	<Value>	214–725

*   When the length indicator value is less than 256, a single octet is used; when the value is greater than 256, 3 octets are used, with the first octet set to binary 1s to indicate that the following 2 octets contain a length between 0 and 65,535.

FIGURE 11.11   Encoding of CN and AC SPDUs

If readers see a potential "chicken and egg" situation regarding the negotiation of maximum transport service data unit size in session connection establishment here, they are to be commended. A maximum of 32 octets of transport user data may be transferred via the T-CONNECT primitives (see Chapter 12); it is thus necessary to first establish a transport connection before the session connect packet can be sent. Now, although the maximum length of transport user data that may be transferred over a transport connection is theoretically unbounded, it's generally a good idea to negotiate the largest possible transport data unit size during transport connection establishment to minimize fragmentation/reassembly, and it would be convenient indeed if the session layer would notify the transport layer of the maximum TSDU size when it requests a transport connection. Unfortunately, the primitives of the T-CONNECT service don't offer a maximum TSDU size parameter, so idication of this useful bit of information is a *local implementation matter.*[7]

A Word about Concatenation   Another truly confusing aspect of the session protocol is the notion of concatenation of session packets (SPDUs) into TSDUs. SPDUs are categorized into three groups:

1. Category-0 SPDUs (give and please tokens SPDUs) are treated as responsible adults; they may be mapped one-to-one onto a TSDU or concatenated with another (category-2) SPDU.
2. Category-1 SPDUs (connect, accept, refuse, finish, disconnect, not finished, give tokens ack, give tokens confirm, exception data, typed data, abort, and prepare SPDUs) are treated as outcasts and must be mapped one-to-one onto TSDUs.
3. Category-2 SPDUs (data transfer, the major/minor/resynchronize, activity, capability, and exception SPDUs) are treated as small children and must be "accompanied by an adult," or category-0 SPDU.

A category-0 SPDU is always the first session packet in a transport service data unit. If basic concatenation is used, a second session packet may be appended to the first if it comes from the set of category-2 SPDUs, and if *extended concatenation* is used, you can piggyback multiple category-2 SPDUs. Here, the rules are so complicated that the session protocol doesn't even attempt to describe them in text; it merely provides a table. Basically, follow these precedence rules: activity management packets precede major/minor synchronization packets, which precede data transfer packets.

Data Transfer   Normal data transfer packets always accompany (at least) a give or please tokens packet. An example of the simplest form of encapsulation is provided in Figure 11.12.

Of course, if a session protocol implementation is *accomplished*, it will be able to parse and process SPDUs concatenated in TSDUs as complex as those illustrated in Figure 11.13.

As a final example, Figure 11.14 illustrates a simple sequence of

---

7.   ISO standards internationally leave out implementation details. This is so orthogonal to the way Internet Requests for Comments are written that one astonished Internetter suggested, "The sum of what falls under 'local implementation matter' in ISO standards could fill an ocean."

Octet No.	SPDUs in TSDU	Meaning/Significance
1	SI = 1	Give tokens SPDU identifier
2	LI = 3	Total length of give tokens parameters
3	PI = 16	Token item parameter identifier
4	LI = 1	Length of token item
5	<Value>	Indicates which tokens are being given by sending SS user
6	SI = 1	Data-transfer (DT) SPDU identifier
7	LI = 255	Indicates that next 2 octets contain "the real LI"
8, 9	LI = 2,001	Length of the DT SPDU
10	PI = 25	Enclosure item parameter identifier
11	<Value octet 1>	Indicates that this is the beginning/middle/end of SPDU
12–2,011	<Value octets 2–2,001>,	User information

FIGURE 11.12   Encapsulation of SPDUs—Simplest Form

session primitives and packets for a session connection in which the activity management, major synchronization, and minor synchronization functional units are used in a half-duplex mode of operation; expedited data transfer is not available, and the exception services were selected but not required. In the example, the requester is assigned all the tokens—major/activity, synchronize-minor, release, data—at connection-establishment time. Also, for illustrative purposes, both confirmed and unconfirmed minor synchronization are shown.

In this example, an activity composed of two dialogue units was transferred from the requester to the accepter. Although quite simple, the exchange represents the way the session service might be used by the OSI Message Handling System to transfer a single mailgram from one mail server to another.

AHA *Rose (1990) calls attention to many of the flaws and weaknesses of the session protocol. His criticism is scathing and complete, and there is little need here to beat a dead horse. To Marshall's credit, however, he didn't just sit on his hands and poke fun; he put together a complete implementation of the session layer in the ISODE, which is probably the most widely used upper-layers implementation in deployment today. Some OSI folks view Marshall as an enemy of the state; considering how much the availability of the ISODE has contributed to OSI deployment today, they might consider looking past the bluster and hype and appreciate all the good his OSI implementation has done.*

Final word on the session protocol: it's ugly, but then, so are the UNIX awk *command, the Report Program Generator Language (RPG), and dozens of*

| Give tokens SPDU | Activity-start SPDU | Major synch SPDU | |
| Give tokens SPDU | Activity-start SPDU | Minor synch SPDU | Data-tranfer SPDU |

FIGURE 11.13   Example of SPDUs Concatenated in TSDUs

other technologies. The only thing that matters is whether it helps people do useful work . . .

Putting It All Together

When OSI is presented in a "layer-by-layer" manner, one is inclined to conclude that there are lots of connections, perhaps altogether too many! This perception can be partially attributed to the rigid, formal manner in which layers are defined: after all, seven separate layers must have seven separate connections, right? Well, not necessarily so.

The risk of examining OSI one layer at a time is that interdependencies between layers are often obscured. When a "bottom-up" approach to understanding and interpreting OSI is applied as well—from the physical layer to the application layer—the problem is exacerbated. A bottom-up approach begins by showing how the physical layer schlepps electrons across physical connections and enables carriage of data-link bits through materials like copper and glass, and proceeds to explain how data-link connections recover the unfortunate bits that get smashed along the way. This is followed by explanations of how datagrams are forwarded (temporary respite) or how network connections are set up between computers. Then, a transport connection is established for reliability. Next, a session connection. . . . Soon, you are gently lulled into a rhythm of "another layer, another connection."

Above the Internet layer in TCP/IP, there are only two connections and, with them, two associated "state machines": an "application" connection and an end-to-end connection (transport). An Internet mail application (RFC 822/SMTP mail; see Chapter 8)—the UNIX sendmail command, for example—establishes "mail" connections to other mail applications to forward, deliver, and receive preformatted mail messages. In a UNIX environment, sendmail resides in user space; it operates over TCP connections accessed via the UNIX socket().

In OSI, the same two connections exist: an MHS-based mail application establishes an association for messaging and runs this over a transport connection. Although the situation is somewhat obscured by

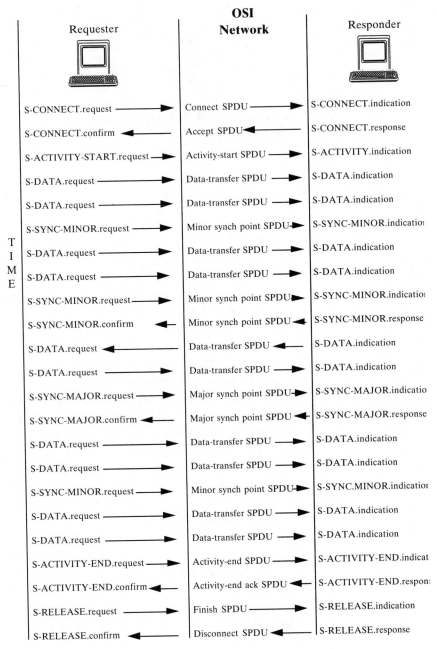

FIGURE 11.14   Sample "Session"

the formal "layer at a time" presentation, close examination of the interaction among the application, presentation, and session service elements

reveals that a single connection state rather than three exists for each end-user application. Association control and presentation connection protocol control information should be piggybacked on session connect and accept packets, effectively creating a pseudoheader for upper layer association management (see Figure 11.15); one software process rather than several can then be invoked to establish or accept an association. (Note: A software process is represented graphically in Figure 11.15 by a round-edged rectangle, itself containing subprocesses or routines similarly represented.) In a UNIX environment, the entire OSI upper layers can be placed in user space, and end-to-end transport can again be accessed via the socket().

In the figure, the fictitious command "Connect (x, y, z)" is used to establish an association between this mail application and another. Once the association is established, control is returned to the application software, which proceeds to send or receive data through some software process responsible for managing data transfer; here, the fictitious operators "Send()" and "Recv()" are invoked to exchange messages. (Note that the association management software process will "sleep" until it is called upon to terminate the association or handle errors.)

Under the direction of the data transfer manager, a mail message is transferred as an activity within the association. Session layer "jimmies"[8] like major and minor synchronization may be used by the mail application if the message is large and recovery from temporary loss of the presentation connection with minimal retransmission is desirable. Semantically, the state of the application service elements is tightly coupled to the session connection when services such as these are invoked (you know the drill: reliable transfer service says, "Do that funky synch thing" to presentation, which echoes it to session, while MHS waits patiently for a confirmation before proceeding to the next activity); syntactically, this merely introduces additional bits in the information streamed across the single end-user connection.

The ISODE (Kille and Robbins 1991) is an example of how one might implement the OSI upper layers as a set of C libraries consisting of the "core ASEs," presentation, and session that are loaded with end-user application programs such as the OSI Directory, Message Handling System, and FTAM, which can then be run over TCP or any equivalently featured end-to-end transport using a transport convergence protocol

---

8.   Jimmies are ant-shaped bits of candy sprinkled over ice cream—i.e., add-ons to an already tasty treat. Here, the term is used to indicate that extra degrees of control can be exercised over information exchange by invoking session services.

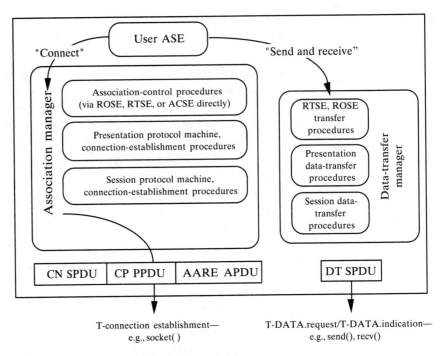

FIGURE 11.15   Association Management

such as RFC 1006. (In the Wisconsin ARGO 1.0 and 4.3 BSD RENO UNIX kernels, an end-to-end OSI transport connection is accessed via sockets as well, using extensions to this interprocess communication mechanism that accommodate a "sequenced-packet delivery"; see Chapter 12).

The Future of OSI Upper Layers

Since 1983, experts have claimed that (1) the organization of the OSI upper layers as described in the OSI reference model is a mess, and (2) the subsequent reconsideration of the application layer architecture (described in Chapter 6) yielded a structure that was more promising. Recently, ISO has extended the application layer structure to allow a single control function (CF) to supervise a set of application service elements, and a revision of the entire upper layer architecture is under consideration, which will essentially allow implementations to slice the upper layers "vertically" and may ultimately collapse the upper layers into a single, object-oriented "service layer" (Day 1992).

The *extended application layer structure* (XALS) and revised OSI upper layer architecture under study in ISO define *application service objects* (ASOs) that will contain multiple application service elements, some of these formed by grouping session functional units into application service elements and eliminating the session layer entirely. The existing presentation layer functionality will be subsumed within a new association control service element, which will offer an A-DATA service, and the presentation layer will be removed from the OSI reference model as well. The extended A^{2}CSE (ASO association control service element) will then be bolted directly on top of the transport layer.

These changes affect a number of OSI standards, including the reference model, and they won't happen overnight. The current wisdom/optimism is that these moves will resolve some of the frequently criticized upper layer implementation difficulties. OSI upper layer implementations are criticized for having considerable overhead. The ISODE 7.0 implementation, for example, binds the entire session service library to each application process at run time; a possible result of rearchitecting the upper layer structure might be that future OSI-based programs/processes would be smaller, since the new ASOs would have only a subset of session functional units (basic synchronization and basic combined subsets rise from the ashes!).

·AHA· *There is, of course, a downside to these proposals; namely, the tremendous impact they would have on the few daring vendors that have ventured forth into OSI upper layers product deployment. Since, for reasons of efficiency already noted, OSI upper layer implementations tend to be closely coupled with the application service element, reorganization and reimplementation will be painful. Also, eliminating a layer of protocol header will wreak havoc on interoperability—the original and continuing goal of OSI, remember?—and require an extensive migration and coexistence plan. The moral? Prototype and measure, until a truly worthwhile "skinny-stack" approach emerges that supports a business case for transition from existing OSI upper layers to the new world.*

Conclusion

This chapter concludes the discussion of the OSI upper layers. Having first examined application services at a conceptual and "features" level in Chapters 7, 8, and 9 (introducing directories, e-mail, and network management), the authors then discussed the service elements on which distributed applications rely to provide such end services—in particular, application connection establishment, remote operations, and reliable transfer. This chapter has demonstrated how certain functions that application service elements provide to user elements or "specific" application service elements—the checkpointing, turn management, and activity management services that constitute reliable transfer—are performed at the session layer and how these are accessed via "pass-through" services provided by the presentation layer. Having completed a layer-by-layer description of the OSI upper layers, the authors "put it all together" and discussed how the existence of seven layers is not a mandate for (at least) seven connections—the interdependencies between the OSI upper layers may be exploited in prudent implementations, and everything in OSI "from session and above" can be implemented as a single connection. The chapter concludes with some insights into how implementation experience and hindsight may contribute to future refinements in the OSI upper layer structure.

PART FOUR

MIDDLE LAYERS

12

THE TRANSPORT LAYER

The transport layer is the basic end-to-end building block of host networking. Everything above the transport layer is distributed-application–oriented; everything below the transport layer is transmission-network–oriented. In the work on OSI, the upper layers have tended to be the province of people with a computer systems (particularly operating systems) background; the lower layers, of people with an electrical engineering (particularly transmission systems) background. The imperfect alignment of the very different perspectives of the "computer people" and the "telecommunications people" has led to the definition of five different classes of transport protocol in OSI, each one tailored to a particular vision of the way in which hosts are properly interconnected by networks. The work on TCP/IP, on the other hand, was carried out by a relatively small group of people who managed to avoid being identified as "upper layer" or "lower layer" until long after the fact. This group agreed on a single model for network interconnection and defined a single transport protocol (TCP).

The OSI reference model explains the purpose of the transport layer in the following terms:

> "To provide transparent transfer of data between session entities and relieve them from any concern with the detailed way in which reliable and cost effective transfer of data is achieved."
> "To optimize the use of available network service to provide the performance required by each session entity at minimum cost."
> "To provide transmission of an independent, self-contained transport-service-data-unit from one transport-service-access-point to another in a single service access." (ISO/IEC 7498: 1984)

In plain-speak, this means that the OSI transport layer provides a reliable data pipe for the upper layers as part of a connection-oriented service, and simple datagram delivery as part of a connectionless service. In the TCP/IP protocol suite, the reliable connection-oriented service is provided by the transmission control protocol [TCP] and the simple datagram service by the user datagram protocol UDP. During connection-oriented operation, the data stream submitted to the transport layer by transport user A must be delivered to transport user B without loss. There may be no duplication of any of the octets in the data stream, and the octets must be delivered in the same order as that in which they were submitted (end-to-end sequence control). The transport layer must also provide end-to-end error detection and recovery: the detection of (and recovery from) errors introduced into the data stream by the network (data corruption).

In both connection-oriented and connectionless modes, the transport layer must also do what it can to optimize the use of the network's resources, given quality of service objectives specified by the transport users. For example, if a local session entity requests a transport connection to a remote host, and the transport layer recognizes that a network connection already exists to that host, *and* the quality of service objectives for both the existing and newly requested transport connections can be satisfied, the local transport entity can decide to multiplex both transport connections onto a single network connection.

Some applications transfer large amounts of data and don't want any of those data lost; they want reliable transport connections. For some applications, however, loss of individual data elements is either irrelevant or annoying but not disruptive; and some applications prefer to provide reliability themselves. For these applications, the reliability provided by transport connections is redundant, and the connectionless transport service is the better choice. The first part of this chapter describes the connection-oriented transport services and protocols of OSI and TCP/IP in detail; their connectionless counterparts are described much more briefly (since they are much simpler) at the end of the chapter.

OSI's Connection-oriented Transport Service

The OSI transport service definition (ISO/IEC 8072: 1993) identifies the functions associated with the connection-oriented transport service (COTS), the transport service primitives and parameters used to define the service, and the parameters used to define transport quality of service.

The following *end-to-end* functions are elements of the connection-oriented transport service:

- *Multiplexing* of transport connections onto network connections (and demultiplexing of them at the destination).
- *Sequence control* to preserve the order of transport service data units submitted to the transport layer.
- *Segmenting* transport service data units into multiple transport protocol data units (and reassembling of the original transport service data units at the destination).
- *Blocking* multiple transport service data units into a single transport protocol data unit (and unblocking it into the original transport service data units at the destination).
- *Concatenating* multiple transport protocol data units into a single network service data unit (NSDU) (and separating it into the individual transport protocol data units at the destination).
- *Error detection* to ensure that any difference between the data submitted to the transport layer at the source and the data that arrive at the destination is detected.
- *Error recovery* to take appropriate action when errors are discovered by the "error-detection" function.
- *Flow control* to regulate the amount and pacing of data transferred between transport entities and between the adjacent session and transport layers.
- *Expedited data transfer* to permit certain transport service user data to bypass normal data flow control. (Similar to "urgent data" in TCP which is examined later in this chapter).

The primitives and parameters of the connection-oriented transport service are depicted in Table 12.1.

TCP/IP's Reliable Stream Service

TCP provides a reliable connection-oriented transport service. RFC 793 describes TCP as providing "robustness in spite of unreliable communications media" and "data transfer that is reliable, ordered, full-duplex, and flow controlled." The end-to-end functions of TCP include:

- *Multiplexing* of multiple pairs of processes within upper-layer protocols.
- *Sequence control* to preserve the order of octets submitted to TCP.
- *Flow control* to regulate the flow of data across the transport connection.

TABLE 12.1   OSI Transport Service Primitives and Parameters

Primitives		Parameters
T-CONNECT	request indication	Called address, calling address, expedited data option, quality of service, TS user data
T-CONNECT	response confirmation	Responding address, expedited data option, quality of service, TS user data
T-DATA	request indication	TS user data
T-EXPEDITED-DATA	request indication	TS user data
T-DISCONNECT	request indication	TS user data TS user data, disconnect reason

- *Push,* whereby a sending upper-layer protocol process can force both sending and receiving TCP processes to deliver data to the receiving upper-layer protocol process.
- *Urgent data,* an interrupt data service whereby a sending upper-layer protocol process may request that data marked "urgent" be processed quickly by the receiving upper-layer protocol process.

RFC 793 serves as both protocol specification and service definition, specifying the interaction between upper-layer protocol (ULP) processes and TCP (Tables 12.2 and 12.3), the format of the transport protocol, and its operation.

Interfaces to Transport Services

The formal interaction that takes place between a service user and the service provider for connection establishment, data transfer, expedited data transfer, and connection release is the same for the transport layer as it is for the upper layers which have already been discussed. It is perhaps more interesting to consider how an interface to the transport service might be implemented in a representative UNIX implementation, such as Wisconsin ARGO[1] 1.0 (*Wisconsin ARGO 1.0 Kernel Programmer's Guide for Operating Systems 4.3*), and 4.3 RENO UNIX (*RENO 4.3 UNIX Operating System*).

Socket Interface for OSI Transport Service

In ARGO 1.0 UNIX, the OSI upper layers are implemented in user space—that portion of the UNIX operating system available for application programming—making the application service elements accessible to application developers through library/procedure calls rather than system calls. OSI's transport layer is implemented in the UNIX kernel along with most of OSI's network layer; some network-layer functions, and the data link and physical-layer components appropriate for the transmission technologies supported (e.g., a LAN or serial interface), reside in network interfaces (see Figure 12.1).

The transport service is implemented as an extension to the UNIX interprocess communication that supports TCP and UDP. Like TCP and UDP, OSI transports are accessed via *sockets* (type *sock-seqpacket*). The

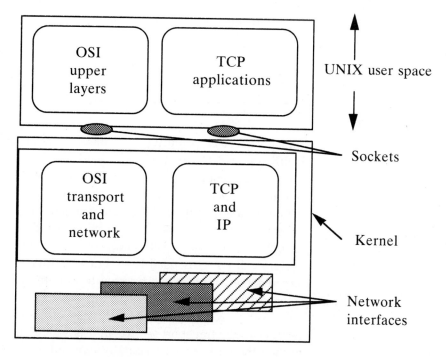

FIGURE 12.1   ARGO 1.0

---

1.   *ARGO* stands for "A Really Good OSI" implementation.

TABLE 12.2   TCP service primitives (from ULP to TCP)

Request Primitives	Parameters
Unspecified Passive Open	source port, ULP_timeout, ULP_timeout_action, precedence, security_range—actually, if IP, any IP option supported
Fully Specified Passive Open	source port, destination port, destination (IP) address, ULP_timeout, ULP_timeout_action, precedence, security_range
Active Open	source port, destination port, destination (IP) address, ULP_timeout, ULP_timeout_action, precedence, security_range
Active Open with data	source port, destination port, destination (IP) address, ULP_timeout, ULP_timeout_action precedence, security_range, data, data length, PUSH flag, URGENT flag
Send	local connection name, data, data length , PUSH flag, URGENT flag, ULP_timeout, ULP_timeout_action
Allocate	local connection name, data length
Close	local connection name—graceful
Abort	local connection name—disruptive
Status	local connection name

transport service primitives and parameters are mapped onto a set of UNIX system calls (see Table 12.4).

Greatly abbreviated, the process of establishing a transport connection in ARGO 1.0 is as follows. The UNIX system call *socket()* creates a communication endpoint. The parameters of the *socket()* system call used to establish an OSI transport connection include the address format (AF-ISO), type (sock-seqpacket), and protocol identifier (ISO TP). The UNIX system call *bind()* is used to assign an address to a socket. This now addressable endpoint can be used to initiate or listen for an incoming transport connection.

A transport user—a session entity or an application that runs directly over the transport service, in user space—initiates a transport connection by issuing the *connect()* system call to another transport user. If the called transport user is also located on a UNIX machine running ARGO 1.0, it must have already issued a *socket()* system call (to create its own communication endpoint) and *bind()* to assign an address to the

TABLE 12.3   TCP Service Primitives (from TCP to ULP)

Request Primitives	Parameters
Open Id	local connection name, source port, destination port, destination (IP) address
Open failure	local connection name
Open success	local connection name—completion of one of the open requests
Deliver	local connection name, data, data length, URGENT flag—data have arrived across the named connection
Closing	local connection name—remote ULP issued close, TCP has delivered all outstanding data
Terminate	local connection name—indication of remote reset, service failure, or connection closing by local ULP
Status response	local connection name, source port, source (IP) address, destination port, destination (IP) address, connection state, amount of data local TCP willing to accept, amount of data allowed to send, amount of data waiting acknowledgment, amount of data pending receipt by local ULP, urgent state, precedence, security, ULP_timeout
Error	local connection name, error description—indication that

TABLE 12.4   Mapping of Transport Service Primitives to UNIX System Calls

TS Primitives		UNIX System Calls
T-CONNECT	request	socket(), bind(), connect(), setsockopt()
	indication	Return from accept(), getsockopt(), following socket(), bind(), listen()
	response	(No applicable system calls)
	confirmation	Return from connect()
T-DATA	request	recv(), sendv(), (new calls)
	indication	Return from recv(), sendv(), select()
T-EXPEDITED-DATA	request	sendv() with MSG_OOB flag set
	indication	SIGURG, getsockopt() with TPFLAG-XPD, return from select()
T-DISCONNECT	request	close(), setsockopt()
	indication	SIGURG, error return, getsockopt()

socket. The transport service user on the called machine must have also initiated a *listen()* system call to passively await an incoming transport connection request. When a request arrives, the called transport user uses the *accept()* system call to accept or reject the request. The time-sequence diagram in Figure 12.2 illustrates the flow of UNIX calls and the transport connection-establishment primitives implied by the calls. (It is safe to assume that the relevant parameters of the transport service primitives are conveyed in the UNIX system calls. Both ARGO 1.0 and RENO 4.3 UNIX use new system calls—*sendv()* and *recvv()*—for data transfer (these correspond to the T-DATA.request and T-DATA.indication, re-spectively). These are scatter-gather or "vectored data" system calls: an array of pointers and lengths describe areas from (or to) which data will be gathered (or scattered). An indication of the end of a transport service data unit is provided using the flags parameter, which allows processing of a

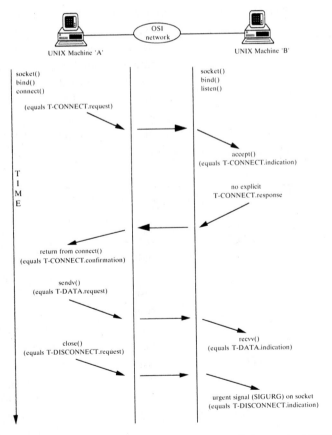

FIGURE 12.2   Transport Connection Establishment in ARGO 1.0

transport service data unit to span multiple system calls. A sending user process distinguishes transport expedited data from normal data by setting the MSG_OOB flag in the *sendv()* call; the receiver is notified of the arrival of expedited data via a UNIX signal mechanism (SIGURG, interpreted as an "urgent condition on the socket"). User processes initiate transport connection release using the *close()* system call. An application process is notified of a peer transport user (or transport provider) initiated release via an urgent condition on the socket (or via an error return on other primitives), whereupon the socket is closed.

The X/OPEN Transport Interface

Like sockets, the X/OPEN Transport Interface (XTI) offers a programmatic interface to OSI transport protocols. Specifically, the X/OPEN Transport Interface allows transport users (user processes) to request transport classes 0, 2, and 4 over network connections and transport class 4 over network datagrams. The X/OPEN Transport Interface supports transport protocol class selection, expedited data, quality of service, orderly release, and variable-length transport addresses and supports both *synchronous* and *asynchronous* communication. With *synchronous* communication, the calling transport user attempts to connect and waits for an accept; similarly, a called transport user will wait and listen for an incoming transport connection (passive). With *asynchronous* communication, the calling transport user attempts to connect and goes off to do other things until notified that the transport connection has been accepted (active); a transport user awaiting an incoming transport connection may listen as a background activity and attend to other operations.

Synchronous communication is the default mode of communication for the *t_connect()* system call. The transport connection-establishment process is similar to the UNIX socket interface: a transport user creates a transport endpoint using the *t_open()* system call, then binds a transport address to the endpoint using the *t_bind()* system call. An active open is invoked via the *t_connect()* system call, followed by a call to *poll()* with time-out value to await confirmation. A passive open is invoked via the *t_listen()* system call. All active processes must create a listening endpoint; a separate responding endpoint is created for each transport connection. A listening transport user accepts an incoming transport connection by invoking the *t_accept()* system call; to reject an incoming transport connection, a listening transport user returns a *t_snddis()* system call rather than the *t_accept()*.

If the transport connection is accepted, the transport users exchange data using the *t_snd()* and *t_rcv()* system calls. In the synchronous mode, a sending transport user waits if flow is constrained; in the asynchronous mode, explicit flow restrictions are signaled via [TFLOW] errors, a flow-control constraint error signaled in the *t_snd()* call return. If expedited data are to be sent, a flag (T-EXPEDITED) is set in the *t_snd()* call request. The *t_rcv()* system calls are used to receive partial or complete TSDUs; if a partial TSDU is received, a flag (T-MORE) is set, reflecting the arrival of an *end of TSDU* indication in the transport protocol. If expedited data are to be received, a flag (T-EXPEDITED) is set among the *t_rcv()* system call parameters.

The transport connection is released upon completion of a *t_snddis()* and *t_rcvdis()* system call sequence. Figure 12.3 illustrates the entire sequence of events associated with a transport connection in which a single transfer of data is performed.

For asynchronous communication, transport users create endpoints but set the O_NONBLOCK flag in the *t_open()* system call. Again, both the calling and called transport users bind a transport address to the endpoint using the *t_bind()* system call. The calling user process (transport user) invokes the *t_connect()* system call, which returns immediately. The calling process may perform other operations while the transport connection-establishment process proceeds.

The listening or passive user process calls:

- *poll()* with a time-out value to await an incoming event

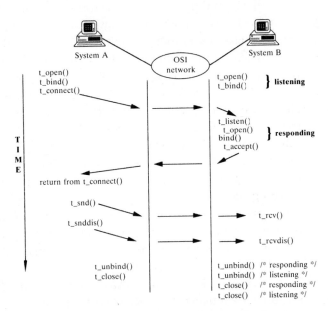

FIGURE 12.3   XTI: Synchronous Communication

- *t_look()* to obtain details about incoming events (in this case, an incoming transport connect request indication)
- *t_listen()* to obtain the information that describes the incoming transport connection request
- *t_accept()* to notify the calling transport user that the connection will be accepted

The calling transport user, periodically calling *poll()*, learns of an incoming event, then calls *t_look()* to check whether the event is a confirmation of the transport connection request it has made. The calling transport user determines the results of transport connection negotiation (described later in this chapter) from the information returned in the *t_rcvconnect()* system call.

The only "twist" on sending and receiving data in asynchronous mode is that user processes must *poll()* for incoming events, then *t_look()* to determine that a particular event is incoming data prior to performing the *t_rcv()* system call. The same twist applies for connection release: a "release event" is returned through *t_look()*. Figure 12.4 illustrates the entire sequence of events associated with asynchronous communication.

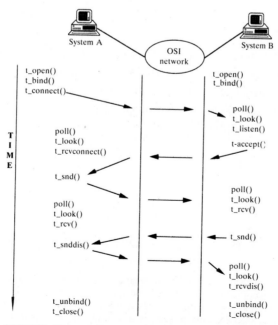

FIGURE 12.4   XTI: Asynchronous Communication

Transport Addressing

In the set of UNIX system calls used to establish interprocess communication between TCP/IP applicatons, a set of *Internet port numbers* is used to differentiate users of the stream and datagram services provided by the transport layers. There are, for example, well-known or "assigned" numbers for the Internet standard applications servers (e.g., FTP, SMTP, SNMP, TELNET). For OSI-based interprocess communication in UNIX, ARGO 1.0 uses a separate address space, *transport service access point identifiers*,[2] to name the interface between the transport service users and the transport entities in the kernel. Like ports, transport service access point identifiers are a particularly important set of names, since they are often visible to program interfaces such as the UNIX socket.

The parameters of the *socket()* system call used to establish an OSI transport connection include the address family/format (AF-ISO), type (sock-seqpacket), and protocol identifier (ISO TP). The transport service access point identifier assigned to a socket using the *bind()* system call usually takes the following form:

```
struct sockaddr_iso {
  short siso_family;           /* address family is iso */
  u_short  siso_tsuffix;       /* the TSAP identifier  */
  struct iso_addr  siso_addr;  /* the NSAP address */
  char siso_zero[2];           /* unused */
}
```

The transport service access point address is represented as the concatenation of the network service access point address and a transport selector. The C programming-language data structure and the data structure used to assign an Internet port/address when establishing a socket (type stream) are very similar; e.g.:

```
struct sockaddr_in {
  short  sin_family;        /* address family is internet */
  u_short  sin_port;        /* the internet port */
  struct in_addr  sin_addr; /* the IP address, a.b.c.d */
  char  sin_zero[8];        /* unused */
}
```

In TCP/IP, ports identify upper-level protocol entities or processes,

---

2.   The full address of a transport service access point consists of a network service access point address and a transport service access point identifier. The term "transport service access point address" refers to this full address; where only the identifier part (sometimes called a "transport selector") is meant, the term "transport service access point identifier" or simply "transport identifier" will be used.

and pairs of endpoints identify TCP connections. Specifically, the pair {IP address, port number} roughly corresponds to the OSI transport service access point address, which is the pair {network service access point address, transport selector}, and two of these {IP address, port number} pairs uniquely identify a TCP connection. Internet port number assignment follows a *client/server* paradigm. A server process binds to a well-known port number and listens at {server-IP-address, well known-tcp-port} for connection requests from any source; i.e., from {any-IP-address, any-port}. A client process binds to {client-tcp-port, client-IP-address}, where client-tcp-port is dynamically allocated from unused ports on the client's system. When a client process initially connects to a server process, the endpoints of the transport connection are {client-IP-address, client-tcp-port} and {server-IP-address, well known-tcp-port}, but when the server accepts an incoming request, it creates a second socket and binds the incoming call to this new socket; the resulting endpoints of the transport connection are {client-IP-address, client-tcp-port} and {server-IP-address, server-tcp-port}. Once the server process has mapped the transport connection onto this new pair of endpoints, it continues to listen at {server-IP-address, server-tcp-port} for requests from any source; i.e., from {any-IP-address, any-port}.

A Comparison of Internet Ports and OSI TSAPAs

Internet port numbers are always 16 bits. OSI allows for variable-length transport service access point identifiers, up to a maximum length of 64 octets. ARGO 1.0 accommodates the assignment of extended transport identifiers through the use of the *getsockopt()* or *setsockopt()* system calls following the call to *bind()*. Another difference between OSI transport service access point identifiers and Internet port numbers is that, generally speaking, a set of Internet port numbers are globally and uniquely assigned to represent a well-known application; transport service access point identifiers are frequently derived from the presentation address attribute of an application entity title (see Chapters 5, 7, and 11).

Five Classes of OSI Transport Protocol

The *Connection Oriented Transport Protocol Specification* (ISO/IEC 8073: 1986) defines five classes of procedures for the connection-oriented OSI transport protocol. The transmission control protocol (TCP), on the other hand, has no concept of "class"; it simply defines one standard way in which to provide a connection-oriented transport service.

The answer to the question "why five classes of transport protocol in OSI?" lies not in the transport layer but in the network layer. If one's model of the world has end-user equipment (hosts) attached to specific individual networks, then one is likely to design a separate transport protocol for each individual network, optimized for the particular characteristics of that network. If one's model of the world has end-user equipment attached to a global internet, consisting of an arbitrary number of interconnected individual networks, then one is likely to design a single transport protocol that provides an end-to-end service with respect to the internet as a whole and makes few (if any) assumptions about the characteristics of individual networks (which, as part of the internet, are not individually visible to the transport protocol). Each of the OSI transport protocol classes 0 through 3 is intended to be used with a particular type of connection-oriented network, according to the probability of signaled and unsignaled errors on that network. Class 4, like TCP, is intended to be used in internets and is not defined with respect to any particular network type.

Class 0: The Simple Class

Class 0 is designed to have "minimum functionality." It provides only the functions necessary to establish a transport connection, transfer data (well, it can segment transport service data units), and report protocol errors. Class 0 relies on the underlying network connection to provide all of the end-to-end capabilities of the transport layer, including sequencing, flow control, and error detection. It was designed with the expectation that the underlying network connection would provide a virtually error-free data-transfer service; for example, in those subnetworks in which a protocol such as CCITT X.25-1984 is used. Class 0 does not provide multiplexing capabilities, and it is so resolutely simple that it does not even have its own disconnection procedures: when the underlying network connection goes away, transport class 0 goes with it.

| ·AHA· | *Class 0 adds no value whatsoever to the underlying network service, which is just the way some network service providers like it. ("Our network service is absolutely splendid. How could you end users possibly imagine that any further work is necessary on your part to obtain a reliable end-to-end connection?") Class 0 is equivalent to the transport protocol defined for the CCITT Teletex service; it persists because it has been written into the CCITT X.400-series recommendations for message handling systems as the required protocol class for connection to public network messaging systems.[3]* |

---

3.   The CCITT X-series recommendations differ from ISO standards in that each service definition identifies *precisely* the protocol that must be used to provide the service; e.g., the

Class 0 does have one redeeming feature: it is used to create an OSI transport service on TCP/IP networks, enabling OSI applications to run over TP/IP. RFC 1006, *ISO Transport Services on Top of the TCP*, specifies a widely used convention for operating OSI applications over TCP/IP networks. TCP, complemented by a simple 4-octet packetization protocol, provides the essence of the connection-oriented OSI network service across TCP/IP networks (in fact, it does so better than the OSI connection-oriented network protocol, X.25), and OSI transport protocol class 0 provides two service features—the transfer of transport addresses and transport service data unit delimiting—to complete the OSI transport service.

Class 1: The Basic Error Recovery Class

Transport class 1 is a small improvement over class 0, providing error recovery following a failure signaled by the network service, expedited data, and an explicit transport connection release (distinct from network connection release). Class 1 could almost be called "the apologist's transport protocol." It recognizes that no connection-oriented network in the real world is truly perfect. Where class 0 says, "Trust me, the network will never do anything bad," class 1 says, "The network will never do anything bad without telling me about it, and if it does, I'll take care of it."

Several error recovery procedures are included in class 1:

- *Retention until acknowledgment:* Following a signaled failure, copies of outstanding transport protocol data units are retained until receipt of an indication that the remote transport entity is alive, at which time resynchronization procedures are invoked.
- *Reassignment after failure:* If the underlying network connection signals a Disconnect, class 1 can map the existing transport connection onto a new network connection.
- *Resynchronization:* Following a recoverable failure signaled by the network connection (e.g., a reset; see Chapter 13) or a reassignment after failure, both transport entities retransmit unacknowledged transport protocol data units and resynchronize the data stream.

Class 1 can recover only from errors explicitly signaled by the network service provider. Errors not detected and reported by the network service provider will also go undetected by the transport protocol.

CCITT Recommendation T.70 for teletex terminals *must* be used to provide the OSI transport service when connecting to a public MHS. ISO service-definition standards describe only the features of a service, implying that a number of protocols might be used to provide that service.

Class 2: The Multiplexing Class

The experts who introduced class 0 were quite pleased about having identified a minimally functional, low-overhead transport protocol until they realized that they had failed to consider one very important aspect of subscriber access to an X.25 public data network: for economy, subscribers often multiplex data streams from more than one piece of data terminal equipment over a single network connection provided by an X.25 network to maximize use of the throughput available over that network connection. The most obvious way to correct this oversight would have been to extend the functionality of class 0. Class 0 "protectionists," while acknowledging that multiplexing was useful, argued for stability and consistency between the ISO transport protocol standard and CCITT Recommendation T.70, the transport protocol for teletex terminals. (It should also be noted that the folks who work for carrier networks were not as keenly interested in multiplexing as were end users.) Thus was born Class 2.

The following functions are present in class 2:

- *Reference numbers* enable two communicating transport entities to distinguish the transport protocol data units associated with one transport connection from those associated with a different transport connection.
- *Explicit flow control*, when selected, allows the transport entities to regulate the amount and pacing of data transferred between them.
- *Expedited data transfer* permits the transmission of up to 16 octets of user data that are not subject to normal flow-control procedures.
- *Extended transport protocol data unit numbering*, when selected, allows transport entities to use a larger sequence number space (31-bit, rather than the normal 7-bit) for transport protocol data unit numbering and acknowledgments. This increases the number of transport protocol data units that a sender can transmit (the "send window") before it must wait for explicit acknowledgment of reception by the receiver. Normally, the use of a larger window increases throughput. Increasing the size of the sequence number space is also necessary to eliminate the possibility of sequence numbers "wrapping"; for example, if the sequence space were {1 . . . 10}, and a window of 15 were allowed, a sender could transmit packets in sequence {1 . . . 10, 1, 2, 3, 4, 5}. Receiving this sequence of packets, the receiver would be unable to determine whether the second transport protocol data unit received containing the sequence number 1 was a duplicate of a transport protocol data unit received earlier with sequence number 1 or a new transport protocol data unit with the same "wrapped" sequence number.

Curiously, class 2 adds only those functions necessary to support multiplexing; in particular, the error-detection capabilities of class 1 are missing from class 2.[4]

Class 3: The Error Recovery and Multiplexing Class

When the work on OSI transport-layer standards began in the late 1970s, most of the people involved approached the job with a particular type of network in mind—an X.25 packet-switching network, for example, or an X.21 circuit-switching network—each of which suggested different design criteria for a corresponding transport protocol. Lacking the inter-networking perspective of the people who designed TCP/IP, the ISO experts proceeded to deal with each of the available network services on a case-by-case basis, accommodating differences in reliability and features not by designing a single, highly resilient, and competent transport protocol but by *introducing one after another.*

So it came to pass that yet another group of experts studied the existing set of transport protocols and—feeling either remorse, concern, or both—decided that at least one transport protocol should combine all of the features of the existing transport protocols. Class 3 represents the union of the functions and capabilities of classes 0 through 2 and then some; the transport protocol standard describes class 3 as having ". . . the characteristics of Class 2 plus the ability to recover from network disconnect or reset." Specifically, transport protocol class 3 provides the multiplexing functions of class 2 plus the error recovery functions of class 1.

Class 4: The Error-Detection and Recovery Class

Implicit in the design of the first four OSI transport protocol classes is the assumption that any errors that might occur in the transfer of data across a network connection will be detected by the network service provider and signaled to the transport entities. Prior to the introduction of class 4, transport protocol design was based on a "network-centric" view of the world: like the dial tone in the telephone system, the OSI network service would in all configurations be provided by one or more common carriers, and service uniformity and homogeneity would be the rule rather than the exception. Further, compelling political and economic arguments existed that made perpetuating the notion that the bulk of end-to-end functionality could be provided at the network layer a standards imperative.

---

4.   Many implementers who are initially appalled by the fact that there are five distinct classes of transport protocol in OSI comfort themselves with the assumption that at least they will be able to implement them by incrementally adding functions to lower classes to create successively higher ones. They are truly aghast when they discover that this is not the case.

Technically speaking, the "network is everything" school of thought views the service provided from network entry to network exit as having *end-to-end* significance. In implementation and practice, however, the networking protocols and interworking among those protocols in fact provide only *edge-to-edge* significance. As will be seen in Chapter 13, the provision of network services, like all human endeavor, is fallible, and variability exists. This is particularly true when multiple providers and diverse technologies are involved in the process. Humans tolerate variability in the voice network because they intuitively apply error-detection and recovery mechanisms; computers lack intuition, so the protocols they use to transfer data must be designed to recognize a variety of failures and recover from them. Until the introduction of transport protocol class 4 (generally referred to as "TP4"), many of the necessary *reliability* functions were absent.

Several years prior to the OSI transport standardization effort, research in the United States questioned the premise that reliability could be assured by establishing uniformity across all networking services. Practical experience gained in the implementation and use of research networks such as the U.S. Department of Defense Advanced Research Projects Agency (DARPA) Internet Research Project (RFC 791), the Livermore Interactive Network Communication System (LINCS; Watson 1982), and the Ethernet-oriented architecture developed at the Xerox Palo Alto Research Center (Xerox Corporation 1981) demonstrated the benefits of incorporating *all* end-to-end reliability functions into a single protocol that operated in host computers (end systems) and relying on the network to perform only the functions essential to the forwarding and delivery of information from source to destination. Since the transport layer takes nothing for granted in this model, the variability of service quality among interconnected networks becomes a non-issue. An entirely different axiom was espoused: *"Sadly, it is a fact of networking life that bits get smashed, octets and packets arrive out of order, some arrive twice, and some do not arrive at all."* Host protocols must therefore be prepared to deal with these problems. From this "host-centric" school of thought, transport protocols such as TCP and OSI transport protocol class 4 emerged.

The OSI transport protocol standard describes class 4 as having ". . . the functionality of class 3 plus the ability to detect and recover from lost, duplicated, or out of sequence transport protocol data units." This is somewhat misleading, since the mechanisms to provide reliability in class 4 differ substantially from those in class 3. It is more accurate to say that transport protocol class 4 provides the multiplexing functions of class 2 and explicit flow control, plus error detection and error recovery based on the "positive acknowledgment and retransmission" paradigm of TCP. The functions of TP4 include those of class 2 plus:

- A *checksum* computed on the transport header and user data. A 16-bit arithmetic checksum based on Fletcher (1982) is computed to detect bit-level errors in the data stream.
- *Resequencing,* which enables a receiver to determine when transport protocol data units have arrived out of order and provides a means of correctly ordering the octet stream before passing it up to the transport service user.
- *Inactivity control,* which enables a transport connection to survive the (temporary) unsignaled loss of network layer connectivity.
- *Splitting* and *recombining,* which enable a transport connection to transfer data simultaneously over multiple network connections to increase throughput or provide resiliency from single network connection failure.
- *Detection* and *recovery* of *lost* and *duplicate transport protocol data units.*

TP4 is genetically closer to TCP, Xerox's RTP, and their proprietary networking relatives (e.g., the reliable transports in Digital Equipment Corporation's DECnet and Burroughs Network Architecture) than the "Tinkertoy" classes that do not provide an actual end-to-end transport service. Later in this chapter we will demonstrate just how similar TCP and TP4 are.

How Do You Choose the Right One?

Having five transport protocols to choose from is clearly a problem for both implementers and users. The way in which the OSI standard describes how to choose which of the transport protocols to use in a given configuration only adds to the confusion. So how do you choose one? The transport protocol standard recommends that a transport protocol class be chosen to support a given transport connection based on the *type of network connection* available at the time of connection establishment and the *quality of service* requested by the transport service user. Since no meaningful guidelines for the specification or interpretation of quality of service parameters have ever been produced for OSI, class selection relies almost entirely on the underlying network type. The standard identifies three types of network connection:

1. *Type A:* a network connection with an acceptable residual error rate and an acceptable rate of signaled errors.
2. *Type B:* a network connection with an acceptable residual error rate but an unacceptable rate of signaled errors.

3. *Type C:* a network connection with an unacceptable residual error rate.[5]

This, of course, begs the question of how the service quality of network connections can be known in advance. Good question, and also one left unanswered by the standard. Like Pilate, the transport protocol standard washes its hands of the responsibility, saying only that "It is assumed that each transport entity is aware of the quality of service provided by particular network connections . . . ." An immediate reaction by any right-thinking individual is that this is a joke. It is impossible to imagine how any individual host could know *a priori* the type and characteristics of all the network connections that might be available to connect to all the host machines in a small, private network, much less a global OSI network! The transport standard's assumption of this nature belies the notion of typing altogether, since it is meaningful only if service uniformity is assumed across every possible set of interconnected networks. (Such uniformity cannot be guaranteed even in the global voice network, which is far more homogenous than any conceivable global data network.)

| ·AHA· | *In fact, the typing of network connections was merely a convenient premise for the existence of multiple transport protocol* |

classes, which served a different purpose altogether. The political realities of the time demanded that each of several existing public network services be characterized within OSI as having at least the potential to be the cornerstone of the pervasive worldwide network, connecting all hosts everywhere. Each of these must, perforce, have its own specially optimized transport protocol. But since compromise and consensus are supposed to be the essence of standardization, it would hardly do to have several separate incompatible standards. The solution was to talk not about specific existing networks but about "types" of networks, with which different "classes" of a single protocol standard could be associated. Achieving this "compromise" made some of the standards developers very happy, while creating a legacy of confusion and incompatibility for OSI implementers and users. Thankfully, at least one of the five classes was based on the practical realization that all of these subnetworks—along with LANs, MANs, spaghetti-nets, and future-nets—would someday be interconnected.

---

5.   In the early stages of OSI transport protocol development, only the connection-oriented network service existed. The connectionless network service and a corresponding addendum to the transport protocol describing how to operate transport protocol class 4 were introduced later. For reasons unknown, networks that offered a connectionless service were considered to offer service functionally equivalent to type-C NCs.

The whole notion of typing network connections was myopic, ill-advised, and ultimately destructive. Ironically, by insisting on a menu of "tailor-made" transport protocols, the "network-centric" individuals who had compelling political and economic motivations to promote a uniform network service accomplished just the opposite, exposing how diverse even publicly provided network services were!

Conformance

What happens when you have more than one choice of protocol? In the case of OSI transport, every delegation, liaison body, even individuals within delegations championed a different protocol. It was popular, for example, but not mandatory, to champion the protocol that one's delegation introduced. The phrase "spirit of compromise" was at first eagerly embraced and subsequently worn extremely thin during the joint ISO/CCITT meetings at which the issue of determining the conformance clause for the OSI transport protocol was discussed.

Combinations were popular, especially if the combination included the protocol one championed. In fact, once combinations were recognized as instrumental in proceeding, the joint committees quickly agreed to eliminate two of the possible combinations (support none and support all). Eventually, it became clear that under no circumstances would the network-centric community agree to abandon support for TP0, and hell would freeze over before the host-centric community would consider anything other than TP4 sufficient for its purposes. The resultant conformance clause is a travesty, a *status quo ante openum*: To claim conformance to the standard, you must implement class 0 or class 2 or *both*. Further, if you implement class 1, you must implement class 0. If you implement class 3 or class 4, you must implement class 2. Confused? There's more. You can operate only class 4 over the connectionless network service.

⊡AHA⊡ *The solution? If you are implementing OSI transport for use with an internetworing protocol (such as CLNP), it's easy—class 4 is the only class that will work at all over a connectionless network service. To cover all possible cases, including those in which your system will operate directly over a connection-oriented network (such as an X.25 network) with no internetwork protocol, implement classes 0, 2, and 4. It's no big deal adding classes 0 and 2, since both are no-brainers. Notwithstanding what must have seemed like good arguments in their favor at the time, classes 1 and 3 have no modern constituency and can safely be ignored. If you are an end user, and you care about reliability, you should insist on class 4; tell your vendors "No discussion—just do it."*

Comparing TP4 to TCP

A 1985 study performed jointly by the U.S. Defense Communications Agency and the National Academy of Sciences (National Academy of Sciences Report 1985) concludes that TCP and TP4 are functionally equivalent and provide essentially similar services. Table 12.5 compares the functions provided by the two protocols.

Table 12.5   Comparison of TP4 and TCP Functions

Function	TCP	TP4
Data transfer	Streams	Blocks
Flow control	Octets	Segments
Error detection[6]	Checksum	Checksum
Error correction	Retransmission	Retransmission
Addressing	16-bit ports	Variable TSAPA
Interrupt service	Urgent data	Expedited data
Security	Not available	Variable in TP
Precedence	Not available	16 bits in TP
Connection termination	Graceful	Nongraceful

6.   The TCP and TP4 checksum functions are both intended to detect errors that may be introduced into the data stream between two transport users, but they do not operate in the same way. The TP4 checksum computation is carried out on the transport packet (header and user data) only, and it may be disabled (by explicitly selecting the "nonuse of checksum" option during connection establishment; the default is to use checksums). The TCP checksum is carried out on the combination of the transport packet (header and user data) and a prepended "pseudoheader" consisting of the source and destination IP addresses, the IP PROTO field, and the TCP segment length, and it may not be disabled. The TP4 checksum is also slightly more complicated (both to generate at the sender and to verify at the receiver) than the TCP checksum, although the additional complexity does not make TP4 significantly more resistant to undetected errors than TCP. An excellent discussion of how to efficiently implement the TP4 checksum is contained in Sklower (1989); a similar analysis for TCP may be found in RFC 1071, Clark (1989), and RFC 1141.

TP4 and TCP are not only functionally equivalent but operationally similar as well. This is best understood by examining the process of establishing a transport connection, providing reliable data transfer through the use of retransmission on time-out mechanisms, and connection termination of each protocol.

OSI Transport Connection Establishment

In the OSI reference model and the transport service definition, establishing a transport connection is described as a process of matching the transport service user's requested quality of service with available network services. One dubious aspect of this process is network service selection—connection-oriented or connectionless. In many end-system configurations, this decision process may not exist; for example, many LAN-based OSI systems will support only TP4 operating over a connectionless network service, and teletex-based systems that are only configured to access a public message-handling service via an X.25 public data network will support only TP0 over X.25. In configurations in which both a connection-oriented and a connectionless network service are available, the transport layer supposedly determines which type of network service to select on the basis of quality of service information submitted along with the T-CONNECT.request, information either stored in a user-defined configuration file or retrieved from a directory, or some set of operating system parameters.

During the exchange of transport protocol data units used for connection establishment, parameters that characterize the nature of the transport connection are negotiated by the two transport entities,[7] including:

- *TP class:* Since we have "choices," both transport entities must agree on the class of protocol to be used. (Successful negotiation of a transport connection implies that the two transport entities share at least one protocol that is sufficient to provide the transport service requested by the initiating application.) The calling transport entity selects a *preferred TP class* and may indicate *alternative TP classes* it is willing to use if the called transport entity does not support the preferred class.

---

7.   The current standards for OSI transport define only two-party connections. New work in ISO on multiparty transport connections had been under way for a year when this book went to press and is expected to result in amendments to the OSI transport protocol standard to support connections in which more than two transport entities participate as peers.

- *TSAP IDs:* Both the calling and called transport service access point identifiers are encoded in the *connect request* transport protocol data unit.

> ⟦·AHA·⟧ The transport protocol standard states that encoding of the transport service access point identifiers in the connect request transport protocol service access point is sufficient to specify the data unit is optional and may be omitted when "either network address unambiguously defines the transport address" (that is, the transport service access point adress can be specified by the network service access point alone, without the additional information provided by the transport service access point identifier). This is an unfortunate artifact of the incorporation of the T.70 teletex transport protocol into OSI; despite what the standard says, the identifiers are indeed necessary!

- *Options:* Options are defined for each transport protocol class. If class 1 is selected, both parties must agree to either use or not use receipt confirmation (see Chapter 13), and expedited data transfer provided by the network layer. If class 2 is selected, both parties must agree whether to use or not use explicit or implicit flow control. If classes 2, 3, or 4 are selected, both parties must agree to use normal or extended transport protocol data unit numbering and to use or not use transport expedited data. If class 4 is selected, both parties must agree on whether or not to perform a checksum on transport data packets and which checksum algorithm they will use.
- *Transport protocol data unit size:* The OSI transport protocol uses a fixed maximum packet size ranging (in powers of 2) from 128 octets to 8,192 octets,[8] including the header.
- *QOS parameters:* The calling transport entity may include values of quality of service parameters indicating the throughput, transit delay, and residual error rate expectations of the end-user application initiating the communication. In theory, these values assist the called transport entity in deciding whether a transport connection can be established that satisfies the end-user criteria for communication.

---

8.   An amendment to the OSI transport protocol that allows for the negotiation of much larger maximum packet sizes in much smaller increments was recently adopted by both ISO and CCITT. The new "preferred maximum TPDU size" parameter is encoded as a variable-length field of up to 32 bits that gives the maximum data packet size in units of 128 octets, allowing for the negotiation of any maximum data packet size from 128 octets to 2^{36} octets in increments of 128 octets.

Other parameters exchanged during transport connection establishment include the called and calling transport service access point identifiers, the value of the *initial credit* (how large a window the called transport entity will offer), and timer values germane to the operation of specific protocol classes. For example, if TP4 is selected as the preferred class, an *acknowledgment time* is exchanged by the called and calling transport entities. This timer value is used during data transfer as an approximation of the amount of time a transport entity will delay following reception of a data packet before sending an acknowledgment packet. For classes 1, 3, and 4 operating over a network connection, the value of *reassignment time* (how long before the called transport entity will attempt to reassign this transport connection to another network connection following a network connection failure) is exchanged.

To establish a transport connection, a transport entity composes a *connect request* packet (CR TPDU) and submits it to the network layer for delivery to the destination transport entity. The destination transport entity is identified by the network address indicated in the network service primitive that conveys the connect request packet (an N-CONNECT.request or N-UNITDATA.request; see Chapter 13). Figure 12.5 shows the composition of the CR TPDU.

Transport protocol classes 2, 3, and 4 provide the ability to multiplex many transport connections onto a single network connection. To distinguish one transport connection established between a given pair of transport entities from another, two 16-bit *references* fields are used. In

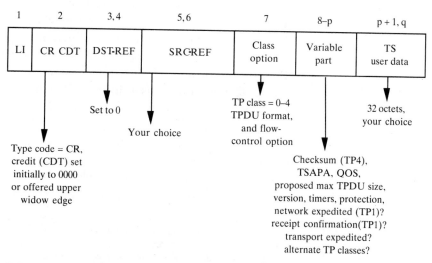

FIGURE 12.5   Connect Request Packet

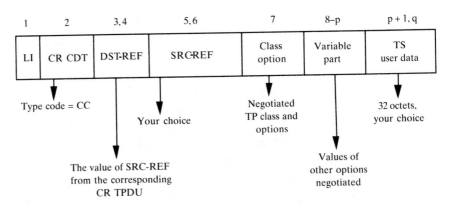

FIGURE 12.6   Connect Confirm Packet

the connection request package, the calling transport entity encodes a value for the *source reference* (SRC-REF in Figures 12.5 and 12.6) field; *a destination reference* (DST-REF in Figures 12.5 and 12.6) field is set to 0, to be determined by the called transport entity. The called transport entity encodes its own source reference in the source reference field of the *connect confirm packet* (CC TPDU) and places the value from the source reference field of the connect request packet into the destination reference field of the connect confirm packet. The pair of references uniquely identifies this transport connection between this pair of transport entities. The selection of the values for references is a *local matter.*[9] Typically (e.g., for simplicity), references are assigned sequentially.

Upon reception of a connect request packet, the called transport entity parses the packet and determines whether it can support the *preferred TP class* indicated; if it cannot, it determines whether it can support any of the *alternative TP classes* identified. If it cannot support any of the TP classes indicated, it must reject the connection (see "Connection Release (Connection Refusal) in the OSI transport protocol"). Table 12.6 illustrates the permissible combinations of preferred and alternative TP class parameter encodings.

The called transport entity next determines which options it can support among those selected by the calling transport entity. The rules governing the response to options selected are straightforward. If the calling transport entity proposes the use of an option—i.e., by setting the flag

---

9.   ISO/IEC 8073 defines a "local matter" as "a decision made by a system concerning its behaviour in the Transport Layer that is not subject to the requirements of this protocol." In plain-speak, use any value you please, so long as you can guarantee its uniqueness for the duration of time during which references are to be *frozen.*

Table 12.6   Combinations of Preferred/Alternative TP classes

Preferred class	Alternative class					
	0	*1*	*2*	*3*	*4*	*None*
0	Not valid	Not valid	Not valid	Not valid	Not valid	TP0
1	TP1 or TP0	TP1 or TP0	Not valid	Not valid	Not valid	TP1 or TP0
2	TP2 or TP0	Not valid	TP2	Not valid	Not valid	TP2
3	TP3, TP2, TP0	TP3, TP2, TP1, TP0	TP3 or TP2	TP3 or TP2	Not valid	TP3 or TP2
4	TP4, TP2, TP0	TP4, TP2, TP1, TP0	TP4 or TP2	TP4, TP3, TP2	TP4 or TP2	TP4 or TP2

representing the option to 1—the called transport entity may agree to use the option by leaving the flag set to 1, or it may refuse to use the option by setting the flag to 0. If the calling transport entity does not propose the use of an option, the called transport entity may not propose its use.

The called transport entity must also determine whether it can support the maximum packet size indicated or whether it must indicate that a *smaller* maximum packet size should be used, and whether it can maintain the QOS indicated.

Once these decisions are made, and assuming that a transport connection can be successfully negotiated, the called transport entity returns a connect confirm packet, indicating what choices it has selected from the negotiable parameters (see Figure 12.6).

The called transport entity also records values of parameters relevant to the operation of the transport protocol that may have been sent in the connect request transport protocol data unit; e.g., the values of either the *acknowledgment time* or the *reassignment time*, and the *initial credit*. These values are used during the data-transfer phase and for error recovery purposes.

Three-Way Handshake

The process of establishing a transport connection is only partially completed when the calling transport entity receives a connect confirm packet unit from a called transport entity; the calling transport entity has parsed the connect confirm packet, and it knows that the called transport entity is indeed willing to establish a transport connection. The calling transport entity also knows the characteristics that the called transport entity has *negotiated* for the transport connection (the called transport entity has indicated these in the connect confirm packet it has composed). Like the called transport entity, the calling transport entity will have recorded values of parameters relevant to the operation of the transport protocol that may have been sent in the connect confirm packet—the values of either the acknowledgment time or the reassignment time, and the initial credit.

At this point, however, the called transport entity hasn't a clue whether the negotiated characteristics for the transport connection are acceptable or even whether the connect confirm packet has been delivered to the calling transport entity. The calling transport entity thus has the additional responsibility in the transport connection-establishment process of providing the called transport entity with an indication of whether transport connection establishment succeeded or failed. Assuming that the transport connection has been successfully negotiated, the calling transport entity has two choices:

1. Return an *acknowledgment* packet (AK TPDU).
2. Start sending data.

The first mechanism is always available to the calling transport entity. Figure 12.7 shows the format of the acknowledgment packet.

Reception of an acknowledgment packet by the called transport entity following transmission of a connect confirm packet provides the called transport entity with an explicit acknowledgment that the calling transport entity accepted the transport connection with the negotiated characteristics. Confirmation that the transport connection is successfully negotiated in this manner is called a *three-way handshake*. Figure 12.8 provides a simplified illustration of this process.

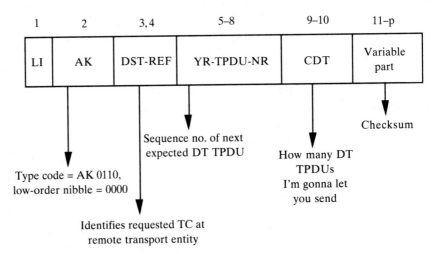

FIGURE 12.7   Acknowledgment Packet

Relevant information encoded in the acknowledgment packet includes:

- *Destination reference,* which contains the value of the calling transport entity's reference number.
- *Your transport protocol data unit number* (YR-TPDU-NR), which contains the value of the next expected sequence number (n), implicitly acknowledging the receipt of all transport protocol data packets up to and including sequence number $n-1$ (modulo 2^7 arithmetic if normal formats, modulo 2^{31} if extended formats). Sequence numbers are used in the data-transfer phase of a transport connection to distinguish packets containing normal data from one another and to assist in determining whether data packets have arrived in order or have been lost or duplicated. The OSI transport protocol begins every transport connection with an initial sequence number of 0; since no data have yet been transferred, YR-TPDU-NR here contains a value of 1.
- *CDT* contains the *initial credit* allocated by the calling transport entity to the called transport entity (the number of transport protocol data packets I'll allow you to send before you must wait for me to acknowledge that I've received them).
- Other parameters, including a checksum computed on the acknowledgment packet and an *acknowledgment sequence number* (see "Normal Data Transfer in OSI transport protocols," later in this chapter).

A second mechanism is available for situations in which the called transport entity has indicated a non-0 initial credit value in the connection packet. The calling transport entity then has the option of immediately sending any normal or expedited transport service user data waiting for transfer; the first *data* packet (DT TPDU) or *expedited data* packet (ED TPDU) received by the called transport entity in this case is interpreted as a completion of the three-way handshake (again, refer to Figure 12.8).

Setting It All to Unix

If one were to trace the OSI transport connection-establishment process through the UNIX system calls described earlier in this chapter and the associated transport protocol state machine, then trace the packets that traversed the network while the process took place, and assuming that

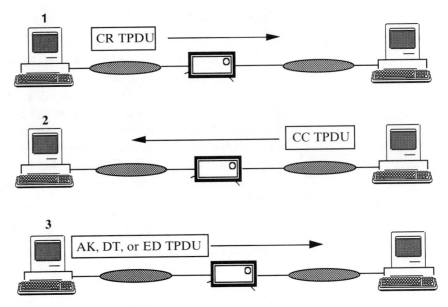

FIGURE 12.8   Three-Way Handshake

both transport users are on ARGO 1.0 UNIX, the time sequence of events might look like the one shown in Figure 12.9.

In the figure, transport user A invokes the UNIX system call *sock-et(AF-ISO, sock-seqpacket, ISO TP)* to create a local communication endpoint. Transport user B does the same. Both parties invoke the UNIX system call *bind()*, which is used to assign a transport service access point address to their respective sockets. Transport user A requests a transport connection by issuing the *connect()* system call. The transport entity composes a CR packet, requesting TP class 4 and indicating that the reference number it will use for this transport connection is 5 (SR in the first step of Figure 12.9). The network layer is called upon to transfer the CR packet.

The called transport entity at B receives the CR packet (transport user B has invoked system calls to passively await an incoming transport connection—i.e., it has issued a *listen()*. It agrees that TP class 4 is a wonderful choice and agrees with all the rest of the choices the calling transport entity has indicated. It composes a CC packet reflecting consent to all these selections. The called transport entity copies the source reference from the CR packet into the destination reference field (DR in the second step of Figure 12.9) and indicates that the reference number it will use for this transport connection is 2 (SR in the second step of Figure 12.9); the pair of reference numbers {5, 2} now distinguishes this trans-

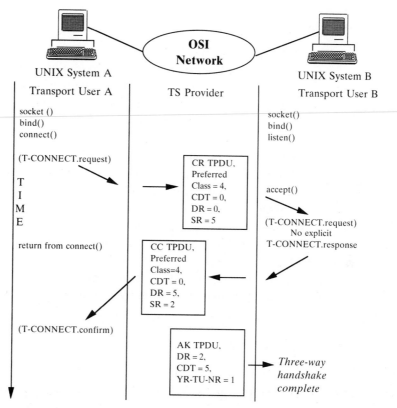

FIGURE 12.9   Setting Connection Establishment to UNIX

port connection from others established between transport service users A and B. In the example, the called transport entity also indicates an initial credit (CDT) of 0. The called transport entity then calls upon the network layer to transfer the CC packet.

The calling transport entity receives the CC packet, noting with great enthusiasm that the called transport entity has accepted all proposed transport connection selections. It composes an acknowledgment packet, setting the destination reference field to 2, the value identified by the called transport entity for this transport connection; offers a credit of 5; and indicates that the next expected sequence number (YR-TPDU-NR) is 1. The network layer is again called upon to transfer the AK packet. A return from *connect()* completes transport connection establishment for transport service user A. The called transport entity receives the AK packet, which completes the three-way handshake. A return from the *accept()* call completes transport connection establishment for transport service user B.

Frozen References

An important consideration when using references is providing a mechanism to avoid reuse of a reference to identify a new transport connection while a packet associated with a previous use of the same reference may still be "trollicking"[10] along a network connection or bounding its way along as a connectionless NPDU. A reference would be reused when the value of the 16-bit reference counter "wraps" in modulo 2 arithmetic; although the circumstances under which this might occur seem extraordinary, betting the ranch that it won't isn't a very good idea. A procedure called *frozen references* offers some guidance to the implementer on how to deal with this phenomenon. In TP4, one way to bound the time (L) to freeze a reference is to wait a minimum of the computed or estimated *round-trip time*—the sum of the time required to transfer an NSDU from the local transport entity to the remote transport entity (M_{LR}) and back again (M_{RL})—plus the value of *acknowledgment time* the remote transport entity indicated in the CR transport protocol data unit (A_R), plus the value of what is known as the *persistence time (R)*, which is how long the local transport entity will try to resend an unacknowledged transport protocol data unit before "giving up." The formula is:

$$L = M_{LR} + M_{RL} + R + A_R$$

Like all simple things, however, this formula has its weaknesses (see "Timers and Open Transport Protocols," later in this chapter). In practice, this value of L may be too large; better too large, however, than too small! One must remember the purpose of the timer and choose a value that can be lived with.

TCP Connection Establishment

The *synchronize stream (SYN)* process of TCP is functionally equivalent to connection establishment in the OSI transport protocol. TCP operates as a pair of independent streams of (octets of) data between upper-layer protocols. The synchronization process establishes the beginning of the byte stream in both directions of information flow. During SYN process-

---

10.   "Trollicking" is derived from the word *trundle*, meaning "to roll on little wheels; to bowl along," and *frollicking*, meaning "dancing, playing tricks, or frisking about." Any transport packets remaining in a network connection during a "frozen references" time period clearly could only be there to cause mischief . . .

ing, information is exchanged between TCP processes that is similar to the information negotiated (or implied) during OSI transport connection establishment:

- *Addressing:* The *named sockets* (source and destination port addresses) for the upper-layer protocol pairs that will use the TCP connection are exchanged during the SYN phase.
- *Initial sequence number (ISN):* All OSI transport protocol classes begin a transport connection using an initial sequence number of 0. TCP offers greater latitude, allowing TCP entities to identify the initial octet sequence number in the SYN segment.
- *Data offset:* contains the number of 32-bit words in the TCP segment header; and therefore points to the first octet of user data.
- *Window:* Similar to OSI TP's credit, the value in the window field indicates the number of bytes of information the originator of the SYN is willing to accept.
- *Checksum:* A 16-bit arithmetic checksum is computed on the header and data of all TCP segments.
- *Maximum segment size (MSS):* Upper-layer protocols negotiate the maximum transport segment size (in octets). The default value on the Internet for TCP maximum segment size is 536 bytes (RFC 879).[11]

Unlike OSI's transport protocol, all TCP segments have the same format.[12] Figure 12.10 illustrates the encodings of fields significant for the SYN segment.

Many of the option facilities negotiated in OSI TP connection establishment are nonoptions in TCP. For example, *urgent data*—the closest thing to OSI's expedited data transfer—is a service that is always available in TCP connections. TCP always uses explicit flow control. TCP is only operated over a datagram service. And TCP wouldn't know receipt confirmation if it were bitten by the warty little beast.

To confirm the establishment of a TCP segment, the responding

11. Extensions to TCP by Van Jacobson, R. Braden, and D. Borman (RFC 1323) describe how large segment sizes and windows are negotiated by TCPs; like the amendment to the OSI transport protocol, this mechanism allows TCP entities to negotiate and use very large TCP packets, necessary for networks that exhibit high bandwidth but have long round-trip delays. Van Jacobson and company have colloquially termed such transmission facilities "long fat networks (LFNs)," pronounced "elephan(t)s."
12. The Internet convention for illustrating protocol headers in its standards is to depict the fields in 32-bit sequences. In this chapter, the authors have elected to draw both OSI transport protocol and TCP headers according to ISO conventions (with apologies to the Internet community).

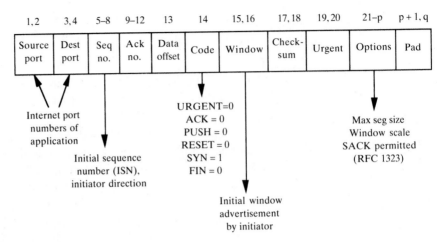

FIGURE 12.10   TCP SYN Segment

TCP entity *acknowledges* receipt of the SYN segment by generating a TCP segment with the code field bits SYN and ACK set to 1. The responding TCP entity acknowledges receipt of the initiator's SYN and attempts to synchronize the byte stream in the responder-initiator direction in a single TCP segment. This process, called *piggybacking*, improves protocol efficiency in several ways. Since only one segment must be created and transmitted to accomplish two tasks, less processing is devoted to protocol composition/decomposition. Fewer bytes of protocol header information are required, so less bandwidth is required. And since two tasks are accomplished in one transmission, overall delay is improved.

Setting the ACK bit in the code field indicates that the *acknowledgment number* field is significant. In the case of a SYN/ACK segment, the responding TCP entity should encode this field with the value of the ISN derived from the originator's SYN packet, incremented by 1. The values of the source and destination ports are encoded in reverse order (i.e., the called TCP entity is the source of the SYN/ACK segment, and the calling TCP entity is the destination). The responding TCP entity synchronizes sequence numbers by encoding the ISN for the responder-to-initiator direction of information flow. Figure 12.11 illustrates the encoding of the fields significant to the SYN/ACK segment.

A three-way handshake is common to OSI's transport protocol and TCP. In TCP, the three-way handshake is completed when the initiator returns a TCP segment with the ACK bit of the code field set to 1 (see Figure 12.12). A TCP segment containing an acknowledgment can also contain user data (another use of piggybacking); thus, if the responder

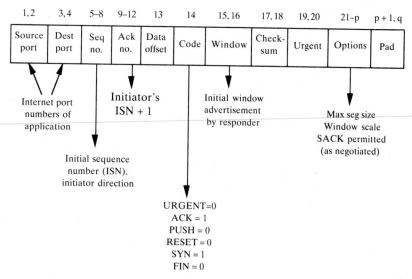

FIGURE 12.11   SYN/ACK Segment

indicated a non-0 initial window in the SYN/ACK segment, the initiator can send up to "responder's initial window" number of bytes of data in the SYN/ACK segment.

Figure 12.13 sets TCP connection establishment to UNIX in much the same fashion as Figure 12.9 does for OSI TP4.

In the figure, a client process (ULP A) on host A creates a socket, binds a port number to that socket, and attempts to connect to ULP B on host B. A's TCP entity composes a TCP segment with the SYN flag set and sets the ISN to 200. A server process (ULP B on host B has also created a socket and has bound a port number to that socket, and is awaiting

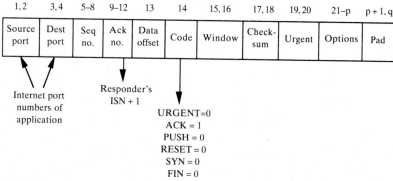

FIGURE 12.12   ACK Segment Encoding

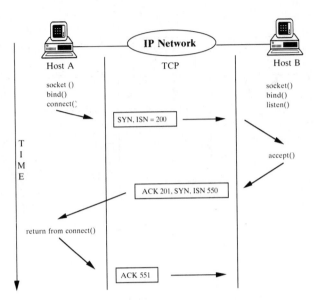

FIGURE 12.13   Setting TCP Connection Establishment to UNIX

incoming connect requests at a well-known port number). The SYN packet arrives, is processed by host B's TCP entity, and the server process at B is notified of the incoming connect request. ULP B accepts the connection (managing TCP endpoints as described earlier in this chapter). Host B's TCP entity composes a TCP segment with both the SYN and ACK flags set and with an ISN of 550. The ACK flag indicates that the acknowledgment field is significant, and it is set to the value of the ISN received in A's SYN packet plus 1 (i.e., 201). When the SYN/ACK segment arrives at host A, ULP A is informed, and A's TCP entity attempts to complete the three-way handshake by returning a segment to host B with the ACK flag set, indicating that the acknowledgment field is significant in this segment (and set to the value of the ISN received in the SYN/ACK packet plus 1; in this case, 551). If host B had offered an initial window, host A could have piggybacked data along with the acknowledgment.

"Keep Quiet"— TCP's "Frozen References"

TCP also worries about reusing a sequence number before its time (well, chronologically speaking, TCP worried first!). To prevent sequence numbers from a previous incarnation of a TCP connection from being mistaken for segments of a new connection, RFC 793 suggests that TCP send no segments for a time equal to the maximum segment lifetime (MSL). The recommended value for MSL in RFC 793 is 2 minutes, al-though this is an *engineering choice* (a cousin to OSI's "local matter").

Normal Data Transfer in OSI Transport Protocol

Once a transport connection has been established, transport service user data may be transferred bidirectionally between communicating session entities (transport service users). The OSI transport service allows corresponding transport service users to submit arbitrarily large (theoretically unbounded) transport service data units. In the context of providing reliable transfer, the sending transport layer performs segmentation of transport service data units into transport protocol data units up to the *maximum transport protocol data unit size* negotiated during transport connection establishment and submits the transport protocol data units to the network layer for forwarding and delivery to the destination transport entity.

The means by which a sending transport entity determines whether transport protocol data units arrived without mishap at their destination varies depending on the transport protocol class negotiated. Mechanisms are provided in class 4 to assure that individual transport protocol data units are explicitly acknowledged and that the transport service data units are reassembled correctly into the original transport service data unit prior to delivery to the destination transport service user. The lesser or *invertebrate* transport protocol classes rely mainly on gimmicks, chicanery, hand waving, and the network layer to provide all or nearly all aspects of reliable data transfer.

In transport classes 0 and 2, for example, transport service data units are segmented and submitted to the network layer for in-sequence transfer, and the network service is relied upon to detect (but not correct for) loss. Users of a transport connection supported by TP0 or TP2 act in blind faith; unless the underlying network connection signals an error, they continue to submit transport service data units and assume that they will be delivered correctly. If, however, an error is signaled by the network service provider, the transport connection is abruptly terminated, and both transport service users are left to fend for themselves. TP2 users are left multi- and per-plexed, and the upper layers are left to clean up the mess.

Transport classes 1 and 3 provide error recovery following a failure signaled by the network service using *reassignment after failure, retention until acknowledgment,* and *resynchronization* functions, as follows:

- If the underlying network connection signals a disconnect, TP1 can map the existing transport connection onto a new network connection. Copies of unacknowledged data packets are retained by a sending transport entity until a new network connection is opened. The retained packets are then retransmitted by the sending transport entity (remember, information flow across a transport connection is bidirectional, so both parties may act as senders) and explicitly acknowledged by the receiver, thus resynchronizing the information flow of the transport connection.[13]

- If the underlying network connection signals an error (a reset), transport entities retransmit unacknowledged data packets to resynchronize the data streams in both directions (over the same network connection).

Remember, these Mickey Mouse mechanisms are considered to be sufficient because *acceptable* levels of service quality are purportedly provided by the network service; in the real world, they are probably adequate when both transport service users subscribe to the same public network provider or are attached to the same physical subnetwork. Since you can't be too careful these days, it's better to practice "safe networking" than to deny the possibility of network connection failures and say, "Well, it won't happen to me."

Flow Control

A major concern in maintaining service quality in a network is seeing that information flows into the network at a manageable rate. Just as a highway can handle only so many automobiles before traffic initially slows and then comes to a stop, networks can only switch a finite number of packets before experiencing similar *congestion*. To prevent traffic jams on major California highways surrounding Los Angeles, for example, traffic signals are positioned on the entrance ramps. These allow automobiles to enter the roadway at intervals that vary according to the amount of traffic already present on the roadway. By regulating the flow of automobiles onto the roadway, congestion is temporarily avoided.[14] Of course, roads are rarely built to handle peak loads (rush hours), and under these conditions, highway congestion inevitably occurs (sometimes the traffic lights at entranceways are turned off, a visible sign of surrender or *congestion collapse*).

Similar techniques are used in networks to avoid congestion. The

---

13.   Copies of connect request and connect confirm TPDUs—and for reasons unknown, TPDUs used for connection release (DR and DC TPDUs)—are retained in the same fashionto permit completion of transport connection establishment or release if the network connection disconnects during that phase of operation.

14.   Los Angelenos may deny that this works at all, but the fault lies in the fact that congestion-avoidance mechanisms have been applied to highways that have existed in a congested state for decades.

rate of information flow into a network (incoming packets) is regulated according to the network's ability to switch packets. Flow control is a classic networking problem, and a variety of *flow-control* techniques have been employed to avoid congestion. Of these, OSI employs both implicit and explicit flow-control techniques in its transport protocol classes.

In a public network service, users subscribe to and expect a certain rate of throughput (often, a negotiated quality of service characteristic); thus, it is no surprise to find that transport classes 0 and 1 are designed to rely entirely on the network service provider to regulate the flow of transport protocol data units. This *implicit flow control*[15] is straightforward (and autocratic): the sending transport entity submits transport protocol data units to the network service (in the form of NSDUs); the network layer accepts the NSDUs and forwards them *at a rate it chooses,* typically one consistent with maintaining some degree of uniform service quality for all subscribers. Transport service users continue to submit transport service data units, and TP0 and TP1 faithfully continue to create transport protocol data units and submit them to the network layer until the local buffer pool allocated to the transport layer is exhausted. TP0 and TP1 then halt and accept no transport service data units from the session layer; the effect of halting percolates through the upper layers and has the same *back-pressure* effect on information flow that (gradually) closing a faucet has on the flow of water. Normal user data cease to flow out of the end system until the back-pressure condition is eased; i.e., until the network layer accepts a sufficient number from the queue of previously submitted NSDUs to allow the flow of information to continue.

A shortcoming of this form of flow control is that although the network layer is somewhat insulated from congestion, an end system receiving packets has no explicit means of indicating that it cannot accept packets at the incoming rate. TP0 and TP1 again rely upon the network service to deal with this situation; protocols used to provide the OSI connection-oriented network service (e.g., X.25) have facilities that enable an end system to signal that it is temporarily unable to receive incoming packets (there are no explicit network service primitives to signal "congestion"; how the transport layer indicates an "unable to receive" state is a local matter).

Flow control is no less important in private internets; the mechanisms, however, are more democratic. All transport entities are expected

---

15.   Implicit flow control is optionally available in TP2 and must be negotiated during connection establishment.

to participate in an explicit flow-control process. TP4, for example, uses a *sliding window* mechanism; very simply stated, this form of flow control proceeds as follows:

1. Each transport entity indicates a number of data packets that it is able to receive; this is called the *credit* (CDT). The initial credit value is exchanged during connection establishment. During data transfer, CDT is added to the value of the highest sequence number acknowledged (called the *lower window edge* [LWE], initially 0) to create the *send window*. This sum is called the *upper window edge* (UWE).
2. A sending transport entity sends a number of transport protocol data units equal to the credit, then waits for an explicit acknowledgment packet before continuing to send.
3. Upon reception of an acknowledgment packet, a sending transport entity extracts the value of the sequence number (YR-TPDU-NR) from the AK packet and uses this value as the new LWE; it also extracts the value of CDT from the AK packet and adds this to the new LWE to determine the new UWE.

As steps 2 and 3 are repeated, the sequence numbers are incremented using modulo 2 arithmetic, and the send window "slides." By increasing or decreasing the value of CDT, the size of the send window increases or decreases. This is also called opening or closing the send window.

Different policies are applied to determine the appropriate value of CDT. One simple policy for determining the initial value of CDT is to divide the number of bytes of buffer space available for the receiver side of the transport protocol by the maximum transport protocol data unit size to yield an integer value for CDT; for example, if there are 4,096 octets of receive buffer available, and the maximum transport protocol data unit size negotiated for this transport connection is 1,024, then CDT could be set initially to 4.

Reliability Mechanisms to Deal with the Real World

Of the OSI transport protocol classes, only TP4 was developed to deal with real-world situations in which, despite the best efforts exerted by the network layer, bad things happen to transport protocol data units on their way from source to destination: specifically, transport protocol data units may get lost, multiple copies of the same transport protocol data unit may be delivered, transport protocol data units may be delivered to the wrong end system, bits of the transport protocol data unit header and (worse) user data may get corrupted, and the transport protocol data units may arrive out of order. TP4 deals with these errors as follows:

- Receipt of each data packet is explicitly acknowledged using an acknowledgment packet; absent an explicit acknowledgment for a data packet sent, the sender assumes that it has been lost (or misdelivered).
- Destination transport connection reference information encoded in each data and acknowledgment packet is used to distinguish the data and acknowledgments of one transport connection established between a pair of transport service access points from those of another and to determine whether a data packet has been misdelivered.
- Transport protocol data unit numbers encoded in the data and acknowledgment packet headers are used to detect out-of-order arrival and duplicate arrival.
- Adaptive timer mechanisms are used to avoid injection of duplicate packets into the network.
- When selected, an arithmetic checksum computed on the user data of each data packet is used to detect bit-level corruption.

An important function performed by sending TP4 entity is determining that loss has occurred and correcting for the error; this mechanism is called *retransmission on time-out* in OSI (see Figure 12.14). Each

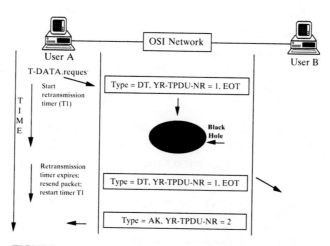

FIGURE 12.14   Retransmission on Time-out

time a TP4 entity sends a DT transport protocol data unit, it runs a retransmission timer *(T1)*; if the explicit acknowledgment of receipt of the data packet is not received by the sender prior to the expiration of the T1 timer, the sender assumes that the data packet is lost and retransmits it.

The detailed manner in which the sender and receiver cooperate to achieve reliability through retransmission is best understood by examining each separately.

Sender TP4 Responsibilities

Like the lesser transport protocol classes, the sending TP4 transport entity segments transport service data units into data packets (if necessary); the data packets are often a fixed size (except the last segment of a packet), up to the maximum packet size negotiated during connection establishment.[16] A sequence number is assigned to each data packet (YR-TPDU-NR in Figure 12.14); the initial value of the YR-TPDU-NR field is always 0, and YR-TPDU-NR is incremented by 1 for all subsequent data packets transferred in the transport connection. The combination of DST-REF and YR-TPDU-NR is used to differentiate transport protocol data units of different transport connections multiplexed between the same pair of transport entities. If multiple transport protocol data units are required to transfer a single transport service data unit, the *end of transport service data unit* (EOT) bit in the data packet header is set to 0 in all but the packet containing the final segment of the transport service data unit (indicating that there are more user data to come); the EOT bit is set to 1 in the data packet containing the final segment of the transport service data unit (see Figure 12.15).

Initially, the sending TP4 entity may send one or more data packets, up to the value indicated in the CDT field of

- The connect request packet if the sender was the responder during connection establishment.
- The connect confirm packet if the sender was the initiator during connection establishment.

The sender retains a copy of each data packet sent. It also maintains information about the number of transport protocol data units it has sent, as well as the *sequence numbers of* those packets, and the sequence number of the next data packet the receiver expects[17] (the lower window edge).

---

16.   In practice, the maximum packet size should be less than or equal to the maximum NSDU size offered by the network layer between the source and destination end systems.

17.   Sequence numbers in acknowledgment packets are interpreted as meaning "I acknowledge receipt of all data packets, in sequence, up to but not including the sequence number indicated in the YR-TPDU-NR field."

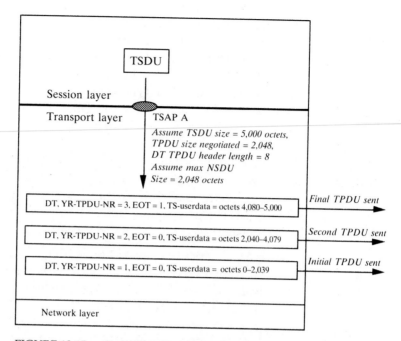

FIGURE 12.15   Example of Transport Segmentation/Reassembly[18]

The sender adds the value of the credit indicated by its peer transport entity to the lower window edge, creating the new upper window edge. These two values determine the new send window; acknowledgments containing sequence numbers outside this window are as-sumed to be duplicates.

Retransmission Timer

A retransmission timer is run for each data packet, or for a set of data packets forming a contiguous sequence (send window). If an acknowledgment is received containing a sequence number within the send window, the sender safely assumes that all data packets having sequence numbers up to (but not including) this value have been received. The value of YR-TPDU-NR from the acknowledgment packet becomes the new lower window edge, the value of CDT in the acknowledgment packet is added to the lower window edge to arrive at a new upper window edge, and the new send window is recomputed.

If the retransmission timer expires, several implementation alterna-

18.   To avoid situations in which dividing the transport user data into maximum length packets would result in an exceedingly small "final" TPDU, algorithms that determine the optimal segmentation based on available network maximum data unit size are applied.

tives are available to the sender; for example, it can update the lower window edge and retransmit only the data packet whose YR-TPDU-NR is equal to the value of the lower window edge, or it can retransmit all or a part of the reevaluated send window (from new lower window edge to old upper window edge). (The value of the retransmission timer is discussed separately; see "Timers and Open Transport Protocols," later in this chapter.)

Receiver TP4 Responsibilities

The primary responsibilities of the receiver are to explicitly acknowledge correct receipt of individual data packets using an acknowledgment packet, correctly reassemble data packets into transport service data units (when necessary), and deliver transport service data units to the called transport service user. Acknowledgment packets are generated

- Upon successful receipt and processing of a data packet.
- When advertised credit is reached (the window is full).
- To *allocate credit*; i.e., to increase or reduce the upper window edge (to open or close the window) and thus identify the number of data packets the receiver is willing to handle. (Often, the initial value is a simple calculation of available receive buffer size divided by the negotiated maximum packet size.)

A receiver TP4 entity also returns an acknowledgment packet upon

- Receipt of a duplicate data packet.
- Expiration of the window timer (see "Timers and Open Transport Protocols").

When the receiver determines that a transport service data unit is arriving in segments (multiple data packets), it must also worry about correct reassembly of the transport service data unit. The retransmission procedures assure that the sender will resend data packets the receiver does not acknowledge (they were not received or were received and failed the checksum computation), and the receiver weeds out duplicate data packets using the TPDU numbering and reference fields of the data packet, but transport protocol data packets may still arrive out of order. One possible strategy that a receiver may use to correctly order data packets that have arrived out of order is to maintain

- An in-order list, containing data packets units of a partially reassembled transport service data unit that arrive in sequence.
- An out-of-order list, containing data packets of a partially reassembled transport service data unit that arrive out of sequence.
- A next expected transport protocol data unit number (NEXT-EX-

PECTED-TPDU-NR) variable, containing the value of the next expected TPDU sequence number (i.e., the sequence number of the data packet that would sequentially follow the last data packet in the in-order list).

When a data packet arrives, if the value of YR-TPDU-NR transport protocol data unit NR is not the same as the value of next expected transport protocol data unit number, the receiver adds this data packet to the out-of-order list, *in order* with respect to the rest of that list. If a data packet arrives and the value of YR-TPDU-NR is the same as the value of *next expected transport protocol data unit number*, the receiver adds the data packet to the tail of the in-order list, checks the out-of-order list for one or more data packets that follow the newly arrived data packet in sequence, and moves these to the in-order list. If at any time in this process a data packet is encountered containing the final segment of the transport service data unit (EOT = 1), the process is stopped; otherwise, the receiver adjusts *next expected transport protocol data unit number* to contain the value of the sequence transport protocol data unit number of the next expected data packet. Alternatively, the receiver can maintain only an in-order list and discard without explicitly acknowledging any data packets received out of order; the sender will dutifully retransmit these data packets according to the retransmission on time-out procedures.

The receiver has an explicit mechanism—setting the value of CDT—for controlling the number of transport protocol data units it is expected to be able to receive at a given time. The receiver can increase or decrease credit (open or close the send window) as necessary to exercise some control over the way its local resources are used. Suppose, for example, that a transport implementation has 64K of buffer space. If a maximum packet size of 1K is negotiated for a transport connection, a theoretical credit of 64 is available; anticipating that multiple transport connections to multiple destinations may be established, an implementation may allocate an initial credit of 8 for up to eight transport connections, then reduce the credit for all transport connections as additional transport connections share the buffer space. (It is expected that some rational value for the maximum number of concurrent transport connections is applied in all implementations; certainly, here, the value must be less than 65!)

Sequencing Acknowledgment Packets in OSI TP4

Like data packets, acknowledgment packets can also be lost, duplicated, corrupted, or delivered out of order. Failing to correct these errors for data packets will corrupt user data; failing to correct these errors for acknowledgment packets will cause the transport protocol to misbehave.

Lost or corrupted acknowledgment packets are recovered as part of the retransmission or window resynchronization processing. Acknowledgment packets are retransmitted when a data packet is received that contains a sequence number outside the send window (lower than the lower window edge or greater than the upper window edge) or when the window timer expires (see "Timers and Open Transport Protocols," later in this chapter). It is also important to be able to determine whether an acknowledgment packet is a duplicate or an indication of a new credit value (a window update). Acknowledgment packets thus often have a *subsequence number* encoded in the variable part of the transport protocol header. This number is used to order acknowledgment packets to ensure that the same credit value is used by both the sending and receiving parties (i.e., that both have the same understanding of what the window looks like).

Transport Protocol Data Unit Concatenation— Piggybacking Acknowledgments, ISO-style

To improve protocol performance, especially in multiplexing scenarios, OSI TPs may group multiple transport protocol data units into a single NSDU. The rules are straightforward: any number of acknowledgment, expedited acknowledgment, reject, error, or disconnect confirmation packets from any number of transport connections may be prepended to a single connect request, disconnect request, connect confirm, data, or expedited data packet; i.e., only one packet from the latter set may be present, and it must be the last transport protocol data unit in the NSDU. In the case of TP4, the most common occurrence of concatenation is likely to be that of a single acknowledgment packet with a data packet for the same transport connection (see Figure 12.16). For TP2 and TP4 over a net-

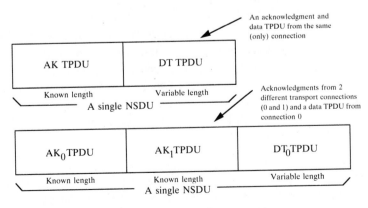

FIGURE 12.16   Examples of TPDU Concatenation

work connection, concatenation has additional benefits: one can, for example, concatenate acknowledgments from different transport connections with a single data packet, send a single large NSDU, and save "turnaround time." Compared to the TCP piggyback mechanisms, in which one need only set the TCP acknowledgment AK flag to true and populate the TCP acknowledgment sequence number, this admittedly is overhead and overkill—another demonstration that flexibility costs.

Data Transfer in TCP—More of the Same

TCP's name for retransmission on time-out is *positive acknowledgment and retransmission*. Mechanisms exist in TCP for detecting and correcting the same set of errors as in TP4. What distinguishes TCP from TP4 in data transfer is *encoding* rather than *functionality*; for example:

- TCP transfers octet streams, not fixed blocks of user data. The 32-bit sequence number in a TCP segment represents the number of the octet in the stream, not the number of the TCP packet.
- The TCP acknowledgment number indicates the next expected *octet*, as opposed to the next expected TCP segment.
- The acknowledgment flag may be set to true to indicate that the acknowledgment sequence number (and window) is significant in data segments in the return stream (piggybacking).
- The 16-bit TCP window indicates in octets the amount of data the receiver is willing to accept in the next TCP segment(s); this value is added to the acknowledgment sequence number to determine the send window. Thus, window is TCP's octet equivalent of TP4's credit.
- A *push* bit in the code field of the TCP segment may be used to decrease delay; i.e., its use overrides TCP's attempt to fill a maximum segment sized packet before sending. (Although it can be misused, push is not intended to be a delimiter of segments as is OSI's EOT bit.)

Figure 12.17 depicts two TCP scenarios—successful transfer with positive acknowledgment and loss followed by retransmission. Many of the sender and receiver responsibilities and strategies described for TP4 were

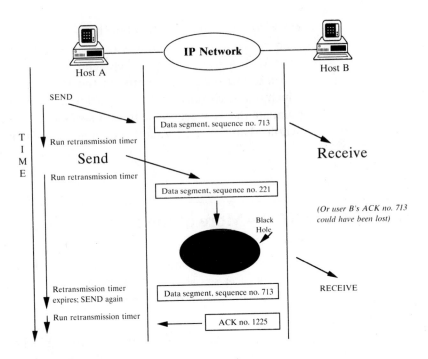

FIGURE 12.17   Data Transfer, TCP-style

derived from the operation of TCP, so these will be familiar to readers.

The sending TCP entity collects data from the upper-layer protocol process and sends those data "at its convenience" (seriously, that's what RFC 793 says . . .). Typically, the sender attempts to fill a maximum segment size (MSS) packet before sending (unless a PUSH is invoked). The default maximum segment size is 536 octets, which allows for a standard TCP header and 512 octets of user data and fits neatly into the default IP packet of 576 octets, assuming an IP header of 40 octets (RFC 879).

The sending TCP entity runs a retransmission timer for each TCP data segment. If the retransmission timer expires and no acknowledgment packet has arrived indicating successful delivery of the segment to the receiver, TCP assumes the data segment is lost, arrived corrupted, or was misdelivered; resends the data segment; and restarts the retransmission timer for this segment. RFC 793 suggests two resend strategies: if the retransmission timer expires, TCP may resend the next unacknowledged segment ("first-only" retransmission), or it may resend all the data segments on the retransmission queue ("batch" retransmission).

The receiving TCP entity may apply one of two acceptance strategies. If an "in-order" data-acceptance strategy is used, the receiving TCP entity accepts only data that arrive in octet-sequence order and discards all other data. The receiving TCP entity returns an acknowledgment to the sender and makes the octet stream available to the upper-layer protocol process as it arrives. If an "in-window" data-acceptance strategy is employed, the receiving TCP entity maintains segments containing octets that arrive out of order separately from those that have arrived in order and examines newly arrived data segments to determine whether the next expected octet in the ordered stream of octets has arrived. If so, the receiving TCP entity adds this segment's worth of octets to the end of the octet stream that had previously arrived in order and looks at the out-of-order stream to see whether additional octets may now be appended to the end of the in-order stream. The TCP entity returns an acknowledgment and makes the accumulated stream of in-order octets available to the upper-layer protocol process.

An explicit acknowledgment is returned in a TCP segment (potentially "piggybacked" with data flowing in the opposite direction). The *acknowledgment sequence number X* indicates that all octets up to but not including X have been received, and the next octet expected is at sequence number X. The *segment window* indicates the number of octets the receiver is willing to accept (beginning with sequence number X). Acknowledgment packets reflect only what has been received in sequence; they do not acknowledge data packets that arrived successfully but out of sequence.

When an acknowledgment packet arrives, the sending TCP entity may choose to resend all unacknowledged data from sequence number X up to the maximum permitted by the segment window. In theory, applying the "batch" retransmission strategy results in more traffic but possibly less delay. The sending TCP entity may resend only the data segment containing the first unacknowledged octet. This negates a large window and may increase delay, but it is preferred because it introduces less traffic into the network. Batch retransimssion strategies are generally regarded as bad ideas, since their excessive retransmission of segments is likely to contribute to network congestion.

Window Considerations for TP4 and TCP

Managing the send and receive windows is critical to the performance of OSI and TCP networks. Every network has a finite forwarding capacity, and absent constant monitoring of network "busy-ness," transport entities can easily submit packets faster than the network can forward and deliver them, even if they are all dutifully abiding by the windows advertised for their respective transport connections (this is simply a case in which the sum of the advertised windows exceeds the capacity of the network). Networks that become too busy or congested do unkind things such as discard packets. Since congestion has the undesirable effect of causing retransmission (either because delays increase and transport entities presume loss and retransmit or because the network is in fact discarding packets due to congestion) and retransmission results in delay, it is important that transport implementations try their best not to retransmit unless they are very sure they must. On the other hand, too much caution will also cause delay; an overly conservative retransmission timer will wait too long before causing genuinely lost packets to be retransmitted. The trick, evidently, is to wait long enough, but not too long.

A number of different mechanisms are available to deal with this conundrum, most of them applicable to both TCP and TP4. One of the most successful is called "slow-start" (Jacobson 1988). Slow-start is a simple mechanism and follows a simple philosophy: as new transport connections are established, they shouldn't upset the equilibrium that may exist in a network by transmitting large amounts of data right away. In other words, transport connections should not be opened with large windows (or credits); rather, the window (or credit) should initially be small and should grow as evidence of the network's ability to handle more packets is returned in the form of acknowledgments for each packet sent. Slow-start recognizes that a receiver advertises a window or credit of a certain size based on the receiver's ability to handle incoming packets, which is closely related to the availability of buffers and processing cycles at the receiver but has nothing whatsoever to do with congestion in the network. It does not follow, therefore, that the most appropriate strategy for the sender is to immediately fill the window offered by the receiver; the sender must also take into account the effect of its behavior on the network.[19] Slow-start couples *flow control* (ensuring that a sender

---

19.   A variation of the familiar "tragedy of the commons" applies to the behavior of hosts sending traffic into an internetwork, since most of the algorithms that have been devised for congestion avoidance and control in internetworks depend on a "good network citizen" collaboration among host transport protocol implementations to globally maximize the traffic that can be handled by the network without congestion collapse. An unscrupulous host can attempt to take advantage of its well-behaved neighbors by deliberately sending traffic into the network at a rate that would produce serious congestion but for the willingness of other hosts to "back off" as the overall network load rises. This problem has been addressed by a combination of legislation (the Internet standards require, for example, that all Internet TCP implementations use Jacobson's slow-start algorithm) and negative reinforcement (operating the internetwork in such a way that "selfish host

does not send faster than its receiver can receive) with *congestion control* (ensuring that the traffic generated by all senders does not overwhelm the capacity of the network).[20]

A transport implementation using slow-start maintains two windows that govern the rate at which it sends packets: the normal "usable" window (the difference between the window or credit offered by the receiver and the amount of outstanding [unacknowledged] data that are already in the window) and a separate "congestion" window, which is a running estimate of how much data can be sent without congesting the network. The transport protocol then uses the congestion window, rather than the usable window, to control the rate at which it sends new data. (Correct operation of the transport protocol requires, of course, that the size of the congestion window never exceed the size of the usable window.)

Slow-start divides the lifetime of a transport connection into "phases." The first phase begins when the connection is established. The congestion window at the beginning of a phase is always set to 1 packet (for TCP, this is the maximum segment size; for OSI transport, 1 transport protocol data unit); thereafter, as long as no packets are lost, the congestion window is increased by 1 packet every time an acknowledgment packet is received, subject to an upper bound of either the current usable window (which the congestion window must never exceed) or the current "slow-start threshold" (which is half the value of the congestion window at the end of the previous phase). This has the effect of opening the congestion window rapidly[21] until a threshold (or absolute upper bound) is reached or a packet loss occurs (which suggests that the window may have been opened too far).

The detection of a packet loss, which triggers retransmission of the lost data, ends a phase. The next phase begins with the congestion window back at 1 and a new slow-start threshold of half the congestion-window value that was in effect when packet loss terminated the previous

---

behavior is punished—for example, by using "fair queuing" in routers, so that individual hosts see the effects of congestion [dropped packets and increased transit delay] caused by their own traffic as well as by the total traffic load on the network).

20.   It is important to understand that flow control is strictly an element of the host-to-host transport protocol (in which the network does not participate), whereas congestion control has both host-based and network-based elements.

21.   The congestion window value grows exponentially during this part of the slow-start procedure, since every time a window of N data packets is sent, N acknowledgments are received in return, increasing the window by N (1 for each acnowledgment); starting at $N = 1$, the progression (assuming there is no packet loss) is 1, 2, 4, 8 . . . .

phase.[22] This "be more conservative next time" strategy, which halves the maximum congestion window every time a packet is lost, would by itself eventually shrink the window to 1 packet—solving the congestion problem, to be sure, but also reducing the transport protocol to an inefficient send-and-wait mode of operation. To avoid this, slow-start is paired with a strategy that Jacobson (1988) calls "congestion avoidance," which allows the congestion window to grow past the threshold—but much more slowly. After the congestion window has reached the slow-start threshold, it is incremented by its reciprocal (rather than by 1) each time an acknowledgment packet arrives.

The slow-start/congestion-avoidance algorithm has been widely implemented in TCP but has only recently found its way into TCP's counterpart in OSI, TP4. In OSI networks based on TP4 and the connectionless network protocol CLNP, it is also possible to detect and signal network congestion by using the *congestion experienced* flag in the QOS Maintenance field of the CLNP header (see Chapter 13) and the base credit-management and retransmission strategies on the work of Raj Jain (1985, 1986a, 1986b, 1990); in fact, Jacobson's congestion-avoidance strategy is nearly identical to Jain's, which differs primarily in its use of a smaller window-shrinking factor when congestion is signaled.

OSI's Expedited Data

OSI transport expedited data is an entirely separate data flow packet. It is not subject to normal data flow control and has its own packet type, acknowledgment, and sequence space (see Figure 12.18). In theory, transport expedited data is used when user data of great urgency must be transferred. Expedited data reminds one of the childhood practice of cutting ahead in line: an expedited data packet is placed at the head of the outbound queue, and although it is not expected to overtake any previously submitted data packets, it must be delivered before any data packet is submitted after it. Expedited data can cut in line, but it may not really be processed with the urgency it expects and may well end up being transferred no more quickly than if it had been submitted as normal data.

Expedited data is highly constrained. Only one expedited data packet

---

22.   The actual formula for calculating the new threshold value is not really as simple as "half the old threshold," but it is close enough for the purposes of this discussion. Not all the details (such as doubling the value of the retransmission timers for unacknowledged packets waiting in the window when a phase-ending packet loss occurs) are covered here; implementers should see Jacobson (1988) and Zhang (1991).

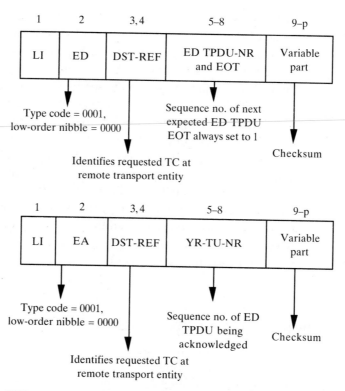

FIGURE 12.18   ED and EA Transport Protocol Data Units

may be outstanding (unacknowledged) at a time; each expedited data TSDU maps onto a single *expedited data* packet (EDT PDU) and it can be used only to transfer 16 weenie little octets.[23] Another curious bit of protocol encoding is the presence of an EOT bit that is always set to 1.

TCP's Urgent Data

TCP's notion of urgent data is somewhat more flexible. TCP allows an upper layer protocol to mark data in the stream as *urgent* for the receiver. The sender TCP does so by setting the URG bit in the code field of the

---

23.   The 16-octet limit to user data in expedited data packets is a consequence of attempting to map expedited data packets at the transport layers onto a single X.25 *interrupt* packet, which offers only 32 octets of user data at the network layer. Substract the maximum protocol overhead of an expedited data packet (16 octets), and only 16 octets remain for user data.

TCP segment to 1, indicating that the URGENT field is significant. The value of the URGENT field represents the number of priority delivery octets in this TCP segment (and perhaps in subsequent segments, if the number of octets in this segment is less than the value of the current field). This value is added to the segment sequence number to assist the receiver TCP in identifying the last octet of urgent data. When the TCP segment containing the URG bit arrives, the receiver TCP notifies the upper-layer protocol that urgent data are coming. Although not explicitly stated in RFC 793, it is assumed that the upper-layer protocol will begin processing the urgent data; when the last octet of urgent data arrives, the receiving TCP delivers the urgent data in the TCP segment and notifies the upper-layer protocol that normal data transfer has resumed. (It has been suggested that the urgent data capability is roughly equivalent to the session layer's *activity interrupt* or *capability data* services. Some say this is a stretch.)

Timers and Open Transport Protocols

The most fundamental thing you can say about TP4 and TCP is that they are timer-based: to operate correctly, both protocols rely on the certainty that either an expected event will occur or a timer will expire. This characteristic is responsible for the robustness and flexibility of both of these protocols. The dependence on timers, however, means that the performance of TP4 or TCP is highly sensitive to the choice of timer values and to the way in which the values of different timers are related. It's not terribly difficult to choose reasonably good (initial) timer values or to build implementations that can dynamically adjust them, but the consequences of choosing bad values, or building implementations that either cannot adapt or adapt inappropriately, are much more serious with TP4 and TCP than they are with protocols that do not depend as heavily on timers.

The OSI transport protocol specification provides rudimentary guidelines for establishing initial values for some of the many timers that transport class 4 relies on for correct operation. If network-service behavior were uniform and stable, these guidelines might be sufficient. Unfortunately, the behavior of real-world networks is anything but uniform and stable. The practice of adjusting timer values to react correctly to change in the behavior of networks is fundamental to correct and efficient transport implementations, be they OSI TP4 or TCP. What must be taken into consideration for many of these timers is described in a general way in the following subsections and is, for the most part, applicable to all retransmission and timer-based transport protocols.

Retransmission Timer

Almost every TP4 packet (or TCP segment) must be either explicitly or implicitly acknowledged. When a transport packet is first assembled and transmitted, it is associated with a retransmission timer. If the expected acknowledgment of the packet is not received before the timer expires, the packet is retransmitted and the timer is restarted (using either the same or a different value for the time-out period); when the acknowledgment is received, the timer is canceled. Until the acknowledgment is received (or the transmission attempt is abandoned after "too many retries"), the sending system must retain enough information to be able to retransmit the original packet if necessary. Dealing with timers and timer-generated events and holding information about packets for some period after they have been sent represent a significant load on the resources of a TP4 or TCP-based system. One of the most important goals of an efficient transport protocol implementation is therefore to minimize this overhead.

The basic problem with retransmission timers is choosing the right time-out interval. An overly sensitive timer will cause the unnecessary retransmission—duplication—of packets that were in fact received and acknowledged correctly; a sluggish timer will respond too slowly to the actual loss of a packet or its acknowledgment, increasing the delay associated with error detection and recovery. Ideally, a retransmission timer should expire only when it is actually the case that a packet or its acknowledgment has been lost or discarded. In practice, however, there is no way to be certain whether or not this has happened—that's why the timers are there.

The realistic goal is to pick (or dynamically approach) a time-out interval that allows the protocol to recover quickly when a packet has been lost (the timer value must not be too large) but reduces below some acceptable threshold the number of occasions on which a packet that was in fact correctly received is retransmitted because the acknowledgment did not arrive before the expiration of the time-out interval (the timer value must not be too small). In any environment in which the loss or corruption of packets is not a rare occurrence, the performance of TP4 and TCP is extremely sensitive to these timer values.

The internet over which TP4 and TCP operates may contain paths with very different delay and throughput characteristics, which may change dramatically during the lifetime of a transport connection, and the timer-based behavior of the transport implementation at the other end of a transport connection cannot be completely predetermined. Because of this variability, one cannot simply pick an "average" value for any retransmission timer (except in very limited, static configurations); there will always be configurations in which the protocol will not operate at all with such a static value, much less operate efficiently. These timers must adapt dynamically to the actual, observed (or inferred) delay characteristics of each individual transport connection.

The timer-value problem has two parts. To maximize performance, the interval between the initial transmission of a packet and its first retransmission should be tuned as finely as possible, with an adaptive granularity small enough to keep the value close to its theoretical ideal. To ensure that the protocol will nevertheless operate correctly when the attempt to maximize performance leads to the choice of a much-too-small initial timer value for the connection-establishment phase and to allow it to cope with sudden, relatively large transient or persistent changes in end-to-end delay during the data-transfer phase, the interval must be increased for the second and subsequent retransmissions (when necessary) in such a way that a sufficiently large interval is allowed to expire before the transmission attempt is deliberately abandoned ("too many retries").

Choosing and Adjusting Retransmission Timer Values

If it were possible to periodically measure the actual end-to-end delay between two transport connection endpoints, the corresponding retransmission timer values could be adjusted up or down accordingly. Unfortunately, TP4's normal data packets and their acknowledgments cannot always be used for delay measurement, since a single acknowledgment packet can acknowledge more than one data packet, and the use of a selective acknowledgment strategy by the receiver can artificially skew round-trip delay measurements. TP4 expedited data packets, which must be acknowledged immediately and individually, could be used for this purpose, but the expedited data option is not always selected, and even when it is, there is no guarantee that expedited data will flow regularly enough (or in some cases, even over the same path) to provide the necessary dynamic delay information.

Although it is not feasible to obtain a direct measurement of end-to-end delay, the first part of the timer-value problem can be solved successfully by using a trial-and-error technique that adjusts the timer value based on observed retransmission behavior: crank the retransmission time-out interval down until the number of retransmissions per measurement interval starts to climb and then gently bump the time-out value back up until the number of retransmissions drops just below some acceptable threshold. When the number of retransmissions rises above the threshold, the retransmission interval is increased; when it drops below the threshold, the interval is decreased. The goal is to maintain an equilibrium just below the threshold.[24]

This "adaptive retransmission" scheme assumes that "false" retransmissions caused by a too-short retransmission time-out interval can be distinguished from "real" retransmissions caused by the actual loss of data packets—that when the retransmission interval is reduced below a certain threshold, the resulting increase in the number of "false" retransmissions will be detectable against the fluctuating background of "real" retransmissions. Since there is no objective way to determine whether any individual retransmission is "real" or "false," this scheme depends on recognizing patterns in the observed retransmission behavior that can be related to deliberate adjustments of the retransmission time-out interval. The basic technique, described earlier, is simply to raise the time-out value when the number of retransmissions increases and lower it when the number of retransmissions decreases, in an attempt to keep the number of retransmissions at some "optimal" level (the threshold).

For most real-world configurations, this basic technique is much too simplistic. It works only if changes in round-trip delay are the only significant cause of changes in the number of retransmissions per measurement interval; the "threshold" number of "real" retransmissions must be known in advance and must not change significantly. Even when these conditions are met, the retransmission timer value will oscillate whether or not the retransmission behavior changes, unless a longitudinal damping function is used to stabilize it. There are a number of ways to im-prove the basic adaptive retransmission scheme. A smoothing function that accounts for recent history (one or two measurement intervals back) can be used to damp oscillation of the time-out value around the threshold. A simple first-order smoothing function might operate to ensure that the time-out value is adjusted only when a change in retransmission behavior has persisted for two or more consecutive measurement intervals. A second-order function (which accounts for changes in the rate of change of the number of retransmissions) can be used to damp oscillations even further, depending on how widely the number of "real" re-transmissions is expected to fluctuate and on how firmly these oscillations must be damped to provide acceptable perfor-

---

24. Although they are discussed separately in this chapter, the dynamic adjustment of retransmission timers and the sliding window flow-control strategy (introduced earlier) will be closely coupled in any actual transport protocol implementation.

mance. No damping function, however, can prevent performance-killing inflation of the re-transmission time-out interval or of the "threshold" number of retransmissions that are interpreted as "real" (and therefore acceptable).

Consider, for example, the following scenario. A change in the characteristics of the end-to-end path over which packets are flowing causes an increase in the number of packets that are lost and/or corrupted; this causes a corresponding increase in the number of packets that must be retransmitted. These are "real" retransmissions, but neither of the transport protocol machines involved has any way of knowing this; as far as they can tell, the observed increase in the number of retransmissions might just as well be caused by premature expiration of the re-transmission timer due to an increase in the end-to-end transit delay. If this condition persists, the retransmission time-out will be adjusted upward until the number of retransmissions per measurement interval stops increasing (if the condition disappears fast enough, and the number of retransmissions drops back to its former level within the granularity of the damping function, the retransmission time-out will not be changed). The increase in the number of retransmissions had nothing to do with the value of the retransmission timer, but the adaptive retransmission algorithm thinks that its action in raising the time-out value is responsible for halting the increase in the number of retransmissions (because when the time-out interval was raised, the increase in the number of retransmissions stopped—Piaget would love this algorithm). If the algorithm's analysis goes no further than this, the time-out interval will stabilize at a new (higher) value and will be driven back down only if the number of retransmissions starts to decline. Just when efficient retransmission behavior is most important (to minimize the adverse effects of the increase in the number of lost and/or corrupted packets), the retransmission time-out interval is inflated, increasing the time it takes the protocol to recover from errors. This is not good.

In principle, the retransmission time-out interval should be adjusted only to account for changes in transit delay; changing the time-out interval will not affect the number of retransmissions that are due to other causes (such as a change in the number of lost or corrupted packets). But because it is not possible to distinguish "real" retransmissions (due to loss and/or corruption of packets) from "false" ones (due to premature retransmission timer expiration, caused by a mismatch between the time-out value and the actual end-to-end transit delay), the inflation just described cannot be prevented. It can, however, be corrected after it has occurred by making the basic adaptive retransmission algorithm more sophisticated. When the number of retransmissions per measurement interval changes spontaneously, the algorithm has no choice but to change the retransmission timer value accordingly (damping small oscillations). When the number of retransmissions is stable, however, the algorithm can deliberately alter the retransmission time-out: increase it to see whether the number drops or decrease it to see whether the number rises. By periodically challenging a stable timer value, the algorithm can correct inflation of the time-out interval and can also correct a too-short time-out interval that is producing an unnecessarily high (but stable, and therefore unprovocative) number of retransmissions.

Adapting retransmission timer values to cope with variable delay is certainly not unique to OSI; it has been observed and managed in TCP networks for many years. In RFC 793, it is recommended that the retransmission time-out be based on *round-trip time* (RTT), which is computed by recording the time elapsed between sending a data segment and receiving the corresponding acknowledgment and by sampling frequently. The algorithm used to compute the round-trip time is:

```
smoothedRoundTripTime = (å* oldRoundTripTime) + ((1 - å)*newRoundTripTime)
```

where å, a weighting factor, is selected such that $0 < å < 1$.

A small å responds to delay quickly; a large å, slowly. The time-out value should be greater than the round-trip time but within reason; for example:

```
time-out = minimum(upperBound, ß*smoothedRoundTripTime)
```

where ß, a delay variance factor, is selected such that $1.3 < ß < 2$.

Some deficiences have been identified and corrected in this initial algorithm. Karn and Partridge (1987) observed that retransmitted segments cause ambiguities in the round-trip time computation; specifically, if the sender cannot determine whether the acknowledgment corresponds to an original data packet or a retransmission, it cannot determine the correct round-trip time for that packet. The Karn/Partridge algorithm computes the round-trip time only for packets that are not retransmitted and increases the retransmission timer by a multiplicative factor (2 is suggested) each time a segment is retransmitted.

Further study showed that limiting ß in the manner described in RFC 793 will fail if delays vary widely, and Jacobson (1988) proposes that estimates for both the average round-trip time and the variance should be provided and that the estimated variance be used in place of ß. These algorithms work as well in TP4 implementations as in TCP implementations.

Connection-Establishment Timers

During OSI transport connection establishment, two timers govern the re-transmission of the connect request and connect confirm packets. These packets are sent out before there has been any opportunity to observe or infer the end-to-end round-trip delay; and in general, no reliable "pregenerated" information about the probable delay to a given destination is available (although when it is, it can be used to guide the selection of initial CR and CC timer values). The end-to-end delay over a single subnetwork (link) might be anywhere from 1 or 2 milliseconds (for a LAN) to 250 milliseconds (for a satellite link), and there could be almost any number of these links, in various combinations, in the actual end-to-end path. The round-trip delay also includes processing time in the two end systems and in an unpredictable number of intermediate (gateway) systems. Under these circumstances, the probability of correctly guessing the optimal timer value (or even something acceptably close to it) is very small.

There is an alternative to simply picking a timer value at random. As long as the retransmission interval is increased substantially for second and subsequent retransmissions (when necessary), a very small initial time-out value (on the order of 250–500 milliseconds) can be used. This will give good performance when the actual delay is small (and configurations with small end-to-end delay are precisely the ones in which high performance is likely to be most important). The possible unnecessary retransmission of one or more connect request or connect confirm packets when the actual delay is larger than the small initial value chosen for the timer is usually acceptable, occurring as it does only during the connection-establishment phase. Incrementally backing off the retransmission timer each time it expires (using, for example, a 500-millisecond increment) and setting the "maximum number of retries" threshold fairly high (at 15, for example) can ensure that very few (if any) connection-establishment attempts are abandoned (timed out) prematurely (see "Backing Off for Subsequent Retransmissions," later in this section).

Data Retransmission Timer Value

A simple way to pick a starting value for an adaptive data packet retransmission scheme is to measure, during the connection-establishment phase, the delay between sending a connect request and receiving the corresponding connect confirm (or at the other end, between sending a connect confirm and receiving the corresponding acknowledgment or first data packet). Because the connect request and/or connect confirm packets may be retransmitted, and because processing delays associated with connection establishment are usually greater than those associated with normal data flow, this value cannot be used as a constant for the data packet retransmission time-out value; it is likely to be accurate enough, however, to ensure that an adaptive retransmission algorithm quickly converges on a satisfactory value. An adaptive retransmission scheme is most useful either when no prior information about the round-trip delay variance is available or when the available information suggests that the delay variance could be large. When it is possible to expect that the delay variance will be relatively small, better performance can be obtained from a well-chosen constant value for the data retransmission time-out value, based on a slight overestimate of the expected maximum round-trip delay (this is especially true for operation of TP4 over a network connection). The retransmission timer associated with expedited data packet can be managed in the same way as the timer associated with normal data packets.

Backing Off for Subsequent Retransmissions

No matter how cleverly the initial value for a retransmission timer is chosen, there will be circumstances in which the timer expires, the associated packet is retransmitted, and the timer must be reset. A simple approach to choosing a new timer value is to reuse the initial value. This approach will produce a series of retransmissions at evenly spaced intervals, which will terminate when the retransmission timer is canceled by the arrival of an appropriate ac-knowledgment or the maximum number of retries is reached. If the initial time-out value is not too far off the mark, or the maximum number of retries parameter is very large, this approach will work. If the initial time-out value is much too short, however, either the maximum number of retries will be exhausted before any acknowledgment has had time to arrive, or a large number of unnecessarily retransmitted packets will be pumped out of the sending system before the acknowledgment arrives. In the former case, the transport connection or connection-establishment attempt will be aborted when the sender's give-up timer expires (the value of the give-up timer depends on the retransmission timer value and the maximum number of retries, as discussed in the following subsection). In the latter case, adaptation of the initial time-out interval (as described earlier) will eventually correct the problem for data packets, but the situation will persist for connect request and connect confirm packets, for which no adaptive adjustment of the retransmission timer value is possible.

Using an equal-interval approach to retransmission constrains the choice of an initial retransmission timer value: if the two pathological situations just described are to be avoided, the time-out interval cannot be reduced below a certain "safety threshold." In configurations in which the mean transit delay is low but the delay variance is relatively high, this constraint limits the effective performance of the protocol.[25]

An algorithm that backs off geometrically for each retransmission rather than linearly eliminates this constraint. When a packet is first transmitted, the corresponding retransmission timer is set to the appropriate initial value for that packet (which is either a constant, for connect request and connect confirm packets, or a dynamic value determined by an adaptive retransmission scheme, for packets). If this timer expires, the packet is retransmitted, and the retransmission timer is set to a value that is the sum of the initial value and a fixed increment (the "back-off" increment). If this timer expires, the packet is again retransmitted, and the retransmission timer is set to a value that is the sum of the initial value and twice the back-off increment. This continues until the timer is canceled by the arrival of a suitable acknowledgment (or the transmission attempt is abandoned after "too many retries"). Each retransmission interval is therefore longer than the one before it. When the retransmission interval is increased in this way after each retransmission, the partial sums that represent the accumulated time since the first transmission of a packet grow geometrically rather than linearly. This allows a transport protocol to recover quickly from the choice of a too-small initial timer value, without falling into either of the two traps described earlier. The initial retransmission interval can be made as small as necessary to achieve good performance, relying on the geometric algorithm to back the value off safely if something goes wrong.

For the algorithm just described, the aggregate retransmission time is a function of the constant parameters for the maximum number of retries and the back-off increment. Without making the function too complicated, we can also allow the first-retransmission interval to be different from the back-off increment. Letting x be the maximum number of retries, y the interval between the initial transmission of a data packet and its first retransmission, and z the fixed increment by which the retransmission time is increased for each retransmission after the first, we obtain the following formula:

```
aggregate = y(x + 1) + [zx(x + 1)/2]
```

Note: The value of y for data packet retransmission will change dynamically if an adaptive retransmission scheme is used.

As an example, assume an implementation that has chosen $x = 5$,

---

25.   If the delay variance is low, the probability of either of the two pathological conditions' occurring is also low, and the "safety threshold" can be set as low as necessary to avoid this performance limit.

y = 500 milliseconds, and z = 1 second. At most, 18 seconds will elapse between the first transmission of a packet and the expiration of the last retransmission timer ("too many retries"). This value sets a lower bound on the value of the give-up timer.

Give-Up Timer

Associated with each OSI transport connection is a "give-up" timer, which is started (or restarted) whenever the first incarnation of a data packet is sent out (that is, it is not reset when a data packet is retransmitted, as is the data packet retransmission timer). Whenever an acknowledgment covering all outstanding data packets is received, the give-up timer is canceled.[26]

The give-up timer establishes an upper bound on the amount of time that can elapse between the first transmission of a packet and the receipt of an acknowledgment that covers that transport protocol data unit. The expectation of an acknowledgment can remain unfulfilled for no more than the give-up time-out interval before TP4 decides that its peer is either dead, disabled, or malfunctioning; if the give-up timer expires, the corresponding transport connection is torn down.

The give-up timer value should be large enough so that it includes any reasonable combination of end-to-end processing and transmission delays (including the maximum number of retransmissions). It must, however, be less than the value of the reference timer in all other transport protocol machines with which a given implementation will communicate, to ensure that no retransmission can occur after a remote peer has decided that it is safe to reuse a transport connection reference (see "Reference Timer," later in this section). When, for whatever reason, a transport protocol machine stops receiving the packets that are being sent by its peer, the operation of the give-up timer in the sending system ensures that the sender will not inject a packet into the pipe that might (if the pipe eventually clears) arrive at the receiver after the expiration of the receiver's reference timer.

The value of the give-up timer must be greater than the maximum aggregate data retransmission time and less than the value of the reference timer in all other transport systems. In the example described in the previous subsection, the aggregate data retransmission time is 18 seconds. A typical reference timer value (again, see "Reference Timer") is 100 seconds. Within these bounds, a reasonable give-up timer value would be 40 seconds.

---

26. Whenever the expedited data option is implemented, there are actually two separate give-up timers: one for normal data TPDUs and one for expedited data TPDUs. They operate independently, but in the same way.

Inactivity Timer

On every transport connection, each of the two transport protocol machines involved must regularly demonstrate both existence and sanity to its peer, by sending a correctly formed packet. This is true whether or not the peers have any user data to exchange; in the absence of data flow, the peers exchange acknowledgment packets in response to the expiration of their window timers (discussed later in this section). The protocol depends on this "I'm OK, you're OK" form of phatic communion to maintain connectivity and to detect its loss. Silence, therefore, is an abnormal (and eventually fatal) condition.

The inactivity timer detects silence. It is started when a connection is first established and is reset whenever any valid packet is received for that connection. It expires, therefore, only when a period of silence has persisted for long enough that the local transport protocol machine must assume that its peer has either died or become disabled. The expiration of an inactivity timer results in termination of the corresponding transport connection.

The value of the inactivity timer is chosen to reflect the most appropriate compromise between the desire to keep a sick transport connection open as long as there is a reasonable hope that it can be revived (within the "quality of service" constraints, if any, specified by the transport user) and the desire to recognize a genuinely dead connection as quickly as possible. Since the value of the window timer is directly related to the value of the inactivity timer in all other transport implementations, the inactivity timer value must be chosen carefully.

Window Timer

Whenever there is two-way data traffic on a transport connection, the corresponding flow of acknowledgments in both directions ensures that both transport machines have up-to-date window (flow-control) information. If data packets flow in only one direction, or if there are no data packets flowing in either direction (there are no user data to send, or one or both of the transport protocol machines has closed its receive window), this information must be exchanged by some other mechanism.

The window timer generates a flow of acknowledgment packets that depends only on the existence and health of the sending transport protocol machine; even when there is no need to acknowledge a data packet, an acknowledgment packet will be sent at regular intervals as the window timer expires. This serves two essential purposes: it prevents the remote peer's inactivity timer from expiring in response to a long stretch of silence (that is, it convinces the remote peer that its partner is still alive and well), and it conveys up-to-date window information (credit), which may change whether or not there is current data traffic. To understand the importance of the latter function, consider that when a receive window closes, a potential sender—which can't send into a closed window, of course, and therefore will not be getting new acknowledgments as a result of having sent new data—will never learn that the receive window has reopened unless the receiver sends an "unprovoked" acknowledgment containing a new credit.

Because one of the roles of the window timer is to prevent the expiration of the inactivity timer in a remote peer, its value must be chosen with respect to the value of the inactivity timer in other transport protocol machines. Since acknowledgments, like other packets, can be lost, the value of the inactivity timer is usually chosen to allow one or two "window" acknowledgments to be generated and lost without risking expiration of the inactivity timer. A typical value for the window timer allows for three window time-outs within an interval that is slightly smaller than the inactivity time-out interval.

Reference Timer

When an OSI transport connection is closed (normally or abnormally), a *reference timer* is started; until it expires, the local connection reference number that was used for the old connection cannot be reused for a new one. The reference timer ensures that a new connection based on a previously used connection reference number cannot be opened until it is certain that all packets generated during the lifetime of the old connection have disappeared.

The reference timer is designed to cope with situations such as the one described in the following scenario. Two transport protocol machines establish a transport connection and start exchanging data packets. At some point, congestion in the path between the two transport peers causes a data packet (and its subsequent retransmissions) to be delayed long enough for the give-up timer in the sending transport protocol machine to expire, terminating the connection. Eventually, however, the congestion clears, and the packet (and/or one or more of its retransmissions) arrives at its destination. If the reference number that was used for the original transport connection has been reused in the interim to establish a new connection, the late-arriving packet could be (mis)interpreted as belonging to the new connection.

It is important to note that no value of the reference timer is large enough to guarantee, by itself, that the confusion just described cannot arise. It is also necessary for the underlying internetwork protocol to operate in such a way that internetwork protocol data units, which carry packets, are discarded after a specific "packet lifetime" is exceeded. The OSI connectionless network protocol includes this function (see Chapter

13). A local system-management function must ensure that the reference time-out value associated with each transport connection is greater than the packet lifetime specified in the network protocol packets that carry data for that transport connection.

Approximately 2^{16} reference numbers are available for use with transport connection endpoints associated with a single NSAP (network) address. Most transport implementations—assuming that even under the most extreme circumstances, it will take at least a couple of milliseconds to set up and tear down a transport connection—will use a value of about 2^7 or 2^8 seconds for the reference timer. If it is very important to recover the local system resources dedicated to a transport connection quickly after the connection is closed, a smaller value will be used. A value of 100 seconds is about the lowest that can be used safely in a general-purpose implementation.

Connection Release (Connection Refusal) in the OSI Transport Protocol

There are actually two circumstances that dictate the release of an OSI transport connection. The first, *connection refusal*, occurs when the called transport entity cannot satisfy one or more of the conditions of transport connection establishment conveyed in the connection request packet, or when the connect request packet received is in error. To refuse a transport connection, the called transport entity composes and returns a *disconnect request* packet (DR TPDU) (Figure 12.19) containing the reason for refusing the connection. The expected reasons for refusing a connection are identified (negotiation failed, reference overflow, transport service access point address unknown), and several more creative reasons for refusing a connection are provided (congestion at transport service access point, session entity not attached to transport service access point).

If the connection is refused due to an inability to parse the connect request packet, the called transport entity returns an error packet (ER TPDU), indicating the reason for refusal. This form of connection refusal typically reflects an error in implementation (e.g., an invalid parameter or parameter value was encountered) or detection of a bit-level error as a result of computing the checksum on the connect request packet. All of the octets of the connect request packet that caused the rejection are returned in the variable part of the error packet.

Connection release is an extremely mundane phase of operation. To

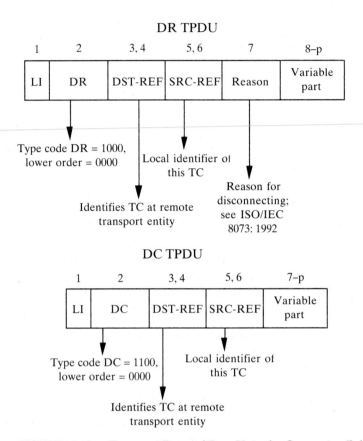

FIGURE 12.19   Transport Protocol Data Units for Connection Release

the degree that one finds transport connections interesting, all of the interesting things have already occurred: both parties have negotiated the characteristics of a connection, meaningful information transfer has taken place, and for those readers old enough to remember, "Now it's time to say goodbye . . . to all our com-pah-nee."[27] The process is especially mundane in the OSI transport protocol since no effort is made to ensure that all data transmitted in both directions have been acknowledged before the transport connection is released (according to the letter of the law as prescribed by the OSI reference model, if a graceful or orderly release is desired, it will be performed by the session layer, when the orderly release functional unit is selected; see Chapter 11, whether

---

27.   For those too young to remember, these are the first words of the closing song of the "Mickey Mouse Club" television show of the fifties.

the functionality implemented at the session layer is equivalent to TCP's graceful close is a subject of ongoing debate).

Essentially, OSI transport connection release is a process of abruptly announcing one's departure from the conversation: one party—the calling or called transport entity, either as the result of an explicit request by a transport service user (a T-DISCONNECT.request) or as a local matter—issues a *disconnect request* packet (DR TPDU) (see Figure 12.20). Following transmission (or reception) of the disconnect request packet, there's lots of tidying up to do:

- All timers related to this transport connection are stopped. For TP4, this may include the retransmission, inactivity, and window timers.
- The receiver composes and returns a *disconnect confirm* packet (DC TPDU) (see Figure 12.19) to the initiating transport entity, and notifies the transport user via a T-DISCONNECT.indication primitive.
- Both parties freeze reference numbers (see "Timers and Open transport Protocols," earlier in this chapter).

Upon expiration of the timer bounding the use of references, the transport entities consider the transport connection closed.

Connection Release (Refusal) in TCP

The circumstances that dictate the release of an OSI transport connection exist for TCP as well. *Connection refusal* occurs in TCP when the responding TCP entity cannot establish a TCP connection or when the SYN packet received is in error. To refuse a TCP connection, the called TCP entity sets the RST and ACK bits in the code field of the TCP packet to 1, and

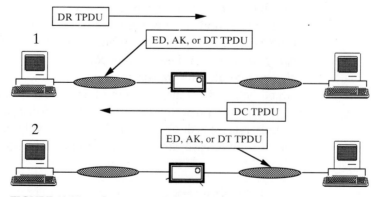

FIGURE 12.20   Connection Release, TP4

sets the acknowledgment sequence number to the initiator's ISN, incremented by 1; unlike the OSI transport protocol, no reason for refusing the connection is indicated in the RST/ACK segment. (A quick examination of the OSI reason codes suggests that this is no great loss.)

TCP offers two forms of *connection release*: abrupt and graceful. Abrupt release indicates that something seriously wrong has occurred. Again, the RST bit of the code field is set to 1; depending on the current state of the TCP entity that receives the RST segment, the sequence-number and acknowledgment sequence number fields may be significant. Graceful close in TCP is an orderly shutdown process. All information transmitted in both directions must be acknowledged before the TCP connection is considered "finished" and may be closed. When an upper-layer protocol has finished sending data and wishes to close the TCP connection, the TCP entity indicates this state to its peer by sending a TCP segment with the FIN bit of the code field set to 1. The sequence-number field is set to the value of the last byte transmitted. The receiver of the FIN segment must acknowledge receipt of the last octet but is not required to close its half of the connection; it may continue to transfer data, and the initiator of the FIN segment must dutifully acknowledge all data received until it receives a TCP segment with the FIN and ACK bits of the code field set to 1 and an acknowledgment number set to the sequence number of the last octet received from the FIN segment initiator. Upon receiving the FIN/ACK segment, the FIN initiator returns an ACK segment, completing a three-way "good-bye," as illustrated in Figure 12.21.

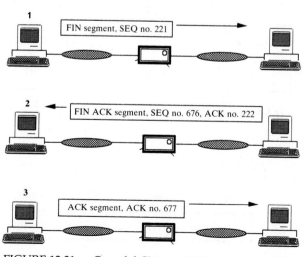

FIGURE 12.21   Graceful Close in TCP

Datagram Transport Protocols—CLTP and UDP

Both OSI and TCP/IP support connectionless (datagram) operation at the transport layer as an alternative to connections for upper-layer protocols that do not need the reliability and other characteristics of a transport connection. The service model is simple unconfirmed best-effort delivery (see Figure 12.22). Formally, the OSI connectionless transport service (ISO/IEC 8072: 1993) is supported by the OSI connectionless transport protocol (ISO/IEC 8602: 1987). Like TCP/IP's user datagram protocol (UDP; RFC 768), the primary purpose of which is to differentiate user-level processes identified by the port number, the primary purpose of the OSI connectionless transport protocol is to differentiate transport service users identified by the transport service access point identifier of the transport service access point address.

The differences between the two are unremarkable (see Figure 12.23). OSI connectionless transport supports variable-length transport service access point addresses, whereas the upper datagram protocol supports 16-bit port numbers. Both provide user data-integrity checks by means of a 16-bit checksum; in both protocols, if the checksum verification fails, the packet is dropped with no indication to the upper layer process (transport service user).

The user datagram protocol is used to support a number of widely used applications in TCP/IP networks: Sun's Network File System/ Remote Procedure Call, the Domain Name System, the Simple Network Management Protocol, even a routing protocol (the Routing Information

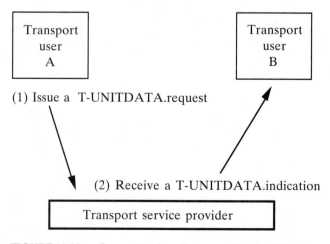

FIGURE 12.22   Connectionless Transport Service Primitives

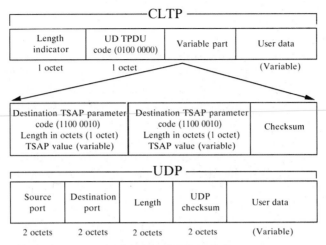

FIGURE 12.23   CLTP and UDP Formats

Protocol; see Chapter 14). The OSI connectionless transport protocol is ostensibly used by OSI connectionless upper layers, but to date, no application service elements have been developed to use these. Sun's Network File System is run over the OSI connectionless transport protocol today, and in dual-stack environments the Simple Network Management Protocol may be operated over it to manage CLNP-based networks in those configurations in which the managed agent does not support the User Datagram Protocol—i.e., those configurations in which an OSI-only host or router is present in an otherwise dual-stack topology (RFC 1418). (Network operators may also find it convenient to use the Simple Net-work Management Protocol over the OSI connectionless transport protocol in certain network diagnostic/debugging modes, in which it is useful to have management information traverse the same logical topology as data packets.)

Socket Interfaces to Datagram Transport Services

In ARGO 1.0 and RENO UNIX, the user datagram protocol and the OSI connectionless transport protocol are accessed via sockets (type *sock-dgram*). The Internet address family is used for UDP, and the ISO address family for CLTP. Both UDP and CLTP sockets support a best-effort datagram service via the *sendto* and *recvfrom* system calls. (In certain applications, the *connect()* call can be used to "fix" the destination address, and subsequent packets can be sent/received using the *recv()*, *read()*, *send()*, or *write()* system calls.)

Conclusion

The transport layer plays the same critical role in both the OSI and TCP/IP architectures: it defines the concept of "host" or "end system," in which applications live, and distinguishes these end-user hosts from systems that are concerned only with the "intermediate" functions (routing, relaying, switching, and transmission) of networking. As it is typically deployed at a real boundary between facilities belonging to end users and facilities belonging to the network, transport is the host's opportunity to ensure that its applications get the data pipe that *they* want, regardless of what the *network* is prepared to provide. The OSI transport protocol fudges this a bit by defining classes 0 through 3 in such a way that the end-to-end reliability seen by applications in fact depends very much on what the network is able to provide; but class 4, and TCP, support a genuinely network-independent transport service, which can be provided as reliably over connectionless internets as over connection-oriented networks. For applications that do not require the reliability of a transport connection, OSI and TCP/IP provide connectionless (transport datagram) alternatives as separate protocols.

Much has been written about the differences between TCP and the OSI class-4 transport protocol in an effort to prove that one or the other is "better." There is ample fuel for this debate: TCP is octet-sequenced, TP4 is packet-sequenced; TCP has graceful close, TP4 does not; TCP's port numbers are fixed at 16 bits, TP4's are variable-length. The list is long, but it contains no "killer argument" in favor of either protocol. Readers interested in pursuing this question will find a convincing argument for the essential irrelevance of this "which is better?" debate in Chapin (1990).

13 THE NETWORK LAYER

Like all the other OSI layers, the network layer provides both connection-less and connection-oriented services. The upper layers and transport provide these two types of service to satisfy a broad range of application and end-user needs. This is universally recognized as a "good thing." In the network layer, the presence of two types of service is generally considered to be a "bad thing." The reason for this is simple: everything above the network layer is host-specific and can be tailored to suit a particular application running among some set of mutually consenting hosts without affecting the communications of other hosts using the same internetwork; the network layer, however, provides the fundamental connectivity without which no communication of any kind can take place among hosts. Most people agree that having one type of service at the network layer would be preferable to having two; as always, though, the problem stems from having to decide *which one*.[1]

The TCP/IP architecture, which from the beginning was based on an "internetworking" model of the network layer,[2] avoided this controversy entirely; the TCP/IP network layer is exclusively connectionless.[3]

---

1.   There are people who attempt to justify a "diversity of needs" at the network layer, but their sense of what constitutes *interoperability* is quite different from ours.

2.   The best (and certainly the most succinct) description of the fundamental architectural premise of the TCP/IP network layer is the one that Vint Cerf uses to describe the TCP/IP internetworking model: "I P on everything."

3.   The requirement to support new types of service in the Internet, such as real-time service for voice and video, may change the traditional "datagrams-only" model of the TCP/IP network layer. The new concept of a "flow," which is neither a connection nor datagrams, promises to make the TCP/IP network layer a bit more complicated (but also a bit more useful) in the near future (Partridge 1992).

The issues surrounding a "choose one" decision at the network layer were of such a highly charged political, economic, and emotional nature that convergence on a single networking solution for OSI was, and remains, a pipe dream. Compounding the problem, there is no generally recognized way to interwork between connection-oriented and connectionless networks. ISO/IEC 8648: 1987, *Internal Organization of the Network Layer*, does not provide a solution; however, demystifying its contents does provide meaningful insight into the problem, so it is a logical place to begin.

Architecture: The Internal Organization of the Network Layer

It is virtually impossible to understand the purpose and contents of the *Internal Organization of the Network Layer* standard without a historical perspective. In the abstract, the OSI network layer provides *the* switching fabric over which end systems communicate. The notion of a single, open networking environment for data is a powerful one, since it implies a very broad scale of connectivity. In fact, it is not hard to imagine (and even easier to desire) an *open* data network that is as ubiquitous as the voice network.

The postal, telephone, and telegraph (PTT) administrations of many national governments[4] have long been committed to standards as processed for telephony under the CCITT. A strong political incentive existed at the time of OSI network-layer standards development to institute a single, uniform network service standard for data. Publicly, advocates of this *network-centric* view claimed that a single service, modeled after the voice network, would scale well—the voice network certainly did. A framework for multiorganizational administration existed for nasty issues like addressing and interworking. Moreover, they continued, similar service characteristics could be expected irrespective of the location of the source and target applications. Privately, these parties hoped that by bringing computer communications further under the administration of the PTTs, they would "contracept" further expansion of the private networking offered by large multinational computer vendors. By so doing, they hoped to promote the interests of their native (especially European) com-

---

4. Some countries, including the United States and the United Kingdom, do not have a single "national" public network agency. To accommodate these countries, the CCITT considers that *recognized private operating agencies* (RPOAs), such as British Telecom and AT&T, have standing equivalent to the PTTs of countries with national public network agencies.

puter vendors and strengthen both their own domestic and international markets. In short, they hoped to expand the market for public networking services, helping their home computer companies in the process.

OSI network-layer development also began when data communication was, by today's standards, in its infancy. Turnkey remote job entry and terminal-to-mainframe communications were the principal applications. Local area networks were fledgling and pricey technologies. On-premises terminal connectivity was achieved by a hodgepodge of largely proprietary asynchronous "poll-select" technologies, and wide-area bandwidth was expensive, even for modest kilobit-rate services, so applications (and end users) were made to tolerate delay. Compared to even the smallest of today's regional TCP/IP networks, private networking was a small-scale, predominantly mainframe-to-mainframe enterprise, and the wide area network was the center of the universe.

When the price of local area network (LAN) technology dropped, the "public network is everything" paradigm was shattered forever. On-premises bandwidth was cheap and plentiful; applications and processing were distributed among large numbers of increasingly powerful yet smaller computers, initially across local area networks, but soon across higher-bandwidth wide area services. Thus, two paradigms for network service—local area network and wide area network—collided precisely at the time of the development of standards for the OSI network layer.

Renegades from the community of local area network equipment manufacturers and consumers rose to challenge the network-centric view of the world. Unlike voice service, they argued, for which the service characteristics necessary to support the primary application (speech) have remained constant for a century, the characteristics of network services necessary for computer-to-computer communications vary widely from application to application. Terminal access to remote computers requires only low bandwidth and can tolerate delay, whereas networked file services like Sun's Network File System (Sandberg 1988) require high bandwidth and low delay, but only for short periods or *bursts*. Other applications (electronic mail, file transfer) have requirements somewhere between these extremes.

Applications also have varying requirements for data integrity, reliability in data transfer, and other characteristics. The local area network proponents argued that true distributed applications needed LAN-like characteristics across a wide area. These can best be provided by adopting the internetworking protocol concepts demonstrated in the Defense Advanced Research Projects Agency experiments and deployed in proprietary architectures such as Xerox Network Systems (XNS), Digital

Network Architecture (DNA), and Burroughs Network Architecture (BNA). Privately, vendors of host computers, routers, and other computer-communications equipment hoped to use OSI as a means of penetrating hitherto single-vendor "closed-shop" environments held by the industry giants: in an open platform, smaller, nimbler manufacturers could compete for market share by specializing rather than offering a comprehensive micro-to-mainframe line of computers. The industry giants contributed their proprietary solutions to universal networking problems in an attempt to ease the inevitable transition. Computer vendors big and small—hereafter referred to as *host-centrics*—had a common objective: they wanted a solution that would enable them to sell more communications as well as host equipment.

The OSI network layer is thus *where net-worlds collide.* Two substantially different views of the way in which network service should be provided had been defined. Champions for both causes stepped forward, lines were drawn in the sand, and battles ensued. The *Internal Organization of the Network Layer* was to become the demilitarized zone of the "police action" initiated to unify the OSI network layer. Within this standard, it was expected that differences would be reconciled and a framework for interconnectivity would be defined.

The *Internal Organization of the Network Layer* began as a microarchitecture document for the OSI network layer. It was to provide a functional description of the network layer that related the OSI architectural model of the network layer to the "real-world" networks, switches (routers and bridges, but also carrier network packet switches), and host computers that comprised the OSI environment (for a historical perspective, see Hemrick [1984]). It was gradually transformed into a means of describing how to retrofit the OSI reference model view of the network layer onto existing real-world networks.

⸻

▮·AHA·▮ *All discussions concerning "architecture" begin with the seemingly innocent question, "What is X?" Questions of this nature are the very essence of why, in many OSI standards meetings, a great deal is said and little is done. The ISO group responsible for producing the* Internal Organization of the Network Layer *spent no less than three meetings fine-tuning the definition of a subnetwork so that all parties could point to their individual "collection of equipment and physical media which forms an autonomous whole and which can be used to interconnect real systems for purposes of communication" (ISO/IEC 8648: 1987) and say, "Now that's a real subnetwork."*

The *Internal Organization of the Network Layer* spends lots of time explaining the real world. Real subnetworks, particularly those that provide a public service tariffed by a common carrier, have a specific protocol that *data terminal equipment* (DTE) uses to access the packet-switching equipment of the public network provider; such protocols are called *subnetwork access protocols* (SNAcPs). Local area network medium access control (MAC) protocols, accompanied by logical link control (LLC) procedures and protocol, can also be said to be subnetwork access protocols.[5] There are consequently many subnetwork access protocols in the real world, providing a wide range of subnetwork services; in fact, creation of subnetwork access protocols is something of an annual event in the standards community.

Most or all of the subnetwork access protocols used in real-world subnetworks don't provide the OSI network service: some functions—for example, the ability to convey the very long and variable-length OSI network service access point addresses—were neither anticipated nor provided for in protocols such as CCITT Recommendation X.25-1980 or the TCP/IP internet protocol (RFC 791).

The proposition put forth in the *Internal Organization of the Network Layer* is that the (presumably small) discrepancy between the OSI network service and the service provided by each subnetwork can be fixed by adding functionality to "enhance" the subnetworks and the equipment connecting them (and connected to them) in one of several ways.

Hop-by-Hop Harmonization

One alternative is to pile functions and protocols on top of each individual subnetwork access protocol, one by one, so that each one is elevated to the level of the OSI network service. This is a case-by-case solution; hence, the term *hop by hop*. This method involves identifying those elements of the OSI network service that are missing from a given subnetwork access protocol and *adding* them. According to this strategy, if subnetwork A could provide all of the OSI network service features except the ability to signal a RESET, one could incorporate a RESET capability into subnetwork A's subnetwork access protocol, and the enhanced subnetwork A would then be capable of providing the OSI network service. If another subnetwork, B, could provide all but the ability to convey OSI network-layer addressing, one could extend the addressing capabilities of subnetwork B's sub-

---

5. By the time the ISO network-layer committee decided upon the term *subnetwork access protocol*, all of the straightforward acronyms containing the letters *SNA* were taken. In particular, it was obviously inappropriate to use *SNA protocol*, and the IEEE 802.1 committee had only recently devised the logical link control subnetwork access protocol (LLC/SNAP); hence, it was necessary to include a lowercase *c* in ISO's acronym.

network access protocol, and the enhanced subnetwork B would then be capable of providing the OSI network service as well. One could then plug subnetworks A and B together, and real end systems attached to subnetwork A could use the OSI network service to communicate with real end systems attached to subnetwork B.

In the real world, making modifications ("enhancements") to every subnetwork access protocol would require changes in far too many end systems, and end-user reaction to such an effort would be ugly indeed (Q: "Why did it take God only six days to create the world?" A: "He didn't have to worry about the installed base . . ."). Better to pile stuff on top of a handful of the most important network protocols to make them support the OSI network service, which is exactly what ISO and CCITT did. The *Internal Organization of the Network Layer* prescribes the use of a protocol *between* the transport protocol and the subnetwork access protocol to convey the missing elements of the OSI network service. As an example, the ability to carry big addresses was missing from the 1980 version of the X.25 packet-level protocol; specifically, the called and calling address fields of the *call request* packet were too small to convey jumbo OSI network service access point addresses. Oh so clever bit-twiddlers devised a way to employ the *call user data* facilities field of the call request packet to convey OSI network service access point addresses and other missing elements of the OSI connection-oriented network service, and thus extend the life of the data circuit-terminating equipment (DCE) in those public networks in which X.25-1984 availability was not imminent. Since the use of this particular technique was unique to X.25-1980, and similar techniques could be devised to operate over other existing subnetwork access protocols with shortcomings, the notion of a *subnetwork-dependent convergence protocol* (SNDCP) was born. (See Figure 13.1.)

In theory, this process could be applied to all subnetworks over which the OSI network service might be provided; in the extreme case, all the subnetworks in the world. Thus, the degree to which this approach can be successfully applied is directly related to just how many subnetwork access protocols one must modify and how many subnetwork-dependent convergence protocols one must create; i.e., how *heterogeneous* the existing subnetwork environment is. Since the network-centrics' view of the world was that there was considerable *homogeneity* among carrier data networks, this seemed to them that the number would be manageably small.

Internetworking Protocol Approach

Host-centrics approach the problem of subnetwork interconnection with a radically different perspective. The host-centric view of the problem

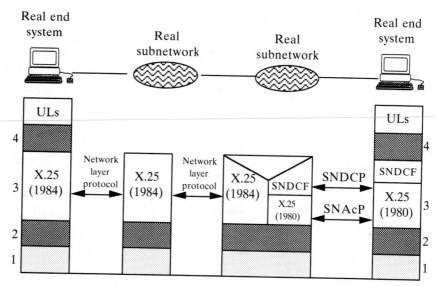

FIGURE 13.1   Hop-by-Hop Harmonization

reflects what folks who deal with LAN-based networks see every day:

- There are many different types of subnetworks in the world.
- They will inevitably be connected together.
- Trying to make them all look exactly alike is hopeless.[6]

For the heterogeneous environments encountered in the real world every day, the practical thing to do is to define one protocol that assumes minimal subnetwork functionality and place it firmly on top of every subnetwork access protocol; i.e., define a *subnetwork independent convergence protocol* (SNICP).

Technically, it is relatively simple to design a subnetwork-independent convergence protocol: treat every subnetwork and data-link service as providing a basic data pipe. Each pipe should support a service data unit large enough to accommodate the header of the subnetwork-independent convergence protocol and a reasonable amount of user data. This is the IP or OSI connectionless network protocol (CLNP) model of networking. In Figure 13.2, CLNP operates in end and intermediate systems in the same manner as IP operates in hosts and routers. Every subnetwork and data-link service that is to provide an underlying, supporting

---

6.   In fact, electrical engineers have demonstrated that they can invent new networking technologies much faster than international standards bodies can develop and approve new subnetwork dependent convergence protocol standards.

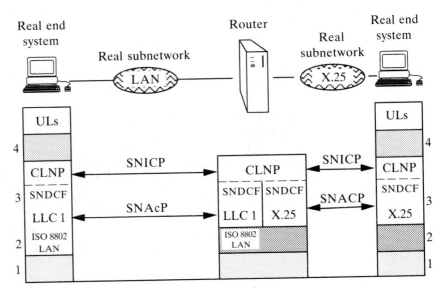

FIGURE 13.2   Internetworking Protocol Approach

service to CLNP must be capable of transferring 512 octets of data.

These minimal requirements are easily accommodated over ISO/IEC 8802 local area networks[7] without introducing convergence protocols; in such cases, CLNP packets are mapped directly onto the ISO/IEC 8802-2 logical link control (ISO/IEC 8802-2: 1990) service data units. The mapping is called a *subnetwork-dependent convergence function* (SNDCF). With different subnetwork dependent convergence functions, CLNP can also be run over connection oriented subnetworks like X.25 public data networks, X.21 circuit-switched data networks, or switched data links. However, the subnetwork-dependent convergence functions are more complex, since they must deal with *subnetwork connection management*. (See "Use of X.25 to Provide a Subnetwork Service in OSI Networks," later in this chapter.)

Hop-by-hop harmonization is something of a bottom-up approach: you look at what your subnetwork lacks and pump it up so that it offers the OSI network service. Internetworking is more of a top-down approach: begin with the assumption that the transport protocol will do what it is supposed to do, define a simple data-transmission service at the network layer, and write a protocol that allows you to forward packets over any underlying bit pipe.

---

7. The ISO/IEC standards for local area networks, consisting of multiple parts of ISO/IEC 8802 (8802-2, 8802-3, etc.), are equivalent to the corresponding IEEE local area network

| AHA | *Although the use of CLNP to provide a uniform connectionless network service over any combination of underlying "sub"networks seems natural to anyone familiar with the internetworking architecture that underlies the TCP/IP Internet (and many vendor-proprietary networks), it was politically naive to propose it as an alternative to hop-by-hop harmonization in the early years of OSI development. Why? The answer may be found in the phrase "placing it firmly and uniformly on top of every subnetwork access protocol," which suggests that those subnetwork access protocols—the pride and joy, not to mention the economic staples, of many large public network service providers—are somehow deficient, not up to the demands of providing the OSI network service. To recognize themselves as providers only of edge-to-edge service (from subnetwork entry-point to subnetwork exit point) rather than end-to-end service (from end user to end user), the public networks would have had to abandon their claims of networking omnipresence and omniscience. Naturally, they were initially unwilling to do this. With hindsight, however, it can be seen that their reluctance to recognize the importance of internetworking delayed the completion of work on the OSI network layer for at least five years and is one of the reasons why OSI networking today is more of a "missed opportunity" than a reality.* |

As if to prove that history repeats itself even in fields with the comparatively brief history of networking, the basic mistake of many X.25 proponents of the late 1970s—believing that a single network technology could be extrapolated into a monolithic global data network—is being replayed in the 1990s by some extremist proponents of asynchronous transfer mode (ATM), who argue that "internetworking" is obsolete, because they can build a worldwide ATM-everywhere wide area network that will "seamlessly" interconnect ATM local area networks, and there won't be any need to have Ethernets, token rings, fiber-distributed data interfaces, or any other "old" network technology. And nothing better will ever be invented. Ever. Really.

Connections or Connectionless?

Before we close the subject of OSI network layer architecture, it will be useful to examine the issues that can be debated when political hats are removed and the technical pros and cons of connection-oriented networks and datagram networks are examined.

Network connections generally have the following characteristics:

- Once a network connection is established, all data packets travel along the same path. Network connections thus offer low routing

---

standards, consisting of multiple parts of IEEE 802 (802.2, 802.3, etc.).

overhead, but they are not resilient; if one link in the path breaks, the connection is broken.

- Network connections provide fixed paths with guaranteed quality of service characteristics (bandwidth, delay, residual error rate); during connection establishment, resources are reserved at each "hop" to minimize quality of service variability. Although this is good for the established network connections, the reserved resources cannot be used by or for other network connections while an established network connection is idle.
- Network connection state must be maintained at every intermediate "hop."
- Network connection-establishment overhead is unacceptable for bursty data. Some applications require very high bandwidth for a very brief spurt or "burst." For example, if a user of a distributed file service attempts to retrieve a file from a remote server across a local area network, that user wants the read completed as quickly as if the file were stored locally (see Sandberg, 1988). The network service must exhibit both high throughput *and* low latency. Network connection establishment is more time-consuming than sending a datagram and in these circumstances is ill-advised; consider how difficult it might be for a file server to reserve a virtual circuit having the bandwidth necessary to read a 4-megabyte file in some measure of milliseconds and do so for many clients.

Connectionless data transfer has its own set of strengths and weaknesses:

- Datagrams are a best-effort delivery; reliability mechanisms, if required, must be provided at the transport layer.
- State machine handling of datagrams at intermediate hops is greatly simplified when compared to network connections.
- Since each packet is routed independently, routing overhead is imposed at each hop. In most routing systems, however, routing is adaptive in the face of failures.
- Resources are used as needed (no resource reservation per network connection); however, to minimize quality of service variability, multilevel congestion-management mechanisms and possibly type of service routing may be required.
- There is no connection setup. Resources are allocated as needed or "on demand." Connectionless data transfer is better suited for supporting bursty data applications.

A colleague (Winston Edmond, who works with one of the authors at Bolt Beranek and Newman) has suggested a useful thumbnail description of the difference between datagrams and connections:

- *Datagrams:* The hosts don't tell the network anything about the traffic they are about to send. In this case, the best the network can do is to monitor the dynamic behavior of the hosts and hope that past history is a guide to future behavior (and that the network designer has provisioned the network so as to accommodate most, if not all, such behavior).
- *Connections:* The hosts tell the network what they want to do and ask for guarantees (bandwidth, maximum delay, maximum error rate, etc.). In this case, there is an actual setup phase during which the required resources are allocated (if possible; explicit connection setup also provides the network with the opportunity to refuse service entirely in situations in which it cannot provide the requested guarantees), and the success or failure of the setup is reported to the hosts before actual data exchange begins.

(Edmond goes on to compare these two types of network service with a hybrid called "flows," in which the hosts tell the network what they are about to do but don't ask for any guarantees—thereby enabling the network to improve somewhat its otherwise poorly informed anticipation of their future behavior without forcing it to preallocate its resources in order to be sure of meeting static per-connection performance criteria. See Partridge [1992] for a discussion of "flows.")

There are more pros and cons for both types of service, to be sure. Some of these are bit niggling (e.g., datagrams require more "header stuff" than network connections once the connection is established) and some religious (but we've *always* offered connections!). Although not exhaustive, these lists provide readers with enough insight to appear to be "in the know" the next time the issue of "connections or datagrams" comes up during polite dinner conversation.

⟦·A·H·A·⟧ The *"Connections versus Connectionless" standoff is often cited as the ultimate tragi-comedy in OSI. But although the OSI environment is certainly partitioned into connection-oriented and connectionless worlds at the network layer, and different transport protocols are used over both types of network service, there remains hope for reunification. Several alternatives exist:*

- *Build network relays. These are truly awful beasts. They constrain topologies, and are difficult to build. And they most often rely on the operation*

of a common transport protocol (class 4); but the presence (or absence) of
TP4 is one among many other bones of contention that caused the parti-
tioning of the network layer in the first place!

- Build transport relays rather than network relays. These, too, are difficult
  to build; they violate the OSI reference model (transport functions are supposed to operate end-to-end); and they are generally considered to be broken. For example, if you attempt to relay protocol mechanisms designed to
  support certain transport functions (e.g., security provided by transport
  protocol encryption), you break them.
- Provide interworking between connection-oriented and connectionless networks. The solutions offered to date are both complex and constraining.
- Support both services in all end and intermediate systems. This is generally
  perceived to be prohibitively costly to end systems.
- Build transport bridges. These have been demonstrated to be better alternatives than transport relays, especially when two useful transport protocols—TCP and TP4—play roles in the bridging mechanism. Transport
  bridges are often the only practical solutions.
- Pray that, over time, attrition will eventually reduce all the useless combinations to a single network service and a single transport protocol. A good
  place to start would be the elimination of all the OSI transport protocol
  classes except class 4 (TP4).

Bridges and attrition are the best bets. Many of the same issues exist for
multiprotocol (TCP/IP and OSI) networking and are discussed in Chapter 16.

Connection-oriented Network Service

An OSI network connection has the same three fundamental phases of
operation—connection establishment, data transfer, release—as all previously described connection-oriented services. The primitives and parameters provided at the network layer for a connection-oriented service
are illustrated in Table 13.1.

Again, the network connection is modeled after a telephone conversation: dial the phone, talk, hang up. However, a couple of astonishing
perturbations are introduced:

- Any party can decide that it has lost track of the conversation (reset).
- The phone company will tell you whether or not the party you called
  heard what you said (receipt confirmation).

Where did these come from? Welcome to the world of grandfather-

TABLE 13.1   CONS Primitives

Primitives		Parameters
N-CONNECT		
	request indication	Called address, calling address, expected data option, QOS, recept confirmation option, NS-userdata
	response confirm	Called address, responding address, expedited data option, QOS, receipt confirm option, NS-userdata
N-DATA		
	request indication	NS-userdata, confirmation request
N-DATA-ACKNOWLEDGE		
	request indication	
N-EXPEDITED-DATA		
	request indication	NS-userdata
N-RESET		
	request indication	Reason
	response confirm	Originator, reason
N-DISCONNECT		
	request indication	Reason, NS-userdata, responding address (Originator, reason, NS-userdata, responding address)

ing existing protocol features into new service definitions. In principle, a service definition provides the template for protocol design and development. Services are identified, functions required to support those services are defined, and a protocol capable of performing the functions and providing the services is specified.

In practice, some of the principle was lost. OSI's *Connection-oriented Network Service Definition* (ISO/IEC 8348: 1987), is a marvelous example of reverse service engineering. CCITT Recommendation X.25 for public packet-switching networks was published before the development of the connection-oriented network service. It had already been deployed by PTTs and common carriers to support *CCITT applications* (e.g., the

TABLE 13.2   Correspondence between Connection-oriented Network Service
Primitive and X.25 Packets

CONS Primitives		X.25 Packet
N-CONNECT	request	Call request
	indication	Incoming call
	response	Call accepted
	confirm	Call connected
N-DATA	request, indication	Data
N-EXPEDITED-DATA	request, indication	Interrupt
N-RESET	request	Reset request
	indication	Reset indication
N-DISCONNECT	request	Clear request
	indication	Clear indication

"triple-X" recommendations—X.3, X.28, X.29 [CCITT Recommendations
X.1–X.32 1989]—that support terminal application protocols), and for
many, the use of X.25 to support the OSI network service was an expedient and politically correct solution.

   To take advantage of as many features in X.25 as possible, advocates adopted a Machiavellian attitude toward the OSI connection-oriented
network service: manipulate the service to conform to the service offered
by X.25. This "Never let an architecture stand in the way of your implementation" approach is best illustrated by the nearly one-to-one correspondence between OSI connection-oriented network service primitives
and X.25 packets, illustrated in Table 13.2.

**X.25 Packet Level
Protocol—OSI's
Connection-ori-
ented Network
Protocol**

Although ISO and CCITT devote reams of paper to codifying the operation of network connections (ISO/IEC 8208: 1987; ISO/IEC 8878: 1987;
ISO/IEC 8881: 1989), it is rather easy to describe how the OSI network
service is provided by the X.25 packet level protocol without descending
to the bit level of detail.

   The ISO/IEC standard for X.25 defines two interfaces:[8]

1. Between a computer (data terminal equipment, or DTE) and a carrier network node (data circuit-terminating equipment, or DCE)
2. Between two computers without an intervening public network
   (DTE/DTE)

---

8.   CCITT Recommendation X.25 deprives only the DTE/DCE interface.

The DTE/DCE physical interface can be leased or switched. The DTE/
DTE physical interface can be a leased line, a switched circuit, or a local area
network (ISO/IEC 8881: 1989). Both virtual-circuit and permanent virtual-
circuit modes of operation are accommodated in the virtual-circuit mode
of operation, a connection must be set up, used, and disconnected. With a
permanent virtual-circuit arrangement, a subscriber has facilities and
resources permanently assigned between two DTEs by a carrier (the call
is "always there"). These alternatives are illusrated in Figure 13.3.

Figure 13.4 illustrates (in the abstract) the three phases of a network
connection established across a switched (VC mode of operation) X.25
circuit.[9] An N-CONNECT.request primitive causes DTE A to issue an
X.25 *call request* packet. The DCE receives this request, and the network
constructs a path between DTE A and DTE B, allocating and reserving
resources of packet switches that comprise the path along the way. The

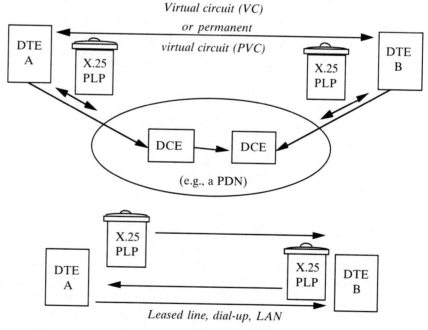

FIGURE 13.3   X.25 Interfaces

9.   The procedures for operating the X.25 packet-level protocol between DTEs without
an intervening public network are virtually identical. This description only covers those
aspects of X.25 VC operation relevant to the packet level of operation. At the data-link
level, both leased-line and circuit-switched access to a DCE are provided by many carrier
networks. CCITT Recommendation X.32 describes additional packet-level considerations
(e.g., user identification) typically required for switched access to a public network.

terminus DCE issues an *incoming call* packet to DTE B, which causes an N-CONNECT.indication. DTE B issues a *call-accepted* packet, and DTE A eventually receives a *call-connected* packet from the DCE. All X.25 *data* packets exchanged during this virtual call are forwarded along the path created by the DCEs during network connection establishment. When the network service user at DTE A elects to close the network connection, it issues an N-DISCONNECT.request, causing DTE A to issue a *clear request* packet. This is processed by the DCE and results in the generation of a *clear indication* packet to DTE B. DTE B acknowledges receipt of the clear indication by returning a *clear confirmation* packet. This packet eventually makes its way back to DTE A, causing the generation of an N-DISCON-NECT.confirmation. Network connection disconnection is described in ISO/IEC 8348 as "unconditional and possibly destructive" (honest, this is what it says, you can look it up).

During the data phase, the X.25 packet level protocol provides sequence control, flow control, expedited data (using the *interrupt* facility and packets), and error notification. *Reset*, carefully distinguished as a feature rather than an error notification, offers a means by which a network connection "can be returned to a defined state and the activities of two network service users synchronized."[10] Reset can be network service provider– or network service user–initiated. Negotiation and use of the *D-bit* facility enables the *receipt confirmation* function of the OSI network service. Receipt confirmation allows a network service user to request end-to-end acknowledgment of the delivery of data it is transmitting. In its implementation, receipt confirmation signals to the network service user that the X.25 data packets transmitted have been acknowledged. Although this is a clear violation of the OSI reference model (the internal machinations of an [N]-layer protocol should be hidden from an [N]-service user), the facility was "grandfathered" into the OSI connection-oriented network service over the protests of purists, largely because it was a tariffed facility

Use of X.25 to Provide a Subnetwork Service in OSI Networks

When a connectionless network service is provided to communicating transport entities in OSI, the X.25 packet-level protocol plays the role of a

---

10.   ISO/IEC 8348 does not provide a definition of "defined state," nor does it describe what activities the network service users "synchronize." From personal experience, we may say that defined state is "Some of your data are lost; I hope someone was keeping track . . ." The synchronization activities are transport protocol–dependent; for example, upon receipt of a reset indication, transport classes 0 and 2 give up and disconnect (big help . . .), but classes 1 and 3 initiate resynchronization procedures (see Chapter 12). TP4 is completely resilient to reset indication, treating it like any other error . . . er, feature.

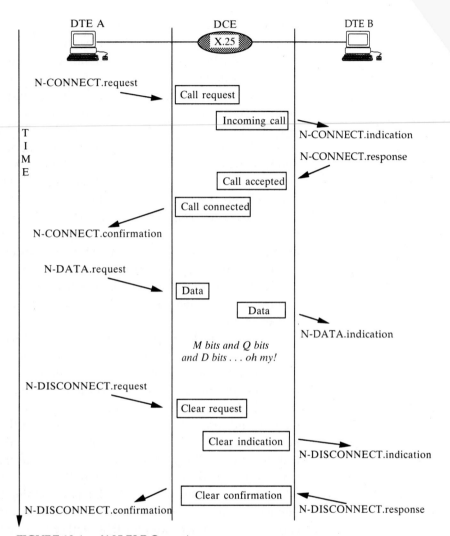

FIGURE 13.4   X.25 PLP Operation

subnetwork access protocol operating beneath an internetworking protocol (i.e., an SNICP; see Figure 13.2), and each X.25 virtual circuit serves
as a simple bit pipe. OSI network datagrams (CLNP packets) are mapped
onto these subnetwork connections and transferred between communicating CLNP network entities. A minimal subnetwork service is expected
from X.25 networks operating in the subnetwork role; essentially, virtual
circuits must be capable of handling a maximum service data unit size of
no less than 512 octets. Many of the reliability features of the X.25 packet-
level protocol remain useful across this single internetwork "hop"

(although the authors know of no implementations that make use of receipt confirmation when X.25 plays this role), but unnecessary. When X.25 virtual circuits are used to provide a subnetwork service to CLNP, subnetwork-dependent convergence functions specific to X.25 are used to set up, transfer data over, and tear down "subnetwork connections" between communicating CLNP network entities. The subnetwork connection-management functions for X.25 are described in ISO/IEC 8473 (the standard for CLNP), and the description is generic enough to apply to a family of switched, connection-oriented network services, including packet-mode Integrated Services Digital Networks (ISDN), Frame Relay, and new "cell-relay" services (see Chapter 15).

Subnetwork connection management begins as a relatively simple process. To send a CNLP packet across an X.25 public data network, for example, an X.25 virtual circuit must be established. If the CNLP packet is the first to be sent to a particular destination reachable via the X.25 public data network, the X.25 call-setup procedures must be initiated (connection establishment) and a virtual circuit must be established. Subsequent CLNP packets can be sent over the same virtual circuit.[11] The process is relatively simple if there is no cause to tear down the X.25 virtual circuit; if, however, there is a cost associated with X.25 call duration (for example, one is charged for how long one remains on a telephone regardless of whether one talks constantly or not), it may be more economical to tear down the virtual circuit when there are no longer any data to send (trading the cost of call duration for the cost of call setup the next time a packet must be sent to that destination). Determining *when* to tear down the X.25 virtual circuit is tricky; like telephones, the virtual circuit is full-duplex, and one party may think the conversation has ended while the party at the other end still has something to say. Timers are recommended to impose a maximum idle time on a virtual circuit; i.e., the expiration of a timer indicates that neither party has said anything for a while, so it's presumably safe to clear the virtual circuit. But timers alone do not en-tirely solve the problem of synchronization, which may require additional protocol interaction on behalf of the parties sharing the virtual circuit (i.e., one computer would ask permission to tear down the call, and would only do so if granted by its peer).

TCP/IP Use of X.25

In the Internet architecture, X.25 is not considered to be a protocol of the

---

11.   Can be, but need not be; the standards permit considerable flexibility in the way in which virtual circuits are managed, so as to accommodate the wide variety of tariffs that govern the use of public networks.

network layer. X.25 is one of many network interfaces on top of which IP is run. Both DTE/DTE and DTE/DCE modes of operation are supported (Defense Communications Agency 1983; RFC 877). A more recent Internet RFC describes multiprotocol interconnection over X.25 and ISDN in the packet mode (RFC 1356). It doesn't change X.25's role in TCP/IP; rather, it corrects some of the errors and ambiguities in the RFC 877 text and aligns it with ISO and CCITT standards that have been written since RFC 877 was published. One important change to the IP encapsulation is that RFC 1356 recommends an increase in the allowed IP datagram maximum transmission unit from 576 to 1,600 octets, to facilitate local area network interconnection.

Connectionless Network Service

Both OSI and TCP/IP support a connectionless network service: OSI as an alternative to network connections and TCP/IP as the only game in town (TCP/IP networking can use connections to transfer IP datagrams, but IP offers only a connectionless service to its users). The OSI standards attach great importance to the way in which transport connections are bound to network connections when the OSI connection-oriented network service is used, because in OSI, the connection-oriented network service represents, in fact, an attempt to perform some of the functions of the transport layer in the network layer. When the connectionless network service of OSI or TCP/IP is used, the coupling of connections is not an issue, and neither service attempts to pass any of the connection-oriented features that may be present in underlying subnetworks through to the transport layer.

OSI's connectionless network service (CLNS) (ISO/IEC 8348: 1993) is a best-effort-delivery service. Like a letter one submits to the postal service, each network service data unit submitted to the OSI connectionless network service contains all the addressing and service quality information necessary to forward the packet from its source to its destination, over potentially many intermediate "hops" along the way (see Figure 13.5).

Datagram Service in OSI

The details of the OSI connectionless network service can be found in ISO/IEC 8348. A "datagram" primitive (N-UNITDATA) is used to describe the process of submitting user data to and receiving user data from the connectionless network service provider (see Table 13.3). The service definition is quite simple; after all, how much can one say about a datagram?

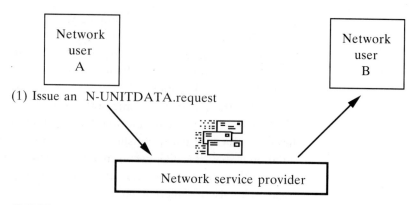

(1) Issue an N-UNITDATA.request

FIGURE 13.5   Connectionless Network Service

TABLE 13.3 Comparison of CLNP to IP

Function	ISO CLNP	IP
Version identification	1 octet	4 bits
Header length	1 octet, represented in octets	4 bits, represented in 32-bit words
Quality of service	QOS maintenance option	Type of service
Segment/Fragment length	16 bits, in octets	16 bits, in octets
Total length	16 bits, in octets	—Not present
Data unit identification	16 bits	16 bits
Flags	Don't segment, more segments, suppress error reports	Don't fragment, more fragments
Segment fragment offset	16 bits, represented in octets	13 bits, represented in units of 8 octets
Lifetime, time to live	1 octet, represented in 500-millisecond units	1 octet, represented in 1-second units
Higher-layer protocol	—Not present	Protocol identifier
Lifetime control	500-millisecond units	1-second units
Addressing	Variable length	32-bit fixed
Options	Security	Security
	Priority	Precedence bits in TOS
	Complete source routing	Strict source route
	Partial source routing	Loose source route
	Record route	Record route
	Padding	Padding
	—Not present	timestamp
	Reason for discard (ER PDU only)	—

⌈·AHA·⌉ *Actually, a lot. ISO/IEC 8348 is embellished by a great deal of explanatory material, since connectionless networking enjoyed a heretic's notoriety ten years ago that is difficult to imagine today. One of the more amusing parts of the standard describes the "queue model" for a connectionless service, which portrays the connectionless network service provider as nothing less than a reprehensible scoundrel who may "discard objects, duplicate objects . . . change the order of objects in the queue," as if such actions were performed deliberately as part of a malicious effort to subvert the true and proper goal of networking—which is of course embodied to its fullest extent only in the connection-oriented network service . . .*

Where are the OSI network-layer protocols in a representative UNIX implementation? Following the model for TCP/IP, the ARGO 1.0/RENO network services, connection-oriented and connectionless, are accessed via procedure calls within the kernel (for debugging purposes, the "raw" socket may be used to access the connectionless service). To support two services, different transport layer to lower layer interfaces are provided. The CLNP and X.25 protocol-control blocks coexist under one transport layer, and the transport protocol-control block is separated from the network-layer protocol-control blocks to allow both CLNP and OSI transport protocols to interface to X.25 in the same way (see Figure 13.6).

Datagram Service in TCP/IP

RFC 793 describes the underlying service that TCP expects to receive from the internet layer (who says we have no architecture in the Internet?) In keeping with the TCP/IP design principle of end-to-end reliability provided by an end-to-end transport protocol, TCP's expectations are minimal: data transfer with nonzero probability of arrival, during which

- Data may be lost.
- Data may arrive in an order different from the order in which they were sent.
- The data that are received may not be precisely the same as the data that were sent.
- Data may be delivered to the wrong destination.

TCP expects the underlying service[12] to select a route and forward

---

12. In most implementations of TCP, the underlying service is provided by IP, but RFC 793 does not require that this be the case; in principle, any protocol that provides the same essential service as IP could be operated under TCP. This is the basic premise for the work that is being done under the name of "TUBA" (TCP and UDP with bigger addresses) in the Internet Engineering Task Force, which substitutes OSI's CLNP for IP as TCP's "underlying

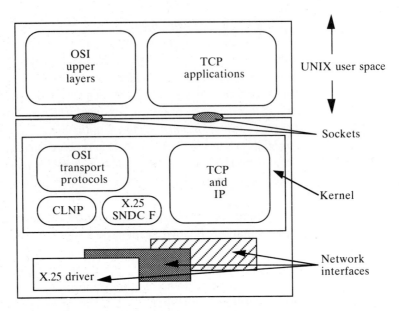

Figure 13.6   OSI Network Layer in a Representative UNIX Implementation

a packet based on the globally unique address it provides. The underlying service must also be capable of transferring maximum TCP segment size of at least 536 octets (see RFC 879).

RFC 793 also formally describes the send and receive operations. For send (NET_SEND), TCP submits the following parameters to the underlying service:

- Source and destination addresses
- Protocol identifier (identifying the service user as TCP)
- Type-of-service indicators—precedence, reliability, delay, throughput
- A "don't fragment" indicator
- A recommended "time to live" value
- The length of the data being sent, in octets
- A data identifier that distinguishes this unit of data from others sent by the same upper-layer protocol (TCP user)
- Options—a selection from the menu of options offered by IP or an equivalent underlying service
- Data

service" but keeps all the other TCP/IP protocols. A description of TUBA may be found in RFC 1347 and in Ford (1993), which is part of a special issue of IEEE *Network* magazine devoted to protocols that are proposed as successors to IP in the Internet.

For a receive operation (NET_DELIVER), TCP receives the following parameters from the underlying service:

- Source and destination addresses
- Protocol identifier
- Type-of-service indicators—precedence, reliability, delay, throughput
- The length of the data received in octets
- Options selected by the sender
- Data

In a TCP/IP implementation, only one transport–to–lower-layer interface is required (see Figure 13.6).

Internetworking Protocols

OSI's CLNP (ISO/IEC 8473: 1993) is functionally identical to the Internet's IP (RFC 791), so the two internetworking protocols—subnetwork-independent convergence protocols in *Internal Organization of the Network Layer* jargon—can be discussed in parallel. Both CLNP and IP are best-effort-delivery network protocols. Bit niggling aside, they are virtually identical. The major difference between the two is that CLNP accommodates variable-length addresses, whereas IP supports fixed, 32-bit addresses. Table 13.4 compares the functions of CLNP to those of IP. Figures 13.7 and 13.8 illustrate the header formats of CLNP and IP, respectively.

The functions performed by the two protocols are also closely related as indicated in the following subsection (see also Postel, Sunshine, and Cohen [1981] and Piscitello and Chapin [1984]).

Header Composition Function   This function[13] interprets the Ns-UNIT-DATA.request parameters and constructs the corresponding CLNP data unit. In IP, this amounts to IP's processing the upper-layer protocol's send (NET-SEND) parameters and constructing the corresponding datagram.

Header Decomposition Function   This function interprets the header

---

13.   CLNP has a silly protocol function called "header format analysis," which amounts to examining the first octet of the protocol (the network-layer protocol identifier, or NLP/ID) to determine whether CLNP or the brain-damaged "inactive network layer protocol" is present. The inactive network layer protocol is an abomination; a single octet of 0 may be encoded in the NLP/ID field to denote "There's no network layer protocol present."

TABLE 13.4   Comparison of CLNP to IP

Function	ISO CLNP	IP
Version identification	1 octet	4 bits
Header length	1 octet, represented in octets	4 bits, represented in 32-bit words
Quality of service	QOS maintenance option	Type of service
Segment/fragment length	16 bits, in octets	16 bits, in octets
Total length	16 bits, in octets	Not present
Data unit identification	16 bits	16 bits
Flags	Don't segment, more segments, suppress error reports	Don't fragment, more fragments
Segment/fragment offset	16 bits, represented in octets	13 bits, represented in units of 8 octets
Lifetime, time to live	1 octet, represented in 500-millisecond units	1 octet, represented in 1-second units
Higher-layer protocol	Not present	Protocol identifier
Lifetime control	500-millisecond units	1-second units
Addressing	Variable-length	32-bit fixed
Options	Security Priority Complete source routing Partial source routing Record route Padding Not present	Security Precedence bits in TOS Stricter source route Loose source route Record route Padding Timestamp

information of the received datagram and creates the corresponding NS-UNITDATA.indication. For IP, this amounts to extracting the receive (NET-DELIVER) parameters to be passed to the upper-layer protocol along with the data.

Lifetime-Control Function   This function limits the amount of time a datagram may remain in the network. The originator of the CLNP or IP packet determines how long it should take the datagram to reach its destination and places this value in the datagram header (using 500-millisecond units for CLNP, 1-second units for IP). This value is decremented by each of the intermediate systems/gateways that subsequently process the datagram. The datagram is discarded if the *lifetime* field (time to live in IP) reaches a value of 0 before the datagram is delivered to the destination.

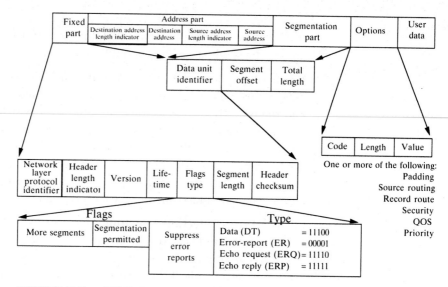

FIGURE 13.7   CLNP Data Unit Format

The CLNP lifetime-control function is a combination of hop count and time. The amount by which the value is to be decremented is the sum (in milliseconds) of the estimated or measured transit delay in the subnetwork from which the CLNP packet was received and the delay within the intermediate system that processed the CLNP packet. The lifetime field must be decremented by at least 1 by each intermediate sys-

Version	Header length	Type of service	Fragment length		
Identification			Flags	Fragment offset	
TTL		Protocol	Header checksum		
Source IP address					
Destination IP address					
Options			Padding		

FIGURE 13.8   IP Datagram Format

tem.[14] IP's time to live (TTL) operates on a time basis; the upper-layer protocol provides a maximum datagram lifetime in 1-second units among the send parameters submitted to the datagram service.

Route PDU and Forward PDU Functions The *route PDU* function determines the network entity to which the datagram must be forwarded and the underlying service (i.e., the link) over which the datagram must be sent to reach this "next hop." The *forward PDU* function submits the datagram to the underlying service selected by the route PDU function for transmission to the next hop (it is here that subnetwork-dependent convergence functions might be invoked—for example, to establish an X.25 virtual circuit to transmit the CLNP packet).

Header Error-Detection Function This function protects intermediate systems from undetected (bit) errors in the protocol-control information of each datagram. An example of such an error is the misdelivery of a datagram as a result of the corruption of the destination address field. A 16-bit arithmetic *checksum* based on Fletcher (1982) is employed in the CLNP; a similar mechanism protects the IP header from transmission errors.

The rules for processing the CLNP header checksum are as follows:

- *Generate* the checksum only once, when the initial packet is created.
- *Check* it at each intermediate system, using a separate algorithm from the one used for checksum generation.
- Do not recompute the checksum, but *adjust* it (again, using a separate algorithm) when modifying the header. (Fields of the CLNP header may be modified by an intermediate system when it performs lifetime control and segmentation and when it performs certain optional functions, such as recording of route or setting the congestion-experienced bit in the QOS maintenance option.)

The rules for processing the IP header checksum are the same as those for CLNP: generate the checksum when the IP segment is created and check it at each router. In IP, the checksum is either adjusted without full recomputation (as for CLNP) if only the time to live field in the header is changed, or completely recomputed if any other header fields are changed.

Segmentation/Fragmentation Functions The terms *segmentation* and *fragmentation* both refer to the process whereby an IP or a CLNP packet of

---

14. Appendix B of ISO/IEC 8473 provides reasonable implementation guidelines for determining datagram lifetime and reassembly lifetime control.

size N is broken up into smaller pieces if and when it becomes necessary to transmit the packet over a subnetwork for which the maximum packet size is less than N. The OSI standards prefer *segmentation* and the TCP/IP standards *fragmentation*, but in most of what follows, the two terms (and other variations of the roots *segment* and *fragment*) are used interchangeably.

Segmentation is the process of composing two or more new *derived* CLNP packets—segments—from an initial CLNP packet.[15] Segmentation can be performed only if the segmentation-permitted flag is set to 1; otherwise, an intermediate system that receives a CLNP packet requiring segmentation must discard that packet.

CLNP segments are identified as being from the same initial packet when they have the same source and destination address pair and the same *data unit identifier*. The value of the *total length* field in all segments of a given initial packet remains the same as the value originally specified in the initial packet. This value may be used by a system to allocate buffer space for the entire CLNP packet regardless of which segment (the first, any of the middle ones, or the last) is received first. The *segment offset* of each CLNP segment is set to the octet at which the segment begins with respect to the beginning of the initial packet (see Figure 13.9). The *more segments flag* is set to 0 if the final octet of the initial packet is contained in this segment; otherwise, it is set to 1.

All header information from an initial CLNP packet *except* the values of the segment length, segment offset, and checksum fields is copied into the header of all segments derived from that packet by fragmentation. The value of the checksum field must be adjusted to reflect the changes in the values of the segmentation part of the CLNP header, lifetime field reductions, and changes to options (if any).

The IP *fragmentation* process is nearly identical to CLNP segmentation. The protocol header of a fragment is copied or derived from the original IP datagram, including its options. IP fragmentation can be performed only if the *don't fragment flag* is set to *may fragment* (0); otherwise, a gateway that receives an IP datagram requiring fragmentation must discard it. Fragments are identified as being from the same IP datagram when they have the same values for the following fields: datagram iden-

---

15. The "initial" CLNP packet is the one constructed by the original sender of the packet in the source end system. When an incoming packet is broken up into segments for transmission over the "next-hop" subnetwork, each segment is transmitted as a CLNP packet, which becomes the "incoming" packet at the next-hop system on the path—where it may have to be fragmented again. An "initial" packet, therefore, really means either the initial packet emitted by the source or any incoming packet (datagram or datagram segment) that is "initial" with respect to the operation of CLNP in the system to which it is "incoming."

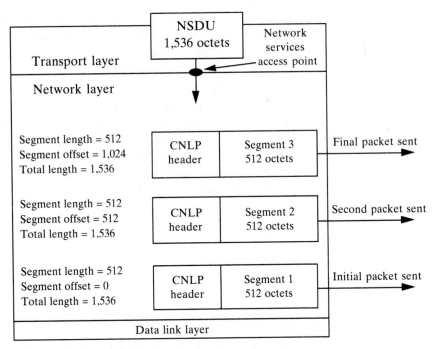

FIGURE 13.9   CLNP Segmentation (Conceptual)

tification, source and destination addresses, security, and protocol. The value of the *fragment offset* field is set to the octet at which the segment begins with respect to the beginning of the initial IP datagram. The value of the *total length* field is set to the length of the IP fragment. (The IP header does not include a field that gives the total length of the initial packet.) The more fragments flag is set to *last fragment (0)* if the final octet of the IP datagram is contained in this fragment or to *more fragments (1)* if fragments containing additional octets from the initial packet follow those contained in this fragment.

IP fragmentation differs from CLNP segmentation in the following ways:

- Data must be fragmented on 8-octet boundaries.
- The value of the fragment offset represents the position of this fragment relative to the beginning of data in 8-octet groups.
- The total length of the initial IP datagram is not encoded in the IP header.

Fragmentation and reassembly have a direct bearing on overall network performance. Experience demonstrates that it is nearly always better for the source end system to compose and send one large datgram rather than lots of little "micrograms," but a poorly implemented fragmentation strategy can cause serious problems if that large initial packet must later be fragmented to cross a subnetwork that cannot swallow it whole (Kent and Mogul 1987). CLNP implementers can benefit by studying and extracting the directly relevant information recorded during the nearly 20 years of practical experience in implementing IP and observing its behavior. For example, Clark discusses IP datagram reassembly algorithms in RFC 815. Clark also provides a marvelous explanation of how transport and internetwork protocols can be efficiently implemented in RFC 817. And the host and gateway requirements documents RFC 1122 and RFC 1009 provide Internet guidelines for the implementation of fragmentation and reassembly procedures.

Discard and Error-reporting Functions   As a last resort, both CLNP and IP discard datagrams when things go bad; e.g., when

- A protocol error is detected.
- A checksum computation fails to yield the value indicated in the checksum field of the datagram header.
- Buffers are not available to store the datagram.
- A datagram arrives that must be segmented (fragmented) before it may be forwarded, but the flag settings don't allow segmentation (fragmentation).
- Conditions for processing options cannot be satisfied.
- The lifetime of a datagram expires.
- The time allotted for reassembly of a datagram expires.

The "Internet-Control Message Protocol" (ICMP; RFC 792) provides an elaborate mechanism for reporting errors in IP datagram processing at hosts and gateways. [16] Equivalent functions are provided for CLNP using a *reason for discard option* conveyed in the CLNP error report. ICMP messages are encapsulated in IP datagrams and are distinguished from other upper-layer protocols conveyed in IP datagrams by the value 1 in the *protocol* (PROTO) field, whereas CLNP error reports are distinguished from CLNP data packets by assigning a value of 1 to the *type* field of the CLNP header.

ICMP messages and CLNP error reports are both datagrams, and delivery of these messages is not guaranteed; generation of error-report messages, however, is mandatory in both protocols when certain errors

---

16.   Error reporting is not the only function of ICMP; see "TCP/IP and OSI Control Messages" later in this chapter.

occur. The header of a discarded CLNP packet and as much of the data as can be accommodated without segmentation is returned in the CLNP error report. Similarly, every ICMP error message includes the IP header and at least the first 8 data octets of the IP datagram that caused the error. More than 8 octets may be sent, so long as the ICMP datagram length remains less than or equal to 576 octets.

The errors reported by ICMP and CLNP are compared in Table 13.5; for TCP/IP, however, it is always useful to refer to "Requirements for Internet Hosts—Communication Layers" (RFC 1122) for the precise circumstances that precipitate the generation of an ICMP error message.

The process of generating error reports and ICMP messages is virtually the same. One never generates an error message about an error occurring during the processing of a CLNP error report or an ICMP message. ICMP messages are generated only when an error is detected in the fragment whose fragment offset is set to 0 (the first chunk of the datagram); since no such restriction is explicitly stated in CLNP, one should conclude that it is appropriate to generate an error report PDU about an error occurring in any segment of a CLNP data unit.

Options   Both CLNP and IP have lots of options. The sets of options defined for the two protocols are virtually identical, but the processing is slightly different (as, of course, are the bits). Table 13.6 compares CLNP and IP options, and provides a brief explanation.

The composition of CLNP error reports is affected by the options present in the discarded CLNP data packet; specifically, the CLNP error report must have the

- Same priority and QOS maintenance (if these options are supported).
- Same security. If this option is not supported, the CLNP error report should not be generated.
- Reversed complete source route. If this option is not supported, the CLNP error report should not be generated.

Padding, partial source routing and record route may be specified by the intermediate system generating the CLNP error report if these options are supported.

ICMP and IP are completely independent protocols; however, which options from the discarded IP datagram are copied into the datagram that conveys the ICMP error message datagrams remains an issue in the Internet Engineering Task Force. Currently, the IP datagram that is used to carry an ICMP message must set type of service to 0, and any ICMP message returned in response to a packet that contains an IP security option should include a security option identical to that found in the discarded IP datagram.

TABLE 13.5   Comparison of ICMP Messages and CLNP Error Reports

Category	CLNP Error Report	ICMP Message
General	Reason not specified	Parameter problem
	Protocol procedure error	Parameter problem
	Incorrect checksum	Parameter problem
	PDU discarded—congestion	Source quench
	Header syntax error	Parameter problem
	Segmentation needed, not permitted	Fragmentation needed, but don't fragment flag is set
	Incomplete PDU received	Parameter problem
	Duplicate option	Parameter problem
Addressing-related	Destination address unreachable	Network unreachable*
	Destination address unknown	Host unreachable
Source routing	Unspecified source-routing error	Source route failed
	Unknown address in source-routing field	Source route failed
	Path not acceptable	Source route failed
Lifetime	Lifetime expired while data unit was in transit	Time to live exceeded in transit
	Lifetime expired during reassembly	Reassembly time exceeded
PDU discarded	Unsupported option, unspecified error	Parameter problem
	Unsupported protocol version	Parameter problem
	Unsupported security option	Parameter problem
	Unsupported source-routing option	Parameter problem
	Unsupported record-route option	Parameter problem
Reassembly	Reassembly interference	Reassembly time exceeded

*Gateways and hosts that generate ICMP destination unreachable messages are encouraged to "choose a response code that most closely matches the reason why the message is being generated." RFC 1122 identifies an expanded list of reason codes.

TABLE 13.6   CLNP and IP Options

CLNP Option	*Corresponding IP Option*	*Comments*
Complete source routing allows the originator of a packet to dictate the entire and only route (i.e., every router) a packet can take.	*Strict source and record routing* enables a ULP to name the IP modules that must be visited.	In both cases, all segments/fragments must follow the same route (option is copied into all fragments).
Partial source routing allows the originator to provide a partial list of routers (pointing the packet in the right direction).	Like CLNP's option, *loose source and record routing* allows a ULP to provide "hints" (the "inverse" route is recorded along the way).	CLNP options are copied into every segment; loose source and record routing is only present in fragment 0.
Partial route recording records the list of intermediate systems visited by a packet, in order of traversal.	*Record route* records the list of gateways a datagram visits.	Each router that forwards the packet records its address in the header (and updates the checksum). The size of the option is fixed by the originator, and the packet may continue even when space for recording is exhausted.
Complete route recording is a restricted variation of partial route recording.		A complete route must be recorded or else the packet is discarded and an error report is generated.
Priority indicates relative priority of this data packet with respect to other data packets.	*Precedence* denotes the importance or priority of the datagam with respect to other datagrams.	Assumes that routing information will assist in ordering packets for forwarding.
QOS maintenance provides information intended to influence routing decisions.	*Type of service* provides information intended to influence routing decisions. (see RFC 1349)	**Examples:** maintain sequence to the extent possible (follow the leader); take the route with the lowest error rate; take the path with the smallest transit delay; take the path with the least cost.
	Timestamp provides a list of timestamps (and optionally, the addresses) from the gateways traversed by the datagram.	
Padding is used to lengthen the header to a convenient length.	*Padding* is the last field of the datagram and is used to ensure that the IP header ends on a 32-bit boundary.	Padding is used to align user data to machine word sizes.
A code point for a *security* option is reserved but is as yet undefined.	Security provides a means of conveying security level, compartmentation, handling restriction codes, and user group parameters. (See RFC 1108)	In many implementations, and in the absence of OSI standards for security, RFC 1108 is encoded in the CLNP security option.

TCP/IP and OSI Control Messages

ICMP defines messages other than error reports. The *source quench* message serves as a coarse congestion-notification mechanism, providing routers with the means to tell hosts to reduce the rate at which they are sending IP packets. The same function is accomplished in OSI using a CLNP error report with the *reason for discard* field set to the value that means "congestion experienced." The ICMP *echo request* and *echo reply* messages are useful in determining whether a remote IP entity is "alive and well." A host issues an echo request and determines from the receipt of a corresponding echo reply message that the remote IP entity is able to process IP (and ICMP) packets. This is accomplished in a nearly identical manner in OSI using CLNP *echo request* and *echo reply* packets, which have been adopted as part of the second edition of ISO/IEC 8473. The ICMP *redirect* message is used by router A when it receives an IP datagram from a host "foo" and determines from its local routing information that router B offers a better (shorter) path to the destination IP address "bar." Router A will forward the original datagram toward its destination and also return a redirect message advising foo to forward future packets destined for bar to router B. (Redirection is accomplished in OSI through the use of the end-system to intermediate-system routing protocol, which is described in Chapter 14.) ICMP also offers a *timestamp* request and reply function, which is used to determine round-trip-times across an internet, and an information request and reply function, which may be used by a host to determine its IP network number. (Currently, OSI has no corresponding capabilities defined for CLNP.)

OSI Protocol Combinations

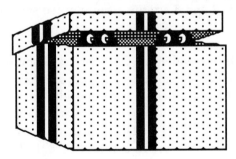

IONL was Pandora's box . . .
ISO/IEC 8880 explains what to do once you've opened it!

The *Internal Organization of the Network Layer* describes the relationships among the real-world components that might be used (individually or collectively) to provide the OSI network service. In a rash moment of pragmatism, it was decided that far too many combinations of real-world protocols existed and a weeding-out process was needed. ISO/IEC 8880: 1990, *Protocol Combinations to Provide and Support the OSI network Service, Part 1—General Principles*, describes the weeding-out process; Parts 2 and 3 describe the combinations that survived the initial cut. To avoid the embarrassing accusation of lacking vision, Part 1 also includes *"Criteria for Expansion of ISO 8880."*[17]

Parts 2 and 3 describe *protocol combinations* (e.g., CLNP over ISO/IEC 8802 LANs, or X.25 packet level protocol over the data link service provided by ISO/IEC 7776), *environments* (LAN, PSDN, CSDN, point-to-point subnetwork), and the obligatory *conformance* for a given environment. Part 2 is devoted to provision of the connection-oriented network service, Part 3 to the connectionless network service. (In keeping with accepted practice in OSI, the issue of interworking between the two types of network service is finessed.)

Inclusion in the protocol combinations and environments was something of a popularity contest. The combinations considered broadly applicable are included. Since there is a clause covering expansion, it is inevitable that additional combinations will be considered and incorporated in the future. The aspect of ISO/IEC 8880 that is both amusing and disappointing is that Parts 2 and 3 are merely *pointer documents*: they identify the ISO/IEC standards included in a given protocol combination/environment but provide little in the way of implementation guidelines beyond that which is contained in the cited documents. The illustrations of the protocols and combinations to support the OSI network service in Parts 2 and 3 are the essence of the standard (Figures 13.10 and 13.11).

TCP/IP Protocol Combinations

The TCP/IP equivalent of OSI's protocol combinations is a series of much more practical documents that describe the mundane but essential details of IP encapsulation and other idiosyncratic behavior associated with IP protocol operation over the many network interfaces (IEEE 802 LANs, Ethernet, SMDS, FDDI, amateur packet-radio link-layer protocol, point-to-point links—see RFC 1042, RFC 894, RFC 1209, RFC 1188, RFC 1226, and RFC 1171, respectively).

Network-layer Protocol Identification

Given that there are potentially lots of protocols in the OSI network layer, and they are sometimes stacked together, how do you distinguish

---

17.   Rather than expanding ISO/IEC 8880, the standards developers decided in early 1993 to replace all 3 parts with an omnibus technical report entitled "Provision of the OSI Network Service" (ISO/IEC 13532: 1993).

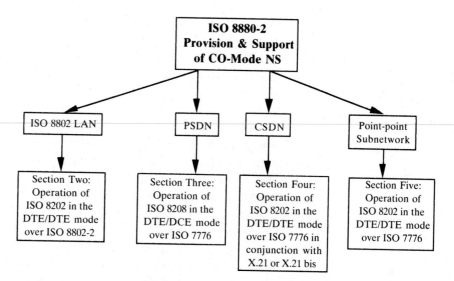

Source: ISO/IEC 8880 (1990), "Protocol Combinations to Provide and Support the OSI Network Service, Part 2—Provision and Support of Connection-mode Network Service."

FIGURE 13.10   Provision and Support of Connection-oriented Network Service

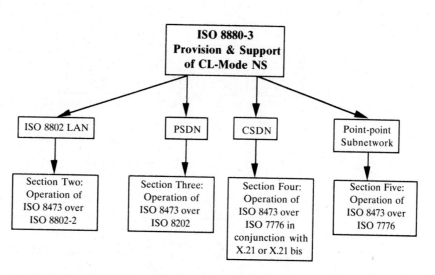

Source: ISO/IEC 8880 (1990), "Protocol Combinations to Provide and Support the OSI Network Service, Part 3—Provision and Support of Connectionless Network Service."

FIGURE 13.11   Provision and Support of Connectionless Network Service

one from the other? By convention (ISO/IEC 9577: 1990), all OSI net-work-layer protocols must reserve the first octet as the *initial protocol identifier* (IPI); the first octet of CLNP, for example, is binary 1000 0001. Thus, the first octet of the data link service data unit identifies which of the OSI network-layer protocols is conveyed (Figure 13.12).

It should come as no surprise that the X.25 packet level protocol treatment of this octet is an exception. The first octet of X.25 packets is a combination of the *general format indicator* (GFI) and the upper 4 bits of logical channel identification—so X.25 hogs dozens of network-layer protocol identifier bit assignments (Figure 13.13).

In OSI, X.25 is a beast of many burdens; it can carry CLNP, OSI routing protocols for CLNP, triple-X protocols, or OSI transport protocols. This multiple role for X.25 necessitates the use of a *subsequent protocol identifier* (SPI) to indicate "what's in the X.25 data packets." The subsequent protocol identifier is the first octet of the call user data field in the X.25 *call request* packet; if the call user data in the X.25 PLP call request packet is absent, then it is assumed that the OSI transport protocol is present in X.25 data packets.

(Note that in theory, one could encapsulate X.25 in CLNP or TCP or the OSI transport protocol: "Tunneling" X.25 is an increasingly common practice in multiprotocol routers]; CLNP does not yet have an option identified for a subsequent protocol identifier or IP PROTO field.)

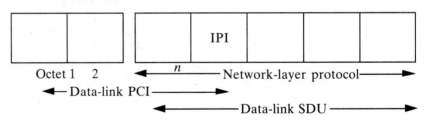

FIGURE 13.12   Initial Protocol Identifier

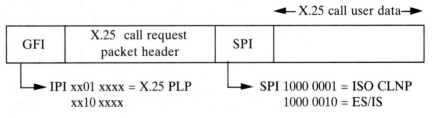

FIGURE 13.13   Subsequent Protocol Identifier

Network-Layer Protocol Identification in TCP/IP and Multiprotocol Environments

With some cooperation from ISO/IEC, IP protocol identification has recently been expanded to accommodate coexistence with OSI and other network-layer protocols on X.25 and ISDN networks. This work obsoletes RFC 877. Network-layer identification for multiprotocol internets combines the scheme described in ISO/IEC TR 9577 and the IEEE subnetwork access protocol (SNAP) technique.

For multiprotocol internets, especially dual-stack internets, some of the relevant values of the initial protocol identifier and subsequent protocol identifier are :

- For IP, binary 1100 1100 (hex CC, Internet decimal 204)
- For CLNP, binary 1000 0001 (hex 81, Internet decimal 129)
- For the *End System to Intermediate System Routeing Exchange Protocol for Use in Conjunction with ISO 8473* (ISO/IEC 9542: 1988; see Chapter 14), binary 1000 0010 (hex 82, Internet decimal 130)
- For the *Intermediate System to Intermediate System Routeing Protocol for Use in Conjunction with ISO 8473* (ISO 10589: 1992; see Chapter 14), binary 1000 0011 (hex 83, Internet decimal 131)

The binary value 1000 0000 (hex 80, Internet decimal 128) identifies the use of the IEEE 802 subnetwork access protocol to encapsulate and identify a non-OSI network-layer protocol in X.25 (see Figure 13.14). The

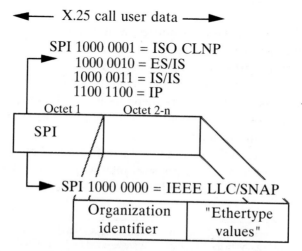

FIGURE 13.14   Relevant IPI/SPI Values for Multiprotocol Internets

IEEE 802 SNAP is a five-octet header consisting of an *organization identifier*, which is set to the value of the Internet Ethernet address block number (see RFC 1340, *Assigned Numbers*), and the *ethertype value* that identifies the encapsulated protocol (e.g., IP, ARP).

Network Layer Addresses

Network-layer addresses identify the hosts (end systems) attached to TCP/IP and OSI networks. IP and OSI network service access point (NSAP) addresses share several common attributes:

- They are globally unique—address administrations and policies exist to ensure that no two host machines use the same network address.
- They accommodate (and prescribe) hierarchies, which enable groups of hosts to be associated with a specific domain (and possibly subdomains within that domain).
- They convey information that is used to determine routes between hosts, across potentially many (sub)networks.

Network addressing in the Internet accommodates a single network service; network addressing in OSI must accommodate not only multiple network services but a very large number of public numbering and private addressing plans. In the following subsections, readers should consider how Internet and OSI network addressing are influenced by differences in scope and in the expectations that have been imposed on them.

Internet (IP) Addresses

The Internet network address is more commonly called the "IP address." It consists of 32 bits, some of which are allocated to a high-order *network-number* part and the remainder of which are allocated to a low-order *host-number* part. The distribution of bits—how many form the network number, and how many are therefore left for the host number—can be done in one of three different ways, giving three different *classes* of IP address (see Figure 13.15).[18]

The network number identifies a real subnetwork, and the host number identifies a physical interface to that subnetwork. Whereas the OSI network-layer address identifies the abstract service access point

---

18.   In fact, there are two other IP address classes which are not discussed here; class-D addresses, which begin with the bit pattern 1110, are reserved for IP multicasting, and class-E addresses, which begin with the bit pattern 1111, and are reserved for experimental use.

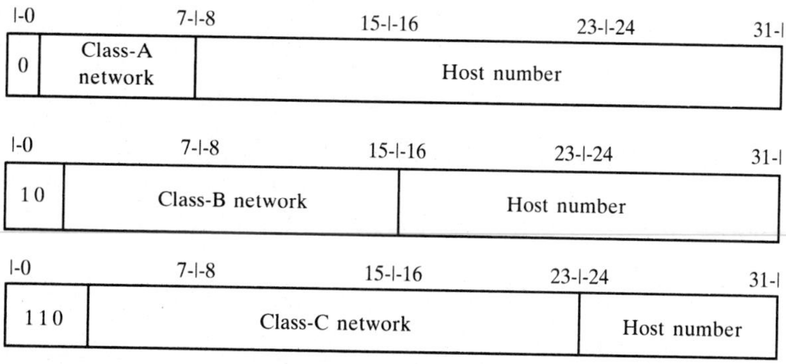

FIGURE 13.15   Class-A, Class-B, and Class-C IP Addresses

between the transport and network layers, the Internet address identifies the actual point of attachment of a computer system to a real subnetwork (the "network interface"). In OSI, this would be referred to as a "subnetwork point of attachment address," which is not at all the same thing as an NSAP address (see "OSI Network Layer Addressing," later in the chapter).

IP Subnetting   Internet addressing inherently accommodates a two-level hierarchy (network and host), and all of the bits in the address are useful for routing. Additional levels of hierarchy can be created within a single class-A, class-B, or class-C network by applying the notion of *subnetting*, which is accomplished by borrowing bits from the host portion of an Internet address. (The Internet Standard subnetting procedure is defined in RFC 950.) Subnetting is visible only within the physical network in which it is applied; hosts and routers outside the physical network do not (in fact, must not) know that the host portion is partitioned into subfields. Routers and hosts within a subnetted network distinguish a *subnet number* from a host number by applying a *bit mask* (see Figure 13.16).

Applying Subnetting to Accommodate Growth   Given the original scope of the ARPANET, it is easy to forgive the developers of IP for having failed to anticpate the success of the Internet. Once a single network with 4 hosts, the Internet now consists of well over 10,000 individual networks with more than a million hosts and is approximately doubling in size every year. The 32-bit IP address space cannot withstand such a growth rate for much longer. By March 1993, nearly 32 percent of the available IP network numbers had been assigned, including:

• Aproximately 39 percent of the 128 class-A network numbers,

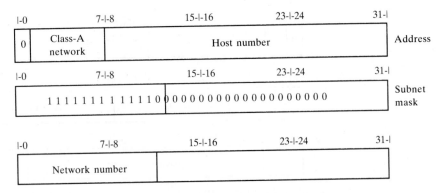

Interpretation

FIGURE 13.16   Subnetted Internet Address

which represent half of the total address space. (Sixty-four of the class-A numbers have been reserved by the Internet Assigned Numbers Authority and are therefore "unassigned"; the number of unreserved class-A network numbers that are available for assignment is therefore much smaller than the 39 percent figure would suggest.)

- Just over half of the 16,384 class-B network numbers, which represent one-fourth of the total address space. (Class-B addresses are by far the most popular, as they provide for a large number of hosts per network, with considerable room for subnetting within the 16-bit host-number space.)
- Approximately 6 percent of the 2,097,152 class-C network numbers, which represent one-eighth of the total address space.
- All of the class-D network numbers, which are reserved as "multicast" addresses, representing one-sixteenth of the total address space.
- All of the class-E network numbers, which are reserved by the Internet Assigned Numbers Authority, representing one thirty-second of the total address space.

The net result is that a significant fraction—a bit more than 42 percent—of the network-number space had already been either allocated (classes A, B, and C) or reserved (classes D and E) by March 1993 (not counting the 654 reserved class-A network numbers, which could in principle be released by the Internet Assigned Numbers Authority):

$$(1/2)*.39 + (1/4)*.51 + (1/8)*.06 + (1/16) + (1/32) = .42375$$

Clearly, we cannot continue to assign new IP network numbers at an annual growth rate of 100 percent for much longer! Fortunately, there appears to be at least a short-term solution to the problem, based on the observation that the depletion of the IP network-number space has been artificially accelerated by a mismatch between the number of hosts per network allowed by the fixed class-B and class-C partitions (64K and 8K, respectively) and the number of hosts that are typically attached to real-world networks (something in between, but often much smaller than 64K). One way to add years to the life of the existing IP address space is to extend the practice of IP subnetting and take advantage of the large number of unassigned class-C network numbers. An RFC in progress 1500 recommends that the rigidly fixed octet boundaries that define the three classes of IP address be broken (ignored) and that more flexible bit-level masks be used to distinguish the network number from the host number. The classless interdomain routing (CIDR) strategy would permit blocks of contiguous class-C network numbers to be assigned to sites that would ordinarily need a class-B network number (to accommodate more than 256 hosts). Although this strategy clearly does not increase the total supply of network numbers, it encourages more efficient (denser) use of the host-number space associated with each network number (or set of contiguous network numbers), thereby slowing the rate at which new network numbers must be assigned.

By itself, the assignment of a block of class-C network numbers rather than a single class-B network number creates a problem that is potentially much worse than the problem it attempts to solve: if routers must advertise each of the class-C network numbers individually, the "not enough addresses" problem has been solved at the expense of creating a new "too many routes" problem. Internet routers cannot efficiently maintain the very large routing tables that would result from the advertisement of many tens of thousands of networks. The classless interdomain routing scheme therefore requires the development and deployment of interdomain routing protocols that summarize ("aggregate") routing advertisements, so that a single routing table entry can be maintained for a set of networks that share a common IP network-number prefix and routing metrics (see Chapter 14). Rather than maintaining an entry for each network number (as would be the case with current interdomain protocols), sites with multiple contiguous class-C network numbers would be routed in the interdomain system using a single routing table entry.

It is in fact necessary for this aggregation to occur recursively at the transit routing domain boundaries (for example, the boundaries between the National Science Foundation backbone NSFnet and the NSFnet regionals; between NSFnet and the European backbone network EBONE; or between the Nordic regional network NORDUnet and the commercial network Alternet) in order to arrest the growth of routing tables in transit domain routers. This requires greater coordination in the assignment of network numbers: sites that are topologically "close" with respect to transit domain routing must be allocated network-number blocks with adjacent prefixes. Making intelligent choices when assigning network numbers in this way is likely to be possible (if it is possible at all) only if the assignment authority is delegated to the organizations that are responsible for coordinating international and interorganizational routing. Classless interdomain routing may not be effective if network-number assignment remains centralized.

Classless interdomain routing will require Internet network operators to use one of the two interdomain routing protocols that currently support variable-length subnet masks (see Chapter 14, "Interdomain Routing") in place of the popular "exterior gateway protocols" (see Chapter 14, "Interdomain Routing in TCP/IP"). It will also be the case that networks that do not default external routes to a major transit network will be unable to continue using an intradomain routing protocol that does not support variable-length subnet masks, because incoming route advertisements representing aggregated sets of network addresses would have to be expanded, resulting in what would eventually be unsupportable increases in the amount of router memory required to store all of the routes individually.

The expected "time to impact" for classless interdomain routing is two to three years, given the time it takes to implement and deploy a new routing protocol and the network-operation adjustments that will be required. Routing experts do not agree on the question of whether classless interdomain routing buys enough time to wait for a completely new Internet routing and addressing architecture or only breathing room for the deployment of a near-term functionally equivalent replacement for IP. However, there is general agreement that classless interdomain routing is worth doing in either case, and the Internet Engineering Steering Group has begun the process of approving an Internet standard that will mandate the use of classless interdomain routing in the Internet.

A Real-World Example of IP Address   Internet address data structures may be represented in a UNIX environment in the following manner:

```
typedef char in_addr[4] /* 4-octet IP address */
struct sockaddr {
```

```
        short      sa_family;    /* address family, e.g., internet */
        char       sa_data (14); /* space for the address */
}
struct sockaddr_in {
        short      sin_family;   /* address family is internet */
        u_short    sin_port;     /* the internet port   */
        in_addr    sin_addr;     /* the IP address a.b.c.d */
        char       sin_zero[8];  /* unused */
}
```

OSI Network Layer Addressing

Like every networking architecture that preceded it, OSI needed addresses to identify hosts and gateways so that routes could be computed and packets could be forwarded. By the time OSI network-layer addressing was considered, however, OSI had already succumbed to a political compromise that demanded the accommodation of multiple solutions to providing the network service. By the rules of this bargain, X.25 public data networks, X.21 circuit-switched data networks, and CLNP-based enterprise networks were all equally capable of providing (and all equally entitled to provide) the OSI network service. This all but eliminated the opportunity to design a logical network-layer addressing scheme from scratch; the common carriers providing X.25 packet-switching service or X.21 circuit-switched service naturally wished to continue to use the CCITT X.121 numbering plan for public data networks or the CCITT E.163 numbering plan for the public switched telephone network, and simply call the X.121 or E.163 numbers "OSI NSAP addresses." Integrated services digital networks (ISDNs) would use the CCITT E.164 *Numbering Plan for the ISDN Era*; these numbers, too, had to be OSI NSAP addresses.[19] CLNP-based networks, on the other hand, would benefit from NSAP addresses structured like the IP addresses of the Internet, so that routing topology information could be derived from the composition of the address and efficient routes could be computed. The OSI standards community briefly considered subsuming all OSI network-layer addressing under the administration of one of the existing numbering plans, but the existence of a half-dozen eager candidates for this role put a quick end to this alternative. After protracted debate, it was finally agreed that the only way forward was to "embrace them all" in a grand compromise that gave the appropriate recognition and status to each of the contenders.

Hemrick (1985) provides an excellent historical account of the

---

19. Addressing plans such as these are sensitive first to administrative needs, and the routing information that can be derived from such addresses is typically limited to geographic locality.

development of the OSI network-layer addressing scheme. Briefly, the foremost issue confronting the standards bodies ended up being not how to define "bits to route with" but how to administer the use within OSI of the many pre-OSI addressing and numbering plans that went into the compromise solution. OSI network-layer addressing therefore focuses primarily on the administrative aspects of address allocation and assignment and leaves the issue of defining the "bits to route with" to the routing and interworking standards.

The OSI Network Addressing Architecture   The network-layer addressing standard contained within the network service definition (ISO/IEC 8348 1993) defines a hierarchically structured, globally unambiguous network addressing scheme for OSI. The *global network addressing domain* is composed of multiple subdomains called *network addressing domains*. An addressing *authority* exists for each network addressing domain; it is responsible for assigning addresses and assuring the uniqueness of the assigned addresses within the domain. The addressing authority also determines the rules for specifying addresses within the domain (*abstract syntax*), provides a human-readable representation of addresses that could be obtained from directories (*external reference syntax*), and describes how the addresses are to be conveyed in network-layer protocols (*encoding*).

The concept of network addressing domains is recursive; an individual network addressing authority may further subdivide its domain into subdomains, and each subdomain would again have its own authority to determine rules of address syntax and administer addresses. An example of a domain hierarchy is shown in Figure 13.17.

ISO/IEC and CCITT jointly administer the global network addressing domain. The initial hierarchical decomposition of the NSAP address is defined by (ISO/IEC 8348) and is illustrated in Figure 13.18. The standard specifies the syntax and the allowable values for the high-order part of the address—the *initial domain part* (IDP), which consists of the *authority and format identifier* (AFI) and the *initial domain identifier* (IDI)—but specifically eschews constraints on or recommendations concerning the syntax or semantics of the *domain specific part* (DSP).

The value used for the authority and format identifier establishes both the format of the initial domain identifier (its syntax and the numbering plan or identifier assignment system on which it is based) and the abstract syntax (the syntax in which values are allocated by a registration authority, as opposed to the concrete syntax in which the value might actually be represented in a protocol header or in a table within an OSI

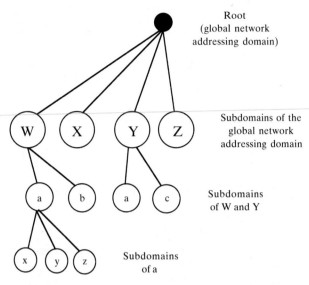

FIGURE 13.17   Hierarchies (Inverted Tree Diagram)

system) of the domain-specific part. The two-digit authority and format identifier is always encoded as a single binary-coded decimal (BCD) octet. The AFI specifies

- The addressing authority that governs the allocation of the initial domain identifier (i.e., the authority that administers this branch of the address tree), such as CCITT's X.121 public data network numbering plan.[20]
- Whether or not leading 0s in the encoding of the initial domain identifier are significant.[21]
- The abstract syntax of the domain-specific part (discussed later in this section).

---

20.   The "authority" identified by the value of the authority and format identifier is typically a numbering plan or other coding system, defined by a specific standard or set of standards, rather than a person or agency. The authority is the standard that specifies the numbering plan or coding system, not the organization that developed the standard or the agency that administers it.

21.   Some of the initial domain identifier formats are based on existing numbering plans that allocate numbers of varying length. In these cases, it is necessary to distinguish between numbers for which leading 0s are significant and those for which leading 0s are not significant, so that leading 0s can be included in or excluded from the standard encoding scheme that produces binary encodings of the decimal-digit parts of the NSAP address. In Table 13.7, where two authority and format identifier values are shown in a single table cell, the first value is used when leading 0s in the initial domain identifier field are not significant, and the second value is used when leading 0s in the initial domain identifier field are significant.

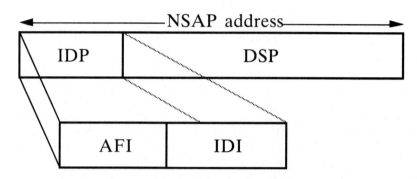

FIGURE 13.18   Structure of the NSAP Address

The available initial domain identifier formats, and the authority and format identifier values that select them, are shown in Table 13.7, which also shows the domain specific part syntax (decimal digits, binary octets, ISO 646 characters, or a nationally standardized character set) selected by each of the possible values.

The initial domain identifier identifies the addressing authority that allocates the bytes of the domain-specific part. It consists of a value selected from the numbering plan or other coding system specified by the value of the authority and format identifier; for example, if the

TABLE 13.7   AFI Values and IDI Formats

IDI Format \ DSP Syntax	Decimal	Binary	Character (ISO 646)	National Character
X.121	36, 52	37, 53	—	—
ISO DCC	38	39	—	—
F.69	40, 54	41, 55	—	—
E.163	42, 46	43, 57	—	—
E.164	44, 58	45, 59	—	—
ISO 6523-ICD	46	47	—	—
Local	48	49	50	51

authority and format identifier value specifies the "ISO data country code (DCC)" format for the initial domain identifier (AFI value of 38 or 39), then the values of the initial domain identifier are selected from the ISO standard for data country codes (ISO/IEC 3166)—e.g., "840" (which is the ISO/IEC 3166 country code for the United States).

The composition of the domain specific part is the responsibility of the individual authority identified by the value of the initial domain identifier (in the preceding example, it would be the responsibility of the authority associated with the ISO/IEC 3166 data country code "840" [United States], which is the American National Standards Institute [ANSI]). Although some of the initial domain identifier formats use up more of the available octets in an NSAP address than others, the upper bound of 20 octets for the length of an NSAP address ensures that there is ample room in the domain-specific part for authorities to create further subdivisions (subhierarchies) if necessary (see Table 13.8).

The ANSI Standard NSAP Address Structure The American national standard for the structure and semantics of the domain-specific part of the subset of NSAP addresses for which ANSI is responsible (see the preceding section) provides an example of the way in which authorities may decide to define the domain-specific part (which is deliberately not specified by any ISO/IEC or CCITT standard). American National Standard X3.216-1992, *Structure and Semantics of the Domain Specific Part of the Network Service Access Point Address*, applies to those NSAP addresses that use the "ISO DCC" format, in which the value of the authority and format identifier is (decimal) 39 and the value of the initial domain identifier is (decimal) 840.

ISO/IEC 8348 does not require that the domain-specific part of the

Table 13.8 Maximum DSP Lengths

IDI Format	Decimal (Maximum Length of DSP in Decimal Digits)	Binary (Maximum Length of DSP in Binary Octets)
X.121	24	12
ISO DCC	35	17
F.69	30	15
E.163	26	13
E.164	23	11
ISO 6523-ICD	34	17
Local	38	19

NSAP address be specified by any international or national standard. The objective of ANS X3.216-1992 is to facilitate the operation of OSI routing functions, by enabling those functions to recognize a relationship between the hierarchical structure of the domain-specific part of the NSAP address and the hierarchical structure of routing domains and areas. This capability is particularly valuable when intradomain routing information is exchanged among intermediate systems (ISs) using the *Intermediate System to Intermediate System Intra-domain Routeing Information Exchange Protocol for Use in Conjunction with ISO/IEC 8473*,[22] defined in ISO/IEC 10589 (see Chapter 14).

The domain-specific part structure specified by American National Standard X3.216-1992 is illustrated in Figure 13.19. The specific way in which this format is used to facilitate routing is covered in great detail in Chapter 14. X3.216-1992 also specifies the way in which the numeric form of the "organization name" allocated and assigned by the ANSI-administered U.S. Registration Authority (see Chapter 5) is used as the "org" component of NSAP addresses constructed according to the standard.

For the purposes of OSI routing, the individual fields of the domain specific part illustrated in Figure 13.19 are interpreted as follows:

- *IDP*: The two subfields of the *initial domain part* are allocated and assigned according to ISO/IEC 8348 and are not affected in any way by X3.216-1992.
- *DFI*: the *domain specific part format identifier*, which specifies the version of the X3.216 standard. The value of this field is binary 1000 0000 (shown in Figure 13.19 as decimal 128).
- *org*: an *organization* name allocated and assigned by the ANSI-administered U.S. Registration Authority for OSI organization

IDP			DSP					
AFI	IDI	DFI						
39	840	128	org	res	rd	area	system	sel
1	2	1	3	2	2	2	6	1

FIGURE 13.19   ANSI Structure of the DSP

---

22.   "Routeing" is in fact the internationally accepted spelling of the word when it is used in the context of computer networking (see Chapter 14).

names (see "The USA Registration Authority," in Chapter 5). The U.S. Registration Authority allocates numeric organization names as decimal numeric values. The value of this field is the binary value obtained by encoding the numeric organization name according to the "network address encoding" procedure defined in ISO/IEC 8348.

- *res*: *reserved*. The value of this field is 0.
- *rd*: the portion of the NSAP address up to and including the "rd" (routing domain) field constitutes a *routing domain prefix*, which summarizes information about some or all of the area addresses within a routing domain. This enables the border intermediate systems in a routing domain to advertise one or more prefixes, in lieu of an enumeration of the corresponding individual area addresses, for the purposes of interdomain routing information exchange (see Chapter 14).
- *area*: an identifier for the *area* within a routing domain to which the NSAP address belongs. The portion of the NSAP address up to and including the area field constitutes an *area address* in the sense in which the term is used (and defined) by ISO/IEC 10589. In the ISO/IEC 10589 context, level-1 intermediate systems report only area addresses, and level-2 intermediate systems exchange among themselves only area address information (and thus route only on the basis of area addresses).
- *system*: an identifier for the individual end system (in the case of an NSAP address) or intermediate system (in the case of a network entity title) with which the NSAP or network entity title is associated. The internal structure, value, and meaning of the *system* field are not specified or constrained by X3.216-1992.
- *sel*: the "NSAP selector," which serves to differentiate multiple NSAP addresses associated with the same network entity. The value of the *sel* field in a network entity title is 0.

A Real-World Example of OSI NSAP Addresses   What in the real world are NSAP addresses? In UNIX implementations, under a socket address family "ISO," an NSAP address could be viewed as the equivalent of a TCP/IP "Internet address." As described in Chapter 12, the C data structure *sockaddr*, OSI-style, looks like this (again, from ARGO 1.0 RENO):

```
struct sockaddr {
    short       sa_family;      /* address family, ISO */
    char        sa_data (14);   /* space for the address */
    }
```

```
struct sockaddr_iso {
    short      siso_family;    /* address family is iso */
    u_short    siso_tsuffix;   /* the TSAP Address   */
    iso_addr   siso_addr;      /* the NSAP Address */
    char       siso_zero[2];   /* unused */
    }
```

Many systems, especially routers, will find it necessary to accommodate multiple NSAP address formats. These might be encoded in the following manner:

```
struct iso_addr {
    u_char     isoa_afi;     /* authority/format identifier */
    union {
        struct addr_37      addr_37;      /* x.121 */
        struct addr_39      addr_ansi;    /* ISO DCC IDI *
        struct addr_47      addr_6523icd; /* ISO 6523 ICD*/
    }
    isoa_u;    u_char
    isoa_len;  /* length */
```

in which "addr_ansi" from the earlier example would appear as follows:

```
struct addr_ansi {
    u_char    ansi_dfi;      /* DSP format identifier   */
    char      ansi_org (3);  /* organization code       */
    char      reservd (2);   /* not used yet            */
    char      domain (2);    /* routing domain          */
    char      area (2);      /* area within domain      */
    char      systemid (6);  /* possibly a 48-bit
                                IEEE 802 MAC address     */
    u_char    NSAPsel;       /* NSAP selector           */
};
```

OSI NSAP Addresses in the Internet   With so many NSAP addressing formats to choose from, which should be used in a multiprotocol Internet supporting (at least) OSI and TCP/IP? *Guidelines for OSI NSAP Allocation in the Internet* (RFC 1237) describes the administrative requirements for obtaining and allocating NSAP addresses and for distributing the assignment authority among the Internet's backbone and midlevel networks. It also explains how to construct and assign the various parts of the NSAP address to achieve efficient OSI and dual-stack (OSI and IP) routing and how to apply NSAP addressing to achieve the OSI equivalents of existing IP topological entities—backbones, regionals, and site and campus networks—in the Internet.

Conclusion

Because of the inability of the OSI standards community to decide between a network-centric or host-centric model of global networking, the OSI network layer is really several layers trying to look like one, as if for the sake of architectural appearances. *The Internal Organization of the Network Layer* is a convenient fig leaf, but the international networking community would be much better served by a forthright recognition of the internet/subnet split within the network layer. The TCP/IP architects avoided this problem entirely—their network layer is actually called the "internet" layer, and it sits on top of clearly distinguished subnetworks ("network interfaces").

┌─────────┐
│ ·AHA· │ *Although this is often characterized as a "failure" on the part*
└─────────┘ *of the OSI standards developers, it is important to realize that the host-centric/network-centric conflict was not played out in purely abstract terms. Network-centric arguments make more sense in the real-world context of national regulation, monopolistic common carriers, and the economics of public data networks and their tariffs. The host-centric argument has always been that diversity—in networks as in everything else— is an inescapable fact of life and that no amount of regulating (or standards making) can or should limit the range of choices from the menu of networking technologies that makes internetworking essential. The conflict has by no means been resolved within OSI, but few people today would bet on anything other than internetworking as the most likely model of the future global data network.*

The apparent incompatibility of the connection-oriented and connectionless network services in OSI is not an interworking problem and would not be solved by the invention of a magic gateway that could convert one type of service into the other. It is a fundamental architectural problem, reflecting two very different models for interconnecting a world's worth of networked hosts. The TCP/IP community has been fortunate to avoid this issue long enough to firmly establish TCP/IP's connectionless-internetworking architecture as the unchallenged centerpiece of the global Internet.

14 ROUTING

"Rōo´•ting" is what fans do at a football game, what pigs do for truffles under oak trees in the Vaucluse, and what nursery workers intent on propagation do to cuttings from plants. "Rou´•ting" is how one creates a beveled edge on a tabletop or sends a corps of infantrymen into full-scale, disorganized retreat. Either pronunciation is correct for *routing*, which refers to the process of discovering, selecting, and employing paths from one place to another (or to many others) in a network.

◊AHA◊ *The British prefer the spelling* routeing, *perhaps to distinguish what happens in networks from what happened to the British in New Orleans in 1814. Since the* Oxford English Dictionary *is much heavier than any dictionary of American English, British English generally prevails in the documents produced by ISO and CCITT; wherefore, most of the international standards for routing protocols use the* routeing *spelling. Since this spelling would be unfamiliar to many readers, we use* routing *in this book, with apologies to our friends in the British Standards Institute.*

A simple definition of routing is "learning how to get from here to there."[1] In some cases, the term *routing* is used in a very strict sense to refer *only* to the process of obtaining and distributing information ("learning"), but not to the process of using that information to actually get

---

1.   This is an application of the classic definition of a route by Schoch (see Chapter 5), augmented by Radia Perlman's (1992a) very practical observation that routes are both source- and destination-*dependent*: knowing how to get there isn't enough; you have to know where you are starting from ("here") as well as where you are going ("there").

from one place to another (for which a different term, *forwarding*, is reserved). Since it is difficult to grasp the usefulness of information that is acquired but never used, this chapter employs the term *routing* to refer in general to all the things that are done to discover and advertise paths from here to there and to actually move packets from here to there when necessary. The distinction between routing and forwarding is preserved in the formal discussion of the functions performed by OSI end systems and intermediate systems, in which context the distinction is meaningful.

Source Routing and "Hop-by-Hop" Routing

The routing operations of finding out how to get from here to there, and then actually getting from here to there, can be done in two (very different) basic ways. In *source routing*, all the information about how to get from here to there is first collected at the source ("here"), which puts it into the packets that it launches toward the destination ("there"). The job of the intervening network (with its collection of links and intermediate systems) is simply to read the routing information from the packets and act on it faithfully. In *hop-by-hop routing*, the source is not expected to have all the information about how to get from here to there; it is sufficient for the source to know only how to get to the "next hop" (perhaps an intermediate system to which it has a working link), and for that system to know how to get to the *next* hop, and so on until the destination is reached. The job of the intervening network in this case is more complicated; it has only the address of the destination (rather than a complete specification of the route by the source) with which to figure out the best "next hop" for each packet.

Consider an example, in which "here" is your home in Hopkinton, Massachusetts (U.S.A.), and "there" is Blueberry Hill Inn in Goshen, Vermont. If you sit down at home with a set of road maps and figure out exactly which roads and highways connect Hopkinton and Goshen, plotting the route you will follow along this road to that interchange to this junction (etc.), and then get in your car and actually drive along precisely that route to Blueberry Hill, you are performing source routing: if you were a packet, an ordered list of identifiers for links (roads) and intermediate systems (junctions and interchanges) would be encoded in your protocol header (see Chapter 13). If, on the other hand, you simply climb into your car and begin driving, stopping at every intersection to ask directions or examine the signposts, you are performing hop-by-hop routing: if you were a packet, the identification of your origin (Hopkinton) and final destination (Blueberry Hill) would be encoded in your protocol header. In the first case, your ability to actually get to Blueberry Hill depends on the accuracy of the maps you used and whether or not any of the roads you have selected are closed for repairs; in the second case, it depends on finding enough information at every intersection to enable you to pick the right road to follow to the next.

For the most part, routing in OSI and TCP/IP networks today is hop-by-hop. Source routing has recently emerged as an important component of a new set of routing capabilities (for both OSI and TCP/IP networks) that support complex *policies* governing the paths that packets are permitted to take when more than one organization owns or administers the equipment and facilities that intervene between "here" and "there." These issues are, however, beyond the scope of this chapter, which concentrates on the current hop-by-hop architecture of OSI and TCP/IP routing, and which also omits the very different concerns of routing in virtual-circuit (connection-oriented) networks. For a detailed and comprehensive description of the theory and practice of routing, including the topics that are beyond the scope of this book, readers are encouraged to consult *Interconnections: Bridges and Routers* (Perlman 1992a).

Routing Principles

The principal criterion of successful routing is, of course, *correctness* (you do in fact want to get to Blueberry Hill, not Cranberry Bog), but it is not the only criterion. You might prefer to take the most direct route (the one that takes the least time and uses the least fuel), the most reliable route (the one that is not likely to be closed by a heavy snowfall), the most scenic route (the one that follows pleasant country roads rather than busy highways), the least expensive route (the one that follows freeways rather than toll roads), or the safest route (the one that avoids the army's missile testing range). In its most general form, *optimal* routing involves forwarding a packet from source to destination using the "best" path. What constitutes the "best" path can, of course, become quite a complicated question, as this example shows; networks, like the highway system, have variable costs, transit restrictions, delay characteristics, and residual error rates, and all of these can be more or less important in the determination of what "best" means for a particular source and destination or for a particular packet.

The principal objective of an open systems routing architecture is not, therefore, to achieve "optimal" routing—such a thing does not exist in the abstract. Such an architecture must nevertheless be based on principles that account for what is happening in the real open systems world of today and tomorrow, in which computers are being connected to networks at a rate that more than doubles the number of systems connected to the worldwide (OSI and TCP/IP) Internet each year. These computers will be connected using a variety of local, metropolitan, and wide area networking technologies; the topology of interconnection will change as computers and the links between them are added and deleted; the networks will cross every conceivable national and international boundary; and the computers and networks will be administered by different organizations, both public and private, each of which may impose rules (policies) governing (and safeguarding) their use.

These observations suggest that an open systems routing architecture should

- Scale well
- Support many different subnetwork types and multiple qualities of service
- Adapt to topology changes quickly and efficiently (i.e., with minimal overhead and complexity)
- Provide controls that facilitate the "safe" interconnection of multiple organizations

It is not likely that the manual administration of static routing tables (the earliest medium for the maintenance of internetwork routes, in which a complete set of fixed routes from each system to every other system was periodically—often no more frequently than once a week—loaded into a file on each system) will satisfy these objectives for a network connecting more than a few hundred systems. A routing scheme for a large-scale open systems network must be dynamic, adaptive, and decentralized; be capable of supporting multiple paths offering different types of service; and provide the means to establish "trust, firewalls, and security" across multiple administrations (ISO/IEC TR 9575: 1990).

OSI Routing Architecture

The architecture of routing in OSI is basically the same as the architecture of routing in other connectionless (datagram) networks, including TCP/IP. As usual, however, the conceptual framework and terminology of OSI are more highly elaborated than those of its roughly equivalent peers, and thus, it is the OSI routing architecture that gets the lion's share of attention in this chapter. Keep in mind that most of what is said about the OSI routing architecture applies to hop-by-hop connectionless open systems routing in general.

The OSI routing scheme consists of:

- A set of *routing protocols* that allow end systems and intermediate systems to collect and distribute the information necessary to determine routes
- A *routing information base* containing this information, from which routes between end systems can be computed[2]
- A *routing algorithm* that uses the information contained in the routing information base to derive routes between end systems

End systems (ESs) and intermediate systems (ISs)[3] use routing protocols to distribute ("advertise") some or all of the information stored in their locally maintained routing information base. ESs and ISs send and receive these routing *updates* and use the information that they contain (and information that may be available from the local environment, such as information entered manually by an operator) to modify their routing information base.

The routing information base consists of a table of entries that identify a *destination* (e.g., a network service access point address); the subnetwork over which packets should be forwarded to reach that destination (also known as the *next hop*, or "next-hop subnetwork point of attachment address"); and some form of *routing metric*, which expresses one or more characteristics of the route (its delay properties, for example, or its expected error rate) in terms that can be used to evaluate the suitability of this route, compared to another route with different properties, for conveying a particular packet or class of packets. The routing information base may contain information about more than one "next hop" to the same destination if it is important to be able to send packets over different paths depending on the way in which the "quality of service" specified in the packet's header corresponds to different values of the routing metric(s).

The routing algorithm uses the information contained in the routing information base to compute actual routes ("next hops"); these are collectively referred to as the *forwarding information base*. It is important to recognize that the routing information base is involved in computations that take place in the "background," independent of the data traffic

---

2.   Like the directory information base, the routing information base is an abstraction; it doesn't exist as a single entity. The routing information base can be thought of as the collective (distributed) wisdom of an entire subsystem concerning the routing-relevant connectivity among the components of that subsystem.

3.   The terms *end system* and *intermediate system* will appear so frequently in this chapter's discussion of routing that the authors feel justified in resorting for the most part to the use of the acronyms *ES* and *IS* in their place.

flowing between sources and destinations at any given moment; but the forwarding information base is involved in the real-time selection of an outgoing link for every packet that arrives on an incoming link and must therefore be implemented in such a way that it does not become a performance-killing bottleneck in a real-world intermediate system (router).

Figure 14.1 illustrates the decomposition of the OSI routing function as it is represented in ISO/IEC TR 9575.

No system—certainly not an end system, which is supposed to be devoted primarily to tasks other than routing—can maintain a routing information base containing all the information necessary to specify routes from any "here" to any "there" in the entire global Internet. Neither is it possible to design a single routing protocol that operates well both in local environments (in which it is important to account quickly for changes in the local network topology) and in wide area environments (in which it is important to limit the percentage of network bandwidth that is consumed by "overhead" traffic such as routing updates). The OSI routing architecture is consequently hierarchical, and is divided into three functional tiers:

1. *End-system to intermediate-system routing* (host-to-router), in which the principal routing functions are discovery and redirection.
2. *Intradomain intermediate-system to intermediate-system routing* (router-to-router), in which "best" routes between ESs within a single administrative domain are computed. A single routing algorithm is used by all ISs within a domain.

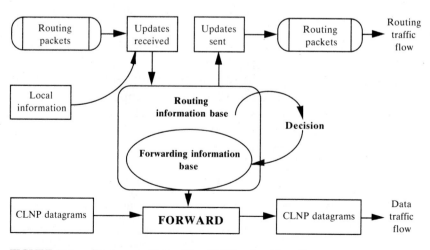

FIGURE 14.1   Decomposition of the OSI Routing Function

3. *Interdomain intermediate-system to intermediate-system routing* (router-to-router), in which routes are computed between administrative domains.

In Figure 14.2, end systems discover and communicate with the intermediate systems to which they are directly connected (by dedicated or dial-up point-to-point links or by multiaccess local or metropolitan area networks) in the outermost level of the hierarchy; intermediate systems communicate with other intermediate systems within a single routing domain in the levels of the hierarchy next closest to the center; and in the center, intermediate systems communicate with other intermediate systems across routing domain boundaries.

The decomposition illustrated in Figure 14.2 is not arbitrary. At each level of the hierarchy, a different set of imperatives governs the choices that are available for routing algorithms and protocols. In the OSI routing architecture, end systems are not involved in the distribution of routing information and the computation of routes, and hence, the participation of end systems in routing is limited to asking and answering the question "Who's on this subnetwork with me?" (On broad-

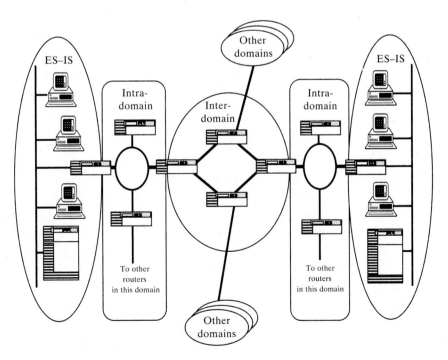

FIGURE 14.2   OSI Routing Architecture

cast subnetworks such as most local area networks, this inquiry typically begins with the more or less Cartesian assertion "I broadcast [multicast], therefore I am . . .")

Within a single routing domain, the hegemony of a single administration (and a correspondingly consistent set of routing policies) argues in favor of using a single routing protocol which provides every intermediate system with complete knowledge of the topology of the routing domain. (See "Intradomain Routing in OSI," later in this chapter.) Between routing domains that may be controlled by different (possibly even antagonistic) administrations, issues of security (including control over the extent to which information about the topology of one domain is propagated to other domains) outweigh most others, and the argument in favor of distributing complete topology information to all intermediate systems, so compelling when selecting an intradomain routing protocol, misfires for the very reason that concealing or witholding information is often as important as distributing it. It is important to recognize that the analysis that leads to one conclusion in the intradomain context does not necessarily hold when it is transplanted to the interdomain context.

| ·AHA· | *Fortunately, with respect to routing, it has not been difficult to refute the simplistic argument that if link-state routing is the* |

best choice for the intradomain level of the routing hierarchy it must be the best choice for the interdomain level. Ten years ago, however, a similarly simplistic argument destroyed the opportunity for OSI to standardize one of the best features of the TCP/IP internetwork architecture—the combination of a connectionless (datagram) internetwork protocol (which could be operated efficiently over any underlying network technology, whether based on datagrams or virtual circuits) with a connection-oriented end-to-end transport protocol (which made everything "come out even" at the hosts, or end systems). The OSI position at that time was that a connection-oriented service at the transport layer "naturally" mapped to a connection-oriented service at the network layer, as if this were something inherent in the very architecture of a layered model. The OSI community wasted years dealing with this red herring, which was intended to divert attention from the fact that a large segment of the OSI community believed that the service provided by the network layer was an end-to-end transport service. The TCP/IP community, unencumbered by such nonsense, happily expanded to fill the resulting vacuum.

End System to Intermediate System Routing   "ES-IS" routing establishes connectivity and reachability among ESs and ISs attached to the same (single) subnetwork. Limiting the scope of routing in this manner allows an ES to play a simple role in the overall routing process and leaves most of the ES's resources available to support end-user applications (which is, presumably, the *raison d'être* of an ES). ESs are commonly attached to *multiaccess subnetworks*, such as IEEE 802 local area networks (LANs) and metropolitan area networks (MANs), creating topologies that are both highly connected and densely populated (with ESs); the protocols and algorithms that are appropriate for routing in this environment are very different from those that are appropriate for routing in the wide area environments served by intermediate system to intermediate system routing.

At this level of routing, the two critical (closely related) concerns are discovery (who is out there?) and reachability (with whom is it possible to communicate?). Within a single subnetwork, an ES is one "hop" away from any ES or IS connected to the same subnetwork, so the only information an ES needs in order to reach either destination ESs on the same subnetwork or ISs that will forward packets to destination ESs on other subnetworks is the "hardware interface" or *subnetwork point of attachment* (SNPA) addresses of the ESs and ISs attached to the subnetwork.

Intradomain Intermediate System to Intermediate System Routing   "IS-IS" routing establishes connectivity among intermediate systems within a single authority, the *administrative domain*. An administrative domain is composed of one or more *routing domains*. Each routing domain consists of a set of ISs and ESs; ISs within a routing domain use the same routing protocol, routing algorithm, and routing metrics.

At this level of routing, the critical concern is the selection and maintenance of best paths among systems within the administrative domain. ISs are concerned about route optimization with respect to a variety of metrics and about the trade-off between (1) the cost of distributing and maintaining routing information (which increases as the granularity of the information approaches "a separate route for every source/destination pair for every value of the routing metric[s]") and (2) the cost of actually sending data over a particular route (which increases if the available routing information causes data to be sent over a "suboptimal" route).

Interdomain Intermediate System to Intermediate System Routing   Interdomain IS-IS routing establishes communication among different administrative domains, enabling them to control the exchange of information "across borders." In most circumstances, it is common to think of routing as something that tries to make it "as easy as possible" for two systems to communicate, regardless of what may lie between them. Interdomain routing, on the other hand, plays the paradoxical role of facilitating communication among open systems for which communication is a (politically) sensitive activity, involving issues of cost, accountability, transit authorization, and security that can produce highly counterintuitive answers to what look like simple technical questions.[4]

At this level of routing, the critical concern is the maintenance and enforcement of policies that govern, for example, the willingness of an administrative domain to (1) act as a transit domain for traffic originating from and destined for other administrative domains, (2) receive information from sources outside the administrative domain and deliver them to destinations within the administrative domain, and (3) forward information from within the administrative domain to destinations outside the administrative domain. Policies concerning 1, 2, and 3 can be derived on the basis of cost, access control, and regulatory concerns.

The hierarchical relationship of the OSI routing protocols is depicted in Figure 14.3.

Within the OSI routing framework, it is possible for different routing domains within a single administrative domain to run different

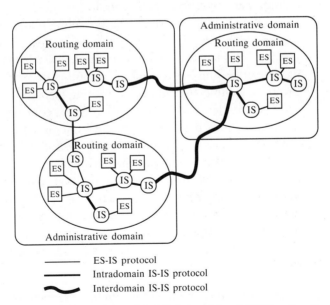

———	ES-IS protocol
———	Intradomain IS-IS protocol
～～	Interdomain IS-IS protocol

FIGURE 14.3   Hierarchical Relationship of OSI Routing Protocols

---

4.   Within the purview of a single network administration, it is considered to be a very good and useful thing for the network to automatically reconfigure itself to route traffic around a failed link onto an alternate path. In an interdomain configuration involving mu-

intradomain routing protocols, and it is also possible to operate different ES-IS protocols within different areas of the same routing domain. At present, however, OSI defines only one standard routing protocol for each of the three levels of the hierarchy.

TCP/IP Routing Architecture

Through a process of evolution—in which some of the ideas that led to features of the OSI routing architecture originated with TCP/IP, developed into OSI standards, and returned to be adopted by the TCP/IP community—the TCP/IP routing architecture today is almost identical to the OSI architecture. The TCP/IP world began with a single network (which didn't require much in the way of routing), and grew into the "core"-based ARPANET, with individual networks connected to a single backbone (composed of "core gateways") as "stubs" (RFC 888; RFC 904). Multiple organizations began offering IP transit services, and for a time, it was difficult to tell whether the Internet was a "mesh" of backbone networks or a hierarchy. A three-tier hierarchy was gradually introduced as the NSFnet[5] grew and supplanted the ARPANET: the NSFnet served as a national backbone, and midlevel networks or ("regionals") provided transit services to and from the IP networks whose directly connected hosts served as the sources and sinks of Internet traffic.

Today, the TCP/IP routing architecture looks very much like the OSI routing architecture. Hosts use a discovery protocol to obtain the identification of gateways and other hosts attached to the same network (subnetwork). Gateways within *autonomous systems* (routing domains) operate an *interior gateway protocol* (intradomain IS-IS routing protocol), and between autonomous systems, they operate *exterior* or *border gateway protocols* (interdomain routing protocols). The details are different but the principles are the same.

---

tually suspicious network administrations, however, it may be the worst possible thing for the network to switch traffic to an alternate path "automatically" without first clearing the change with the legal departments of both parties. This conundrum has led one of the authors to claim that the only large-scale interdomain routing protocol that is likely to be deployed in the near future will be implemented as an army of lawyers on bicycles.

5. The National Science Foundation network (NSFnet) is the principal wide area backbone network for the Internet in the United States.

Routing Protocols

Over the past two decades, there have been more than a dozen routing protocols in operation in various parts of the Internet: HELLO, RIP (succeeded by RIP II), EGP, GGP, and BGP (which has gone through several versions, of which the most recent is BGP-4).[6] This is largely due to the fact that the Internet has been so successful that it has encountered—more than once!—a fundamental (architectural) limit to the ability of its prevailing routing technologies to cope with its increased size and extent. OSI benefited enormously from these years of experience with TCP/IP networks and can boast today that its routing protocols have been designed "from the beginning" to scale into the foreseeable future of billion-node internets. The boast is empty, of course, since the same lessons have been factored into a new generation of TCP/IP routing protocols; in some cases, in fact, the two communities are close to adopting the same routing protocol (much to the dismay of protocol-stack isolationists, but much to the relief of network operators and users!).

It is impossible to cover each of the TCP/IP routing protocols in detail in this chapter. However, it is instructive to compare a single TCP/IP routing protocol at each level of the routing hierarchy with an equivalent OSI protocol. The remainder of the chapter considers each of the three levels of the hierarchy (which is a common feature of both the OSI and the TCP/IP routing architectures) in turn, examining the OSI protocol (for which there is just one at each level) in some detail and comparing with it the currently recommended TCP/IP counterpart.

Reachability and Discovery in OSI—The ES-IS Protocol

In OSI, the discovery paradigm is *announcement*. An end system uses the *end system hello message* (ESH) of the ES-IS protocol (ISO/IEC 9542)[7] to announce its presence to intermediate systems (and end systems) connected to the same subnetwork. Any end or intermediate system that is listening for ES hello messages gets a copy; intermediate systems will store the NSAP address and the corresponding subnetwork address pair in routing tables. ESs may do so if they wish, or they may wait to be informed by intermediate systems when they need such information.

The announcement process is most effective when operated over a

---

6.   RIP: routing information protocol; EGP: exterior gateway protocol; GGP: gateway-to-gateway protocol; BGP: border gateway protocol.

7.   ISO often carries descriptive naming too far. The full title of the ES-IS standard is *End System to Intermediate System Routeing Exchange Protocol for Use in Conjunction With the Protocol for Providing the Connectionless-mode Network Service (ISO 8473)*. No wonder everyone refers to it simply as "ES-IS"!

multiaccess, connectionless subnetwork such as an IEEE 802 local area network. ISO/IEC 9542 refers to such facilities as "broadcast subnetworks." ES-IS can, however, operate quite nicely over X.25 public (or private) data networks and over newer wide area network services such as switched multimegabit data service (SMDS; Perlman 1992b).

The protocol operates over an IEEE 802 local area network as follows. An end system periodically composes an ES hello—inserting its NSAP address(es), subnetwork point of attachment address, and a *holding time* into the ES hello packet—and sends this packet to the 48-bit multicast medium access control (MAC) address whose value has been defined to mean *all intermediate system network entities* (Figure 14.4). This aspect of the protocol is called the *report configuration* function.[8]

The frequency of these announcements is determined by the value of a locally administered *configuration timer* (CT). Why periodically? On LANs especially, computer systems are powered on and off frequently, sometimes for hours or more. LAN-based computers are also moved from office to office, and depending on how LANs are administered, NSAP addresses may remain associated with the computer or the office. Since resources for storing addressing information at intermediate systems are precious, it is important for ISs to know whether such information remains useful and accurate. Periodic transmission of ES hellos also

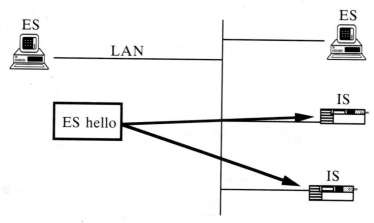

FIGURE 14.4   Report Configuration by End Systems

---

8.   Over multidestination subnetworks such as SMDS, in which a form of multicast or group addressing is offered, configuration information can be announced to any set of individual subnetwork addresses that are collectively identified by a "group address" (see Chapter 15, "Emerging Digital Technologies").

allows a new router on a subnetwork to obtain configuration information about ESs on the subnetwork without explicitly asking for it and allows a router that has "crashed," lost state, and reinitialized to do so as well. The configuration time is used by the originators of hello messages to compute a *holding time* (HT). The holding time is encoded in the hello messages and tells recipients of hello messages how long the addressing information encoded in this hello message should be treated as accurate. Clearly, the shorter the configuration time (and accordingly, the holding time), the more accurate the addressing information, but the accuracy has to be weighed against the amount of traffic on the LAN and the resources consumed by recipients who must process each ES hello.

Upon receiving an ES hello, an intermediate system records the configuration information (NSAP addresses, subnetwork point of attachment address, holding time) contained in the message and holds the addressing information for the period of time indicated in holding time. If holding time elapses and no ES hello messages are received from this ES, the intermediate system discards the configuration information it has maintained for this ES, and assumes that the ES is no longer reachable. This aspect of the ES-IS protocol is called the *flush old configuration* function. Holding time is always greater than configuration time and is typically set at the source to at least twice the configuration time (with this value, even if every other ES hello is lost, ISs should hear a hello message, and thus, the presence of the ES on the LAN will be known and its configuration information will continue to be maintained by ISs).

An intermediate system performs nearly the same report configuration function (see Figure 14.5). An IS composes an *intermediate system hello*

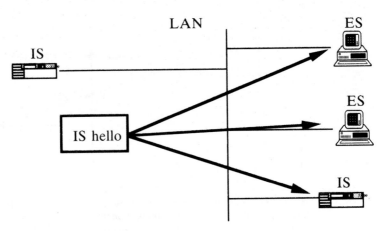

FIGURE 14.5   Report Configuration by Intermediate Systems

message (ISH) and announces its configuration information to intermediate systems and end systems alike connected to the same broadcast subnetwork. Like the ES hello, the IS hello message contains the addressing information for the IS (network entity title, subnetwork point of attachment address) and a holding time; optionally, IS hellos may encode a *suggested ES configuration time*, which recommends a configuration timer to end systems. This may be used by a LAN administrator to coordinate (distribute) the announcement process across all ESs that will report configuration to an IS. The announcement process over IEEE 802 LANs is again accomplished by issuing the IS hello message to a 48-bit multicast destination MAC address, but here, the value indicates *all OSI network entities* (so that both ESs and ISs may listen for the messages).

Upon receiving an ISH, an end system records the configuration information contained in the message and holds that information for the period of time identified in the holding time parameter. Again, if holding time elapses and no IS hello messages are received from this IS, the end system discards the configuration information it has maintained for this IS and assumes that the IS is no longer reachable. If this was the only (or last remaining) IS the end system had discovered, it may no longer be able to communicate with end systems other than those attached to its own subnetwork. ISs also listen for ISH messages for initial configuration information prior to operating the IS-IS intradomain routing protocol.

Redirection   Both IP and OSI have a redirection capability, and the two are functionally the same. In IP, redirection is part of the Internet-control message protocol (ICMP, see Chapter 13, "Internet and OSI Control Messages"); in OSI, the redirect function, and the *redirect message* (RD), are part of the ES-IS protocol.

In OSI, redirection proceeds as follows. When an IS receives a CLNP data packet from an ES, it processes the packet and forwards it to the next hop toward its destination. If the IS determines that the destination is on the same LAN as the originator of the datagram, it returns a redirect message to the end system, indicating the *better next-hop subnetwork point of attachment address* to that destination, which is the subnetwork point of attachment address (BNSPA) of the destination NSAP address itself (Figure 14.6). Note that a holding time is also associated with redirect configuration information.[9]

Absent any further information in the redirect message, an end sys-

---

9.   ISO/IEC 9542 Annex B describes important timer considerations and optimizations for redirection that are too detailed to describe here. These are discussed extensively in Perlman (1992b).

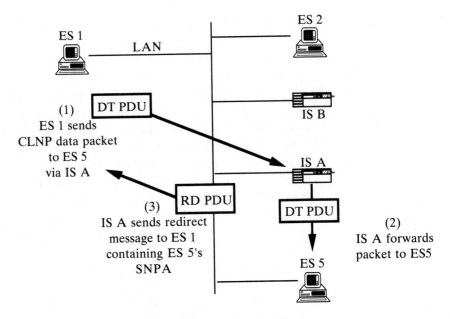

FIGURE 14.6   Redirection of One IS to Another IS

tem can only conclude that a better path to a given destination NSAP address exists through an IS identified by the network entity title and BSNPA encoded in the redirect message. For those situations in which the identified IS provides a better route to a larger set of destinations—or as ISO/IEC 9542 says, "an equivalence class of NSAP addresses to which the same redirection information applies"—an IS can include an *address mask* parameter, which indicates just how widely the redirection information can be applied. The address mask is composed from the destination NSAP address that caused the redirection, with binary 1s identifying how much of the NSAP address is the mask. For example, the bits representing the entire initial domain part and the first 16 bits of the domain-specific part of the mask might be set to binary 1s, and the remaining bits of the domain-specific part set to binary 0s. This signals to the end system that anytime it receives a request to send a data packet to a destination that has the identical initial domain part and the same initial 16 bits of domain-specific part as this NSAP address, it should forward the packet to the IS identified in the redirect message.

AHA   *One can't help but notice the similarity between the actions of ESs and ISs in this protocol and the actions of the citizens of* Whoville *in Dr. Seuss's* Horton Hears a Who, *who, attempting to save their world, proclaim loudly and frequently, "We are here! We are here! We are HERE!" (Giesel 1971).*

Reachability and Discovery in TCP/IP — ARP and Friends

The original *Address Resolution Protocol* (ARP; RFC 826) was designed to be used over a single Ethernet to solve a very simple routing problem: determine the 48-bit Ethernet hardware address associated with a specific Internet address. It has since been extended to operate over many local area network and metropolitan area network technologies and services, including SMDS (RFC 1209), frame relay (RFC 1293), and FDDI (RFC 1188).

The paradigm for the address-resolution protocol is *request/reply*. To discover the binding between IP addresses and the interface addresses of other hosts, a host issues address resolution protocol requests over the Ethernet "broadcast" address (or its equivalent for non-Ethernet networks). All hosts listening for the broadcast address will receive a copy of the request; in its simplest form, the host whose IP address corresponds to that encoded in the request will return a reply to identify its hardware address. In another form, a router may listen for address resolution protocol requests for a set of IP addresses (i.e., addresses of hosts for which it provides routing service) and, acting as an agent or "proxy," will reply on their behalf ("proxy ARP").

In either case, ARP processing proceeds as follows. A TCP segment is submitted to IP for forwarding. The IP packet is created, and the routing process looks up the destination IP address in a routing table to determine the Internet address of the next hop (the destination address itself or the IP address of a router). Associated with this IP address is an address for the interface over which the packet is to be forwarded. This is called the *hardware address*—in this case, a 48-bit Ethernet address. When the routing process looks for the hardware address associated with a "next hop" and finds none, it builds an *ARP request* packet, placing the destination IP address from the IP packet into the request packet.[10] The request packet is "broadcast" over the local area network (step 1 in Figure 14.7). A copy of the packet is received by each station on the local area network that is listening for broadcasts. If the destination address in the ARP request packet doesn't match any of the local IP addresses, it is discarded. If a match is found, a reply packet is composed from the request; in particular, the source and destination IP address fields are reversed, the source hardware address is copied into the destination hardware address field, and the local hardware address is copied into the source hardware

---

10.   In most instances, the routing process attempts to hold the IP packet until the ARP request is resolved; a system can drop the IP packet under circumstances enumerated in the Host and router Requirements RFCs (RFC 1122, 1989), RFC 1123, 1989).

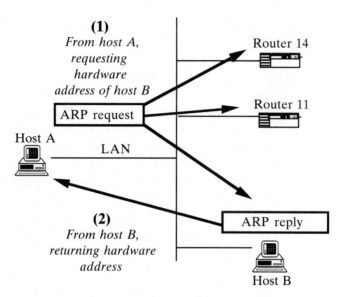

(1)
From host A,
requesting
hardware
address of host B

Router 14

ARP request

Router 11

Host A

LAN

(2)
From host B,
returning hardware
address

ARP reply

Host B

FIGURE 14.7   Address-Resolution Protocol Request/Reply Sequence

address field of the reply packet. The ARP reply packet is then returned directly to the originator of the ARP request packet (step 2 in Figure 14.7). The requester now has the necessary information (IP address, hardware address pair) for routing to this destination.

As for the ES-IS protocol, a configuration or lifetime is associated with address information obtained via the address resolution protocol. Few details on how to implement this are provided in the address resolution protocol RFCs; Comer (1991) provides an example of how to implement the address resolution protocol and associated cache management.

Which Is Better?   There are pros and cons to both discovery protocols. ES-IS was designed to be media-independent; all ESs and ISs use it, irrespective of the medium to which they are connected. The address resolution protocol has been extended to accommodate network interfaces other than the original Ethernet. The address resolution protocol is used "on demand," whereas ES-IS is operated periodically. The address resolution protocol uses a broadcast address (partly a consequence of its having been developed for the experimental Ethernet rather than the IEEE 802.3 local area network). This causes interrupts to occur at systems that are not IP-based, so all end systems must look at the packet. ES-IS uses multicast addresses, which restrict interrupts (and packet processing) to only those systems that are listening to OSI-specific 48-bit multicast addresses. In any event, both these discovery protocols are a whole lot better than static tables.

Intradomain Routing in OSI

The OSI intradomain IS-IS routing protocol (ISO/IEC 10589) operates within a routing domain to provide every IS with complete knowledge of the topology of the routing domain. Generally speaking, within a single routing domain, small convergence time and simplicity of operation are more important than trust and fire walls. Thus, the main design goals of IS-IS are to

- *Accommodate large routing domains*: IS-IS is designed to handle 100,000 NSAP addresses and 10,000 ISs in a single routing domain.
- *Converge quickly*: When a change in topology in the routing domain occurs, IS-IS converges to correct routes quickly and without oscillation.
- *Provide operational "simplicity"*: In the OSI routing architecture, the role of ESs in routing is extremely simple, and with IS-IS, the configuration and parameter tuning of ISs is also relatively simple. IS-IS is relatively simple to maintain as well.
- *Support multiple subnetwork types*: IS-IS is designed to operate over local area networks, metropolitan area networks, point-to-point links, and X.25 networks. These subnetworks have widely differing delay, bandwidth, and operational characteristics (e.g., some offer connections, and some run datagrams), yet IS-IS is immune to the differences.

To accommodate large routing domains, IS-IS is organized as a two-level hierarchy. The subdomains that comprise level 1 of the hierarchy are called *areas*, and level-1 ISs within an area maintain routes only to destinations within their area. Routes to destination areas within the same routing domain (and routes to areas in other routing domains absent any policy restrictions—e.g., shortest paths to destination routing domains) are maintained at the second level of the hierarchy, by *level-2 ISs* (note that ISs designated as "level-2 ISs" maintain both level-1 and level-2 routes).

To converge quickly on the best (shortest) routes, IS-IS uses both a link-state routing algorithm based on the "new ARPANET" algorithm developed by McQuillan, Richter, and Rosen (1980), and the fault-tolerant broadcast mechanism developed by Radia Perlman (1983). IS-IS computes routes using the Dijkstra *shortest path first* (SPF) algorithm. Link-state routing avoids the "count-to-infinity," oscillatory behavior exhibited by many distance-vector algorithms such as the *routing information protocol* (RIP RFC 1058, 1988). In a *distance-vector routing* environment, each router passes to its neighbors information about routes to destinations that the router has computed based on information it has received from other neighbors; since the information being distributed is filtered through the route-computation process of each router, each router has only a partial map of the topology of a routing domain. In a *link-state routing* environment, each router broadcasts to every other router in the domain complete information about all of its links to adjacent routers; every router thereby acquires information describing the complete topology of the routing domain and uses that information to compute its own best routes to every destination. Paul Francis aptly described the difference between the two protocols by saying that "distance-vector routing is rumor-based, while link-state routing is propaganda-based.[11] Consider the topology of a single routing domain illustrated in Figure 14.8, in which all the links in the topology conveniently have equal costs, and the routing metric is hop count. Conceptually, distance-vector routing information received by router Dave from router Deborah would tell Dave, "I

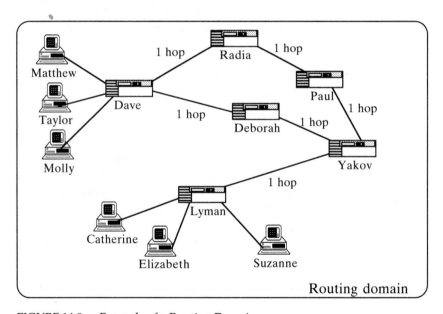

FIGURE 14.8   Example of a Routing Domain

---

11.   To appreciate how link-state routing might be related to propaganda, readers must first refrain from assuming that propaganda is bad; in fact, propaganda is "the dissemination and the defense of beliefs, opions, or actions deemed salutary to the program of a particular group." Routing information fits this definition nicely. Each router announces (disseminates information describing) its own neighbors, links, and link costs, effectively saying "it is so" (the "defense of beliefs" component); and indeed, all the routers that listen to the announcements believe them to be true. Each router is therefore a *propagandist*, devoting itself to "the spread of (a) system of principles or set of actions" (Webster's , 1977).

(Deborah) hear that I can get to Lyman, so you can get to Lyman through *me*, but it will cost you 2 hops"; the routing packet would be a bit more succinct, saying perhaps in this case that Deborah has a 2-hop route to Lyman. Dave would add the cost of the link he shares with Deborah (1 hop) and conclude that the cost of the path through Deborah to Lyman is 3 hops. Dave, hearing from Radia that she hears she can reach Lyman in 3 hops, would add the cost of the link he shares with Radia and conclude that the best path to Lyman is through Deborah (3 hops) rather than through Radia (4 hops).

Link-state routing information is distributed quite differently, and paints a *very* different conceptual picture of the topology. Deborah would announce ("advertise") a list of neighboring routers (Dave, Yakov) over each of her links; Yakov would announce his list (Deborah, Paul, Lyman), Radia her list (Dave, Paul), Paul his list (Radia, Yakov), and Lyman his list (Suzanne, Katherine, and Elizabeth—perhaps collectively referred to as "the Chapins", and Yakov). (Dutifully, Dave would announce his list as well (Molly, Matthew and Taylor—the "Piscitellos"—Deborah, and Radia).[12]

This information is flooded through the entire routing domain; everyone hears about everyone else's links, neighbors, and link costs. Dave waits until it's quiet, then deduces from the collection of announcements that "I can get to Deborah (1 hop); Deborah can get to Yakov (1 hop); Yakov can get to Lyman (1 hop); therefore *I* can get to Lyman over the link to Deborah in 3 hops!" (Having the entire set of announcements, Dave also deduces that he can get to Lyman over the link to Radia in 4 hops, and elects to use the path through Deborah; of course, since Radia was kind enough to offer Dave an *alternative* path, he keeps this in the back of his mind—just in case Deborah goes away, or becomes very busy).

│·AHA·│ *The selection of a standard IS-IS protocol for OSI began in the United States in 1987 and is remembered as the "late, great, OSI routing debate." Two routing protocols were introduced as candidates— one from Digital Equipment Corporation and one from Burroughs (Unisys). Both protocols scaled well and offered hierarchical, multiple–quality of service routing with partition repair. The principal difference was that the DEC protocol was a link-state or "new ARPANET" protocol, and the Burroughs protocol*

---

12.   Distance-vector and link-state routing share the notion of *neighbor greetings exchange*, in which each router identifies itself to its neighbors when a link comes up or its status changes.

was a distance-vector or "old ARPANET" protocol.

The most damning fault of distance-vector routing is that it converges too slowly following topology changes. The Burroughs protocol, based on the Burroughs Integrated Adaptive Routing Algorithm System (BIAS) used in the Burroughs Network Architecture (BNA) (Piscitello and Gruchevsky 1987; Rosenberg, Piscitello, and Gruchevsky 1987), incorporated many improvements (Jaffe and Moss 1982; Kamoun and Kleinrock 1977; Tajibnapis 1977) to the original Bellman-Ford algorithm that dramatically reduced the seriousness of the problem, but it could not converge as quickly as the DEC link state protocol, and this difference proved to be the deciding factor.

A generic description of the IS-IS protocol follows. Initially, routers begin by learning about other routers to which they share direct connectivity; i.e., a router X learns first about those routers that are attached to the same subnetworks as X, often by using the IS hellos described earlier). This process is called neighbor greeting, or neighbor initialization. Each router then constructs a *link-state packet* (LSP), which contains a list of the names of its *neighbors* and its *cost*[13] to reach each of those neighbors. Routers then distribute these link-state packets to all the other routers. When all the link-state packets have been propagated to all the routers, each router will have received a complete map of the network topology in the form of link-state packets; each router uses these link-state packets to compute routes to every "destination" in the network using Dijkstra's *shortest path first* algorithm.[14]

All of the OSI NSAP address formats (see Chapter 13) can be used with the IS-IS routing protocol. For the purpose of computing routes, an NSAP address is always interpreted by IS-IS as having three fields: an area address, a system identifier, and an NSAP selector. The *area address* identifies an area within a routing domain; the *system identifier* unambiguously identifies a system or "host" within that area; and the *NSAP selector* identifies an entity within the system (a transport entity in an ES or a network entity in an IS; the NSAP selector is the OSI functional equivalent of the protocol identifier in IP). The relationship between the gen-

---

13.   IS-IS uses non–traffic-based *metrics* to compute route costs. The metrics are insensitive to traffic, so IS-IS is able to avoid unnecessary recomputation of routes when traffic patterns on links oscillate. The default metric is capacity (a measure roughly equal to bitsper second); however, IS-IS computes routes based on transit delay, cost (incremental expense, such as a charge per packet), and error (a measure of the probability of undetected errors on a circuit) so that CLNP datagrams originated with the QOS maintenance bits set (see Chapter 13) can be forwarded as requested by the originator.

14.   Details of link-state packet distribution schemes and computation of Dijkstra's SPF algorithm as applied in IS-IS routing are described in Perlman (1992a).

eral structure of OSI NSAP addresses and the way in which NSAP addresses are interpreted by IS-IS for routing purposes is illustrated in Figure 14.9.[15]

The IS-IS interpretation of the domain-specific part (DSP) of the NSAP address, which has been standardized in the United States as American National Standard X3.216-1992, allows 1 octet for the NSAP selector, 6 octets for the system ("host") identifier,[16] and the remaining (leftmost) octets for the low-order part of the area address. The system identifier must be unique among all the NSAPs in the same area; it need not be globally unique, and it need not be an IEEE 802 medium access control address (it is, however, often convenient for a network administrator to use actual MAC addresses for the values of the system identifier as a simple way to ensure uniqueness). The IS-IS standard refers to the leftmost domain-specific part octets (the ones that form the low-order part of the area address) as the *LOC-AREA* field. The LOC-AREA value must be unique among NSAPs with the same initial domain part. In general, the procedures associated with level-1 routing look only at the contents of the system identifier field; the procedures associated with level-2 routing look only at the contents of the area address field.[17]

This address structure reflects the two-level hierachy of IS-IS routing, illustrated in Figure 14.10. In this figure, the notation "<number>.

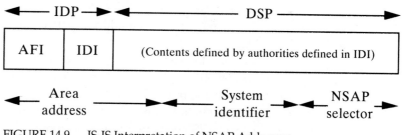

FIGURE 14.9   IS-IS Interpretation of NSAP Addresses

15.   See Chapter 13 for a detailed description of the way in which the IS-IS interpretation of the NSAP address structure has been formalized as American National Standard X3.216-1992.

16.   Readers who read "6 octets" and immediately thought, "I'll bet that the system identifier is expected to be a 48-bit IEEE 802 medium access control (MAC) address," are right—but they might also think about consulting a good obsessive/compulsive disorder specialist . . . The 6-octet size of the system identifier field was indeed chosen so as to make it possible to use a MAC address as a system identifier field value, but none of the ISO/IEC standards requires that this be the case.

17.   An intermediate system that is configured to operate as a level-2 IS may also be configured to participate in level-1 routing in areas to which it is directly connected; that is, a single hardware component (what one would ordinarily recognize as a "router box") may participate in both level-1 and level-2 routing.

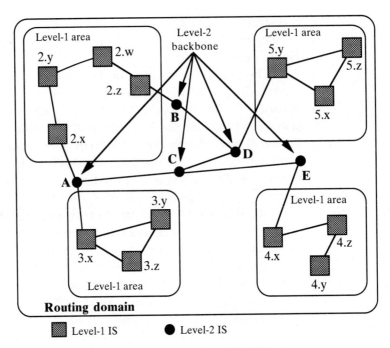

Level-1 IS   ●Level-2 IS

FIGURE 14.10   Two-Level Hierarchy of IS-IS Routing

<lowercase letter>" is used for the area address and system identifier parts of the network entity titles of level-1 ISs; the notation "<uppercase letter>" is used for the area address part of the network entity titles of level-2 ISs.

A level-1 IS needs to know only about the ESs and other level-1 ISs in its own level-1 area and about the "nearest" level-2 IS which it can use to forward traffic out of its own area. The level-1 "view" of the routing domain depicted in Figure 14.10 is illustrated in Figure 14.11.

A level-2 IS needs to know only about other level-2 ISs in its own routing domain, the location of level-1 areas, and the "best" exit level-2 IS to use for traffic destined for other routing domains. The level-2 "view" of the routing domain depicted in Figure 14.10 is illustrated in Figure 14.12.

The existence of and distance to other routing domains is administratively configured into level-2 ISs that share links with ISs in other routing domains. The other routing domains are included in level-2 link-state updates and propagated to all other level-2 ISs. When an interdomain routing protocol is present (see "Interdomain Routing in OSI," later in the chapter), it may be possible for border level-2 ISs to learn about other routing domains dynamically.

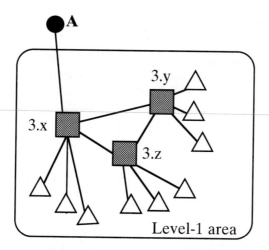

FIGURE 14.11   Level-1 View of a Routing Domain

Once NSAP addresses and routing metrics are configured, IS-IS runs automatically: "best" routes are automatically calculated and recalculated upon topology change without manual intervention.

The IS-IS Link-State Algorithm: A Closer Look   The idea behind link-state routing is that each IS obtains a full topology map of the network—a complete description of how the ISs and ESs are connected. Using this map, each IS can generate a next-hop forwarding table by calculating the shortest path to all ESs. As long as all ISs have identical topology maps

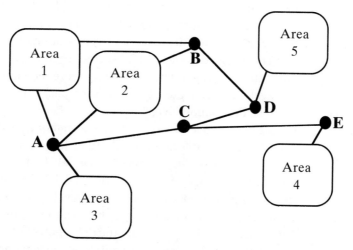

FIGURE 14.12   Level-2 View of a Routing Domain

and use the same algorithm to generate the next-hop forwarding table, routes will be computed correctly.

The topology maps constructed by each IS are distributed among and collected by ISs using a directed form of flooding. Each IS generates a link-state update consisting of the list of ISs (in the case of a level-2 IS) or of ESs and ISs (in the case of a level-1 IS) to which it is connected, along with the metric associated with each link to an ES or IS in the list. The link-state update—consisting of a set of link-state packets (LSPs)—is flooded to all neighbor ISs, which flood it to their neighbor ISs, and so on (with the proviso that a link-state packet is *not* propagated back to the neighbor from which it was received). ISs designated as level-1 ISs propagate link-state packets to other level-1 ISs in their area; level-2 ISs propagate level-2 link-state packets to other level-2 ISs throughout the routing domain. Sequence numbers are used to terminate the flood and to distinguish old link-state updates (duplicates) from new ones. Every IS receives link-state updates from every other IS, and from these, it builds a full topology database. When the connectivity of an IS changes, it floods another link-state update.

The Two-Level Hierarchy Level-2 ISs form a backbone that connects different level-1 areas. The IS-IS protocol assumes that the level-2 ISs are *connected*; that is, that any level-2 IS can reach any other level-2 router by going through only level-2 routers. Note that this does not imply that "mesh" connectivity must exist as depicted in Figure 14.10; in fact, any of the three links between the level-2 ISs in Figure 14.10 could be removed and the notion of "connected" would be preserved. As depicted, the three links simply provide resiliency of the level-2 "backbone."

Although routing hierarchies can be built without this sort of backbone configuration, it simplifies the operation of both level-2 and level-1 ISs. The connection of level-2 ISs frees routers designated as "level-1 ISs only" from having to know anything more than how to route to the nearest level-2 IS (see Figure 14.10). Once a packet reaches a level-2 IS, it can reach its destination level-1 area (or another routing domain entirely) via level-2 IS routing exclusively. If this were not true, then level-1 ISs would need to know the location of all other level-1 areas to prevent loops as the packet was sent from level-2 ISs to level-1 ISs and back to level-2 ISs. Another advantage of the connected level-2 "backbone" is that it simplifies routing protocol evolution. Since level-1 ISs need not know the level-2 routing protocol or topology, changes can occur at level 2, or in other level-1 areas, without affecting the operation of other level-1 ISs.

Two penalties are incurred as a consequence of the "backbone" simplification. The first is the restriction on the topologies that can be constructed (since all the level-2 ISs must be directly connected without using level-1 paths). Considering that many routing domains have or require a backbone topology anyway, and that any level-1 IS can be administratively upgraded to a level-2 IS if necessary to connect the backbone, this restriction is at most a minor inconvenience.

The second penalty is a potential increase in path length. To illustrate, consider again the topology depicted in Figure 14.10, and imagine that all the links have the same metric value. Assume that a message from an ES attached to level-1 IS {2.w} is destined for an ES attached to {3.x}, outside its local area. Level-1 IS {2.w} must forward the packet to its nearest level-2 IS; based on the topology information that {2.w} keeps, the packet will be forwarded to level-2 IS B via {2.z}. Level-2 IS B will forward it over the level-2 backbone to IS A, which will deliver it to level-1 IS {3.x}. The path chosen is six hops long—two hops more than the shortest path via level-1 IS {2.y}.

Area Partitions   One of the problems associated with an area hierarchy is the possibility of an area *partition*. For instance, if the link between level-1 ISs {2.y} and {2.w} in Figure 14.10 is lost (see Figure 14.13), then level-1 IS {2.y} will not be able to deliver packets to {2.z} even though a physical path exists (via level-2 ISs). Why? As a level-1 IS, {2.y} keeps routing information only about the area in which it resides and about the nearest level-2 IS. Knowing from previous link-state updates that {2.z} is in its area because of the area address part of its address and that {2.w} provided a route to {2.z}, and knowing also that its link to {2.w} is lost,

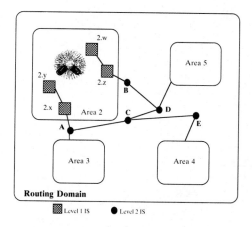

FIGURE 14.13   Area Partition

{2.y} would not be able to route packets within the area to {2.z} because of the partition. In fact, some packets forwarded to {2.z} coming from the backbone would be delivered to {2.y} because they had entered the "wrong" partition segment of the area. This is called a level-1 partition.

Level-2 partitions are also possible. For instance, if the link between level-2 ISs C and D breaks, packets coming from area 3 will not get to area 5 even though a physical path exists (through area 2; see Figure 14.14). IS-IS dynamically repairs level-1 partitions but not level-2 partitions. The partition-repair mechanism works entirely in level-2 ISs. Level-2 ISs discover the partition because they get inconsistent information from level-1 ISs, telling which level-2 ISs are attached to an area, and from level-2 ISs, telling which level-1 areas can be reached (recall that all level-2 ISs that are attached to an area are also level-1 ISs in that area, giving them access to the level-1 IS information required to know which ESs are in their partition segment). When a partition is discovered by level-2 ISs, all of the level-2 ISs "elect" a *partition designated level-2 IS* in each partition segment to execute a repair (the winner of the election is the "partition-repair-capable" level-2 IS with the numerically lowest system identifier). Partition designated level-2 ISs build a level-1 repair path between them by establishing a virtual level-1 link between them using level-2 ISs and passing level-1 routing updates over the level-1 virtual link. CLNP datagrams, error reports, and link-state updates travel across the virtual link as encapsulated CLNP datagrams.[18] The level-1 ISs do not know that the virtual level-1 link passes through level-2 ISs—they see it

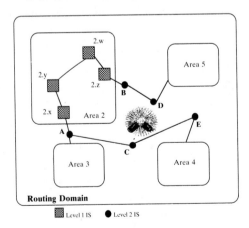

Figure 14.14   Level 2 Partition

---

18.   Every packet that must traverse the level-1 repair path is encapsulated within another CLNP packet with its own header. The source and destination address information in the

as no different from a "real" level-1 link.

For example, consider again the case in which the level-1 link in Figure 14.10 between {2.y} and {2.w} is lost. Level-2 ISs A and B will discover the partition and, following the election, will be recognized as partition designated level-2 ISs. A and B will establish a virtual link between themselves and pass level-1 IS updates between themselves encapsulated as CLNP datagrams. Now assume that an ES attached to level-1 IS {4.x} has a packet destined for an ES attached to level-1 IS {2.z}. The packet will initially be routed to level-2 IS A, since it is the shortest path to that area (again assuming that all links shown have identical metric values). Level-2 IS A will recognize that it cannot deliver the packet via level-1 links and so will encapsulate the packet in a CLNP header addressed to level-2 IS B. The packet will backtrack to level-2 IS B, which will decapsulate the packet and deliver the original CLNP packet from {4.x} to level-1 IS {2.z}. The level-1 repair path for this example is illustrated in Figure 14.15.

No IS other than level-2 ISs A and B is aware that a partition exists and was repaired. The penalties for the advantage of localizing the repair effort are suboptimal paths and the extra burden of encapsulation and decapsulation. The gain, of course is, the preservation of connectivity.

Routing Metrics   In the examples used so far, all of the metric values have been assumed to be the same. Typically, metric values are assigned to help control the flow of traffic over individual links. The default metric for IS-IS is a 1-octet parameter that represents a measure of capacity/throughput of a link. The "length" of a path is the sum of the metric

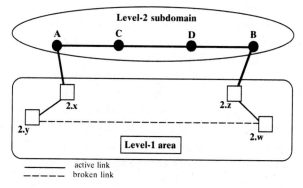

FIGURE 14.15   Level-1 Repair Path

additional header is populated with the network entity titles of the level-2 routers providing the partition repair.

values for the links on that path. One octet was chosen because it gives adequate granularity and allows for an efficient implementation of the shortest-path-first route calculation—i.e., it allows ISs to generate the forwarding table from the topology map efficiently and quickly.[19]

IS-IS optionally computes routes based on metrics for transit delay, cost, and error rate, so that CLNP datagrams originated with the quality of service maintenance bits set can be forwarded as requested by the originator over appropriate routes. ISs that compute routes based on optional metrics report these metric values for links in link-state packets (in which a separate octet is identified for each optional metric). ISs compute quality of service routes by using only link-state packets that contain values for a given metric; for example, to compute a "cost" route, an IS will run the shortest-path-first algorithm using only those link-state updates that indicate a value for the cost metric and only if the IS itself has a link with a cost metric associated with it.

Partial Routing Updates   Since the purpose of a routing protocol is to assist in directing traffic, and not to consume resources that might otherwise be employed to forward user data, it is always desirable to keep routing updates small while still keeping track of which neighbors are reachable and which are not. IS-IS routing updates originally conveyed which neighbors were reachable by listing them and which neighbors were not reachable by not listing them; if a neighbor was listed in a previous routing update but was not in the latest routing update, that neighbor was assumed to be unreachable. As a result, all existing neighbors were listed in all routing updates.

The more neighbors a router had, the larger its routing updates. Large updates had to be fragmented and reassembled by CLNP, which slowed down the entire update process (since the fragments had to be reassembled at each hop during flooding). IS-IS now uses *partial updates* to circumvent this problem.

With partial updates, the otherwise complete routing update is split into multiple updates, and each update indicates the numerical range of neighbors that are covered by the update. This way, the semantics of explicitly listing reachable neighbors and implicitly listing unreachable neighbors is preserved. If a partial routing update does not list a neighbor that is in the range covered by the update, then it is assumed that the neighbor is unreachable. The various partial updates each maintain their

---

19.   An implementation of the shortest path first algorithm used by IS-IS is likely to assume that an IS maintains an intermediate table of entries, ordered by distance; by limiting distance values to 1 octet, this intermediate table is bounded to a reasonable size.

own sequence numbers. If the status of a neighbor changes, only the partial update covering that neighbor must be sent.

Pseudonodes   IS-IS defines another method of limiting the size of routing updates for those configurations in which many ISs populate a broadcast subnetwork (such as a local area network). On these subnetworks, and using the general case principles, each IS is a neighbor of all the other ISs attached to the same subnetwork. If each of the N ISs on a broadcast subnetwork were to send full routing updates, then N ISs would each send a routing update describing $N-1$ neighbors, burdening the subnetwork with the exchange of order $N^{(N-1)}$ routing information. To prevent this, one IS on the subnetwork is elected as the *pseudonode* or LAN desigated router, see (Perlman, 1992a). The pseudonode advertises all the other ISs (including itself) as its neighbors, but all the other ISs advertise *only* the pseudonode as their neighbor. With the pseudonode, a logical star configuration with N links is formed rather than the original fully connected "mesh" configuration with $N^{(N-1)}$ links. To maintain the correct metric values, the metric value from the pseudonode to the (real) ISs is 0.

Operation over X.25 Subnetworks   When operating over an ISO/IEC 8208 (X.25) subnetwork, IS-IS distinguishes virtual circuits established by administrative procedure (static) from virtual circuits established because of the receipt of a CLNP packet (dynamically allocated, as described in the CLNP standard). Among the dynamically allocated circuits, IS-IS also distinguishes those for which the NSAP addresses reachable via the neighbor are learned from routing updates from those for which the NSAP addresses reachable via the neighbor are locally administered. The latter case allows the use of X.25 subnetworks without requiring that the virtual circuits be left open solely for the purpose of exchanging routing updates. Depending on the tariffs associated with a particular X.25 network service, call duration may be an expensive proposition, and this optimization leaves such links open only when they are needed.

"Integrated IS-IS"   The OSI standard for IS-IS (ISO/IEC 10589 1992) deals only with the provision of routing information to support the forwarding of CLNP packets. Internet RFC 1195 augments the base standard by describing how IS-IS can be used to route both CLNP *and* IP datagrams. RFC 1195 specifies how ISs distribute information about the TCP/IP destinations they can reach in addition to the OSI destinations they can reach, simply by adding more information to the IS-IS link-state packets. The mechanism extends naturally to environments that include other protocol stacks as well; for example, the techniques described in

RFC 1195 could be used to build routes to XNS/IPX[20] destinations by adding IPX-specific information to link-state packets.

The term used to describe the operation of a single intradomain routing protocol to support the forwarding of traffic associated with multiple protocol stacks is *integrated routing*. The alternative to integrated routing, of course, is to run a separate intradomain routing protocol for each protocol stack (OSI, TCP/IP, XNS/IPX, etc.). Advocates of integrated IS-IS cite the advantages of fewer protocols to operate, fewer resources devoted to the routing process, and simpler management. Advocates of the alternative (which is called "ships in the night," or "S.I.N.," by members of the Internet community) cite the advantages of intradomain protocols that are custom-tailored to their corresponding protocol stacks, noninterference of one protocol stack (and its routing concerns) with others, and the ability to configure ISs with only those intradomain routing functions that are needed for the stack(s) that will be supported.

Intradomain Routing in TCP/IP

A variety of different intradomain routing protocols are operated in the Internet today. The most commonly used is the *routing information protocol* (RIP; RFC 1058). RIP is the routing protocol "we love to hate"; its main problem is that today's Internet is far too big and diverse for it to handle. The routing information protocol operates as an application over the user datagram protocol (UDP), computes routes using a distance-vector algorithm, and uses a hop-count metric that reflects distance but not link speed, efficiency, or congestion. The routing information protocol is vulnerable (as are all distance-vector routing protocols) to loops; to avoid them, it uses a variety of more or less effective techniques, including a maximum hop count of 16 to indicate "no path" or "link down." This limits the network diameter to a maximum of 15 hops, which is small by today's standards.[21]

⟦AHA⟧ *HELLO is another open routing protocol that has seen better days; but seriously, how can you hate something called "HELLO"? It's simply easier to rip RIP.*

The new kid on the block is an intradomain routing protocol called the *Open Shortest Path First Protocol* (OSPF; RFC 1247). Open shortest path

---

20.   XNS: Xerox Network Systems; IPX: Internet packet exchange.
21. A version 2 of RIP that deals with these and other limitations has been published as a proposed standard (RFC 1388).

first is a close relative of the OSI intradomain IS-IS routing protocol, tailored specifically for the TCP/IP (only) environment.

How is OSPF like IS-IS? Both OSPF and IS-IS are link-state routing protocols that compute routes using Dijkstra's shortest path first algorithm and distribute link-state information (OSPF calls this information "link-state advertisements," or LSAs) using Perlman's fault-tolerant broadcast technique. OSPF has a two-level hierarchy: a backbone and attached areas. It is capable of providing multiple types of service routing as indicated in the IP header. It handles area partitions and provides pseudo-node (designated router) optimization over local area networks.

How does OSPF differ from IS-IS? Mostly, in the way in which some of the detailed operations of the protocol are performed. OSPF is encapsulated in IP datagrams; IS-IS operates directly over the individual underlying data link (or subnetwork) protocols. The two protocols also differ in how they deal with link-state updates that are very large and may require fragmentation. IS-IS puts all the link-state update information into a single link-state packet with a single header, and ISs fragment the link-state packet if it is too large, using a single fragment number to identify and order the fragments of the link-state packet. OSPF builds separate link-state advertisements for each destination (i.e., multiple packets) and combines these into a single IP datagram. The OSPF encoding is optimized for a scenario in which incremental updates may be frequent, and hence, the savings in link utilization will be great. The tradeoff is an increased consumption of memory to accommodate the overhead of many separate link-state advertisements rather than one link-state packet.

OSPF and IS-IS also differ in their philosophies of "route granularity." OSPF propagates link-state advertisements between areas, so that a level-1 IS can choose which level-2 IS offers the best path to destinations outside its own area. In the OSPF scheme, the advantage of having more refined routes is traded off against the disadvantage of increased usage of memory and link resources. When used for routing CLNP packets, IS-IS has no way of telling ISs about addresses in other areas, and hence, it is assumed that IS-IS imposes a strict separation of area information. When integrated IS-IS is used, however, IP addresses look the same, regardless of whether they are from inside or outside the area, so the same granularities can be achieved using either integrated IS-IS or OSPF.

OSPF and IS-IS also handle level-1 (area) partitions differently. Level-1 partitions are repaired automatically by IS-IS; they are not repaired at all in OSPF, except by manual reconfiguration of OSPF's level-2 address summaries after a partition has occurred. IS-IS requires that level-2 ISs be connected only through other level-2 ISs, and therefore, partition repair always involves encapsulation (tunneling). OSPF provides network administrators with the ability to manually configure routes or "virtual links" to circumvent level-2 partitions.

It is possible to debate the pros and cons of IS-IS and OSPF much more passionately than the authors have done here (see, for example, Coltun [1989]; Tsuchiya [1989]; Perlman [1991a, 1991b]; Medin [1991]). The fact that IS-IS can be used in both OSI-only and dual-stack roles in parts of the Internet may be important, perhaps increasingly so as CLNP deployment increases and as the Internet community deals with scaling issues such as IP address exhaustion (see Chapter 16). However, a recently published Internet applicability statement[22] (RFC 1370) specifies the use of OSPF for intradomain routing in TCP/IP-only domains of the Internet, leaving the future of "integrated IS-IS" in doubt. There is nevertheless at least one thing on which the proponents of OSPF and the proponents of IS-IS strongly agree—*both* of these protocols are better than their predecessors!

Interdomain Routing in OSI

The OSI *interdomain routing protocol* (IDRP;[23] ISO/IEC 10747) views the global OSI internetwork as an arbitrary interconnection of routing domains (RDs) connected to each other by subnetworks and by "border" intermediate systems (BISs), which are located in routing domains and attached to these subnetworks. Each border IS resides in a single routing domain and may simultaneously participate in both the interdomain routing protocol and an intradomain routing protocol of the domain (e.g., IS-IS).

IDRP calculates interdomain routes as a sequence of *path segments*. A path segment consists of a pair of border ISs and a link that connects them. If a pair of border ISs are attached to a common subnetwork, then the link between them is called a *real link*. Links between border ISs in different routing domains are always real. Within a single routing domain, however, a link that connects two border ISs may be constructed and maintained by intradomain routing protocol procedures; such links

---

22. *Applicability statements* are a type of Internet standard, distinct from technical specifications in that they describe the way in which a protocol or mechanism shall be used in a particular configuration or context, not the details of the protocol or mechanism itself; see Chapter 2.

23. The curse of "acronymania" has fallen with particularly cruel force on the field of interdomain routing. Two very different interdomain routing protocols—the OSI interdomain routing protocol (IDRP) and the Internet's interdomain policy routing (IDPR) protocol—are commonly referred to by their almost identical acronyms, neither of which is readily "pronounceable"!

are called *virtual links*.

To illustrate the role of IDRP, consider how a packet leaves an end system in one domain and travels to an end system in some other domain. First, the packet is forwarded by the ES to the nearest IS in its "home" domain. The packet will be forwarded by this and possibly other ISs via intradomain routing to a border IS in the home domain. The border IS uses information obtained via IDRP to determine a path to a border IS in an adjacent domain lying on a route to the destination and forwards the packet across the path segment toward the first-"hop" border IS in the interdomain path, which lies in the next domain. When the packet arrives at the next domain, the border IS in that domain forwards it through that domain toward a border IS located in the next hop or domain along the interdomain route. (Note that the path segment within this or any domain transited may be constructed either by IDRP alone or by a combination of IDRP and the intradomain routing procedures.) The process will continue on a hop-by-hop basis (with hops being expressed in terms of domains) until the packet arrives at a border IS in the domain that contains the destination end system. Here, the packet will be forwarded to its destination via the intradomain routing procedures of the destination routing domain.

As an illustration, consider the interdomain topology shown in Figure 14.16, and assume that the path between ESs in routing domains A and F goes through routing domains B, C, and E. A packet originated by

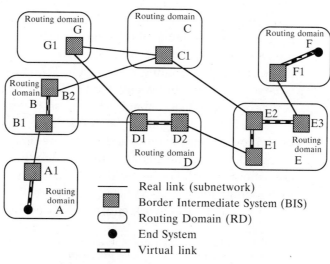

FIGURE 14.16   Example of Interdomain Topology.

an ES located in routing domain A and destined for an ES located in routing domain F will first be routed by means of routing domain A's intradomain routing procedures to border IS A1. Border IS A1 uses information obtained via IDRP to determine that the next border IS on the path is B1, which is located in the next domain along the route. Since border ISs A1 and B1 share a common subnetwork, border IS A1 can forward the packet directly to border IS B1 over a real link. Border IS B1 uses information obtained via IDRP to select border IS B2 as the next border IS along the path. (Note that the link between B1 and B2 is a virtual link; hence, the forwarding of the packet along this link is accomplished using domain B's intradomain routing procedures.) The process continues through border ISs C1, E2, and E3, until the packet finally reaches border IS F1, which is located in the routing domain (F) that contains the destination end system. The packet is forwarded to the destination ES within routing domain F by means of domain F's intradomain routing procedures.

The IDRP Routing Algorithm   The routing algorithm employed by IDRP bears a certain resemblance to distance-vector (Bellman-Ford) routing. Each border IS advertises to its neighboring border ISs the destinations that it can reach. The IDRP routing algorithm augments the advertisement of reachable destinations with *path attributes*, information propagated in IDRP routing control packets that describes various properties of the paths to these destinations. To emphasize the tight coupling between the reachable destinations and the properties of the paths to these destinations, IDRP defines a route as a unit of information that consists of a *pairing* between a destination and the attributes of the path to that destination. A path, expressed in terms of the domains that the routing information has traversed so far, is carried in the *RD_PATH* attribute of the IDRP packets that distribute the routing information. Therefore, one may call IDRP a *path-vector* protocol, in which a border IS receives from each neighboring border IS a vector that contains paths to a set of destinations.[24]

The IDRP routing algorithm is distributed: each border IS maintains partial routing information, and routes are determined through the exchange of information among border ISs and through local computations carried out in each border IS. The IDRP routing algorithm assumes that each routing domain has a globally unique *routing domain identifier* (RDI), which is simply a network entity title,[25] and that the NSAP addresses

---

24.   The term *path-vector protocol* bears an intentional similarity to the term *distance-vector protocol*, in which a border IS receives from each of its neighbors a *vector* that contains *distances* to a set of destinations.

25.   A routing domain identifier always identifies a particular domain for the purposes

assigned to ESs within the routing domains that participate in IDRP exchanges are unique and unambiguous as well. Although this is a general characteristic of NSAP addressing, and is also assumed by the OSI intra-domain routing protocol, it is mentioned explicitly here because IDRP has no mechanism to enforce either of these two assumptions or even to detect whether they have been violated (which may result in incorrect protocol operation).

Loop-free Routing in IDRP   IDRP is designed to ensure that, during steady-state operation (i.e., no interborder IS topological changes have occurred), routes computed by the border ISs participating in IDRP are loop-free. Since data packets flow in a direction opposite to the direction in which IDRP routing information flows, one way to satisfy this design objective is to ensure that routing information does not loop. Because the RD_PATH attribute contains a list of routing domains expressed in terms of the routing domain identifiers of the domains that routing information has traversed so far, suppressing routing information looping is straightforward: a border IS that receives a route must examine the RD_PATH attribute of the route and check whether the routing domain identifier of the border IS's own routing domain is present in the attribute. If it is, the border IS must not use this route.

As an illustration of how the loop-suppression mechanism works, consider a flow of routing information (route) that advertises reachable destinations within routing domain F (see Figure 14.17). Assume that routes are selected in such a way that routing domain C prefers to reach destinations in routing domain F via routing domain E, routing domain B prefers to reach destinations in routing domain F via routing domain C (then via routing domain E), and routing domain D prefers to reach destinations in routing domain F via routing domain B (then via routing domains C and E). Denote the routing domain identifiers of the participating domains by B, X, Δ, E, and Φ. Border IS F1 originates the route and propagates it to border IS E3. At this point, the RD_PATH attribute associated with the route contains only one routing domain identifier—namely, the routing domain identifier of F (RD_PATH is $< \Phi >$). Border IS E3 propagates this information to the other border ISs within its own domain—namely, E1 and E2. As E2 propagates the route to border IS C1, it updates the RD_PATH attribute by appending to it the routing domain identifier of its own routing domain (RD_PATH becomes $< \Phi, E >$). Likewise, when C1 propagates the route to border IS B2, it appends the routing domain

---

of IDRP but does not necessarily convey any information about the NSAP addresses of the end systems within the domain.

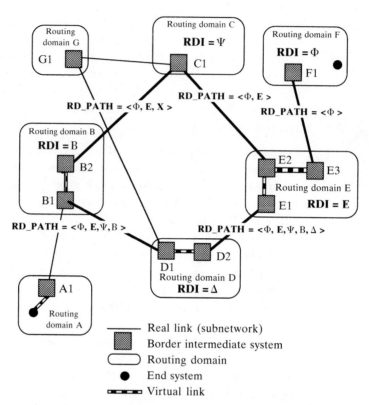

FIGURE 14.17   Interdomain Topology with Routing Domain Identifiers

identifier of its own routing domain, C, to the RD_PATH attribute (RD_PATH becomes < Φ, E, X >). Since border ISs B2 and B1 reside within the same routing domain, propagation of the route from B2 to B1 does not result in any changes to the RD_PATH attribute. Border IS B1 propagates the route to border IS D1 and appends routing domain B's own routing domain identifier to the RD_PATH attribute (RD_PATH becomes < Φ, E, Ψ, B >). Border IS D1 propagates the route to border IS D2 (without any modification to the RD_PATH attribute). However, when border IS D2 propagates the route to border IS E1, E1 detects that it cannot use it, since the RD_PATH attribute of the route already contains routing domain E's own routing domain identifier, E (RD_PATH of the route that border IS D2 propagates to border IS E1 is now < Φ, E, C, B, Δ >).

Even when connectivity between border ISs F1 and E3 is disrupted, thus making the original route unusable, none of the border ISs within domain E can switch to a route that was advertised by border IS D2 (since such a route would involve routing information looping). (Note that we have only traced one flow of routing information in this example. Readers are encouraged to trace other flows to acquire a feel for how the routing process converges.)

Selecting an Optimal Route IDRP does not require all routing domains to have identical criteria (policies) for route selection. IDRP does not even have a notion of a globally agreed upon metric that all the domains must use for route selection. Moreover, the route-selection policies used by one routing domain are not necessarily known to any other routing domain. To maintain the maximal degree of autonomy and independence among routing domains, each routing domain that participates in IDRP may have its own view of what constitutes an optimal route. This view is based solely on local domain route-selection policies and the in-formation carried in the path attributes of a route.

Note that when presented with exactly the same set of possible routes to a given destination, different routing domains may choose different routes from the set. As an example, consider again the interdomain topology shown in Figures 14.16 and 14.17 and assume that routing domains C and D both have a route to destinations in routing domain F (both of which go through domain E). When routing domains C and D advertise this information to routing domains B and G, routing domain B may select the route offered by C, whereas routing domain G may select the route offered by D, despite the fact that C advertises exactly the same route to both B and G.

The following essential properties of the IDRP algorithm make it possible to provide loop-free steady-state routing even in the presence of independent route-selection policies that need not be known outside a domain:

- Routing information distribution is preceded by the computation over the information.
- Only the results of the computation are distributed to other border ISs.
- Suppression of routing information looping does not depend on the presence of a globally agreed upon, monotonically increasing metric.

Thus, the only thing that is needed to provide consistent operation across multiple routing domains is to standardize the mechanism used to exchange the results of the route-selection procedure (the results of the route computation) while allowing the policies that affect route selection to be of local significance only (nonstandard).[26]

---

26.   This elegant and succinct observation was made by Ross Callon.

Restricting Transit Traffic   Providing ubiquitous connectivity within the global OSI internetwork implies that a domain may need to share its own transmission and switching facilities (links, subnetworks, and ISs) with other domains, as well as rely on the willingness of other domains to share theirs. Of course, once sharing exists, the ability to control it becomes an important issue; there is always a cost associated with deploying and managing transmission and switching facilities, and the administrator responsible for these facilities must be able to control and account for their use, particularly by parties outside the scope of his or her own local user base.

One such control mechanism is the ability to restrict transit traffic, or prohibit it entirely, for a particular set of domains or for all other domains. In such cases, a domain is said to employ *transit restrictions* (*transit policies*) as a way of controlling the use of its facilities.[27]

Transit Policies Supported by IDRP   The fundamental technique used by IDRP in support of transit policies is controlled distribution of routing information. This technique is based on a simple observation: when a packet's flow is determined by the routing information present in border ISs, the direction of this flow is opposite to the direction of the routing information flow between the border ISs. Controlling routing information flows allows restriction of packet flows, which, in effect, imposes transit policies.[28] (In the extreme case in which there are no routes over which a packet may be forwarded, the packet is discarded.)

Selective Advertisement of Routing Information   IDRP provides several mechanisms with various degrees of granularity and sophistication that allow a routing domain to control the distribution of routing information, thus providing control over its own transit traffic. The simplest mechanism is to have a border IS within a domain announce only a subset (or possibly none) of the routes that it uses to any border ISs in adjacent domains. Note that a border IS may announce a different subset to border ISs in different adjacent domains, so as to grant to some routing domains a specific set of transit privileges and to others none.

To illustrate how this mechanism can be applied in the context of the topology illustrated in Figure 14.16, consider the following example. If border IS B1 has a route to destinations in routing domain F (which

---

27.   Examples of domains that rely heavily on transit policies are the backbone networks sponsored by agencies of the U.S. federal government, such as the Energy Sciences Network (ESnet), the NASA Science Internet (NSI), and the National Science Foundation Network (NSFnet).

28. This technique was pioneered in the NSFnet backbone phase II (RFC 1104; RFC 1092).

may traverse, for example, routing domains C and E), but does not announce this route to border IS A1, then no packets originated from an ES in routing domain A and destined for an ES in routing domain F will traverse the facilities that are under the control of routing domain B. This imposes a transit policy that prevents transit traffic from routing domain A to routing domain F from flowing through routing domain B. The same border IS B1 may, however, announce a route to destinations in routing domain F to border IS D1, thus allowing transit traffic flowing between routing domains D and F to traverse routing domain B. Furthermore, by making the distribution of routing information depend on the contents of the RD_PATH attribute, this mechanism may be extended to take into account not only the origin and the destination of traffic but the intervening path (in terms of routing domains) as well.

This mechanism works well if one wants to restrict transit traffic between sources that are within routing domains immediately adjacent to one's own routing domain and destinations that are in some other (and not necessarily adjacent) routing domain. However, to impose a more general transit policy, IDRP provides another mechanism, one that explicitly controls the distribution of routing information, thereby enabling a domain to restrict the scope of potential recipients of the routing information that flows through it. The scope may be specified by using a *distribution inclusion list* (DIST_LIST_INCL) path attribute, which allows the enumeration of the potential recipients of the routing information (identified by their routing domain identifiers), or a *distribution exclusion list* (DIST_LIST_EXCL) path attribute, which allows the enumeration of the domains that shall be excluded from receiving the routing information. The mechanism provided by the DIST_LIST_INCL and DIST_LIST_EXCL path attributes imposes no restrictions on the relative placement of the source and destination domains of the transit traffic that must be restricted.

Referring again to Figure 14.16, suppose that routing domain C is willing to carry transit traffic destined for any ES in routing domain F, as long as the traffic does not originate from any of the ESs in routing domain A. To impose such a transit policy, border IS C1 must attach a DIST_LIST_EXCL path attribute that contains A's routing domain identifier to the route that it advertises to border IS B2 (DIST_LIST_EXCL of the advertised route shall be < A >). Border IS B2 will propagate this route, together with the DIST_LIST_EXCL attribute, to border IS B1. Although B1 may now propagate this route to border IS D1, it may not send it to border IS A1, since A1 belongs to the routing domain A, which is listed in the DIST_LIST_EXCL attribute of the route.

⸢·AHA·⸣ *The ability to control the distribution of routing information provides an organization with corresponding control over the way in which its resources may be used, while facilitating the interconnection of multiple organizations—thereby satisfying a major objective of OSI routing. It remains to be seen whether the controls that are available in IDRP are sufficient or whether the deployment of a more elaborate control system, such as that provided by the source-routed interdomain policy routing (IDPR) protocol, will be necessary.*

Routing Domain Confederations   To achieve good scaling characteristics, IDRP provides a mechanism that allows a set of connected routing domains to be grouped together and treated as a unit. Such a grouping of domains, called a *routing domain confederation* (RDC), is defined and established by means that are beyond the scope of IDRP.[29] From the outside, a routing domain confederation (hereafter, simply "confederation") looks like a single routing domain: routing domains outside the confederation cannot tell whether the confederation is just a single domain or a collection of domains. This mechanism is inherently recursive, so that a member of a confederation may be either a routing domain or a set of routing domains that themselves form a confederation. Confederations may be nested, disjoint, or overlapped. The protocol does not place any topological restrictions on the way in which confederation boundaries are defined, nor on the number of confederations to which a single domain may belong.

Routing domain confederations are identified by *routing domain confederation identifiers* that are taken from the same address space as the routing domain identifiers used to identify individual routing domains. The protocol assumes that all the border ISs that belong to a confederation are statically preconfigured with both the routing domain identifier of their routing domain and the routing domain confederation identifier of the confederation. If a routing domain belongs to more than one confederation, then the static information must include information about the nested/disjoint/overlap relationships that exist between each pair of confederations. No other requirements are imposed on the confederation members. For example, different confederation members may advertise different routes to a given destination—there is no need to have consistent route-selection policies for all the members of a confederation. Different members may also impose different transit policies—there is no

---

29.   Specifically, IDRP does not suggest or recommend any principles, operating procedures, or policies that might be used by administrative domains which attempt to establish bilateral or multi-organizational routing relationships.

need for an *a priori* agreement on the transit policies that will be imposed by individual members.

Note that *how* one establishes a routing confederation is outside the scope of the protocol; however, the protocol explicitly recognizes a confederation's boundaries by taking specific actions when routing information enters and exits a confederation. Specifically, routing information that enters a confederation is marked by appending a special RD_PATH path segment (either ENTRY_SET or ENTRY_SEQUENCE), followed by the routing domain confederation identifier of the entered confederation, to the RD_PATH attribute.[30] As routing information exits a confederation, the RD_PATH attribute is scanned in the reverse direction: the protocol searches for the ENTRY_SET or ENTRY_SEQUENCE path segment that contains the routing domain confederation identifier of the confederation that is about to be exited. Exiting a confederation results in removing all the domains within the confederation that the routing information traversed, leaving only the routing domain confederation identifier, thereby reducing the amount of information carried in the RD_PATH attribute.

The ability to group routing domains into confederations provides a powerful mechanism for routing information aggregation and abstraction, which, in turn, makes IDRP scalable to a practically unlimited number of routing domains. The formation of confederations can keep the RD_PATH information from growing beyond a manageable size (and from preserving topological details that may be irrelevant in a very large internetwork). Similarly, transit policies may be expressed in terms of confederations rather than individual domains.

Using Confederations to Support Transit Policies   Relations between confederations—expressed in terms of nesting, disjoint, or overlap—may be used to impose certain types of transit policies that otherwise would be difficult to support. Such policies are imposed via a "two-phase" rule that states that once routing information enters a confederation, it cannot exit the confederation. To record the fact that routing information has entered a confederation, IDRP uses the HIERARCHICAL_RECORDING path attribute. The distribution of the routing information is determined by the value of the attribute and by the flow of the information. Specifically, if a

---

30.   Recall that the RD_PATH attribute is defined as a sequence of path segments. IDRP supports four distinct types of path segments: RD_SEQ (an ordered set of domains or confederations), RD_SET (an unordered set of domains or confederations), ENTRY_SEQ (an ordered set of entered but not exited confederations), and ENTRY_SET (an unordered set of entered but not exited confederations).

given border IS chooses to advertise routing information whose HIERAR-CHICAL_RECORDING attribute is equal to 1, it may advertise it to a border IS located in any adjacent routing domain as follows:

- If it is necessary to enter a confederation in order to reach the adjacent border IS, then the advertising border IS shall set the value of the HIERARCHICAL_RECORDING to 0.
- If the adjacent border IS can be reached without entering any confederation, then the advertising border IS shall not change the value of the HIERARCHICAL_RECORDING.

If a border IS chooses to advertise routing information whose HIERARCHICAL_RECORDING attribute has a value of 0, it may advertise this information only to border ISs that can be reached without exiting any confederation to which the advertising border IS belongs.

To illustrate how this mechanism can be applied, consider the topology shown in Figure 14.18, in which solid dots represent individual routing domains and rectangular boxes represent the boundaries of routing domain confederations. Routing domains E and F form confederation X; routing domains G and H form confederation Y; and routing domains A through H form confederation Z. Routing domain A's transit policy is such that it is willing to carry transit interdomain traffic that originates in L, D, C, B, or A and is destined for K, provided that the traffic does not traverse any of the domains in either confederation X or Y. Routing domain A is also willing to carry transit interdomain traffic that originates in any domain within confederations X or Y and is destined for K. Such a transit policy may be supported by requiring border ISs in A that are connected to border ISs in B and E to attach the HIERARCHICAL_RECORDING path attribute with the value of 1 to the routing in-

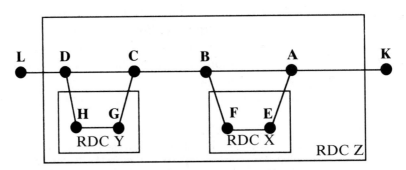

FIGURE 14.18   Example of the use of the HIERARCHICAL_RECORDING Attribute

formation that they receive from border ISs in K prior to propagating this information to border ISs in routing domains B or E. As a result, routing domain F would not be allowed to propagate routing information to routing domain B that traversed routing domains A and E. Likewise, routing domain H would not be allowed to propagate routing information to routing domain D that traversed routing domains A, B, C, and G. That leaves routing domain B with routing domain A as the only possible route to K, and leaves routing domain C as the only possible choice that goes via B and A, and routing domain D as the only possible choice that goes via C, B, and A.

Using the HIERARCHICAL_RECORDING path attribute in conjunction with the formation of routing domain confederations as a way of implementing transit policies creates an environment that significantly enhances an administrator's ability to assess the effect of changes in interdomain connectivity on interdomain routing. For example:

- Changes in the connectivity between domains that are located in a region in which two or more routing domain confederations overlap will not affect routing between domains outside the overlap. This is because border ISs located in routing domains within the overlap cannot propagate routes between domains located outside the overlap.

- Changes in the connectivity between routing domains within a confederation cannot affect routing between domains outside the confederation, since routing domains that form a confederation cannot be used for transit traffic between routing domains outside the confederation.

- Changes in the connectivity between a border IS that belongs to a domain within a confederation and a border IS that belongs to a domain outside the confederation have no effect on routing between the domain outside the confederation and any other domain outside the confederation.

Handling Reachability Information   Recall that in the context of IDRP, a route is defined as a pairing between a set of reachable destinations and the attributes of the path to those destinations. The set of reachable destinations is called *network layer reachability information* (NLRI).

IDRP expresses network layer reachability information in terms of NSAP address prefixes. Such an encoding provides a flexible and concise mechanism for describing a set of reachable destinations. A set covered by an NSAP address prefix may be as small as a single end system or as large as a collection of all end systems within a confederation consisting of multiple routing domains. If NSAP addresses are assigned in a hierarchical fashion, and the address assignment hierarchy is congruent with interdomain topology, the ability to express network layer reachability information in terms of NSAP address prefixes provides a powerful tool for reducing the amount of reachability information that must be carried and processed by the protocol. This reduction, accomplished by IDRP's route-aggregation procedures, allows IDRP to combine several routes into a single route. Part of the route-aggregation procedure involves the aggregation of network layer reachability information, in which a set of longer address prefixes is aggregated into a single shorter address prefix.

Supporting Multiple Routes to a Destination   IDRP allows a border IS to support multiple routes to a destination, based on the ability of CLNP to carry quality of service and security parameters (see Chapter 13). A pair of border ISs may exchange not one, but multiple "path vectors" to the same destination, with each vector being tagged by its distinguishing path attributes. This tagging allows a border IS to construct multiple forwarding tables, one for each set of distinguishing attributes associated with individual path vectors. When a border IS needs to forward a packet, it checks for the presence of quality of service or security parameters in the packet and, if any are present, maps them into a corresponding set of distinguishing attributes. To determine the next hop on a path to a destination, the border IS uses the forwarding table tagged with the appropriate distinguishing attributes. To ensure consistent forwarding across multiple domains, IDRP standardizes on the mapping between quality of sevice and security parameters supported in CLNP and the distinguishing attributes that are defined in IDRP.

Conceptually, one may think of a set of distinguishing attributes defined in IDRP as a set of "route colors." Similarly, one may think of the quality of service and security parameters defined in CLNP as a set of "packet colors." Tagging path vectors with appropriate distinguishing attributes may be viewed as "route coloring"; specifying quality of service or security parameters in CLNP packets may be viewed as "packet coloring." Consistent mapping between a route's colors and a packet's colors across domains ensures correct forwarding.

Like the quality of service and security parameters in CLNP—which permit the use of source-specific, destination-specific, and global parameter values—route and packet colors also have a scope. Specifically, the meaning of a color may be defined only within the scope of a source or destination ES, or a color may have global significance. The scope of the source- and destination-specific quality of service and security *distin-*

guishing attributes in IDRP with respect to their significance for forwarding is determined by the source addresses and destination addresses, respectively. The scope of such distinguishing attributes as cost, residual error rate, and capacity is global; that is, their significance for forwarding does not depend on the source or destination addresses in the CLNP packets.

IDRP requires all the border ISs within a single domain to agree on the supported distinguishing attributes. However, the protocol does not require all the domains within the global OSI environment to support the same set of distinguishing attributes. In other words, the decision to support or not support a particular set of distinguishing attributes is left to a domain's local administration.

Having the ability to support multiple routes to a destination provides IDRP with a flexible and powerful scheme for supporting various forwarding granularities, including source- and destination-sensitive forwarding.

| AHA | *Support for multiple routes to a destination allows IDRP to take into account factors such as the cost or quality of service associated with different routes; because "someone is paying," support for such features is critical to interdomain routing.* |

Routing Information Exchange   IDRP packets (IDRP PDUs) are carried in the data field of CLNP packets. A border IS that participates in IDRP exchanges routing information (routes) with its neighboring border ISs in the form of *IDRP update packets.*

The set of neighbors is partitioned into two categories: internal and external. The internal neighbors are the border ISs that belong to the same routing domain as the local border IS. The external neighbors are the border ISs that belong to different routing domains but share a common subnetwork with the local border IS.

IDRP requires all border ISs within a domain to maintain pairwise connections with each other, in effect creating a complete mesh of border-IS to border-IS connections. Although this appears to be a significant burden, careful analysis shows that such a mesh has no impact on overhead, other than maintaining state information for each of the border ISs within a domain. This overhead will usually be negligible compared to the amount of interdomain routing information that a border IS needs to handle.

Routing information exchange in IDRP may be modeled as a two-phase procedure. A border IS first selects the best route among the routes received from all its external neighbors and advertises this route to all its internal neighbors. In the second phase, a border IS selects the best route from all the routes received from all its neighbors, both external and internal, and advertises this route to all its external neighbors (subject, of course, to constraints on dissemination of routing information). To achieve consistency between border ISs within a domain, a border IS that sends a route to an internal neighbor attaches the LOC_PREF path attribute to the route. This attribute carries the metric that the border IS assigns to that route. The receiving border IS may use this information to check whether its own route selection policies are consistent with the one of the sending border IS.

The IDRP routing information dissemination algorithm that controls the exchange of routing information (update packets) between border ISs is based on the technique of *incremental* updates, in which after an initial exchange of complete routing information, a pair of border ISs exchange only changes to that information. This technique helps to conserve a significant amount of resources (processor cycles and bandwidth), which is critical when dealing with an environment consisting of a large number of domains. Support for incremental updates requires reliable information exchange between participating border ISs. IDRP supports this reliability by a combination of sequence numbers assigned to update packets, explicit acknowledgments, and retransmission of unacknowledged update packets. In addition to incremental updates, IDRP provides a mechanism to perform a complete update of the routing information in either solicited or unsolicited mode (this is done by using refresh packets).

The IDRP routing information dissemination procedure is completely event-driven and dynamic. The two possible events that may trigger the dissemination of (new) routing information are the establishment of a new session with a neighboring border IS and the selection of new routes by the local border IS as a result of either receiving an update packet from one of its neighbors or the deletion of all the routes received from a neighbor due to loss of the neighbor.

IDRP in Large Public and Private Data Networks   For domains that employ general mesh topology subnetwork technology, such as X.25 or Switched Multimegabit Data Service networks (see Chapter 15), IDRP avoids the use of border ISs within such domains for packet forwarding altogether; rather, IDRP uses border ISs solely as a mechanism to put transit and route-selection policies in place. To accomplish this, a border IS is allowed to pass a route to another border IS located in an adjacent domain that contains the NSAP of the next hop on a path to a destination that is different from the NSAP of the border IS that sends the update packets (this information is conveyed in an update packet and encoded in the NEXT_HOP path attribute). In such circumstances, the border IS acts as a *route server*, whose sole responsibility is to participate in the protocol without forwarding any packets.

Using this technique, a routing domain that forms a large public or private data network may need to deploy only a handful of border ISs that would maintain border-IS to border-IS connections with a large number of external border ISs located in domains that are attached to that network. Packet forwarding between these domains through the network will be accomplished solely by the border ISs in these domains without any direct participation of border ISs within the network. Moreover, in order to receive routing information from all the domains attached to such a large data network, an external border IS needs to maintain border-IS to border-IS connection only with the border ISs that act as route servers rather than with all other external border ISs.

Figure 14.19 illustrates IDRP operation in a large data network (straight lines denote border-IS to border-IS connections). Routing domain X, which forms the network, has only two border ISs deployed within its boundaries. All the border ISs of the domains that use routing domain X as a transit have border-IS to border-IS connections with either of these two border ISs. Some of them may be connected to only one border IS in routing domain X; some, for redundancy, may be connected to

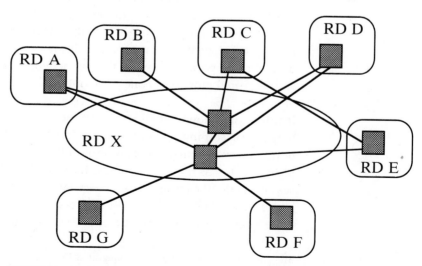

FIGURE 14.19   Example of IDRP in a Large Data Network

both. If a border IS in routing domain A advertises to a border IS in routing domain X a route to a destination, then the border IS in routing domain X may readvertise this route to border ISs in other domains, like border ISs in routing domains C or G, with the NSAP of the border IS in routing domain A, rather than its own, as the next hop. Thus, when the border IS in routing domain G needs to forward a packet to that destination, it may send it directly to the border IS in routing domain A. To facilitate forwarding, the information about the next-hop NSAP may be further augmented with the list of SNPAs associated with that NSAP. Observe that although border ISs in the domains attached to routing domain X have sufficient routing information to send packets directly to each other through routing domain X, distribution of this information does not require these border ISs to have border-IS to border-IS connections with each other. Instead, the distribution is accomplished as a result of maintaining border-IS to border-IS connections with only border ISs in routing domain X.

Interdomain Routing in TCP/IP

In the terminology of TCP/IP routing, "interdomain" routing becomes "interautonomous system" routing. The first *exterior gateway protocol* (RFC 904) assumed a tree structure for the Internet: lots of midlevel networks branching off the core or backbone autonomous system, and lots of networks branching off the midlevel networks. In principle, leaf networks forwarded IP packets to midlevels if they didn't know how to get to a destination, midlevels forwarded IP packets to the core if they didn't know how to get to a destination, and the omniscient core dealt with forwarding IP packets out through the branches to the leaves.

All well and good, right? Well, not exactly. First, the deployed Internet topology did not conform to the model: links were deployed and used to route packets between the leaf networks and between midlevels, and (horrors!) more backbones were introduced! (So much for the notion of a "core.") Second, and equally disconcerting, the EGP model required that the core know everything about the connectivity of the topology (a major shortcoming of EGP was the fact that it functioned as both an intra- and interdomain routing protocol). EGP always distributed complete updates: as the Internet grew, the size of EGP "updates," which are sent in single IP packets, became very large, and IP reassembly became a bottleneck.[31] EGP really didn't address the issue of policy; "policies" were manually introduced by operators and applied as *filters* to EGP

---

31.   Recall that both OSPF and integrated IS-IS try to avoid IP fragmentation and reassembly by allowing incremental (partial) updates.

routing updates as they were received. Finally, and most damaging of all, EGP couldn't detect loops (it insisted that the topology have none). In short, EGP simply could not cope, nor could the network administrators using it.

Enter the *border gateway protocol* (first specified in RFC 1105; subsequent versions, denoted BGP-1 through BGP-3, have appeared in RFC 1163 and RFC 1267). Incrementally, versions of BGP have freed and will free the Internet from the restrictive notion of a tree-based topology for inter-AS routing. BGP versions 3 and 4 (an RFC in preparation) offer a subset of the features for IP that IDRP offers for CLNP (not particularly suprising, since it is the ancestor of the ISO IDRP [Rekhter 1991; Tsuchiya 1991]). Like IDRP, BGP uses a path/distance-vector method of route computation and distribution: at start-up, BGP *speakers* (the equivalent of border ISs in IDRP) exchange their complete routing information bases and subsequently distribute incremental updates of in-use autonomous system paths only. Like IDRP's RD_PATH, which is composed of routing domain identifiers of real and virtual paths between border ISs, an *autonomous system path*, composed of Internet network numbers, may be real or virtual; however, the terms used in BGP are *external* or *internal paths*. As BGP speakers distribute reachability information, including path attributes, they compose and forward a complete list of autonomous systems that have already forwarded this routing information; like IDRP's compilation of the RD_PATH, this is done to avoid looping. Whereas IDRP operates point-to-point between border ISs over CLNP and supports reliability by a combination of sequence numbers, explicit acknowledgments, and retransmission of unacknowledged update packets in IDRP proper, BGP speakers operate pairwise over TCP connections and leave reliability to TCP.

Final Comments on Policy Routing

Interdomain routing protocols like BGP and IDRP are fine for most forms of traffic enforcement, especially those that can be generally applied to a majority of users to facilitate routing domain interconnection; in such cases, the routing overhead—interdomain distribution and route computation—is more than justified, since these policies are widely used. Both BGP-4 and IDRP are expected to scale well enough to accommodate general needs for the foreseeable future.

There are other types of interdomain routes, however, that merit special consideration. For example, a research branch of one company may collaborate with another, perhaps even a competitor, to advance a particular technology. In cases such as these, it may be important to offer connectivity between the research laboratories of the two companies, but it remains equally important to both administrations that they retain the ability to prohibit access to other parts of their enterprise networks. Another example is one in which a company maintains networks in several countries; quite often, international law frowns on such companies' providing intertransit services to third parties. In small doses, policies such as these can be managed by IDRP or BGP, but it is quite obvious that dealing with every policy eccentricity of every interdomain pairing of communicating hosts with hop-by-hop routing will quickly tend toward unmanageability; IDRP and BGP don't scale that well! In other words, there is a need for "exception-case" interdomain routing.

The *interdomain policy routing* (IDPR) architecture and protocol (RFCs in preparation) provide the means whereby special restrictions on interdomain routes may be specified or "demanded" at the source; hence, the name *source-demand routing*. The current version of IDPR uses link-state routing to distribute interdomain reachability and policy information between *policy gateways*, which, like IDRP's border ISs and BGP's speakers, are routers that are directly connected across administrative domains (here, the relationship is called a *virtual gateway*). The policy gateways in each domain receive interdomain link-state advertisements and calculate routes based on the topology map they have received according to whatever policies the administration wishes to enforce. When a packet is to be forwarded with certain policy considerations, it is forwarded to a policy gateway within the routing domain of that packet's source. This "source" policy gateway calls upon a route server to assist in setting up a route determined by the source policy gateway; a *route-setup* packet that describes the interdomain path selected by the source policy gateway is forwarded to all the policy gateways that must maintain the route in the transit (and destination) routing domains. A path or flow identifier is assigned to this interdomain route, and all packets that are to be forwarded across this route are encapsulated in an IP datagram that carries the flow identifier as additional header information.

"Unified" Interdomain Routing   Note that these two different methods of interdomain routing overlap, in the sense that nearly the same types of controls can be imposed on interdomain traffic using either method (RFC 1322 1992). However, it is not necessary to choose between the two methods of interdomain routing; rather, each has its respective merits. RFC 1322, A *Unified Approach to Inter-domain Routing*, suggests that in a robust interdomain routing architecture, these two methods are complementary. "Hop-by-hop" or *node-routing* interdomain protocols are important because they allow administrations to set policies for the largest percentage of interdomain traffic and from the largest number of sources; i.e., policies for the masses. Of course, since the node-routing protocols are expected to support the masses, they must maintain routes that are operational and under some administrative control, and they must also be able to adapt to topology changes, to keep the interdomain traffic flowing in the face of failures (IDRP and BGP have these characteristics).

Source-demand routing protocols like IDPR are important because they allow administrations to build special routes that could be supported by the "hop-by-hop" protocols, but at considerable routing expense/ overhead. Having both methods available allows administrations to put in place policies that are generally needed while accommodating exceptional circumstances. Balancing between the two is an important operational matter. Since the routes maintained by source-demand routing protocols are supposedly "special," there is an assumption that they will be used sparingly; indeed, if they become widely used, then the routing information should be distributed by node-routing protocols.

Conclusion

This chapter has discussed the routing principles, architecture, and protocols of OSI and TCP/IP—in the process, illustrating how OSI routing has benefited from what has been learned from the considerable experimentation and field experience with IP routing. The IP community has developed a hierarchy of routing functions and protocol in an evolutionary fashion, by necessity (a consequence of its success) increasing the robustness and reach of its protocols and architecture to scale to millions of hosts. The resulting IP routing architecture locates discovery and reachability among hosts and gateways in one functional tier, providing best paths between hosts within a single routing domain in a second tier, and providing methods for routing between domains in a third tier. The OSI community readily adopted this functional hierarchy, defining the three functional tiers of ES-IS, intradomain IS-IS, and interdomain IS-IS routing. The benefit to the OSI community is that it won't have to undergo many of the growing pains that have been endured by the IP community and that it can support a routing environment that scales at least as well as that of IP. The OSI community—and of course, the "tweeners"—have attempted to return the favor by defining some useful improvements in OSI routing protocols that can be applied in IP-only or integrated routing protocols as well.

15 DATA LINK AND PHYSICAL LAYERS

Below the network layer, the architectural uniformity of the OSI reference model partially breaks down. According to the OSI reference model, the role of the data link layer is to "provide for the control of the physical layer, to detect and where possible, correct errors which may occur in a physical connection established for bit transmission" (ISO/IEC 7498: 1993). There is, however, a small problem: at the data link layer, things get very technology-specific. All sorts of technologies are used to connect computers, and there is an astonishingly large number of standards for the data-link and physical layers that describe a trillion or so modem and electrical interface standards. Some have been around for decades. Consider the venerable high level data link control (HDLC). Having provided nearly two decades of wide-scale deployment and service over kilobit transmission facilities (the equally venerable V-series modems), HDLC is enjoying something of a rejuvenation in the form of frame relay services.

Later technologies—notably, local area networks—improved on earlier technologies by introducing shared-medium, multipoint communication; significantly higher bandwidth; low latency; and very low error rates. Metropolitan area network (MAN) technologies, the *asynchronous transfer mode* (ATM) platform for broadband integrated services, and the *synchronous optical network* (SONET) technology are expected to further expand the role of the data link layer, introducing constant bit rate and isochronous services (for voice and real-time video) and even greater (potentially gigabit) bandwidth.

This technology advance wreaked havoc on the poor souls responsible for providing service definitions for the data link and physical layers of OSI (ISO/IEC 8886: 1992; ISO/IEC 10022: 1990). Ultimately, the parties involved quite literally threw their hands up in exasperation and provided definitions that can be viewed as at best a "for completeness's sake" effort. Truthfully, this is nothing to lose sleep over: given how frequently technologies are introduced, the data link– and physical layer service definitions offer a snapshot of what these layers looked like at the time of standardization, but they absolutely should not be interpreted as the final word on what the data link and physical layers should be.

Some technologies—for example, point-to-point and HDLC-based links—fit conveniently into the OSI reference model's notion of a data link. Advocates of local area networks, however, opined that LANs were richer in function than mere data links—they had globally unique addressing, and it could even be argued that Medium Access Control included routing functions. For a brief time, LANs led a truly schizophrenic existence: eventually, the "it's a subnetwork technology" folks were beaten into submission by the "it's a data link" folks, and LANs were placed at the data link layer, along with point-to-point protocols like ISO/IEC 7776, *high level data link* control, and CCITT Recom-mendation X.21*bis*, *Use on Public Data Networks of Data Terminal Equipment Designed for Interfacing to Synchronous V-series Modems*, etc. Metropolitan area networks—fiber distributed data interface (FDDI) and the distributed queue dual bus (DQDB)—will undoubtedly share the same fate as LANs, and since politics will most certainly play a role in *broadband integrated services digital networks* (BISDN), it is inevitable that one or more broadband services will contend for roles in the network layer.

Not to worry: it will be possible to run IP and CLNP over *all of them*.

Taxonomy of Data Link Standards

Consistent with Tanenbaum's (1988) taxonomy, data link– and physical-layer standards for OSI generally fall into two categories:

1. *Point-to-point connection standards* describe the use of HDLC procedures (ISO/IEC 3309: 1991; ISO/IEC 4335: 1991; ISO/IEC 7809: 1991) as a means of framing data for transmission over various physical media in single- and multilink configurations (ISO/IEC 7478: 1984; ISO/IEC 7776: 1986).[1]
2. *Multi access channel standards* describe logical link control proce-

---

1.   There are more data link– and physical layer standards that apply to OSI, to be

dures (ISO/IEC 8802-2: 1990) as well as physical access methods and medium specifications for local and metropolitan area networks: *carrier sense multiple access with collision detection* (CSMA/CD; ISO/IEC 8802-3: 1992), *token-passing bus* (ISO/IEC 8802-4: 1990), and *token ring* (ISO/IEC 8802-5: 1990). *Fiber distributed data interface* (ISO/IEC 9314-2: 1989) and *distributed queue dual bus* (IEEE 802.6 1990) MAN complete the list.

These categories apply equally well to the Internet architecture. Although the nomenclature differs slighty—Internetters prefer the term *network interfaces* over *data link layer*—the Internet community wisely elected to treat anything and everything that IP could conceivably be run over as a network interface.

Point-to-Point Connection Standards

HDLC-based protocols remain the most common form of link-level framing for point-to-point connection technologies; connection-oriented and datagram transmission (a.k.a. *unnumbered information* frames, or UI) are described among the HDLC classes of procedures. Both perform error detection using a 16- or 32-bit cyclic redundancy check.

Point-to-point subnetworks play an important role in both TCP/IP and OSI network connectivity. The standard for encapsulation of Internet datagrams over point-to-point links is RFC 1331, the *point-to-point protocol* (PPP). RFC 1331 describes a convention for encapsulating network-layer protocols in full-duplex, asynchronous or synchronous links, using HDLC framing. The default 8-octet frame format defined in the PPP (Figure 15.1) accommodates a maximum frame size of 1,500 octets and specifies a 16-bit *frame-check sequence*. PPP uses an address-extension mechanism available in HDLC to specify a protocol field, which is used to identify network-layer protocols in a multiprotocol (OSI, TCP/IP, AppleTalk®, XNS/IPX, etc.) environment. PPP also describes a *link control protocol* that can be used, for example, to negotiate maximum receive frame size, to indicate that authentication must be performed using the specified authentication protocol, and to indicate to a peer that the link quality is to be monitored using the specified protocol. Finally, PPP provides a framework for the development of a set of *net-*

---

sure. Folts (1991) devotes entire volumes of a multivolume compendium of OSI standards to the CCITT V-series and X-series recommendations. Halsall (1988) provides a college-text-level primer on these layers. And of course, there is always Tanenbaum (1988).

PPP Field	No. of Octets
Flag (01111110)	1
Address	1
Control	1
Protocol ID	2
User data	<Variable, up to 1,500 octets>
Frame-check sequence	2
Flag (01111110)	1

FIGURE 15.1   Point-to-Point Protocol Frame

work control protocols (NCPs), which deal with the behavior and idiosyncracies of individual network-layer protocols operating over point-to-point links. (At the time of this book's publication, network control protocols for OSI, DECnet, AppleTalk®, IP, and IPX were available only as Internet drafts and RFCs in preparation and thus did not yet have any official standards status.)

Systems using PPP establish and negotiate the characteristics of the link and specify the set of network-layer protocols that will share the link using configuration packets of the link control protocol, then proceed through authentication (if specified), and finally process the network-centricities of the protocols that will share the link using the appropriate network control protocols (if specified). The OSI standards do not describe multiprotocol issues; thus, it should be expected that PPP will eventually be used in many multiprotocol environments that include IP and CLNP.

The corresponding description of encapsulation of CLNP into point-to-point subnetworks was originally drafted as an addendum to ISO/IEC 8473 and was then incorporated into ISO/IEC 8473 prior to its publication as an international standard. The standard only describes the minimum maximum service data unit size required and assumes that network layer protocol identification is sufficient to distinguish one network layer protocol from another; i.e., it relies on some other (data link) demultiplexing mechanism to distinguish protocols that have as their initial octet an initial protocol identifier (see "Network Layer Protocol Ident-ification," Chapter 13) from those that do not.

Multiaccess Channel Standards

Several local area network technologies—the Ethernet/IEEE 802.3 CSMA/CD MAC, the IEEE 802.4 token-bus MAC, and the IEEE 802.5 token-ring MAC—have been around for better than a decade: descriptions abound, and there is little left to say that has not already been said. One aspect of the IEEE 802/ISO 8802 LAN architecture that should be considered within the context of OSI and TCP/IP, however, is IEEE 802.2/ISO 8802-2, *logical link control* (LLC).

Logical Link Control—The Nether-Layer

A perturbation introduced in the IEEE 802 LAN architecture, perpetuated by OSI, and eventually finding its way into TCP/IP, logical link control is primarily used to demultiplex higher-layer protocols (well, to placate frame zealots, there *are* type-1 connectionless and type-2 connection-oriented LLCs, and even a type-3 acknowledged connectionless LLC, but thankfully, OSI and TCP/IP both use type 1). To indicate that the protocol encapsulated in the LLC information field is an OSI network layer protocol, the originator of an LLC frame sets the destination and source service access points (DSAP, SSAP; see Figure 15.2) to the hexadecimal value FE. The receiver examines the first octet of the information field (the initial protocol identifier; see Chapter 13) to distinguish which of the many OSI network-layer protocols this might be.

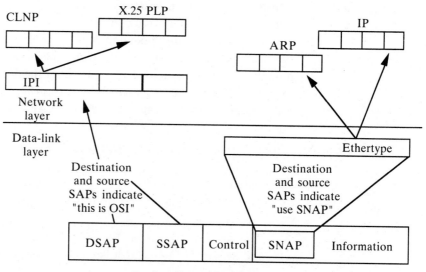

Logical link control PDU

FIGURE 15.2   LLC and Protocol Identification

·AHA·　*When Ethernet was first developed, the last 2 octets of the MAC frame (the ethertype field) were used to identify higher-layer protocols. When the technology was introduced into the IEEE 802 committee so that it might become a standard LAN technology, the ethertype field of the MAC frame was abandoned in favor of a MAC frame-length field (ostensibly, the ethertype field was specific to Ethernet; given that the IEEE 802 committee was attempting to standardize multiple MAC technologies, it seemed more appropriate to have a MAC-independent means of identifying higher-layer protocols—i.e., logical link control). The dual role of these octets would cause considerable difficulty if stations with IEEE 802.3 CSMA/CD and Ethernet MACs were to attempt to communicate if not for the fact that the values of the field are nonoverlapping: the maximum value of the length field in the IEEE 802.3 MAC frame is slightly more than 1,500 octets, and the ethertype values are, conveniently, integers greater than this value. Most implementations now recognize both techniques. Even though interoperability is accommodated, a rift was formed between the Ethernet and IEEE 802 communities that persists today.*

Initially, IEEE intended that values other than hexadecimal FE would be assigned to deserving organizations; it didn't take long, however, to realize that a single octet (255 values) would not suffice to identify all organizations requiring protocol/organization identifiers. Rather than expand the length of the LLC SAP fields, the IEEE 802.1 committee adopted what is called the *subnetwork access protocol* (SNAP). The SNAP is itself identified by populating the destination and source service access point fields with the hexadecimal value AA. This value indicates that an additional 5 octets are appended to the 3-octet LLC type-1 frame to convey a 3-octet *protocol identifier/organization identifier* field and a 2-octet organization-specific field. The existence of the SNAP doesn't come close to smoothing the feathers ruffled during the "ethertype versus IEEE 802.3 frame length" debates; however, SNAP does have two redeeming virtues:

1. For IP encapsulation in IEEE 802.x LANs (RFC 1042 1988), switched multimegabit data service (RFC 1209 1991), and fiber distributed data interface (FDDI) (RFC 1188), the protocol identifier/organization identifier field is set to 0, and the *ethertype* field is conveyed in the remaining 2 bytes.

2. The addition of 5 octets to the 3-octet LLC type-1 field word-aligns the header of the encapsulated network protocols for both 16- and 32-bit machines.

Emerging Digital Technologies

Several *new* technologies—in some cases, applications of these technologies—have emerged only recently, among these the FDDI and DQDB metropolitan area networks, the HDLC-based frame-relay technology, and broadband ISDN. These technologies are discussed here because they are expected to provide much-needed high-bandwidth/low-latency platforms for Internet and OSI-based applications over a wide geographic extent. A related physical layer technology, synchronous optical network (SONET), is also discussed.

Metropolitan Area Networks: FDDI and IEEE 802.6 DQDB

Metropolitan area network technologies extend the characteristics of LANs that provide a favorable environment for distributed computing—high bandwidth, low latency, large information payloads—beyond the distance constraints of existing LAN technologies. MAN services are likely to be extended over very wide areas and hence encompass more than what intuitively comes to mind when the term *metropolitan* is applied.

Another characteristic that continues to be associated with MANs is the ability to integrate services—particularly real-time voice and data—over the same physical transmission facilities. Also, with the virtually boundless promise of bandwidth offered by fiber-optic transmission systems, real-time video will inevitably enter the picture. Services other than real-time broadcast television and video conferencing—image transfer and recognition systems, collaborative work and education, virtual reality—are more likely to play a prominent role once their potential as ubiquitous applications is realized. In many respects, the term *MAN* is apropos; like *homo sapiens*, a MAN is a multifaceted beast:

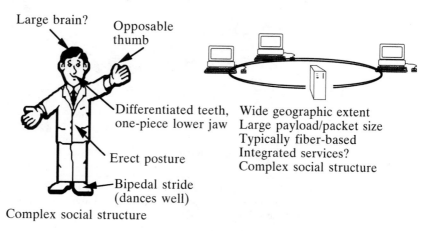

Large brain?

Opposable thumb

Differentiated teeth, one-piece lower jaw

Erect posture

Bipedal stride (dances well)

Complex social structure

Wide geographic extent
Large payload/packet size
Typically fiber-based
Integrated services?
Complex social structure

**Fiber-Distributed
Data Interface**

FDDI is a very-high-bandwidth (100 Mbps) LAN technology. It is typically deployed as a dual ring, with one ring enabling transmission "clockwise," the other "counterclockwise" (see Figure 15.3).

Stations may be attached to one or both rings, or via a concentrator to allow "trees" to be branched off a central dual ring (see Figure 15.4). Attachment to both rings is a reliability consideration:[2] when a link be-

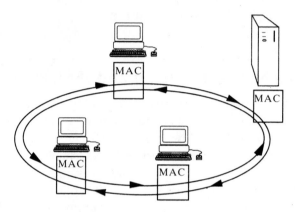

FIGURE 15.3   FDDI Deployed as a Dual Ring

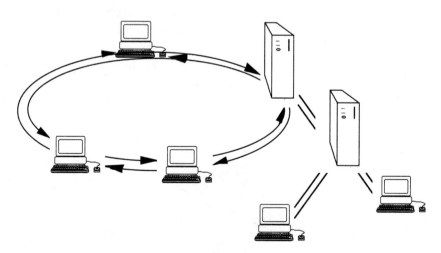

FIGURE 15.4   FDDI Trunk Ring and Tree

---

2.   Contrary to claims made by an overzealous (albeit well-intentioned) sales force during an early FDDI marketing presentation, dual attachment does not double the available bandwidth.

tween two stations fails, dual-attached stations can reverse their direction of transmission and take advantage of the healthy ring; if a station fails, stations adjacent to the failed station can reconfigure (wrap) the dual ring so that the single logical ring survives (see Figure 15.5).

Like the IEEE 802.5 token ring LAN, the FDDI MAC protocol uses a token-ring medium access method. A station must acquire a MAC control frame called a *token* before it can transmit data. Once a station has transmitted a MAC data frame, it generates and writes a new token to the ring from which it acquired the token. Each station reads every frame off the ring and checks to see whether the destination address in the MAC frame is the same as its respective MAC address. If the address is not a match, a station repeats the frame (downstream); if it is a match, the station copies the frame off the medium and passes it up to the logical link control function for protocol demultiplexing, etc.

Each 4 bits of binary data in a MAC data frame are encoded into a 5-bit pattern called a *symbol* prior to submission to the physical layer. A 32-bit *cyclic redundancy check* (CRC) is computed over the frame-control, information, and CRC fields to detect bit errors on the data symbols. Control frames (e.g., the token) are also encoded as a (separate) sequence of symbols (see Figure 15.6).

Priorities are implemented by restricting a station's ability to acquire the token. A station is responsible for determining when a frame it has generated has traversed the entire ring (i.e., it has returned to its origin) and for *stripping* these frames; a *frame status* encoded in the MAC

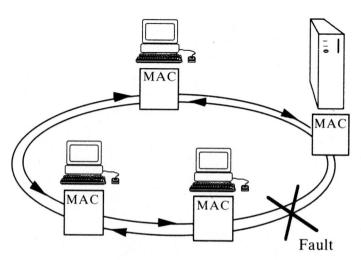

FIGURE 15.5   FDDI Ring Wrap

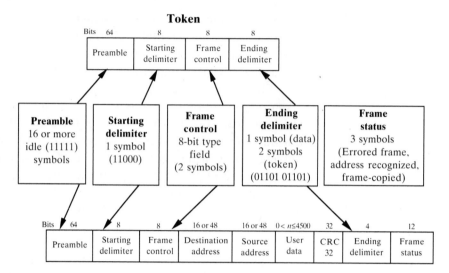

FIGURE 15.6   FDDI MAC Frame Formats

frame header indicates whether the transmission has been successful.

The FDDI MAC frame can accommodate 4,500 octets of user data. Typically, 48-bit (Ethernet) addressing is used (see IEEE 802.1; ISO/IEC 8802-2); 16-bit addressing may also be used. A *timed token-rotation* (TTR) *protocol* is used by stations to establish a uniform token-rotation time. The token-rotation time can be set to a large value to allow very high ring utilization under heavy load (e.g., many stations distributed over a large ring perimeter), or it can be set to a small value to guarantee band-width for delay-sensitive applications such as packetized voice or video.

FDDI was originally designed to operate over multimode optical fiber. This limited the distance between stations to 2 kilometers. FDDI has since been extended to operate over single-mode fiber-optic cable; with single-mode fiber, a maximum perimeter of 60–100 kilometers can be achieved for the dual ring. The specification of a *single-mode fiber phys-ical-layer medium-dependent* (SMF-PMD) and an FDDI-to-SONET physi-cal-layer mapping (FDDI-SPM) function is significant, since single-mode fiber is used by telecommunications carriers and can be leased and used between facilities to extend individual links between FDDI stations over metropolitan area networking distances.

IP encapsulation over FDDI is described in RFC 1188; like encapsu-lation of IP in IEEE 802 subnetworks, RFC 1188 prescribes the use of the LLC/SNAP, described earlier in this chapter, and both ARP and routing protocols are operated over FDDI networks in the same manner as IEEE 802 LANs. Encapsulation of OSI CNLP in FDDI frames is not the subject of a standard but in practice is accommodated by using LLC type 1 in the fashion described earlier in this chapter for IEEE 802.3 and IEEE 802.5 subnetworks.

Distributed Queue Dual Bus

The *distributed queue dual bus subnetwork* (IEEE 802.6 1990) is a high-speed MAN technology that operates over two unidirectional, contraflowing buses over a variety of transmission rates. The MAN can be deployed in two topologies (see Figure 15.7):

1. In an *open* topology, stations providing a *head-of-bus* function generate fixed-length data *slots* and management control information over both buses. The slots are used to compose variable-length MAC frames.

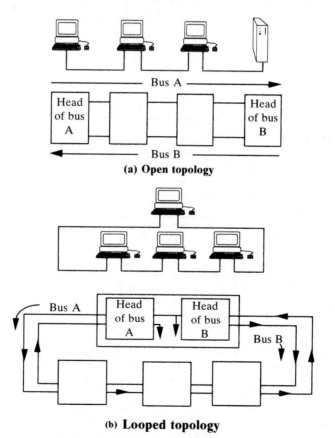

(a) Open topology

(b) Looped topology

FIGURE 15.7   Topologies of a DQDB MAN

2. In a *looped* topology, the heads of bus are colocated in a single station, and the topology can be configured to be self-healing in the face of failure.

The DQDB MAN provides:

- A connectionless data-transmission service
- A connection-oriented, isochronous service, suitable for voice and video applications
- A connection-oriented, nonisochronous service alternative for data communications

The functional model of a DQDB node to support these services is depicted in Figure 15.8. Both the connection-oriented and connectionless MAC services submit data through a segmentation and reassembly (SAR) function to "atomize"[3] variable-length frames into fixed-length *slots* consisting of an access-control octet, a 4-octet segment header, and a 48-octet segment payload (for the connectionless data service, 4 octets are taken from the segment payload for "adaptation" functions; see Figure

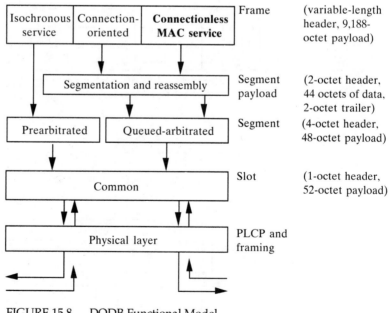

FIGURE 15.8   DQDB Functional Model

---

3.   Both the DQDB MAN and broadband ISDN use fixed-length micro-packets (slots, cells). The term "atomize" is pejorative, derived from "ATM-ize," or "to make into ATM-like cells" (origin unknown).

15.9). Standards for call signaling and bandwidth management for iso-chronous services have yet to be developed.

In the *queued-arbitrated* mode of operation, MAN stations can send and receive variable-length, connectionless MAC frames (up to 9,188 octets). The *prearbitrated* mode of operation, still under study in IEEE 802.6, provides support for digitized voice and other isochronous services. The DQDB connectionless MAC frame permits the use of 16-, 48-, and 60-bit MAC addresses. Addresses are encoded in fixed-length, 8-octet source and destination address fields; the most significant "nibble" of the address fields identifies the address type, followed by 60 bits of padding and addressing (44 bits of padding precede a 16-bit address, 12 bits of padding precede a 48-bit address, and 60-bit addresses require no padding). An optional 32-bit *cyclic redundancy check* is selected by setting the *CRC indicator bit* in the *initial MAC protocol header* (see Figure 15.9). The *beginning-end tags, buffer allocation size,* and *length* fields of the initial MAC protocol header and trailer are used by the sending and receiving stations for error detection and control functions (see Figure 15.9).

IMPDUs are segmented into 44-octet segment payloads, and each payload has a 2-octet header and trailer (see Figure 15.10). These 4 octets are aligned with the broadband ISDN ATM adaptation layer, type 4 (see "Asynchronous Transfer Mode and Broadband ISDN," later in this chapter). The segment header contains a segment type indicator—beginning of message (BOM), continuation of message or "middle" (COM), and end of message (EOM)—and a single-segment message type indicator (SSM). A sequence number is used to detect lost, misordered, or inserted segments.[4] A *message identifier* (MID) assists in the identification of seg-

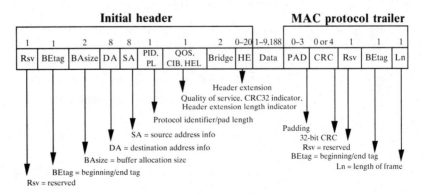

FIGURE 15.9   DQDB Initial MAC Protocol Data Unit (IMPDU)

4.   The usefulness of performing cell sequence checking, particularly over dual-bus

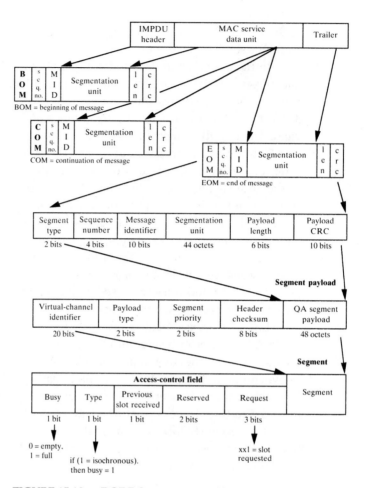

FIGURE 15.10   DQDB Segmentation, Slot Decomposition

ments of the same IMPDU during reassembly. The payload-length field contains either the value 44 (BOM or COM) or the number of octets in an EOM or SSM, and the *payload cyclic redundancy check* is optionally used for single-bit error detection on the segment payload.[5]

topology, is questionable, especially since the sequence space is too small to uniquely identify all segments of an IMPDU that is segmented into 16 or more slots. This bit twiddling is another fine example of last-minute standards chicanery: rather than reopen the question of whether the length and composition of the ATM cell/DQDB slot was correct, the IEEE 802 and CCITT folks decided it would be easier and subtler to whittle away 4 octets from the segment payload for adaptation-layer functions.

5.   The DQDB MAC protocol stack is replete with checksums of one sort or another (see Figures 15.9 and 15.10). During the joint development of the ATM cell/DQDB slot by CCITT and IEEE 802.6, the network-centrics viewed the slot as the unit of significance for

Connectionless MAC stations operate in what is called *queued-arbitrated* (QA) mode. Heads of bus A and B continuously generate/forward 53-octet queued-arbitrated slots on their respective buses, composed of a 1-octet *access control field* (ACF) and a 52-octet payload (see Figure 15.10). The operation of the distributed queue access protocol is predicated on the values of two fields of the ACF: the *busy* bit indicates whether the slot is empty (available) or full (taken). The *request* bits indicate whether slots have been queued for access (i.e., that a station has requested a slot). Each station maintains two *request counters*, one for each bus (logically, one for each direction of information flow). A station in the idle state (i.e., one with nothing to send) decrements the request counter for each empty slot it sees on bus A and increments the same request counter by 1 for each request bit set on bus B; i.e., it constantly checks how many slots have been queued on bus A. In so doing, a station establishes its position in the distributed queue, relative to other stations wishing to send on bus A (a similar computation occurs simultaneously for bus B).

When a station wishes to send on bus A, it writes a request on bus A; i.e., it writes a binary 1 to the request bit in the access-control field of the first slot that has not already been used by downstream stations to request slots. The station copies the current value of the request counter from bus B into a *countdown counter*, then decrements the countdown counter each time an empty slot passes by on bus A; i.e., a station waits until all the stations that have queued requests to send on bus A ahead of it have satisfied their requests (sort of like children in a classroom raising their hands and waiting their turn). When the countdown counter reaches 0, the station copies the next empty slot from bus A, fills the payload with user data, marks the slot busy, and writes it back to bus A. The process is the same if a station wishes to send a slot on bus B; here, the station queues a request on bus B, copies the current value of the request counter from bus A into the countdown counter, and waits until all the stations that have queued requests to send on bus B ahead of it have satisfied their requests.

The DQDB MAN MAC protocol was developed in a physical-transmission-facilities-independent fashion; i.e., the MAN can operate over a variety of physical transmission systems, including those currently used

---

all broadband services and insisted that error detection and recovery be performed on a cell-by-cell basis. Host-centrics pointed to the IEEE 802.1a LAN architecture standard and claimed that to be consistent with *all* the MACs that preceded IEEE 802.6, error detection—in the form of a 32-bit CRC—should be performed on the initial MAC protocol data unit. Who won? Everybody . . . sort of. There are *optional* error-detection functions for the entire IMPDU and optional error-correction functions for the slot header.

by telephony providers in the United States, throughout Europe, and Asia, as well as the emerging SONET transmission system, described later in this chapter. Borrowing (perhaps subliminally) from the principles of convergence described in the *Internal Organization of the Network Layer* (see Chapter 13), *physical layer convergence procedures* (PLCPs) have been defined to describe how to map DQDB slots onto physical-layer framing provided by a variety of standard telephony transmission systems (Brandwein, Cox, and Dahl 1990). PLCPs enable the DQDB MAN MAC to operate over existing telephony digital transmission hierarchies at rates of 1.544 Mbps (DS1) and 44.736 Mbps (DS3) in North America and at rates of 2.048 Mbps (E1), 34.368 Mbps (E3), and 139.264 Mbps (E4) in Europe and Asia, as well as over SONET (discussed later in this chapter). This, combined with the fact that the length and encoding of DQDB segments is intentionally aligned with the ATM "cell" of the broadband ISDN under study in CCITT, makes IEEE 802.6 attractive for a public network service. Two such services are currently under trial and early deployment in the United States and several European countries: switched multimegabit data service (SMDS) and the European Telecommunications Standards Institute's MAN project (ETSI MAN).

Fast Packet Services and Technologies

The term "fast packet" has emerged from the telecommunications industry as a way to collectively refer to transmission technologies that may be used in wide area network as well as local area network and campus configurations. These technologies may be operated over existing telecommunications digital transmission facilities to provide public data networking services that offer higher bandwidth and lower delay characteristics than their "narrowband" predecessors, ISDN and X.25. In the following sections we describe the most prominent of these emerging "broadband" services—SMDS and its European cousin, ETSI MAN, frame relay, and ATM—and a relatively new and promising fiber-optic transport system, SONET.

Switched Multimegabit Data Service

SMDS is a public, packet-switched datagram service. The service is often described as "LAN-analogous" (Bellcore Technical Requirement TR-TSV-000772 1991), meaning that the features of the public service—high bandwidth, low delay, large packet sizes, multicasting, address screening/filtering—emulate characteristics of LANs. The interface protocol to the public network (SMDS interface protocol, or SIP) is based on the IEEE

802.6 MAN. The SMDS interface protocol is described as a three-level protocol exchanged across the *subscriber network interface* (SNI) between a switching system within a public carrier network—in the United States, a local exchange carrier, an independent exchange carrier, or an interexchange ("long-distance") carrier network—and the customer communications equipment (in Figure 15.11, the router and host B). In the United States, an open DQDB topology will be applied; i.e., separate physical transmission facilities will be dedicated to each subscriber site.

The SIP level-3 packet corresponds to the IEEE 802.6 initial MAC frame. Most of the IEEE 802.6 protocol control information is interpreted exactly as defined in the IEEE standard. SMDS uses 60-bit publicly administered addresses. The most significant 4 bits of the destination address field are used to indicate whether the 60-bit address is an individual or a group address (a group address is functionally similar to a multicast Ethernet address); the remaining bits of the source and destination address fields are used to convey the SMDS address. The address format is ten BCD-encoded decimal digits, imitating the format used for telephone numbers in the United States. In hosts, bridges, or routers attached to the dual bus, these addresses are used the same way that 48-bit Ethernet addresses are used for communication over LANs; in the public

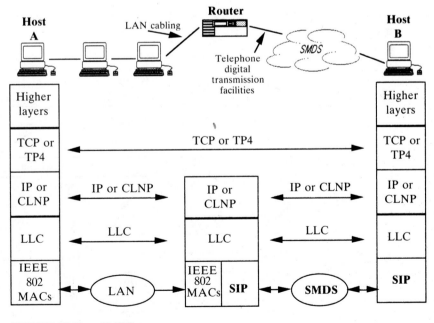

FIGURE 15.11   SMDS

network, however, the addresses are used for routing between switches. The header extension field provides a means to support carrier selection for interexchange ac-cess (to long-distance carriers).

SMDS provides several supplementary services: *source address screening* allows subscribers to filter traffic originating from unwanted sources on the public network, and *destination address screening* allows subscribers to limit the destinations to which traffic may be forwarded across the public network. *Group addressing* allows subscribers to create the equivalent of a multicast capability across the public network. Essentially, a subscriber identifies a set of SMDS addresses that should all receive copies of a group-addressed packet, and the SMDS network provider assigns the subscriber a 60-bit group address. Thereafter, any SMDS packet that is submitted to the SMDS network having that group address as its destination address will be copied to all members of the group address list submitted by the subscriber.

The SIP level-2 protocol data unit corresponds to the IEEE 802.6 DQDB slot. SIP level 2 provides framing and segmentation for the variable-length SIP level-3 packets through the use of fixed-length slots and also provides an error-detection capability through a 10-bit payload CRC in the level 2 trailer (see Figure 15.12).

SMDS will be deployed over existing digital transmission facilities of the public telephone network over a metropolitan or wide area by telecommunications providers. SIP level 1 describes a physical interface

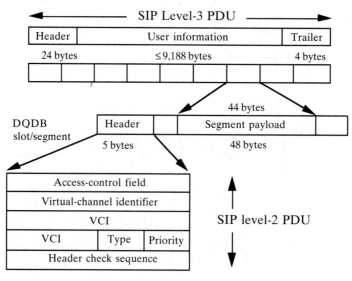

FIGURE 15.12   SIP Level-2 PDU

to the digital transmission network. Currently, two access rates are defined. A PLCP is defined for DS3, which provides a transfer rate of 44.736 Mbps, and for DS1, which provides a transfer rate of 1.544 Mbps. The DS1 physical interface uses the *extended superframe* format (ESF). SMDS is described in a series of Bellcore Technical Requirements (TR-TSV-000772 1991; TR-TSV-000773 1991).

There will be a number of subscribers who may want to benefit from the low latency offered by the DS3 access for bursty data applications but whose sustained information rates are expected to be much lower than 45 megabits per second. *Access classes* allow customers to subscribe to what are essentially "fractions" of bandwidth for both bursty and sustained data transmission. The mechanism is straightforward. A customer selects an access class (separate access class tariffs are expected for sustained information rates of approximately 4, 10, 16, and 25 Mbps, accompanied by maximum burst rates of approximately 10, 13, 18, and 34 Mbps, respectively). A *credit manager* monitors the rate at which SIP level-2 protocol data units are sent to the network. If the rate at which the subscriber sends SIP level-2 protocol data units into the network exceeds either the subscribed-to *sustained information rate* or the *maximum burst rate,* the network provider will discard the excess (see Bellcore Technical Requirement TR-TSV-000772 [1991] for more details on this "leaky bucket" or credit manager algorithm).

SMDS will be used primarily for local area network interconnection. The unusual (unprecedented) combination of local area network characteristics and telephony-style numbering in SMDS makes the service suitable for a number of interenterprise (multiorganizational) as well as intraenterprise applications (this is touted as "any-to-any communication"). Early trial and field experience has demonstrated that SMDS can be used as a "gathering net" for commercial IP networks (it may also be used as part of the backbone network). In this scenario, the commercial IP provider subscribes to "fat" DS3 SMDS pipes and recommends SMDS access at DS1 rates to its customers. The DS3 SMDS access provides an aggregation point for the IP provider and reduces the number of interfaces the IP provider must manage and pay for.

SMDS can also be used by disaster recovery service providers (people who provide data center redundancy—i.e., exact duplicates of an organization's data-processing environment and database) to simplify and reduce the cost of cutover procedures following a catastrophic failure. In this scenario, the disaster recovery service provider recommends SMDS for wide area service; if an earthquake destroys a company's data center, cut-over to the duplicate data center is a matter of "entering a different telephone number" in routing tables across the company's internetwork. This is considerably simpler and faster than reprovisioning private lines and virtual-circuit services and cheaper than subscribing to additional private lines to the disaster recovery service provider.

SMDS makes it convenient and economical for organizations to have many temporary communications partners (commercial IP providers do this as well, but incredible as it may seem, there are folks who do not use them). For example, medical centers may routinely distribute X-ray, magnetic resonance, and positive tomography images to affiliated medical schools and attending physicians, but on occasion, they may wish to distribute them to specialist and other medical centers. In these circumstances, SMDS may offer an attractive alternative to constructing and operating a private network.

To accommodate those enterprises that want SMDS but cannot justify the cost of DS1 access to all locations, *frame-based access* at 56 and 64 Kbps—in many instances, on frame-relay interfaces—will be offered by local and interexchange carriers. In these configurations, the SMDS level-3 packet is encapsulated in an HDLC frame rather than segmented (at such low rates, the packetization into IEEE 802.6 slots is impractical). SMDS will eventually be offered over SONET interfaces (discussed later in this chapter) and, as broadband switching is introduced into public networks, over ATM as well.

ETSI MAN

Like SMDS in the United States, the ETSI MAN responds to the European consumer demand for multimegabit communication services. An enabling vehicle for broadband ISDN, ETSI MAN is slightly more ambitious than SMDS, encompassing

- A "packet-oriented" MAC service of ISO 8802 LANs, suitable for bursty data communications
- A connection-oriented isochronous service, suitable for voice and video applications
- A connection-oriented, nonisochronous service alternative for data communications

Like SMDS, ETSI MAN applies the DQDB MAN MAC protocol for the connectionless MAC service. Because the regulatory environment in many parts of Europe differs from that in the United States, single- or multisubscriber access facilities may be provided, and both open and looped topologies are anticipated. Two forms of interface are described in the ETSI MAN architecture ("ETSI Metropolitan Area Network" 1991). The *user MAN interface* is similar to SMDS; the public network provides a physical transmission facility with access rates of 2.048, 34.368, and 139.264 Mbps (i.e., over E1, E3, and E4 transmission facilities), and the subscriber attaches a host, bridge, or router. Network providers may also offer encapsulation, bridging, or routing via a *user service interface* at access rates of 4, 10, or 16 Mbps; in such configurations, subscribers attach their IEEE 802.x LANs directly into network equipment (see Figure 15.13).

Many SMDS features are present in the ETSI MAN: 60-bit, telephony-style addressing and supplementary services (e.g., address screening). Since both SMDS and ETSI MAN are early broadband ISDN applications, compatibility between the service offerings is both desirable and essential.

RFC 1209 describes IP encapsulation and operation of the address resolution protocol (ARP) over SMDS. IP datagrams are encapsulated in the 8-octet LLC/SNAP frame in exactly the same manner as for IEEE 802 LANs. ARP is performed over what are called "logical IP subnetworks"; essentially, a set of hosts whose IP addresses share a common IP network/subnet number and whose SMDS addresses are all identified as recipients of the same group address send ARP requests using the group address in the same manner as they would use a 48-bit broadcast address over an Ethernet or IEEE 802 LAN. ARP replies are directed back to the source using the 60-bit address of the ARP request originator.

RFC 1209 is suitable for IP over ETSI MAN as well; only the aspects of group addressing for the purposes of using ARP require additional consideration. Encapsulation of CNLP (ISO/IEC 8473-1: 1993) is not the subject of a standard but, in practice, is again accommodated by using LLC 1 in the fashion described for IEEE 802.3 and IEEE 802.5 subnetworks in ISO/IEC 8802-3.

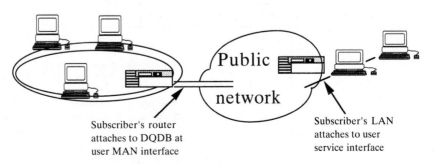

Subscriber's router attaches to DQDB at user MAN interface

Subscriber's LAN attaches to user service interface

FIGURE 15.13   ETSI MAN, UMI, and USI

Frame Relay Technology

By OSI standards, frame relay is a hybrid. It offers aspects of connection-oriented services that hint of the X.25 packet-level protocol—for example, frame relay service is provided over permanent and switched virtual circuits—but forgoes the protocol and processing overhead of the level-3 error handling of X.25. Since the X.25 reliability mechanisms are omitted, frame relay offers higher throughput than X.25 and is less expensive than X.25 and equivalent private-line solutions.

From a technology standpoint, frame relay is nothing new: it is a juiced-up or "fast-packet" technology based on HDLC. It can be deployed as a shared, common-access WAN in a public or private networking environment. From a services perspective—applying nomenclature from the architecture of the *integrated services digital network*, CCITT Recommendation I.122-(1989)—frame relay is a packet-mode bearer service. The access protocol is based on HDLC and on the link access protocol developed for signaling over the D channel of narrowband ISDN (LAP-D; CCITT Recommendation Q.921 1989). Variable-length HDLC frames (up to 1,600 octets) are packet-switched on the basis of a 10-bit *data link connection identifier* (DLCI; see Figure 15.14). Although the data link connection identifier can be locally or globally administered, a 10-bit DLCI is already viewed as a major shortcoming of the protocol; an address extension indicator in both octets of the header can be used in later versions of frame relay to extend the header to 3 or 4 bytes. A *frame check sequence* (FCS) is computed on the entire frame prior to its submission to the frame relay network.

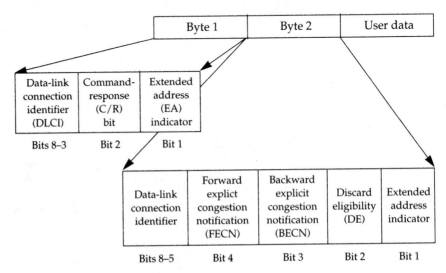

FIGURE 15.14   Frame Relay Header

Network (switch) processing of incoming frames is as follows. If the frame check sequence check is successful, the data link connection identifier is used as an index into a table of trunks over which frames are forwarded (relayed) to (toward) their destinations. If the FCS check fails, the frame is discarded. At the ingress point, the DLCI encoded in the incoming frame indicates the destination; however, the DLCI is modified by the network prior to transmission across the egress link so that the DLCI in the outgoing frame contains the source (the switch thus recomputes or adjusts the FCS as part of the processing of each frame).

Internal to frame relay networks, frame relay providers apply the concepts of *statistical multiplexing:* every user is not expected to use all of the bandwidth subscribed to every minute of every day, so resources (switching equipment, trunk lines between switches) are allocated to handle what is determined to be a reasonable load under normal conditions. As with highways, anticipated traffic loads can be exceeded, and congestion can occur. In a frame relay network, congestion is alleviated by discarding frames. Frame relay offers *explicit congestion notification* (ECN) mechanisms that are similar to that of OSI CLNP (see Chapter 13), but bidirectionally: forward and backward indications—FECNs and BECNs —are defined. Computers attached to frame relay circuits are thus notified that the network is discarding packets.

Frame relay provides another mechanism to maintain fairness among multiple senders. A *discard eligibility* indicator can be set by a sender or the network to indicate that certain frames are sacrificial lambs; i.e., if frames must be discarded, throw away the frames that have the DE flag set.

In theory, the DE bit may be used to guarantee some level of service (especially, throughput) to individual data link connections; i.e., the DE bit might be set in all frames of a given data link connection, but not set in the frames sent over a second data link connection, effectively assigning a higher priority of service to the users of the second data link connection. Under an arrangement such as this, an IP or CLNP network administrator can bias much of the *committed information rate* negotiated between the subscriber and network provider toward the (privileged) users of one data link connection. (Committed information rate is a subscription time parameter used by public frame relay providers that is an estimate of the user's "normal" throughput needs and a measure of the amount of data the public network promises to deliver.)

 The "features" of congestion notification and discard eligibility are often promoted imprudently in frame relay marketing. As

an indicator in an end-to-end datagram network-layer protocol like CLNP, a congestion-experienced notification can be conveyed to the transport layer, where mechanisms exist to reduce the rate of traffic introduced into a network by a source end system. Beyond the obvious marketing value of being able to say, "We notify you of congestion," the usefulness of these indicators in a data link protocol is questionable. Unless additional mechanisms are introduced in the network layer protocol operating over a frame relay service to propagate congestion-status information of the frame relay link back to all sources—for example, mapping the value of a BECN/FECN received across a frame relay link into the congestion-experienced bit of the CLNP header—the notification is an annoying no-op. (Well, not quite; routers that have SNMP agents can now count the number of FECNs and BECNs received, so one at least knows whether the frame relay network is overworked). And unless transport protocol entities operating at traffic sources "behave" and actually slow down the rate at which they introduce traffic, FECNs and BECNs have absolutely no effect on the rate of packet flow into the frame relay network. Finally, in multiprotocol environments (OSI, TCP/IP, etc.), relying on single-bit congestion notification can be dangerous: unless all network layer protocols propagate congestion notices, and all end system transport implementations react to this information by changing their rates of transmission uniformly, it is quite possible that those end systems that behave well will be penalized (they will slow down) and those that ignore the information will benefit (since others have slowed down, they may be able to continue at their present rate without penalty).

It's easy to sum up the "truthful" aspects of advertisement regarding discard eligibility: discard eligibility relies on cooperation on the part of all senders, all of whom will responsibly identify which of their data aren't important.

Both CNLP and IP implementations will treat frame relay as a point-to-point network. RFC 1294 describes IP encapsulation and operation over frame relay as part of a multiprotocol identification and encapsulation scheme. Each protocol that is to be transmitted across a frame relay circuit is identified using a 1-octet network layer protocol identifier (see Chapter 13), which must be the first octet encoded in the frame relay frame. Values assigned by ISO and CCITT distinguish among the OSI network layer protocols, and code points in the NLPID are also used to identify the encapsulated protocol as IP and the IEEE 802.1 SNAP. The NLPID value for SNAP is used for bridging purposes and also to indicate that the ethertype value is to be used to distinguish among the protocols that do not have an NLPID assigned to them[6] (see *Assigned Numbers*, RFC

---

6.   It seems that history is forever repeating itself. Standards makers, failing to heed the

1340). Encapsulation of CNLP over frame relay is not the subject of a standard, but in multiprotocol environments, it is expected that RFC 1294 will be applied. RFC 1294 also prescribes maximum packet sizes for frame relay networks and describes a means of negotiating a maximum frame size, a retransmission timer, and a maximum number of outstanding information frames, using HDLC exchange identification (XID) frames. Some frame relay networks (the switches, actually) support a maximum frame size of only 262 octets; since this is much smaller than the default maximum IP segment size of 576 octets, RFC 1294 defines a "convergence protocol" that must be used to segment IP packets before they are forwarded across such networks.

Address resolution over frame relay networks is a matter of associating a data link connection identifier with the IP address of a station on "the other side" of a permanent virtual circuit. The *inverse address resolution protocol* (INARP; RFC 1293) proceeds as follows. An IP station performs address resolution by (1) constructing an ARP request packet, (2) encapsulating the packet in a frame relay packet, and (3) sending it directly to the target DLCI (note that there is no notion of broadcast or group addressing of ARP requests over frame relay). The INARP request packet is essentially the same format as other ARP requests: the source IP address is provided, and the target IP address field is 0-filled; however, in the case of frame relay, the requesting station inserts DLCIs rather than conventional 48-bit LAN addresses in the source and target hardware address fields. Upon receiving an INARP request, the called, or target, station will typically place the requester's {IP address, DLCI} mapping into its ARP cache. The target station then composes an INARP reply using the source DLCI and IP addresses from the INARP request as the target addresses for the INARP reply and using its own DLCI and IP addresses to populate the source hardware and network protocol addresses, respectively. When the requesting IP station receives the INARP reply, it uses the {IP address, DLCI} address information from the INARP reply to complete its ARP cache.

Like SMDS, frame relay will be used primarily for local area network interconnection. It is a direct and cheap replacement for private lines. When switched virtual circuits are offered, frame relay will provide the virtual-circuit equivalent of any-to-any connectivity; until then, it is best suited for intraenterprise topologies.

---

lessons from the service access point debacle of the logical link control, also made the OSI NLPID a single-octet field and may again find themselves with insufficient code points to identify all the protocols that might be identified using the NLPID demultiplexing scheme.

Frame relay allows companies to supplant existing private lines with statistically multiplexed services at a lower cost per access line. This is attractive because it gives subscribers some interesting cost-performance trade-offs:

- Replace the existing private-line topology with corresponding frame relay permanent virtual circuits and reduce monthly communications costs. In this scenario, a network administrator would replace the private topology with permanent virtual circuits forming an identical virtual topology.
- Replace existing private lines with frame relay permanent virtual circuits and use the savings to enrich the topology by adding permanent virtual circuits. frame relay tariffs often have an access-connection component, an information-transfer (switching) component, and per permanent virtual circuit charges. The permanent virtual circuit charges are relatively low, so some or all of the savings accrued by converting to a switched service could be used to add permanent virtual circuits between routers, especially between routers where no private lines existed. They would improve overall network performance by eliminating one hop.
- Replace existing private lines with frame relay permanent virtual circuits and use the savings to enrich the topology by subscribing to higher-rate access connections. The reduction in monthly communications costs may be significant enough over a given topology to justify the use of a DS1 facility (or fraction thereof) rather than a 56 Kbps or 64 Kbps access connection.

Like SMDS, frame relay services are likely to be offered over increasingly higher-bandwidth access connections. If there is a market pull for it, 45 Mbps frame relay access will undoubtedly be offered.

There are currently two schools of thought regarding the evolution or migration of frame relay services to a broadband ISDN environment. School 1 recommends that the relatively straightforward process of mapping data from one virtual circuit onto another be used. Here, an interworking unit—a data link service bridge—will maintain a logical relationship between frame relay data link connection identifiers and broadband ISDN virtual circuit identifiers and will forward encapsulated data (e.g., IP or CLNP packets) between the two networks. School 2 recommends that the frame relay bearer service operate on the asynchronous transfer mode platform that supports all broadband ISDN services (see "Asynchronous Transfer Mode and Broadband ISDN," later in this chapter). Here, frame relay frames operate over asynchronous transfer mode and eventually SONET facilities as a native rather than an interworked service.

> *Why are fast packet services like SMDS, ETSI MAN, and frame relay more economical than private lines? The answer usually provided by packet-switching pundits is that they offer individual subscribers the economies of a switched environment, in which the resources are shared among the entire population of subscribers rather than dedicated to each individual subscriber. Historically, this sharing took place more often at what network-centrics call "the customer's premises"; private networks use routers to reduce the number of dedicated links they must pay for, handcrafting topologies that offer end users acceptable service while lowering the enterprise's monthly telecommunications costs (see Figure 15.15[a]). Fast packet services attempt to move more of the successful and profitable form of switching back into the telephone "central office" and apply the same logic. Providing a private line between two computers requires that the network provider dedicate and maintain a physical transmission facility from one customer site to the central office, then out again to a second customer site, for each private line; thus, computers that act as packet switches (routers) have multiple line terminations (see Figure 15.15[b]). With a fast packet service, a public service provider must dedicate only one link to each router—from the subscriber's site to the fast packet switch inside its central office (this link is often called a "tail"), thereby saving the cost of maintenance and provisioning for the "other tail" (see Figure 15.15[c]). Since maintenance of transmission facilities is a very large part of the cost of offering a telecommunications service, carriers can propose attractive rates to those who set tariffs. (Note that if the subscriber actually needs the aggregate bandwidth offered by multiple links, a higher access class [committed information rate] or higher-bandwidth transmission facility may be used instead.)*

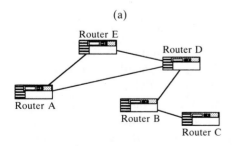

(a)

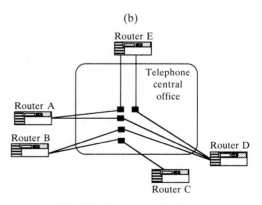

(b)

■ Central office line termination

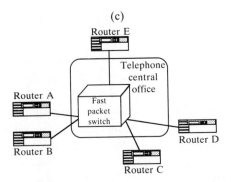

FIGURE 15.15   Anatomy of Router Interconnection Alternatives

Asynchronous Transfer Mode and Broadband ISDN

The DQDB MAN technology offers isochronous and queued-arbitrated services over the same physical medium; broadband ISDN promises this and more. Both DQDB MAN and BISDN accomplish this multiservice integration by using "cell" technology. In broadband ISDN, the chunks are called ATM cells (CCITT Recommendation I.361 1989); like DQDB slots, they are composed of a 5-octet header and a 48-octet payload. In a broadband integrated services environment, bandwidth can be flexibly allocated to support several forms of communications simultaneously, even when different amounts of bandwidth are required for each form. The network provides a steady stream of ATM cells, and stations attached to the network (multimedia stations) acquire ATM cells—on an as-needed basis, one at a time—to transmit voice, video, or data. From the available bandwidth, a station may acquire cells at fixed intervals to support voice calls and video (typically, 64 Kbps is required for a single voice call, whereas NTSC-quality video requires between 30 and 45 Mbps, and high-definition television may require anywhere from 140 to 500 Mbps) and on an as-needed basis to support a bursty datagram service like SMDS or a circuit-switched data service like frame relay.

Synchronous Transfer Mode and Asynchronous Transfer Mode   To understand the current popularity of ATM, it is useful to compare it with its predecessor, synchronous transfer mode (STM, also known as synchronous time division multiplexing). Synchronous transfer mode networks divide the bandwidth of a transmission line into units of time rather than cells. Every connection C that is multiplexed over an STM link is given one or more fixed time slots S for transmission over the link. At any instant in time, there can be at most C times S slots used; thus, a large value of S for a connection C assigns a large fraction of the total bandwidth of the STM link to C and correspondingly reduces the total number of connections that may share the link with C. Conversely, large values of C reduce the fraction of bandwidth that may be assigned to any given connection. If a single time slot represents 64 Kbps, for example, and 1 connection on a DS1 link is assigned 6 slots, then the bandwidth available for that connection is 384 KBps. The remaining bandwidth—approximately 1.1 megabits—can be assigned to other connections (there could be up to 17 connections having a bandwidth of 64 Kbps or 3 more connections having a bandwidth of 384 Kbps, etc.).

What's wrong with this scheme? Once time slots are assigned to a connection, the bandwidth represented by those time slots cannot be used to support other connections even if the connection is idle. This scheme is too inflexible if the transfer mode is to support a variety of applications (real-time data, voice and video, "bursty" data applications, etc.) that demonstrate different peak and average rates of transmission over a common medium; too much bandwidth must be reserved to accommodate the peaks, especially when the very high peak-to-average transmission ratio is considered.

Since synchronous transfer mode fell short of the expectations, folks turned to packet-switching techniques as a means of accommodating a wider range of transmission rates and unpredictable traffic loads. *Fixed-length* packets were selected so that constant bit rate channels could be emulated using a packet-switching technique. Small packets were selected to minimize delay. The resulting "microgram" is illustrated in Figure 15.16.

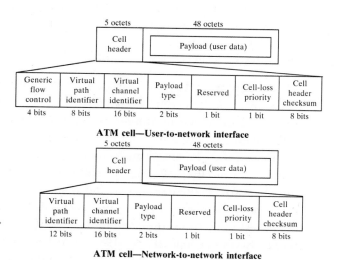

FIGURE 15.16   ATM Cell Structure

ATM Cell Structure   Actually, there are two forms of the microgram: the cell submitted by and delivered to customer communications equipment (i.e., across the *user-to-network interface [UNI]* and the cell that is transferred betwen ATM networks (i.e., across a *network-to-network interface [NNI]*). The initial field of the ATM user-to-network interface cell is a *generic flow indicator* (4 bits), which will be used for end-to-end flow control between ATM stations. A *virtual-path identifier* (8 bits) identifies the path between a source and destination ATM station pair, and a *virtual-channel identifier* (16 bits) defines a connection within the virtual path. A *payload type* (3 bits) identifies the contents of the payload (currently only one value, 0, for user information) and provides congestion notification. A *cell loss priority* (1 bit) is like the discard eligibility bit in frame relay. An 8-bit *cell header checksum* can be used to detect and in some cases correct errors in the cell header. The ATM network-to-network in-terface cell is identical in all but one respect to the ATM user-to-network interface cell: the UNI generic flow indicator is not present in the NNI cell and the virtual-path identifier is extended an additional 4 bits.

⟦·AHA·⟧   *To accommodate voice and perhaps real-time video without echo effects, the current wisdom is that fixed (or predictable) delay between cells/slots must be maintained. After considerable debate over packetization delay and packet length, CCITT, T1, and IEEE 802.6 converged on a chunk/cell/slot length of 53 octets (5 for the header, 48 for the payload). The number 48 is notable because it is a fine example of the standards process in action. There is little technological substance in the decision to use 48 octets; it is a compromise between the 64-octet payload originally specified in the DQDB MAN standard and the 32-octet payload preferred by CCITT and T1. "I like 32, you like 64. Let's meet somewhere in the middle . . ."*

ATM Adaptation Layers   Although they will be multiplexed/interleaved over the same cell/slot fabric, voice, video, and data services will use fixed-length cells in different ways; for example, a data service like SMDS could be implemented over a broadband ISDN platform and requires an IMPDU-to-cell mapping and SAR functions similar to those provided in the IEEE 802.6 architecture. The functions and protocols required to provide these services to the MAC layer (and similar services for voice and video) are placed at what is called the BISDN *ATM adaptation layer* (AAL; CCITT Recommendation I.362-1989), and there are several (CCITT Recommendation I.363-1989): AAL1 is provided for voice, AAL2 for video, AAL3 for mapping frame relay onto a cell fabric, and AAL4 is nearly identical to the IEEE 802.6 DQDB (see Figures 15.8 and 15.10). A recent addition to the ATM adaptation layer famly, AAL type 5, is the encapsulate of choice for IP. This adaptation layer provides IP packet delimiting and a 32-bit CRC error check, effectively providing the same framing as a local area network MAC frame (see Clapp [1992] for a complete description of ATM adaptation layers). An RFC in preparation will describe multprotocol encapsulation over ATM, including CLNP.

ATM is likely to appear in several offerings (see Figure 15.17). Speculating a bit, the authors suggest that these offerings are likely to appear in the following chronological order:

1. *Local ATM, or ATM LANs*: In this configuration, an ATM switch acts as a hub for communication between workstations in ATM work groups. The switch will provide dedicated bandwidth to each station, initially in permanent virtual circuit arrangements and later, when signaling is available, in a switched environment.
2. *Campus ATM*: Here, ATM switches compete against FDDI and other MAN technologies. The campus ATM network is shared by dedicated-bandwidth users and users who wish to interconnect local area networks over high-bandwidth, low-delay networks.
3. *Seamless ATM*: Here, ATM hubs interconnect campuses using private lines and provide ATM services across a wide area topology.
4. *Broadband ISDN and cell-relay services*: Public network providers offer permanent virtual circuit and switched cell-relay services. Subscribers will have access to constant and variable bit rate services, distinguished at subscription or call-setup time by interpacket arrival guarantees and cell loss probability.

ATM is most likely to succeed if (1) there is a LAN-based ATM "presence" in the workplace and an established need for very high bandwidth over the wide area; (2) the wide area cost is reasonable; (3) wide area ATM service is a ubiquitous and uniform offering (hard lessons learned from narrowband ISDN); and (4) there is a graceful migration from early broadband services like frame relay and SMDS to broadband ISDN. ATM is a seductive technology, but it is also very much a fledgling technology—a packet-switching technology having nearly all the complexities and baggage associated with scaling as IP and CLNP. To succeed, ATM will have to live up to some very ambitious market expectations (see especially Nolle [1993]).

Synchronous Optical Network (SONET)

SONET (ANSI T1. 105A-1990) is a fiber-optic transport system. The system combines a basic signal rate of 51.840 Mbps (synchronous transport signal—level 1, or STS-1) with a byte-interleaved multiplexing scheme to

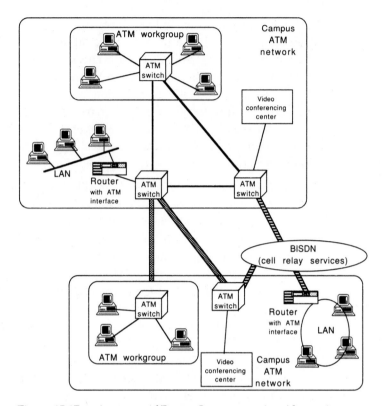

Figure 15.17   Anatomy of Router Interconnection Alternatives

create a hierarchy of higher-rate signals, with each higher-rate signal providing an integer multiple of the STS-1 signal. The convention for denoting these higher rates is STS-N, where $N = \{1, 3, 9, 12, 18, 24, 36, 48\}$; with transmission rates *beginning at* 51+ Mbps and defined for up to 2.5 Gbps, the SONET physical layer will play an important role in the much-heralded gigabyte networking strategies for the 1990s.

STS-1 frames (810 bytes, 6,480 bits) are transmitted at a rate of 8,000 frames per second (1 every 125 microseconds). *Transport overhead* bytes (those that deal with framing, synchronization, and the multiplexing of the STS-1 signal) and *payload overhead* bytes (those that deal with framing, synchronization, and the multiplexing of services) account for 36 bytes, leaving a payload of 774 bytes (6,192 bits) per frame, or 49.536 Mbps (see Figure 15.18). This is sufficient to convey an existing DS3 signal and will minimize the impact of this new technology on embedded digital transmission facilities.

STS-N signals are formed by interleaving bytes of N STS-1 signals.

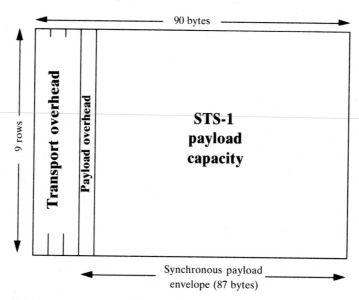

FIGURE 15.18   SONET STS-1 Frame

In the United States, STS-3 (155.52 Mbps) and STS-12 (622.08 Mbps) are expected to be offered as subscriber access rates. For broadband services such as SMDS (super-rate services), the synchronous payload envelopes of the constituent STS-1 frames will be concatenated (only one set of payload overhead bytes is used; see Figure 15.19, an example of an STS-3c frame).

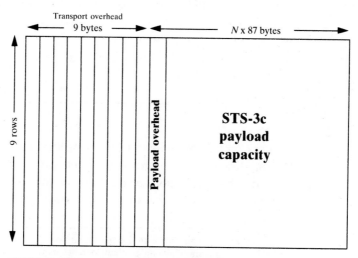

FIGURE 15.19   SONET STS-3c Frame

The impact of SONET will be more economical than technological. The existence of a standard for optical transmission systems will eventually make optical-to-electrical equipment a commodity, and commodity pricing will speed the deployment of fiber-based facilities by public telecommunications providers.

Very High Bandwidth as an Enabling Vehicle for OSI

It is often suggested that the protocol overhead associated with OSI's upper layers is so great that very high bandwidth is needed simply to establish an OSI application association; there are, for example, T-shirts that proclaim OSI to be "same-day service in a nanosecond world".[7] True, OSI's upper layers have lots of header bits, and the ASN.1 syntax hardly qualifies as a bit-economical form of data transfer, but (1) in a multimegabit environment, the overhead is not nearly so significant as it is in kilobit environments; (2) the flexibility introduced to the application writer may be worth the overhead; and (3) end users care about the net result of the application, not how it is encoded. And one simply cannot overlook the fact that ATM itself is hardly the model for packetizing efficiency. The fact remains that if ATM technology succeeds at providing very high bandwidth, and the cost is at or near the "willingness to pay," ATM platforms offer the potential to remove some encumbrances from distributed applications; if "bandwidth on demand" becomes the transmission norm, full-color imaging, recorded and real-time video, and high-fidelity audio can be integrated into distributed applications. OSI's upper layers provide standard tools to develop such applications, over OSI and Internet transport services; ATM/SONET facilities provide enough transport that standard tools may be worth the overhead.

Conclusion

Network architects sometimes imagine that networking happens from the "top down," because that is how network architectures are often constructed—the applications at the top are, after all, presumably the *raison d'être* of any network, so it makes sense to start with the requirements of

---

7.   Van Jacobson came up with this particular poke at OSI, which appears on the T-shirt just below a graphic in which an elephant perches happily, if precariously, on a telephone wire stretched between sagging poles.

distributed applications and let those determine the functions that must be provided by successively lower layers. OSI demonstrates this approach in its alternation of service definition and protocol specification at each layer; in the OSI standards community, the generally accepted practice has been for the group working on one layer to ask for "requirements" from the group working on the layer just above and to use those requirements to decide what should and should not be in the service definition for its layer. In the real world, however, things are not nearly so simple.

The technologies that populate the data link and physical layers of a network architecture do not arise in response to "requirements" expressed by standards developers working in the network layer. The research and engineering that produce a new communications technology—fiber-optic transmission systems, for example, or token-ring local area networks—are driven by a broad range of scientific and economic forces that are far stronger than the voices of standards developers (or network architects) calling for the inclusion of a particular function in "the data link layer" or a particular feature in "the data link service" because it will help them to design network-layer protocol standards. It is important, therefore to pay attention not just to what the service definitions for the two lower layers say *ought* to be provided but also to the actual capabilities of the link-level transmission technologies that have been and are constantly being applied to the construction of new data networks. In an open system standards context, the right question to ask about SMDS or ATM, for example, is not "Does it (or can it) provide the OSI data link service?" but "Could it be used as a subnetwork with an appropriate internetwork protocol?" No one who discovers a promising new data link transmission or switching scheme is likely to abandon it because "it doesn't provide the OSI physical or data link service!" The real story of the data link and physical layers, therefore, is not how they accommodate "requirements" from above but how they embrace and express within a networking architecture the communication capabilities that are perpetually welling up from the real world.

PART FIVE

THE FUTURE OF OPEN
SYSTEMS NETWORKING

16 MULTIPROTOCOL OPEN SYSTEMS

The world of open systems networking does not look the way industry pundits predicted it would less than a decade ago. The great open-system sirens of the eighties—homogeneity, uniformity, transition—are now largely silent; the new age of networking must embrace and accommodate what appears to be a permanently heterogeneous mix of technologies and standards. Having examined OSI and TCP/IP side by side and in some detail, it is instructive for us to discuss their present status in the real world and to speculate on their future.

The Myth of "OSI Migration"

By the mid-1980s, OSI was widely heralded as the gospel of a "new age" networking religion that would use the power of international standards to achieve for data networks the same ubiquitous, multivendor connectivity that is enjoyed by users of the international telephone network. Even proprietary network architectures that explicitly eschew "openness" in favor of "optimal performance" began applying the language of the OSI reference model to describe the way in which their protocols and services are organized (a favorite claim across the industry at that time was, "Our architecture conforms to the OSI reference model"). Industry pundits of the eighties predicted that OSI would eventually dominate the world of open systems networking, and the widely accepted inevitability of OSI at that time forced the issue of network evolution into a narrow box: specifically, how to manage a "transition," or "migration," from whatever one currently had to OSI.

Just as the evolution of a species is influenced by external conditions—climate, in particular—network evolution toward a single open systems networking technology has been affected by the climate of the information-processing marketplace, which has too many networking choices. TCP/IP, DECnet, IPX, SNA, and AppleTalk are "durable, if incompatible, and they just won't die peacefully."[1] At the same time that OSI was being touted as the networking technology of the future, network administrators were dealing with a major change in culture, as society embraced electronic mail, distributed file service, and LAN operating systems as part of its daily routine: networks were growing and the demands of users were changing, and a wholesale shift to a new technology was not a high priority in the field. Vendors seized the opportunity to extend the life cycle of existing technology rather than invest in a new one, and the standards process provided them with a convenient excuse: "critical-path" standards—notably, routing and management—were not yet completed, so many vendors decided to wait for closure before tackling OSI. Thus, the real networks of the world are running the bulk of their traffic over something other than OSI—SNA, DECnet, TCP/IP, or one of a host of LAN protocols (often referred to as "LAN operating systems").

Many real networks are running something best described as "all of the above and then some." In terms of deployment, the market presence of TCP/IP dwarfs that of OSI and is likely to continue growing at a rapid pace for many years, no matter how many GOSIPs (government OSI procurement regulations) are adopted by national governments. TCP/IP is now widely available and understood; it works; and it has benefited enormously from decades of steady improvement in both the protocols and their implementations. And it has carefully attended to the protection of the installed base: more often than not, changes are introduced only after lengthy evaluation of how those changes will affect TCP/IP networks already in operation.

The assertion that TCP/IP is fine for universities but will never make it in the commercial world—a myopic OSI bigot once called the Internet an "academic toy"—has been proved wrong: in 1990, 56 percent of the sales of TCP/IP-based networking equipment and software were in the traditional commercial market, and this figure is projected to rise to 77 percent by the end of 1993. It is important to recognize, too, that the

---

1.   A quote fron Dan Lynch, founder and chairman of Interop, Inc., and former member of the ARPANET team that assisted in the transition from NCP protocols to TCP/IP in the early 1980s, found in *Update: Interop '92 Spring*. If anyone would know about the difficulties of transitioning a network, it would be Dan.

strengths of OSI are for the most part also the strengths of TCP/IP; from a technical standpoint, the rationale for deployment of TCP/IP networks is no less compelling than the rationale for deployment of OSI networks. TCP/IP developers who recognize that there are useful lessons to be learned from the evolution of OSI (particularly in the upper layers) will be building and selling TCP/IP networks long after OSI has established itself in the marketplace.

It is also important to recognize that the TCP/IP marketplace itself is dwarfed by the cumulative share held by LAN operating systems such as Novell Netware and Banyan Vines and that proprietary networking solutions continue to hold a formidable share as well. These alternatives won't die peacefully either. They play an important role in mainstream distributed processing and will continue to do so despite bureaucratic efforts to the contrary.

OSI Is an Alternative, Not a Substitute

As a practical matter, perfect network homogeneity is no longer viewed as attainable or necessarily desirable. Marshall Rose's "D-day conjecture" was anything but farfetched: TCP/IP-based networks already offer OSI application services alongside TCP applications (Rose 1990, 551). The change in climatic conditions now forces the issue of network evolution onto an open field: the truly interesting issue is not how to provoke every conceivable network architecture through a "transition to OSI" but how to accommodate heterogeneity within a *multiprotocol* network architecture. OSI is no longer the only alternative; it is one among many, and it will have to survive by the virtue of its own strengths.

So what *are* OSI's strengths? Although it is often most harshly attacked, one strength of OSI is its status as an international standard. This is of relatively small importance to a considerable proportion of the Internet community which tends to exclude the politics and diplomacy of international networking from its list of valid concerns; however, for others, the imperatives driving the international acceptance of OSI were —and remain—impressive. OSI standards represent a powerful international alignment of computer vendor and telecommunication carrier interests in market stability and predictability, augmented by the emergence of GOSIPs, which may ultimately have the political effect of making OSI the norm, rather than the exception, in many large contract bids. Whether networking technology should be determined by political fiat is not at issue here; it is simply a fact that certain organizations will (perhaps dogmatically) accept OSI because they feel they must. It should also be noted that a lucrative marketplace for OSI continues to exist among companies that believe that OSI is a strategic imperative—for example, telecommunications equipment and service vendors, which constitute a huge market for OSI to support public directory and message-handling services as well as internal "operations" (management services).

Another of OSI's strengths is its applications infrastructure. From a technical standpoint, the elaborate OSI upper-layer architecture—often maligned as unnecessarily complex and a performance-stifling burden— will be increasingly important as sophisticated distributed-processing applications enter the computing mainstream. Much of this is in evidence today, as the Internet community experiments with the OSI directory and message-handling applications over ISODE, RFC 1006, and TCP/IP. The OSI Directory has become an increasingly important tool to the Internet; efforts to improve the response time for directory queries, complemented by efforts to reduce the overhead of directory user agents so that they can run easily on desktop computers, will undoubtedly make the OSI Directory a finer tool.

Because this book discusses OSI and TCP/IP together, it is inevitable that the future of OSI will be highly colored with the perspective of "the future of OSI in the Internet." But advocacy for OSI message-handling and directory services exists outside the Internet community to an even greater extent than within. It is instructive to note that corporate internets that have little or no connectivity to the Internet (due, in some cases, to a conscious effort to ensure complete privacy and security) and that have, in some cases, little or no TCP/IP (especially environments in which PC and mainframe OSs are pervasive and UNIX is virtually nonexistent) see OSI message-handling and directory services as providing a welcome reprieve from the proliferation of PC, proprietary, and homebrew mail gateways and directory services. Not surprisingly, the absence of a single, dominant mail system like the Internet's SMTP and a universal name system like the DNS in these environments has played to the advantage of OSI.

OSI's lower layers are also often treated with disdain, primarily because of the exaggerated "connections versus connectionless" interworking problem, but also because of performance. Both of these criticisms will disappear over time. OSI's strength in the lower layers is that in architecture and implementation, it is very similar to TCP/IP. A very positive side effect of GOSIPs is that they have forced system designers, implementers, and users to build and use "first-generation" OSI products, if only to satisfy a checklist item on a "request for proposal" from a government agency. As a consequence of being coerced into implementing or, worse still, *using* OSI, implementers have begun to realize that the widely advertised problems of performance and resource utilization are not due to some inherently threatening "OSI baggage"; instead, they discover that OSI's lower layers can benefit from the experience and engineering expertise that have come gradually with TCP/IP. It is easy to forget that TCP/IP as it stands in 1993 is the result of nearly two decades of improvement and refinement. And as with TCP/IP, experiments to trim fat from OSI will happen only after the fat has been distinguished from the muscle. The process of improving OSI performance will accelerate as the expertise acquired by TCP/IP engineers is applied to the implementation and refinement of OSI protocols—assuming, of course, that the TCP/IP engineers continue to overcome their initial disdain for OSI and that the OSI developers pay attention to what the TCP/IP engineers have to say.

It is a small matter of time and experience before improvements to OSI's underlying transport service and solutions to the "connectionless versus connection-oriented" interworking problem make these nonissues as well. Implementations of OSI's transport class 4 have already been improved by the use of slow-start algorithms, dynamic window-adjustment mechanisms, and other forms of congestion avoidance and control that are commonplace in TCP implementations. Implementers are also beginning to understand that in some cases—notably, the issue of efficiency in checksums—"apples are not being compared to apples"; the checksum used in TCP is faster, but the one used in TP4 is stronger.

The "connections versus connectionless" debate may also end soon. Although ISO has developed and adopted a technical report describing a recommended means of interworking between connection-oriented and connectionless networks (ISO/IEC TR 10172: 1991), and the very fine work of folks like Jeremy Onions has provided us with useful transport service bridges, the authors speculate that attention to the "Tinkertoy transports and X.25" will wane as the decade closes, even among PTTs and public network providers, and that the application of TP4 over ISO CLNP as *the recommended* underlying transport service will be widespread. This speculation is based partly on the authors' conviction that this is technically the right choice, also on the steadily increasing interest in IP and connectionless metropolitan-area network services throughout Europe and North America.

In the minds of some, OSI will never be acceptable, in any form; and although it is unlikely ever to be the universal panacea for networking, it most certainly will do useful work for a sizable population. In the

Internet, it coexists alongside TCP/IP today and will continue to do so for the forseeable future.

OSI and TCP/IP Coexistence: Networking Détente

If integration, rather than migration, has become the issue, the question remains "how to make it happen." To date, several alternatives have been deployed with varying degrees of success. Some of these were introduced and discussed in Marshall Rose's *Open Book* in the context of "transition to OSI"; here, the authors examine these alternatives with the luxury of hindsight, considering whether and how each has been applied or extended and also placing the discussion in the context of "coping with a multiprotocol environment."

Dual and "Multiple" Stacks

The simplest solution to the problem of multiple protocol architectures in the Internet is to run each protocol "stack" independently in each system. Figure 16.1 illustrates how OSI and TCP/IP can be deployed as "dual stacks," but the principle applies for multiple stacks as well. In the dual-stack approach, OSI and TCP/IP applications and protocols coexist but do not interoperate—although they may be engineered to share the avail-

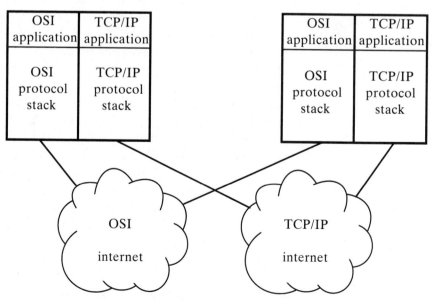

FIGURE 16.1   The Dual-Stack Approach

able underlying physical transmission resources (link drivers, repeaters, and cables) and switching resources (bridges and multiprotocol routers) when economies result from their doing so.

The dual-stack approach is sometimes called *ships in the night,* or S.I.N. The metaphor of ships "passing in the night"—independently and without interaction—captures the sense of multiple protocol suites communicating over the same network links, ostensibly without interference, in much the same way as independent telephone conversations can be carried over a common set of telephone wires and switches. It should be noted that multiple protocol stacks have operated over LAN technologies such as Ethernet for years: with the advent of multiprotocol routers, the multistack approach has become nearly ubiquitous in the Internet today. The NSFnet has been capable of switching both CLNP and IP datagrams since 1990. Many regional, national agency, international, and connected ("stub") subnetworks now offer CLNP as well as IP connectivity to both single- and dual-stack hosts. (Figure 16.2 depicts the approximate CLNP connectivity across the Internet as of March 1993.) Member sites in these networks are piloting, experimenting with, or have in production one or more OSI application services, including file transfer (FTAM), virtual terminal, electronic mail (X.400), and directories (X.500).

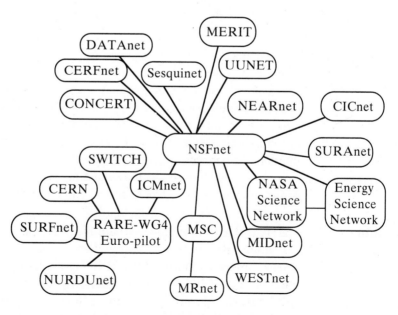

FIGURE 16.2   Internet CLNP Connectivity
("Stub" Networks Not Illustrated)

Dual (multiple) stacks are often the only way to accommodate more than one protocol suite within a single system. However, the drawbacks discussed in the *Open Book* remain in evidence today:

- The dual-stack (multiple-stack) approach is *expensive*, since it requires "two (many) of everything": network management, software, protocol overhead, on-call systems-engineering expertise, and administration of addresses, operation, software and equipment updates, and access control. This solution is expensive in the traditional interpretation as well, as it often requires more CPU, more memory, and more storage to operate.
- It *affects all systems*. Hosts, in particular, must have two (many) of everything, and where multiprotocol switching systems (routers, bridges) cannot be deployed, parts of the infrastructure must be duplicated (multiplied).
- It often affects *performance*. Absent a perfect "memory and CPU are cheap" utopia, running two or more protocol stacks costs.
- It is difficult to achieve transparency. The UNIX *socket()* interface provides access to both OSI and TCP/IP, but the services are distinct. The same is true for the X/Open Transport Interface (XTI) and various application program interfaces (APIs); transparency is an elusive target.
- Unless all systems have dual (multiple) stacks, there will not be complete interoperability.

Unless the protocol suites are implemented and deployed very carefully, it may not be possible to avoid interference. When both protocol suites are operated over the same transmission facilities, for example, and both do not subscribe to the same philosophy of congestion avoidance, the effectiveness of such feedback mechanisms as explicit "congestion-experienced bits" is compromised. Even when it is possible to prevent direct interference between two different protocol suites, the metaphorical ships cannot pass obliviously, as they must be subject to at least some form of common system-management and resource-utilization arbitration.

Application Gateways

The dual-stack (multiple-stack) approach typically accommodates diversity among protocol suites everywhere except at the very bottom of the stacks, where common physical interconnections among systems can often be shared (this includes common data-link layer framing as well). Although this permits different protocol suites to share transmission resources (with the constraints and compromises noted earlier), it does not provide for any interaction among them—although systems running different stacks may be able to communicate at the level of their common links, their applications cannot interoperate. This adversely affects end users who are unfortunate (or wise) enough to have a single-stack host, since they cannot run the same distributed applications everywhere and to everyone; it also affects those fortunate enough to have a dual-stack host, because they must distinguish the end users reachable over one stack from those reachable over the other. Rose (1990) and others describe a sort of meta-application to deal with this sticky business—i.e., to hide the decision-making uglies from the end user—but this involves even more software (a directory service or a local cache-inquiry mechanism) and administration.

Adding an "application gateway" to a dual-stack configuration addresses the problem of application interoperability by establishing well-defined (and accessible) points at which the intrinsic semantics of an application—electronic mail, for example, or file transfer—can be extracted from the protocols of one stack and translated into the corresponding protocols of another stack (see Figure 16.3). This approach permits applications within each protocol suite to interoperate homogeneously with applications of their own kind (e.g., X.400 [1984] MHS with X.400 [1988] MHS), yet also bridges the gap to a foreign protocol suite by passing through a gateway that preserves the essential semantics of the application (e.g., electronic mail) while converting or translating the application protocols into alternatives that are compatible with the foreign protocol suite (e.g., Internet mail *à la* SMTP). This is a widely practiced

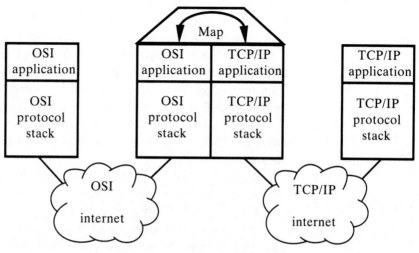

FIGURE 16.3   The Application Gateway Approach

method of interconnecting users in the Internet today.

Application gateways are natural for some applications, such as store-and-forward electronic mail, that are designed to pass through application-relay points in the normal course of events even in a homogeneous environment. The results are much less satisfying for other distributed applications—networked operating systems, file systems, distributed database systems—where the paradigm for such distributed systems may differ radically: an application gateway situated between clients and servers of AT&T's Remote File Service and Sun's Network File System is decidedly more complicated than one involving X.400–to–RFC 822 mail; the entire paradigm for a distributed filestore differs more than one would ever hope to reconcile in a gateway.

Application gateways also permit network managers to establish and monitor a strong administrative boundary between a local application environment (the campus mail network, for example) and the rest of the Internet; this is sometimes referred to as "outside-world contraception." And in some cases, of course, an application gateway is the only way to glue two otherwise oblivious environments together without changing an operating system software in which the lower-layer protocol implementations are embedded.

The unavoidable "least-common-denominator" effect of an application gateway is its worst drawback; users whose electronic mail traverses an X.400-1988–to–RFC 822 mail gateway, for example, may only be able to send transparent ASCII text in the interpersonal message (and similarly, MIME users to X.400-1984 MHS). Users will generally have to be keenly aware of the presence of the gateway (especially true when one is dealing with electronic mail addresses), and conduct their communications accordingly, in order to achieve success. Every type of application, of course, requires its own special type of application gateway, and the problem is exacerbated each time another stack is introduced—a separate gateway or extension is then required for every pair of *like* applications (an X.400 MHS–to–RFC 822 mail gateway is a separate ordeal from an SMTP to PC LAN-based mail/messaging gateway); this is exactly the situation in which many corporate internets having no "core" TCP/IP service find themselves.

Because the gateway must perform a fairly complicated transformation on the data flowing through it, it often represents a performance bottleneck (for some applications, such as electronic mail, the performance degradation is unobtrusive). Users must ensure that only one application gateway intervenes between the source and destination systems, since it is generally true that application gateways do not chain well. If an

FTAM-to-FTP gateway is used to transfer a file, for example, and the original FTAM virtual filestore was other than one of the file structure/data representations handled by FTP, a gateway will make a best effort at matching the virtual filestore, but without altering FTP, some information about the original filestore will be lost. If that file passes through a (subsequent) FTP-to-FTAM gateway, it won't be possible to reconstruct the file in the original filestore, and so despite the fact that the file originated from and was delivered to an FTAM application, the original file will differ from the one delivered.

Finally, the proliferation of application gateways tends to carve up the Internet into xenophobic nation-states with heavily guarded border crossings and long lines at customs and immigration—quite different from the "universal connectivity" goal of most network designers.

Transport Service Bridge

It is, of course, not strictly necessary to go all the way up the protocol stack to the application before establishing a point at which translation from the protocols of one suite into those of another can be made. In the "transport service bridge" approach, the end-to-end characteristics of the transport service of a given protocol suite (e.g., the OSI transport service) are provided using the transport protocol of another protocol suite (e.g., TCP [RFC 1006). (See Figure 16.4 as well as Chapter 12.) End users may then use the same applications despite having different underlying transports.

The appeal of the transport service bridge approach lies in the fact that it requires no changes to host (end-system) software—as long as all

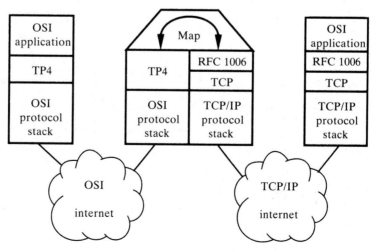

FIGURE 16.4   The Transport Service Bridge Approach

the systems that wish to communicate (1) mimic the same (OSI) transport service and (2) run the same (OSI) application. The transport service bridge is essentially an "interworking unit" in OSI terminology. Rather than relaying the OSI network service, the transport service bridge relays transport service primitives (see Figure 16.5); when, for example, an OSI application residing on the pure-stack OSI system "brady" attempts to establish an association with an OSI application on the hybrid-stack system "bunch" (in which TCP/IP provides the OSI network service), the following primitive sequence occurs:

1. The application on "brady" initiates an association; the upper-layers connection requests are composed, and a T-CONNECT.request is issued. Assuming for this example that TP4 and CLNP are used, the connect request packet is forwarded to a network address associated with the transport service bridge (rather than to the actual destination network address). A T-CONNECT.indication is passed up to the transport service bridge junction (denoted as event 1 in Figure 16.5).

2. The transport service bridge examines the TSAP address information (contained in the T-CONNECT.indication) and determines

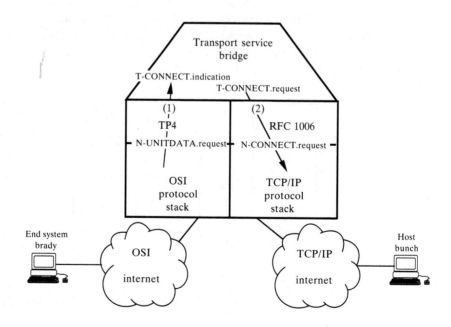

FIGURE 16.5   Transport Service Bridge

from a local "transport-bridging table" that an RFC 1006 host is the target for this connection. Extracting the actual destination TSAP address, port, and IP number from the table, the transport service bridge generates a T-CONNECT.request and attempts to establish a transport connection between itself and a transport server on "bunch" (denoted as event 2 in Figure 16.5).

3. Per RFC 1006, the T-CONNECT.request results in the establishment of a transport connection between the transport server at "bunch" and the transport service bridge using a protocol functionally identical to OSI transport protocol class 0 over TCP.

4. When the transport connection to "bunch" has been established, the transport service bridge confirms the establishment of the transport connection between itself and "brady."

5. The upper-layer connection-establishment protocol packet is transferred from "brady" to the transport service bridge in TP4 data packets; at the bridge, the upper-layer protocol packet is forwarded over the TCP connection to "bunch" using the packetization scheme described in RFC 1006. The upper-layer connection-acceptance protocol packet is returned over the reverse path. Following completion of the upper-layer connection-establishment process, data exchanges follow the same course.

The transport service boundary is often implemented as a programmatic interface between user programs and the host operating system. Chapter 12 describes how multiple transport stacks are accommodated in UNIX by extending the set of *socket()* types to include "sequenced packet" (seqpacket); other operating systems offering direct access to transport services can apply similar extensions. The text description of the transport server in RFC 1006 is a mere 8 pages; one might suspect that transport service bridges similar to the one that makes use of RFC 1006 can easily be defined for other non-OSI protocol architectures as well.

In fact, a transport service bridge offers a more attractive and simpler method of solving the problem of connection-oriented versus connectionless interworking in OSI than the transport relay described in ISO/IEC TR 10172: 1991, since it easily accommodates scenarios in which hosts using TP4 over CLNP wish to communicate with hosts using TP0 over X.25. The transport service bridge approach today is a deployed and expedient choice for users who would like to introduce OSI applications into an existing internet gradually and with little or no disruption of day-to-day operations as well as users who have to cope with multiple OSI network services.

The transport service bridge approach succeeds more often than the application gateway approach in preserving not merely the essential semantics but all semantics of end-user applications. As one might expect, however, the transport service bridge approach is not without its problems. The transport service bridge terminates the transport protocol on either side, interrupting the end-to-end transport features of flow control, error detection and correction, and congestion avoidance (the latter usually a collaboration with underlying network protocols). It also completely breaks any security mechanisms that rely on cryptographic protection of transport protocol header information (such as sequence numbers). A transport service bridge represents a single point of failure in an otherwise dynamically adaptive internetwork. Also, because it must "spoof" the network addresses (so that each party thinks it is talking to the other, when in fact it is talking to the transport service bridge), it makes it much more difficult to diagnose routing problems in the internet.

|·AHA·| *Contrary to popular belief, the operation of a packetization protocol over TCP described in RFC 1006 is not the only (nor the first) example of using a transport protocol to provide the OSI connection-oriented network service. In the mid-1980s, United Kingdom representatives to ISO introduced a variation of OSI TP4 called "network protocol 4 (NP4)" and proposed it as an alternative to further modifying X.25 PLP for use in providing the connection-oriented network service over connectionless local area networks. NP4 was a TP4 clone capable of conveying OSI NSAP addresses rather than TSAP addresses and could run over CLNP or IEEE 802 LANs (encapsulated in logical link control type 1 frames). NP4 would interwork at the network layer (between a private and public network) with the X.25 packet level protocol. It failed to catch on for the simple reason that it was not X.25, and not CLNP, and so had no natural constituency in the standards-development community.*

Hybrid Stacks

The big win for transport service bridges (and transport relays, although with greater complexity) is that they accommodate a "mix and match" of applications across multiple transport fabrics. In principle, and with appropriate transport service bridges, one can run OSI applications over TCP/IP, AppleTalk, etc. The transport service bridge most widely used today is the OSI transport service bridge based on RFC 1006; however, with a transport service bridge designed to provide TCP's stream service, one could certainly run TCP/IP applications over OSI transports.

Encapsulation

In some cases, the problem of multiprotocol interoperability is not how to talk to a foreign host or application but simply how to transit a network that doesn't support a given protocol stack to reach a compatible host or application on the other side. A specific example of such a scenario is one in which the path between two OSI networks is an IP-based network. One way to solve this problem is for the IP-based network to play the role of a "subnetwork" for an OSI network (Figure 16.6). The IP-based network—perhaps the entire TCP/IP Internet—is treated as a point-to-point subnetwork (link), and CLNP data units are simply "encapsulated" in IP datagrams in order to "tunnel" to the friendly system on the other side.

This approach, of course, works equally well if the roles of CLNP and IP are reversed, or if other network protocols are encapsulated for the purpose of tunneling AppleTalk, XNS/IPX, etc. In such configurations, a CLNP network provides a point-to-point link for IP. The principal advantage of this approach is its near transparency—neither network needs to be aware of the protocols of the other, since one network is acting as a simple point-to-point link between two systems belonging to the other. Hosts are unaffected (actually, they have no idea what's going on), and the integrity of transport services is preserved.

Encapsulation does not solve the host interoperability problem; hosts communicating over a path that includes a tunnel lack awareness of the existence of hosts in the network providing the tunnel and do not have the wherewithal to talk to them. Routing is collectively more complicated, since it is taking place independently at two different levels

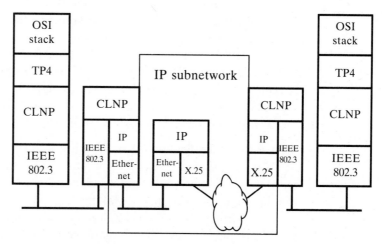

FIGURE 16.6   The Encapsulation Approach

(network and "subnetwork") for paths that include a tunnel (good news for router vendors). Over some paths—if one tunnels across the Internet using the standard 576-octet IP datagram maximum segment size, for example—link efficiency goes to hell in a handbasket.

At present, no standard exists for operating OSI's connectionless network protocol (CLNP) over TCP/IP's internetwork protocol. Although conceptually straightforward, details such as the identification of "encapsulated" protocols, efficient route selection, the use of IP addresses as "subnetwork addresses," segmentation efficiency, and packet size negotiation must be considered. Tunneling, however, is widely practiced across the Internet and is not restricted to the network layer; IBM SNA traffic is frequently encapsulated in TCP/IP packets, and AppleTalk traffic is conveyed using IP encapsulation (and vice versa in AppleTalk networks).

Bringing OSI into a Network

For some, the question remains, "Given these alternatives, how do I bring OSI into my network?" Here, then, is a practical scenario.

Step 1: Introduce OSI Applications in a "Hybrid-Stack" Environment
Bring OSI applications to TCP/IP hosts by (1) using the RFC 1006 techniques to run the OSI upper layers over the TCP transport interface provided by the host operating system software and (2) using application gateways (particularly for electronic mail) to tie together OSI and TCP/IP application environments that cannot be changed. The benefit of this method of introduction is that end users get to play with OSI applications while the network infrastructure remains the same (see the network administrator smile). End users also don't have to completely cut over to new applications—the existing applications remain available. OSI applications still don't talk to TCP/IP applications, but needs in this area can be satisfied with gateways. Note that by applying the RFC 1006 principles, this strategy can be employed in corporate internets that have "core" transport services other than TCP/IP.

Step 2: Build TS Bridges Use TS bridges to bring new OSI-only hosts into the TCP/IP network as they become available. Dual-stack hosts may be configured to use either transport service; the choice will depend on the direction the "internet" is taking (e.g., if there is to be an eventual cutover to primarily OSI service, it might be desirable to bring dual-stack hosts onto the OSI backbone). Again, note that by applying the transport service bridge principles, this strategy can be employed in corporate internets that have "core" transport services other than TCP/IP.

Step 3: Expand the Network Infrastructure to Include OSI   As OSI-only or multiprotocol routers (which can route both OSI and TCP/IP traffic) replace or complement IP-only routers in the network, begin to use OSI transport services as host operating system software with embedded OSI transport comes on line. If absolutely necessary, carry TCP/IP-only hosts along with IP-over-CLNP encapsulation.

If homogeneity is an absolute must for a given enterprise network, and OSI is an imperative, routers initially placed to switch both CLNP and IP datagrams can be gradually configured to switch only CLNP data units, and traffic from TCP/IP hosts can be tunneled using CLNP. This is a highly unlikely scenario for the Internet; rather than solving interoperability problems, it merely swings the pendulum to the left rather than the right.

Step 4: Learn to Rely on Names, Not Numbers   Wherever possible, rely on a centrally administered (if operationally distributed) directory service to keep track of the mappings between names and the attributes associated with them.

Why Is This Scenario Practical?

OSI has been—and continues to be—successfully introduced into parts of the existing Internet, alongside TCP/IP using steps 1 through 3 (step 4 is coming). OSI applications appeared first in the Internet over ISODE and RFC 1006, and gateway experiments followed shortly thereafter. From the gateway experiences, the Internet community learned to appreciate the transport service bridge approach and has popularized it.

The evolution toward a "dual-stack" Internet (step 3) has proceeded in the same fashion as ripples spreading out from a stone thrown into a pond. The NSFnet staff introduced CLNP alongside IP in the backbone while most end users were busily going about their business running applications over IP, and others were experimenting with ISODE and OSI applications over RFC 1006. Several regional and commercial IP subnetworks are now proceeding with their introduction of CLNP in the same manner, and the attached "stub" networks, encouraged by the presence of backbone CLNP connectivity, are likely to follow suit. Applications running on OSI and dual-stack hosts can reach IP-only hosts of the Internet via transport service bridges and application gateways.

Are the Instrumentation and Expertise Available to Operate OSI Networks?

Network administrators who remain skeptical or unconvinced will ask, "What problems can I expect to run into when I introduce OSI into my network?" OSI demonstrations at Interop and continued OSI testing across the Internet have revealed a great deal of what one can expect when integrating OSI alongside TCP/IP (Hares92, Connexions). Initially, there will be a limited pool of network operators and engineers familiar with OSI protocols. Tools for diagnosing problems with OSI protocols exist, but not for all products. Fortunately, the Network OSI Operations (NOOP) Working Group in the IETF, along with working groups in RIPE and RARE, are preparing the way for OSI operations staff in emerging OSI environments. There is, for example, an OSI equivalent to *ping* (RFC 1139), which has been incorporated into the second edition of CLNP. There is also an OSI *traceroute* that uses increasing values of the CLNP lifetime field of the echo packet in the same manner as IP trace-route uses time-to-live. Implementations will gradually offer utilities such as routing table dumps. Multiprotocol systems in particular may use TCP/IP's Simple Network Management Protocol over OSI (RFC) to collect routing information from the CLNS management information base (RFC 1238), while purist-stack OSI implementations may use the OSI common management information protocol (CMIP) to accomplish the same feats.

Many of these problems may all but disappear if the Network Layer OSI Operations working group of the IETF is successful in establishing a permanent, readily available OSI test bed within the Internet. The Internet community has benefited for years from the practice of using the resources of the community—the Internet protocols and applications—to understand how networks work, and the community has openly shared its experiences conducting daily IP operations. There is no reason to assume that the same recipe should not succeed for OSI.

Conclusion

The Internet becomes more commercialized each day. The cost of "Internet access" through electronic mail is in some places comparable to the cost of plain old telephone service. Even "host access" is within reach of small-business and residential consumers. On-line information available via the Internet is no longer confined to science, engineering, and technology, and information retrieval tools make navigating through the "maze of data" child's play. You can even send electronic mail to the White House; more importantly, the White House can send electronic mail to Congress!

Whether any of the competing technologies now deployed throughout the Internet or in enterprise networks is "best" has become a largely irrelevant question. The Internet *is* multiprotocol, and is likely to remain so for the forseeable future, if not forever. The application of gateways, hybrid stacks, service bridges, and tunneling described in this chapter will inevitably grow as people who neither know nor care what protocol stack they use make the Internet as fundamental to their daily lives as the telephone.

17

AN ARCHITECTURAL ALTERNATIVE FOR THE INTERNET

A common thread and an inherent weakness among the existing alternatives for bringing OSI and other protocols into the Internet is that they approach the problem in a patchwork fashion. A potential alternative to the four methods described in Chapter 16 for accommodating multiple protocols in the Internet has emerged from a series of workshops sponsored by the Internet Architecture Board. Consideration of the way in which the concept of "the Internet" has evolved since its inception has led to the formulation of a proposal that might be called "a new multiprotocol architecture for the Internet." In this chaper, the authors present a brief and highly speculative look into the possible future of the Internet.[1]

What Is "the Internet"?

It is very difficult to deal constructively with the issue of "the multiprotocol Internet" without first determining what "the Internet" is (or should be). In this context, it is important to distinguish the Internet (a set of communicating systems) from the Internet community (a group of people and organizations). Most people would accept a loose definition of the latter as "the group of people who regard themselves as being part of the Internet community"; however, no such "sociological" definition of the Internet itself is likely to be useful.

---

1.   These ideas emerged at the Internet architecture workshop held at the San Diego Supercomputer Center in June 1991. The participants in that workshop deserve much of the credit—such as it may be—for the contents of this chapter; see RFC 1287.

The scope of the Internet has traditionally been defined by the existence of IP connectivity. IP and ICMP were and remain the only "required" Internet protocols. It has been relatively easy to identify a host or router as a participant in the Internet; namely, if my host (router) could ping your host (router) and yours could ping mine, then we were both on the Internet. From this relatively simple test, a very satisfying, and eminently workable, definition of the Internet—transitive closure of IP-speaking systems (see Figure 17.1)—is thus constructed.

Until recently, the IP-connectivity model clearly distinguished systems that were "on the Internet" from those that were not. As the Internet has grown, and the technology on which it is based has gained widespread commercial acceptance, the notion of what it means for a system to be on the Internet has expanded to include the following:

- Any system that runs the TCP/IP protocol suite, whether or not it is actually accessible from other parts of the Internet
- Any system that can exchange RFC 822 mail (without the intervention of mail gateways or mail object transformations)
- Any system with E-mail connectivity to the Internet, whether or not a mail gateway or mail object transformation is required

These definitions of "the Internet," however, remain limited, for they are still based on the original concept of connectivity and merely percolate the addressing upon which connectivity is based up the stack to a "host" level rather than an IP level (e.g., if I can somehow convey enough information in an E-mail address to identify my host unambiguously to the recipient of my mail, there's a good chance the recipient will find a reciprocal path, be it through BITNET, UUCP, RFC 822 mail, or whatever).

A new definition of "the Internet" has been proposed, one that is

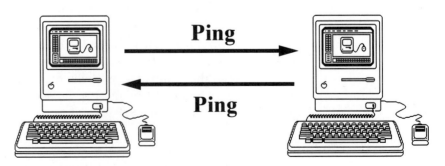

FIGURE 17.1   The "ping" Model of the Internet

based on a more powerful and *unifying* concept. Whereas the "old Internet" concept relied on IP connectivity—in which the IP address served as the fundamental, organizing principle and provided a common network address space—the "new Internet" is based on the notion of application name space. Specifically, the organizing principle is the existence of the domain name system and directories; viz., the ping test for connectivity becomes a name game.

A Naming-based Concept of Internet Connectivity

In the "new Internet," the idea of "connected status"—traditionally bound to the IP address—is coupled to the names (and related identifying information) contained in the distributed Internet directory (see Figure 17.2).

A naming-based definition of "the Internet" implies a much larger Internet community and a much more dynamic (and unpredictable) operational Internet. This argues for an Internet architecture based on adaptability to a broad spectrum of possible future developments. Rather than specifying a particular "multiprotocol Internet," comprised of a predetermined number of specific protocol architectures, the proposal instead presents a process-oriented model of the Internet, which accommodates different protocol architectures—new members—according to the traditional "protocols and combinations that do useful work" principle that permeates the Internet community and keeps the Internet itself from falling to pieces.

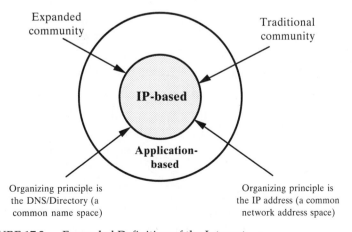

FIGURE 17.2   Expanded Definition of the Internet

The process-oriented model of the Internet asserts that there is no *steady-state* "multiprotocol Internet." Protocols and combinations may be added to the Internet as their usefulness, openness, and widespread use are demonstrated (in this model, it is also conceivable that a protocol or combination that ceases to be useful may be weeded from the Internet). A major assumption here is that everyone would agree that it is better to adapt and be connected than to be isolated or partitioned from the global community.

This seems to suggest that the forces driving the evolution of the Internet are pushing it toward multiprotocol diversity. Not so. Although we may never adopt a single "pure" stack, we may achieve a catholic notion of protocol-stack uniformity by adaptation and hybridization of stacks. Current wisdom suggests that the tendency of the Internet is to evolve toward what may be described as a "thermodynamically stable" state, defined through four components of the process-based Internet architecture (see Figure 17.3).

Component 1: The "Core" Internet Architecture

The traditional TCP/IP-based architecture will remain the "magnetic center" of Internet evolution. This is not a statement of superiority but merely a recognition that (1) having something that people can point to as the common thread that holds the Internet together is good, and (2) IP connectivity remains that common thread. The argument here is as follows. The success of the Internet has stretched IP to its limits, and IP by itself can no longer be the lone measure of connectivity. For the Internet to extend further, other protocols must coexist; however, regardless of whether or not the actual state of IP ubiquity can be achieved in practice

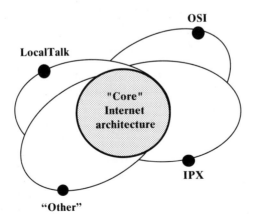

FIGURE 17.3   The Process Model of the Internet

in a global operational Internet, it is generally recognized that "getting there using IP" is a good thing.

Two additional components of the new Internet architecture express the ways in which the scope and extent of the Internet have been expanded.

Component 2: "Link Sharing"

Physical resources (transmission media, network interfaces) will be shared by multiple, noninteracting protocol suites. The necessity and convenience of coexistence at this level is not at issue; issues of how common resources are to be managed, how to minimize the degree to which protocol suites interfere with each other, and how to create "equal access" in real Internet systems are critical to the continued success of the Internet. The Internet cannot grow without new controls or the means to extend existing controls across a multiprotocol platform; without these, prospects for a multiprotocol Internet would be grim.

What controls are needed and for what resources? Currently, there are communities interested in providing type of service routing, effective implementation of the notions of IP precedence, CLNP priority, and OSI's embarrassingly vague QOS within the framework of the existing "best-effort delivery," datagram environment of the Internet. There is a desire to introduce alongside these improvements an effective means of allocating or reserving resources so that applications such as packet voice, video, and teleconferencing might be supported across the Internet. These imply capabilities that are not currently accommodated in the Internet (there is a tendency to conclude that applications such as these require "connections," but it isn't necessarily the case that these connections must adhere to the traditional model of the "telephone call").

Beyond these controls, there are additional levels of control that are equally important: policy, access control, and accounting must all be improved.

Component 3: Application Interoperability

In those circumstances in which it is not possible to achieve interoperability among (all) the underlying protocol stacks, it is still possible to achieve application ubiquity, through the deployment of gateways. The ultimate role of the Internet is to serve as a basis for communication among applications. At a minimum, the Internet should enable communities of end users sharing a common application "objective"—among these, the exchange of electronic mail, files, documents, images, and access to remote resources—but having diverse applications as "tools" to operate and migrate from one underlying protocol suite to another without unacceptable loss of functionality.

The scope of the Internet and the size of the Internet community are expanded considerably by these changes, but at a cost. The Internet may become harder to administer from backbone to individual hosts. The cost of multiprotocol hardware, software, and support and administrative staff increases as well. Accounting, accountability, and security are no longer merely important but essential. The changes are unavoidable, but they are not painless, and each time functionality is lost, or additional system complexity and costs are endured in order to expand the scope of the Internet, the decision to grow out from the "warm and comfy" world of IP connectivity will be subjected to renewed harsh scrutiny. In a perfect world, however, the Internet would evolve and expand without these penalties; there is a tendency, therefore, for the Internet to evolve in favor of the homogeneous architecture represented by component 1, and away from the compromised architectures of components 2 and 3. Component 4 expresses this tendency.

Component 4: Hybridization/ Integration

This component expresses the tendency of the Internet, as a system, to attempt to return to the original "state of grace" represented by the uniform architecture of component 1. It is a force acting on the evolution of the Internet rather than a process whereby the Internet actually returns to a uniform state at some point in the future. Component 4 recognizes the desirability of integrating similar elements from different Internet protocol architectures to form hybrids that reduce the variability and complexity of the (central) Internet system. It also recognizes the desirability of leveraging the existing Internet infrastructure to facilitate the absorption of "new stuff" into the Internet, applying to "new stuff" the established Internet practice of test, evaluate, adopt.

The result is something akin to bombarding the nucleus of an atom with neutrons (the neutrons here being complementary or replacement protocols for the existing "core" stack). According to this dynamic model, running X.400 mail over RFC 1006 on a TCP/IP stack, integrated IS-IS routing, transport bridges, and the development of a single common internetwork protocol successor to IP and CLNP are all examples of "good things"[2]— they represent movement away from the nonuniformity of components 2 and 3 in the direction of greater homogeneity, under the influence of the "magnetic field" asserted by component 1, following the hybridization dynamic of component 4. Thus, homogeneity is accommodated not through adoption of a single, "pure" stack but through widespread implementation

---

2.   The authors wish to emphasize that these are merely examples and are not intended to suggest that the very fine work done to produce MIME and OSPF should be set aside!

of the protocols and combinations that compose the "core."

What protocols and combinations will (initially) comprise the "core" remains highly speculative. Certainly, the existing TCP/IP "stack" will remain in the core (including ARP, OSPF, and BGP-something); these are likely to be complemented by CLNP and integrated IS-IS routing, the OSI directory and message-handling applications, and the RFC 1006 transport service bridges. Because of its virtual ubiquity among IP-based systems, the simple network management protocol (SNMP) is likely to remain the fundamental management component; it now runs over an OSI stack, as will its heir apparent, SNMP version 2.

This is, of course, highly speculative and considers only the complementing items from OSI. Depending upon stakeholders' interest in making other networking technologies "open," and their willingness to do so, the "core" may be complemented by applications and services of current, proprietary, or *de jure* networking architectures.

18 A READING FROM THE BOOK OF GENEBITS

If a history of computer networking were to be written in the form and fashion of the King James Bible, the book of Genesis (Genebits . . .) might describe the final 40 years of the present millennium in this manner:

In the beginning, God created the heavens and the earth. He performed wonders of every sort and created Man in His own image. Unfortunately, Man screwed up big time, and God sent him packing (Gen. 1, 2). Generations followed generations (Gen. 3–10), and Man frequently crossed the line and God doled out punishment accordingly.

Through these generations, all men used the same language and the same words. One sunny morning, Man aspired to reach the heavens and began to build towers and such. God said, "Not!," confused the language of the whole earth, and towers have by and large been modest efforts since then (Gen. 11).

Man ever after sought to have the whole earth use the same language and the same words. He struggled ages upon ages until he discovered electricity and mined copper, and wed the two together with devices of a curious nature, and conducted the electricity over copper wire in every manner and kind until finally Man said, "Let there be carrier."

And Man saw that carrier was good and that digits of binary could ride the carrier. The "bits" were formed into words, first in the language of Morse and later of Baudot, which enhanced the language. And the devices were telexes and wondrous indeed. But the language was constraining, the bits numbering only 5, and Man saw that more bits were needed and saw also that the bits must travel *faster*.

But Man saw also that the carrier had not the strength, for bits were indeed lost or destroyed as they traveled over the copper wire—verily, at the dizzying rates of 300–1,200 bits per second—so Man grouped the bits into 8, and *framed* the bits first with start bits and stop. After a time, the 8-bit *bytes* themselves framed the bits of good and noble use, and the framing bytes were called *header* and the noble bits *user data*, respectively, and Man saw that this, too, was good. And the devices were mainframes and wondrous indeed. Now copper connected the mainframes, two by two, and the whole earth used very nearly the same language and the same words, for the mainframes were but either blue or from the BUNCH.

And Man used the language, and the language grew and yet more bits were needed, and no longer could the mainframes be connected two by two, for amongst the devices were now minis and micros, and they were plentiful indeed, and the bandwidth of one copper pair was indeed too small, and copper pairs continued to be added, and the copper became a real mesh (sorry . . .), and among Men there were sorcerers and apprentices—Roberts, Cerf, Postel, Crocker, Kahn, and more—who created *more header* and caused IMPish devices to *switch,* and the devices and the copper were one and the one was called *network,* and it was wondrous indeed. Now among the devices, there were those that computed routes and switched *packets* or *circuits* (for among Men, there remained those who thought circuits were better, but switching was generally recognized as a good thing, so Men agreed to disagree for a time, but this was not a good idea, as was later revealed).

And so the networks grew. But the whole earth no longer used the same language and the same words, and Man was saddened, deflated, but not yet defeated. So Man caused there to be interconnection, relay, and translation among the networks in various, sundry, and occult forms and thereby concealed the differences for a time (where Man could not conceal the differences, he made them tolerable), and Man saw that this was not as good as he had hoped, but it was OK.

And Man used the languages for more and diverse purposes, and the purposes were good (mostly). But the bits of noble use became lost and arrived out of order, and the users complained. Now *more header* was applied, and among Men there now came sorcerers—Karn, Nagle, Clark, Jacobson, and more—who brought with them windows, timers, and positive acknowledgments. These were applied *end-to-end* and the transport of bits was *reliable* and sources were quenched, and Man saw that this, too, was *really* good (although there remained still purposes for which this was not an issue, and so Man agreed that along with reliable transport, datagrams should be universal and both were indeed good).

Above the transports, the purposes became more potent indeed. Now messaging grew, and the applications multiplied and became distributed. The devices were now PCs and workstations and transaction-processing machines, and they were more plentiful still. Ever more bandwidth was needed and copper yielded to fiber and the network grew and was divided into occasionally manageable and always autonomous pieces of many and diverse names, and Man used the languages, and the languages grew, and the network became an interconnected set of networks, and it was called first a catenet and later an internet. (Among Men, there persisted those who believed in circuits, and their networks were public, and these, too, were subsumed within the Internet, and the role they played was good, for they too were links among many.)

Yet Man aspired still to have the whole earth use the same language and the same words, though the differences in the languages of the networks were not small. Carried away once more, Man proclaimed, "Let us build for ourselves a model and a tower with seven layers whose top will reach into heaven, and let us make for ourselves an *open network*, lest our mail and files and databases be scattered abroad over the face of the whole earth" (Gen. 11:4). And those among Men who saw this to be good labored to make it so, some honestly and some not, since there remained among them Men with agendae obscura, and policy and compromise often burdened the Men of technology. The labor continued, but the progress was slow, indeed so much so that among Men, many turned to the language of DARPA, for it was open *de facto*, and the language of PARC nearly equally so, for it was novel (sorry . . .). And for a period of time, there was much acrimony and contempt, which caused much sadness indeed. Even those among Men who studied not rocket science saw that this was not good at all.

After a time, intellectual curiosity infected even the most zealous and extreme of the varied communities of Man, and among Men, those called implementers began to share and cooperate, and gossip had less effect on these than on others, and with abandon, they *implemented* so that they could know more. They took from the language of the open network one whose syntax was abstract, and among them came Four who asserted that Simple was better and repetition was key, and so made the technology tractable rather than common. And network operators embraced the fruit of their efforts and made the technology *available*, and the Internet grew and the languages became strong. Now others joined, and the languages used were both pure and hybrid, for the words of one became the words of the others, especially the simple ones. Doing useful work took precedence even over purity of religion, and so the languages grew. Man saw that this was actually far better across the whole earth than one language and one word, and agreed that the network should embrace the many and useful languages, and the network should be multiprotocol indeed.

Among Men, there are now those who believe that the whole earth doesn't really have to use the same language and the same words after all; they must merely share one word, and that word is *cooperation*. And the Lord looked upon Man and said, "Truly, this is what they began to do, and now nothing which they propose to do will be impossible for them" (Gen. 11:6).

This historical account is, of course, allegorical and largely whimsical. Much of the actual histories of OSI and TCP/IP are interrelated, and for better or worse, their futures are now inextricably intertwined. It may be that by the end of the millennium, we will all know just how farfetched the final verses of "Genebits" truly were. It will be our collective good fortune if the future of open systems networking is guided by open-mindedness, and one purpose of this book has been to contribute to that goal.

A NETWORKING ACRONYMS

AAL	ATM adaptation layer
AARNet	Australian Academic Research Network
ACE	advanced computing environment
ACERLI	Association Française des Centres d'Essais pour les Reseaux Locaux Industriels
ACET	Advisory Committee on Electronics and Telecommunications (of IEC)
ACID	atomicity, consistency, isolation, durability (properties of transaction processing)
ACM	Association for Computing Machinery
ACSE	association-control service element
ACSNET	Australian Computer Science Network
ACTAS	Alliance of Computer-based Telephony Application Suppliers
ADAPSO	Association of Data Processing Service Organizations (superseded by ITAA)
ADCCP	advanced data communication control procedure
ADCU	Association of Data Communications Users
ADDMD	administration directory-management domain (for X.500 directory system)
ADMD	administration (public) management domain (of MHS)
AE	application entity
AEF	address extension facility (of X.25 [1984])
AET	application entity title
AFI	authority and format identifier (of NSAP address)
AFII	Association for Font Information Interchange

AFIPS	American Federation of Information Processing Societies
AFNOR	Association Française de Normalisation
AIA	Aerospace Industries Association
AIAG	Automotive Industry Action Group
AIIM	Association for Information and Image Management
AIS	alarm indication signal (of SONET)
ANS	Advanced Network and Services (Corporation)
ANS	American national standard
ANSI	American National Standards Institute
AOSIP	airline OSI profile
AOWS	Asia–Oceanic (OSI) Workshop
AP	application process
APCC	American Public Communications Council
API	application-program(ming) interface
APIA	Application Programming Interface Association (for X.400)
APP	applications (area of the IETF)
ARGO	A really good OSI
ARP	address-resolution protocol
ARPA	Advanced Research Projects Agency (of the Department of Defense)
AS	autonomous system
ASC	ANSI-accredited standards committee
ASCII	American Standard Code for Information Interchange
ASE	application service element
ASN.1	Abstract Syntax Notation One
ASO	application service object
ASTM	American Society for Testing Materials
ATM	asynchronous transfer mode
BAS	basic activity subset (of the OSI session service)
BCD	binary-coded decimal
BCS	basic combined subset (of the OSI session service)
BDT	Bureau of Telecommunications Development (of the ITU)
BECN	backward explicit congestion notification (of frame relay)
BEITA	Business Equipment and Information Technology Association (U.K.)
BER	basic encoding rules (of ASN.1)

BER	bit error rate
BIAS	Burroughs Integrated Adaptive Routing System
BIND	Berkeley Interactive Name Demon
BISDN	broadband ISDN
BITNET	"Because It's Time" Network
BNA	Burroughs Network Architecture
BNF	Backus-Naur Form
BOC	Bell Operating Company (22 local telephone companies)
BPS	bits per second
BSD	(University of California at) Berkeley Software Distribution
BSI	British Standards Institute
BSR	(ANSI) Board of Standards Review
BSS	basic synchronized subset (of the OSI session service)
BT	British Telecom
CALS	Computer-aided Acquisition and Logistic Support (of U.S. DOD)
CAT	common authentication technology
CATV	community antenna television
CBEMA	Computer and Business Equipment Manufacturers' Association
CC	connect confirm (PDU)
CCH	Harmonization Coordination Committee (CEPT)
CCH/SP	Permanent Secretariat of the CCH (CEPT)
CCIA	Computer and Communication Industry Association
CCIR	International Radio Consultative Committee
CCIRN	Coordinating Council on International Research Networks
CCITT	International Telegraph and Telephone Consultative Committee (Comité Consultatif International Télégraphique et Téléphonique)
CCR	commitment, concurrency, and recovery
CCTA	Central Computer and Telecommunications Agency (U.K. treasury department)
CD	carrier detect
CD	committee draft (ISO) (formerly DP)
CDT	credit (field of ISO transport protocol class 4)
CEC	Commission of the European Community
CEN	Comité Européen de Normalisation (European

	Committee for Standardization, Joint European Standards Institution)
CENELEC	Comité Européen de Normalisation Electrique (European Committee for Electrotechnical Standardization)
CEP	connection endpoint
CEPT	Comité Européen des Administrations des Postes et des Télécommunications (European Conference of Postal and Telecommunications Administrations)
CERN	European Center for Nuclear Research
CERT	computer emergency response team
CIGOS	Canadian Interest Group on Open Systems
CIR	committed information rate (of frame relay)
CIX	commercial Internet exchange
CL	connectionless
CLNP	connectionless network protocol (ISO IP)
CLNS	connectionless network service
CLTS	connectionless transport service
CMIP	common management information protocol
CMIS	common management information service
CMISE	common management information service element
CMOT	common management information protocol over TCP/IP
CNET	Centre National d'Etudes des Télécommunications (of the French PTT)
CNMA	Communications Network for Manufacturing Applications (ESPRIT project 955)
CO	central office (telephone)
CO	connection-oriented
CoA	(RARE) Council of Administration
COCOM	Coordinating Committee for Multilateral Export Control
COMSEC	communications security
CONCERT	Communications for North Carolina Education, Research, and Technology
CONS	connection-oriented network service
COS	Corporation for Open Systems (International)
COSINE	Cooperation for Open Systems Interconnection Networking in Europe
COSN	Consortium for School Networking
COST	Cooperation Européene Scientifique et Technique

COTS	connection-oriented transport service
CPE	customer premises equipment
CR	connect request (PDU)
CRC	cyclic redundancy check
CREN	Corporation for Research and Educational Networking (parent of BITNET)
CSA	Canadian Standards Association
C/SCC	Computer/Standards Coordinating Committee (of the IEEE Computer Society)
CSCW	computer-supported cooperative work
CSDN	circuit-switched data network
CSELT	Centro Studi e Laboratori Telecommunicazioni S.p.A. (Italy)
CSMA	carrier sense multiple access
CSMA/CD	carrier sense multiple access with collision detection
CSMC	Communications Services Management Council
CSNET	(U.S.) Computer Science Network
CSPDN	circuit-switched public data network
CSPP	Computer Systems Policy Project
CSTO	[DARPA] Computer Systems Technology Office
CSU	channel service unit
CTIP	Commission on Computing, Telecommunications, and Information Policies (of the ICC)
CTNE	Compañía Telefónica Nacional de España
CTRG	Collaboration Technology Research Group
CWI	Centrum voor Wiskunde en Informatica (the Dutch computer science and mathematics institute)
DA	destination address
DAD	draft addendum (ISO) (now DAM)
DAM	draft amendment (ISO) (formerly DAD)
DAP	directory-access protocol
DAP	document application profile (of ODA)
DARPA	Defense Advanced Research Projects Agency
DARTnet	(U.S.) Department of Defense Advanced Research Testbed Network
DASS	Design Automation Standards Subcommittee (of IEEE)
DBMS	database-management system
DCA	(U.S. Department of) Defense Communications Agency (now DISA)
DCC	data country code

DCE	data circuit-terminating equipment
DCE	distributed computing environment (OSF)
DCEC	(U.S. Department of) Defense Communications Engineering Center
DCS	defined-context set (in presentation)
DDN	Defense Data Network
DDP	distributed data processing
DDS	digital data service
DES	data-encryption standard (FIPS PUB 46 1-15-77)
DESIRE	Directory of European Information Security Standards Requirements
DFN	Deutsches Forschungsnetz (German research network)
DIB	directory information base
DIGI	Deutsche Interessengemeinschaft Internet (German Internet users' group)
DIN	Deutsches Institut für Normung
DIS	draft international standard (ISO)
DISA	(U.S. Department of) Defense Information Systems Agency (formerly DCA)
DISERF	Data Interchange Standards Education and Research Foundation
DISN	(U.S. Department of) Defense Information Systems Network
DISP	draft international standardized profile
DIT	directory information tree
DLCI	data-link connection identifier (of LAP-D)
DME	distributed management environment
DMZ	demilitarized zone
DN	distinguished name (of X.500 directory service)
DNA	Digital Network Architecture (DEC)
DNIC	data network identification code
DNS	domain name system
DOD	(U.S.) Department of Defense
DOE	(U.S.) Department of Energy
DP	draft proposal (ISO) (now CD)
dpANS	draft proposed American national standard
DQDB	distributed queue dual bus (802.6 MAN)
DS	directory service
DS0	digital signal level 0 (64 Kbps)
DS1	digital signal level 1 (1.544 Mbps)
DS3	digital signal level 3 (44.736 Mbps)

DSA	directory system agent
DSAP	destination (link) service access point
DSP	directory system protocol
DSP	domain-specific part (of NSAP address)
DSSSL	Document Style, Semantics, and Specification Language
DSU	digital service unit
DT	data (PDU)
DTAM	document transfer, access, and manipulation
DTE	data terminal equipment
DTI	(U.K.) Department of Trade and Industry
DTR	data terminal ready
DTR	draft technical report (ISO)
DUA	directory user agent
EARN	European Association of Research Networks
EASINet	European Academic Supercomputer Initiative Network
EBCDIC	Extended Binary-coded Decimal Interchange Code
EBONE	European (Internet) Backbone
EC	European Community (or Commission)
ECMA	European Computer Manufacturers' Association
ECSA	Exchange Carriers Standards Association
ECTEL	European Conference of Telecommunications and Electronics Industries
ECU	European currency unit
EDI	Electronic data interchange
EDIA	Electronic Data Interchange Association (supersedes TDCC)
EDICUSA	EDI Council of the United States
EDIF	electronic data interchange format
EDIFACT	electronic data interchange for finance, administration, commerce, and transport
EDIMS	EDI messaging system
EEC	European Economic Community
EEMA	European Electronic Mail Association
EEPG	European Engineering Planning Group
EFT	electronic funds transfer
EFTA	European Free Trade Association
EGP	exterior gateway protocol
EIA	Electronic Industries Association

EIES	ESPRIT Information Exchange System (now ROSE)
EIUF	European ISDN Users' Forum
ELAN	ESPRIT Local Area Network
EMI	electromagnetic interference
EMUG	European MAP/TOP Users' Group
ENS	European Nervous System (ETSI-sponsored backbone project)
ENTELEC	Energy Telecommunications and Electrical Association
EOTC	European Organization for Certification and Testing
ER	error (PDU)
ES	end system
ESF	extended superframe format (24-bit framing for T1)
ESH	end-system hello (PDU of ISO 9542)
ES-IS	end-system to intermediate-system (routing protocol)
ESnet	Energy Sciences Network
ESPRIT	European Strategic Project for Research on Information Technology
ETCO	European Telecommunications Consultancy Organization
ETCOM	European Testing for Certification of Office and Manufacturing Equipment
ETSI	European Telecommunications Standards Institute
EWICS	European Workshop on Industrial Computer Systems
EWOS	European Workshop for Open Systems
FACT	Federation of Automated Coding Technologies
FADU	file access data unit (of FTAM)
FAIS	factory automation interconnection system
FARNET	Federation of American Research Networks
FCC	(U.S.) Federal Communications Commission
FCCSET	Federal Coordinating Council on Science, Engineering, and Technology
FCS	frame-check sequence
FDDI	fiber-distributed data interface
FDT	formal description technique
FECN	forward explicit congestion notification (of frame relay)
FED-STD	federal standard
FEPG	Federal Engineering Planning Group
FIPS	federal information-processing standard
FIPS PUB	federal information-processing standard publication
FIRST	Forum on Incident Response and Security Teams

FIX	Federal Internet Exchange
FNC	Federal Networking Council
FOPG	FNC OSI Planning Group
FOTS	fiber-optic transmission system
FOX	field operational X.500
FR	frame relay
FREDMAIL	Free Educational Electronic Mail (network)
FRF	Frame Relay Forum
FRICC	Federal Research Internet Coordination Committee (superseded by FNC)
FSTG	Functional Standardization Taxonomy Group
FTAM	file transfer, access, and management
FTP	file-transfer protocol (DOD)
FTSC	Federal Telecommunications Standards Committee
FTZ	Fernmeldetecnisches Zentralamt (Deutsche Bundespost)
GAO	(U.S.) Government Accounting Office
GDAP	government document application profile (GOSIP)
GDMI	generic definition of management information
GDMO	guidelines for the generic definition of managed objects
GGP	gateway-to-gateway protocol (Internet)
GNMP	government network-management profile
GOSIP	government OSI profile (United Kingdom and United States)
GSA	General Services Administration
GSLB	Groupe Special Large Bande (CEPT Special Group on Broadband Communications)
GUI	graphical user interface
GUS	guide to the use of standards (SPAG)
HDLC	high-level data-link control
HDTV	high-definition television
HEMS	high-level entity-management system
HEPNET	High-Energy Physics Network
HPCA	High Performance Computing Act (of U.S. Congress)
IA5	International Alphabet 5 (CCITT V.3), (ISO 646)
IAB	Internet Architecture Board (formerly Internet Activities Board)
IAC	International Advisory Committee (of X3)
IANA	Internet Assigned Number Authority

IAPP	(ANSI) Industrial Automation Planning Panel
ICA	International Communications Association
ICC	International Chamber of Commerce
ICI	interexchange carrier interface
ICMP	Internet-control message protocol (ARPA)
ICN	International Cooperating Network
ICOS	International Club for Open Systems
ICP	initial connection protocol (ARPA)
ICST	Institute for Computer Science and Technology (of NIST)
ID	Internet draft
IDCMA	Independent Data Communication Manufacturers' Association
IDI	initial domain identifier (of NSAP address)
IDP	initial domain part (of NSAP address)
IDPR	interdomain policy routing
IDRP	interdomain routing protocol (ISO/IEC 10747)
IEC	interexchange carrier
IEC	International Electrotechnical Commission
IEEE	Institute of Electrical and Electronics Engineers
IEEE-USA/ CCIP	IEEE (U.S.A.) Committee on Communications and Information Policy
IEN	Internet engineering note (ARPA)
IEPG	Intercontinental Engineering Planning Group
IES	information exchange system (of ESPRIT)
IESG	Internet Engineering Steering Group
IETF	Internet Engineering Task Force
IFIP	International Federation of Information Processing Societies
IFOBS	International Forum on Open Bibliographic Systems
IFRB	International Frequency Registration Board (of the ITU)
IGES	initial graphics exchange specification (from NIST)
IGOSS	industry and government open systems specification
IGP	interior gateway protocol
IMP	interface message processor
InARP	inverse address-resolution protocol
INCA	integrated network communication architecture
INFOSEC	information systems security
INMARSAT	International Maritime Satellite Organization
INTAP	Interoperability Technology Association for Information Processing (Japan)

INTUG	International Telecommunications Users' Group
IONL	"Internal Organization of the Network Layer" (ISO 8648)
IP	Internet protocol (DOD IP or ISO 8473)
IPC	interprocess communication
IPDU	internetwork protocol data unit
IPI	initial protocol identifier (ISO 9577)
IPM	interpersonal messaging (of MHS)
IPSIT	International Public Sector Information Technology (group)
IPMS	interpersonal message system
IPX	Internet packet-exchange (protocol) (Novell)
IRSG	Internet Research Steering Group
IRTF	Internet Research Task Force
IS	intermediate system
ISDN	integrated services digital network
ISH	intermediate-system hello (PDU of ISO 9542)
ISI	Information Sciences Institute
IS-IS	intermediate system to intermediate system (routing protocol)
ISO	International Organization for Standardization
ISOC	Internet Society
ISO/CS	ISO Central Secretariat
ISODE	ISO Development Environment
ISP	international standardized profile
ISPT	Instituto Superiore Poste e Telecommunicazioni (Italy)
ISSB	Information Systems Standards Board (of X3)
ISSO	Information Systems Security Organization (of the NSA)
ISTE	International Society for Technology in Education
IT	information technology
ITAA	Information Technology Association of America (formerly ADAPSO)
ITAEGS	Information Technology Ad Hoc Experts' Group on Standards
ITAEGT	Information Technology Ad Hoc Experts' Group on Private Telecommunication Networks
ITAR	International Traffic in Arms Regulations
ITCC	Information Technology Consultative Committee (of ANSI)
ITI	Industrial Technology Institute

ITRC	Information Technology Requirements Council
ITS	Institute for Telecommunication Sciences (of NTIA)
ITSB	Image Technology Standards Board (of ANSI)
ITSC	Interregional Telecommunications Standards Conference
ITSEC	Information Technology Security Evaluation Criteria (EC)
ITSTC	Information Technology Steering Committee
ITU	International Telecommunications Union
ITUA	Independent T1 Users' Association
IWU	interworking unit
IXI	international X.25 infrastructure (RARE)
JANET	(U.K.) Joint Academic Network
JBIG	Joint Bilevel Imaging Group
JEMA	Japanese Electric Machinery Association
JIPS	JANET IP Service
JNT	(U.K.) joint network team
JPEG	Joint Photographic Experts' Group
JRAG	(JTC1 TAG) Joint Registration Advisory Group
JTC1	Joint (ISO/IEC) Technical Committee 1
JTM	job transfer and manipulation
KDD	Kokusai Denshin Denwa (Japanese telephone company)
LAN	local area network
LAP	link access procedure
LAP-B	link access procedure–balanced
LAP-D	link access procedure (for ISDN D channel)
LATA	local access and transport area
LCN	logical channel number
LEC	local exchange carrier
LI	length indicator
LLC	logical link control
LLC1	logical link control type 1
LLC2	logical link control type 2
LLSIG	Lower Layer Special Interest Group (of the OSI Implementers' Workshop)
LME	layer-management entity
LSAP	link service access point
LTE	line-terminating entity (of SONET)

LU	logical unit (SNA)
LWSP	logical white space
MAC	medium access control
MAC	multiplexed analog components (EC HDTV)
MAN	metropolitan area network
MAP	manufacturing automation protocol
MASE	message administration service element
MAU	medium attachment unit
MD	message digest 5
MDSE	message delivery service element
MRSE	message retrieval service element
MHS	message-handling system(s)
MIB	management information base
MICR	magnetic ink character recognition
MIL-STD	(U.S.) military standard
MIME	multipurpose Internet mail extensions
MITI	Ministry of International Trade and Industry (Japan)
MMFS	manufacturing message format standard (MAP)
MNP	Microcom Networking Protocol
MOCS	managed-object conformance statement
MOTIS	message-oriented text-interchange system
MPDU	message protocol data unit
MRI	Magnetic Resonance Imaging
MS	message store (of MHS)
MSS	Maritime Satellite Service
MSSE	message submission service element
MTA	message-transfer agent (of MHS)
MTBF	mean time between failures
MTP	message-transfer protocol (of MHS)
MTS	message-transfer system (of MHS)
MTSE	message-transfer service element
MUX	multiplexer
MX	mail exchanger
NAC	Network Applications Consortium
NACHA	National Automated Clearing House Association
NADF	North American Directory Forum
NAK	Negative Acknowledgment
NAMAS	National Measurement Accreditation Service (U.K.)
NAMTUG	North American MAP/TOP Users' Group (part of COS)

NAPLPS	North American Presentation Level Protocol Syntax (for videotex)
NARUC	National Association of Regulatory Utility Commissioners
NASA	(U.S.) National Aeronautics and Space Administration
NASTD	National Association of State Telecommunications Directors
NATA	North American Telecommunications Association
NBS	National Bureau of Standards (now NIST)
NC	network connection
NCC	National Computing Centre Ltd. (U.K.)
NCS	national communications system
NCS	Network Computing System (Apollo)
NCSA	National Center for Supercomputing Applications
NCSL	(NIST) National Computer Systems Laboratory
NCUG	National Centrex Users' Group
NE	network element
NE	network entity
NEMA	National Equipment Manufacturers' Association
NET	European Telecommunication Standard (CEPT)
NFS	network file system (Sun)
NIC	Network Information Center
NIKHEF	Nationaal Institut voor Kernfysica en Hoge-Energiefysica (Dutch institute for high-energy physics)
NIST	National Institute of Standards and Technology (formerly NBS)
NMF	Network Management Forum (OSI)
NMS	network-management station
NOC	network operations center
NOOP	network OSI operations
NP	(ISO/IEC) new project (formerly NWI)
NPDU	network protocol data unit
NPTN	National Public Telecomputing Network
NREN	National Research and Education Network
NRS	(U.K.) name-registration scheme
NRZI	Non return to Zero Inverted (binary-encoding scheme)
NSA	(U.S.) National Security Agency
NSAP	network service access point
NSEP	National Security Emergency Preparedness (DOD)
NSF	National Science Foundation
NSFnet	National Science Foundation (-sponsored) Network

NSI	NASA Science Internet
NTIA	National Telecommunications and Information Agency
NTSC	National Television System Committee
NUA	Network Users' Association
NVLAP	National Voluntary Laboratory Accreditation Program (NIST)
NWI	new work item (now new project) (ISO)
NYSERNet	New York State Education and Research Network
OAM&P	operations, administration, maintenance, and provisioning
OASIS	Online Access to the Standards Information Service (of ANSI-accredited Standards Committee X3)
OC	optical carrier
ODA	office document architecture
ODETTE	Organization for Data Exchange by Tele-Transmission in Europe
ODIF	office document interchange format
ODP	open distributed processing
OECD	Organization for Economic Cooperation and Development
OFTEL	(U.K.) Office of Telecommunications
OID	object identifier
OIW	(NIST) OSI Implementers' Workshop
OLTP	on-line transaction processing
OMG	object-management group
ONC	Open Network Computing (Apollo/HP)
O/R	originator/recipient (name in MHS)
ORWG	Open Routing Working Group (of IETF)
OS	open system
OS	operating system
OS	operations system
OSE	open systems environment
OSF	Open Software Foundation
OSI	open systems interconnection
OSI	OSI integration (area of the IETF)
OSIE	OSI environment
OSInet	OSI (experimental) Network (sponsored by NIST)
OSITOP	European TOP Users' Group
OSPF	open shortest path first (routing algorithm and protocol)

L. I. H. E.
THE BECK LIBRARY
WOOLTON RD., LIVERPOOL, L16 8ND

OSTC	Open Systems Testing Consortium (successor to CTS/WAN)
OSTP	Office of Science and Technology Policy (of the U.S. government)
OTA	Office of Technology Assessment
PAEB	Pan-American EDIFACT Board
PAGODA	Profile Alignment Group for ODA
PCI	protocol-control information
PDAD	proposed draft addendum (ISO) (now PDAM)
PDAM	proposed draft amendment (ISO)
PDAU	physical delivery access unit
PDISP	proposed draft international standardized profile (ISO)
PDN	public data network
PDTR	proposed draft technical report (ISO)
PDU	protocol data unit
PEM	privacy-enhanced mail
PGI	parameter group identifier
PI	protocol identification (PDU)
PICS	protocol implementation conformance statement
PID	protocol identifier
PIP	"P" Internet protocol
PLP	(X.25) packet-level protocol (ISO 8208)
PMD	private management domain
POSI	Promoting Conference for OSI (Japan)
POTS	plain old telephone service
PPP	point-to-point protocol
PRDMD	private directory-management domain (of X.500 directory system)
PRMD	private management domain (of X.400 MHS)
PSAP	presentation service access point
PSC	Public Service Commission
PSDN	packet-switched data network
PSI	Performance Systems International
PSPDN	packet-switched public data network
PSRG	Privacy and Security Research Group (of the IRTF)
PSTN	public switched telephone network
PTE	path-terminating entity (of SONET)
PTK	Peter T. Kirstein (of UCL)
PTNX	private telecommunications network exchange
PTT	postal, telephone, and telegraph (agency)

PUC	public utility commission
PVC	permanent virtual circuit
PVC	polyvinyl chloride
QOS	quality of service
RA	registration authority
RACE	R&D in Advanced Communications Technologies in Europe (CEC)
RARE	Réseaux Associés pour la Récherche Européene
RARP	reverse address-resolution protocol
RBHC	Regional Bell Holding Company
RBOC	Regional Bell Operating Company (7 regional telephone companies)
RDA	remote database access
RDN	relative distinguished name (in X.500 directory service)
REC	RARE Executive Committee
REUNA	Red Universitaria Nacional Chilena (Chilean academic and research network)
RFC	request for comments
RIP	routing information protocol
RIPE	Réseaux IP Européens (literally, "Research IP for Europe")
RISC	reduced instruction set computing
RISE	Retrieval and Interchange of Standards in Europe
RJ	reject (PDU)
RJE	remote job entry
RM	(OSI) reference model
ROER	remote operations error
ROIV	remote operations invoke
RORJ	remote operations reject
RORS	remote operations result
ROS	remote operations service
ROSE	remote operations service element
ROSE	Research on Open Systems for Europe (of ESPRIT)
RPC	remote procedure call
RPOA	recognized private operating agency (CCITT)
RSA	Rivest, Shamir, Adelman (public-key encryption scheme)
RSO	regional standards organization
RTC	RARE technical committee
RTS	reliable transfer service

RTSE	reliable transfer service element
RTT	round-trip time
RWCC	Regional Workshop Coordinating Committee
SA	source address
SACK	selective acknowledgment
SAFENET	Survivable Adaptable Fiber Optic Embedded Network (U.S. Navy)
SAP	service access point
SAR	segmentation and reassembly
SASE	specific application service element
SC	subcommittee (ISO)
SCSI	small computer systems interface
SCTR	system conformance test report
SDE	submission-delivery entity
SDH	synchronous digital hierarchy (SONET in Europe)
SDLC	Synchronous Data Link Control (IBM)
SDO	standards development organization
SDSAF	Switched Digital Services Applications Forum
SEAL	simple and efficient (ATM) adaptation layer (equivalent to AAL5)
SEC	security (area of the IETF)
SECAM	Système Électronique Couleur avec Mémoire (French TV system)
SG	study group (of CCITT)
SGFS	Special Group on Functional Standardization (of ISO/IEC JTC1)
SGML	Standard Generalized Markup Language
SGMP	simple gateway-monitoring protocol
SI	SPDU identifier
SIA	stable implementation agreements (of the OIW)
SIG	special interest group
SIGCOMM	(ACM) Special Interest Group on Data Communications
SIP	SMDS interface protocol
SITA	Society for International Telecommunications for Aeronautics
SLIP	synchronous line Internet protocol
SMAE	system-mangement application entity
SMC	Secretariat Management Committee (of X3)
SMDS	switched multimegabit data service

SME	Society of Manufacturing Engineers
SMI	structure of management information
SMIS	specific management information service
SMISE	specific management information service element
SMP	simple management protocol (successor to SNMP, now SNMPv 2)
SMS	service-management system (of AIN)
SMTP	simple mail-transfer protocol (RFC 821)
SNA	system network architecture (IBM)
SNAcP	subnetwork access protocol
SNARE	subnetwork address-resolution entity
SNDCP	subnetwork-dependent convergence protocol
SNI	subscriber-network interface
SNICP	subnetwork-independent convergence protocol
SNMP	simple network-management protocol
SNPA	subnetwork point of attachment
SOG-T	Senior Officials' Group for Telecommunications (of CEPT)
SONET	synchronous optical network
SPAG	Standards Promotion and Applications Group
SPARC	Standards Planning and Review Committee (of X3)
SPDL	Standard Page Description Language
SPDU	session protocol data unit
SPE	synchronous payload envelope (of SONET)
SPI	subsequent protocol identifier (ISO 9577)
SQL	Standard Query Language
SSAP	session service access point
SSAP	source (link) service access point
STE	section-terminating equipment (of SONET)
STEP	standard for the exchange of product model data (for EDI)
STM	synchronous transfer mode
STM	synchronous transport module (of SONET)
STS	synchronous transport signal (of SONET)
SVC	switched virtual circuit
SWG	special working group (ISO)
SWIFT	Society for Worldwide International Financial Telecommunications
SWITCH	Swiss Academic Research Network
TA	terminal adapter (in ISDN)

TAC	terminal access controller
TAG	technical advisory group
TC	technical committee
TC	transport connection
TCP	transmission-control protocol
TCSEC	Trusted Computer System Evaluation Criteria (of the U.S. Department of Defense)
TDCC	Transportation Data Coordinating Committee (superseded by EDIA)
TDM	time division multiplexing
TDMA	time division multiple access
TE	terminal equipment
TELNET	Internet virtual terminal protocol
TERC	Technology Education Research Center
TERC	Telecommunications Equipment Remarketing Council
TFTP	trivial file-transfer protocol
TG	task group
THEnet	Texas Higher Education Network
TIP	terminal interface processor
TLI	transport-layer interface
TLMA	telematic access unit
TLV	type-length-value (format for parameter encoding in PDUs)
TMP	test-management protocol
TNIC	transit network identification code
TOP	technical and office protocols
TOS	type of service (routing)
TP	transaction processing
TP	transport protocol
TP0, TP1, etc.	transport protocol (ISO/IEC 8073) class 0, class 1, etc.
TPDU	transport protocol data unit
TPI	transport protocol interface (streams)
TR	(Bellcore) technical reference
TR	technical report (ISO)
TRAC	Technical Recommendation Application Committee (of CEPT)
TS	transport service
TSAP	transport service access point
TTC	Telecommunications Technology Council (of the Japanese Ministry of Posts and Telecommunications)
TTCN	Tree and Tabular Combined Notation

TT-CNMA	Testing Technology for Communications Network for Manufacturing Applications (ESPRIT II project)
TTL	time to live
TWA	two-way alternate (in session)
TWS	two-way simultaneous (in session)
UA	user agent (in MHS)
UAOS	User Alliance for Open Systems
UCL	University College, London
UCS	uniform communications standard
UD	UnitData (PDU)
UDP	user datagram protocol (ARPA)
UI	UNIX International
UI	unnumbered information (frame)
UKRA	U.K. (United Kingdom) registration authority
UL	Underwriters' Laboratories
ULA	upper-layer architecture
ULCC	University of London Computing Centre
ULP	upper-layer process
UNI	user-network interface (of ISDN)
UPS	uninterruptable power supply
UPT	universal personal telecommunications
USITA	United States Independent Telephone Association
USNC	United States National Committee
USO	UNIX software operation
USRA	Universities Space Research Association
USV	user services (area of the IETF)
UTC	universal time coordinate
UUCP	UNIX-to-UNIX copy
VADS	value-added data services
VAN	value-added network
VC	virtual circuit
VCI	virtual channel identifier (of SONET)
VMTP	versatile message transaction protocol
VPI	virtual path identifier (of SONET)
VPN	virtual private network
VT	virtual terminal
VT	virtual tributary (of SONET)
VTP	virtual terminal protocol
WAIS	wide area information service (or server)

WAN	wide area network
WATS	wide area telephone service
WD	working draft
WG	working group
WIN	Wissenschaftsnetz (German scientific network)
WINCS	WWMCCS Intercomputer Network Communication Subsystem
WINDO	Wide Information Network for Data Online (of U.S. Government Printing Office)
WINS	warehouse information network standard
WP	working party (of CCITT study group)
WWW	World Wide Web
WWMCCS	Worldwide Military Command and Control System (DOD)
XALS	extended appliation-layer structure
XDR	external data representation (Sun)
XID	exchange identification (PDU)
XMH	X mail handler
XNS	Xerox Network Systems
XPG	X.400 Promotion Group
XPG	X/Open Portability Guide
XTP	express transfer protocol

Readers will encounter many more acronyms and abbreviations in this list than the authors dared use in the text. These are provided as a hedge against the inevitable; if you read further about open systems networking, you will eventually encounter all of these acronyms, and many more.

B SOURCES

How and Where to Obtain Useful Information

No book, no matter how large, could possibly contain all the information that is available about open systems networking; even a casual interest in the subject will sooner or later give rise to questions that either are not answered in this book or are answered without the additional detail or context that the reader's interest requires. Fortunately, the world of open systems networking is, for the most part, genuinely "open" with respect to access to documentation; with few exceptions, any information about TCP/IP or OSI that is not found in this book can be obtained with little difficulty from one of the sources listed in this appendix.

At the time this is being written, it is still the case that the primary sources of information about the TCP/IP architecture and protocol suite are available at essentially no cost[1] to anyone with any kind of access to the Internet (including, for example, anyone with a commercial electronic mail account with MCI or CompuServe,[2] in addition to those who are fortunate enough to have a direct connection to the Internet), but the primary OSI sources—the ISO/IEC and CCITT standards—are not. The standards-development activities of the Internet are almost entirely subsidized by the United States government and (very recently) by the Internet Society; the standards-development activities of ISO/IEC and

---

1. "Essentially" because even though there is no explicit charge for retrieving documents by file transfer or electronic mail over the Internet, someone, somewhere is paying for the network access that makes it possible.
2. See the discussion of mail gateways later in this appendix for a list of some of the ways in which electronic-mail access to Internet information can be obtained when no direct Internet connection is available.

CCITT (and their associated national standards bodies in individual member countries), on the other hand, are funded in large part by the sale of (printed) standards. This situation is likely to change soon, so readers are advised to ask about alternative sources (particularly on-line archives) for OSI standards before buying them.

⟨AHA⟩ *Many people in the Internet community use the fact that Internet documents are "free" and OSI documents are not as a prime example of the superiority of the Internet way of doing things, notwithstanding the behind-the-scenes government largess that makes it possible. However, this is more than just a matter of smug satisfaction for members of one group at the other's expense; the difficulty and expense of obtaining the OSI standards and related documentation, particularly in light of the apparent ease and freedom with which similar documentation for the Internet standards can be obtained, has effectively blocked the widespread acceptance of OSI as the basis for open systems networking. From a marketing perspective, the way in which the OSI standards community has packaged and promoted its products could not have been better designed to ensure the success of the alternative (TCP/IP). TCP/IP information is free and is available (in electronic form, instantly, "over the net") everywhere; OSI information is absurdly expensive and can be obtained (by postal mail, on paper) only from a very small number of authorized sources. If the success of a standards-development activity is the extent to which its results (standards) are actually used, then it is not hard to conclude that in the case of OSI, the ISO/IEC and CCITT standards bodies have actively—and it appears, successfully—labored mightily to ensure their own failure.*

Information about TCP/IP and the Internet

In order to tap into the vast reservoir of information about the Internet and its technology[3] that is available "on-line," one must first figure out a way to be "on-line" oneself. This can be accomplished in one of two ways: by connecting to the Internet directly or by connecting indirectly through an electronic-mail gateway.[4]

---

3.   There is also, of course, a wealth of information available through the Internet about things other than the Internet itself; except for those people for whom the Internet itself is the primary subject of interest, these other information resources are naturally much more important and are ultimately the reason for having an Internet in the first place. They are not, however, the point of this appendix.

4.   A wealth of additional information about the way in which networks around the world are interconnected, and how to navigate the maze of different address formats and

Direct connection simply means that one's computer system—personal computer, workstation, time-sharing computer, etc.—is equipped with the protocols (usually, TCP/IP) necessary to exchange information directly with similarly equipped systems and that the local network to which one's system is attached (local area network, dial-up access network, etc.) is itself attached by communication links to other networks as part of the worldwide Internet "network of networks." If this is the case, and local policy constraints do not prohibit doing so,[5] one can use the TCP/IP file-transfer protocol (FTP) to obtain files directly from sites that maintain "anonymous FTP" archives—"anonymous" because they allow anyone to log in to the site with the user name "anonymous" and any password.[6] The way in which one uses FTP to do this varies from one system and software package to another; one must check with the local system or network administrator.

The information contained in many (but not all) Internet archives can also be obtained by users who do not have a direct connection to the Internet but do have some sort of electronic-mail capability (such as MCImail, CompuServe, or BITNET). *Mail gateways* between the Internet and many electronic-mail systems (including virtually every commercial mail system) allow messages to be sent from a system that is not directly connected to the Internet to an Internet archive and for that archive (if it is equipped to do so, as many are) to send back, in reply, one or more files that were named in the message. The two main drawbacks are that (1) one must know precisely which file or files one wants (so as to be able to give the precise file name in the request message), and (2) many mail gateways impose a limit on the size of mail messages that may pass through them, which effectively denies access to files above a certain size. Commonly used mail gateways include the BITNET/Internet gateway at `cunyvm.cuny.edu`, the UUCP/Internet gateway at `uunet.uu.net`, and the MCImail gateway at `mcimail.com`.

RFCs and Internet Drafts

Internet requests for comments (RFCs) and the working documents of Internet Engineering Task Force (IETF) working groups (Internet drafts) are available from four primary (and many secondary) archives distrib-

---

usage conventions, may be found in three excellent reference books: *The Matrix: Computer Networks and Conferencing Systems Worldwide*, by John S. Quarterman (1990); *Users' Directory of Computer Networks*, edited by Tracy L. LaQuey (1990); and *!%@:: A Directory of Electronic Mail Addressing and Networks*, by Donalynn Frey and Rick Adams (1989).

5. Some sites, concerned about the security of their local networks, do not allow direct access to the Internet, even though they are capable of providing it.

6. In practice, many sites will ask that an anonymous user provide his or her electronic-mail name (e.g., "lyman@bbn.com") as the password; other sites will accept any password.

uted around the world:

1. `nic.ddn.mil` `(192.112.36.5)`, maintained by the Internet Network Information Center, on the East Coast of the United States
2. `ftp.nisc.sri.com` `(192.33.33.22)`, maintained by the Network Information Services Center at SRI International, on the West Coast of the United States
3. `munnari.oz.au` `(128.250.1.21)`, maintained by the Australian Academic and Research Network (AARNet), in Australia
4. `nic.nordu.net` `(192.36.148.17)`, maintained by the Network Information Center of the Nordic Universities Network (NORDUnet), in Europe

RFCs and Internet drafts are also available by electronic mail. They can be obtained be sending a message to `mail-server@nisc.sri.com` and typing, in the body of the message

SEND <name of RFC or Internet draft>

For example, a copy of the Internet draft entitled "draft-iesg-roadplan-01.txt" can be obtained by sending a mail message containing the following line:

SEND draft-iesg-roadplan-01.txt

Additional information about even more ways to obtain RFCs and Internet drafts may be obtained by sending an electronic-mail message to `rfc-info@isi.edu` containing, in the message body, the line "help: ways_to_get_rfcs." To receive announcements of the posting of new RFCs, a mail message can be sent to `rfc-request@nic.ddn.mil`.

Anyone may submit a document to the RFC editor and request that it be published as an informational RFC. Prospective RFC authors should read RFC 1111, "Instructions to RFC Authors." Submissions should be sent to `rfc-editor@isi.edu`.

Internet Mailing Lists

Whereas participation in the OSI standards-development community generally requires that one attend meetings and collect reams of paper, participation in the Internet community is mediated largely by the exchange of electronic mail. One of the first things that happens when a new Internet-based activity (including all standards-making activities) is begun is the establishment of an electronic-mail distribution list to which anyone who is interested in the topic may subscribe; mail messages sent to the distribution list are then copied to each of the subscribers automatically, creating a highly dynamic "community of interest."

Some of the most important mailing lists are those that support the activities of the IETF and its working groups. The most basic of these is the *ietf-announce* list, to which the IETF Secretariat posts announcements of IETF meetings and other activities, reports of administrative actions, and other messages of general interest. Interested parties can join the list by sending a mail message to `ietf-announce-request@nri.reston.va.us`.[7]

SRI International publishes two useful guides for Internet users: *Internet: Getting Started*, edited by April Marine (1992), is (as its title suggests) a primer for beginners (and a handy reference for more experienced Internet users); and *Internet: Mailing Lists*, edited by Edward Hardie and Vivian Neou (1993), contains an extensive list of Internet mailing lists and bulletin boards (including a brief description of the purpose of each).

IP Network-Number and Domain Name Registration

The assignment of IP network numbers and the registation of Internet domain names is the formal responsibility of the Internet Assigned Numbers Authority, but the actual operations of assignment and registration are carried out by the Internet Network Information Center, which is managed by Government Systems, Inc.:

Internet Network Information Center
Government Systems, Inc.
14200 Park Meadow Drive
Suite 200
Chantilly, Va. 22021
U.S.A.

+1 703 802 4535 (or 800 365 3642 within North America)
+1 703 802 8376 (fax)
electronic mail: `hostmaster@nic.ddn.mil`

In 1992, the Network Information Center began to distribute the job of assigning and registering network numbers and domain names to organizations outside of North America. The Network Coordination Center of the Réseaux IP Européens (RIPE) is responsible for those parts of the Internet that are located within Europe:

---

7.   By the time this book is published, the mail address for the ietf-announce list may have been changed; if a message to the address given in the text is rejected, try `ietf-announce-request@isoc.org` instead.

RIPE Network Coordination Center
NIKHEF (Nationaal Institut voor Kernfysica en Hoge-Energiefysica)
Kruislaan 409
NL-1098 SJ Amsterdam
Netherlands

electronic mail: `ncc@ripe.net`

Information about OSI

From modest (but never humble!) beginnings, the world of OSI standards has grown to truly daunting proportions; very few corners of the information technology field have escaped the broad reach of OSI standardization efforts. A comprehensive list of the current OSI standards published (or under development) by ISO/IEC and CCITT is published semiannually by the Association for Computing Machinery's Special Interest Group on Data Communication (ACM SIGCOMM) in its technical journal *Computer Communication Review*. To find out how to join SIG-COMM[8] or obtain a specific issue of *Computer Communication Review*, readers can send an electronic-mail message to `sig-services@acmvm.bitnet` (from the Internet, or another mail network that is not part of BITNET, messages can be addressed to `sig-services%acmvm@cunyvm.cuny.edu`) or contact the SIG Services department of ACM by mail, phone, or fax:

Association for Computing Machinery
Office of SIG Services
1515 Broadway
New York, NY 10036-9998

212 626 0500
212 302 5826 (fax)

Obtaining OSI Standards

The ISO/IEC standards for OSI are most readily obtained from the national standards bodies of the countries that participate in the information technology standardization activities of ISO/IEC Joint Technical Committee 1 (JTC1). In the United States, for example, requests for OSI

---

8.   Membership in SIGCOMM, which includes a subscription to the quarterly *Computer Communication Review*, is by far the least expensive way to keep track of the status of OSI standards!

standards documents (which are available either as printed documents or in page-image format on CD-ROM) should be addressed to the American National Standards Institute (ANSI):

American National Standards Institute
Document Sales Department
11 W. 42d St.
New York, N.Y. 10036

212-642-4918
212-302-1286 (fax)

ANSI, unfortunately, has no electronic-mail address to which requests for documents could be sent, nor does it have any automated (electronic) means of distributing them. This situation-—which, as the authors have noted before, has done little to encourage the adoption of OSI standards by potential users—may have changed (for the better!) by the time this book is published.

CCITT recommendations can be ordered from the International Telecommunications Union Secretariat in Geneva:

ITU Secretariat
Place des Nations
1211 Geneva
Switzerland

+41 22 730 5338
+41 22 730 5337 (fax)

In the United States, they can also be ordered from:

National Technical Information Service
5285 Port Royal Rd.
Springfield, Va. 22161

703-487-4600

and from:

United Nations Bookstore
Room GA 32B
United Nations Plaza
New York, N.Y. 10017

The ITU has recently begun to make some of its documentation available on-line through the Teledoc document-distribution service. The first available interface is the Teledoc Auto-answering Mailbox (TAM), an X.400-based document server. Electronic-mail messages can be sent to the TAM at either the X.400 address `S=teledoc;P=itu;A=arcom;C=ch` or the Internet address `teledoc@itu.arcom.ch`. Commands to the TAM must be placed in the body of the mail message (not in the subject field). The commands are simple; for example:

> HELP
> LIST CCITT
> LIST CCITT/REC

will send the TAM HELP file and a list of the contents of the CCITT and CCITT Recommendations sections of the ITU database. The HELP file describes how to retrieve individual documents. A welcome feature of TAM is its recognition that it is a robot and may not understand what a human user is trying to say to it. The command HUMAN, followed by any message, will cause TAM to stop processing commands and automatically forward the message to a human operator at the ITU. For example:

> HUMAN
> I am having trouble locating a document concerning standards for the aromatic properties of madeleines. Could you please tell me where it is available?
> Thank you,
> Marcel

Additional information about Teledoc may be obtained from the Teledoc project coordinator, Robert Shaw, at the address and phone number listed earlier for the ITU Secretariat, or at the electronic-mail address `shaw@itu.arcom.ch` (Internet) or `G=robert;S=shaw;P=itu;A=arcom;C=ch` (X.400).

Authors' Electronic Mail Addresses

The authors can be reached at the following Internet electronic-mail addresses:

| David Piscitello | `dave@mail.bellcore.com` |
| Lyman Chapin | `lyman@bbn.com` |

REFERENCES

Alberi, J. L., and Pucci, M. F. 1987. "The DUNE Distributed Operating System." Piscataway, N.J.: Bell Communications Research (December).

ANS T1.105A-1990. "American National Standard for Telecommunications: Digital Hierarchy—Optical Interface Rates and Formats Specification."

ANS X3.216-1992. "American National Standard for Information Processing Systems: Data Communications—Structure and Semantics of the Domain Specific Part (DSP) of the OSI Network Service Access Point (NSAP) Address."

ANS Z39.50-1988. "Information Retrieval Service Definition and Protocol Specification for Library Applications."

Bellcore Technical Requirement TR-TSV-000772. 1991. "Generic Requirements for Network Elements in Support of Switched Multi-megabit Data Service" (May).

Bellcore Technical Requirement TR-TSV-000773. 1991. "Local Access System Requirements in Support of Switched Multi-megabit Data Service" (June).

Berrino, C., and Manuello, D. 1992. "Y-NET—The Esprit Pan-European Community OSI Network." *Computer Networks and ISDN Systems* 25: 554–560. Elsevier Science Publishing, North Holland.

Brandwein, R.; Cox, T.; and Dahl, J. 1990. "The IEEE 802.6 Physical Layer Convergence Procedures." *IEEE LCS Magazine* (May): 29–34.

Brim, S. 1989. "IP Routing between U.S. Government Agency Backbones and Other Networks" (on-line report). Ithaca, N.Y.: Cornell University (December).

CCITT Recommendation E.163. 1985. "Numbering Plan for the International Telephone Service." CCITT Red Book, Volume II, Fascicle II.2. Geneva, Switzerland.

CCITT Recommendation E.164. 1985. "Numbering Plan for the ISDN Era." CCITT Red Book, Volume II, Fascicle II.2. Geneva, Switzerland.

CCITT Recommendation F.69. 1985. "Plan for Telex Destination Codes." CCITT Red Book, Volume II, Fascicle II.4. Geneva, Switzerland.

CCITT Recommendation I.122. 1989. "ISDN Architecture." CCITT Blue Book, Volume III, Fascicle III.7. Geneva, Switzerland.

CCITT Recommendation I.361. 1989. "ATM." CCITT Blue Book, Volume III, Fascicle III.8. Geneva, Switzerland.

CCITT Recommendation I.362. 1989. "B-ISDN ATM Adaptation Layer (AAL) Functional Description." CCITT Blue Book, Volume III, Fascicle III.8. Geneva, Switzerland.

CCITT Recommendation I.363. 1989. "B-ISDN ATM Adaptation Layer (AAL) Specification." CCITT Blue Book, Volume III, Fascicle III.8. Geneva, Switzerland.

CCITT Recommendation Q.921. 1989. "Link Access Protocol Developed for Signalling over the D-Channel of Narrowband ISDN (LAP-D)." CCITT Blue Book, Volume VI, Fascicle VI.10. Geneva, Switzerland.

CCITT Recommendation Q.931. 1989. "ISDN User-Network Interface Layer 3 Specification for Basic Call Control." CCITT Blue Book, Volume VI, Fascicle VI.11. Geneva, Switzerland.

CCITT Recommendation T.62. 1988. "Control Procedures for Teletex and Group 4 Facsimile Services." CCITT Blue Book, Volume VII, Fascicle VII.3. Geneva, Switzerland.

CCITT Recommendations X.1–X.32. 1989. "Data Communication Networks: Services and Facilities, Interfaces" (Study Group VII). See Recommendations X.3, X.28, X.29. CCITT Blue Book, Volume VIII, Fascicle VIII.2. Geneva, Switzerland.

CCITT Recommendation X.25. 1981. "Interface between Data Terminal Equipment (DTE) and Data Circuit Terminating Equipment (DCE) for Terminals Operating in the Packet Mode and Connected to Public Data Networks by Dedicated Circuit." CCITT Yellow Book, Volume VIII, Fascicle VIII.2. Geneva, Switzerland.

CCITT Recommendation X.25. 1985. "Interface between Data Terminal Equipment (DTE) and Data Circuit Terminating Equipment (DCE) for Terminals Operating in the Packet Mode and Connected to Public Data Networks by Dedicated Circuit." CCITT Red Book, Volume VIII, Fascicle VIII.3. Geneva, Switzerland.

CCITT Recommendation X.121. 1985. "Numbering Plan for Public Data Networks." CCITT Blue Book, Volume VIII, Fascicle VIII.3. Geneva,

Switzerland.

Cerf, V., and Cain, E. 1983. "The DOD Internet Architecture Model." *Computer Networks and ISDN Systems* 7, no. 10: 307–318.

Chapin, A.L., and Piscitello, D., "TCP and TP4: Moving Forward." 1990. *ConneXions: The Interoperability Report* 4, no. 9 (September).

Clapp, G., and Zeug, M. 1992. "Components of OSI: Asynchronous Transfer Mode (ATM) and ATM Adaptation Layers." *ConneXions: The Interoperability Report* 6, no. 4 (April): 22–29.

Clark, D. D.; Jacobson, V.; Romkey, J.; Salwen, H. 1989. "An Analysis of TCP Processing Overhead." *IEEE Communications*, June 1989, pp. 23–29.

Cohen, D., and Postel, J. 1983. "The ISO Reference Model and Other Protocol Architectures." In *Information Processing '83: Proceedings of the 9th World Congress of the International Federation for Information Processing*. Paris (September).

Coltun, R. 1989. "OSPF: An Internet Routing Protocol." *ConneXions: The Interoperability Report* 3, no. 8 (August): 19–25.

Comer, Douglas. 1991. *Internetworking with TCP/IP*. 2d ed. Englewood Cliffs, N.J.: Prentice-Hall.

Craigie, J. A. I. 1988. "Migration Strategy for X.400(84) to X.400(88)/ MOTIS: COSINE Specification Phase 8.2." RARE (Réseaux Associés pour la Recherche Européene).

Day, J. 1992. "Finishing the Upper Layer(s) of the OSI Reference Model: Part 2 of the ULA Charter." Author's courtesy copy from Bolt Beranek and Newman Communications Division (January 6).

Defense Communications Agency. 1983. "DDN X.25 Host Interface Specification" (December).

Diffie, W., and Hellman, M. 1976. "New Directions in Cryptography." *IEEE Transactions on Information Theory* IT-22, no. 6 (November).

ECMA 75. 1982. "Session Protocol Specification." European Computer Manufacturers Association. Geneva, Switzerland.

ETSI Man. 1991. "ETSI Metropolitan Area Network: Principles and Architecture." European Telecommunications Standards Institute, ETSI NA5 WP MAN (February).

Fletcher, J. 1982. "An Arithmetic Checksum for Serial Transmission." *IEEE Transactions on Communications* COM-30, no. 1 (January).

Folts, H., (ed.). 1991. "McGraw-Hill's Compilation of Open Systems Standards," 4th ed. Hightstown, NJ: McGraw-Hill.

Ford, P., and Katz, D., "TUBA: Replacing IP with CLNP." 1993. *IEEE Network*, May 1993 (no page numbers available).

Forum 006. 1992. "OMNIpoint 1 Definitions." *Network Management*

Forum, Forum Library, vol. 4, issue 1.0 (August).

Frey, Donalynn, and Adams, Rick. 1989. *!%@:: A Directory of Electronic Mail Addressing and Networks*. Newton, Mass.: O'Reilly and Associates (August).

Giesel, Theodore (a.k.a. Dr. Seuss). 1971. *Horton Hears a Who*. New York: Random House. (unpaged)

Halsall, F. 1988. "Data Communications, Computer Networks and OSI." 2d ed. Wokingham, England: Addison-Wesley.

Hardcastle-Kille, S. 1992. "The QUIPU Directory Implementation." *ConneXions: The Interoperability Report* 6, no. 9 (September): 10–15.

Hardie, Edward, and Neou, Vivian, eds. 1993. *Internet: Mailing Lists*. Englewood Cliffs, NJ: Prentice-Hall.

Hares, S. 1992. "Lessons Learned for OSI at INTEROP '91 Fall." *ConneXions: The Interoperability Report* 6, no. 3. (March).

Hemrick, C. 1984. "The Internal Organization of the OSI Network Layer: Concepts, Applications, and Issues." *Journal of Telecommunications Networks* 3, no. 3 (Fall): 222–232.

Hemrick, C. 1985. "The OSI Network Layer Addressing Scheme, Its Implications, and Considerations for Implementation." NTIA Report 85-186. Boulder, Colo.: National Telecommunications and Information Administration (November).

IEEE 802.6. 1990. "Distributed Queue Dual Bus Metropolitan Area Network Standard." Institute of Electrical and Electronic Engineers.

ISO/IEC 3166. 1988. "Codes for the Representation of Names of Countries." 3d ed.

ISO/IEC 3309. 1991. "Information Technology—Telecommunications and Information Exchange between Systems—High Level Data Link Control (HDLC): Frame Structure." 4th ed. June 1, 1991.

ISO/IEC 4335. 1991. "Information Processing Systems—Data Communications—HDLC: Consolidation of Elements of Procedures." 4th ed. Sept. 15, 1991.

ISO/IEC 6523. 1984. "Data Interchange—Structure for the Identification of Organizations." 1st ed.

ISO/IEC 7478. 1984. "Information Processing Systems—Data Communications—Multi-link Procedures." 3d ed. July 1, 1984.

ISO/IEC 7498-1. 1993. "Information Processing Systems—Open Systems Interconnection—Basic Reference Model." Also published as CCITT Recommendation X.200.

ISO/IEC 7498-3. 1989. "Information Processing Systems—Open Systems Interconnection—Basic Reference Model, Part 3: Naming and Addressing. Also published as CCITT Recommendation X.650. March 1, 1989.

ISO/IEC 7498-4. 1989. "Information Processing Systems—Open Systems Interconnection—Basic Reference Model, Part 4: Management Framework." Also published as CCITT Recommendation X.700. Nov. 15, 1989.

ISO/IEC 7776. 1986. "Information Processing Systems—Data Communications—HDLC—Description of the X.25 LAPB-compatible DTE Data Link Procedures." Dec. 15, 1992.

ISO/IEC 7809. 1991. "Information Processing Systems—Data Communications—HDLC—Consolidation of Classes of Procedures." 2d ed. (Sept. 15, 1991).

ISO/IEC 8072. 1993. "Information Processing Systems—Open Systems Interconnection—Transport Service Definition." Also published as CCITT Recommendation X.214.

ISO/IEC 8073. 1992. "Information Technology—Telecommunications and Information Exchange between Systems—Protocol for Providing the Connection-mode Transport Service." Also published as CCITT Recommendation X.224.

ISO/IEC 8208. 1993. "International Standards Organization—Data Communications—X.25 Packet Layer Protocol for Data Terminal Equipment." 3d ed.

ISO/IEC 8326. 1987. "Information Processing Systems—Open Systems Interconnection—Basic Connection Oriented Session Service Definition." (Aug. 15, 1987). Also published as CCITT Recommendation X.215.

ISO/IEC 8326 Addendum 1. 1987. "Information Processing Systems—Open Systems Interconnection—Addendum 1: Session Symmetric Synchronization."

ISO/IEC 8326 Addendum 2. 1987. "Information Processing Systems—Open Systems Interconnection—Addendum 2: Incorporation of Unlimited User Data."

ISO/IEC 8327. 1987. "Information Processing Systems—Open Systems Interconnection—Basic Connection Oriented Session Protocol Specification." Also published as CCITT Recommendation X.225.

ISO/IEC 8327 Addendum 1. 1987. "Information Processing Systems—Open Systems Interconnection—Addendum 1: Session Symmetric Synchronization."

ISO/IEC 8327 Addendum 2. 1987. "Information Processing Systems—Open Systems Interconnection—Addendum 2: Incorporation of Unlimited User Data."

ISO/IEC 8348. 1993. "Information Processing Systems—Data Communications—Network Service Definition." Also published as CCITT

Recommendation X.213.

ISO/IEC 8473-1. 1993. "Information Technology—Protocol for Providing the Connectionless-mode Network Service, Part 1 Protocol Specification." Also published as CCITT Recommendation X.233.

ISO/IEC 8602. 1987. "Information Processing Systems—Open Systems Interconnection—Protocol for Providing the Connectionless-mode Transport Service." Dec. 15, 1987. Also published as CCITT Recommedation X.234.

ISO/IEC 8613. 1989. "Text and Office Systems—Office Document Architecture and Interchange Format." (Sept. 1, 1989).

ISO/IEC 8648. 1987. "Information Processing Systems—Data Communications—Internal Organization of the Network Layer." (Feb. 15, 1988).

ISO/IEC 8649. 1988. "Information Processing Systems—Open Systems Interconnection—Service Definition for the Association Control Service Element." (Dec. 15, 1988). Also published as CCITT Recommendation X.217.

ISO/IEC 8650. 1988. "Information Processing Systems—Open Systems Interconnection—Protocol Specification for the Association Control Service Element." (Dec. 15, 1988). Also published as CCITT Recommendation X.227.

ISO/IEC 8802-2. 1990. "Information Processing Systems—Data Communications—Local Area Networks, Part 2: Logical Link Control." (July 16, 1990).

ISO/IEC 8802-3. 1992. "Information Processing Systems—Data Communications—Local Area Networks, Part 3: Carrier Sense Multiple Access with Collision Detection—Access Method and Physical Layer Specification." 3d ed. (March 20, 1992).

ISO/IEC 8802-4. 1990. "Information Processing Systems—Data Communications—Local Area Networks, Part 4: Token-passing Bus Access Method and Physical Layer Specification." (Aug. 17, 1990).

ISO/IEC 8802-5. 1990. "Information Processing Systems—Data Communications—Local Area Networks, Part 5: Token Ring Access Method and Physical Layer Specification."

ISO/IEC 8822. 1988. "Information Processing Systems—Open Systems Interconnection—Connection Oriented Presentation Service Definition." (Aug. 15, 1988). Also published as CCITT Recommendation X.216.

ISO/IEC 8823. 1988. "Information Processing Systems—Open Systems Interconnection—Connection Oriented Presentation Protocol Specification." (Aug. 15, 1988). Also published as CCITT Recommendation X.226.

ISO/IEC 8824. 1990. "Information Processing Systems—Open Systems Interconnection—Specification of Abstract Syntax Notation 1 (ASN.1)." (Dec. 15, 1990). Also published as CCITT Recommendation X.208.

ISO/IEC 8825. 1990. "Information Processing Systems—Open Systems Interconnection—Specification of Basic Encoding Rules for Abstract Syntax Notation 1 (ASN.1)." (Dec. 15, 1990). Also published as CCITT Recommendation X.209.

ISO/IEC 8859. 1987. "Information Processing—8-Bit Single-Byte Coded Graphic Character Sets."

ISO/IEC 8878. 1987. "Information Processing Systems—Data Communications—Use of X.25 to Provide the OSI Connection Oriented Network Service." (Sept. 1, 1987). Also published as CCITT Recommendation X.223.

ISO/IEC 8881. 1989. "Information Processing Systems—Data Communications—Use of the X.25 Packet Level Protocol in Local Area Networks." (Dec. 1, 1989).

ISO/IEC 8886. 1992. "Information Processing Systems—Data Communications—Data Link Service Definition." (June 15, 1992). Also published as CCITT Recommendation X.212.

ISO/IEC 9040. 1990. "Information Processing Systems—Virtual Terminal Service: Basic Class."

ISO/IEC 9041. 1990. "Information Processing Systems—Virtual Terminal Protocol: Basic Class."

ISO/IEC 9066-1. 1989. "Information Processing Systems—Open Systems Interconnection—Reliable Transfer, Part 1: Model and Service Definition." (Nov. 15, 1989). Also published as CCITT Recommendation X.218.

ISO/IEC 9066-2. 1989. "Information Processing Systems—Open Systems Interconnection—Reliable Transfer, Part 2: Protocol Specification." (Nov. 15, 1989). Also published as CCITT Recommendation X.228.

ISO/IEC 9314-2. 1989. "Information Processing Systems—Data Communications—Fiber Distributed Data Interface, Part 2: Medium Access Control." (May 1, 1989).

ISO/IEC 9542. 1988. "Information Technology—Telecommunications and Information Exchange between Systems—End System to Intermediate System Routeing Exchange Protocol for Use in Conjunction with the Protocol for Providing the Connectionless-mode Network Service." (Aug. 15, 1988).

ISO/IEC 9545. 1989. "Information Processing Systems—Open Systems

Interconnection—Application Layer Structure." (Dec. 15, 1989). Also published as CCITT Recommendation X.207.

ISO/IEC 9545 Amendment 1. 1993. "Extended Application Layer Structure."

ISO/IEC TR 9575. 1990. "Information Processing Systems—Telecommunications and Information Exchange between Systems—OSI Routeing Framework." (June 1, 1990).

ISO/IEC TR 9577. 1993. "Information Technology—Telecommunications and Information Exchange between Systems—Protocol Identification in the OSI Network Layer." 2d ed.

ISO/IEC 9579. 1993. "Information Technology—Database Languages—Remote Database Access, Part 1: General Model, Service and Protocol; Part 2: SQL Specialization."

ISO/IEC 9594. 1990. "Information Technology—Open Systems Interconnection—The Directory, Part 1: Overview of Concepts, Models, and Services; Part 2: Models; Part 3: Abstract Service Definition; Part 4: Procedures for Distributed Operation; Part 5: Protocol Specifications; Part 6: Selected Attribute Types; Part 7: Selected Object Classes; Part 8: Authentication Framework." Also published as CCITT Recommendations X.500 (part 1), X.501 (part 2), X.511 (part 3), X.518 (part 4), X.519 (part 5), X.520 (part 6), X.521 (part 7), and X.509 (part 8).

ISO/IEC 9595. 1991. "Information Technology—Open Systems Interconnection—Common Management Information Service Definition." (June 1, 1991). Also published as CCITT Recommendation X.710.

ISO/IEC 9596-1. 1991. "Information Technology—Open Systems Interconnection—Common Management Information Protocol, Part 1: Specification." (June 1, 1991). Also published as CCITT Recommendation X.711.

ISO/IEC 9804. 1990. "Information Technology—Open Systems Interconnection—Service Definition for the Commitment, Concurrency, and Recovery Service Element." Also published as CCITT Recommendation X.851.

ISO/IEC 9805. 1990. "Information Technology—Open Systems Interconnection—Protocol Specification for the Commitment, Concurrency, and Recovery Service Element." Also published as CCITT Recommendation X.852.

ISO/IEC 9834. 1991. "Information Technology—Open Systems Interconnection—Procedures for the Operation of OSI Registration Authorities." Also published as CCITT Recommendation X.660.

ISO/IEC 10021. 1990. "Information Processing Systems—Open Systems

Interconnection—Message-oriented Text Interchange System (MOTIS), Part 1: System and Service Overview; Part 2: Overall Architecture; Part 3: Abstract Service Definition Conventions; Part 4: Message Transfer System—Abstract Service Definition and Procedures; Part 5: Message Store—Abstract Service Definition; Part 6: Protocol Specifications; Part 7: Interpersonal Messaging System." Also published as CCITT Recommendations X.400 (part 1), X.402 (part 2), X.407 (part 3), X.411 (part 4), X.413 (part 5), X.419 (part 6), and X.420 (part 7).

ISO/IEC 10022. 1990. "Information Technology—Telecommunications and Information Exchange between Systems—Physical Service Definition." (Aug. 1, 1990). Also published as CCITT Recommendation X.211.

ISO/IEC 10026. 1992. "Information Technology—Open Systems Interconnection—Distributed Transaction Processing, Part 1: Model; Part 2: Service Definition; Part 3: Transaction Processing Protocol Specification; Part 4: PICS Proforma; Part 5: Application Context Proforma and Guidelines When Using DSI TP; Part 6: Unstructured Data Transfer." Also published as CCITT Recommendations X.860 (part 1), X.861 (part 2), X.862 (part 3), and X.863 (part 4).

ISO/IEC 10026. 1992. "Information Technology—Open Systems Interconnection—Distributed Transaction Processing, Part 1: Model; Part 2; Service; Part 3: Protocol."

ISO/IEC 10040. 1992. "Information Technology—Open Systems Interconnection—Systems Management Overview." (Nov. 1, 1992). Also published as CCITT Recommendation X.701.

ISO/IEC 10164. 1992. "Information Technology—Open Systems Interconnection—Systems Management, Part 1: Object Management Function; Part 2: State Management Function; Part 3: Attributes for Representing Relationships; Part 4: Alarm Reporting Function; Part 5: Event Report Management Function; Part 6: Log Control Function; Part 7: Security Alarm Reporting Function; Part 8: Security Audit Trail Function; Part 9: Objects and Attributes for Access Control; Part 10: Accounting Meter Function; Part 11: Workload Monitoring Function; Part 12; Text Management Function; Part 13: Measurement Summarization Function; Part 14: Confidence and Diagnostic Test Categories." Also published as CCITT Recommendations X.730 (part 1), X.731 (part 2), X. 732 (part 3), X.733 (part 4), X.734 (part 5), X.735 (part 6), X.736 (part 7), X.740 (part 8), X.741 (part 9), X.742 (part 10), X.739 (part 11), X.745 (part 12), X.738 (part 13), and X.737 (part 14).

ISO/IEC 10165. 1992. "Information Technology—Open Systems Interconnection—Structure of Management Information, Part 1: Management Information Model; Part 2: Definition of Management Information; Part 4: Guidelines for the Definition of Managed Objects; Part 5: Generic Management Information; Part 6: Requirements and Guidelines for Management Information Conformance Statement Proformas." Also published as CCITT Recommendations X.720 (part 1), X.721 (part 2), X.722 (part 4), X.723 (part 5), and X. 724 (part 6).

ISO/IEC TR 10172. 1991. "Information Technology—Telecommunications and Information Exchange between Systems—Network/ Transport Protocol Interworking Specification." (Sept. 15, 1991).

ISO/IEC 10589. 1992. "Information Technology—Telecommunications and Information Exchange between Systems—Intermediate System to Intermediate System Intra-domain Routeing Information Exchange Protocol for Use in Conjunction with the Protocol for Providing the Connectionless-mode Network Service." (June 15, 1992).

ISO/IEC 10733. 1993. "Information Technology—Telecommunications and Information Exchange between Systems—Specification of the Elements of Management Information Relating to OSI Network Layer Standards."

ISO/IEC 10737. 1993. "Information Technology—Telecommunications and Information Exchange between Systems—Specification of the Elements of Management Information Relating to OSI Transport Layer Standards."

ISO/IEC 10737-1. 1993. "Information Technology—Telecommunications and Information Exchange between Systems—Elements of Management Information Relating to OSI Transport Layer Standards."

ISO/IEC 10747. 1993. "Protocol for Exchange of Inter-Domain Routeing Information among Intermediate Systems to Support Forwarding of ISO 8473 PDUs."

ISO/IEC ISP 11183-2. 1992. "Information Technology—International Standardized Profiles AOMn—Management Communication Protocols, Part 2: AOM12, Enhanced Management Communications" (September).

ISO/IEC ISP 11183-3. 1992. "Information Technology—International Standardized Profiles AOMn—Management Communication Protocols, Part 3: AOM11, Basic Management Communications" (September).

ISO/IEC TR 13532. 1993. "Information Technology—Telecommunications and Information Exchange between Systems—Provision of the

OSI Network Service."

Jacobson, V. 1988. "Congestion Avoidance and Control." *Proceedings of ACM SIGCOMM '88.* Stanford, Calif. (August): 314–329.

Jaffe, J., and Moss, M. 1982. "A Responsive Distributed Routing Algorithm for Computer Networks." *IEEE Transactions on Communications* COM-30 (July): 1758–1762.

Jain, R. 1985. "CUTE: A Timeout-based Congestion Control Scheme for Digital Networking Architecture."

———. 1986a. "Divergence of Timeout Algorithms for Packet Retransmissions." *Proceedings of the Fifth IEEE Phoenix Conference on Computer Communications.* Scottsdale, Ariz. (March): 174–179.

———. 1986b. "A Timeout-based Congestion Control Scheme for Window Flow-Controlled Networks." *IEEE Journal on Selected Areas in Communication* SAC-4, no. 7 (October): 1162–1167.

———. 1990. "Congestion Control in Computer Networks: Issues and Trends." *IEEE Network* 4, no. 3 (May): 24–30.

Kamoun, F., and Kleinrock, L. 1977. "Hierarchical Routing for Large Networks." *Computer Networks* 1: 155–174.

Karn, P., and Partridge, C. 1987. "Improving Round-Trip Time Estimates in Reliable Transport Protocols." *Proceedings of ACM SIGCOMM '87.* Stowe, Vt. (August): 2–7.

Kent, C. A., and Mogul, J. C. "Fragmentation Considered Harmful." *Proceedings of ACM SIGCOMM '87.* Stowe, Vt. (August): 390–401.

Kille, S. E. 1984a. "Gatewaying between RFC 822 and JNT Mail." JNT Mailgroup Note 15 (May).

Kille, S. E., ed. 1984b. "JNT Mail Protocol (Revision 1.0)." London: Joint Network Team, Rutherford Appleton Laboratory (March).

Kille, S., and Robbins, C. 1991. *The ISO Development Environment: Users Manual (Version 7.0)* (July). ISODE Consortium, P.O. Box 505, London SW11 1DX, United Kingdom.

Landweber, L. 1992. "International Connectivity." *Internet Society News* 1, no. 3 (Summer): 40.

LaQuey, Tracy L., ed. 1990. *Users' Directory of Computer Networks.* Bedford, Mass.: Digital Press (July).

McQuillan, J.; Richter, I.; Rosen, E. 1980. "The New Routing Algorithm for the ARPANET." *IEEE Transactions on Communications* (May): 711–719.

Marine, April, ed. 1992. *Internet: Getting Started.* Menlo Park, Calif.: SRI International.

Martin, James. 1976. *Telecommunications and the Computer.* 2d ed. Englewood Cliffs, N.J.: Prentice-Hall.

Medin, M. 1991. "The Great IGP Debate—Part Two: The Open Shortest Path First (OSPF) Routing Protocol." *ConneXions: The Interoperability Report* 5, no. 10 (October): 53–61.

National Academy of Sciences Report. 1985. *Transport Protocols for Department of Defense Data Networks: Report to the Department of Defense and the National Bureau of Standards.* Washington, D.C.: National Academy Press (February).

Nolle, T. 1993. "A Reality Check on ATM." *Business Communications Review.* (January): 55–59.

Partridge, C., and Trewitt, G. 1988. "High Level Entity Management System (HEMS)." *IEEE Network* 2, no. 2 (March).

Perlman, R. 1983. "Fault Tolerant Broadcast of Routing Information." *Computer Networks* (December): 93–102.

Perlman, R. 1991a. "A Comparison between Two Routing Protocols: OSPF and IS-IS." *IEEE Network* (September): 18–24.

———. 1991b. "The Great IGP Debate—Part One: IS-IS and Integrated Routing." *ConneXions: The Interoperability Report* 5, no. 10 (October): 46–52.

———. 1992a. *Interconnections: Bridges and Routers.* Reading, Mass.: Addison-Wesley.

———. 1992b. "Specification for Implementation of Connectionless OSI over SMDS." SMDS Interest Group Document TWG-1992/028 (November).

Piscitello, D., and Chapin, L. 1984. "An International Internetworking Protocol Standard." *Journal of Telecommunications Networks* 3, no. 3 (Fall): 210–221.

Piscitello, D., and Gruchevsky, S. 1987. "The Burroughs Integrated Adaptive Routing System (BIAS)." *ACM SIGCOMM Computer Communication Review (CCR)* 17, nos. 1–2 (January–April): 18–34.

Plattner, B.; Lanz, C.; Lubich, H.; Muller, M.; and Walter, T. 1991. *X.400 Message Handling: Standards, Interworking, Applications.* Wokingham, England: Addison-Wesley.

Postel, J. B.; Sunshine, C. A.; and Cohen, D. 1981. "The ARPA Internet Protocol." *Computer Networks* 5: 261–271.

Quarterman, John S. 1990. *The Matrix: Computer Networks and Conferencing Systems Worldwide.* Bedford, Mass.: Digital Press.

Radicati, S. 1992. "The 1992 Extensions to X.500." *ConneXions: The Interoperability Report* 6, no. 9 (September): 2–9.

Reijs, V. 1992. "RARE/COSINE Connectionless-mode Network Service Pilot." *Computer Networks and ISDN Systems* 25: 426–430. Elsevier Science Publishing, North Holland.

Rekhter, Y. 1991. "The Border Gateway Protocol." *ConneXions: The Interoperability Report* 5, no. 1 (January): 24–29.

RENO 4.3 UNIX Operating System. On-line help.

RFC 123. 1971. Crocker, S. D. "Proffered Official ICP." Internet Request for Comments 123. (April).

RFC 475. 1973. Bhushan, A. K. "FTP and Network Mail System." Internet Request for Comments 475. (March).

RFC 768. 1980. Postel, J. B. "User Datagram Protocol." Internet Request for Comments 768. (August).

RFC 780. 1981. Sluizer, S., and Postel, J. B. "Mail Transfer Protocol." Internet Request for Comments 780. (May).

RFC 791. 1981. Postel, J. "Internet Protocol." Internet Request for Comments 791. (September).

RFC 792. 1981. Postel, J. "Internet Control Message Protocol." Internet Request for Comments 792. (September).

RFC 793. 1981. Postel, J. "Transmission Control Protocol." Internet Request for Comments 793. (September).

RFC 815. 1982. Clark, D. D. "IP Datagram Reassembly Algorithms." Internet Request for Comments 815. (July).

RFC 817. 1982. Clark, D. D. "Modularity and Efficiency in Protocol Implementation." Internet Request for Comments 817. (July).

RFC 821. 1982. Postel, J. B. "Simple Mail Transfer Protocol." Internet Request for Comments 821. (August).

RFC 822. 1982. Crocker, D. "Standard for the Format of ARPA Internet Text Messages." Internet Request for Comments 822. (August).

RFC 826. 1982. Plummer, D. C. "A Standard for Transmission of IP Datagrams over Ethernet Networks." Internet Request for Comments 826. (November).

RFC 871. 1982. Padlipsky, M. A. "A Perspective on the Arpanet Reference Model." Internet request for Comments 871. (September).

RFC 877. 1983. Korb, J. T. "Standard for the Transmission of IP Datagrams over Public Data Networks." Internet Request for Comments 877. (September).

RFC 879. 1983. Postel, J. B. "TCP Maximum Segment Size and Related Topics." Internet Request for Comments 879. (November).

RFC 882. 1983. Mockapetris, P. V. "Domain Names: Concepts and Facilities." Internet Request for Comments 882. (November).

RFC 883. 1983. Mockapetris, P. V. "Domain Names: Implementation Specification." Internet Request for Comments 883. (November).

RFC 888. 1984. Seamonson, L., and Rosen, E. C. "'STUB' Exterior Gateway Protocol." Internet Request for Comments 888. (January).

RFC 889. 1983. Mills, D. L. "Internet Delay Experiments." Internet Request for Comments 889. (December).

RFC 894. 1984. Hornig, C. "Standard for the Transmission of IP Datagrams over Ethernet Networks." Internet Request for Comments 894. (April).

RFC 904. 1984. Mills, D. L. "Exterior Gateway Protocol Formal Specification." Internet Request for Comments 904. (April).

RFC 950. 1985. Mogul, J. and Postel, J. "Internet Standard Subnetting Procedure." Internet Request for Comments 950. (August).

RFC 954. 1985. Harrenstien, K.; Stahl, M. K.; and Feinler, E. J. "NICNAME/WHOIS." Internet Request for Comments 954. (October).

RFC 987. 1986. Kille, S. E. "Mapping between X.400 and RFC 822." Internet Request for Comments 987. (June).

RFC 1006. 1987. Rose, M. "ISO Transport Services on Top of the TCP." Internet Request for Comments 1006. (May).

RFC 1009. 1987. Braden, R. and Postel, J. "Requirements for Internet Gateways." Internet Request for Comments 1009. (June).

RFC 1014. 1987. Sun Microsystems. "XDR: External Data Representation Standard." Internet Request for Comments 1014. (June).

RFC 1021. 1987. Partridge, C., and Trewitt, G. "High-level Entity Management System (HEMS)." Internet Request for Comments 1021. (October).

RFC 1022. 1987. Partridge, C., and Trewitt, G. "High-level Entity Management Protocol (HEMP)." Internet Request for Comments 1022. (October).

RFC 1026. 1987. Kille, S. E. "Addendum to RFC 987 ('Mapping between X.400 and RFC 822')." Internet Request for Comments 1026. (September).

RFC 1034. 1987. Mockapetris, P. V. "Domain Names—Concepts and Facilities." Internet Request for Comments 1034. (November).

RFC 1035. 1987. Mockapetris, P. V. "Domain Names—Implementation and Specification." Internet Request for Comments 1035. (November).

RFC 1042. 1988. Postel, J. B., and Reynolds, J. "Standard for the Transmission of IP Datagrams over IEEE 802 Networks." Internet Request for Comments 1042. (February).

RFC 1057. 1988. Sun Microsystems. "RPC: Remote Procedure Call Protocol Specification: Version 2." Internet Request for Comments 1057. (June).

RFC 1058. 1988. Hedrick, C. "Routing Information Protocol." Internet Request for Comments 1058. (June).

RFC 1071. 1988. Braden, R.; Borman, D.; and Partridge, C. "Computing the Internet Checksum." Internet Request for Comments 1071. (September).

RFC 1072. 1988. Jacobson, V., and Braden, R. T. "TCP Extensions for Long-delay Paths." Internet Request for Comments 1072. (October).

RFC 1085. 1988. Rose, M. "ISO Presentation Services on Top of TCP/IP-based Internets." Internet Request for Comments 1085. (December).

RFC 1092. 1989. Rekhter, J. "EGP and Policy-based Routing in the New NSFNET Backbone." Internet Request for Comments 1092. (February).

RFC 1094. 1989. Sun Microsystems. "NFS: Network File System Protocol Specification." Internet Request for Comments 1094. (March).

RFC 1095. 1989. Warrier, U. S., and Besaw, L. "CMIP over TCP/IP (CMOT)." Request for Comments 1095. (April).

RFC 1102. 1989. Clark, D. D. "Policy Routing in Internet Protocols." Internet Request for Comments 1102. (May).

RFC 1104. 1989. Braun, H. W. "Models of Policy-based Routing." Internet Request for Comments 1104. (June).

RFC 1113. 1989. Linn, J. "Privacy Enhancement for Internet Electronic Mail: Part I—Message Encipherment and Authentication Procedures." Internet Request for Comments 1113. (August).

RFC 1114. 1989. Kent, S. T., and Linn, J. "Privacy Enhancement for Internet Electronic Mail: Part II—Certificate-based Key Management." Internet Request for Comments 1114. (August).

RFC 1115. 1989. Linn, J. "Privacy Enhancement for Internet Electronic Mail: Part III—Algorithms, Modes, and Identifiers." Internet Request for Comments 1115. (August).

RFC 1118. 1989. Krol, E. "Hitchhiker's Guide to the Internet." Internet Request for Comments 1118. (September).

RFC 1122. 1989. Braden, R. T., ed. "Requirements for Internet Hosts—Communication Layers." Internet Request for Comments 1122. (October).

RFC 1123. 1989. Braden, R. T., ed. "Requirements for Internet Hosts—Application and Support." Internet Request for Comments 1123. (October).

RFC 1125. 1989. Estrin, D. "Policy Requirements for Inter-administrative Domain Routing." Internet Request for Comments 1125. (November).

RFC 1137. 1989. Kille, S. E. "Mapping between Full RFC 822 and RFC 822 with Restricted Encoding." Internet Request for Comments 1137. (October).

RFC 1139. 1990. Hagens, R. A. "Echo Function for ISO 8473." Internet Request for Comments 1139. (January).

RFC 1141. 1990. Mallory, T., and Kullberg, A. "Incremental Updating of the Internet Checksum." Internet Request for Comments 1141. (January).

RFC 1155. 1990. Rose, M., and McCloghrie, K. "Structure and Identification of Management Information for TCP/IP-based Internets." Internet Request for Comments 1155. (May).

RFC 1157. 1990. Case, J.; Fedor, M.; Schoffstall, M.; and Davin, C. "Simple Network Management Protocol." Internet Request for Comments 1157. (May).

RFC 1171. 1990. Perkins, D. "Point-to-Point Protocol for the Transmission of Multi-protocol Datagrams over Point-to-Point Links." Internet Request for Comments 1171. (July).

RFC 1188. 1990. Katz, D. "Proposed Standard for the Transmission of IP Datagrams over FDDI Networks." Internet Request for Comments 1188. (October).

RFC 1189. 1991. Warrier, U. S.; LaBarre, L.; and Handspicker, B. D. "CMIP for the Internet." Internet Request for Comments 1189. (October).

RFC 1209. 1991. Piscitello, D., and Lawrence, J. "Transmission of IP Datagrams over the SMDS Service." Internet Request for Comments 1209. (March).

RFC 1213. 1991. McCloghrie, K., and Rose, M. "Management Information Base for Network Management of TCP/IP-based Internets: MIB II." Internet Request for Comments 1213. (March).

RFC 1214. 1991. Labarre, L. "OSI Internet Management Information Base (OIM MIB-II)." Internet Request for Comments 1214. (April).

RFC 1226. 1991. Kantor, B. "Internet Protocol Encapsulation of X.25 Frames." Internet Request for Comments 1226. (May).

RFC 1232. 1991. Baker, F., and Kolb, C. P., eds. "Definitions of Managed Objects for the DS1 Interface Type." Internet Request for Comments 1232. (May).

RFC 1233. 1991. Cox, T., and Tesink, K., eds. "Experimental Definitions of Managed Objects for the DS3 Interface Type." Internet Request for Comments 1233. (May).

RFC 1237. 1991. Colella, R.; Gardner, E.; Callon, R. "Guidelines for OSI NSAP Allocation in the Internet." Internet Request for Comments 1237. (July).

RFC 1238. 1991. Satz, G. "CLNS MIB for Use with Connectionless Network Protocol (ISO 8473) and End System to the Intermediate

System (ISO 9542)." Internet Request for Comments 1238. (June).

RFC 1247. 1991. Moy, J. "The Open Shortest Path First Protocol (OSPF)—Version 2." Internet Request for Comments 1247. (July).

RFC 1267. 1991. Lougheed, K., and Rekhter, Y. "A Border Gateway Protocol 3 (BGP-3)." Internet Request for Comments 1267. (October).

RFC 1283. 1991. Rose, M. "SNMP over OSI." Internet Request for Comments 1283. (December).

RFC 1287. 1991. Clark, P.; Chapin, L.; Cerf, V.; Braden, R.; and Hobby, R. "Towards the Future Internet Architecture." Internet request for Comments 1287. (December).

RFC 1288. 1991. Zimmerman, D. "The Finger User Information Protocol." Internet Request for Comments 1288. (December).

RFC 1292. 1992. Lang, R., and Wright, R., eds. "A Catalog of Available X.500 Implementations." Internet Request for Comments 1292. (January).

RFC 1293. 1992. Brown, C. "Inverse Address Resolution Protocol." Internet Request for Comments 1293. (January).

RFC 1294. 1992. Bradley, T.; Brown, C.; and Malis, A. "Multiprotocol Interconnect over Frame Relay." Internet Request for Comments 1294. (January).

RFC 1310. 1992. Chapin, L. "The Internet Standards Process." Internet Request for Comments 1310. (March).

RFC 1321. 1992. Rivest, R. "The MD5 Message-Digest Algorithm." Internet Request for Comments 1321. (April).

RFC 1322. 1992. Estrin, D.; Rekhter, Y.; and Hotz, S. "A Unified Approach to Inter-domain Routing." Internet Request for Comments 1322. (May).

RFC 1323. 1992. Jacobson, V.; Braden, R.; and Borman, D. "TCP Extensions for High Performance." Internet Request for Comments 1323. (May).

RFC 1327. 1992. Kille, S. E. "Mapping between X.400(1988)/ISO 10021 and RFC 822." Internet Request for Comments 1327. (May).

RFC 1328. 1992. Hardcastle-Kille, S. E. "X.400 1988 to 1984 Downgrading." Internet Request for Comments 1328. (May).

RFC 1331. 1992. Simpson, W. "The Point-to-Point Protocol (PPP) for the Transmission of Multi-protocol Datagrams over Point-to-Point Links." Internet Request for Comments 1331. (May).

RFC 1340. 1992. Reynolds, J. K., and Postel, J. "Assigned Numbers." Internet Request for Comments 1340. (July).

RFC 1341. 1992. Borenstein, N., and Freed, N. "MIME (Multipurpose Internet Mail Extensions) Mechanisms for Specifying and Describing the Format of Internet Message Bodies." Internet Request for Comments 1341. (June).

RFC 1347. 1992. Callon, R. "TCP and UDP with Bigger Addresses (TUBA): A Simple Proposal for Internet Addressing and Routing." Internet Request for Comments 1347. (June).

RFC 1349. 1992. Almquist, P. "Type of Service in the Internet Protocol Suite." Internet Request for Comments 1349. (July).

RFC 1351. 1991. Davin, J.; Galvin, J.; and McCloghrie, K. "SNMP Administrative Model." Internet Request for Comments 1351. (December).

RFC 1352. 1991. Galvin, J.; McCloghrie, K.; and Davin, J. "SNMP Security Protocols." Internet Request for Comments 1352. (December).

RFC 1353. 1992. McCloghrie, K.; Davin, J.; and Galvin, J. "Definitions of Managed Objects for Administration of SNMP Parties." Internet Request for Comments 1353. (January).

RFC 1356. 1992. Malis, A.; Robinson D.; and Ullmann, R. "Multiprotocol Interconnect on X.25 and ISDN in the Packet Mode." Internet Request for Comments 1356. (August).

RFC 1360. 1992. Postel, J., ed. "IAB Official Protocol Standards." Internet Request for Comments 1360. (September).

RFC 1363. 1992. Partridge, C. "A Proposed Flow Specification," Internet Request for Comments 1363. (September).

RFC 1418. 1993. Rose, M. "SNMP over OSI." Internet Request for Comments 1418. (March).

RFC 1422. 1993. Kent, S. "Privacy Enhancement for Internet Electronic Mail: Part II—Certificate-based Key Management." Internet Request for Comments 1422. (February).

RFC 1423. 1993. Balenson, D. "Privacy Enhancement for Internet Electronic Mail: Part III—Algorithms, Modes, and Identifiers." Internet Request for Comments 1423. (February).

RFC 1424. 1993. Kaliski, B. "Privacy Enhancement for Internet Electronic Mail: Part IV—Key Certification and Related Services." Internet Request for Comments 1424. (February).

Rose, M. T. 1991. *The Simple Book*. Englewood Cliffs, N.J.: Prentice-Hall.

Rose, Marshall. 1990. *The Open Book*. Englewood Cliffs, N.J.: Prentice-Hall.

Rosenberg, J.; Piscitello, D.; and Gruchevsky, S. 1987. "Adaptive Routing in Burroughs Network Architecture." *Proceedings of ACM SIGCOMM '87*. Stowe, Vt. (August). 173–184.

Ross, F.; Hamstra, J.; and Fink, B. 1990. "FDDI—A LAN among MANs." *ACM SIGCOMM Computer Communication Review* 20, no. 3 (July): 16–31.

Sandberg, R. 1988. "The Sun Network File System: Design, Implementation, and Experience." Mountain View, Calif.: Sun Microsystems.

Schoch, J. 1978. "Inter-Network Naming, Addressing, and Routing." *Proceedings of IEEE COMPCON* (Fall): 72–79.

Schoch, J.; Cohen, D.; and Taft, E. 1980. "Mutual Encapsulation of Internetwork Protocols." *IEEE Communications* (July): 1–11.

Sklower, K. 1989. "Improving the Efficiency of the ISO Checksum Calculation." *ACM SIGCOMM Computer Communication Review* 18, no. 5 (October): 32–43.

Steedman, Douglas. 1990. *Abstract Syntax Notation One (ASN.1): The Tutorial and Reference.* Great Britain: Technology Appraisals, Ltd.

Steenstrup, M. 1991. "An Introduction to Policy Routing." *Connexions: The Interoperability Report* 5, no. 1 (January): 2–29.

Stevens, W. Richard. 1990. *UNIX® Network Programming.* Englewood Cliffs, N.J.: Prentice-Hall.

Tajibnapis, W. 1977. "A Correctness Proof of a Topology Information Maintenance Protocol for Distributed Computer Networks." *Communications of the Association for Computing Machinery* 20 (July): 477–485.

Tanenbaum, Andrew. 1981. *Computer Networks.* Englewood Cliffs, N.J.: Prentice-Hall.

———. 1988. *Computer Networks.* Englewood Cliffs, N.J.: Prentice-Hall. Second edition.

Thatcher, A., and McQueen, A., eds. 1977. *The New Webster Encyclopedic Dictionary of the English Language.* Chicago: Consolidated Book Publishers.

Tsuchiya, P. 1989. "Components of OSI: IS-IS Intra-domain Routing." *Connexions: The Interoperability Report* 3, no. 8 (August): 40–45.

———. 1991. "Inter-Domain Routing in the Internet." *Connexions: The Interoperability Report* 5, no. 1 (January): 2–9.

U.S. Department of Commerce. 1987. "Codes for the Identification of the States, the District of Columbia and Outlying Areas of the United States, and Associated Areas." U.S. FIPS-5 (May 28).

Walden, D. C. 1975. "Host-to-Host Protocols." Internal BBN paper. Cambridge, Mass.: Bolt Beranek and Newman.

Walker, B., et al. 1983. "The LOCUS Distributed Operating System" (June): 49–70.

Wallace, B. 1992. "OSI Migration." *Computer Networks and ISDN Systems* 25: 540–545. Elsevier Science Publishing, North Holland.

Watson, R. 1982. "An Overview of the Livermore Interactive Network Communication System (LINCS) Architecture." Lawrence Livermore Laboratories Report UCID-19294 (April).

Wisconsin ARGO 1.0 Kernel Programmer's Guide for Academic Operating Systems 4.3. On-line document, available from the Computer Science Department, University of Wisconsin (Madison).

Xerox Corporation. 1981. "Internet Transport Protocols." Xerox System Integration Standard 028112 (December).

"X/Open Management Protocol API." 1992. Draft 5. X/Open Company (May).

Zhang, L.; Shenker, S.; and Clark, D. 1991. "Observations on the Dynamics of a Congestion Control Algorithm." *Proceedings of ACM SIGCOMM '91.* Zurich, Switzerland. (September). 133–147.

INDEX